BETTER BUSINESS

SECOND EDITION

Michael R. Solomon
Contributing Editor

Mary Anne Poatsy

Kendall Martin

Prentice Hall
Boston   Columbus   Indianapolis   New York   San Francisco   Upper Saddle River
Amsterdam   Cape Town   Dubai   London   Madrid   Milan   Munich   Paris   Montreal   Toronto
Delhi   Mexico City   São Paulo   Sydney   Hong Kong   Seoul   Singapore   Taipei   Tokyo

Editorial Director: Sally Yagan
Editor in Chief: Eric Svendsen
Acquisitions Editor: James Heine
Director of Development: Steve Deitmer
Development Editor: Shannon LeMay-Finn
Director of Editorial Services: Ashley Santora
Assistant Editor: Karin Williams
Editorial Assistant: Jason Calcano
Director of Marketing: Patrice Lumumba Jones
Senior Marketing Manager: Maggie Moylan
Marketing Assistant: Ian Gold
Senior Managing Editor: Judy Leale
Production Project Manager: Jacqueline A. Martin
Senior Operations Supervisor: Arnold Vila
Senior Art Director: Kenny Beck
Cover and Interior Designer: LCI Design
Cover Images: Red eared Slider/Velychko/Shutterstock; Brown hare/scattoselvaggio/Shutterstock; Carrot and stick/ajt/Shutterstock; Autumn landscape/Kostyantyn Ivanyshen/Shutterstock
Lead Media Project Manager: Lisa Rinaldi
Media Editor: Joan Waxman
Full-Service Project Management: S4Carlisle Publishing Services
Composition: S4Carlisle Publishing Services
Printer/Binder: R.R. Donnelley/Roanoke
Cover Printer: Phoenix Color Corp., Hagerstown
Text Font: 10.5/13 Palatino

Credits and acknowledgments borrowed from other sources and reproduced, with permission, in this textbook appear on appropriate page within text (photo credits appear on page 583–584).

Microsoft® and Windows® are registered trademarks of the Microsoft Corporation in the U.S.A. and other countries. Screen shots and icons reprinted with permission from the Microsoft Corporation. This book is not sponsored or endorsed by or affiliated with the Microsoft Corporation.

Many of the designations by manufacturers and seller to distinguish their products are claimed as trademarks. Where those designations appear in this book, and the publisher was aware of a trademark claim, the designations have been printed in initial caps or all caps.

Library of Congress Cataloging-in-Publication Data

Solomon, Michael R.
  Better business / Michael R. Solomon, Mary Anne Poatsy, Kendall Martin. —
2nd ed.
      p. cm.
  Rev. ed. of: Better business / Mary Anne Poatsy, Kendall Martin. 2010.
  Includes bibliographical references and index.
  ISBN-13: 978-0-13-249669-8
  ISBN-10: 0-13-249669-0
1. Industrial management. 2. Business. 3. Entrepreneurship. 4.
Commerce. I. Poatsy, Mary Anne. II. Martin, Kendall. III. Poatsy, Mary
Anne. Better business. IV. Title.
  HD31.P555 2011
  658—dc22
                                                                    2010043083

Prentice Hall
is an imprint of

PEARSON

www.pearsonhighered.com

10 9 8 7 6 5 4 3 2 1
ISBN 10: 0-13-249669-0
ISBN 13: 978-0-13-249669-8

Dedication

To Rose
Michael R. Solomon

For my husband, Ted, who unselfishly continues to take on more than his fair share to support me throughout this process; and for my children, Laura, Carolyn, and Teddy, whose encouragement and love have been inspiring.
Mary Anne Poatsy

For all the teachers, mentors, and gurus who have popped in and out of my life.
Kendall Martin

Brief Contents

Contents

About the Authors

Michael R. Solomon, Ph.D., *Contributing Editor*

Michael R. Solomon is Professor of Marketing and Director of the Center for Consumer Research in the Haub School of Business at Saint Joseph's University in Philadelphia. He also is Professor of Consumer Behaviour at the Manchester School of Business, The University of Manchester, U.K. Professor Solomon's primary research and consulting interests include consumer behavior, branding, and marketing applications of virtual worlds. He has written several textbooks and trade books; his *Consumer Behavior* text is the most widely used in the world. Michael often speaks to business groups about new trends in consumer behavior and marketing strategy.

Mary Anne Poatsy, MBA, CFP

mpoatsy@mc3.edu

Mary Anne Poatsy is an adjunct faculty member at Gwynedd Mercy College and senior adjunct faculty member at Montgomery County Community College, teaching various business, management, and computer application and concepts courses in face-to-face and online environments. She holds a BA in psychology and education from Mount Holyoke College and an MBA in finance from Northwestern University's J. L. Kellogg Graduate School of Management.

Mary Anne has been teaching since 1995 at a variety of elementary and secondary institutions, including Gwynedd Mercy College, Montgomery County Community College, Muhlenberg College, and Bucks County Community College, as well as training in the professional environment and presenting at several conferences. Before teaching, she was a vice president at Shearson Lehman Hutton in the Municipal Bond Investment Banking Department.

Kendall Martin, Ph.D.

kmartin@mc3.edu

Kendall Martin has been teaching since 1988 at a number of institutions, including Villanova University, DeSales University, Arcadia University, Ursinus College, County College of Morris, and Montgomery County Community College, at both the undergraduate and graduate levels.

Kendall's education includes a BS in electrical engineering from the University of Rochester and an MS and a Ph.D. in engineering from the University of Pennsylvania. She has industrial experience in research and development environments (AT&T Bell Laboratories) as well as experience with several start-up technology firms.

At Ursinus College, Kendall developed a successful faculty training program for distance education instructors. She makes conference presentations throughout the year.

Acknowledgments

Like any good business, this project could not have been completed without the dedicated efforts of a talented group of people to whom we are eternally grateful. The authors would like to take this time to thank the many colleagues, friends, and students who have contributed toward our vision of an introductory textbook that excites and challenges students.

From the very conception of *Better Business*, 2nd edition, to the last page produced, a remarkable board of reviewers at schools across the nation has guided us with wise counsel. Our joy in working with such talented and student-centered faculty is deep. We extend our sincerest gratitude to our reviewers.

The division of Business Publishing at Prentice Hall has been incredible in devoting time and resources to the creation of the *Better Business*, 2nd edition, learning system. We are indebted to Jodi McPherson, our former executive editor, who had the vision for a new introduction to business textbook system that engages and excites students, and our current acquisitions editor, James Heine, whose guidance provided the foundation for this second edition. Without their vision, passion, dedication, and drive, this textbook would not exist. Our thanks also extend to our project manager, Karin Williams, who diligently kept us on track with only gentle threats when we went astray! Karin's fine management skills enabled this complex project to be completed on time—a feat not easily accomplished. We are also grateful to Shannon LeMay-Finn, our development editor, for her advice, keen eye, and calming support. Her input ensured that the many components of this project met a high standard of excellence and quality that most products have a hard time matching. Maggie Moylan-Leen, senior marketing manager, has been very instrumental in shaping the message of the book. We are so appreciative of her ardent attention to all the marketing details that are so important in a successful new launch. We're also appreciative for the dedication of the media team of Cathi Profitko, Joan Waxman, and Josh Keefe, who were instrumental in the development of all the multimedia products that comprise **my*biz*lab**, and for their efforts to ensure that it works seamlessly with the textbook. Additionally, we would like to thank Kenny Beck, Judy Leale, and Jacqueline Martin for their efforts in the design and production of *Better Business*, 2nd edition. Lastly, our thanks to Jerome Grant, president of business publishing, and Eric Svendson, editor in chief, who had faith in our vision and backed this project with the necessary financial and human resources to make our vision a reality.

We would be completely negligent if we did not acknowledge all the incredibly talented and devoted designers, permissions researchers, and others who contributed to the project and to whom we extend our sincerest thanks.

Additionally, we would like to thank the many supplement authors for this edition: Claire Hunter, Brandi Hollier, Christina McCale, Patricia Lanier, and the teams at PreMediaGlobal and ANSRSource.

Everything we do is inspired by the experiences we have in the classroom. We want to thank and encourage our students, whose experiences, struggles, victories, and honesty have shaped this project turn by turn. May *Better Business*, 2nd edition, serve our students as a stepping-stone to meaningful careers and lives.

Last, but not least, close to home, our families have sacrificed much to let us focus on the project. We appreciate their patience and support over the last several years.

Reviewers

Wendi Achey, *Northampton Community College*
Joni Anderson, *Buena Vista University*
Lydia Anderson, *Fresno City College*
Natalie Andrews, *Sinclair Community College*
Sally Andrews, *Linn Benton Community College*
Roanne Angiello, *Bergen Community College*
Brenda Anthony, *Tallahassee Community College*
Maria Aria, *Camden County College*
Corinne Asher, *Henry Ford Community College*
Susan Athey, *Colorado State University*
Michael Aubry, *Grossmont College*
David Bader, *Columbus State Community College*
Mazen Badra, *Webster University*
Michael Baran, *South Puget Sound Community College*
Ruby Barker, *Tarleton State University*
William Barrett, *University of Wisconsin*
Denise Barton, *Wake Technical Community College*
Dick Barton, *El Camino College*
Crystal Bass, *Trinity Valley Community College*
Jeffrey Bauer, *University of Cincinnati*
Christine Bauer-Ramazani, *Saint Michael's College*
Leslie Beau, *Orange Coast College*
Gayona Beckford-Barclay, *Community College of Baltimore County*
Robert Bennett, *Delaware County Community College*
George Bernard, *Seminole Community College*
Patricia Bernson, *County College of Morris*
Rick Bialac, *Georgia College and State University*
Danielle Blesi, *Hudson Valley Community College*
Chuck Bowles, *Pikes Peak Community College*
Malcolm Bowyer, *Montgomery Community College*
Steven Bradley, *Austin Community College*
Charles Braun, *Marshall University*
Edwin Breazeale, *Midlands Technical College*
Sharon Breeding, *Bluegrass Community Technical College*
Richard Brennan, *North Virginia Community College*
Robert Bricker, *Pikes Peak Community College*
Lisa Briggs, *Columbus State Community College*
T. L. Brink, *Crafton Hills College*
Dennis Brode, *Sinclair Community College*
Katherine Broneck, *Pima Community College*
Harvey Bronstein, *Oakland Community College*
Deborah Brown, *North Carolina State University*
Sylvia Brown, *Midland College*
Janet Brown-Sederberg, *Massasoit Community College*
Lesley Buehler, *Ohlone College*
Barry Bunn, *Valencia Community College*
Carroll Burrell, *San Jacinto College*
Marian Canada, *Ivy Technical Community College*
Diana Carmel, *Golden West College*
John Carpenter, *Lake Land College*
Deborah Carter, *Coahoma Community College*

Tiffany Champagne, *Houston Community College*
Glen Chapuis, *St. Charles Community College*
Bonnie Chavez, *Santa Barbara City College*
Sudhir Chawla, *Angelo State University*
Lisa Cherivtch-Zingaro, *Oakton Community College*
Desmond Chun, *Chabot College*
John Cicero, *Shasta College*
Michael Cicero, *Highline Community College*
Subasree Cidambi, *Mount San Antonio College*
Joseph Cilia, *Delaware Technical & Community College*
Mark Clark, *Collin County Community College*
William Clark, *Leeward Community College*
Paul Coakley, *Community College of Baltimore County*
Ken Combs, *Del Mar College*
Jamie Commissaris, *Davenport University*
Rachna Condos, *American River College*
Charlie Cook, *University of West Alabama*
Solveg Cooper, *Cuesta College*
Douglas Copeland, *Johnson County Community College*
Julie Couturier, *Grand Rapids Community College*
Brad Cox, *Midlands Technical College*
Diane Coyle, *Montgomery County Community College*
Chad Creevy, *Davenport University*
Geoff Crosslin, *Kalamazoo Valley Community College*
H. Perry Curtis, *Collin County Community College*
Dana D'Angelo, *Drexel University*
Mark Dannenberg, *Shasta College*
Jamey Darnell, *Durham Tech*
Shirley Davenport, *Prairie State College*
Helen Davis, *Jefferson Community Technical College*
Peter Dawson, *Collin County Community College*
David Dearman, *University of Arkansas*
Sherry Decuba, *Indian River Community College*
Andrew Delaney, *Truckee Meadows Community College*
Kate Demarest, *Carroll Community College*
Donna Devault, *Fayetteville Tech*
Susan Dik, *Kapiolani Community College*
Michael DiVecchio, *Central Pennsylvania College*
Gerard Dobson, *Waukesha County Technical College*
Kathleen Dominick, *Bucks County Community College and University of Phoenix Online*
Ron Dougherty, *Ivy Technical Community College*
Karen Drage, *Eastern Illinois University*
Nelson Driver, *University of Arkansas*
Allison Duesing, *Northeast Lakeview College*
Timothy Durfield, *Citrus College*
David Dusseau, *University of Oregon*
Dana Dye, *Gulf Coast Community College*

C. Russell Edwards, *Valencia Community College*
Karen Edwards, *Chemeketa Community College*
Stephen Edwards, *University of North Dakota*
Stewart Edwards, *North Virginia Community College*
Susan Ehrfurth, *Aims Community College*
Patrick Ellsberg, *Lower Columbia College*
Susan Emens, *Kent State University*
Karen Emerson, *Southeast Community College*
Theodore Emmanuel, *State University of New York Oswego*
Kellie Emrich, *Cuyahoga Community College*
Vince Enslein, *Clinton Community College*
Steven Ernest, *Baton Rouge Community College*
Mary Ewanechko, *Monroe County Community College*
Marie Farber-Lapidus, *Oakton Community College*
Geralyn Farley, *Purdue University*
Janice Feldbauer, *Schoolcraft College and Austin Community College*
Mary Felton-Kolstad, *Chippewa Valley Technical College*
Louis Ferracane, *University of Phoenix*
David Fitoussi, *University of California*
Joseph Flack, *Washtenaw Community College*
Jacalyn Flom, *University of Toledo*
Carla Flores, *Ball State University*
Carol Flowers, *Orange Coast College*
Jake Flyzik, *Lehigh Carbon Community College*
Thomas Foley, *Kent State University*
Craig Fontaine, *Northeastern University*
Joseph Fox, *Asheville-Buncombe Technical Community College*
Mark Fox, *Indiana University–South Bend*
Victoria Fox, *College of DuPage*
Charla Fraley, *Columbus State Community College*
John Frank, *Columbus State Community College*
Leatrice Freer, *Pitt Community College*
Paula Freston, *Merced College*
Fred Fry, *Bradley University*
Albert Fundaburk, *Bloomsburg University*
William Furrell, *Moorpark College*
Michael Gagnon, *Kellogg Community College*
Wayne Gawlik, *Joliet Junior College*
George Generas, *University of Hartford*
Vanessa Germeroth, *Ozarks Technical Community College*
Gerald GeRue, *Rock Valley College*
John Geubtner, *Tacoma Community College*
Katie Ghahramani, *Johnson County Community College*
David Gilliss, *San Jose State University*
Eric Glohr, *Lansing Community College*
Constance Golden, *Lakeland Community College*
Gayle Goldstone, *Santa Rosa Junior College*
Alfredo Gomez, *Broward Community College*
Phillip Gonsher, *Johnson County Community College*
Robert Googins, *Shasta College*
Karen Gore, *Ivy Technical Community College–Southwest*

Carol Gottuso, *Metropolitan Community College*

Gretchen Graham, *Community College of Allegheny*

Selina Griswold, *University of Toledo*

John Guess, *Delgado Community College*

Kevin Gwinner, *Kansas State University*

Peggy Hager, *Winthrop University*

Lawrence Hahn, *Palomar College*

Semere Haile, *Grambling State University*

Lynn Halkowicz, *Bloomsburg University*

Clark Hallpike, *Elgin Community College*

Paula Hansen, *Des Moines Area Community College*

Frank Harber, *Indian River Community College*

LaShon Harley, *Durham Technical Community College*

Jeri Harper, *Western Illinois University*

Deborah Haseltine, *Southwest Tennessee Community College*

Carol Heeter, *Ivy Tech Community College*

Linda Hefferin, *Elgin Community College*

Debra Heimberger, *Columbus State Community College*

Dennis Heiner, *College of Southern Idaho*

Cheryl Heitz, *Lincoln Land Community College*

Charlane Held, *Onondaga Community College*

Rebecca Helms, *Ivy Tech Community College*

Heith Hennel, *Valencia Community College*

Dorothy Hetmer-Hinds, *Trinity Valley Community College*

Linda Hoffman, *Ivy Technical Community College–Fort Wayne*

Merrily Hoffman, *San Jacinto College*

Gene Holand, *Columbia Basin College*

Phillip Holleran, *Mitchell Community College*

Robert Hood, *Chattanooga State Technical Community College*

Sheila Hostetler, *Orange Coast College*

Larry Hottot, *North Virginia Community College*

William Huisking, *Bergen Community College*

Lynn Hunsaker, *Mission College*

Steven Huntley, *Florida Community College at Jacksonville*

Johnny Hurley, *Iowa Lakes Community College*

Kimberly Hurns, *Washtenaw Community College*

Holly Hutchins, *Central Oregon Community College*

Linda Isenhour, *Eastern Michigan University*

Katie Jackson, *Columbus State Community College*

Linda Jaeger, *Southeast Community College*

Dolores James, *University of Maryland University College*

Pam Janson, *Stark State College of Technology*

Larry Jarrell, *Louisiana Technical University*

Joe Jenkins, *Tarrant County College*

Brandy Johnson, *Columbus State Community College*

Dennis Johnson, *Delaware County Community College*

Floyd Johnson, *Davenport University*

M. Gwen Johnson, *Black Hawk College*

Carroll Jones, *Tulsa Community College*

Jeffrey Jones, *The College of Southern Nevada*

Kenneth Jones, *Ivy Technical Community College–Central Indiana*

Gayla Jurevich, *Fresno City College*

Alex Kajstura, *Daytona Beach College*

Dmitriy Kalyagin, *Chabot College*

Radhika Kaula, *Missouri State University*

John Kavouras, *Ohio College of Massage Therapy*

Dan Keating, *Fox Valley Technical College*

Albert Keller, *Dixie State College of Utah*

Ann Kelly, *Georgia Southern University*

Jeffrey Kennedy, *Broward Community College*

Jeffrey Kennedy, *Palm Beach Atlantic University*

Daniel Kipley, *Azusa Pacific University*

William Kline, *Bucks County Community College*

Susan Kochenrath, *Ivy Technical Community College*

Linda Koffel, *Houston Community College Central*

Todd Korol, *Monroe County Community College*

Jack Kraettli, *Oklahoma City Community College*

Jim Kress, *Central Oregon Community College*

John Kurnik, *St. Petersburg College*

Paul Laesecke, *University of Denver*

Martha Laham, *Diablo Valley College*

Mary LaPann, *Adirondack Community College*

Deborah Lapointe, *Central New Mexico Community College*

Rob Leadbeater, *Mission College*

David Leapard, *Eastern Michigan University*

Denise Lefort, *Clemson University*

Ron Lennon, *Barry University*

Angela Leverett, *Georgia Southern University*

Sue Lewis, *Tarleton State University*

Kathleen Lorencz, *Oakland Community College*

Mark Lowenstein, *College of St. Joseph*

John Luke, *Delaware County Community College*

John Mago, *Anoka-Ramsey Community College*

Jan Mangos, *Valencia Community College*

Christine Marchese, *Nassau Community College*

James Marco, *Wake Technical Community College*

Suzanne Markow, *Des Moines Area Community College*

Gary Marrer, *Glendale Community College*

Calvin Martin, *Davenport University*

James Martin, *Washburn University*

Kathleen Martinez, *Red Rocks Community College*

Thomas Mason, *Brookdale Community College*

Marian Matthews, *Central New Mexico Community College*

Kelli Mayes-Denker, *Carl Sandburg College*

Kevin McCarthy, *Baker University*

Gina McConoughey, *Illinois Central College*

Lisa McCormick, *Community College of Allegheny*

Patrick L. McCormick, *Ivy Tech Community College*

Pamela McElligott, *Meramec Community College*

Edward McGee, *Rochester Institute of Technology*

Donna McGill-Cameron, *Yuba College*

Vince McGinnis, *Bucks County Community College*

Allison McGullion, *West Kentucky Community & Technical College*

Lorraine McKnight, *Eastern Michigan University*

Bruce McLaren, *Indiana State University*

Juan Meraz, *Missouri State University*

Miriam Michael, *American River College*

Jeanette Milius, *Iowa Western Community College*

Carol Millard, *Scottsdale Community College*

John Miller, *Pima Community College*

Linda Miller, *Northeast Community College*

Pat Miller, *Grossmont College*

Morgan Milner, *Eastern Michigan University*

Diane Minger, *Cedar Valley College*

Susan Mitchell, *Des Moines Area Community College*

Theresa Mitchell, *Alabama A&M University*

Joseph Molina, *MiraCosta College*

Carol Moore, *California State University*

Wayne Moore, *Indiana University of Pennsylvania*

Richard Morris, *Northeastern State University*

Jennifer Morton, *Ivy Tech Community College of Indiana*

David Murphy, *Madisonville Community College*

Gary Murray, *Rose State College*

John Muzzo, *Harold Washington College*

Mark Nagel, *Normandale Community College*

Conrad Nankin, *Pace University*

Kristi Newton, *Chemeketa Community College*

Steven Nichols, *Metropolitan Community College*

Simon Nwaigwe, *Baltimore City Community College*

Mark Nygren, *Brigham Young University*

Asmelash Ogbasion, *Southwest Tennessee Community College*

Cynthia L. Olivarez Rooker, *Lansing Community College*

David Olson, *California State University*

Anthony O'Malley, *Baruch College*

Lori Oriatti, *College of Lake County*

Robert O'Toole, *Crafton Hills College*

Mary Padula, *Borough of Manhattan Community College*

Esther Page-Wood, *Western Michigan University*

Lauren Paisley, *Genesee Community College*

Dyan Pease, *Sacramento City College*

Jeffrey Pepper, *Chippewa Valley Technical College*

Clifford Perry, *Florida International University*

Melinda Phillabaum, *Indiana University–Purdue University*

Rose Pollard, *Southeast Community College*

Jackie (J. Robinson) Porter, *Eastfield College*

Kathleen Powers, *Henry Ford Community College*

Dan Powroznik, *Chesapeake College*

Sally Proffitt, *Tarrant County College*

Joe Puglisi, *Butler County Community College*

James Pullins, *Columbus State Community College*

Kathy Pullins, *Columbus State Community College*

Bobby Puryear, *North Carolina State University*

Martha Racine Taylor, *College of the Redwoods*

Anthony Racka, *Oakland Community College*

Robert Reck, *Western Michigan University*

Philip Regier, *Arizona State University*

Delores Reha, *Fullerton College*

David Reiman, *Monroe County Community College*

Robert Reinke, *University of South Dakota*

New to the Second Edition

We have invested a great deal of work creating the second edition of *Better Business* to give students and instructors a powerful learning and teaching tool that captures the evolving issues and opportunities of business. Enhancements for the second edition follow:

- All of the end-of-chapter materials have been reviewed, and we have modified over 50% of these materials to include the most recent events and trends in the business environment. With continuing economic shifts, changes in technologies, and ever-increasing globalization, the business world is evolving quickly. The second edition of *Better Business* provides instructors with wide-ranging choices for discussion topics, assessment questions, and group activities that cover the most current and timely topics in the business community.

- One of the most significant shifts in the business environment since the first edition of *Better Business* is the explosive growth of social media in all parts of business. The second edition of *Better Business* features social media strategies and technologies in over 85% of its chapters.

- Every chapter and all special features of *Better Business* have been rewritten to better match student vocabulary and student reading abilities. The second edition introduces an increased focus on metaphors and stories to pull students into the material.

- All of the time-sensitive material has been updated. Stories and examples from the first edition that have continued to evolve have been updated and placed in the most current context. Over 90% of the endnotes were replaced with more current references. Timely examples have replaced older material, giving the second edition a more up-to-date feel that resonates with students.

- Feedback from the first edition of *Better Business* indicated that the "Top Ten" lists not only interested students but also pushed them to go more deeply into the body of the text. For the second edition, we updated several Top 10 lists and added new ones that reflect current market trends, with a focus on selecting topics that would appeal to students.

- The Business Plan Project exercise is often the capstone experience in the Introduction to Business survey course. For the second edition of *Better Business*, we reviewed and revised the entire Business Plan Project presentation and related exercises based on in-classroom feedback from both professors and students. It is now featured as an appendix at the end of this text, and a sample business plan and other supporting documents are available in the Instructor's Manual as well as online at **my*biz*lab**.

Letter from the Authors

When we set out on this project, we had several goals in mind . . . and one guiding philosophy. We wanted to have a conversation with our students, not merely write a book that we hoped they would read. We wanted to change the expectations we have that students will come to class unprepared. Why can't they come ready for class, with a desire to know about business? Why can't we have a little fun with the course while teaching students about the lighter side of business? We think we can.

To that end, we worked tirelessly on selecting our topics and our resources to help you, the student. We incorporated a "Question & Answer" format throughout to get you to want to know the answer and see more . . . and not simply because it will be on the test. We paid more attention to the details because that is where the course often comes together for you.

In each chapter, the *On Target* and *Off the Mark* features illustrate positive and negative outcomes of business ventures related to the chapter material. These features, along with the various "Top 10" lists, can fuel in-class dialogue.

Mini Chapters are five special sections in the book that give you additional information on key topics in business: Special Issues in Online Business, Constructing an Effective Business Plan, Business Communications, Finding a Job, and Personal Finance.

Better Business, 2nd edition, offers the content you need for a solid overview of business, but in a *better* way. By presenting the material in a stimulating way, *Better Business* encourages you to come to class prepared to have better conversations and a truly engaging classroom experience.

Better Business, 2nd edition, is tightly integrated with **my**biz**lab**, Pearson's revolutionary online learning system that combines assessment, reporting, and personalized study, all in ONE place. **my**biz**lab** gives your instructor easy access to a variety of media, homework, and activities to get you interacting with business and not just reading about it. Throughout *Better Business*, you are encouraged to use **my**biz**lab** for immediate review and reinforcement of the material. With **my**biz**lab**, you won't just read about business, you will INTERACT with it through business simulations and other engaging exercises.

The end result is a ***better experience*** . . .

BizChat boxes can spark thoughtful discussions in class or virtual discussions via **my**biz**lab**. *BizChat* boxes explore "hot topics" in business to help you connect the chapter material with what's going on in business today.

mybiz**lab** offers multiple ways of reviewing each chapter, including a *Study Plan, Self-Tests, PowerPoints, Flash Cards* and *Critical-Thinking Questions*. Multiple activities are also provided to get you interacting with the material: *Web Cases, Video Cases and Exercises, Document Makeovers, Regional Examples*, and *BizSkills Simulations*.

BizSkills are real-world scenarios that invite you to assume the role of a decision maker at a company and apply the concepts you have just learned. You are scored on the five-minute simulation and then directed to quizzes to help reinforce the concepts.

mybiz**lab** offers a pre-test that will generate a personalized *Study Plan* where you see exactly the topics that require additional practice. The *Study Plan* links to multiple learning aids, such as videos, the eText, and flashcards, for additional help. After you work through the learning aids, you can take a post test to check your improvement.

The *Video Library* features a variety of topical business videos that correspond to each chapter topic.

Document Makeovers ask you to analyze and correct business documents such as e-mail messages, letters, memos, blogs, and resumes. Immediate feedback is provided.

my*biz***lab** also includes the complete set of *Business Plan Project* documents, written to accompany the Business Plan Mini Chapter and Business Plan Project Appendix.

The Ten Easy Steps for *Better Business* Success

Step 1: It's all up to you.

You've heard that before, right? You've bought textbooks, and read some of the materials, but maybe still haven't ended up with the grade you wanted. So the key to success is not just buying the book or simply reading it. Instead, your success depends on three skills:

- finding,
- understanding, and
- applying the information found within this textbook and all of its resources.

The following steps will help you succeed in this course, and if you apply some of these steps outside the classroom, you may also succeed in business and in life.

Step 2: Go to class with intent.

How do your classes go for you? Are you generally able to follow what the instructor and your classmates are saying in lecture and class discussions? Are you able to actively participate in a group discussion, or do you simply observe other group members? Your attitude and the plan you have for using class time can change the entire experience for you. Try these quick tips to make sure your classroom experience is as rich and fulfilling as possible:

"You should know the material so well you can explain it to others so that they understand it—even your mom."

—*Brett Neslen*, student

Review the Syllabus

If you have trouble speaking up in class, try this strategy. The syllabus is one of the most important documents in the course. It acts as a binding contract between you and the professor. Read the syllabus in detail as soon as it comes out. Then, in the next class, ask at least one question about it. It will show the professor you're serious about meeting your responsibilities in class—and will get you in the habit of speaking up in class.

Show Up!

As Woody Allen says, "Eighty percent of success is showing up." It's basic advice, but many students lose sight of how important it is to come to class. You should be punctual, if not early; be attentive; and be noticed. Sit near the front and ask good questions so that the professor gets to know your face and name. It's just as important that the professor knows you as it is that you know your professor (see Step 3).

Ask Questions

If you're confused during class, ask a question right then. Don't think, "I'll look really dumb if I ask this," or "I'll probably understand it after I read the text," or "I'll wait to ask someone else, or go to office hours tomorrow." Asking now will save you time and effort and will probably help other students in the room. You'll learn so much more if you ask questions in class. If you do need to contact your instructor after class to clarify a point, stop by during office hours rather than asking the question electronically or over the phone. Keep in mind, face-to-face visits trump e-mail or voicemail. Now, aren't you glad you invested some time earlier to get to know your instructor (**Step 3**)? After all, it's easier to ask for help from someone with whom you already feel comfortable.

Write a One-Minute Review

Immediately at the end of class, take one minute and write all that you can recall from today's lecture. Try to identify what the main take-away points are by highlighting key ideas. Forcing yourself to be quick and brief helps you to capture the main ideas without the smaller details providing distraction.

Write Down Your "Muddiest" Point

When class is finished, also take a quick moment to write down two sentences that describe the most confusing part of today's lecture. Keep this in one specific part of your notebook—it's a great thing to bring along to your study group or to office hours. It will also work well in creating your own personalized study guide for the next exam.

Step 3: Connect with people.

Business is all about people. Right now, your business is getting a great grade in this class. As in any business, there are many people available to provide help: instructors, fellow students, and school staff. Look around for these people—and then enlist their help.

Get to Know Your Instructor: Go to Office Hours

Your teachers can be your most helpful contacts on campus. Not only can they become mentors, but as you near graduation, they can write job recommendations or references. They can't do that unless you get to know them beyond the focus of the course. So plan to make a couple of trips to office hours—even if you know everything.

Create or Join a Study Group

Find study buddies early. In the first few days of class, try to get acquainted with at least two classmates in every course. Watch the people in your class to figure out who seems to know what's going on, who seems dependable, and who you could work well with. Approach those people and ask if they wouldn't mind forming a study group. You don't need to meet all the time—the group can be available on an "as needed" basis. But it's good to have a group of connected students who can help you prep for exams, confirm or clarify points made during class, and exchange notes if you miss a class. (Trust us: it's much better to have a buddy give you the information you missed than to ask the instructor, "Did I miss anything important?")

"When studying for a test, I've found that it's very helpful to use a partner and a study guide. I like to come up with a study guide full of questions relating to every important topic that I think will be on the test, and write the answers directly below them. Then, my partner and I go through the study guide and quiz each other. This way we can read aloud all of the main ideas and begin to remember key concepts. After we have gone through the study guide a couple times, we quiz each other from memory. Once we've memorized small concepts, it's easier to understand the bigger picture."

—*Mallory Hensel,* student

Use the People Around You

Do you know students who already took this class? Spend some time with them and ask the right questions. What sections of the course will demand more time out of your schedule? What tools in the library helped them out with their projects?

Be sure to look around the class for older students. Many colleges are seeing a large influx of people returning to college after successful careers. These people have that precious thing you may lack: real-world experience. Buy someone a cup of coffee and ask him or her for advice that helps you in the course or in finding a job.

Use All the Resources the School Provides

The faculty and staff at your school want you to succeed—we all take pride in our students' accomplishments! So be sure to investigate all the resources available to you at your school. Talk to your advisor about services such as the following:

Writing Support

Many schools provide special clinics that can help you with your writing. Some also provide writing labs where you can get assistance in editing and proofreading your work.

Support Services

Look for support services that offer help with note-taking techniques, strategies to combat stress in test taking, and workshops on helping you organize and manage your time. If you discover that you have a pattern of specific struggles (for example, you always underperform on tests), see if free screening for learning disabilities is offered. You may need specific testing accommodations (such as additional time or larger-print exams), or you may be eligible for help with an in-class notetaker. The key is to become your own best advocate. Be informed—know how your mind works and what conditions make you perform your best.

Step 4: Explore the world of business in real time.

While this text book intends to apply business concepts to current situations, the examples cannot be as current as those that are exposed in the business press. Until now, you may not have been interested in picking up the *Wall Street Journal*, *Financial Times*, *BusinessWeek*, or the *Economist* because you did not have the necessary background or interest. Try the following technique. Every day, go online and read the lead story in the *Wall Street Journal*. Keep a log that notes the theme of the article (e.g., the economic situation in the United States or some other part of the world, a government action that impacts business, an acquisition by a major company, trends in the workplace, the stock market, a new technology, etc.). Also, rate how easy it was for you to understand the article, with "1" being the easiest and "10" being the most difficult. Similarly, rate how interesting the article was, with "1" being absolutely fascinating and "10" being massively boring. Note any questions about the article, and how it relates to material being covered in class, or note from the syllabus or table of contents where it might apply to future class content. As the end of your course approaches, review your log. You should see that the articles are becoming easier to understand, and perhaps more interesting. Plus, you will also have created an informal study of the current business landscape, including the hottest business trends. For example, if you see that a significant percent of the articles are about government actions, it is fair to assume that governments are taking a more active role in business and the economy for some reason. But, above all, this exercise will demonstrate that business—once you really understand it—is far more fascinating than you ever imagined, and it will also help you develop the exceedingly valuable habit of reading the business press regularly, a habit that will serve you well in both life and business.

Step 5: Experience Business.

Business is about people. If you want to be a business success, leave your house and find someone who runs a small business (a restaurant, a print shop, a car wash, etc.) where you are a regular customer because you value the quality of their products. It doesn't matter if you don't have aspirations to work in this line of business, as you are just trying to understand the foundations of any small business that seems successful to you. Ask the owner or manager if you can interview them. Ask them how they spend their time, what is most important to the success of their business, and what their most troublesome problems are. Perhaps, you can even volunteer a few hours per week to do odd chores for them, so you can observe first-hand how they manage the business and continue to ask questions. It may start with meaningless errands, but one day you'll appreciate the foundation when a real opportunity arrives. Until that day, you'll be learning by watching a successful businessperson run a company.

Step 6: Know your learning style.

Determining what kind of learner you are will help you apply the most appropriate resources to create a successful learning program. Knowing your learning style can help you select and use the study strategies that best fit the way you learn.

▼ **Table 1** will help you figure out whether you learn best by seeing (visual), hearing (auditory), or touching/doing (tactile and kinesthetic). Read the word in

▼ **Table 1**

What's Your Learning Style?			
When you . . .	**Visual**	**Auditory**	**Kinesthetic & Tactile**
Spell	☐ You try to see the word.	☐ You sound out the word or use a phonetic approach.	☐ You write the word down to find if it looks right.
Listen	☐ You get easily distracted when asked to listen for a long time.	☐ You grasp the information quickly and easily.	☐ You find yourself doodling as you listen.
Talk	☐ You favor words such as see, picture, and imagine.	☐ You use words such as hear, tune, and think.	☐ You gesture and use expressive movements. You use words such as feel, touch, and hold.
Concentrate	☐ You become distracted by untidiness or movement.	☐ You become distracted by sounds or noises.	☐ You become distracted by activity around you.
Meet someone again	☐ You forget names but remember faces or remember where you met.	☐ You forget faces but remember names or remember what you talked about.	☐ You remember best what you did together.
Contact people for class or business	☐ You prefer direct, face-to-face, personal meetings.	☐ You prefer talking on the phone.	☐ You prefer talking with people while walking or participating in an activity.
Read	☐ You like descriptive scenes or pause to imagine the actions.	☐ You enjoy dialogue and conversation or imagine the characters talking.	☐ You prefer action stories or are not a keen reader.
Do something new at school or work	☐ You like to see demonstrations, diagrams, slides, or posters.	☐ You prefer verbal instructions or talking about it with someone else.	☐ You prefer to jump right in and try it.
Put something together	☐ You look at the directions and the pictures.	☐ You prefer verbal instructions or talking about it with someone else.	☐ You ignore the directions and figure it out as you go along.
Need help with a computer application	☐ You seek out pictures or diagrams.	☐ You call the help desk, ask a neighbor, or growl at the computer.	☐ You keep trying to do it or try it on another computer.
Total			

Source: Adapted from Colin Rose (1987). Accelerated Learning. Source: http://www.chaminade.org/inspire/learnstl.htm

the far left column of the chart and then place a checkmark next to the statement in one of the successive three columns to the right that best describes how you respond to each situation. Count the number of checkmarks in each column, placing the total at the bottom of the table. Your answers may fall into all three columns, but one column will likely contain the most answers which indicate your primary learning style. If one of the remaining columns nears in the number of checkmarks to your primary learning style, that can be considered your secondary learning style.

After you've determined your primary—and perhaps, secondary—learning style, you can best match up the textbook, system, and resources from your instructor to help you achieve a better grade. And, if you can figure out how to succeed in this course, you can apply the same study strategies to succeed in other courses.

Note that your instructor also has a specific style of learning and teaching with which he or she is most comfortable. Watching how your instructor works can be a great clue to helping you succeed in the course. For example, does he or she talk without ever drawing a picture? Or does he or she use visuals to illustrate points? Figure out your instructor's learning style and use it to predict what kinds of interactions he or she wants in the classroom and on your assignments.

Step 7a: Read this book.

What is the best investment you can make in yourself right now? If there were something that could promise you an "A" in this course and that would help you to succeed in college in general, it would be worth paying for, right? There is: this book, plus your time. Really, all you need to succeed in this course is this book and its resources, plus some investment of your own time and energy. Doing well in this course is a good start at getting "A"s in follow-up business courses that you might take in the future. That leads to a great job after graduation, followed by huge wealth, fame, and fortune! (Well, maybe not those last three, but you get the picture.)

Step 7b: Use the system, not just the textbook.

Most likely, when you shelled out the cash to buy your textbook, you thought you were just getting a book, right? As it turns out, you actually bought a "system."

▼ **Table 2** walks you through everything that comes with the purchase of this book. Remembering your learning style, consider how each of these resources can help you study and learn!

▼ **Table 2**

Better Business Resource Guide

Resource	Where is it?	When does it help me?
BizSkills (interactive simulations that let you try out your skills in many common business situations)	On **my***biz*lab.com	For test prep Concept reinforcement
PowerPoint Presentations	On **my***biz*lab.com	Before the chapter starts For test prep
Study Guide	Printed Study Guide or On **my***biz*lab.com	In study groups For test prep Concept reinforcement
Chapter-Specific Videos and Exercises	On **my***biz*lab.com	When you're on the go Concept reinforcement
End of Chapter Exercises	On **my***biz*lab.com or At the end of each chapter	When you're on the go For test prep Concept reinforcement

Step 8: Take awesome notes.

Even if you're a strong auditory learner, you'll benefit from taking notes. Awesome notes are the key when you review and prepare for papers and exams. Take advantage of learning about different types of note-taking strategies. One will certainly work better for your learning style than another. Experiment and see which one best meets your needs. Three popular strategies are outlining, mind mapping, and the Cornell System.

Outlining

You might already use an outlining system. The main points are written down, and any supporting or additional points are indented and listed below the relevant main point. Outlining is a great system for taking notes from a book or PowerPoint presentation since the material has already been organized for you. However, this system may not be as effective to record the points made in a lecture or class discussion, because the hierarchy structure of an outline is not very flexible, and this makes it hard to insert points that are made later on in a discussion but relate to something mentioned earlier.

Mindmapping

A mind map is a graphic representation of the content of a lecture or reading. It is a flexible system, and many visual learners find mindmapping beneficial because it organizes a lecture graphically. ▼ **Figure 1** shows one example.

Mind maps capture main and supporting ideas similar to an outline, but instead of a fixed hierarchy, the structure of a mind-map is more fluid. The main points are captured in a box or circle in the middle of a page. Supporting points, or sub-topics, are then drawn as smaller boxes or circles that radiate from the main circle. If later on another sub-topic needs to be added, then a new branch can be drawn. If there is

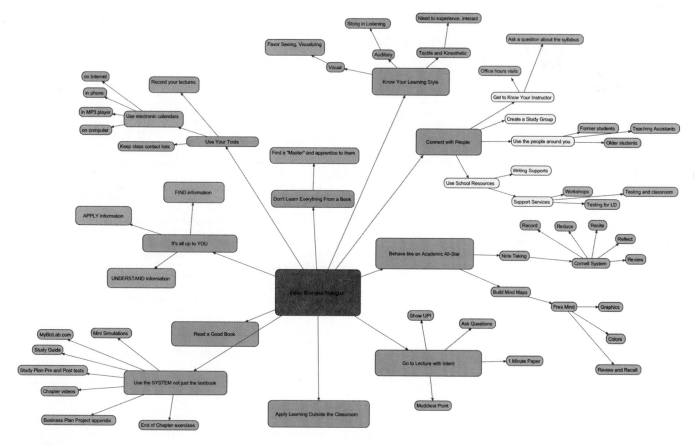

▼ Figure 1
An Example of a Mind Map of this Prologue

anything off-topic that should be noted, it can be recorded in a cloud or circle that is not connected to anything and sits outside the main concept area.

Later on, when reviewing, add colors to connect ideas or concepts that aren't necessarily connected by branches but do share the same theme (such as those topics that your instructor pointed out will be on the test, or that were from a Power-Point presentation, or that should be further explored). As you review for a test or while preparing for a paper, you can use the boxes and colors to help you connect the main ideas of several lectures. Consider creating a *progressive mind map* (separate from individual lecture mind maps) that will express how specific topics relate to the course overall. Many free online resources, including software and templates, can help you begin to use mind maps. One such free product is FreeMind from SourceForge. Even if you just have paper and pencil, you can build useful mind maps.

"I use a mind map to arrange the material before writing a paper. It helps me get all of my ideas on paper and makes the information easier to organize logically."

—*Laura Poatsy,* student

The Cornell System

The Cornell System is a simple and powerful system that, if used correctly, can help with recall and increase the usefulness of your notes. When using the Cornell System, you don't need to rewrite or retype your notes. Instead, you use a specific set-up to define your notes. Begin by setting up your 8½ by 11 inch notepaper as shown in ▼ **Figure 2**. Draw a vertical line 2½ inches from the left side of the page. Next, draw a horizontal line about an inch or so from the bottom of the page for a summary. You can also use a product such as Microsoft One Note, which comes pre-loaded with a Cornell Note System template (see Figure 2).

In the largest and main section of the paper, capture the main ideas of the lecture. You can use an outline or mind mapping system, whichever suites you best. Then, as soon as possible after the lecture, jot down in the skinny column ideas or

▼ **Figure 2**

The One Note Template for the Cornell Note Taking System

Cornell Note-Taking Method

Friday, June 20, 2008
9:12 AM

Cue Column:

As you are taking notes, keep the cue column empty. Soon after the lecture, reduce your notes to concise jottings as clues for reciting, reviewing, and reflecting.

Note-Taking Area:

Record the lecture as fully and as meaningfully as possible.

This format provides the perfect opportunity for following through with the **5 R's** of note-taking:

Record	During the lecture, record in the main column as many meaningful facts and ideas as you can.
Reduce	As soon after as possible, summarize these facts and ideas concisely in the Cue Column. Summarizing clarifies meanings and relationships, reinforces continuity, and strengthens memory.
Recite	Using only your jottings in the Cue Column, say over the facts and ideas of the lecture as fully as you can, not mechanically, but in your own words. Then, verify what you have said.
Reflect	Draw out opinions from your notes and use them as a starting point for your own reflections on the course and how it relates to your other courses. Reflection will help prevent ideas from being inert and soon forgotten.
Review	Spend 10 minutes every week in quick review of your notes, and you will retain most of what you have learned.

This information was taken from the following Web site:
http://www.westshore.edu/webs/ltc/cornell_note_taking_method.htm

Summary Area:

Summarize your notes in a sentence or two.

Extra Tips for the Online Learner

Taking this class online? Here are some additional tips for success:

1. Purchase your textbook and any other course materials before class begins. If you're buying online, allow for delivery time.

2. Check your technology needs. Make sure your computer, software, and Internet connection are sufficient for the requirements of the course before the class starts. Faulty technology is not a good excuse for missing assignments in an online course. Have a backup computer you can use, just in case.

3. Establish a regular study time. Without specific classroom meeting times, it's easy to forget about the class. Time passes quickly and before you know it, your "other life" has taken precedent and you're playing catch-up to meet the requirements of the course. Set a regular study time—one that works with your schedule—when you can log into the class and do whatever work may be required.

4. Be proactive asking questions about assignments. If you have questions on an assignment, remember that sometimes getting answers is not immediate. You should always count on things taking more time than in a classroom.

5. Participate in discussions and ask questions. Your online instructor should provide a way for you to interact with other students and ask questions. Active participation will enable you to grasp the material better—and to know your classmates better.

6. Exchange contact information. Although it's harder to meet and interact with others in an online class, try to get contact information for at least one or two people with whom you can share information and questions.

7. Make sure the instructor knows who you are. Take the time in the first week or so to introduce yourself to the instructor via e-mail or through the class chat room. It's harder for an instructor to get to know you in an online course than in a traditional face-to-face class.

8. Know how to work your class Web site and course management software. Especially know how you can get and submit your assignments, check your grades, and communicate with your instructor, as well as with your classmates.

9. Be organized and don't procrastinate. Especially if the class is self-paced, make sure you know when the big assignments and tests are due. As soon as you get your syllabus, record all assignment due dates on your own personal calendar.

10. Become comfortable expressing your ideas in writing. You'll need to communicate in a professional way about both course content and your future career.

---

key words that will define the main idea of the lecture. Lastly, in the bottom section of the page, summarize the key points in your own words. This forces you to process the information in a new way.

Review

With any of these systems, it will help you to vocalize the key points made as you review your notes. As dorky as it seems, reciting out loud is an effective way to learn, especially if you're an auditory learner, because hearing your thoughts helps you sharpen your thinking process, and stating ideas and facts in your own words challenges you to think about the meaning of the information.

Step 9: Use your tools: cell phone/MP3 player/laptop.

Undoubtedly, you come to class armed with at least a cell phone—and may even have a separate MP3 player and a laptop. Here are a few ideas of how you can use these tools to get you to that "A."

Use a Calendar

Organization is a critical skill for success. Enter assignment deadlines into your cell phone's calendar. You also can use organizational tools such as Microsoft Outlook or Google Calendar to track key due dates and access them from your laptop.

Keep a Class Contact List

Collect the contact information for at least three classmates and for your professor in your cell phone or laptop contact list. Be sure to have it all—home phone, cell phone, IM identity, and e-mail address. This way, you'll have the information at your fingertips when you really need it and don't have your notebook with you. This habit will create all kinds of opportunities for you later in the real world. Successful folks call it "networking"!

Record Audio or Video of the Class

Most MP3 players can be equipped to record audio files, even in stereo. An Apple iPod, for example, can record using a microphone accessory. It could pick up class discussions even if you just sat it by your desk. If your professor is willing to carry yours in his or her pocket and wear a lapel mike, you can be sure to have the best sound quality.

> "Take breaks during a study session—just be sure to come back to the work!"
>
> —*Devin Kownurko*, student

Any cell phone that has a built-in camera can record video. Although the video may be low resolution, it will still be a useful review of what was said back on Tuesday. By adding a larger memory card (many phones now can use 8GB cards) you can record back-to-back lectures with no storage problems.

Laptops equipped with a camera can do the best job of video recording. Cameras such as the Logitech QuickCam Pro 5000 plug right into a USB port and actually track the voice of the lecturer, moving to keep him or her in focus even if he or she walks around the room while lecturing.

Many instructors are now beginning to create their own audio recordings of lectures and deliver them as podcasts to the class. If your instructor is not, ask for permission to record him or her and explain that you are happy to make the files available to him or her or willing to post them to the other students.

Step 10: Apply these rules outside the classroom.

All of these classroom tips also can apply to your career. For example, **Step 7** suggests you find, understand, and apply the information from this textbook system to meet the demands of your instructor. In your working life, you'll need to find out what your boss or client wants and figure out the best way to meet his or her needs. Likewise, **Step 6** encourages you to understand how you best learn. Revisit Table 1—many of the actions apply to a business context as well. Knowing your learning style will help you be successful in business as well as in the classroom.

Because business is all about people, think about how you can apply the strategies in **Step 3** to your job. If you can, get to know your boss or supervisor. They, too, can become your mentors and be instrumental in recommending you for advancement within the company. Bosses don't have office hours, but you can stop by their offices periodically to just say hello or ask to meet them for lunch or coffee every month or so. Get to know the people you work with and develop a contact list. You never know when you may need to contact someone in the office when you're not there, or vice versa. So, get a co-worker's e-mail, home or cell phone numbers, and maybe even his or her IM address. Again, it's much better to have someone in the office to ask, "What did I miss?" or "Can you help me?" than running to your boss (or not having anyone at all) to ask the same questions. Also, don't ignore the other people outside your immediate office. Get to know the cleaning staff, the elevator attendants, and the security guards in your building.

They can help you in a pinch and are more willing to do so if they know your face and name.

To get ahead, follow **Step 2**, and come to work with intent! Don't be afraid to ask questions; good questions indicate that you're thinking about the situation at work and trying to apply it to what you already know. If things don't make sense, or you don't understand something, ask for clarification.

Do you think you won't ever take notes again once you're out of the classroom? Think again. The workday includes attending lots of meetings, even when they occur over the phone. Use your college career and **Step 8** to perfect note taking so when you get to the business world, you'll have that skill down pat. And although you might occasionally get lucky with an instructor that ignores your absences in the classroom, such luck most likely will not follow you into the office. We also suggested ways you can use your cell phone, MP3 player, and laptop in the classroom in **Step 9**. These tools can also be used in the office as well. Again, you need to make sure people know about and agree to your taping/recording them, but having good records of meetings and discussions can be helpful to you and to your colleagues. And because many people are afraid of technology, establishing yourself as someone who is comfortable and innovative with technology can also be a good thing.

Don't stop learning and reading! In **Step 7** we encouraged you to read this book. When you find a career you're interested in pursuing, seek out books for advice and insight about that career. There is no end to learning—it's a lifetime activity, so embrace it. And by following the advice in **Step 4**, you should already have developed a love for reading real-time press. Knowing what is happening in the world around you helps anytime.

Finally, in **Step 5**, we encouraged you to interview a manager or owner of a business, or perhaps even volunteer some of your time. Becoming involved in a business, and learning it from the ground up, puts you in the position of better understanding any business in which you are involved. After all—as we say in **Step 1**: It's all up to you!

We hope you have found these steps to *Better Business* success helpful and hope you will be able to apply them to your academic and professional careers. Good luck in whatever endeavors you pursue!

Business Basics

The Business Landscape

The business landscape in the United States is vast and varied. Steve Chen, Chad Hurley, and Jawed Karim launched the video-sharing Web site YouTube. Meanwhile, the Chang family opened a small Chinese restaurant. What do these seemingly unrelated businesses have in common?

Objective 1 What are profits, and how do for-profit businesses and not-for-profit organizations compare? (pp. 3–4)

Objective 2 What is the difference between a good and a service, and what are the factors of production? (pp. 3–4)

Common Business Challenges and Opportunities

Leroy Washington is the owner of a local deli in Florida. When a Quiznos franchise moved in across the street, Washington had to think creatively to deal with the new competition. How did he manage to keep his small deli in business despite the major franchise across the street?

Objective 3 How do competition, the social environment, globalization, and technological growth challenge and provide opportunities to business owners? (pp. 5–13)

Types of Businesses

Wawa convenience stores are located in the mid-Atlantic region of the United States. Although the chain has over 500 stores, it is still considered a small, regional business. What would Wawa have to do to expand its business and become a national franchise?

Objective 4 What are the four types of businesses? (pp. 14–17)

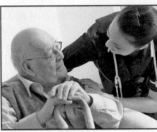

Types of Business Ownership

Estelle Peterson is the sole proprietor of a private-duty nursing business, which she runs out of her home in New York City. She is being harassed by creditors who are trying to seize her personal assets as the result of legal proceedings against her business. Can her creditors legally seize her personal possessions? Can this happen to all business owners?

Objective 5 How do sole proprietorships, partnerships, corporations, and limited liability companies (LLCs) differ from one another as forms of business? (pp. 17–19)

Taking Business Personally

Do you run your life like a business? Managing a business requires many of the same financial and personal skills that you use in your daily life. Understanding how you use business concepts and methods in your life can help you understand how they are used in business.

Objective 6 How do life skills translate to the business environment? (pp. 20–21)

PEARSON **mybizlab**

Adapting to the Economic Environment

As the owner of a chain of regional bakeries, it's your job to stay up to date on business news and keep track of how fiscal and monetary policy changes and other external events might affect your company. Can you make sense of what's going on in the world and keep your company afloat?

Objective 7 Test yourself using my*biz*lab.com to show that you understand the chapter objectives.

The Business Landscape pp. 3–5

n 2005, Steve Chen, Chad Hurley, and Jawed Karim, three 20-something tech company employees, decided to pool their resources and expertise to launch the video-sharing Web site YouTube.[1] The three hatched the idea at a dinner party in San Francisco, and, in less than a year, they developed a Silicon Valley company that became a huge success.

Meanwhile, in a small town in Pennsylvania, the Chang family was developing a plan to open a restaurant. Over three decades ago, the Chang family emigrated from Hong Kong and set out to fulfill their goal of opening a Chinese restaurant. The Changs purchased an existing restaurant from an ad in the local newspaper. Although opening their new business was challenging, the Changs built a reputation for treating people like family and developed a loyal customer base. ■

What do a billion-dollar Web site and a small-town family restaurant have in common? One is a media portal that hosts hundreds of millions of videos, while the other is a family-run eatery in a small town. These organizations represent the varied spectrum of *business* in the United States. In this chapter, you'll learn about the basic skills it takes to run a successful business.

Business Defined

What exactly is a business? Both YouTube and the Changs' Chinese restaurant are **businesses**—entities that offer products to their customers to earn a profit. A **profit** is earned when a company's **revenue** (the money it brings in) is greater than its **expenses** (the money it pays out). When expenses exceed revenue, the company posts a *loss*.

What kinds of products do businesses offer? A product can be either a *good* or a *service*. **Goods** are physical products a business sells. A roast beef sandwich at Arby's, a 42-inch LCD television at Best Buy, and a Honda Civic at your local car dealership are all considered goods because they are tangible items. Conveyer belts, pumps, and sundries sold to other businesses are also goods, even though they are not sold directly to consumers.

On the other hand, a **service** refers to an intangible product that is bought or sold. Services include products such as haircuts, health care, car insurance, and theatrical productions. Unlike a polo shirt on the rack at Hollister, services cannot be physically handled.

Some companies offer products that are both goods *and* services. Take, for example, restaurant franchises like T.G.I. Friday's. When you order a sirloin steak at T.G.I. Friday's, you're paying for the good (a fire-grilled sirloin) as well as the service of preparing, cooking, and serving the steak.

What do businesses do with their profits? More often than not, profit is the driving force behind a business's growth. As more profit is generated, a company can reward its employees, increase its productivity, or expand its business into new areas.

Many not-for-profit organizations, such as the American Diabetes Association, operate like a business but do not pursue profits. Instead, they seek to service their community through social, educational, and political means.

The proprietor of a business is not the only one who benefits from earned profits. A successful business benefits society by providing the goods and the services consumers need and want. Businesses also provide employment opportunities for members of the community. Because they offer desired goods and services, provide employment, and generate income and spending in the economy, successful businesses contribute to people's quality of life by creating higher standards of living for the entire society.

What about not-for-profits? Not-for-profits may operate like a business, but **not-for-profit organizations,** as their name suggests, do not go into business to pursue profits for their owners. Instead, a not-for-profit organization seeks to service its community through social, educational, or political means. Organizations such as universities, hospitals, environmental groups, and charities are not-for-profit organizations because any excess revenue is required to be used to further their stated mission.

The Factors of Production

What do businesses use to create the products they sell? To fully understand how a business operates, you have to consider its **factors of production,** or the resources it uses to produce goods and services. For years, businesses focused on four traditional factors of production: labor, natural resources, capital, and entrepreneurial talent. However, in our twenty-first-century economy, an additional factor has become increasingly important: technology.

- **Labor.** Needless to say, businesses need people to produce goods and provide services. **Labor** is a human resource that refers to any *physical* or *intellectual* work that people contribute to a business's production. Intellectual work refers to the ideas and knowledge contributed by the employees.

- **Natural resources. Natural resources** are the raw materials provided by nature that are used to produce goods and services. Soil used in agricultural production; trees used for lumber to build houses; and coal, oil, and natural gas used to create energy are all examples of natural resources.

- **Capital.** There are two types of capital: *real capital* and *financial capital*. **Real capital** essentially refers to the physical facilities used to produce goods and services, such as office buildings and factories. **Financial capital,** on the other hand, refers to money used to facilitate a business enterprise. Financial capital can be acquired via business loans, from investors, through other forms of fund-raising, or by tapping into personal savings.

- **Entrepreneurial talent.** An **entrepreneur** is someone who assumes the risk of creating, organizing, and operating a business and directs all of a business's resources. Entrepreneurs are a human resource, just like labor, but what sets entrepreneurs apart from labor is not only their willingness to bear risks but also their ability to effectively manage an enterprise. Successful entrepreneurs are rewarded with profits for bearing risks and their managerial expertise.

- **Technology. Technology** refers to items and services such as computers, smartphones, software, and digital broadcasting that make businesses more efficient and productive. Successful companies are able to keep pace with technological progress and harness new knowledge, information, and strategies. Unsuccessful companies often fail because they have not kept pace with the latest technology.

You will learn more about labor (Chapter 9), capital (Chapter 15), entrepreneurs (Chapter 5), and technology (Chapter 10) as you continue to read the text.

Recall the examples of YouTube and the Changs' Chinese restaurant. YouTube provides a service to its users: the ability to use a media platform to exchange video information. The Changs provide goods to their customers in the form of the food they sell. They also provide a service in the form of the preparation and delivery of that food. Although the business models and products offered by these businesses vary considerably, the two businesses are similar because they were both started by creative entrepreneurs determined to make a profit. For Steve Chen, Chad Hurley, and Jawed Karim, these profits came in the form of billions when YouTube was sold to Google for $1.7 billion in 2006.[2] For the Chang family, the profits are much more modest; they make a solid living but are far from seeing a 10-figure profit. Although these two enterprises differ greatly in many ways, both the Changs and the founders of YouTube have realized a dream by starting a successful business. ■

Common Business Challenges and Opportunities pp. 5–14

In 1998, Leroy Washington inherited his family's deli. The deli had a loyal clientele with a regular lunch crowd. However, a Quiznos franchise moved into a building directly across the street. As a national franchise, it had a great deal of name recognition from print ads and commercials. It also had a larger space, more workers and ovens, and a more extensive menu. Leroy found his lunch crowd dwindling as people switched to the national chain with its faster service and greater variety of sandwiches. To be competitive with Quiznos, Leroy had to become creative. Instead of just offering traditional deli choices, his deli expanded its menu to include Cuban pressed sandwiches and an "early bird special" light fare dinner menu. Leroy hoped that the changes would appeal to the large number of Cuban immigrants and senior citizens populating the area. ■

Dealing with competition is just one of the many challenges that business owners such as Leroy Washington face in a twenty-first century economy. However, as Leroy found, confronting these challenges can sometimes lead to opportunities for growth as well. In this section, we'll discuss how competition, the social environment, globalization, and technological change manifest themselves as both challenges and opportunities in the business world.

Competition

How does competition influence business? In a market-based economy, such as that in the United States, there is an emphasis on individual economic freedom and a limit on governmental intervention. In this type of market, competition is a fundamental force. **Competition** arises when two or more businesses contend with one another to attract customers and gain an advantage. The private

enterprise system in the United States is predicated on the fact that competition benefits consumers because it motivates businesses to produce a wider variety of better and cheaper goods and services.

Competition in Today's Marketplace

Customer Satisfaction and Beyond   A competitive environment is where a free-market economy thrives. Competition forces companies to improve their product offerings, lower their prices, aggressively promote their brands, and focus on customer satisfaction. Having to compete for a finite number of consumers usually weeds out less efficient companies and less desirable products from the marketplace. Because profit is the ultimate goal, it is the job of a successful business to convince customers that its product is either better or less expensive than that of its competitors.

For example, consider the explosion in sales of blu-ray players over the last few years. Because more manufacturers and retailers have jumped into the HDTV market, prices for HDTV sets fell drastically in 2008.[3] This created a market of people hungry for blu-ray players to provide high-definition programming for the new sets. In fact, the sales of blu-ray players—once the sole dominion of high-end retailers and manufacturers—increased 72 percent in the first quarter of 2009.[4] Because customers are able to find moderately priced blu-ray players at such diverse retailers as Amazon .com, Costco, and Best Buy, prices have come down because these companies are able to turn over merchandise quickly and in high volume, which allows them to narrow the margin between the price they pay and the price the customer pays. At the same time, consumer electronics specialty stores, such as Audio Vision in San Francisco, compete by offering exceptional customer service and a more personalized buying experience. Audio Vision knows that keeping customers happy is a key to its success.

Social Networking   Sites like Facebook, MySpace, Twitter, Ning, and many others are examples of social-networking sites. **Social networking** describes a set of services focused on building and supporting social relationships among people, for example, connecting old friends or people who share activities. People can quickly communicate with others by posting text, photos, and videos; they are automatically alerted when someone posts new information or comments on their site.

Facebook (Facebook.com) is probably the best-known social-networking site, with over 400 million user accounts. Twitter (Twitter.com) is another social-networking site. Users can choose to follow different Twitter accounts and are automatically alerted if a person they are following posts new information on their Twitter account.

What does all this have to do with business competition? Today more than ever, customers are connected to each other through a great variety of media—e-mail, texting, blogs, and social-networking sites. Companies are therefore increasingly using social networking to connect to their customers. Through these sites, they can promote their products, offer discounts, and build relationships with people interested in their company. Individuals can use social-networking sites to quickly spread the word about very good (or very bad) services or products. If a customer is dissatisfied, word can spread like the speed of light—very fast. Similarly, as we'll see later in the book, a happy customer base can be a powerful marketing tool for a company.

Other social-networking sites are used commonly in business. LinkedIn, for example, connects over 70 million professionals. LinkedIn users exchange résumés and build networking contacts by connecting with old acquaintances, former employers, and coworkers.

Employee Empowerment   In a competitive environment, it is essential for a company to empower workers to feel free to deal with customer needs. This means employers seek workers who have interpersonal, communication, and decision-making

Biz**Chat**

Apple: Taking a Bite Out of Microsoft?

Apple and Microsoft have a history of bitter rivalry revolving around the desire to dominate the personal computer (PC) market. The main point of contention between these companies was the graphical user interface (GUI), which is the user interface for the main program that runs PCs. Apple released the first GUI, which included folders and long file names, in 1983. When Microsoft released Windows 2.0 in 1988, Apple took Microsoft to court, complaining that the "look and feel" of the Windows interface was stolen from the Apple interface. This suit continued until 1992 when Apple finally lost.

Microsoft led the competition in the early 1990s. It became an industry standard to have Windows operating systems preinstalled on most PCs, which were dominating the computer market at the time. The 10-year battle finally ended when Apple announced an official alliance with Microsoft in 1997. Microsoft and Apple agreed to a 5-year deal in which Microsoft would continue to develop Office software for Apple computers and Apple agreed to bundle Microsoft's Internet Explorer in all its operating systems.[5]

So competition can create new partnerships—strange ones at times. Today, Microsoft is actively wooing Apple, trying to place its search engine, Bing, as the default on the Apple iPhone.[6] This would replace the Google search engine the iPhone has always used. What's in it for Apple? Google has become one of Apple's main competitors in the mobile phone market with its Android phone platform. The element of competition between these rival high-tech companies drives them all to keep innovating and produce higher-quality products than if no one challenged them.

For more information and discussion questions about this topic, check out the BizChat feature on my**biz**lab.com.

skills. Companies today need to be more reactive to customers' needs to retain their competitive advantage. Therefore, more companies are placing greater decision-making responsibilities on employees, rather than having decisions trickle down through layers of management. This also means greater employee satisfaction and more career advancement opportunities.

Social Environment

How does the social environment affect businesses? A **social environment** is an interconnected system of different demographic factors, such as race, ethnicity, gender, age, income distribution, sexual orientation, and other characteristics. Social, economic, and political movements and trends cause the social environment in the United States to constantly change. An influx of immigrants can change the racial demographic, or an economic slump can change the income distribution demographic. These changes affect where we live, what we buy, and how we choose to spend our money. To best serve their employees, customers, and the community, businesses must consider the shifts and changes in the social environment when making decisions. Let's discuss three specific issues surrounding the social environment that present potential challenges and opportunities for today's businesses.

An Aging Population

Not only are older Americans living longer, healthier lives, but they are also better educated, are wealthier, and have achieved a higher standard of living than previous generations. *Baby boomers*, the generation born between 1946 and 1964, represent the majority of the aging population in the United States. Not only do the 78 million baby boomers make up the largest population group in the United

States, but they are also the wealthiest. Baby boomers, who in 2011 were between the ages of 47 and 65, have an estimated spending power of over $2 trillion per year. This makes baby boomers a large and lucrative target for businesses. For example, the cosmetics company Garnier is eager to make a profit from the aging population by releasing an antiaging beauty line called UltraLift that is aimed at baby boomer women. Garnier is hoping this keeps its product offerings aligned with the shift in demographics—a change in the social environment.

Although an aging population presents many opportunities for businesses, it also presents challenges for the U.S. economy. Ben Bernanke, chairman of the Federal Reserve, has warned that the nation will be faced with difficult choices as baby boomers reach retirement age. Some potential problems include higher taxes, a reduction in government spending on entitlement programs such as Social Security and Medicare benefits, and a higher federal budget deficit. This is primarily because economic forecasters predict a shift in the demographics of the United States.

Why does this matter? As shown in ▼ **Figure 1.1** in the year 2050, there will be over 80 million Americans age 65 or older. Today, almost 40 percent of the total personal income for senior citizens comes from Social Security payments. Together these trends imply that there will be a decrease in the number of workers and an increase in the demand for social services. Longevity is another aspect of this demographic shift; in 2005, there were 68,000 centenarians (people age 100 or older) in the United States.[7] Projections place that number at 580,000 by 2040. The health-care costs and services required to care for this population will need to be in place.

Along with these challenges, as we noted above, caring for the needs of an older population will present businesses with opportunities for growth, especially for the health-care, pharmaceutical, and travel industries. After all, a bigger population translates to a larger market for these goods and services.

Increasing Diversity

In business, there is no one-size-fits-all method to managing employees and appealing to customers because every person is different. As the United States becomes more diverse, it is important for businesses to mirror that diversity in their workforce. According to the latest data available, the U.S. Census Bureau reports that the minority population in the United States is about 35 percent, making one in three residents a minority. In some companies, minorities account for the majority of the workforce. At the hotel chain Four Seasons, for example, minorities represent 66 percent of the company's 12,600 employees.[8]

However, in today's business climate, increasing and managing a company's diversity involves more than just employing an ethnically diverse workforce. Companies must also develop a diversity initiative that outlines their goals and objectives for managing, retaining, and promoting a diverse workforce. A diversity initiative might include a nondiscrimination policy, a minority network, or diversity education. According to Frank Dobbin, a sociology professor at Harvard University, "To increase diversity, executives must treat it like any other business goal."[9]

Although the inclusion and advancement of racial minorities in the workplace is an important step in establishing a diverse

▼**Figure 1.1**
U.S. Population Age 65 and Over: 1990–2050

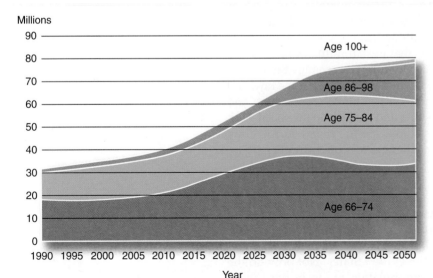

Millions

Age 100+

Age 86–98

Age 75–84

Age 66–74

1990 1995 2000 2005 2010 2015 2020 2025 2030 2035 2040 2045 2050

Year

workforce, it is only part of the process. Today, the term *minority* applies to more than just people of different ethnicities. Minority groups might represent a person's gender, culture, religion, sexual orientation, or disability. Companies must include these minority groups in their diversity initiative to ensure that all minority employees are treated fairly by management and coworkers.

The Green Movement

In a recent United Nations (UN) study, many of the world's most respected environmental scientists reported that the threat of global warming and climate change is real.[10] As environmental anxieties become prevalent throughout society, it is important for businesses to become involved in a **green economy**—one that factors ecological concerns into business decisions. Businesses that manufacture products that contribute to higher emissions of carbon dioxide and consume inordinate amounts of fossil fuels must adapt to this new environmental awareness if they want to be relevant in a green economy.

In the automotive industry, for example, hybrid vehicles, which run on a combination of electricity and gasoline, have become not only hot sellers but also critical to meeting national objectives. In 2009, President Barack Obama proposed a new national fuel economy program. The program ultimately requires an average fuel economy standard from automobile manufacturers of 35.5 miles per gallon (mpg) of gas in 2016 (39 mpg for cars and 30 mpg for trucks), a jump from the current average for all vehicles of 25 mpg. Obama said, "The status quo is no longer acceptable."[11] Almost every major car manufacturer—including Toyota, Honda, and BMW—now offer hybrid models. Hybrids have become part of our popular culture, with references on shows like *Curb Your Enthusiasm* and nightly comedy programming.

A focus on environmental issues also opens up a brand new market that will be increasingly important in the future. The demand for more green products presents new opportunities for entrepreneurs to meet those needs. These "green-collar" jobs can revitalize large swathes of the U.S. manufacturing economy that have been decimated. Creating wind energy turbines, installing solar panels, and landscaping designs that make your microclimate (the climate immediately surrounding your home) energy efficient will be necessary businesses of the twenty-first century.

The Social Environment and You

As a prospective employee, any one of these social issues will probably affect the company for which you end up working. Because workers are increasingly retiring

A focus on environmental issues is opening up markets such as wind turbines that will become increasingly important in the future.

at later ages, competition for certain jobs and career advancement might be fiercer than in years past. On the other hand, the culture of business is constantly shifting to meet the ever-evolving needs of U.S. demographics. This means more opportunity for employees who can navigate a diverse environment. In addition, jobs aimed at responding to the needs of the growing green economy will also likely present new opportunities for job seekers. Entrepreneurial possibilities always exist for those who have the vision and desire to succeed and are willing to take risks.

Globalization

How has globalization affected businesses? You're probably familiar with multinational companies such as Nike, McDonald's, and Coca-Cola. **Multinational enterprises**—companies that have operations in more than one country—are among the leaders of a movement called globalization. **Globalization** is a movement toward a more interconnected and interdependent world economy. This means that economies around the world are merging as technology, goods and services, labor, and capital move back and forth across international borders. For example, FedEx, the world's largest express transportation company, conducts business in more than 220 countries and territories around the world.[12]

The effects of globalization on the business world vary widely, from economic transformation in India to the shutting down of major manufacturing plants in the United States. The Internet and modern technological advances are making it possible for a company of any size from anywhere in the world to compete globally. Lower tariffs and other trade restrictions give U.S. companies the option to export or import goods to and from other countries or conduct their business overseas. Instead of building their products in plants at home, a growing number of companies are relocating their production facilities overseas or subcontracting at least some of the components of their products to foreign companies around the world to achieve lower manufacturing costs. This is called **offshoring.** The low labor costs in countries such as China and India make these countries ideal locations for multinational companies seeking technology services and manufactured products at a low cost.

Although the concept of globalization is essential for many companies, it is still a highly controversial subject for many. Globalization presents both benefits and risks to the U.S. economy. For example, lowered production costs allow prices on consumer products to decrease, meaning that you as a consumer benefit by purchasing goods at lower prices. Yet concerns remain about workers in the United States who lose their jobs to workers overseas. Globalization poses other risks for U.S. companies, including the following:

- Increased competition from international companies
- Fluctuations in the value of the U.S. dollar
- Security and patent protection concerns
- Unstable political climates in foreign countries

Globalization has therefore sparked fierce debates among politicians, businesspeople, and the general public for the past few decades. We'll discuss the controversies surrounding globalization in greater depth in Chapter 4.

Benefits and risks aside, one thing is for sure: Globalization is here to stay. To stay competitive in the global market, companies must work to enhance quality and develop and implement innovative strategies for the long term. The increasingly global nature of business increases the demand for workers who can communicate with international business partners, have up-to-date technological talents, can demonstrate excellent communication and creative problem-solving skills, and possess leadership skills.

Globalization makes it possible for the German company Nivea to manufacture some of its products in Shanghai. These products later turn up on store shelves in the United States and other countries around the world.

Technological Changes

Why does the pace of technological change present challenges to businesses today? Over the past 20 years, advancements in information technology (IT) have been revolutionary. In today's business world, companies must stay on the cutting edge of technology to remain competitive. No matter the business, technology can be used to keep a company flexible, organized, and well connected—either with customers or employees. There is no question that keeping up with the pace of technology is an expensive and time-consuming operation. The rapid pace of technological innovation means that computers are often outdated after three years and obsolete after five.[13] Add to that the cost of applicable software, training, and infrastructure, and it is no wonder that IT is often the single largest expense for many companies.[14] But cost isn't the only challenge to consider. In the same way that robotics completely revolutionized the automotive industry, advancements in computer and telecommunication technology are completely changing the foundation and focus of how many businesses are run.

What benefits does technology provide to business? Technology, when used and implemented effectively, can help streamline businesses and cut costs. For example, many new tools, such as Twitter and Facebook, have been created that promote better communications with customers. Companies can also use new technology systems to increase productivity. Giving employees what they need to get their work done more efficiently and effectively is the simplest way to increase productivity. If employees can get more work done in a shorter amount of time, productivity increases. When employees are more productive, they are more valuable. This, in turn, makes the whole company more valuable. But technological benefits aren't limited to just helping employees; they streamline the internal operations of a business so the entire business can be more effective, efficient, and productive.

> *"The number one benefit of information technology is that it empowers people to do what they want to do. It lets people be creative. It lets people be productive. It lets people learn things they didn't think they could learn before, and so in a sense it is all about potential."*[15]
>
> —Steve Ballmer, CEO, Microsoft

Thirty years ago, businesses were often centrally located, with all employees in one building. Today, this is less common. Technology is making it possible for employees

Technology makes it possible to work from virtually anywhere. Is that a good thing?

to **telecommute,** or work from home or another location away from the office. The virtual global workforce, or telecommuters who work on a global scale, expands the pool of potential employees so that the right employee can be found for the job no matter where he or she works. In fact, the worldwide population of mobile workers is expected to top one billion in 2011.[16] Teleconferencing is keeping CEOs and other corporate representatives from having to travel constantly for meetings. It is also allowing companies to communicate easily, no matter the distance. Both of these advancements are saving money on what used to be necessary expenses. With less travel, there is less money spent on plane tickets, hotel rooms, and food. With more employees telecommuting, many businesses can operate out of smaller offices, which are cheaper and easier to manage. The reduction in travel and other services also has an impact on the environment, consuming less energy and resources.

What role does the Internet play in technological growth? If IT is the tool that is changing the function of business, the Internet is the tool that is changing the scope of business. Although IT by itself would be extremely influential for the business world, the Internet makes it truly revolutionary. In 1995, the Internet was just starting to proliferate. Even though it had been commercially available for years at that point, the Internet had only recently become viable after the advent of the World Wide Web a few years before. Many people were intimidated by this new technology, and there weren't high hopes for companies that operated solely on the Internet. But this changed in 1995 when both eBay and Amazon.com launched. These companies showed that such an endeavor was not only possible but also potentially lucrative. Their high-profile success paved the way for the general acceptance of public e-commerce. We'll discuss business technology in more detail in Chapter 10.

E-commerce

E-commerce primarily consists of two different kinds of business: *business-to-consumer* (B2C) and *business-to-business* (B2B). B2C interactions are the ones you're probably most familiar with, such as buying books at Amazon.com or songs or movies from iTunes. B2C interactions take place between a business and a consumer. B2B interactions involve the sale of goods and services, such as personalized or proprietary software, from one business to another. Although both are fairly similar in many ways, the ways in which they differ are significant. B2B e-commerce often involves large transactions to few customers, customized products and pricing, and numerous managers from both businesses making sure that the transaction is beneficial to both parties. This process is obviously more involved than typical B2C transactions, such as downloading a new ringtone for your cell phone or bidding on an item listed on eBay.

Every year, e-commerce becomes a more significant element of the overall economy. E-commerce has been growing rapidly since the new millennium, forcing many businesses to either adapt or be left in the dust. For example, in 2009, Bob MacDonald, the

CEO of Procter & Gamble (P&G), announced plans to expand electronic sales of its products from $500 million to $4 billion annually, using Amazon.com and the firm's own Web sites.[17] As ▼ **Figure 1.2** shows, over 85 percent of worldwide Internet users have made online purchases. So far this trend shows no sign of stopping. As it becomes easier for consumers to find even the most obscure items at competitive prices, e-commerce will continue to be a driving force in our economy.

It is important to note that the commercialization of the Internet has been around only less than two decades. The Internet, as a medium for sales, has yet to reach its full potential. As the Internet and its influence continue to grow, so will its economic importance and necessity for businesses. This growth will also affect the dangers and concerns that are associated with such prevalence.

Online Security

The widespread access to information that the Internet affords affects businesses in a variety of ways. Personal information such as Social Security numbers, credit card numbers, addresses, and passwords are all accessible online. This sensitive information, even when it is secured, can be vulnerable to hackers. Because businesses often store this and other types of personal information, the responsibility is on them to take measures to protect the online security of all their customers. It's no coincidence that as the number of people and businesses who trade and store personal information online rises, so does the number of people who are victims of **identity theft**— the illegal gain and use of personal information. The *Wall Street Journal* reported in 2009 that 9.9 million Americans fell victim to identity theft in 2009.[18] This was a 22 percent increase, and the loss per incident also rose. The need for more awareness of personal online security and better tools to ensure corporate online security is clear.

Privacy

Privacy is another important issue for businesses. E-mails, internal documents, and chat transcripts all contain private information that is not intended for public viewing. Nevertheless, many of these documents can be accessed online because online storage has become a convenient alternative to hard drives. Web e-mail and Web-based documents are also becoming more common. Even gaining access to your desktop at work or at home from a remote location is a simple process that is becoming more popular. And with all this universal access, it is increasingly difficult to ensure that information remains private. Web-based storage and services offer many benefits to business. Yet privacy and security concerns cannot be overlooked. Over time, technology will continue to introduce challenges.

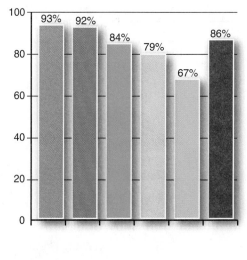

- Western Europe
- North America
- Asia-Pacific
- Latin America
- Eastern Europe, Middle East, and Africa
- Worldwide

▼ **Figure 1.2**
Online Buyers Among Internet Users Worldwide

Review the story about Leroy Washington. When competition from a national franchise threatened his business, Leroy confronted the challenge head-on. To capitalize on the diversity of the area—particularly the sizable populations of both Latinos and seniors—Leroy expanded his menu. His strategy was a success. The Cuban pressed sandwiches became a local favorite. Moreover, the deli was soon packed every day from 3:30 to 5:30 PM, when the "early bird special" fare—consisting of sandwiches, soups, and salads at reasonable prices—was offered. As Leroy Washington demonstrated, challenges and opportunities abound and overlap in the business world. ■

Types of Businesses pp. 14–17

I n 1964, Grahame Wood opened a convenience store in Folsom, Pennsylvania. The business's focus was on providing fresh dairy products and produce and a full-service delicatessen. This marked the beginning of the Wawa chain of convenience stores, which serve the mid-Atlantic region of the United States. The chain now consists of over 570 stores in five states.[19] Although Wawa is certainly successful, it's still a regional company that does not currently serve a national or international market. Regional businesses such as Wawa face unique challenges that don't affect larger businesses, especially involving access to adequate funding and insurance. Wawa continues to expand in the mid-Atlantic region and may one day move into the category of a national business. Is that the best move for this regional chain? ■

What's the difference between a small business and a large corporation? What about everything in between? A small business has different goals and challenges than a large corporation. Small businesses often provide limited goods or services to a small population, such as a local dry cleaner. A large multinational corporation, such as P&G, supplies a wide range of goods or services to many countries. A local or regional business will have very different needs and concerns. In this section, we'll look at the different types of businesses and what constitutes each.

Local and Regional Businesses

What defines local or regional businesses? Take a walk around your town or city, and you'll see a variety of local and regional businesses. Used bookstores, bakeries, shoe repair shops, boutiques, restaurants, and specialty shops are often local businesses. A **local business** is usually one of a kind, and it relies on local consumers to generate business. A company is local if it serves a limited surrounding area. A local catering company in Baltimore, for example, might have one kitchen and cater events in Baltimore and its surrounding suburbs. Local companies generally have a small number of employees and are associated with the town or city in which they are located. **Regional businesses** serve a wider area although, like local companies, they do not serve a national or international market. Wawa is an example of a regional convenience store.

What special challenges do local and regional businesses face? The most common challenge for local and regional businesses is managing money. Poor financial planning, as well as unfavorable economic conditions, can lead to bankruptcy. **Undercapitalization** occurs when a business owner cannot gain access to adequate funding. When a business can no longer afford to produce goods or provide services, it goes bankrupt. The owner must anticipate the cost of doing business and estimate the revenue that the business will generate. To avoid going into debt, the owner should have enough projected revenue to cover expenses for at least the first year. So if the owner of a local catering company has $100,000 in expenses and expects to generate $75,000 in the first year of business, then the owner should have at least $25,000 to fund the company. Even with adequate funding, there is always a chance that the economy will not support the business. Many small businesses fail when the economy slows down because consumers are less likely to spend extra money.

▼ **top**
10 *Forbes'* **Best Small Companies of 2009**[20]

1. Lumber Liquidators
2. Allegiant Travel
3. Quality Systems
4. LHC Group
5. Green Mountain Coffee Roasters
6. Transcend Services
7. Rackspace Hosting
8. NV Energy
9. American Public Education
10. American Science and Engineering

Business owners also have to take taxes and insurance costs into consideration, such as a health insurance plan to cover employees. They also need liability insurance, which will protect the company in the event of stolen or damaged property or if an employee is injured on the job. If a local jewelry store is broken into and jewelry is stolen, liability insurance will cover the cost of the broken window and the stolen property. If the jewelry store is not insured, the business could go bankrupt if the owner can't afford to cover the loss and damages.

National Businesses

Businesses like Old Navy are national businesses in that they have locations throughout the United States but do not serve an international market.

What defines national businesses in the United States? If you drive from New York to Los Angeles, you'll most likely encounter a CVS/pharmacy somewhere along the way. CVS/pharmacy has over 7,000 locations and can be found anywhere in the United States.[21] All CVS/pharmacy locations essentially look alike and carry similar merchandise—all within a similar price range. With companies such as this, the customer knows what to expect. A **national business** has several outlets throughout the country, but it does not serve an international market. It provides goods or services to virtually all U.S. residents, no matter where in the country they live. A car insurance company such as Allstate is another example of a national business. It has offices in 49 states and serves the entire country. National companies have become standard symbols of U.S. business.

What special challenges do national companies face? Like local and regional companies, national companies also have to worry about their budget and managing their finances. But they have other concerns that local businesses don't have. Because laws vary from state to state, national companies must be aware of state laws in every state where they do business. For example, each state has its own tax laws. In most states, retail businesses are required to apply for a state sales tax permit to be able to collect sales tax from their customers. Every state imposes a corporate income tax, but the rate varies across states. And some states, such as New Jersey and Rhode Island, require businesses to pay for temporary disability insurance.[22] These laws can be difficult to keep up with and prevent companies from having standardized operational policies.

Another challenge that national companies face is a longer, more complex supply chain. The **supply chain** is the process by which products, information, and money move between supplier and consumer (see ▼ **Figure 1.3**). The product flows

▼ **Figure 1.3**
The Supply Chain

(a) Supplier (b) Manufacturer (c) Wholesaler (d) Retailer (e) Consumer

from supplier to manufacturer to wholesaler to retailer to consumer. If the product is returned, it flows from the consumer back to the retailer. Information flow includes orders and delivery status, and financial flow includes manufacturing costs, payment, credit terms, and profit.

Let's look at an example of a supply chain. When you go to Target to buy a bottle of Tide detergent, you are a part of the supply chain, as is the Target store itself. Target's stock of Tide was supplied by a distributor, whose supply of detergent came from its supplier, P&G. P&G has its own set of suppliers providing the chemicals and packaging materials required to manufacture the detergent.

The bigger a business is, the longer and more complicated its supply chain becomes. If not managed properly, long supply chains can be inefficient because products and materials have to pass through more warehouses and sustain more shipments. Products may get backed up in long supply chains, which can result in delayed shipments and late payments. A lack of communication among companies in the chain can cause mix-ups and delays, especially if there is a sudden change in the process. A national company must therefore rely on the cooperation of all members of the supply chain to keep the business running smoothly.

Multinational (International) Businesses

What categorizes a company as multinational (or international)?
As we discussed earlier, *multinational businesses* make and/or sell products in several countries. They are businesses that have expanded to provide goods or services to international consumers or serve only one country but have suppliers or production facilities in other countries. For example, you can now find a McDonald's restaurant in more than 119 countries, all serving distinctly U.S. food.[23] However, not every McDonald's restaurant is exactly the same. They have all been adapted to fit the culture of the country in which they are located. For example, if you enter a McDonald's restaurant in some parts of Canada, you'll see a McLobster on the menu. The McAloo Tikki Burger is a vegetarian sandwich made with potatoes, peas, and spices served in McDonald's restaurants in India. Because of the large Hindu population in India, beef is not used in any of their menu items.[24] This is the nature of multinational businesses.

What special challenges do multinational corporations face?
Every country has different corporate laws and business practices, and multinational corporations must be familiar with the laws of the countries in which they operate. Laws concerning the import and export of goods vary greatly from one country to another. Things can get particularly complicated if a product is shipped to one country for assembly, another for packaging, and then yet another country for distribution. Often, several countries are involved in the manufacture of one product, in which case the laws and regulations of all those countries must be adhered to. It might be necessary for a U.S. company to work with the governments of foreign countries if there are strict importing restrictions or a multitude of taxes. Safety regulations, quality control, copyrights, and patent rights are just some of the laws that multinational corporations must keep in mind when doing business in foreign countries.

Cultural differences have as much impact as legal differences on international business. Some of these issues, which we'll discuss further in Chapter 4, include the following:

- Countries may have different business hours or workweek schedules. For example, in Spain, workers tend to take lunch from 1:30 to 3:30 P.M.
- Values and customs relating to business etiquette may vary. For example, timeliness is valued in Germany, but it is less important in Italy.
- Violating local taboos can be a concern, such as the preference for group harmony in many Asian countries.

- Multinational companies may have difficulty determining wages for foreign workers and pricing for international markets.
- The language barrier presents a challenge to businesses that are trying to establish themselves in foreign countries.

Multinational companies also must contend with many important economic differences among countries, such as the different levels of economic development, interest rates, and inflation rates that make international business more complicated than purely domestic business.

The move from being a regional business to a national, or even multinational, business is an exciting one, but it also brings a new set of challenges. Wawa currently deals with those issues that impact a regional company. In fact, the company has reached saturation in the five-state market (New Jersey, Maryland, Pennsylvania, Delaware, and Virginia) it controls. However, recent attempts to expand into nearby states, such as Connecticut, have proved challenging, as Wawa had difficulty finding the right locations and replicating its focus on customer service and teamwork outside its regional base.[25] Instead of expanding toward being a national chain, Wawa has begun moving into gas retailing, creating superstores that include the traditional Wawa convenience center and also a gas station. Clearly, businesses must proceed carefully when making such decisions. ∎

Types of Business Ownership pp. 17–19

Estelle Peterson runs a private-duty nursing business out of her home. She is the sole proprietor of this business, which gives her a great deal of freedom in deciding how her business should be run. While Estelle has been moderately successful in her business for several years, she has recently experienced a series of setbacks. These setbacks are a result of several lawsuits that have been filed against her company, due to the illegal conduct of two nurses on her staff. She is struggling to pay off her growing legal debts, and creditors are calling her with threats of asset seizure. What does she do now? ∎

Every company, no matter how large or small, begins with an idea. When this idea turns into a business, it can take one of several different ownership structures, each with its own advantages and disadvantages. The most common types are *sole proprietorship*, *partnership*, and *corporation*. Let's take a brief look at these types of business formats, as well as *LLCs* (see ▼ **Table 1.1**). We'll discuss them in more detail in Chapter 6.

Sole Proprietorship

A **sole proprietorship** is a business that is owned by one person. A sole proprietorship does not need to register with the state, and it is not legally separated from the owner. This means the company's debts are the responsibility of the owner, and the owner pays personal income tax, rather than corporate taxes, on his or her profits. A sole proprietorship is simpler to operate and is under less government regulation than other businesses, but there is also more risk involved. If the company is

▼ **Table 1.1**

Comparisons of Business Ownership Forms				
	Sole Proprietorship	**Partnership**	**Corporation**	**LLC**
Business Documentation	None	Written or oral agreement	Articles of incorporation	Articles of organization
Risk	Unlimited liability	Unlimited liability	Limited liability	Limited liability
Taxes	Taxed as personal income	Taxed as personal income	Separate filing, double taxed	Taxed as personal income (can vary)
Management	Owner manages entire business	Partners share management	Managed by owners and shareholders	Managed by members

sued, the owner is liable. If the company owes a debt that the business can't afford to pay, the creditors can legally collect personal assets, such as funds from the owner's retirement accounts, property, or cars. A sole proprietorship is not protected by *limited liability*, which would require owners to be responsible only for losses up to the amount they invested. Limited liability safeguards personal assets from being seized as payment for debts or claims.

Partnership

A business owned by two or more people that is not registered with the state as a corporation or an LLC is a **partnership**. The owners of a partnership pay tax on their portion of the business income instead of corporate taxes. Each owner is also responsible for paying off any debts or lawsuits. Therefore, similar to a sole proprietorship, if business assets are not sufficient to meet business debts, debtors can collect personal assets from all business owners. However, unlike a sole proprietorship, profits and liability in a partnership are shared between two or more people.

There are two types of partnerships: general and limited. A **general partnership** is simpler and less expensive to establish and pools the talent of partners, but it carries more risk for all partners because they are all financially liable and are not protected by limited liability. In a general partnership, every partner participates in the daily management tasks of the business, and they all have some degree of control over the decisions that are made. In a **limited partnership,** there is at least one partner who controls business operations and is personally liable. The other partners are limited partners and don't have much, if any, control over management decisions. They contribute capital to the business and are protected by limited liability.

Corporation

A **corporation** is a business that is a legal entity separate from the owner or owners. The business owners have limited liability, so they are not personally responsible for debts incurred by the company. If someone sues Microsoft, for example, the plaintiff can collect money from the corporation but cannot take Bill Gates's car.

◎ On Target Nantucket Nectars: Tom and Tom's Partnership

Tom First and Tom Scott were college buddies who did not want to climb the traditional corporate ladder. After graduating from Brown University, the friends moved to Nantucket, Massachusetts, and started a floating convenience store called Allserve. Based from Tom and Tom's red boat in Nantucket Harbor, the company provided delivery service of almost any item, from newspapers to laundry, to neighboring boats. While Allserve proved to be a modest success, the pair soon had another idea. They decided to sell their own natural juice blend, and Nantucket Nectars was born. Popularity of the juice spread quickly in Nantucket, and Allserve purchased a distribution company to expand the reach of its products. While many national chains are now carrying their products, Tom and Tom maintained their local roots by starting the Juice Guys Juice Bar in Nantucket.[26] This partnership is an example of how a successful business can be started by two eager and driven people. Tom and Tom have come a long way since their days as floating delivery boys in Nantucket Harbor, and they are now running a nationally recognized corporation.

Although incorporating a business protects the business owners from personal bankruptcy, complex paperwork must be filed to establish and run the corporation, which can sometimes make running a business more complicated. When a business incorporates, it must do the following:

1. Keep thorough financial records that detail every transaction the business makes.
2. Report income generated by the business in separate corporate tax returns. If some of the profits are paid to owners (stockholders), then that income to them is taxed again as personal income. So, corporate profits can be taxed twice.

It is up to the business owners to decide whether the advantages of incorporating a business are worth the extra work.

Limited Liability Company

Another business format that is relatively new is called a **limited liability company (LLC),** which blends the characteristics of both corporations and sole proprietorships and/or partnerships. Like corporations, LLCs are companies in which the owners have limited personal liability for the debts and actions of the company. They require complex paperwork to establish and, like traditional corporations, are separate legal entities. However, LLCs provide the advantage of avoiding double taxation often associated with corporations, and the tax forms are much simpler. LLCs are also simpler to maintain than corporations because they are subject to fewer government regulations and reporting requirements. The owners of an LLC are called *members*. In most states, LLCs may be single member, that is, owned by one person. LLCs are a popular choice for many new businesses due to the safety, flexibility, and tax benefits they provide.[28]

▼ top

10 *Forbes'* Largest Private Companies in the United States[27]

Rank	Company	Revenue ($ Billions)
1.	Cargill	$106
2.	Koch Industries	$100
3.	Chrysler	$48
4.	GMAC Financial Services	$35
5.	Bechtel	$31
6.	Mars	$30
7.	Hospital Corporation of America (HCA)	$28
8.	PricewaterhouseCoopers	$26
9.	Publix Super Markets	$24
10.	Ernst & Young	$21

The Players in Business Ownership

Who can be affected by a company's type of business ownership?
A **stakeholder** is someone who is affected by a company's actions or who has an interest in what the company does. Corporate stakeholders include employees, shareholders, investors, suppliers, and society at large. Sole proprietorships usually have fewer stakeholders than large corporations. Partnerships, LLCs, and corporations may have many stakeholders, some who are only remotely affected by the business. Adidas, for example, is an international corporation whose stakeholders include their employees, customers, and foreign laborers, among others. The ownership and the activities of the Adidas corporation affect all of these people.

Review Estelle's story. Because Estelle is the sole proprietor of her nursing business, she is financially and legally responsible for all aspects of the business. This means creditors have a right to seize her personal possessions, and she must pay off her business debts or risk damage to her personal credit. Looking back, Estelle wishes she had chosen an LLC as the format for her business. An LLC would have provided her flexibility in managing her business and easier tax filing. As a single member LLC, though, Estelle would not be personally liable for her business's debts. The selection of business ownership structure is therefore a critical decision in the life of any business. ■

Taking Business Personally pp. 20–21

Taylor Evans is a very organized and orderly person. He prides himself on being efficient and meticulous with his schoolwork, finances, and social life. His friends joke with him about this and tell him that he runs his life like a business. But Taylor doesn't take offense; why shouldn't he run his life like a business? His life is just as complicated. He has revenue, expenses, and assets. He participates in commerce. Taylor even likes to keep up with the latest technology to make sure he runs his life most efficiently. Taylor is always looking for cost-effective ways to operate his life, and any profits (or money he has left over after paying his bills) are set aside for future purchases. In many ways, his life *is* a business. Do you maintain your life like a well-run business? ■

Each of you probably has a different level of familiarity with the basics of business. Some of you may have witnessed the operations of a business firsthand while employed at a part-time job. For others, your business knowledge may be limited to what you've read or seen on television. Regardless of your prior work experience, you all have experience running a business, and that business is your life. Similar to a small company, your life requires careful planning, precise record keeping, and openness to change. To help you understand some of the business concepts discussed in this book, let's look at how you run your "business."

Are you a sole proprietorship or a partnership? If you're a single individual, not married, then you work as a sole proprietorship. You're responsible and liable for all your debts and actions. If you're married, then you work as a partnership. Both you and your partner are responsible for each other's debts and actions.

How do you receive funding? Regardless of whether you have a job or not, you're receiving money from somewhere. It could be from work, a family member, a student loan, or your own savings. You need these funds to secure the necessities of life. Similarly, all businesses need funds to operate. Ideally, a business would produce revenue right away; however, some businesses may operate on funds received from a bank loan, investors, or their owners' capital.

What are your expenses? Rent, clothing, food, tuition—these are expenses whether they are paid for with cash, credit, or a loan. Ultimately, you will want to generate enough revenue, or income, to cover your expenses and have leftover cash. The lives of some students operate a bit like a start-up business; you may have to pay for expenses with loans until you have enough experience to generate a profit.

How does the social environment affect your life? The social environment probably presents similar opportunities and challenges to you as it does to businesses. How do you deal with these opportunities and challenges? Are you open to learn from people who are different from you? Do you embrace diversity? How do you relate to people from an older generation? What about the green movement? Are you finding ways to make your lifestyle more eco-friendly? It is important to address these issues so you can live a more harmonious life and prepare yourself for the modern work environment.

How does globalization affect your life? Not only is the world getting smaller for businesses, but the world is also getting smaller for you. Your favorite music group may be a band from Germany. You might like to chat online about movies with a friend from Japan. Just as businesses now have the opportunity to work with other firms from all over the world, you have the ability to make friends or connections on any continent. You probably purchase items that are designed and/or manufactured in other countries. As the forces of globalization continue, the chances of you working in a foreign country for part of your career continue to climb.

Most e-commerce requires credit cards to complete transactions. How do you keep your online transactions secure?

How do you keep up with new technology? Whether or not you consider yourself to be tech-savvy, chances are you still use some sort of technology to run your life. Perhaps you use online banking or buy things over the Internet. Similar to a business, if you don't keep up with new technology, you may find yourself in trouble.

What sort of e-commerce do you use? E-commerce is a popular form of purchasing goods. What sort of things do you buy online? There are many online clothing stores that let you design the products yourself, like the Sole Brother custom sneaker online store. Perhaps you even sell things over the Internet. Posting old clothing or other unwanted items on eBay might be your way of making a few extra dollars or more room in your closet.

How do you keep your business secure? As businesses work to keep personal information secure, so also should customers. You can help keep your information secure by changing your online passwords on a regular basis, making sure your wireless connections are secure, switching to paperless mail, and removing personal information such as phone numbers or addresses from your Facebook account or other social-networking sites. Keeping your personal information secure can help you avoid identity theft or other dangerous blows to your financial health.

What types of goals do you have? The goals of a business typically revolve around achieving financial success. You, too, might have certain financial goals that you would like to achieve in your life. To reach these goals, you'll need to make informed decisions about how you spend and save your money. Mini Chapter 5 (see p. 544) can help you manage your personal finances and plan for the future.

So when Taylor's friends say he runs his life like a business, maybe that is a compliment! Many of the same concepts and strategies used to run a business can be used to monitor your day-to-day activities. As you learn new business concepts in upcoming chapters, you may find them easier to understand by applying them to your own life. However, not everything in the business world parallels your own life. The business world has its own unique issues and strategies that may not work for your personal life. Think about the material presented in this course carefully, as both a consumer of business goods and services and as a future business leader. ■

Chapter Summary

Are you an active learner?

Go to my*biz*lab.com to master Chapter 1's contents. Chapter 1's interactive activities include:

- Customizable Study Plan and Chapter practice quizzes
- Chapter 1 Simulation, Adapting to the Economic Environment, that helps you think critically and prepare to make choices in the business world
- Chapter 1 Video Exercise, The Flaming Lips: Business Basics, which shows you how textbook concepts are put into practice every day
- Flash Cards for mastering the definition of chapter terms
- Interactive Lessons that visually review key chapter concepts

1. What are profits, and how do for-profit businesses and not-for-profit organizations compare? (pp. 3–4)

- **Profits** (p. 3) are earned when a company's **revenue** (p. 3) exceeds its **expenses** (p. 3).
- A **business** (p. 3) is an entity that offers goods and services to its customers to earn a profit. A **not-for-profit organization** (p. 4) is an organization that does not pursue profits but instead seeks to service its community through social, educational, or political means.

2. What is the difference between a good and a service, and what are the factors of production? (pp. 3–4)

- **Goods** (p. 3) are the physical products offered by a business. **Services** (p. 3) are intangible products, such as a haircut, health care, or car insurance.
- The **factors of production** (p. 4) are the resources used to create goods and services. The five factors of production include **labor** (p. 4), **natural resources** (p. 4), **capital** (p. 4), **entrepreneurs** (p. 4), and **technology** (p. 4).

3. How do competition, the social environment, globalization, and technological growth challenge and provide opportunities to business owners? (pp. 5–13)

- **Competition** (p. 5) arises when two or more businesses contend to attract customers and gain an advantage over one another. Competition forces companies to improve their product offerings, lower their prices, aggressively promote their brand, and focus on customer satisfaction.
- **Social environment** (p. 7) encompasses demographic factors such as race, ethnicity, gender, age, income distribution, sexual orientation, and other characteristics. An aging population, increasing diversity, and the green movement both challenge and pose opportunities to business owners.
- **Globalization** (p. 10) involves the merging of economies around the world as technology, goods and services, labor, and capital move back and forth across international borders. Although globalization provides profitable opportunities, such as increased markets and offshoring, it also leads to greater competition for U.S. businesses and workers.

- **Technology** (p. 4) items and services such as smartphones, computer software, and digital broadcasting make businesses more efficient and productive. E-commerce is well established and still growing, offering even small firms a chance to sell to a global market. At the same time, keeping up with the pace of technology is an expensive and time-consuming operation for many businesses.

4. What are the four types of businesses? (pp. 14–17)

- A **local business** (p. 14) relies on local consumers to generate business.
- **Regional businesses** (p. 14) are companies that serve a wider area than local businesses but do not serve national or international markets.
- A **national business** (p. 15) has several outlets throughout the country, but it does not serve an international market. It provides goods or services to all U.S. residents, no matter where in the country they live.
- **Multinational enterprises** (p. 10), also known as multinational companies or corporations, multinational businesses, or international businesses, are companies that have operations in more than one country. They are among the leaders of a movement called globalization.

5. How do sole proprietorships, partnerships, corporations, and LLCs differ from one another as forms of business? (pp. 17–19)

- A **sole proprietorship** (p. 17) is a business that is owned by one person; it is not registered with the state, and it is not legally separated from the owner.
- A **partnership** (p. 18) is a business owned by two or more people that is not registered with the state as a corporation or an LLC.
  - In a **general partnership** (p. 18), every partner participates in the daily management tasks of the business, and each has some degree of control over the decisions that are made.
  - In a **limited partnership** (p. 18), there is at least one partner who controls business operations and is personally liable.
- A **corporation** (p. 18) is a business that is a legal entity separate from the owner or owners.

- **Limited liability companies** (**LLCs**; p. 19) are companies in which the owners have limited personal liability for the debts and the actions of the company; they also provide owners with tax advantages and management flexibility inherent in sole proprietorship and partnerships.

6. **How do life skills translate to the business environment? (pp. 20–21)**
   - You are either a sole proprietorship or a partnership.
   - You have funds, expenses (p. 3), and profits.
   - You are affected by globalization and technology.
   - You have concerns with security.

Key Terms

businesses   (p. 3)

competition   (p. 5)

corporation   (p. 18)

e-commerce   (p. 12)

entrepreneur   (p. 4)

expenses   (p. 3)

factors of production   (p. 4)

financial capital   (p. 4)

general partnership   (p. 18)

globalization   (p. 10)

goods   (p. 3)

green economy   (p. 9)

identity theft   (p. 13)

labor   (p. 4)

limited liability company (LLC)   (p. 19)

limited partnership   (p. 18)

local business   (p. 14)

multinational enterprise   (p. 10)

national business   (p. 15)

natural resources   (p. 4)

not-for-profit organization   (p. 4)

offshoring   (p. 10)

partnership   (p. 18)

profit   (p. 3)

real capital   (p. 4)

regional business   (p. 14)

revenue   (p. 3)

service   (p. 3)

social environment   (p. 7)

social networking   (p. 6)

sole proprietorship   (p. 17)

stakeholder   (p. 19)

supply chain   (p. 15)

technology   (p. 4)

telecommuting   (p. 12)

undercapitalization   (p. 14)

Self-Test

Multiple Choice You can find the answers on the last page of this book.

1. **Which of the following are the factors of production?**

   a. Labor, natural resources, capital, entrepreneurs, and technology

   b. Labor, capital, entrepreneurs, and motivation

   c. Natural resources, entrepreneurs, profits, and creativity

   d. Labor, profits, natural resources, technology, and motivation

2. **Goods are products a business sells like**

   a. haircuts.

   b. conveyer belts.

   c. car insurance.

   d. health care.

3. **Which of the following is a current sociocultural trend?**

   a. A decrease in the overall U.S. population

   b. An increase in the population of Americans ages 30 to 45 years old

   c. A decrease in the U.S. minority population

   d. An increase in the population of Americans ages 65 and over

4. **Social networking makes it possible for**

   a. companies to better manage their employees.

   b. customers to spread the word about great products.

   c. companies to keep network information secure.

   d. social gatherings to be monitored.

5. **If a firm decides to shift the production of goods or services to an overseas company, this firm is**

   a. diversifying.

   b. offshoring.

   c. telecommuting.

   d. forming a partnership.

6. **Companies are placing greater decision-making responsibilities on**

   a. new layers of management.

   b. the political leadership of foreign countries.

   c. the regulatory commissions of the federal government.

   d. employees directly.

7. **B2B and B2C interactions are**

   a. common now because of the explosive growth of e-commerce.

   b. important only for businesses, not consumers.

   c. two different names for the same thing.

   d. dominated by sole proprietorships.

8. **To avoid debt, a new business owner should have enough projected revenue to cover expenses for the first**

   a. six months.

   b. year.

   c. two years.

   d. five years.

9. **Which of the following is NOT a common challenge facing most national companies?**

   a. Undercapitalization.

   b. A complex supply chain.

   c. Employment laws.

   d. Worker's compensation.

10. **What are the four most common types of business formats?**

    a. Sole proprietorship, partnership, corporation, and limited liability company

    b. Limited partnership, stakeholder, shareholder, and corporation

    c. Sole proprietorship, general partnership, stakeholder, and multinational company

    d. Limited liability company, partnership, corporation, and regional company

Self-Test

True/False You can find the answers on the last page of this book.

1. Businesses are entities that offer goods and services to earn a profit.
   ☐ True or ☐ False

2. Identity theft is no longer a problem because of new Internet security protocols.
   ☐ True or ☐ False

3. The supply chain is the process by which products, information, and money move between a supplier and the consumer.
   ☐ True or ☐ False

4. Globalization poses risks to the U.S. economy because of security and patent protection concerns.
   ☐ True or ☐ False

5. A corporation is a legal entity that defines the relationship between two or more business partners.
   ☐ True or ☐ False

Critical Thinking Questions

1. Consider all the factors of production: labor, natural resources, capital, entrepreneurs, and technology. Is each resource a vital part of the school you attend or the company for which you work? Which factors do you believe are most important to the goods and services provided by your organization?

2. It is increasingly important to businesses to have green practices—reducing their carbon footprint, offering green options for consumers, and so on. What examples can you think of where a company's marketing campaign has highlighted its concern for the environment? What might the costs to a company be for going green? What consequences might a company face if it does not?

3. Most business owners agree that keeping up with the pace of technological change is a challenging task. Imagine you are the owner of a new business and must decide what technology would best suit your needs. From what types of technology would this business benefit? Consider the factors of production, organization, and communication in your decision.

4. Many businesses now maintain both an online presence and a bricks and mortar physical presence. List a few companies that offer their products or services both online and in physical stores. How do they use the two delivery styles to give more value to their customers? In what way does the online store compete with the physical store?

5. Review the various business formats: sole proprietorship, partnership, corporation, and LLC. What do you think are some of the major benefits and challenges of each format? If you were to start a business, what kind of business would it be, and what type of business organization would best suit it and why?

Team Time

The Competitive Edge

You now know that competition arises when two or more businesses contend to attract consumers and gain an advantage over one another. Divide into three groups: Company A, Company B, and Consumers. *Company A and B:* Collectively decide what type of business you want to represent, for example, sports apparel companies, beauty salons, or pet care agencies. Then choose a product or service applicable to that type of business. (Both groups should choose the same type of business and product or service.)

Process

Step 1. **Companies A and B:** Decide how you will present your product to your customers. Focus on the following factors:
- → packaging/presentation
- → price/budget
- → quality

Consumers: Compile a list of what is important to you when choosing this product or service.

Step 2. **Companies A and B:** Provide a brief presentation to your competition and consumers. *Consumers:* Provide in-depth feedback to both companies as to how they could improve; consider your initial list.

Step 3. **Companies A and B:** Use the consumer feedback to alter your product or service to gain advantage over your competition. *Consumers:* Discuss how the two companies compare to real-life companies offering similar products or services. Would you consider purchasing from either of these two companies? Why or why not?

Step 4. **Companies A and B:** Present your product again. Explain why your product or service surpasses that of your competition.

Step 5. **Consumers:** Discuss the changes made by both companies and consider how they accommodated your needs. Did each company effectively incorporate your feedback into its revised presentation? Choose one company that you think gained the competitive advantage.

Step 6. **Entire Class:** Openly discuss the factors real companies must face in competition. Were these factors considered in the challenge?

Ethics and Corporate Social Responsibility

Cultural Awareness: Unwritten Laws

There are many challenges facing multinational companies. Complete the following exercise to experience one challenge.

Process

Step 1. Divide into six groups, each representing one of the following countries: Hong Kong, France, Egypt, Japan, Mexico, and the United States. Examine the cultural practices, customs, and values of the country you will represent. This may be done in class, if you have Internet access, or as homework.

Step 2. Each group should pair together with a second group as follows: United States with Japan, Mexico with Egypt, and Hong Kong with France.

Step 3. Each group should produce one scenario of a business transaction that would be affected by cultural differences found in your research. Fabricate specific companies, characters, interactions, and resolutions.

Step 4. Answer these questions and discuss with the class:
→ What were some challenges encountered in your business scenario and how did you overcome them?
→ Why is it important for multinational companies to research a foreign country with which they intend to conduct business?

Web Exercises

1. **Are You Savvy to Society?**
Imagine you are starting a new business. To what demographic area would you market? Think about the following factors: race, ethnicity, gender, age, income, and sexual orientation. Visit www.census.gov to locate reports on the demographic area you are interested in. Do you believe your business can thrive in this area? If not, what area would be conducive to your future customers?

2. **The Languages of the Global Marketplace**
As globalization increases and the world markets become more intertwined, language barriers become important. Investigate online resources for automated translation tools. What happens if you want to read a Web page posted by a German firm? Can you make online purchases from a company based in Asia? What resources are there for translating telephone conversations in real time? Investigate Babelfish.com and personal interpreter services like LanguageLine.com.

3. **Business Technology On-the-Go**
Mobile devices are evolving quickly and are setting the style of advertising and marketing. Using the site MobileBehavior.com, find one new trend appearing in modern advertising campaigns because of the prevalence of mobile devices. Write a brief summary.

4. **Budget Planning at Your Fingertips**
What tools are available to help a business budget its finances? Type "business budget plans" into any search engine. Using online examples, write a brief budget plan for a start-up company of your choice.

5. **Comparing Companies**
Consider two national companies discussed in this chapter—Old Navy and CVS. What states are each of these based in? Go to www.business.gov to research the laws applicable in the states in which these companies are based. How do the workers' compensation and tax laws differ for each company? Which company do you think was more difficult to establish based on state laws?

Web Case

For more on the importance of innovation and creativity in building a successful business, access the Chapter 1 Web case entitled "Focus on GE: The Imagination of a Successful Business" located in the End of Chapter Assignments section at my*biz*lab.com.

Video Case

For more on the impact of global competition, environmental forces, and market changes on business, access the Chapter 1 Video Case entitled "Liquid Lab: Outshining the Competition" located in the End of Chapter Assignments section at my*biz*lab.com.

2 Economics and Banking

The Basics of Economics

Why does water cost less than diamonds? It's a matter of supply and demand—a problem that Bryan Weirmoyer faces as a sales executive for a real estate development company every day. How can businesses use basic economic concepts to their advantage?

Objective 1 What is economics, and what are the different types of economic systems? (pp. 29–32)

Determining Price: Supply and Demand

For many business owners, weathering shifts in supply and demand is like riding a roller coaster. The levels of supply and demand for a given good or service shift constantly, each influenced by a variety of factors. Consider, for example, the effect of a faster oven on a baker's ability to supply bread or the impact of a low-carb diet craze on the demand for a baker's muffins. From this dynamic economic landscape, a price for goods and services is determined.

Objective 2 What are the principles of supply and demand and the factors that affect each principle? (pp. 32–39)

Degrees of Competition

Once a player owns all the property of the same color in this famous board game, he or she has a monopoly and controls all that happens on that property. Although that's the goal of the board game, large monopolies are rarely allowed in the United States. Microsoft was investigated by the U.S. Department of Justice for illegally holding a monopoly. What is a monopoly? Why are there laws against it? And how does it differ from an oligopoly, monopolistic competition, and perfect competition?

Objective 3 What are the various degrees of competition? (pp. 39–42)

Economic Indicators

Greg Johnson is managing the lumber inventory of a large lumber company. During years of booming housing development, ordering inventory was simple because of the large quantity of new housing starts. These days, he's not sure about his company's direction. Although new housing starts are still high in his immediate area, he's not sure if such high growth will continue. Are there measurements of the economy that he can use to help him make his decision?

Objective 4 How do economic indicators— particularly the gross domestic product (GDP), price indexes, the unemployment rate, and productivity— reflect economic health? (pp. 42–47)

Government and the Economy

Joaquin and Jacinta are looking to buy their first home. What information do they need to make sure they stay within their budget? Can government actions have an effect on what Joaquin and Jacinta do?

Objective 5 What are the four stages of the business cycle? (pp. 47–48)

Objective 6 How does the government use both fiscal policy and monetary policy to control swings in the business cycle? (pp. 48–52)

PEARSON
my**biz**lab

Supply and Demand

You're the owner of a small startup company called Moondogs Coffee, which has plans to set up coffee kiosks across college campuses in the U.S. You're setting up your first kiosk and have to make some tough decisions. Can you make the right moves and survive in the land of Starbucks?

Objective 7 Test yourself using my*biz*lab.com to show that you understand the chapter objectives.

The Basics of Economics pp. 29–32

I t was the third phone call this week, and Bryan Weirmoyer knew it wouldn't be the last. Bryan is the sales executive of a residential and commercial real estate developer in eastern Pennsylvania. As a sales executive, Bryan sells properties to clients for commission. A couple of years ago, he enjoyed taking phone calls that generally ended by closing contracts for the construction of new homes. But now, the phone doesn't ring much, and when it does, it's generally a call to cancel contracts Bryan had worked hard to negotiate. Why were there so many sales a couple years ago and so few this year? ■

Bryan's dilemma of diminishing sales is due to the economic concept of supply and demand. Have you ever wondered why water, a basic commodity that is critical to life, is priced so low, and diamonds, which aren't necessities, are expensive? It might seem that utility would have a large effect on price in that the more useful an item is, such as water, the greater its price. Instead, this paradoxical situation illustrates a different relationship, which is the fundamental concept of economics—supply and demand. Supply and demand determine how goods are priced and exchanged. The exchange of products and services between people, companies, and even countries is the very root of economics. In this chapter, we'll examine the laws of supply and demand, discuss economic indicators, and look at how the government affects the economy. First, let's begin with some economics basics.

Economics Defined

So what is economics? **Economics** is the study of how individuals and businesses make decisions to best satisfy wants, needs, and desires with limited resources. It is about businesses making *goods* (such as books, pizza, or computers) or supplying *services* (such as giving haircuts, painting a house, or installing a home entertainment network) that we want or need to buy.

Because businesses don't have enough tools, money, or products to provide *all* the books, pizza, or haircuts that we want, they must decide what and how much to make. Not everyone will be able to have what he or she wants because of limited resources (such as money, space, or time) and supplies. Therefore, economists look at how resources are distributed in the marketplace and how equitably and efficiently those resources are disbursed. There are two basic studies of economics: *microeconomics* and *macroeconomics*.

For an interactive, real-world example of this topic, access this chapter's **BizSkill** entitled Supply and Demand, located at **my*biz*lab**.com.

Microeconomics

Microeconomics is the study of how individual businesses, households, and consumers make decisions to allocate their limited resources in the exchange of goods and services. When Bryan Weirmoyer tries to determine how a change in prices may help generate sales or analyzes the number of existing houses that are already for sale in the local market, he is using the microeconomic principles of supply and demand.

Macroeconomics

Macroeconomics, on the other hand, looks at the bigger picture. **Macroeconomics** is the study of the behavior of the overall economy. Economy-wide occurrences, such as changes in unemployment, interest rates, inflation, and price levels, are all part of the study of macroeconomics. Macroeconomists, for example, look at how a change in interest rates affects the demand for housing or how a change in the housing market affects the overall economy. The government and individuals in a society also affect the manner in which resources are allocated and define the economic system in which goods and services are allocated.

Different Types of Economic Systems

What are the different types of economic systems? An **economy** is a system that tries to balance the available resources of a country, such as land, capital, and labor, against the wants and needs of consumers. An economy deals with (1) what is produced, (2) how it is produced, and (3) who gets what is produced. The world's different economies are classified into four basic economic systems:

- Traditional economies
- Planned (or controlled) economies
- Market economies
- Mixed economies

Traditional economies were found in earlier agrarian communities, which were primitive in nature and based on a strong social network. Very few traditional economies exist today. Although most economies today represent some form of a mixed economic system or a market economic system, some planned economies exist. ▼ **Table 2.1** summarizes the features of the three most common basic economic systems.

Planned Economic Systems

In a **planned economic system**, the government plays a significant role in determining the goods and services that are provided and how they are produced and distributed. Communism and socialism are examples of planned economic systems.

▼ **Table 2.1**

World Economic Systems

Type of Economy	What to Produce	How to Produce	For Whom to Produce
Planned (Controlled)	The government or other centralized group completely or partially determines what to produce.	The government or other centralized group completely or partially determines and controls the resources and means of production.	The government or other centralized group completely or partially determines wages and sets prices. Resources and products are distributed to the common group.
Market (Capitalism)	Individuals and businesses make decisions based on consumer needs and wants.	Individuals and businesses determine the production methods. The focus is on efficiency and profitability.	Individual income ultimately controls purchasing decisions.
Mixed	A blend of planned and market economies. Individuals and businesses determine what to produce, along with some level of government involvement.	Individuals, businesses, and the government control resources and determine production methods.	The government distributes some goods and services through selected social programs. Individual income determines purchasing decisions for other goods and services.

Communism **Communism** is an economic system in which a state's government makes all economic decisions and controls all the social services and many of the major resources required for the production of goods and services. Karl Marx, the originator of communist principles, envisioned in *The Communist Manifesto* that workers themselves would eventually take over the government's responsibilities to provide services. No communist country has achieved this level of Marx's vision. Existing communist states, including North Korea and Cuba, are failing economically. This is a result of problems that have arisen with communist systems, such as shortages of goods and services. In fact, in the later years of the twentieth century, most former Soviet republic states and Eastern European countries turned from communism-based economies to market economies to combat these problems.

Socialism **Socialism** provides that the government owns or controls many basic businesses and services so that profits can be distributed evenly among the people. In socialist economic systems, governments traditionally run some of the social services, such as education, health care, retirement, and unemployment, as well as other necessary businesses, such as utility companies (e.g., telephone, electric, water, and sewer). The government charges high tax rates to pay for the services it provides. For example, compared with the highest marginal income tax rate in the United States in 2010 (about 35 percent[1]), Finland, a country in which many social services are administered by the government, has a marginal income tax rate of nearly 47 percent.[2] Denmark and Sweden top the list with income tax rates of 60 percent.[3] Although citizens of these countries pay higher tax rates, they benefit from social programs that tax proceeds are used to fund. For example, education at even the best universities in Denmark is free.[4] And recent studies have indicated that Danes rank among the most satisfied people in the world.[5]

Although many feel government-controlled and government-supplied social services provide a fair and equitable distribution of such services, a concern with *true* socialism is a diminishing motivation for workers. In a true socialist system, workers turn over their earnings and profits to the state rather than keep their own earnings, so the incentive to work hard is reduced. Therefore, it is difficult to find purely socialist economies. Many socialist and communist countries are beginning to change their economies into free market economies through the practice of **privatization**—the conversion of government-owned production and services to privately owned, profit-seeking enterprises.

Market Economies

In a **market economy**, individuals are able to make their own economic decisions. For example, there may be several pizza parlors in your town, and each one may sell slices of pizza at different prices. No one is restricting the number of pizza parlors, and no one is controlling what prices they can charge. Similarly, you are free to choose any pizza you'd like to buy. This freedom of choice for both the buyer and the seller defines a free market economy.

Capitalism is an economic system that allows such freedom of choice and encourages private ownership of the resources required to make and provide the goods and the services we enjoy. Capitalism has become a major influence in the Western world's economic system. In a capitalist economy, the production and pricing of goods and services is determined through the operation of a **market**—the mechanism by which buyers and sellers exchange goods and services.

Mixed Economies

Today, most economic systems are **mixed economies,** which are a blend of market and planned economies. Most Western European countries, for example, operate with a mixed economy of privately owned businesses and government control of selected social programs, such as health care. Although the United States is closest to a capitalist economy, there is still government intervention in many industries, with the potential for even greater intervention in the future. For example, a national

Planned Economy								Market Economy
	Cuba	Russia	India	Denmark	United Kingdom	Japan	United States	

▼ **Figure 2.1**
Continuum of Economic Systems: Degree of Government Control[6]

health-care plan was passed into law in early 2010 and places the U.S. government in more control of health-care management. One provision of the bill mandates that most Americans will need to buy health insurance, and the government will provide financial assistance for those in need to pay the premiums. One way to think about the various economies and how they relate to each other is to place them on a continuum, as shown in ▼ **Figure 2.1**.

Business and Economics

Why do business managers need to be concerned with economics?

It's important for business managers and owners to understand the principles of economics because the very nature of business is to provide items or services for purchase in exchange for something, generally money. Businesses need to know how much of their products to produce or services to offer, as well as how much to charge for these products and services. Additionally, business managers need to be aware of the potential impact that government decisions (such as changing interest rates) and the decisions of collective businesses (such as the general level of unemployment) can have on their individual business or industry.

How much to charge for his good and service is one dilemma Bryan Weirmoyer faces as the need for new housing dwindles. His decisions affect other areas of the business, such as land acquisitions and staffing. Bryan watches carefully as the decision to raise or lower interest rates is made because he knows that even the smallest change in interest rates will influence a homebuyer's attitude toward mortgages, affecting Bryan's market directly. So, understanding economics, how prices are determined, the relationship of supply and demand, and the involvement of government is instrumental to operating a successful business. ■

Determining Price:
Supply and Demand pp. 32–39

Rachelle Coleman has finally realized her dream of opening her own gourmet bakery. She successfully launched the business but never realized the ongoing demands of managing it. After a newspaper reporter raved about her bakery, the lines for her cakes and cookies sometimes wrapped around the corner. Rachelle had to either increase staff to keep her baked goods on the shelf at all times or potentially lose business, but how would that affect her prices? Similarly, the increase in cost of the quality ingredients she was insistent on using—such as real butter, fresh fruit, imported cocoa powder, and real vanilla beans—forced her to choose between raising her own prices or using less pricey and lower quality ingredients. What is the relationship between supply, demand, and prices? How can Rachelle use this information to better manage her shop? ■

In the days of bartering, when people traded goods or services without an exchange of money, the price of something was determined by the needs of each person in the bartering exchange and what they were willing to trade. For example, if you wanted milk and had no cow, but you had chickens, you were willing to give up eggs for some milk. You would look for someone who wanted to trade his or her milk for your eggs. At the end of the trade, everyone was happy because you got the milk you needed and the other person got the eggs he or she needed.

However, there were problems with this exchange system. Bartering can be inefficient and inconsistent. What if the person who had the cow didn't need chickens, or what if the cow owner thought his milk was worth a chicken, but you thought it was worth only a dozen eggs? To offset some of the difficulties of bartering, the concept of currency, or money, was developed. **Currency**, a unit of exchange for the transfer of goods and services, provides a consistent standard, the value of which is based on an underlying commodity, such as gold.

In a system using currency, items such as milk, eggs, and chickens were assigned a price, or a value, based on how much the item was worth against a standard. Today, although we do have currency, ultimately the price for a good or service is determined by two fundamental concepts of economics: supply and demand.

Supply and demand is actually a very complicated process because many factors are involved, such as income levels and tastes, as well as the amount of competition in the market. However, if we ignore those factors for the moment (and economists do this all the time—it's called "all else held constant") and examine the fundamentals only, we find that when the need and availability for an item are in balance, or in equilibrium, the **market price** for a good or a service is the price at which everyone who wants the item can get it without anyone wanting more or without any of the item being left over. The need for an item is *demand*, and the availability of that item is *supply*.

The closest real-world example of determining a market price that is based on pure supply and demand is the auction process, like that found on eBay. In an auction process, bidders state the price they are willing to pay for a particular item. The

Currency developed as a means to make the exchange of goods and services more consistent and equitable.

price increases depending on the demand: the greater the demand, the higher the price the bidders are willing to pay. Supply also affects price: If similar or identical items are available for auction, the price is lower. When a unique item is auctioned, prices tend to be higher because demand is higher and supply is lower. Eventually, the winning bid establishes the market price.

Supply

What is supply? Supply refers to how much of a good or a service is available for purchase at any given time. Supply is dependent on the resources that are required to produce the good or offer the service, such as land, labor, and capital (buildings and machinery), and the quantity of similar products that can easily be substituted for the product and that are competing for a customer's attention. However, if all these factors are ignored or held constant, then supply is directly affected by price.

Supply is derived from a producer's desire to maximize profits. The more money a business can get for its good or service, the more of its product it is willing to supply. In economic terms, the amount supplied will increase as the price increases; also, if the price is lower, less of the product is supplied. This is known as the **law of supply.**

Let's look at an example. If Eddie opens a coffee kiosk in the middle of a college campus, he will want to supply more cups of coffee at $2.00 per cup than at $0.50 per cup. The reason for this is obvious: Eddie has a greater incentive to supply more cups of coffee if he can sell them at $2.00 each rather than at $0.50 each. Notice in ▼ **Table 2.2** that Eddie supplies only 10 cups of coffee at $0.50 per cup. However, if Eddie can charge $1.25, he has a greater incentive to supply more cups of coffee and produces 70 cups. Finally, at the price of $2.00, Eddie wants to supply even more cups of coffee, and his supply increases to 115 cups. We can illustrate this relationship between supply and price in a graph, which economists call a **supply curve,** like the one shown in ▼ **Figure 2.2**. You can see that Eddie's desire to supply, or sell, more cups of coffee is affected by price. The more he can charge, the more he will want to supply. However, as you can imagine, the *demand* for coffee has a very different reaction to price.

▼ **Table 2.2**

The Relationship Between Price and Supply	
Price ($)	Coffee Supplied (cups)
0.50	10
0.75	30
1.00	50
1.25	70
1.50	85
1.75	100
2.00	115

▼ **Figure 2.2**
The Supply Curve
The supply curve illustrates the incentive to supply more of an item as prices increase.

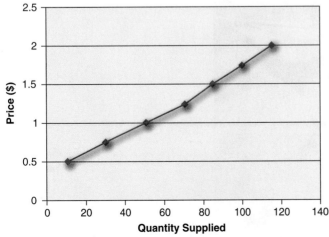

Demand

What is demand? Demand refers to how much of a good or a service people want to buy at any given time. People are willing to buy as much as they need, but they have limited resources (money). Therefore, people will buy more of an item at a lower price than at a higher price. In our coffee example, as shown in ▼ **Table 2.3**, students buy only 12 cups of coffee when Eddie charges $2.00 a cup, but they buy 120 cups at $0.50 a cup. In other words, as price decreases, demand increases. Again, economists illustrate the relationship between demand and price with a graph that they call a **demand curve,** as shown in ▼ **Figure 2.3**.

Factors That Determine Price

What factors determine price? As you've seen with Eddie's coffee kiosk, there is an obvious conflict when setting a price. The higher the price, the more the product is likely to be supplied, but the lower the price, the more

▼ **Table 2.3**

The Relationship Between Price and Demand	
Price ($)	Coffee Demand (cups)
0.50	120
0.75	95
1.00	72
1.25	55
1.50	38
1.75	23
2.00	12

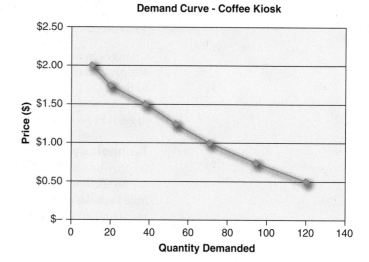
Demand Curve - Coffee Kiosk

▼ **Figure 2.3**
The Demand Curve
The demand curve illustrates that demand increases as prices decrease.

customers will likely purchase, or demand. If these two concepts of pricing are at odds with each other, then what determines the final price?

Holding all other factors constant, prices are set at a point where supply equals demand. The supply-demand relationship is one of the fundamental concepts of economics. At Eddie's coffee kiosk, for example, at some point, supply and demand balance each other out. Although Eddie would love to sell coffee at $2.00 a cup (or even more), he realizes that not too many students are willing to buy coffee at that price. At $2.00 a cup, Eddie would not completely use up his entire supply, and he would end up with unsold product left over, creating a **surplus.**

As Eddie begins to lower his price, he finds that more students are willing to buy his coffee. However, if Eddie lowers his price too much, to $0.50 a cup, for example, then the demand would be so great that Eddie would run out before he was able to satisfy all the students who wanted coffee, creating a **shortage.**

Ideally, Eddie would strive to determine a price at which he is willing to supply the coffee and at which students are willing to buy (demand) the coffee without anyone wanting more or without any coffee being left over. As noted earlier, the price at which supply equals demand is the *market price*. The market price (or **equilibrium price**) is illustrated in a supply-and-demand curve, as shown in ▼ **Figure 2.4.** In this case, 60 cups of coffee is equally demanded and supplied at a price of $1.15.

▼ **Figure 2.4**
The Market Price
The market price is determined at the point where supply equals demand.

Factors That Shift Supply

What makes supply change? Think back to Rachelle's dilemma when the price of the ingredients she used for her bakery increased dramatically. What would happen if she bought a new modern industrial oven that could produce more baked goods faster than her old conventional oven? Both of these occurrences would affect Rachelle's supply. There are many factors that can create a change in supply. These factors, known as the **determinants of supply,** are as follows:

- Technology changes
- Changes in resource prices
- Price expectations

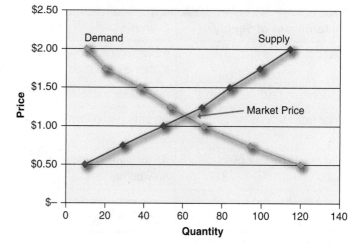
Supply and Demand Curves - Coffee Kiosk

- The number of suppliers
- The price of substitute goods

Changes in any of these factors that help to create a good or a service can affect its supply and shift the supply curve to the left (have a negative impact on supply) or to the right (have a positive impact on supply). ▼ **Table 2.4** summarizes the key determinants of supply and how they might affect the housing industry. Let's look at each in more detail.

Technology Changes
Improvements in technology enable suppliers to produce their goods or services more efficiently and with fewer costs. A baker who purchases a new modern oven is able to make more fresh breads and rolls in less time; a homebuilder who begins to use a nail gun, rather than hammering in nails one at a time, can build homes faster.

Changes in Resource Prices
The price of the resources that are used to produce a good or a service affects the cost of production. An increase in resource prices increases the cost of production and reduces profits, thus lowering the incentive to supply a product. An increase in the cost of flour or butter would raise the price of fresh baked goods at Rachelle's bakery. Likewise, an increase in the price of lumber and other building supplies can increase housing prices, as contractor Bryan Weirmoyer from our first story in the chapter experienced.

Price Expectations
Price expectations reflect the producer's best guess at the *future* price of a good. Current supply may be increased or decreased depending on the expectations of future prices. If prices are expected to increase in the future, the supplier may reduce supply now to supply more at a later time when prices are higher. Similarly, if prices are expected to decrease in the future, the supplier may make every attempt to deplete supplies now at the higher price. From a buyer's perspective, the reverse can be true, as well. For example, if Rachelle is anticipating an increase in the price of sugar because of a plight that affected sugarcane in the summer, she may want to buy more sugar than she needs now at a lower price to continue to keep her prices low, or she will need to consider raising her prices to compensate for the increase in her costs.

Number of Suppliers
The supply of a good or a service increases as the number of competitors increases. It makes sense that the number of suppliers often increases in more profitable in-

▼ **Table 2.4**

Key Determinants of Supply	
Determinant of Supply	**Example**
Technology changes	Continuing improvements in technology result in lower costs of production and create a higher level of productivity, which increases quantity and lowers price.
Changes in resource prices	A decrease in the cost of lumber increases the number of new homes built.
Price expectations	An anticipated lowering of interest rates may indicate a future increase in new housing contracts.
The number of suppliers	An increase in homebuilders increases the supply of new homes and decreases the cost of new homes.
The price of substitute goods	The construction of apartment buildings is an alternate construction project to building new single-family residences.

dustries. Think about what Starbucks has done to the coffee business. Although Starbucks remains the leader in the retail coffee market, there are many companies, such as Dunkin' Donuts and McDonald's, that are marketing to coffee drinkers, thus increasing the supply of coffee. Similarly, as an industry becomes less popular, due to a change in technology or other cause, the number of suppliers decreases. For example, when the digital camera became popular, the number of suppliers of film cameras decreased drastically.

Price of Substitute Goods

The price of comparable substitute goods also affects the supply of a product. If there are other equally comparable goods that are available at a lower price, the supply of goods will be affected. For example, if margarine, a substitute for butter, is priced lower than butter, then the supply of butter may be affected by consumers switching from butter to margarine. A change in any of these determinants of supply will affect the supply of a product and shift the demand curve. If the change is a positive effect, thereby increasing supply, the supply curve shifts to the right. Negative changes decrease supply and shift the supply curve to the left. Again, we are assuming that everything else is held constant.

Factors That Affect Demand

What factors affect demand? Just as there are factors that affect the supply side, there are also factors that affect a product from the demand side. These factors, known as the **determinants of demand**, are as follows:

- Changes in income levels
- Population changes
- Consumer preferences
- Complementary goods
- Substitute goods

A positive change in any of these determinants of demand shifts the demand curve to the right, and negative changes shift the demand curve to the left. ▼ **Table 2.5** summarizes the key determinants of demand. Let's look at each in more detail.

▼ **Table 2.5**

Key Determinants of Demand	
Determinants of Demand	**Example**
Changes in income levels	A job loss will reduce discretionary income and decrease the amount of coffee one buys. A promotion may allow a homeowner to buy a larger house or a house in a better neighborhood.
Population changes	An increase in young, working professionals in a neighborhood may increase the demand for coffee shops and single-family homes.
Consumer preferences	Needs and wants change based on fads and often manipulation by advertisers. A health alert concerning the negative effects of caffeine might reduce the demand for coffee.
Complementary goods	If the construction of new houses is in demand, complementary goods, such as appliances and other home goods, are also in demand. A reduction in new housing would negatively affect these other industries.
Substitute goods	Products or services that can be used in place of another. In the housing industry, modular housing or trailers can be substituted for building a new home from scratch.

Changes in Income Levels

When income levels increase, people are able to buy more products. Conversely, when income levels decrease, most people cut back on spending and buy fewer products. Therefore, as we'll discuss later in this chapter, when the economy enters a recession and people begin to lose their jobs, the demand for some goods and services decreases. An improving economy will bring an increase in spending as more people find jobs and create an increase in demand for some goods and services. A change in income levels is one factor that affects the housing market, for example. With an increase in income, people can afford to buy a home for the first time or can afford to upgrade to a bigger, more expensive home if they already own. On the other hand, if people begin to lose their jobs, they may need to downsize into a smaller home and sell their more expensive home.

Population Changes

Vacation rentals in resort communities experience an increase in demand during the "in" season. Increases in population create a greater demand for utilities (e.g., telephone, electric, sewer, and water) and public and consumer services such as banks, drugstores, and grocery stores. Demographic changes, such as the aging baby boomers, will also affect the demand for certain goods and services.

Consumer Preferences

Demand for a product can change based on what is popular at any given moment. Tickle Me Elmo dolls, Wii game systems, and the Apple iPad are all products that had high initial demand. As the demand for these items increases, there is a shift in the demand curve to the right. As demand begins to wane, the demand curve shifts to the left.

Complementary Goods

Products or services that go with each other and are consumed together, such as the iPod and iTunes, are considered **complementary goods**. The demand for iTunes is great as long as consumers are buying and using iPods and other portable media devices. If a new technology renders portable media devices obsolete, the demand for iTunes also decreases, shifting the demand curve for iTunes to the left. When the new iPad came out, the demand to download content from iTunes increased, shifting the demand curve for iTunes to the right.

Substitute Goods

Goods that can be used in place of other goods, such as Coke for Pepsi or McDonald's Quarter Pounder for Burger King's Whopper, are **substitute goods**. Suppose, for example, someone reported getting violently ill after eating a McDonald's Quarter Pounder. The demand for the Burger King Whopper might increase, shifting the Whopper's demand curve to the right.

So how did Rachelle handle the increase in demand for her bakery goods and determine prices for her goods when her own costs rose? It is merely a factor of supply and demand. A higher demand provides an incentive to supply more baked goods and perhaps to increase prices. Higher costs may also force Rachelle to increase her prices, but this may lower demand for her goods. The simple solution for Rachelle is to set prices at a point at which supply equals demand. Ideally, Rachelle would determine a price at which she is willing to supply various baked goods and at which her customers are willing to purchase the goods without creating either a surplus or a shortage. ■

⊙ On Target Apple iPad

Apple's release of the iPad—a tablet device designed for media engagement and light content creation—was greeted by eager consumers and surging sales. Within a week of the launch of the basic model (without 3G connectivity), an estimated 450,000 units were sold. Analysts project 7.1 million would be purchased in the first year.[7] Compare this to the initial sales for Amazon's e-book reader, the Kindle. The Kindle was introduced to the market nearly 2.5 years earlier and sold approximately 250,000 units in the first year. At the time, the Kindle was deemed a success in its own right.[8] Although the iPad is more than an e-book reader, what else might account for the far-reaching demand of the iPad over Kindle's comparatively modest success?

Consider the factors that led to the high demand for the iPad. For example, has Apple developed the market need for this device with its previous launches of the iPod touch, the iPhone, and corresponding applications? Is Apple's pricing of the device driving the sales, or do you think Apple is taking advantage of an enthusiastic market and pricing it higher than it should be?

Degrees of Competition pp. 39–42

n 1996, Microsoft developed its own Web browser, Internet Explorer, and tried to pressure computer manufacturers and Internet service providers to carry it exclusively. As a result, the U.S. Department of Justice began investigating the corporation for attempting to establish a monopoly over the market. In 1999, a U.S. District Court found Microsoft to be in violation of the Sherman Antitrust Act and ordered the company to break up. In 2001, an appeals court overturned this order but maintained that Microsoft was illegally holding a monopoly. What exactly is a monopoly? And why doesn't the government allow large monopolies to exist in the United States? ∎

Some products or services have no substitutes, whereas others share the market with many similar products. The amount of substitutes for a certain good or service determines the *level of competition*. Various degrees of competition exist:

- Monopoly
- Duopoly
- Oligopoly
- Monopolistic competition
- Perfect competition

Keep in mind that these degrees of competition are four points on a scale, not absolute measures. For example, many industries fall somewhere between a monopolistic competition and an oligopoly.

Monopolies

What is a monopoly? If one company were the sole provider of automobile tires and no other tire manufacturers were available to the automobile industry, that company would be considered a monopoly. Monopolies can also happen in a local or a regional market. For example, if Eddie's coffee kiosk is the only place students can buy coffee on campus, then Eddie has a monopoly on campus coffee sales. A **monopoly** occurs when there is only one provider of a service or a good and no substitutes exist. Without competition, the monopoly supplier can charge a higher price and may be less responsive to consumer needs. In the United States, as well as in other countries, large monopolies are rarely allowed. In fact, the U.S. Federal Trade Commission (FTC) must review mergers between large competitors to determine whether the combined firm would result in a monopolistic situation. For example, the FTC was involved when Gillette and P&G merged in 2005. Because these companies produced several similar personal hygiene products before the merger, P&G was required to sell certain product lines to other companies to avoid creating a near-monopoly by the newly merged company.

In the United States, natural monopolies are an exception. Utility companies, such as those that sell natural gas or water to consumers, may be permitted to hold monopolies in an effort to conserve natural resources. However, the government reg-

Utility companies, such as those that sell natural gas, water, or electricity, may hold monopolies, but the government then regulates the price for the goods and services to protect consumers.

ulates the prices for these goods and services, thus preventing the utility companies from overcharging for their products.

Duopolies and Oligopolies

What happens when another company enters a monopoly? In Eddie's situation, let's say that a bookstore on campus opens a café and sells coffee to students. Students now have a choice to buy coffee at two places—either at the bookstore or Eddie's coffee kiosk. The situation has now changed from a monopoly to a **duopoly.** A true duopoly is where only two suppliers exist, though in reality the definition is generally used to describe situations where only two firms have dominant control over a market. Examples of duopolies include PepsiCo and Coca-Cola in the soft drink market and Intel and AMD in the computer processor market.

However, if the campus cafeteria also begins to sell coffee, then an oligopoly is created. An **oligopoly** is a form of competition in which only a few sellers exist. When there are few sellers in a given market, each seller has a fairly large share of the market. Typically, oligopolies (and duopolies) occur in industries in which there is a high investment to enter, so oligopolies are often major corporations in certain areas such as the airline, automobile, high-tech, pharmaceutical, and tobacco industries.

Because there is little differentiation between products, competition is strong in a duopoly and an oligopoly, and prices differ only slightly, if at all, between the few suppliers. If one company cuts prices, its action is usually matched quickly by the competition. Therefore, competition in duopolies and oligopolies is centered on product differentiation (making one product stand out from another) more than on price.

Monopolistic Competition

What happens when there isn't much differentiation between products? Let's assume that the coffee that the cafeteria begins to offer is perceived among students to be superior to Eddie's and the bookstore's. The added choice of a perceived superior product creates monopolistic competition. **Monopolistic competition** occurs when there are many buyers and sellers and little differentiation between the products themselves (coffee versus coffee), but there is a *perceived* difference among consumers, who thereby favor one product offering over another. Eddie's coffee kiosk faces new competition that is perceived to be better than his product, and demand for his coffee decreases, as shown in ▼ **Figure 2.5**.

Monopolistic competition is everywhere. Think of the traditional strip mall or local shopping center in your neighborhood where most likely there is a pizza parlor, a dry cleaner, a hair or nail salon, a bank, and a dollar store. These mom and pop stores are traditional, monopolistic competitive businesses because there are many buyers and sellers and the products are similar but not identical. Often, the distinction between products is price.

▼ Figure 2.5 Demand and Competition
Increased competition negatively changes coffee demand and moves the demand curve to the left.

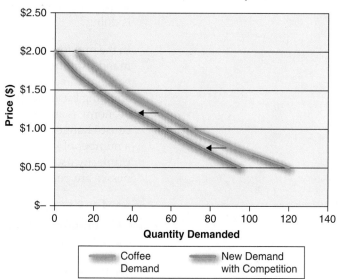

Decreased Demand with Competition

Perfect Competition

What happens when products are almost identical? **Perfect competition** occurs when there are many buyers and sellers of products that are virtually identical and any seller can easily enter and exit the market. When these conditions exist, no single supplier can influence the price. In reality, there are very few, if any, examples of perfect competition. However, agricultural products such as grains, fruits, and vegetables come close. Many of these products appear to be identical, and, because there are many sellers in the market, no single seller can set the price for these products.

Competition encourages businesses to make creative decisions and gives customers options. Because of this need for competition, U.S. businesses face stiff penalties if they are found holding illegal monopolies. Microsoft was punished in 1999 and continued to face the effects of the legal battle years later, with the appeal court's ruling in 2001 and a $611 million fine in 2004 from the European Union (EU).[9] Stiff penalties such as these exist to discourage companies from creating monopolies. By keeping a close watch on monopolies, the U.S. government ensures that no single seller drastically influences the price of a certain service or good. ◼

Economic Indicators pp. 42–47

Greg Johnson needs to decide how much inventory to purchase for his lumber company. He has seen new housing starts decline over the past year, but he knows that if certain conditions change, he could be supplying lumber for another housing boom soon. Similarly, his staffing needs can change as quickly as his inventory supply. Not knowing whether demand might pick up, how is Greg to decide how much inventory to hold or what staff to keep or let go? ◼

The economy plays a big part in business. In Greg's situation, the economy is affecting new housing starts, which in turn affect Greg's lumber sales. Which aspects of the economy should Greg watch to help him make his business decisions? How can he tell how well or how poorly the economy is doing?

In the previous section, you learned about several factors that affect supply and demand. Another factor that affects supply and demand is the overall state of the economy. In a good economy, the demand for most consumer goods will be high, spurring business expansion. In a bad economy, the opposite will be the case. The economy is an indicator of how well or poorly businesses are doing in general. Because changes in the economy can affect a business, managers need to be aware of a number of key **economic indicators** and how they relate to business. Economists primarily use the following three economic indicators to determine how well businesses are performing overall:

- The Gross Domestic Product (GDP)
- Consumer and producer price indexes
- The unemployment rate

We'll look at these economic indicators as well as productivity in this section.

The Gross Domestic Product

How do we determine the health of an economy? The broadest measure of the health of any country's economy is its **gross domestic product (GDP)**. The GDP measures economic activity—that is, the overall market value of final goods and services produced in a country in a year.

It is important to note that only those goods that are actually *produced in* the country are counted in the country's GDP. (Hence the term *domestic* in *gross domestic product*.) For example, Toshiba, a Tokyo-based high-tech company, has a plant in Lebanon, Tennessee, that manufactures color television sets. The value of the television sets produced in the Tennessee plant is counted in the U.S. GDP, not in Japan's GDP.

What's the difference between GNP and GDP? Most countries outside the United States use GDP to measure their economic health. The United States formerly used the **gross national product (GNP)** as its economic yardstick, but in 1991 it changed to the GDP to allow for fairer comparisons between world economies. The GNP attributes earnings to the country where the company was owned, not where the product was manufactured. Therefore, those Toshiba television sets made in Tennessee would not be included in the U.S. GNP, whereas the Nike apparel and footwear produced outside the United States would be included. So the GNP measures the U.S. income resulting from production, whereas the GDP measures production in the United States, regardless of country of ownership.

How does the GDP act as an economic indicator? The GDP is the most widely used indicator of economic growth by countries worldwide. When the GDP goes up, the indication is that the economy is in a positive state. Goods and services are being produced, and businesses are doing well. A downward-moving GDP indicates problems with the economy because fewer goods are being produced, fewer services are being sold, and businesses are not doing as well and may have to lay off employees or shut their doors altogether. Therefore, business owners such as Greg use GDP data to forecast sales and adjust production and investment in inventory.

top 10 Countries by GDP, 2009[10]

Rank	Country	Millions of U.S. Dollars
1.	United States	14,510,000
2.	China	8,791,000
3.	Japan	4,141,000
4.	India	3,561,000
5.	Germany	2,812,000
6.	United Kingdom	2,165,000
7.	Russia	2,117,000
8.	France	2,113,000
9.	Brazil	2,024,000
10.	Italy	1,756,000

Consumer and Producer Price Indexes

What else is used to gauge the health of an economy? There are two price indexes used as economic indicators: the consumer price index (CPI) and the producer price index (PPI). You may not hear about these indicators often, but you've probably heard of inflation and deflation. A consistent increase in either indicator indicates inflation. **Inflation** is a rise in the general level of prices over time. A decrease in the rate of inflation is **disinflation**, and a continuous decrease in prices over time is **deflation**. Later in the chapter we discuss how the government also uses these indicators to make monetary policy decisions to control inflation and deflation.

How are changes in the price of consumer goods measured? The **consumer price index (CPI)** is a benchmark used to track changes over a period of time in the price of goods and services that consumers purchase. The CPI measures price changes by creating a "market basket" of a specified set of goods and services that represent the average buying pattern of urban households. The value of this market basket is determined by the combined prices of these goods and services and is compared to its value in a prior period (generally a month), and the change is noted.

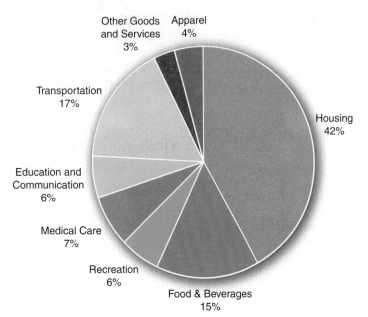

**▼ Figure 2.6
CPI Components**

What goods and services are included in the CPI? The basket of goods and services is evaluated by the U.S. Bureau of Labor Statistics to ensure that it reflects current consumer buying habits. The market basket as of December 2009 was determined by tracking the spending habits of about 7,000 families over 2005 and 2006.[11] The expenditure items are classified into 200 categories, which are further arranged into eight major groups[12] (see ▼ **Figure 2.6**):

- Apparel
- Housing
- Food and beverages
- Recreation
- Medical care
- Education and communication
- Transportation
- Other goods and services (such as tobacco and smoking products, haircuts and other personal services, and funeral services)

Does the CPI measure the change in price of all goods? The CPI measures the change in prices of consumer goods only. It does not measure the change in prices of those resources that are used to create the goods. The **producer price index (PPI)** tracks the average change in prices at the wholesale level (that is, from the seller's perspective). Therefore, the PPI tracks the prices of goods sellers use to create their products, such as raw materials, product components that require further processing, and finished goods sold to retailers. The PPI excludes energy prices and prices for services.

Why are price indices important? The CPI and PPI are important economic indicators because they measure purchasing power and consequently trigger some business decisions. During periods of increasing prices as reflected by the CPI, the purchasing power of a dollar decreases—meaning that less is bought with a dollar today than could have been purchased with the same dollar yesterday. To compensate for such price increases, wages eventually need to be increased. Businesses in turn must eventually increase the prices of their products to compensate for the higher cost of labor. Similarly, if the price to produce goods or services in-

How Much Money Do You Need to Get By?

The cost of living is the average monetary costs of the goods and services required to maintain a particular standard of living. It is closely related to the CPI. In fact, to keep up with inflation, the Social Security Administration calculates automatic cost of living adjustments to So-

cial Security benefits based on annual percentage increases in the CPI. As you can imagine, the cost of living varies greatly by state and city. For example, the cost of living in New York City or San Francisco is much higher than in Topeka, Kansas, or Little Rock, Arkansas. Why do you think these differences exist? What factors account for the differences?

For more information and discussion questions about this topic, check out the BizChat feature on my***biz***lab.com.

creases (as measured by the PPI), businesses may need to pass on those cost increases in the form of higher prices, again decreasing the consumer's purchasing power. Therefore, business leaders watch the CPI and the PPI to determine the rate at which consumer and wholesale prices, respectively, change.

The Unemployment Rate

What other indicators are used to measure the economy? The **unemployment rate** measures the number of workers who are at least 16 years old, who are not working, and who have been trying to find a job within the past four weeks and still haven't found one. Because there are different reasons why people are not working, there are several different measurements of unemployment:

- **Frictional unemployment** measures temporary unemployment in which workers move between jobs, careers, and locations.

- **Structural unemployment** measures permanent unemployment associated when an industry changes in such a way that jobs are terminated completely. Many steel workers and miners lost their jobs when there was a decline in those industries. Likewise, robots have replaced many automobile workers, and computers have replaced many newspaper typesetters. Workers displaced by these types of circumstances can hopefully learn new skills or receive additional training in an effort to keep their jobs or find new ones.

- **Cyclical unemployment** measures unemployment caused by a lack of demand for those who want to work. This generally follows the economy. Companies must cut back their workforce when there is a downturn in the business cycle. Once the demand for goods and services increases, companies begin to hire again.

- **Seasonal unemployment** measures those out of work during the off-season, such as those in snow- or beach-related industries, agriculture, and/or holiday activities.

Why is unemployment an important economic measure?
Businesses, as well as government policy makers, pay close attention to unemployment rates. High unemployment results in an increase in unemployment benefits and government spending on social programs, such as Social Security, welfare (now called Temporary Assistance for Needy Families [TANF]), and Medicare.

"I'd like you to head up the new team of recently let go."

High unemployment can also result in increases in mental stresses and physical illnesses and can bring on increases in crime as well. It is costly for businesses to lay off workers and then, as the economy improves eventually, hire and train new employees. In a declining economy, businesses prefer to reduce their workforce through retirement and natural attrition, which takes planning. Ironically, if the unemployment rate drops too low, meaning the workforce is nearly fully staffed, the concern is that more workers have increased buying power and spend more, which ultimately causes prices to increase, resulting in increasing inflation. Therefore, the challenge is to keep both inflation and unemployment low—a difficult task because they seem to have an inverse relationship to each other.

Productivity

How is the productivity of the workforce measured? In its broadest terms, **productivity** measures the quantity of goods and services that human and physical resources can produce in a given time period. It can be calculated as a physical measure or as a monetary measure. For example, measuring productivity for an automobile assembly plant may be either the total *number* of cars produced in a given period of time (week, month, or year) per worker-hours needed to produce them or as the total dollar *value* of cars produced in a given period per worker-hours needed to produce the cars. As you might expect, the calculation of productivity in the service sector is a bit more complicated. A different calculation is required for those service industries where there is a tangible output, such as meals delivered in a restaurant, than for those service industries where there is a less tangible output, such as in hospitals or banks.

"Productivity—the goods and services produced from each hour of work—is the magic elixir of economic progress. It's why we live better than our grandparents did, without working longer hours." [13]

—Alan Greenspan, former chair of the Federal Reserve Board

Why is measuring productivity important to businesses? No matter how it is measured, productivity is an indicator of a business's health. An increase in productivity indicates that workers are producing more goods or services in the same amount of time. Therefore, higher productivity numbers often result in lower costs and lower prices. Increasing productivity means that the existing resources are producing more, which generates more income and more profitability. Companies can reinvest the economic benefits of productivity growth by increasing wages and improving working conditions, by reducing prices for customers, by increasing shareholder value, and increasing tax revenue to the government, thus improving the GDP. In aggregate, overall productivity is an important economic indicator of an economy's health.

So, how do all these indicators help Greg and his inventory decision? After ensuring there is inventory to fill current needs, Greg keeps a close eye on all economic indicators, especially the CPI and the unemployment rate to help guide his future buying decisions. As explained above, movements in the CPI determine the trend of current prices. Such trends can help Greg determine whether it is better to stock up now at lower prices or wait to buy later if prices are expected to fall.

Equally important is the unemployment rate. Greg's business, like so many others, is tied closely to the new housing industry. Unfortunately, Greg is feeling the pressures of a sagging housing industry and a declining economy. Because there is less for his employees to do, he has already laid off workers. A continued downturn in the housing industry will have a negative effect on the unemployment rate, an indicator for Greg that his inventory might not move quickly. Although none of the indicators can guide Greg's decisions precisely, watching the indicators over time allows Greg to get a feel for future expectations and helps him make better business decisions. ■

Government and the Economy pp. 47–52

Joaquin and Jacinta Robertson have been saving for years to buy their first house. Over the past several years, the interest rate that banks charge for home loans has been at historically low levels. Recently, however, all Joaquin and Jacinta hear on the news is about the rapid changes in the stock market, reports from the chairman of the Federal Reserve Board about changes in interest rates, and debates on how the government might change its tax policies to control the economy. They aren't sure what effects all of this will have on their ability to be approved for a mortgage loan and buy a home. Is now the best time to buy a house? ■

If you or someone you know has tried to buy a house or make any big investment, you may have realized that the state of the economy can have a big impact on your decision. What makes the economy change? How does the government help control the economy? What do you need to be aware of when making decisions on large investments? These are the questions we'll address in this section of the chapter. Let's start by discussing some economic policies.

Economic Policies

Why does the state of the economy change? In 1980, the rate of inflation was at its highest level—nearly 15 percent.[14] Only eight years before and six years after that high inflationary period (1972 and 1986), inflation was hovering around 2 percent.[15] Over time, the economy naturally goes through periodic increases and decreases. Economists refer to these increases and decreases as the **business cycle**.

There are four stages of the business cycle, as illustrated in ▼ **Figure 2.7**.

- **Peak:** This occurs when the economy is at its most robust point. The peak occurs when an expansion ends and a recession begins.
- **Recession:** By definition, a **recession** is a decline in the GDP for two or more successive quarters of a year. In recessionary times, corporate profits decline, unemployment increases, and the stock market reacts with large selling sessions that result in decreasing stock prices. The U.S. economy has experienced seven recessions over the past 40 years; the most recent recession began in late 2007. A very severe or long recession is a

▼ **Figure 2.7**
The Business Cycle

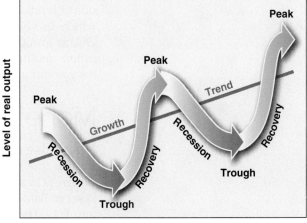

depression. Depressions are usually associated with falling prices (deflation). After the onset of the Great Depression in 1929, the government used policies to control the economy to avoid another such depression.

- **Trough:** A *trough* occurs when the recession hits bottom and the economy begins to expand again.
- **Expansion or recovery:** Eventually, after a recession or even a depression, the economy hits a trough and begins to grow again and therefore enters into an expansionary or recovery phase. Eventually, the recovery will hit a peak, and the cycle begins again.

How does the government control swings in the business cycle?

Ideally, the economy could stay near its peak all the time. But left to its own forces and in reaction to external actions on the economic system, such as wars and variations in the weather, it is inevitable that the economy cycles through recession and recovery. To smooth out the swings in the business cycle, the government influences the economy through its **fiscal policy**, in which the government determines the appropriate level of taxes and spending, and its **monetary policy**, in which the government manages the supply of money.

Fiscal Policy

Why does the government increase taxes to influence the economy?

Threats of *increasing taxes* are a concern to Joaquin and Jacinta. They feel they pay too much already and need as much of their paychecks as possible to make their anticipated mortgage payments. However, they are told that an increase in taxes is necessary to offset rising inflation. Higher taxes translate into consumers spending less money, which in turn slows the growth of businesses and consequently slows down the economy by reducing the amount of money in the system. *Decreasing taxes* does not have quite the opposite effect on the economy as increasing taxes. It would seem that if increasing taxes would slow down an economy, a tax cut would help stimulate the economy. Although that is partially true, the amount of money entering into the system is dependent on how much of the reduction in taxes consumers spend and how much of the tax cut consumers actually save. Money put into savings does not help stimulate the economy immediately. To stimulate the economy faster, the government uses another form of fiscal policy: government spending.

How does government spending help stimulate the economy?

Another tactic in fiscal policy that the government uses to help fuel a lagging economy is increasing government spending. The government spends money on a wide variety of projects, such as infrastructure improvements and those that benefit the military, education, and health care. Government spending increases cash flow to the economy faster than decreasing taxes because it is an immediate injection of funds into the system. Often, government spending creates additional jobs, which also helps stimulate the economy. The huge stimulus plan that President Obama introduced in 2009 included government spending for infrastructure, education, and health care improvements. During periods of high economic growth, the government may decrease its spending, potentially affecting interest rates.

Monetary Policy

What else can be done to control the economy?

The **Federal Reserve System (the Fed)** is the central banking system in the United States. Created by Congress as an independent governmental entity, it includes 12 regional Federal Reserve Banks (see ▼ **Figure 2.8**) and a Board of Governors based in Washington, D.C. The Fed also includes the Federal Open Market Committee (FOMC), which sets the policies of the Fed, including monetary policies. The Fed manages

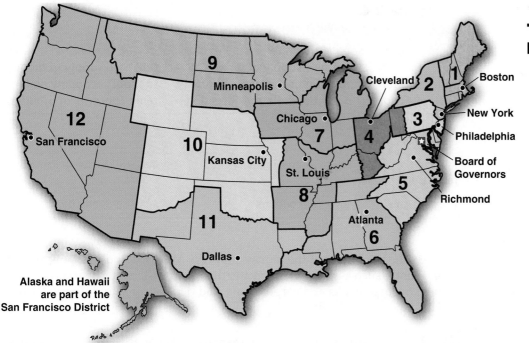

▼ **Figure 2.8**
The 12 Federal Reserve Districts

the country's money supply through its monetary policy to control inflation. It uses three strategies to accomplish this:

- Changing certain interest rates
- Buying and selling government securities
- Trading in foreign exchange markets

The Federal Reserve Banks carry out most of the activities of the Fed.

What is the money supply? When determining the amount of money in our system, it is natural to think of all the coins and bills held by people, businesses, and banks. However, that would represent only a portion of the money supply. **Money supply** is the combined amount of money available within an economy, but there are different components to the money supply (see ▼ **Figure 2.9**).

- **M-1:** Coins and bills (currency), traveler's checks, and checking accounts constitute the narrowest measure of our money supply, which is referred to as **M-1**. M-1 assets are the most liquid in that they are already in the form of cash or are the easiest to change into cash.

- **M-2:** Another part of the money supply is that which is available for banks to lend out, such as savings deposits, money market accounts, and certificates of deposit (CDs) less than $100,000. (You'll learn more about these items in Chapter 16.) This layer of the money supply, in addition to the M-1 layer, constitutes **M-2**.

▼ **Figure 2.9**
Money Supply Measures for M-1 and M-2
Surprisingly, currency is not the biggest component of the U.S. money supply. Savings and other deposits represent the largest component of the money supply. Note: The Federal Reserve Board of Governors stopped publishing M3 data after March 2006.

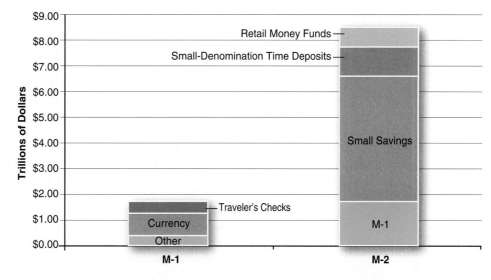

▼ **Table 2.6**

Federal Reserve Bank Monetary Policy		
Federal Reserve System Action	**Increase supply of money to stimulate economy and off-set potential deflation/recession**	**Decrease supply of money to "cool" economy and tame concerns of inflation**
Open market operations	Buy securities	Sell securities
Reserve requirement	Lower reserve requirement	Increase reserve requirement
Discount rate	Lower discount rate	Increase discount rate

- **M-3:** The third layer of the money supply is **M-3**. M-1 and M-2 plus less liquid funds, such as larger CDs (greater than $100,000), money market accounts held by large banks and corporations, and deposits of Eurodollars (U.S. dollars deposited in banks outside the United States) comprise M-3.

Why is the money supply important? Money has a direct effect on the economy: The more money we have, the more we tend to spend. When we as consumers spend more, businesses do better. Demand increases for resources, labor, and capital due to the stimulated business activity, and, in general, the economy improves. However, there can be too much of a good thing. When the money supply continues to expand, eventually there may not be enough goods and services to satisfy demand, and, as was previously discussed, when demand is high, prices will rise. (Remember the demand curve? It shifts to the right.) Inflation results from an increase in overall prices. Economists carefully watch the CPI to monitor inflation, especially because they don't want inflation to go too high.

An opposite effect can also happen when the supply of money becomes limited following a decrease in economic activity. When the economy begins to slow down due to decreased spending, either disinflation (reduced inflation) or deflation (falling prices) results. To help manage the economy from being in the extreme economic states of inflation or deflation, the Fed uses three tools to affect money supply (see ▼ **Table 2.6**):

- Open market operations
- Reserve requirements
- The discount rate

Open Market Operations

What are open market operations? The primary tool the Fed uses in its monetary policy is **open market operations**, buying and selling U.S. Treasury and federal agency bonds on the "open market." The Fed does not place transactions with any particular security dealer; rather, securities dealers compete for federal transactions in an open market. When the Fed buys or sells U.S. securities, it is changing the level of reserves in the banking system. When the Fed buys securities, it adds reserves to the system, money is said to be "easy," and interest rates drop. Lower interest rates help stimulate the economy by decreasing the desire to save and increasing the demand for loans such as home mortgages. Because Joaquin and Jacinta would benefit by obtaining a mortgage with the lowest interest rate possible, they should watch for reports that would indicate what the Fed intends to do with its open market operations.

When the Fed sells government bonds, it decreases the amount of reserves in the system, causing interest rates to increase. Using open market operations is probably the most influential tool the Fed has to alter money supply.

Reserve Requirements

What are reserve requirements? The **reserve requirement**, determined by the Federal Reserve Bank, is the minimum amount of money banks must hold in reserve to cover deposits. Although the Fed rarely uses the reserve requirement as a means of monetary policy, it can increase or decrease the reserve requirement to ease or tighten the money supply, respectively.

To better understand reserve requirements, you need to know something about how banks work. When you deposit money into a bank, the money does not sit in a vault waiting for the time when you want to withdraw it. Instead, banks use your deposited money to make loans to others: people, small businesses, corporations, and other banks. Banks make money by the interest charged on those loans; however, a bank must be able to give you back your money when you demand it. Therefore, banks do not lend out the entire balance of deposits. Banks retain a reserve that is sufficient to cover any demands by their customers for funds on any given day. This includes trips to automatic teller machines (ATMs), the use of debit cards, requests for loans, and the payment of checks that you write. If banks don't have enough funds to cover daily demands, customers might get nervous that the bank may lose their money, and so they will withdraw all their funds. In fact, this concern is what contributed to the bank run in 1929 at the beginning of the Great Depression. At that time, people were so nervous about banks not being able to cover their deposits that the massive withdrawals forced many banks to close.

The Discount Rate

What is the discount rate? The Federal Reserve Bank is the bank's banker, and sometimes the "lender of last resorts." Occasionally, commercial banks have unexpected needs for funds that might put them near their reserve funds. In those instances, banks may turn to the Federal Reserve Bank for short-term loans. When these banks borrow emergency funds from the Fed, they are charged an interest rate, called the **discount rate**. The Federal Reserve has the power to increase or decrease the discount rate in its efforts to control monetary supply. When the Fed lowers the discount rate, commercial banks are encouraged to obtain additional reserves by borrowing funds from the Fed. Commercial banks then lend out the reserves to businesses, thereby stimulating the economy by adding funds into the economic system. However, if the economy is too robust, the Fed can increase the discount rate, which discourages banks from borrowing additional reserves. Businesses are then discouraged from borrowing because of the higher interest rates.

Is the discount rate the same as the Fed Funds rate? The Fed Funds rate is not the same as the discount rate. It is often reported in the news that the Fed intends to change the Fed Funds rate in its efforts to stabilize the economy. The **Fed Funds rate** is the interest rate that banks charge other banks when they borrow funds overnight from one another. (As mentioned above, the Fed requires banks to have so much money on reserve depending on the deposits in the bank and the other assets and liabilities held by each bank. Banks avoid dipping below their required reserves by borrowing from each other.) Despite news reports, the Fed does not control the Fed Funds rate directly. Instead, the Fed Funds rate is the equilibrium price created through the Fed's open market operations and the exchange of securities.

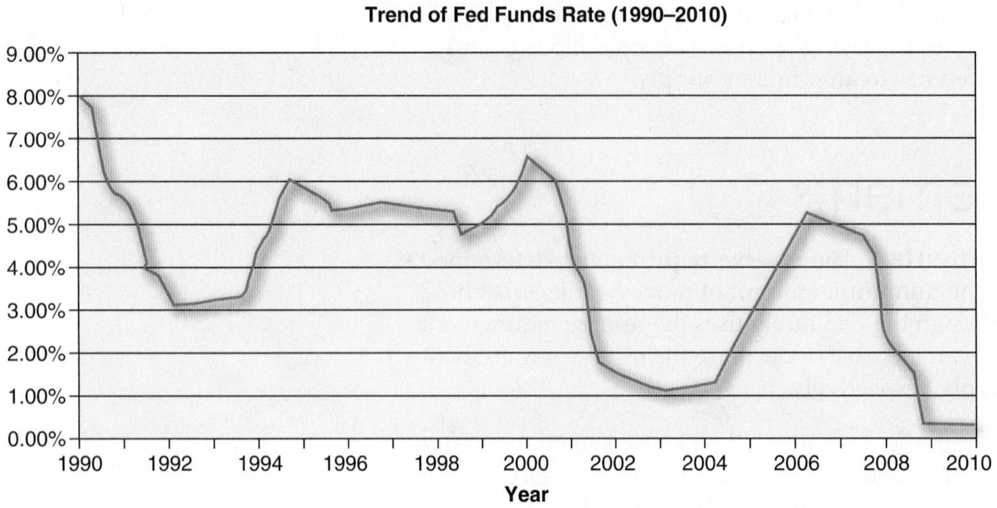

Trend of Fed Funds Rate (1990–2010)

▼ Figure 2.10
Trend of Fed Funds Rate (1990–2010)

The excess reserves that are available to lend between banks come from securities that the Fed buys and sells through its open market operations. If there are many excess reserves on hand, banks have adequate funds to lend to other banks. On the other hand, if excess reserves are not as plentiful, banks lend funds to one another more sparingly. To increase the Fed Funds rate, the Fed sells bonds in the open market. Banks buy the securities, thus reducing their excess reserves available for loans. The decrease in excess reserves increases the Fed Funds rate.

The opposite holds as well. To decrease the Fed Funds rate, the Fed will buy bonds in the open market. Buying securities from banks increases the banks' excess reserves, making money supply more available, which decreases the Fed Funds rate and helps stimulate the economy. ▼ **Figure 2.10** shows the trend of Fed Funds rates over the past several decades.

It is important to be aware of the overall state of the economy when making decisions on large investments. Because the government's actions affect the economy, it's also important to be aware of what these actions are and their effects. Remember Joaquin and Jacinta? In making their decision about whether to buy a home, Joaquin and Jacinta would benefit from paying attention to the Fed's monetary policies. Through open market operations, if the Fed buys securities, it's likely that interest rates for mortgage loans will decrease. Additionally, Joaquin and Jacinta can look to the discount rate and the Fed Funds rate. News about the lowering of the discount rate will signal that banks might have funds available to lend out, at potentially lower rates. And, while the Fed Funds rate does not have a direct impact on mortgage rates, it does have an indirect effect because interest rates respond to economic growth and inflation. Reports on the news that the Fed is striving to change the Fed Funds rate will indicate to Joaquin and Jacinta whether it's likely that interest rates will increase or decrease in the near future. These Federal Reserve tools can help them determine the best time to buy a home. ▪

Chapter Summary

Are you an active learner?

Go to my**biz**lab.com to master Chapter 2's content. Chapter 2's interactive activities include:

- Customizable Study Plan and Chapter 2 practice quizzes
- Chapter 2 Simulation, Supply and Demand, that helps you think critically and prepare to make choices in the business world
- Chapter 2 Video Exercise, Economics and Banking, which shows you how textbook concepts are put into practice every day
- Flash Cards for mastering the definition of chapter terms
- Interactive Lessons that visually review key chapter concepts

1. What is economics, and what are the different types of economic systems? **(pp. 29–32)**

- **Economics** (p. 29) is the study of how individuals and businesses make decisions to best satisfy wants, needs, and desires with limited resources and how efficiently and equitably resources are allocated.
- There are different types of economic systems.
  - A **planned economic system** (p. 30) is a type of economy in which the government has more control over what is produced, the resources to produce the goods and services, and the distribution of the goods and services. **Communism** (p. 31) and **socialism** (p. 31) are planned economic systems.
  - **Market economies** (p. 31), represented by **capitalism** (p. 31), give control of economic decisions to individuals and private firms.
  - Most modern economies in the Western world are **mixed economies** (p. 31), which are a blend of market and planned economies.

2. What are the principles of supply and demand and the factors that affect each principle? **(pp. 32–39)**

- **Supply** (p. 34) refers to how much of a good or service is available. The amount supplied will increase as price increases. Supply is affected by five factors:
  - Technology changes
  - Changes in resource prices
  - Price expectations
  - The price of substitute goods
  - The number of suppliers
- **Demand** (p. 34) refers to how much people want to buy at any given time. The amount demanded increases as price declines. Demand is affected by five factors:
  - Changes in income levels
  - Consumer preferences
  - Changes in population
  - Changes in the prices of substitute or complementary goods
  - Changes in expectations

3. What are the various degrees of competition? **(pp. 39–42)**

- There are several degrees of competition, including **monopoly**, **oligopoly**, **duopoly**, **monopolistic competition**, and **perfect competition** (pp. 40–41).
- In a monopoly, where only one seller supplies a good or service, supply may be limited. Supplies may increase with a duopoly, or an oligopoly, in which two or a few sellers exist, respectively. Monopolistic competition allows for many sellers, increasing the supply and choices for consumers. Similarly, there are many sellers in perfect competition, which also increases the supply of a good or service.

4. How do economic indicators—particularly the GDP, price indexes, the unemployment rate, and productivity—reflect economic health? **(pp. 42–47)**

- The **gross domestic product** (**GDP**; p. 43) measures the overall market value of final goods and services produced in a country in a year. When the GDP goes up, the indication is that the economy is moving in a positive direction.
- The **consumer price index** (**CPI**) and **producer price index** (**PPI**; pp. 43–44) are indicators of **inflation** (p. 43) or **deflation** (p. 43).
  - The CPI tracks changes in prices over time by measuring changes in the prices of goods and services that represent the average buying pattern of urban households.
  - The PPI tracks the average change in prices of those goods the seller uses to create products, such as raw materials, product components that require further processing, and finished goods sold to retailers.
- The **unemployment rate** (p. 45) is watched as an indicator of how productive the workforce is. An increasing unemployment rate generally has a corresponding increase in government spending on social policies (such as welfare and unemployment payments).
- Increasing **productivity** (p. 46) means that the existing resources are producing more, which generates more income and more profitability. Overall productivity is an important economic indicator of the economy's health.

Continued on next page

Chapter Summary (cont.)

5. What are the four stages of the business cycle? **(pp. 47–48)**

- The four stages of the **business cycle** (p. 47) are peak, **recession** (p. 47), trough, and expansion or recovery.

6. How does the government use both fiscal policy and monetary policy to control swings in the business cycle? **(pp. 48–52)**

- The government's **fiscal policy** (p. 48) determines the appropriate level of taxes and government spending. An increase in taxes translates into lower consumer spending and helps contain an economy that is growing too quickly. Lowering taxes will stimulate spending and help boost a lagging economy.

- The government's **monetary policy** (p. 48) manages the **money supply** (p. 49) to control inflation by changing interest rates, buying and selling government securities, and/or trading in foreign exchange markets.

- The **Federal Reserve System** (p. 48) is responsible for the monetary policy and uses **open market operations** (p. 50), manipulations of the **reserve requirements** (p. 51), and changes in the **discount rate** (p. 51) to help keep the economy from experiencing severe negative or positive swings.

Key Terms

business cycle   (p. 47)

capitalism   (p. 31)

communism   (p. 31)

complementary goods   (p. 38)

consumer price index (CPI)   (p. 43)

currency   (p. 33)

cyclical unemployment   (p. 45)

deflation   (p. 43)

demand   (p. 34)

demand curve   (p. 34)

depression   (p. 48)

determinants of demand   (p. 37)

determinants of supply   (p. 35)

discount rate   (p. 51)

disinflation   (p. 43)

duopoly   (p. 41)

economic indicators   (p. 42)

economics   (p. 29)

economy   (p. 30)

equilibrium price   (p. 35)

Fed Funds rate   (p. 51)

Federal Reserve System (the Fed)   (p. 48)

fiscal policy   (p. 48)

frictional unemployment   (p. 45)

gross domestic product (GDP)   (p. 43)

gross national product (GNP)   (p. 43)

inflation   (p. 43)

law of supply   (p. 34)

M-1   (p. 49)

M-2   (p. 49)

M-3   (p. 50)

macroeconomics   (p. 29)

market   (p. 31)

market economy   (p. 31)

Self-Test

Multiple Choice   You can find the answers on the last page of this book.

1. Which of the following is a good example of microeconomics?

   a. how a specific company would maximize its production and capacity so it could better compete in its industry

   b. how an increase in the unemployment rate would affect a country's GDP

   c. how a decrease in taxation affects consumer spending

   d. All of the above

2. There are four pizza parlors in your town. You can choose to buy pizza from whichever shop you want, and the restaurants can charge whatever price they feel is best. This situation defines what kind of economic system?

   a. Communism

   b. Planned economy

   c. Market economy

   d. Socialism

3. DeJean has a successful landscaping business in which he mows lawns, weeds flower beds, and trims hedges. Last summer, he bought a brand new mower and hired a helper. The supply curve for DeJean's business would shift in which direction?

   a. To the right

   b. To the left

   c. No change would occur.

   d. There is a shift along the demand curve only.

4. Which of the following is a determinant of demand?

   a. Technology changes

   b. Changes in income levels

   c. Price of substitute goods

   d. Change in the price of resources

5. Racerback Swimwear, an Australian company, opens a factory near Tallahassee, Florida. The value of the swimsuits produced in the new Florida factory is included in which country's GDP?

   a. Australia

   b. United States

   c. Both Australia and the United States

   d. It is not included in the GDP at all.

6. Which of the following tracks the prices of goods and resources sellers use to create their products?

   a. GDP

   b. CPI

   c. PPI

   d. GNP

7. Jackson Paulson works as a waterskiing instructor at Migis Lodge on Sebago Lake. He claims unemployment from October through April. Jackson experiences which type of unemployment?

   a. Frictional

   b. Seasonal

   c. Cyclical

   d. Structural

8. To smooth out the swings in the business cycle, the government influences the economy by

   a. Increasing or decreasing taxes

   b. Changing certain interest rates

   c. Buying and selling government securities

   d. All of the above

9. What results when the economy begins to slow down due to decreased spending?

   a. inflation

   b. deflation

   c. expansion

   d. depression

10. If the Fed wants to stimulate the economy, which of the following actions would it NOT take?

    a. Buy securities

    b. Lower the discount rate

    c. Lower the reserve requirements

    d. Increase the discount rate

Self-Test

True/False You can find the answers on the last page of this book.

1. Macroeconomics is the study of the behavior of the overall economy.
   ☐ **True** or ☐ **False**

2. The Fed Funds rate is another name for the discount rate.
   ☐ **True** or ☐ **False**

3. Sweden, with its high taxes and widespread government programs, is an example of a market economy.
   ☐ **True** or ☐ **False**

4. An unexpected early snowstorm in the Pocono Mountains will most likely shift the demand curve for ski rentals to the right.
   ☐ **True** or ☐ **False**

5. M-2 includes M-1 as well as savings deposits, money market accounts, and small CDs.
   ☐ **True** or ☐ **False**

Critical Thinking Questions

1. How have the Kindle and the iPad affected the supply and demand for newspapers and other printed material (such as textbooks)? Discuss the impact of technology on those industries that produce printed information.

2. The text discusses the unemployment rate as a measure of economic performance. Another way to gauge economic performance is to count the number of jobs or number of people employed in the economy. Discuss the differences between these two measurements of job creation. Is either measurement better than the other?

3. Look in the newspaper or on the Internet for economic indicators, such as the unemployment rate and the CPI for the past several years. Determine by these factors whether economic state in the United States is improving or deteriorating. Explain your decision.

4. Discuss whether you think the National Football League (NFL) or Major League Baseball (MLB) is a monopoly.

5. The text defines the GDP as a measurement of economic activity. Think about other things that may "help" the GDP that are really not good for our society in general, such as the economic activity required to clean up oil spills or increases in consumer debt to buy more goods. In addition, there are other situations that may "hurt" the GDP by limiting expenditures on items but help the overall good of society, such as reusing plastic bags or installing solar water heaters (thus limiting spending on oil, gas, or electricity). Does the definition of GDP need to be revised?

Team Time

The Great Debate

Your instructor will divide the class into three groups and assign each group one of the following debate topics. Once in your group, divide the group into two smaller groups to prepare stances on your assigned debate issues.

Debate Topics

1. In 2009, the government bailed out several large banks and automotive and insurance firms in an effort to thwart a huge financial crisis. Were the government's actions successful?

2. Minimum wage laws were introduced in the 1930s to protect workers after the Great Depression. In the 2008 presidential election, minimum wage increases were a topic of discussion. What impact does increasing the minimum wage have on unemployment? Does increasing the minimum wage benefit the worker or does it ultimately result in higher unemployment?

3. Taxation and tax cuts are fodder for volatile debate among political leaders. Many propose that tax cuts help strengthen the economy by freeing money to increase spending. Others propose that past tax cuts have not had a positive effect on the economy and have caused greater stress on the government budget and reduced the government's ability to spend on important public needs. Do tax cuts benefit the economy?

Process

Step 1. After dividing your group into two debate sides, meet separately to discuss the issues of the debate.

Step 2. Group members should then individually prepare their responses to their side of the debate issue.

Step 3. Gather your smaller groups and discuss the responses provided by each group member. Develop a single list of responses.

Step 4. Determine who will be the group's primary spokesperson for the debate.

Step 5. Each group will be given five minutes to present its side of the issue. After each group has presented its argument, each team will be given five minutes to prepare a rebuttal and then three minutes to present the rebuttal.

Step 6. Repeat this process with the other groups.

Ethics and Corporate Social Responsibility

Economic Inequality

Economic inequality refers to the differences of assets and income among groups. It has long been the subject for great discussion and can refer to the inequality between individuals, city/rural areas, countries, or economic structures. As a class or on an individual basis, discuss the following:

1. How do you define economic equality? For example, is economic equality simply making sure everyone has equal income, or is it enough to provide all equal opportunity to earn income?

2. Is economic equality feasible? Would other problems result from economic equality?

3. One method used to measure differences in national income equality around the world is the national Gini coefficient. Research the Gini coefficient. Which countries have the most equality? Which have greater inequality?

4. What other methods could be used to measure economic equality?

Web Exercises

1. **Getting Acquainted with Your Local Federal Reserve Bank**
   What Federal Reserve Bank branch is nearest your home or school? Go to the Web site of your local Federal Reserve Bank and outline its latest policies. What kind of information does the Web site give you?

2. **Buying Your Dream Car**
   How much would it cost to finance the car of your dreams? What are the current new car interest rates in your area for three- and five-year loans? Research how much it would cost to buy the car of your dreams. Then find a loan calculator online and calculate the monthly loan payment for the full price of the car with both the three-year and five-year rates. Assume you make a 10 percent down payment on the car. What happens to the loan payments when a down payment is made?

3. **Learning More About Supply and Demand**
   Search on Google to find The Lemonade Stand Game and play a round or two. Using information you learned from this chapter, write a brief paper about your experience.

How much money did you make each time you played the game? What are the important variables? How does this game illustrate the effects of supply and demand?

4. **Pro Sports and the Economy**
   How do professional sports and the economy interact? Play Peanuts and Crackerjacks on the Boston Federal Reserve Bank's Web site and test your knowledge of basic economic principles in the context of professional sports. Write a brief summary of your experience. What did you learn from playing the game?

5. **Monetary Policy: You're in Control**
   How would it feel to be in control of the monetary policy for a country? Go to the Federal Reserve Bank of San Francisco Web site, and under Student Activities, find the Fed Chairman Game. In this game, you act out the role of a fictitious central bank by implementing monetary policy in a simple virtual economy so you can get a feel for the options and limitations of monetary policy. Write a brief summary of your experience. What did you learn from playing the game?

Web Case

For more on reimagining supply in response to shifting market demands, access the Chapter 2 Web case entitled "Focus on GE: Standing the Heat, Staying in the Kitchen" located in the End of Chapter Assignments section at my*biz*lab.com.

Video Case

For a comparison of different economic systems and more on the regulation of the U.S. free-market economy, access the Chapter 2 Video Case entitled "The U.S. Department of Commerce: Leveling the Playing Field" located in the End of Chapter Assignments section at my*biz*lab.com.

Ethics in Business

CHAPTER 3

Ethics: The Basics

Ethics and business—many people consider these terms to be unrelated. How can you maintain your own personal integrity while still fulfilling your business responsibilities? Examining your own personal ethical code is the first step in successfully navigating this potentially tricky terrain.

Objective 1 What are ethics and different ethical systems? (pp. 61–62)

Objective 2 How does someone create a personal code of ethics? (pp. 62–63)

Personal Ethics Meets Business Ethics

Randy Marks had a recipe for success with his pottery business, but it flew in the face of his personal beliefs. What do you do if your own ethics conflict with success in business?

Objective 3 How might personal ethics play a role in the workplace? (pp. 65–67)

Objective 4 How can you evaluate a company's ethical code using available resources, such as a mission statement? (p. 67)

Corporate Social Responsibility

Although the primary focus in business often seems to be on making money, many businesses also make meaningful contributions to the social, environmental, and economic development of the world. Howard Schulz runs Starbucks "to inspire and nurture the human spirit." How could such a lofty goal lead to amazing profits and growth?

Objective 5 How do a company's policies and decisions affect its achievement of corporate social responsibility (CSR)? (pp. 68–71)

Objective 6 What challenges does a company face in balancing the demands of social responsibility with successful business practices? (pp. 71–74)

Dangers of a Weak Ethical Focus

Of course DVDs are copyrighted, but with a big trade show coming up, Lana's project team needed to rip some videos to hard drives for testing. Who would it hurt, after all? Sometimes it seems that if you break ethical standards just a bit, you'll come out ahead. But does it really pay in business to ignore ethics? Or do good guys come out ahead?

Objective 7 What is legal compliance, and how does it affect ethical conduct? (pp. 76–77)

Objective 8 What strategies can a company use to recover from ethical lapses? (pp. 78–79)

Business Opportunities Created by Ethical Needs

Richard Stephenson saw a need—more compassionate medical care that was still state of the art in quality. By creating new markets based on ethical needs, many companies like Stephenson's reap financial rewards, improve employee morale, and make valuable contributions to the world.

Objective 9 How can companies apply ethical standards to create new business opportunities? (pp. 79–82)

How Businesses Develop an Ethical Environment

Unbelievable. There they were—the once-frozen test tubes of samples, leaking all over the back delivery dock. Rashid's heart sank. He needed to manage his client—and his bosses—in an ethical way. But what did that mean exactly?

Objective 10 What approaches can a company use to develop and maintain an ethical environment? (pp. 82–85)

PEARSON
my**biz**lab

Navigating Murky Ethical Waters

You join a start-up company called Sustainable Green, led by an inspirational owner who wants to blend cutting-edge business practices with a passion for corporate social responsibility. As you follow the company's attempts to walk the talk, you quickly discover that even the most sincere efforts to do the right thing can lead to ethical challenges. Can you navigate the murky waters of trying to be both a good company and a successful one?

Objective 11 Test yourself using mybizlab.com to show that you understand the chapter objectives.

Ethics: The Basics pp. 61–64

hen Tracy gets up each morning, he turns on Sirius Radio to listen to the Howard Stern broadcast, laughing along with the quips and jokes about stereotypes. He grabs his keys and heads out the door to school. As he leaves the line in the school cafeteria, he realizes that he received $20 back in change instead of a $1. Should he go back to tell the cashier about her error? He then heads into the photocopy room to duplicate his homework but discovers the answer key to his next exam was left on the machine. He shoves the answer key into his backpack, not sure what, if anything, he'll do with it yet. Before the end of class, the professor compliments him in front of everyone for outstanding writing on his last paper. Tracy knows the writing came from a friend in class but just nods in thanks. That night, he thinks over the day, reviewing the choices he made along the way as he drifts off to sleep. What would you have done if you were in Tracy's shoes? ■

Like Tracy, we all make ethical decisions every day. We decide how we will act, which thoughts we will feed, and which we will dispel. We make these decisions based on a set of beliefs about how the world works and what kinds of behaviors are rewarded. These beliefs can be classified as our set of values. In this chapter, we'll see that businesses are similar in that they also have a set of values that guide their actions. Let's examine how values and beliefs about how the world operates influence our personal and business lives.

For an interactive, real-world example of this topic, access this chapter's **BizSkill** entitled Navigating Murky Ethical Waters, located at **my**bizlab.com.

Ethics Defined

What exactly *is* ethics? Ethics is the study of the general nature of morals and the specific moral choices a person makes.[1] In effect, ethics represents the guidelines you use to make decisions every day. But not all people share the same ethics. Many systems of ethical conduct exist. Some are based on religious systems, some are cultural or national, and some have been passed from generation to generation within a specific ethnic group.

Systems of Ethical Conduct

What are the different systems of ethical conduct? One ethical system is **moral relativism**, a perspective that holds that there is no universal moral truth; instead, there are only people's individual beliefs, perspectives, and values. This means that there is no single view that is more valid than any other; thus, no single standard exists to assess ethical truth. According to moral relativists, each person has his or her own ideas of right and wrong, so who are you to judge anyone else? Imagine trying to organize any group of people—a family, a company, or a country—according to this ethical system.

Another ethical system is **situational ethics**, in which people make decisions based on a specific situation instead of universal laws. Joseph Fletcher, a Harvard Divinity School professor, developed situational ethics because he believed that applying the Golden Rule—treating others as you would like to be treated—was more important in making ethical decisions than applying complex sets of moral rules. Because it challenged the idea that universal rules exist and can be applied to every situation, Fletcher's ethical system was considered very controversial.

Many other ethical systems exist, some of which are defined by religious traditions. For example, **Judeo-Christian ethics** refers to the common set of basic values shared across both Jewish and Christian religious traditions. These include respecting property and relationships, respecting one's parents, and being kind to others.

Of course, people sometimes act in a manner that violates the beliefs they hold or the beliefs of the ethical system they say they follow. **Unethical behavior** is defined as behavior that does not conform to a set of approved standards of social or professional behavior. This is different from **amoral behavior**, in which a person has no sense of right and wrong and no interest in the moral consequences of his or her actions.

Personal Ethics

What are personal ethics? Every day you have thoughts that lead you to say and do certain things. As you choose your words and actions, you're following a set of **personal ethics**, the principles that guide the decisions you make in your life. Sometimes, people have a very clear, well-defined set of principles that they follow. Other times, a person's ethics are inconsistent or are not applied the same way in every situation. Still other times, people have not taken the time to clarify what they value most.

Sometimes, it seems clear that making an unethical decision will produce an immediate benefit. This is when it is most challenging to adhere to your own ethical system. Consider this example: When applying for a dream job, a college senior exaggerates a bit on her résumé about her experiences and responsibilities during an internship to seem more qualified. Is this lying or is it justified behavior?

Now consider how you treat property. Say you bring home a few pads of paper, some pens, and a stack of blank CDs from the supply closet at work. Is this stealing? What if it were just one piece of paper you brought home? Some would say it depends on whether you use the material to do work at home. What if you used some of it on work projects and some on personal projects? What if it wasn't you who was taking office supplies but someone else with whom you work? It's often easy to have one view when you're taking the supplies and another when it's the person you like least in the office.

How can I clarify what my personal ethics are? Taking the time to examine your personal ethical code is of great value. If you have a clear idea of which values are most important to you, it will be easier to handle situations in your personal and professional life that require you to make complex ethical decisions. ▼ **Table 3.1** outlines one way to analyze your own ethical system. Let's look at each step in the process:

1. Write down what kind of person you are. What is your *character*? Would a friend describe you as honest and kind? Ambitious and self-serving? Interested in others' well-being? Be honest in your assessment of yourself.

"Interesting business proposal. We'll have to run it by illegal."

▼ **Table 3.1**

	Question	Examples
Determining Your Code of Personal Ethics		
Base Character	What characteristics would others use to describe you?	Honest, reliable, kind, self-centered, aggressive
Beliefs	What are the most important beliefs you hold and use to make decisions in your life?	"Nice guys finish last."; "Hard work always pays off."
Behavior	How do your relationships reflect your character and beliefs?	"I have mostly shallow relationships because I tend not to follow through on my commitments."; "I have many deep, long-lasting friendships because I value friendship and work to take care of my friends."
Belief Origins	Where did your beliefs and your view of your character come from?	Family, religion, movies, personal experiences, people you admire

2. List the *beliefs* that influence your decision making. For example, would you feel comfortable working in a lab that uses animal testing for medical research purposes? Do you think it is okay to lie? If so, which kinds of lies are acceptable to you and which kinds are not acceptable? Are your answers flexible— that is, are you committed to adhering strictly to your ethical positions?

3. Consider your *behavior* with regard to the places you work, study, and live and how you relate to people around you. Would you like to change anything about your behavior? For example, do you ever find yourself gossiping or speaking in a way that creates a more divisive atmosphere? You may feel justified in the comments you're making, but is your ethical position on gossiping creating the kind of environment you ultimately want?

4. Now that you have your beliefs written down, think about *how you came to believe them*. Life experiences offer all of us opportunities to develop our personal ethics. We also are taught about ethical behavior by our families, places of worship, first-grade teachers, and so on. Sometimes, our experiences lead us to abandon some ethical rules and adopt others. And for some of us, our ethical rules are modified depending on what is at stake. Have you accepted your ethical beliefs without investigation, or do they stand up to the test of real-world experiences in your life?

How can an ethical life get me ahead? Sometimes, ethics feels like an abstract ideal—ideas that would be nice in a utopian world but have no real impact on your life in the here and now. Yet there are some clear benefits from living ethically.

First, society has established its own set of rules of conduct as *laws*. It's no surprise that ignoring or being inconsistent in following laws can have an immediate impact on your life. Because we live in a society of many different cultures, religions, and ethical systems, the laws do not always reflect our personal ethics. Acts of civil disobedience occur when people choose to nonviolently follow their own beliefs even when they go counter to current laws. Whether it is complying with a law about the way you run your business or following laws that affect your personal life, deciding how your own ethics align with a society's laws is critical.

Living ethically may even be good for your health. When your day-to-day decisions are in conflict with the values that you consider most important, you often feel stressed and angry. In situations where constant conflict exists between what you value and what actions you take, a variety of types of mental and physical damage may follow.

For example, Renate Schulster was a vice president for the human resources department at a financial services firm.[2] She was asked to investigate an employee's

BizChat

Can Living Ethically Make You Happy?

Research suggests that happiness itself is a result of living ethically. Psychology has established this as a new focus with the emergence of an area of psychology known as *positive psychology*. Dr. Martin Seligman of the University of Pennsylvania's Positive Psychology Center[3] pioneered this field. He and his colleagues have worked to discover the causes of happiness instead of addressing the treatment of mental dysfunctions. Seligman's research has shown that by identifying your personal strengths and virtues (things like having empathy or a sense of justice) and aligning your life so you can apply your personal strengths and values every day, you will see an increase in happiness (and a decrease in depression) equivalent to the effects of antidepressant medication and therapy. Finding a way to identify and then apply your ethics and virtues to your daily life does indeed have an impact on your happiness.

For more information and discussion questions about this topic, check out the BizChat feature on my*biz*lab.com

PEARSON
my*biz*lab

For an interactive, real-world example of this topic, access this chapter's **BizSkill** entitled Ethics and Social Responsibility, located at **my*biz*lab.com.**

allegation of sexual harassment. Schulster's investigation led her to believe that the CEO of the corporation was guilty of the offense. Her personal ethics dictated following through with the employee's claim, which put her at odds with the company. As pressure from the conflict between her own values and those of the CEO grew, she sought psychological counseling for the emotional impact of the stress. She was eventually able to recover her medical and legal expenses from the employer and left the position. Renate held onto her integrity; however, the battle was not an easy one.*

Personal ethics are a large part of how people define themselves, their roles in society, and their business conduct. Remember Tracy? Like all of us, Tracy will continue to face ethical decisions throughout his life. By truly thinking about his thoughts and actions—that is, by developing a code of personal ethics—he will be in a better position to see what his options are in complex and challenging situations. ■

Personal Ethics Meets Business Ethics pp. 64–68

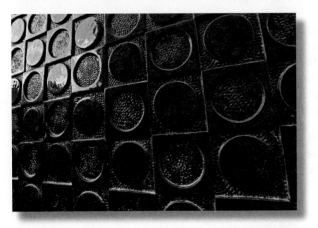

" It was a beautiful glaze," Randy Marks says with a sigh. His small pottery shop depends on orders from individuals and small architecture firms who are looking for authentic, custom pieces of tile to adorn their kitchens, floors, or fountains. "I used copper and a special firing method to give the glaze a stunning crimson color," Randy explains. "It was our best-selling item." An architect in New York City quickly signed the shop to produce a much larger number of tiles for his clients. This meant more hours and more employees hired at the

---

*The character's name in this story was changed from the name used in the original article.

shop to handle this boom. However, part of the production process entailed the introduction of additional copper during firing, producing a thick black smoke laced with toxic copper. As the orders increased, more often than not, the kiln in the back of the workshop spewed this smoke into the air, in contrast to the clean white smoke produced by normal glazes.

Randy had been part of environmental groups in his community for years, so he knew how detrimental to the environment this process was. How could he find a way to stay true to his ethical standards and still be mindful of his responsibilities to his employees and customers? ■

We often find ourselves torn between several choices, and finding a path that works for both you and the company you work for can be challenging. In some settings, the line between right and wrong is difficult to see. Other times, your own personal values just won't align with the company's, and you may wish you had better understood the company's sense of ethical culture early in your career—before you invested your time and effort. Let's review some examples, resources, and techniques to help you navigate ethical conflict in the workplace.

You as a Person and as an Employee

What role does personal ethics have in a business environment❓

Our personal ideas of right and wrong influence our actions, words, and thoughts. But how does that carry over into the work environment? After all, our employer is purchasing our time and energy. As employees, our responsibility is to follow the ethics that the owner or director has established for the business. However, a business owner has no control over or even input into your conduct outside the office.

But is this really true? Perhaps at one time this model applied to life in the United States, but the modern workplace is more complex. Today, off-the-job behavior, integrity, and honesty relate to on-the-job performance. For example, in the modern workplace, workers telecommute, working from home using technologies to connect electronically to office documents and meetings. In this newly expanded workplace, an employer may indeed care if an employee drinks at home during the workday or experiments with drugs recreationally after hours. The business environment is a changing landscape, and the lines of privacy laws are becoming blurred. Do employers really have a say over employees' behavior outside the office if that behavior may affect the company for which he or she works?

Likewise, stockholders (people who own stock in a company) and employees sometimes have a say over the behavior of management outside the office. In 2004, Boeing was recovering from a set of scandals involving how it obtained military contracts.[4] The aerospace leader fired its current CEO and hired a former Boeing employee, Harry C. Stonecipher, to lead the company back to stability. Fifteen months later, Stonecipher, who was married, was discovered having an affair with a female employee. The very same code of ethical conduct that Stonecipher had created and pointed to as a sign of the return of ethical conduct at Boeing was

In 2004, Boeing fired its CEO, Harry Stonecipher, for unethical conduct. Ironically, Stonecipher had been hired to lead Boeing back to stability after a number of scandals had rocked the aerospace company.

used to force his resignation. There were no charges of sexual harassment, and the woman did not work directly for Stonecipher. He never showed her any favored treatment within Boeing. But there still was a conflict between his personal ethics and his role in the business. It took a great toll on him personally as well as the company he was working to restore.

What if you are asked to do something that is outside your understanding of ethical behavior?

It can be challenging to decide whose ethics to follow, yours or your company's, and each path has legal and moral consequences. For example, Andrea Malone[5] was ordered by the president of her company to fire an employee who had a brain tumor because the tumor had lowered the employee's productivity. Andrea knew the Americans with Disabilities Act (ADA) covered such situations and that it was a violation of federal law to fire the employee under these conditions. However, her company insisted she fire the employee and say that it was for other reasons, not the tumor. Andrea chose to leave the company rather than fire the person unfairly, but she has since had difficulty finding other employment. Andrea held to her personal ethics but was not properly prepared for the short-term consequences.*

What if you find you are taking part in unethical activity without realizing that you were doing so? Before Bruce Forest[6] accepted a job offer as a human resources director, he asked the firm about rumors that they hired undocumented immigrants. He was assured that was no longer the case. However, soon after Bruce started to work for the company, reports began arriving that such illegal hiring was a continuing practice. His boss ordered Bruce to stop investigating the situation, saying that the company would prefer the risk of being fined by U.S. Citizenship and Immigration Services. The fine the company would have to pay was "an acceptable business expense," according to Bruce's boss. So now Bruce was complicit in an illegal activity and had to make some tough decisions. Should he move his family, take a pay cut, and lose his promised bonus or stay knowing he's now a party to this deception?*

To stumble unknowingly into unethical and even illegal activity brings the consideration of our own ethics to the forefront. Both inside and outside the office, people can find themselves involved in situations that are difficult for them ethically, but it is especially difficult when your job is on the line.

ADM was at the center of an international price-fixing scandal, meeting with its own competitors to set the price and amount of product it sold. ADM employee Marc Whitacre became an FBI informant for two years to expose the scandal. He was portrayed by Matt Damon in *The Informant*, a dark comedy about these events.

Consider Mark Whitacre, a senior executive with the agricultural giant Archer Daniels Midland (ADM). ADM was involved for years in a multinational price-fixing scheme. **Price fixing** occurs when a group of companies agree among themselves to set a product's prices, independent of market demand or supply. Based on such price fixing, ADM stole millions of dollars from its customers by agreeing with its own competitors to set a product's price. Whitacre was a participant in the illegal activities and was set to

*The character's name in this story was changed from the name used in the original article.

rise to the very top of the organization. His wife, however, became increasingly conflicted with what was happening at ADM and with her own ethical values. She finally threatened to divorce Whitacre unless he found a way to end his involvement. Whitacre then went to the FBI and agreed to record secret meetings at ADM, ultimately capturing over 250 hours of incriminating audiotape and videotape.[7] Whitacre himself ended up spending almost nine years in prison and is now the chief operating officer (COO) of a biotech firm in California. The story is so compelling that it was made into a film starring Matt Damon in 2009—*The Informant*.

Although some people decide they will be flexible with their own ethical standards in the workplace, it can often take a toll on their mental state, relationships, and physical health.

Identifying a Company's Ethics

How do I examine a company's ethics? Some companies may have a written **code of ethics**, or a statement of their commitment to certain ethical practices. Additionally, many companies have a public **mission statement** (sometimes called a *corporate vision*) that defines the core purpose of the organization—why it exists—and often describes its values, goals, and aspirations. Consider the following mission statement of Fetzer Vineyards:

> Enhance the quality of life for our consumers, community, stakeholders, and employees in ways that build great brands thereby giving us a competitive advantage in the wine.[8]

This mission statement has led to 100 percent organic wine production, awards for the conservation of energy, and a companywide English as a Second Language training program offered as part of its education package to employees.

How can I find out the best and worst aspects of a company's ethical conduct? In addition to a company's code of ethics and mission statement, other resources allow you to evaluate the acts of responsibility and legal violations by any given company. For example, you can check the legal compliance of a corporation by researching actual charges that have been filed or cases that have been adjudicated against a company. Web sites such as lawcrawler.findlaw .com help you find relevant case law generated by lawsuits filed by or against many corporations.

There are also organizations, such as the Boston College Center for Corporate Citizenship, that work with corporations to help them define, plan, and institute their corporate citizenship. This center also highlights companies that act in positive ways by publicizing responsible corporate activities and listing on its Web site reports in the general media of ethical issues in business. By doing so, the center works with companies to "leverage their assets to ensure both the company's success and a more just and sustainable world."[9] We'll discuss other ways you can assess a company's ethics and sense of corporate responsibility in the next section.

What did Randy Marks decide to do when his personal ethics and business ethics collided with the production of the special pottery glaze? No one was "watching"; there was no censure from any environmental authority, and no laws were being broken. But the conflict for Randy was too much. "I had campaigned against factory emissions of air pollution for years," Randy said. "The ethical conflict was too great; I had to stop making the glaze." Randy's decision led to difficult times for the shop. The New York architect cancelled his order—the glaze had been the winning factor for his business. The workers in the shop were also frustrated. They loved producing interesting, beautiful pieces, and the new orders meant extra hours and extra earnings. Their shop was so small, they argued, how could a little smoke possibly matter in the big scheme of things?

Although Randy's pottery shop does not have a formal written mission statement, his behavior and willingness to discuss his decision behind discontinuing the popular glaze let each employee see clearly the priorities Randy held for the business. Randy had to be firm, repeatedly explaining that his personal ethics had to be consistent with his workplace ethics and that he was sure that, in the long run, the shop would benefit from his decision. Even though Randy's employees did not easily accept his decision, they felt the larger mission of the business was well defined and respected. ■

Corporate Social Responsibility pp. 68–75

" **N**o matter where you come from, and who you are or what your last name is, whether you have money or you don't, don't let anybody tell you that your dreams can't come true. That is tragic. When you convince yourself that your dreams can come true, dream big dreams. And then after that, dream bigger. This isn't a Hollywood movie— I'm an example! I had some luck and I had some good timing, but I dreamed big dreams and here we are."

—Howard Schulz, *chairman and founder of Starbucks*

"He cares and it's very evident in everything he does, in how he runs his company. He loves helping people understand that they matter."

—Norman Lear, *television producer on Howard Schulz*

Howard Schulz purchased Starbucks, a Seattle storefront that sold fresh-roasted whole bean coffee, in 1987 with the lofty mission "to inspire and nurture the human spirit." Since then, Starbucks has become an entrepreneurial dream business, with over 16,000 stores in over 50 countries. How are the goals of helping communities, protecting the environment, and inspiring employees related to the bottom line of business—profit and growth? ■

Corporate decisions reflect a company's desire to fulfill a sense of corporate social responsibility. Every day, large companies like Gap, Disney, and Shell, as well as medium-sized firms and small local businesses, must make decisions regarding CSR. Let's look at what it means, who it affects, and how companies can achieve it.

The Five Pillars of CSR

What is corporate social responsibility? Corporate social responsibility (CSR) is defined as a company's obligation to conduct its activities with the aim of achieving social, environmental, and economic development. All business organizations, regardless of their size, have a corporate responsibility. By being socially responsible, a company makes decisions in five major areas (see ▼ **Figure 3.1**):[10]

1. Human rights and employment standards in the workplace
2. Ethical sourcing and procurement
3. Marketing and consumer issues
4. Environmental, health, and safety concerns
5. Community and good neighbor policies

Let's look at each of these areas.

Human Rights and Employment Standards in the Workplace

CSR concerns affect the world outside the office in both local and global communities. For example, employment standards—how a company respects and cares for its employees—are reflected locally in the policies a company sets and the impact a company has on the community. As a business interacts more with the global marketplace, a company will have to make decisions about ethical standards on tough issues such as child labor, pollution, fair wages, and human rights. Consider the case of the Vadanta Resources, a mining and aluminum refining company based in the United Kingdom. When Vadanta came into the Indian community of Orissa, it promised great gains in the quality of life for its employees and the entire region. Such gains have not appeared, however, and, because of the refining company's practices, the air is hard to breathe. Meanwhile, the river, the main source of drinking water, is so polluted that bathing in it causes rashes and blisters.[11] What responsibility does Vadanta have to its employees, the people of the area, and company stockholders?

▼ **Figure 3.1**
The Five Pillars of CSR
Corporate social responsibility is the collection of policies covering five major areas and can be the foundation of a business.

Ethical Sourcing and Procurement

Finding a source for raw materials and making agreements with suppliers is an aspect of many businesses. In today's global marketplace, many companies find themselves working with international suppliers. Once a business considers purchasing materials from a supplier in a different country or even a different region of their home country, the company is tied to environmental and social concerns in that area. Consider a company that has an assembly plant in a different country. That company is now tied to the social conditions there. To keep its supplier operating or keep an assembly plant running smoothly, the company has a vested interest in the quality of the schools in that area so that the local workforce is educated.

The banana supplier Chiquita, for example, has a vested interest in other parts of the world where they get their product—bananas. Chiquita has had a decades long reputation of allowing dangerous conditions for its farm workers, contaminating water, and clear-cutting tropical forests. With the threat of these environmental and worker's rights issues endangering the brand, Chiquita began to improve conditions. It constructed housing and schools for employees' families, and now all of Chiquita's farms are certified by the environmental group Rainforest Alliance.[12] A commitment to CSR means that companies must be aware of the ethical impact of their behavior—both at home and in communities far from their shores.

Marketing and Consumer Issues

Marketing can often present ethical challenges. In addition to issues regarding truth in advertising, marketers must consider messages that may be manipulative even if they are not outright lies. For example, *Brigette*, a leading German fashion magazine, recently announced it will no longer accept advertising featuring professional "zero-sized" models.[13] As more medical authorities have linked the viewing of these images with an increase in eating disorders, the publishers were faced with a decision. Editor Andreas Lebert said his staff were "fed up." They decided to begin using "real" women in place of professional models to better connect with their readers. There are many marketing and consumer issues that companies must consider if they are to behave in a socially responsible way. What do you think? Are magazines that use professional models socially irresponsible? How do we judge when responsible behavior turns into irresponsible behavior?

Environmental, Health, and Safety Concerns

Many industries, even small companies, make decisions every day that affect the environment and the safety of their workers or neighbors. From multinational manufacturing giants to the local auto body shop, any industry involved with processes that produce toxic waste must make decisions that directly affect the environment. Meanwhile, the production of toxic materials is moving at a far faster pace than the growth of proper storage facilities and techniques, so disposal becomes more and more expensive. One of the most infamous cases was documented in the award-winning book *A Civil Action* (Vintage, 1996). A high incidence of childhood leukemia appeared in a small Massachusetts town. A civil action lawsuit filed by one boy's mother ultimately found that the town water supply had been poisoned by trichloroethylene dumped by two local businesses. What are the short- and long-term costs of ignoring these concerns? Companies that have a CSR focus concentrate on ways to make such decisions in a socially sound way.

Community and Good Neighbor Policies

Finally, CSR is concerned with how a company affects the community, particularly the surrounding neighborhood. This issue has been a challenge for Walmart for years. In the documentary *Wal-Mart: The High Cost of Low Price*, film director Robert Greenwald argues that Walmart pays its associates so little that the arrival of a Wal-mart outlet in a community actually costs the community.[14] Because workers are paid poorly and are not offered medical benefits to cover their children, Medicaid expenditures increase. In addition, Greenwald argues that many local and smaller businesses cannot compete with the giant and are forced to close. Adding insult to injury, often a community has given Walmart subsidies to attract them to the area. Finding a way to be good corporate neighbor is important to avoid the tensions and bad publicity that Walmart has struggled against.

The Conflict of CSR in the Business Environment

Can a corporation really be socially responsible? The Nobel Prize–winning economist Milton Friedman said, "Asking a corporation to be socially responsible makes no more sense than asking a building to be."[15] He argued that an abstract idea, like a corporation, cannot perform human functions, such as meeting responsibilities. There has long been debate around these ideas. A company has a unique responsibility to its stockholders: They expect a profit at the end of the year. It is difficult to measure how that responsibility interacts with a long-term responsibility to the community or the planet. There can be a conflict between a company's need to produce profit for its shareholders and the demands of quality in the product it delivers to its customers. With so many competing interests, companies must carefully analyze the idea of appropriate social and corporate responsibility.

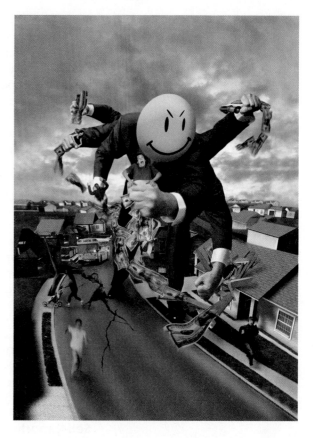

Walmart's impact on a community is debated in the film *Wal-Mart: The High Cost of Low Price.*

The Benefits of CSR

What are the benefits of CSR? Having a strong and clear ethical policy helps a business in a number of ways:[16]

- A company develops a positive reputation in the marketplace with consumers as well as with its suppliers and vendors.
- A company enjoys strong recruitment and retention of the best available talent.
- Efficiency increases when companies use materials efficiently and minimize waste.
- Sales increase through new product innovations and environmentally and ethically conscious labeling.

Although businesses reap benefits while being socially responsible, management at very high strategic levels must have a common vision of how the interests of the business can be supported by an effective CSR policy.

Measuring CSR

Is it possible to measure a company's CSR level? It may seem impossible to measure something as complex as CSR, but there are reports that present a useful picture of the overall strength of a company's CSR effort.

Social Audits

A **social audit** is a study of how well a company is meeting its social responsibilities. It is an internal and systematic examination that measures and monitors what goals a company has set, what progress it has made, and how resources such as funding and labor have been applied to the CSR goals.

Ratings and Rankings

In addition to social audits, companies like the Boston College Center for Corporate Citizenship assess corporate responsibility and publish their findings. And companies like the Calvert Investment Company provide corporate responsibility ratings and reports to consumers. The Calvert Company assigns companies a score based on performance in the categories of environment, workplace, business practices, human rights, and community relations. Investors can use the "Know What You Own®" tool to investigate a fund and check the environmental and social performance of the companies in the fund.

In addition to social audits and the Calvert ratings, various magazines, such as *Fortune*, publish lists of admired companies each year. Other organizations award businesses for superior CSR. For example, as a 2010 recipient of the WorldBlu Most Democratic Workplaces, Chroma Technology Corp., a manufacturer of optical filters, has many innovative practices.[17] In this global company, employees hold all the seats on the board of directors. In addition, the salary structure heavily rewards loyalty, with each employee making a base salary based on occupation that then increases based on seniority.[18]

Another often cited CSR award winner is Clif Bar, Inc., a manufacturer of organic energy bars. Gary Erickson started the company in his kitchen with $1,000. After 10 years of consistent growth, he was about to accept an offer of $120 million for the company. At the last minute, he learned that the purchasers were planning to move Clif Bar out of state and lay off all the current employees. He felt his integrity and vision were at stake, so he canceled the deal and took over the company again.

Self-Reporting

Companies self-reporting their own efforts in addressing ethically complex issues and issues of social responsibility is also becoming more prevalent. For example, every year, Time Warner presents a CSR report to its stockholders that discusses its advances in corporate citizenship, including its focus on journalistic integrity, socially responsible programming (including such issues as the depiction of smoking in films), content accessibility, consumer privacy, content diversity, and child protection.[19]

Corporate Philanthropy

Many companies participate in **corporate philanthropy**, donating some of their profits or resources to charitable organizations. Often companies view such charitable activity as a marketing investment that builds a stronger relationship with the community and their own employees. Consider the Target store chain. The retailer donates 5 percent of its pretax profits to charity, which is about $3 million a week.[20] This is more than twice the average of other American corporations.

Another example is the Bill and Melinda Gates Foundation, started by Microsoft chairman Bill Gates. With an endowment of $33 billion, the Gates Foundation has tackled issues like global infant survival rates, began an initiative for a malaria vaccine, and is working to upgrade public access to technology. Even though the foundation is not directly associated with Microsoft, it has had a positive impact on the public perception of Microsoft.

CSR and Social Networking

What does social networking have to do with CSR? As is the case with many aspects of business, social networking is changing the face of CSR. For example, did you know that PepsiCo did not run a Super Bowl ad during the 2010 game? Why not? The company passed up on this exclusive marketing opportunity in favor of funding its Pepsi RefreshEverything Web site. At refresheverything.com, people from across the country can post their project proposals in different categories of need—$5,000, $25,000, and so on up to $250,000. Over 1,000 ideas per month are accepted at the site, and visitors to the site then vote and comment on the projects. PepsiCo funds the 10 most popular ideas in each category for that month. PepsiCo has pledged to give away $1.3 million a month to community organizations through this initiative. After funding, the winning projects continue to update the site with their results, keeping voters engaged in the final outcome. Project winners for 2010 included an autism classroom in New York, science classrooms in a Wisconsin middle school, and an animal shelter in South Carolina. Besides the main Web page, the Refresh project also maintains a Facebook site and a Twitter channel.

What does PepsiCo get in return for its shifted focus from Super Bowl ads to corporate philanthropy? Perhaps a more positive reputation and increased engagement by its customers. As you can see, the look of CSR is changing as the current tools of social media are incorporated.

The Challenges of CSR

What challenges does CSR pose? It's clear that the many conflicting demands facing businesses today pose numerous ethical challenges. Consider the dilemma facing companies that produce unique products, such as pharmaceutical companies that develop medications to treat AIDS. What is their exact moral and ethical obligation with regard to the AIDS pandemic in sub-Saharan Africa? AIDS killed 1.6 million people in Africa in 2008.[21] Tuberculosis killed approximately 550,000 that same year, and at least 1 million people die from malaria each year, mostly children.[22] Meanwhile, 70 percent of the population exists on less than $2 a day and is unable to pay for the medications at a price point that would reimburse pharmaceutical companies for their research investment. It is a challenge for modern business leaders to balance their need to respond to investors and produce a profit with their desire to alleviate human suffering. There is no fixed training that prepares and equips business decision makers to navigate such difficult decisions.

As noted above, some corporations manage to consistently balance the demands of social responsibility and successful business practices. For example, Intel scores high as an industry leader in its commitment to strong CSR practices.[23] Environmentally, it has decreased the emissions from its operations over the past four years, mitigating its impact on global warming. It has shown a strong commitment to its employees by providing benefits for domestic partners as well as carefully monitoring workers for exposure to hazardous chemicals. The company also has human rights policies in place in each country it operates; it donates computer equipment to many organizations, supports many charitable organizations through monetary donations, and is responsive to community needs.

The Bill and Melinda Gates Foundation commits more than $1.5 billion a year in grants to global health and development projects, such as funding the search for a vaccine to prevent malaria.

The Effects of CSR on Society

How does CSR affect society as a whole? Businesses do not operate separately from society as a whole, so CSR affects us all in many ways.

Environmental Effects

Environmentally, how businesses operate has both local and global effects. For example, people living in the Silicon Valley area near San Francisco rely on groundwater for their main supply of water. This leaves the entire Silicon Valley area dependent on proper industry practices by the many semiconductor manufacturers in the area. If these companies allow chemical contaminants to enter the groundwater system, the entire region suffers.

Businesses raise troubling environmental questions on a global scale as well. Some say that allowing free trade—in which countries produce and sell products anywhere in the world—will export pollution to less developed countries. Would companies move "dirty industries"—those that have a high risk of pollution, danger to workers, or toxic damage of the environment—to a country where environmental regulations are lacking? It is increasingly important for industry leaders to have some structured ethical system to make such complex, long-reaching decisions.

Economic Effects

As an individual, CSR affects you as well. Financially, the long-term consequences of businesses implementing a strong CSR plan have an impact on the prices you pay for products, the products that are available, and the quality of those products. Both short-term savings and long-term investments rely on interest rates that are related to the perception of how stable a business is. Industries that act in ways that jeopardize their own long-term sustainability can create economic ripples that affect the bottom line of individual consumers.

Effects on Employee Morale

Think of your own career. Your potential for advancement, day-to-day work environment, and overall sense of purpose and value are affected by the degree to which the company you work for practices sound CSR. The ethical culture of a company and its leadership has effects on its workers every day. Sometimes, this effect is a positive one. Consider the Kaplan Thaler advertising agency, the fastest-growing advertising firm in the country, started by Linda Kaplan Thaler and Robin Koval.[24] The company, which began as a one-client start-up in 1997 and has reached billings of more than $1 billion, prides itself on creating unique ad campaigns—like the Aflac duck campaign—that grab viewers' attention.

Yet with all of its success, the core philosophy of the company is that it pays to be nice, described in Thaler and Koval's book, *The Power of Nice* (Broadway Business, 2006). After spending years at high-powered, high-pressure firms where "those who eat their young get raises," Thaler and Koval founded a firm dedicated to the principles of being empathetic. They assume that the people around you are there to help you and remember that emotionally, well-adjusted people earn higher incomes, live longer, and have more satisfying lives.[25] The company founders' beliefs affect the employees at Kaplan each and every day.

Even from the initial interview, aspects of a company's CSR plan may be apparent. Some companies find that personality testing of job candidates helps them find employees who match their own corporate values. Tools like the Hogan Personality Inventory assess a candidate in areas such as interpersonal sensitivity, stress tolerance, and learning approach. As a job seeker, you'll want to decide whether you value a company for using these tools or if their use violates your sense of appropriate business and personal privacy boundaries.

The Effects of Individuals on CSR

How can I affect how businesses operate ethically? There are many ways that individuals can work toward a more ethical world filled with more ethical businesses. In addition to contributing by means of your own personal conduct, both at the workplace and outside it, your choices about where and on what to spend your money greatly influence corporate behavior. Companies survive only because consumers buy their products or use their services. If you don't believe in a company's ethics, you can take your business elsewhere.

Meanwhile, if you choose to invest money in mutual funds and the stock market, you have another opportunity to make a statement about corporate ethics. **Socially responsible investing (SRI)** is investing only in companies that have met a certain standard of CSR. This means that fund managers look at the social and environmental behavior of companies to decide which companies to include and exclude from the investment fund portfolio. As a shareholder, you can also use your voice to encourage a company to improve or maintain a high standard of ethics.

Finally, when you choose an employer, you're making a clear statement on ethical conduct by offering the company your valuable time and energy. By agreeing to work for a company, you're saying that you agree with its mission and ethics.

As a boy, Starbucks founder Howard Schulz saw his family lose their home and be driven into public housing because of the financial consequences of his father's illness. He was determined that any company he ran would never let such a thing happen to an employee. When he bought Starbucks in 1987, he immediately extended a company-subsidized health-care package to all full- and part-time employees and their dependents. The deductibles, co-pays, and benefits are the same for all employees. The incredible success of Starbucks could be an accident that happened in spite of the company's commitment to ethics and social responsibility, but Howard Schulz would tell you something different. ■

Dangers of a Weak Ethical Focus pp. 75–79

"To me, it was stealing, and, bottom line, stealing is wrong." The software firm that Lana Phillips worked for had finished developing a program to deliver movie content on-demand to home cable subscribers. Before it could break into the market, however, it needed to test its product and make appearances at big electronics trade shows. To test the program, the company needed data—that is, DVD movies. But DVD movies are copyrighted and protected with specific software encoding schemes so they cannot be copied onto a computer hard drive. As the testing phase approached, word came down from management: purchase some DVDs, break the encoding scheme, and rip them to hard drives to use as testing. After all, the managers reasoned, the company was not going to make money off violating DVD copyrights; it was just

using it to test its software. And if it worked well, it would then run demos for clients and at trade shows using those DVDs. What was the harm?

The company consulted its attorneys, and half felt the use of the DVDs might be illegal and half felt it could be defended. Lana suggested some other solutions: The company could use Hollywood films that were older and not covered by copyright protection or public domain documentaries, which were freely available for public use. Company managers worried what the impact on business would be. Would a product shown running a 30-year-old movie or an unknown documentary grab the attention of buyers on a busy Vegas trade-show floor? The danger on the other side was that a successful product launch by the company might not save it from facing future legal action for copyright infringement. How could Lana and her boss resolve the issue when it wasn't even clear what the correct legal path was?

Depending on the industry, there may be significant legal consequences to business behavior that ignores agreed-on ethical standards. Companies are responsible for following complex sets of laws, and if they violate them, even unknowingly, their businesses may be in jeopardy. Violating the law deliberately may be the result of a lapse in emphasis and an understanding of ethics and will have a serious impact on the future of the people inside the company and the entire business community. In this section, we'll examine some of the business dangers of ignoring ethical conduct.

Legal Regulations and Legal Compliance

How is a company regulated legally? **Legal regulations** are the specific laws governing the products or processes of a specific industry. When enough people feel that a particular ethical standard is important, it eventually becomes law. For example, in 1962, the Consumer Bill of Rights was passed in Congress. This bill made the following ethical standards legal rights:

- The right to safety
- The right to choose
- The right to information
- The right to be heard[26]

Another example is the Organic Seal of the U.S. Department of Agriculture (USDA), which assures consumers of the quality and integrity of organic products. To certify a product as organic, a company must meet stringent conditions set by the USDA, including annual and random inspections to check on standards.

Legal compliance refers to conducting a business within the boundaries of all the legal regulations of that industry. Various government agencies, such as the Equal Employment Opportunity Commission (EEOC) and the Securities and Exchange Commission (SEC), provide guidance to companies to help them maintain legal compliance. The EEOC monitors compliance by investigating complaints of federal law violations on issues such as discrimination, sexual harassment, or violations of the ADA. The ADA of 1990 requires companies to make a reasonable accommodation to the known disabilities of an applicant or employee, as long as it doesn't require undue hardship for the employer. The SEC governs the securities industry, making sure that all investors have the same access to information about companies.

Violations of federal laws can severely damage a company. We mentioned earlier how ADM, the agriculture giant, was involved in a large price fixing scheme in which it bilked its own customers out of millions of dollars. The company was later fined $100 million for its role in the price fixing. Likewise, in 2010, Toyota Motor Sales was fined $16.4 million by the U.S. Department of Transportation to settle claims that it hid potentially dangerous defects from federal highway-safety regulators.[27]

Don't companies often break the law and still make money?

There are plenty of cases in which companies have broken the law and seemed to benefit for a time. Take the case of Enron. With 21,000 staff members in more than 40 countries, Enron had grown to become the seventh largest company in the United States. The company was lauded by *Fortune* magazine as the Most Innovative Company in America many times and was in the top 25 of *Fortune*'s 100 Best Companies to Work For. Enron had published its social and environmental positions, noting that the company made decisions based on three values:[28]

- **Respect:** mutual respect with communities and stakeholders affected by the company's operations
- **Integrity:** examining the impacts, positive and negative, of the business on the environment and society and integrating human health, social, and environmental considerations into the company's management and value system
- **Excellence:** continuing to improve performance and encouraging business partners and suppliers to adhere to the same standards

However, by October 2001, a series of scandals began to emerge when it was discovered that Enron's success had been largely based on fraudulent activities. The company had hidden debts totaling more than $1 billion to inflate its own stock price; manipulated the Texas and California power markets, causing enormous hardship; and bribed foreign governments to win contracts abroad. A few months later, the company dissolved in bankruptcy, and founder Kenneth Lay was convicted on 10 counts of fraud and conspiracy. He later died while awaiting sentencing. CEO Jeffrey Skilling was convicted of 18 counts of fraud and is serving a prison term.

Even the accounting auditor that Enron had hired, the famous firm Arthur Andersen, collapsed as a result of its involvement. Arthur Andersen was convicted of obstruction of justice for destroying thousands of documents relating to its work with Enron and its knowledge of the criminal fraud taking place at Enron. For both Enron and Arthur Andersen, the flagrant violations of ethical conduct led to outside agencies levying huge penalties. It also led to the internal collapse of both companies, with the subsequent loss of each company's management and employees within the firms. Most sadly, it led to the loss of pensions for thousands of employees who had dedicated their lives to the companies, not knowing management was participating in such illegal activities.

To avoid future occurrences such as these, the Sarbanes-Oxley Act of 2002 was enacted. Under this act, CEOs are required to verify their companies' financial statements and vouch for their accuracy with the SEC.

Still, in 2008, one of the largest financial scandals of all time was exposed. Bernie Madoff owned and ran a large investment firm, managing the funds of many clients, including pensions and not-for-profit charities. In December 2008, it was revealed that over $65 billion was missing from client accounts. For years Madoff had been running a massive Ponzi scheme, defined as an investment swindle in which some early investors are paid off with money put up by later ones to encourage more and bigger risks.[29] Madoff was convicted and sentenced to a 150-year prison sentence and a $170 billion fine.

Recovering from Weak Ethical Conduct

What if your company is breaking the law and you want it to stop? Some people risk their positions and future careers to stop corporate abuse when they see it in the workplace. A **whistle-blower** is an employee who reports misconduct, most often to an authority outside the firm. Famous examples include Jeffrey Wigand, a vice president of a tobacco company who revealed on *60 Minutes* in February 1996 that his company was deliberately manipulating the effect of the nicotine in its cigarettes to promote addiction. Another example is Sergeant Joseph Darby, who sent to the U.S. Army Criminal Investigation Command an anonymous note and a set of images of the abuse taking place at Abu Ghraib prison in Iraq. It sparked an investigation that eventually revealed to the public the abuses at Abu Ghraib. Darby later received a John F. Kennedy Profile in Courage award, but he and his wife were forced to live in protective custody in an undisclosed location because of threats made against them.

Legal protection for whistle-blowers varies from state to state and industry to industry. For the people who take such a step, the pressure of the conflict between what they see and their own ethical standards forces them to make sacrifices.

Can a company really recover from an ethical lapse? Companies seeking to recover from publicized ethical lapses often face long battles once customer loyalty and a company's reputation have been lost. Recovery almost certainly requires pervasive change, and usually people who were not involved in the wrongdoing work to forge a new image. For example, a major scandal broke at Tyco International in 2003. An SEC investigation had found that company president Dennis Kozlowski and chief financial officer (CFO) Mark Swartz had swindled more than $170 million in illegal corporate loans and another $430 million by manipulating the company's stock price. Both Kozlowski and Swartz were convicted of fraud charges and later sentenced up to 25 years in prison. Within a few months of being named the new CEO of Tyco, Edward Breen replaced the entire Tyco board and 290 employees.

Companies that are attempting to recover from scandal often follow some common strategies:

1. They work to find a leader who will set an example of the new ethical image of the company.
2. They restructure their internal operation to empower all employees to consider ethical implications of decisions and feel free to speak up when they spot a concern.
3. They redesign internal rewards—for example, restructuring the incentive package for a sales department so that there is a financial reward for building an ongoing relationship with a client rather than just closing a sale one time.

By using creative thinking and adhering to clearly stated ethical principles, a company can actually turn a scandal into something good. For example, in 2004, many shoppers boycotted Target because the chain had a policy of not allowing solicitors to collect money outside its doors, including volunteers collecting for the Salvation Army. In fact, the Salvation Army claimed the ban cost them more than $9 million in possible donations. Target could have responded with a defensive attack on the Salvation Army. Instead, the company chose to work with the charity, first donating the lost $9 million directly and then by creating an online "wish list" that

"Companies do business in an ecosystem. Ultimately you can't have a great reputation unless everyone who comes in contact with you trusts you. And people don't trust you unless they think you do the right thing."[30]

—Dov Seidman, CEO of LRN, a consultant firm specializing in legal compliance and ethical management

shoppers could use to donate toys, clothes, and household items to needy families during the holiday season. By acting together with the Salvation Army in new ways, Target was able to turn a negative situation into something beneficial for both Target and the community.

Think back to Lana Phillips' company and their work of ripping movies from DVDs. Even though Lana's firm was not knowingly committing fraud on the scale of the Enron scandal, many of the same principles were at play. The temptation to ignore existing laws to make a profit, or even the chance for profit, was at the heart of both stories. For Enron officials, the penalties they paid for their unethical actions were devastating to thousands, if not millions, of people. At Lana's firm, future penalties could cripple the company, but the immediate penalty of knowingly violating her own personal code of ethics was the driving force for Lana. She was forced to decide whether she would refuse to work on the project and potentially lose her job, knowing that her manager would assign the work to another employee who would then be breaking the law. Lana decided to make her case to the company, urging it to not use the copyrighted DVDs. Ultimately, the company executives agreed with Lana's argument. They felt that the risk of future copyright infringement lawsuits was too great. Lana's persistence paid off, and she was able to maintain both job security and a personal code of ethics. ■

Business Opportunities Created by Ethical Needs pp. 79–82

In the early 1980s, Mary Stephenson lost her battle with cancer. After her death, her son, Richard Stephenson, tried to explore what options the family might have pursued that would have made his mother's final days with her family of higher quality. He found facilities that were equipped to provide top-notch technical care, but none that provided compassion and nurturing for the whole person who was ill, as well as for his or her entire family. How could he give his mother's death meaning and positively affect the lives of others? Was there a way that the business of health care could be both successful and compassionate? ■

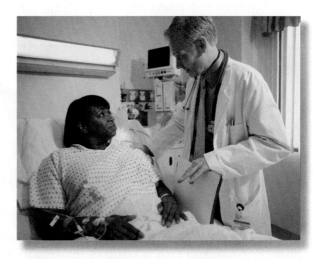

So far we've addressed the extra work and the difficult decisions that are required for conducting business ethically. But there are also opportunities and the potential for gain by understanding and applying ethical standards to a business. Some companies focus on creating new markets with an ethical focus. Others redesign their businesses so that they no longer have a negative impact on the environment. Still others use ethical challenges as a tool to unite and empower employees.

Creating New Markets with an Ethical Focus

How can firms create business by acting ethically? By examining the world with an eye toward social responsibility, many firms have created opportunities with new types of products and services. Let's examine a few examples.

Offering Clean Fuel

Topia Energy, an energy company in Canada, has opened the first chain of alternative fuel stations, named GreenStop, which offer only renewable fuel blends, such as gasoline combined with corn ethanol. The gasoline products can be used in regular cars, and the stations themselves are constructed from renewable, chemical-free products. Inside you won't see the same lineup of cigarettes and candy, but you will have your choice of organic veggie wraps and coffee roasted using solar energy.[31]

Creating Medical Vaccines

Other companies have created business opportunities by addressing the world's most serious medical needs. Malaria kills up to three million people a year, mostly children, and is the leading cause of death in children worldwide, mostly in Africa. The disease is transmitted very easily, whereas the drugs currently used to treat it are becoming increasingly ineffective. Many businesses haven't found a way to balance the tremendous cost of research for creating a malaria vaccine with the anticipated meager profits. Enter Sanaria, a new pharmaceutical company founded by Dr. Stephen Hoffman, whose mission is to create a malaria vaccine. Hoffman remarks, "I haven't spent 25 years working on diseases of the most disadvantaged and neglected people in the world to start a company that's just here to make money."[32] Already the company has secured government grants and a $29.3 million Gates Foundation grant. A malaria vaccine, long considered to be impossible, is now about to enter clinical trials.[33]

Fighting Censorship

Still other companies are creating business opportunities by fighting censorship. The Chinese government maintains a tight rein on the flow of information to its citizens, including controlling the accessibility of certain Internet sites. This policy of censorship garnered the attention of the international business community when, in 2010, after four years of complying with China's system of censorship so that search results were edited before being presented to users, Google did an about-face and announced it would no longer censor search results for China.[34] Google's announcement was met by an announcement from Microsoft that its Bing search engine would continue to abide by Chinese censorship laws.

This censorship left Dynamic Internet Technology (DIT) company founder Bill Xia with a very skewed view of the world when he arrived in the United States

Earth-friendly GreenStop gas stations are popping up in Canada.

from China. "I was a believer of the propaganda," he says.[35] DIT and similar companies provide a service to their clients in an effort to counteract the impact of censorship. When a site is placed on the list of censored sites by the Chinese government, DIT quickly creates a new, uncensored Web address that points users to the same material. A list of the new accessible sites is then e-mailed to Web surfers who want full Internet access. Chinese censors often stamp out the new site within a few days, at which point DIT starts the process again, determined to override censorship through its business. DIT and other companies are showing there are ways to fight censorship and profit from it.

Businesses Going Green

How can businesses benefit by going green? While some businesses are tackling ethical issues and offering consumers more ethical choices through their businesses, others are attempting to reduce the impact they have on the environment. Take Interface, Inc., the world's largest commercial carpet manufacturer. The company was careful to follow all laws and regulations relating to its industry in its first 21 years of business, but it made no special commitment to stewardship of the environment beyond that. Then, in 1994, CEO Ray Anderson read *The Ecology of Commerce* (HarperBusiness, 1994).[36] He was so inspired by the book's message that he began the process of reorganizing his $1.4 billion company using the principles of **sustainability**—the process of working to improve the quality of life in ways that simultaneously protect and enhance the earth's life support systems.[37] Interface has a mission statement, nicknamed Mission Zero, that reads: "Our promise is to eliminate any negative impact Interface has on the environment by 2020."[38]

Interface is considering all aspects of its business in its goal to run its business without having a negative impact on the planet. It is eliminating waste and toxic substances from its products, using renewable energy, and finding how to route its trucks for more efficient transportation routes. The grand goal of Mission Zero has resulted in a shift in the company's principles and the goals and expectations of shareholders.[39]

COOL carpet is one product that demonstrates how Interface now operates. The "cool" part of COOL carpet is that it allows customers to choose to have an impact on global warming. Interface makes sure that all carbon dioxide emissions over the full life cycle of COOL carpet—from its manufacture through its delivery—are offset. Actions like purchasing energy from wind farms and choosing suppliers that are ecologically friendly balance out the necessary carbon dioxide produced in other stages of carpet production. For example, Interface purchases carbon offsets by buying energy from family-owned dairy farms in Pennsylvania and Wisconsin.[40] These farms generate electricity by processing their manure differently, preventing the release of methane, a powerful greenhouse gas. Anderson recognizes the choices Interface makes today will ultimately affect future generations and hopes his customers see the value in these choices and go green themselves.

Another large international company that has worked for over a decade to reduce its environmental footprint is Starbucks. Their corporate Shared Planet progress plan sets clear objectives for the company in recycling, energy and water usage, building, and climate change.[41] In 2009, it convened a summit with local governments, cup manufacturers, and recyclers to identify the steps required to make its cups recyclable. Stores are being designed to have recycling locations in the front, and customers are given

Starbucks discounts coffee if customers bring their own recyclable tumblers. In 2009, 4.4 million people did just that.

$.10 off each cup of coffee served in a reusable tumbler. In 2009, 4.4 million more beverages were served this way than in 2008.

As we have seen, companies can create opportunities based on ethical challenges in a variety of different ways. New businesses are appearing, focused on addressing the ethical issues of our times. For example, a newly diagnosed cancer patient has more options today than ever before. Richard Stephenson responded to his mother's death by founding a network of hospitals called the Cancer Treatment Centers of America (CTCA). At CTCA, providers are guided to treat patients with the "Mother Standard of care," the level of compassion and support that you would want for your own family members. In four hospitals spread across the United States, CTCA treats patients with the latest conventional therapies but also provides a full range of complementary treatment options and access to multidisciplinary team support. Hospital staff members are available for nutritional consults; spiritual support; mind-body counseling; and the latest treatments in chemotherapy, radiation, and surgery. The hospital policies are centered on a model called "Patient Empowerment Medicine," in which both the patient and caregivers play an active role in treatment options. From the pain of his mother's illness and the lack of compassionate, integrated care available for her, Richard Stephenson recognized the opportunity for a more ethical, humane medical system. ■

How Businesses Develop an **Ethical Environment** pp. 82–85

Rashid has seen it all as a project manager at a major clinical laboratory—samples left on the dock over the 4th of July weekend (thawed beyond repair), tests done with old chemicals, and reports delivered late and incomplete. But he knew he'd really be on the hot spot with a client when a lab tech walked in on Friday and announced that three key samples from the testing for a major client were missing. The results for those samples were critical to the report that was being delivered to that client on Monday . . . but now there was no proof for the Food and Drug Administration (FDA) that those data points had ever really existed. As Rashid pondered how to handle the situation, his e-mail inbox was filling up with demands from his supervisors not to say anything to the client until a complete "story" had been developed that would make the lab appear blameless. Some even suggested covering up the whole episode with false data. What would Rashid do? ■

On Target Playing the Ethics Game

A unique approach to ethics training is emerging in the corporate world: games. For example, Cadbury Schweppes, an international confectionery and beverage company, has created a board game called "Ethical Risk" that its employees play to help bridge the gap between the values the company wants to achieve and the day-to-day decision making and practices of its managers.[42] Lockheed Martin uses a computer game called "Gray Matters," which presents a series of ethical dilemmas. Group discussion with a facilitator leads to a better understanding of how to resolve complex ethical issues.[43] Many other companies offer self-paced online training in ethics awareness issues. The use of multimedia and a gaming environment promotes a stronger dialog and builds insight into the practical ways to address the complex issues of corporate ethics and social responsibility.

Almost every business wants to promote an ethical environment, but sometimes managers find it difficult to know how to implement this successfully. Let's look at some different approaches being used by businesses to help their employees and the company decision-making processes become attuned to an emphasis on ethical conduct.

Ethical Focus from the Start

How can a business improve its own culture of ethical and responsible conduct? There are several steps that businesses can take to make sure employees get off to an ethical start:

1. Managers can make sure a strict code of ethics and a meaningful and current mission statement is in place and that both are clearly communicated to employees when they start working at an organization. The code of ethics and mission statement should be posted throughout the workplace.
2. A company can offer orientation programs to new employees to inform them of the ethical standards in place and the conduct expected of them from the beginning of their careers at a company.

Companies should set the right tone at the beginning—show how serious they are about ethics and act with the highest regard to ethical behavior.

Ethical Focus Every Day

How can a business maintain its policy of ethical conduct in the workplace? When employees are faced with unethical situations on a daily basis, adhering to a company's code of ethics can be very difficult. Business leaders must take steps to make sure that all employees are making ethical decisions. This becomes even more of a challenge during tough economic times, such as has been recently experienced in the United States. In recent surveys, however, the majority of U.S. employers say they are keeping their budgets for ethics training and compliance monitoring at the same level or increasing them, despite the economic downturn.[44]

Companies often report doing the following to support ethical conduct:

- Managers check sporadically to determine that the code of ethics is being followed.

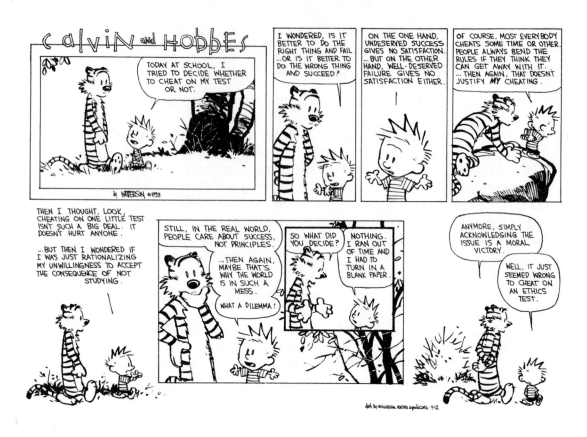

- Managers focus on ethics themselves, setting clear examples for the standards of behavior expected at all levels of the organization.

- Companies employ ongoing **ethics training programs** designed to boost the awareness of their employees about ethical issues. Such training occurs at all levels of the organization. From top management that makes strategic and far-reaching decisions, to frontline managers who use their decision-making skills to put out fires, to salespeople who work with vendors and must navigate ethical questions, to lower-level employees who make decisions regarding whether to follow the advice of their leaders, all levels of employees are involved in ethical training.

- Companies create a hotline for employees to anonymously report violations of the ethics code and make sure the allegations are followed up on.

- Managers communicate with employees regularly about acceptable and unacceptable business practices.

Of course, private sector businesses are not alone in wanting ethics training programs for their employees. State and government organizations face similar challenges. Many law enforcement agencies—including local police, state police, and the FBI—have ethics training programs to help officers deal with cases in which there may be no clear response.[45] For example, when an officer responds to a domestic disturbance call but decides no crime has been committed, does he or she have a responsibility to try to prevent a potential escalation into a future criminal incident? By discussing, role-playing, and writing about these scenarios, the officers are more prepared for the ethical dilemmas facing them on the job.

Developing an ethical environment involves several components and often requires a concentrated investment of time and resources; however, it remains a priority for most businesses. Think back at Rashid's story. What did Rashid decide to do? Although he was pressured by his supervisors not to say anything to the client until a complete "story" had been developed, Rashid knew how he would want to be treated and was willing to live up to his personal ethical beliefs even in this crisis. In doing so, he set an example for his own employees to emulate.

Next he went looking for the company's stated procedure for the ethical handling of a corrective action like this. It turned out there was no such document at this facility, but the company's Salt Lake City lab had a corrective procedures document, so Rashid obtained a copy of it. He then began a series of interviews with all the employees involved, not as a hunt for blame but with a clear message of improving lab performance. Some practices were identified that needed to be changed—for example, scientists often just walked into the lab and took samples they wanted for their own research. It also became clear there was one employee who had been involved in several instances of sample mishandling. It was never proven whether this was due to incompetence or unethical conduct, but the employee was given a "performance improvement plan" to help train him and monitor and improve the situation. As these results were communicated to the client, their trust in the lab began to grow again. Rashid's supervisors begrudgingly saw the value of having made early contact with the client and the corporate policies were modified formally. ▪

Chapter Summary

Are you an active learner?
Go to my*biz*lab.com to master Chapter 3's content. Chapter 3's interactive activities include:
- Customizable Study Plan and Chapter 3 practice quizzes
- Chapter 3 Simulations, Navigating Murky Ethical Waters and Ethics and Social Responsibility, that help you think critically and prepare to make choices in the business world
- Chapter 3 Video Exercise, Patagonia: Ethics and Social Responsibility, which shows you how textbook concepts are put into practice every day
- Flash Cards for mastering the definition of chapter terms
- Interactive Lessons that visually review key chapter concepts

1. What are ethics and different ethical systems? (pp. 61–62)
- **Ethics** (p. 61) are the moral choices people make.
- Ethical systems include the following:
  - **Moral relativism** (p. 61), a perspective that holds that there is no universal moral truth but instead only individuals' beliefs, perspectives, and values
  - **Situational ethics** (p. 61), which encourages people to make ethical decisions based on the circumstances of a particular situation, not on fixed laws
  - Systems defined by religious traditions, such as **Judeo-Christian ethics** (p. 62), which refers to the common set of basic values shared across both Jewish and Christian religious traditions

2. How does a person create a personal code of ethics? (pp. 62–63)
- Determine your base character.
- List all the beliefs that influence your decision making.
- Think about how your behavior reflects these beliefs.
- Now think about where your beliefs and view of your character come from. Why do you hold these beliefs?

3. How might personal ethics play a role in the workplace? (pp. 65–67)
- Having a strong ethical foundation can help you achieve success in business and greater happiness in life.
- In the modern workplace, there is less distinction made between how you conduct yourself inside and outside the office. Telecommuting is one instance when a person's employer may influence how an employee behaves at home.
- Conflicts can emerge when your **personal ethics** (p. 62) are different than those of your company.

4. How can you evaluate a company's ethical code using available resources, such as a mission statement? (pp. 68–71)
- Some companies may have a written **code of ethics** (p. 67), or a statement of their commitment to certain ethical practices.
- Many companies have a public **mission statement** (p. 67) that defines the core purpose of the organization and often describes its values, goals, and aspirations.

5. How do a company's policies and decisions affect its achievement of corporate social responsibility? (pp. 68–71)
- **Corporate social responsibility** (CSR; p. 68) consists of five major areas: employment standards, ethical sourcing, marketing issues, environmental concerns, and community policies.
- A strong CSR plan allows a company to serve its local and global communities well. It also benefits a corporation in direct and indirect ways.

6. What challenges does a company face in balancing the demands of social responsibility with successful business practices? (pp. 71–74)
- Companies must balance their moral and ethical obligations to consumers with their need to respond to investors and produce a profit.
- It's also important for companies to show a strong commitment to their employees (by ensuring workplace safety), the local community (by responding to community needs, for example), and all the countries in which they operate (by upholding human rights policies). At times, it can be difficult to balance these commitments with the need to ensure that the business remains financially successful.

7. What is legal compliance, and how does it affect ethical conduct? (pp. 76–77)
- **Legal compliance** (p. 76) refers to conducting a business within the boundaries of all the legal regulations of that industry.
- Companies that establish and adhere to high ethical standards are more likely to maintain legal compliance.

8. What strategies can a company use to recover from ethical lapses? (pp. 78–79)
- A company can work to find a leader who will set an example of the new ethical image of the company.
- A company can restructure its internal operations to empower all employees to consider the ethical implications of decisions and feel free to speak up when they have concerns.
- A company can redesign internal rewards.

9. **How can companies apply ethical standards to create new business opportunities?** (pp. 79–82)

- While some businesses are tackling ethical issues and offering consumers more ethical choices through their businesses, others are attempting to reduce the impact they have on the environment.

10. **What approaches can a company use to develop and maintain an ethical environment?** (pp. 82–85)

- Managers can make sure a mission statement is in place and set clear examples for the standards of behavior expected at all levels of the organization.
- Companies can offer orientation programs to new employees to inform them of the ethical standards in place.
- **Ethics training programs** (p. 84) can boost the awareness of employees about ethical issues.

Key Terms

amoral behavior   (p. 62)

code of ethics   (p. 67)

corporate philanthropy   (p. 72)

corporate social responsibility (CSR)   (p. 68)

ethics   (p. 61)

ethics training program   (p. 84)

Judeo-Christian ethics   (p. 62)

legal compliance   (p. 76)

legal regulations   (p. 76)

mission statement   (p. 67)

moral relativism   (p. 61)

personal ethics   (p. 62)

price fixing   (p. 66)

situational ethics   (p. 61)

social audit   (p. 71)

socially responsible investing (SRI)   (p. 75)

sustainability   (p. 81)

unethical behavior   (p. 62)

whistle-blower   (p. 78)

Self-Test

Multiple Choice   You can find the answers on the last page of this book.

1. **Ethics are based on**

   a. the current popular culture.

   b. religious, cultural, or ethnic systems.

   c. society's legal system.

   d. each situation and the moral consequences of an action.

2. **A corporation can behave in a socially responsible way by**

   a. having strong policies in place to help the community.

   b. acting to reduce the negative impact a company has on the environment.

   c. being truthful with consumers in its market.

   d. All of the above

3. **Personal ethics collide with business ethics**

   a. whenever there is a claim of sexual harassment.

   b. when a business owner tries to control employees' behavior outside of work.

   c. if employees try to dictate corporate policies.

   d. None of the above

4. **CSR can be measured by**

   a. a company's rate of growth.

   b. organizations that monitor and rank performance on social issues.

   c. the happiness level of employees in a company.

   d. businesses that have a high profit margin and gross sales.

5. **A business is in legal compliance if**

   a. it follows all the laws of which it is aware.

   b. it cannot be proven guilty of violating any laws.

   c. it meets all local, state, and federal regulations.

   d. it only hires employees who do not have criminal records.

6. **A company's ethics can be examined by**

   a. following its stock price.

   b. interviewing employees.

   c. checking documents filed when it was incorporated.

   d. reviewing its code of ethics and mission statement.

7. **A vision statement**

   a. defines the marketing direction for a business.

   b. is a set of principles that defines how to measure the success of a business.

   c. indicates how well a company is doing at meeting its social responsibilities.

   d. is the common set of basic values shared across both Jewish and Christian religious traditions.

8. **Ethical sourcing means that**

   a. people should make ethical decisions based on a particular situation.

   b. there is one accepted source for guiding ethical decision making.

   c. a company follows accepted conduct when acquiring raw materials from suppliers.

   d. companies will not work with international suppliers.

9. **Which of the following strategies is *not* designed to help a company recover from an ethical lapse?**

   a. Ensuring that the whistle-blower faces legal consequences

   b. Working to find a leader who will set an example of the new ethical image of the company

   c. Restructuring internal operations to empower all employees to consider ethical implications of decisions and feel free to speak up when they have concerns

   d. Redesigning internal rewards—for example, restructuring the incentive package for a sales department so that there is a financial reward for building a relationship with a client rather than just closing a sale

10. **The practice of corporate philanthropy _____.**

   a. is only a marketing strategy.

   b. can build stronger relationships with employees and the community at large.

   c. states that success can be found by competing fiercely to provide lowest price.

   d. is a strategy that works only in certain segments of industry where there is a lot of media attention.

Self-Test

True/False

You can find the answers on the last page of this book.

1. A mission statement details the plans of how a company will achieve profitability.

   ☐ **True** or ☐ **False**

2. Minimizing a company's carbon footprint is part of a plan to increase corporate philanthropy.

   ☐ **True** or ☐ **False**

3. Ethics is the study of the general nature of morals and the specific moral choices a person makes.

   ☐ **True** or ☐ **False**

4. Environmental effects from business policies can have global consequences.

   ☐ **True** or ☐ **False**

5. Employee morale is the responsibility of only individual employees.

   ☐ **True** or ☐ **False**

Critical Thinking Questions

1. How can a person determine his or her personal ethical code? What is your personal ethical code? What forces have helped build your personal code of ethics?

2. Do you believe being ethical will lead to a better quality of life for you? Do cheaters win in the real world or does ethical conduct lead to a more satisfying outcome? Are there times you would be willing to compromise your ethics for business gain?

3. How does a corporation's responsibility to shareholders to produce a profit interact with its social responsibility? Name several areas of possible conflict and analyze them from both a short-term view and a long-term view.

4. Which of the five pillars of CSR seems the most important to you? How do the five areas relate to each other?

5. How would an international business be able to devise a common ethical framework that works for employees of different nationalities?

Team Time

One Issue, Three Sides

Divide into three teams, one to represent each of the following:

a. Pharmaceutical company executives

b. People with a catastrophic but treatable illness

c. People identified as having "unique" DNA

Scenario

Are there some things that can't be owned? Leukemia patient John Moore would answer yes. After Moore had his cancerous spleen removed at the University of California at Los Angeles, the university kept the spleen and was eventually granted a patent for DNA removed from the organ. The value of the DNA was estimated to be more than $1 billion. When Moore demanded that his cells be returned, the California Supreme Court ruled against him, saying that he had no right to his own cells after they had been removed from his body. Pharmaceutical researchers, like those at the University of California, often hope to later license the DNA patterns or sell them to other companies so they may use them to develop drugs or tests for the presence of disease. In March 2010, a Maryland state judge ruled that patents on two other genes, BCRA1 and BCRA2, breast cancer markers claimed by the University of Maryland and Myriad Genetics, were invalid. However, the judge chose not to rule on the larger issue of whether people own the genetic information their cells carry.[46]

Does a person or a group of people who have that specific, perhaps unique, gene have ownership? Do they deserve payment? Do they have a right to a voice in the use of their genetic material? Or are their interests trumped by the value of such discoveries to the greater good?

Process

Step 1. Record your ideas and opinions about the issue presented in this scenario. Be sure to consider the issue from your assigned perspective.

Step 2. Meet as a team and review the issue from multiple perspectives. Discuss together what one best policy could be developed to address the concerns of all three groups.

Ethics and Corporate Social Responsibility

Personal and Business Ethics

As you've learned, sometimes a person's personal code of ethics does not fall within the code of ethics used in his or her profession. What is your personal code of ethics? What profession do you hope to have in the future? How does your personal code of ethics match the code of ethics used in that profession? Would you be willing to ignore your personal ethical code for business?

Process

Step 1. Draft your personal code of ethics. Use the steps for analyzing one's own ethical system outlined at the beginning of this chapter.

Step 2. Think about a profession you'd like to have in the future. Visit http://ethics.iit.edu/codes/codes_index.html to find the code of ethics employed in this profession.

Step 3. Compare your personal code of ethics to the profession's code of ethics. Then write a paragraph explaining how the two codes compare.

Web Exercises

1. **Happiness and That New Lexus**
   Do you need a new car every few years to be happy? International studies of happiness suggest that happiness is not tied to income or material wealth. Watch the eight-minute BBC videos "Bhutan's happiness formula" and "The recipe for happiness" (both at www2.newsbbc.co.uk/2/hi/programmes/happiness_formula/default.stm) and see if you think the idea of a Gross National Happiness measurement can be incorporated into organizational decision making.

2. **Identifying Your Strengths**
   Visit the Web site of Martin Seligman's Web site, found at authentichappiness.sas.upenn.edu/Default.aspx, a psychologist who promotes the field of positive psychology. Complete the VIA Survey of Character Strengths. Consider how you can use your strengths each day in the work schedule you have right now.

3. **Socially Conscious: How Do Your Investments Measure Up?**
   When you invest in mutual funds, you can make decisions in different ways. You may want to just put money into funds that had the greatest gain last year or you may want to invest in funds that are collections of socially responsible companies. Find several socially conscious mutual funds. What restrictions do they make on the companies they include? What is their average rate of return?

4. **Determining Your Personality Type**
   Complete the personality test at the 41q.com Web site. Analyze the results to identify your Myers-Briggs personality type. What are your strengths? Are there any areas you would like to develop?

5. **Corporate Social Responsibility with Your Java**
   Visit the responsibility page of Starbucks' Web site. Discuss three different strategies supported by Starbucks to "have a positive impact on the communities we serve." Do any of these cost Starbucks profits? Do you think these policies attract more customers to the store?

Web Case

For more on how one ethical trend is lowering costs and increasing sales, access the Chapter 3 Web case entitled "Focus on GE: Ecomagination" located in the End of Chapter Assignments section at my*biz*lab.com.

Video Case

For more on ethical issues affecting not-for-profits' business decisions, access the Chapter 3 Video Case entitled "The American Red Cross: Lending a Helping Hand" located in the End of Chapter Assignments section at my*biz*lab.com.

Business in a Global Economy

What Is Globalization?

Devin always "buys American"—but what does that mean in the new global marketplace?

Objective 1 What are the implications of the globalization of markets and the globalization of production? (pp. 93–95)

Objective 2 Why has globalization accelerated so rapidly? (pp. 95–96)

International Trade

As foreign companies begin to compete in U.S. markets, there is more competition and more pressure on American businesses. What are the benefits of international trade? What are the costs?

Objective 3 What are the costs and benefits of international trade? (p. 99)

Free Trade and Protectionism

Trying to compete in the world marketplace means using every means available. So when the Miller farm found genetically modified organisms (GMOs) helped to boost their yield, they were thrilled. Now they have discovered they can't sell in 27 countries because they used GMOs. How do free trade agreements affect businesses and members of a community?

Objective 4 What are the different types of trade barriers? (pp. 100–106)

Conducting Business Internationally

When conducting international business, many factors come into play. What are the strategies of international business? How can you enter a foreign market? Which mode is best? Hachimo Isu needs some answers before he expands his business.

Objective 5 What are the three basic strategies of international business? (p. 107)

Objective 6 How can international firms successfully enter foreign markets? (pp. 107–109)

International Business: Economic Factors and Challenges

Exchange rates both encourage and deter countries from trading with one another, and other economic factors play a huge role in what products are exported overseas. Business owners like Rachel Gao are turning to countries with favorable exchange rates, like China, to import goods. How do exchange rates impact a nation's economy? How do exchange rates impact the bottom line for Rachel's jewelry business?

Objective 7 What are exchange rates, and how do they affect international business? (pp. 111–114)

Objective 8 What economic factors and challenges play a role in conducting business on a global scale? (p. 114)

Creating Successful International Businesses

How would you feel if a potential client from Venezuela wouldn't sign with you because you didn't pat him on the shoulder when you first met? Joe lost one account that way and now is headed to Japan to try to sign a new client. What challenges does he face there? Does he bring gifts for the new partners in India that he meets with the week after that? Knowing the answers to such questions is vital to running a successful global business.

Objective 9 What are the sociocultural, political, legal, and ethical challenges to conducting business in a global marketplace? (pp. 115–118)

PEARSON

mybizlab

Going Global

You and a friend have developed an inexpensive battery that recharges itself by sitting in the sun. While you're considering the prospects in the U.S. market, your friend suggests that your opportunities may be greater in emerging markets where electricity is less reliable. The potential global market is huge, but you have to make the right decisions to get in. Are you willing to take the risk?

Objective 10 Test yourself using my*biz*lab.com to show that you understand the chapter objectives.

What Is Globalization? pp. 93–96

Devin is a worldly guy who has traveled globally, including camping in Canada as a child and taking a spring break vacation in Mexico one year. But he is very loyal to American products and tries to buy American whenever he can. So he doesn't even dream of a fancy Italian Maserati. "Italian car? Never! I'd rather buy a good 'ole American Jeep," he says. When it comes to vacationing now, he chooses a weekend in Manhattan over spending money abroad that would go to a foreign company. Politically, he favors high tariffs to make foreign beer sold here more expensive so that American products sell better. "The world is a tough place, and we should do whatever we can to give American companies an edge," he tells his friends. ■

Former President Bill Clinton once said, "Globalization is not something we can hold off or turn off . . . it is the economic equivalent of a force of nature—like wind or water."[1] In recent years, the rise of globalization has made a dramatic impact on the lives of people around the world. People from the United States to Taiwan to Argentina are interconnected and dependent on one another for a variety of goods and services. The United States and other nations are increasingly **importing**, or buying products from other countries, and **exporting**, or selling domestically produced products to other countries. Many products we own were made in countries other than the United States. Not only has globalization affected individual lives, it has also affected the way companies conduct business around the world.

What can people do to enhance their country's ability to compete in the global economy? What can a country do to provide good-paying jobs for its citizens? How can U.S. companies increase their profitability in the face of foreign competition at home or enhance their market share overseas? When the U.S. dollar is stronger or weaker than the currencies of other countries, how does it affect business in the United States? After studying this chapter, you'll be able to answer these and other questions.

top

10 **Most Powerful People in the World**[2]

Do you know every name on this list?

1. Barack Obama
2. Hu Jintao
3. Vladimir Putin
4. Ben S. Bernanke
5. Sergey Brin and Larry Page (tie)
6. Carlos Slim Helu
7. Rupert Murdoch
8. Michael T. Duke
9. Abdullah bin Abdul Aziz al Saud
10. William Gates III

The Effects of Globalization

How does globalization affect the United States? The old sayings "No man is an island." and "It's a small world, after all." can both be used to describe globalization. **Globalization**, the movement toward a more interconnected and interdependent world economy, may be one of the most profound factors affecting people in the United States and around the globe.[3] Why is this? Whatever happens today in the U.S. economy—the world's largest economy—will have a significant impact on people not only in the Unites States but also worldwide. Meanwhile, economic conditions in other countries also affect the U.S. economy, producing changes and challenges for U.S. consumers, businesses, and workers.

One example of this can be seen in the booming economies of India and China. Their growth is a major reason for the increasing global demand for energy. Increased energy demand is a major cause of the world's rising oil prices, which have created higher prices at the gas pump for people around the world. As a result, people have less money to spend on other things, such as eating out. Local restaurants and other local businesses feel the pinch, and their sales fall. In response to lower demand, businesses curtail production and lay off employees. Higher energy prices can also drive up production costs, which, in turn, drive up the prices businesses must charge consumers.

As you can see, globalization means that the behavior of each country has an impact on other countries of the world. Of course, markets have not only become more interconnected but also more reliant on one another. If you inspect the packaging of items you buy, you'll see that many products consumed in the United States today, such as laptop computers and cars, are made from parts that were manufactured in countries around the world. ▼ **Figure 4.1** shows how Ford cars, which many people think are made in the United States, are composed of components manufactured in other countries or assembled outside the United States.

How does globalization offer more marketing opportunities to businesses❓
Globalization has two main components: the *globalization of markets* and the *globalization of production*.[4] The **globalization of markets** refers to the movement away from thinking of the market as being the local market or the national market to thinking of the market as being the entire world. This offers incredible new opportunities for businesses. Companies such as General Electric (GE), Dell, and Toyota are not just selling to customers in Dallas or Atlanta, California or Vermont, or Japan or Europe; they're selling to customers all over the globe. ▼ **Figure 4.2** shows that for Ford Motor Company, the dominant markets in which sales are increasing are overseas markets. Many U.S. corporations are benefiting from the same situation, and even some relatively small companies find it profitable to sell their products abroad.

The globalization of markets has become so widespread that more and more businesses are finding that they must "think globally and act locally." Companies often need to adjust their products or marketing campaigns to suit the unique tastes and preferences of their local customers, wherever they may be. For example, Coca-Cola often must tweak its recipes to appeal to the tastes of consumers in different parts of the world. In India, Coca-Cola adapted its Minute Maid orange soda recipe to suit the taste of the majority of the Indian population, who prefer a sweeter version of the drink than the version sold in the United States.[5] Similarly, many foreign-owned companies advertise or adapt their products for sale in the United States to attract consumers.

How does globalization make it easier to manufacture products❓
The **globalization of production** refers to the trend of individual firms moving production to different locations around the globe to take advantage of lower costs or enhance quality. Globalization of production often involves *outsourcing*. **Outsourcing** is the assignment of certain tasks, such as production or accounting, to an outside company or organization. Currently, much outsourcing is **offshore outsourcing** (or **offshoring**), a term that describes the movement of production from a domestic site to a foreign location. Companies may decide to relocate at least some of their production to another country to realize lower costs so they can offer customers lower prices.

▼ **Figure 4.1**
Made in the USA?
Many brand name products are composites of components manufactured around the world. For example, most people think that Ford cars are made in the United States. But is it really "made in the USA" if most of its components are manufactured in other countries or assembled outside the United States?

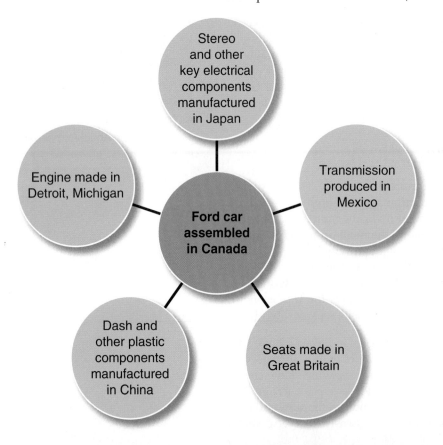

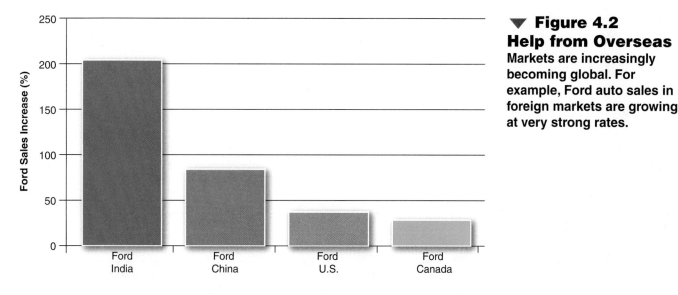

▼ **Figure 4.2**
Help from Overseas
Markets are increasingly becoming global. For example, Ford auto sales in foreign markets are growing at very strong rates.

Reasons for the Rise in Globalization

Why has globalization accelerated so rapidly? Two main factors underlie the trend toward greater globalization:[6]

1. **A dramatic decline in trade and investment barriers.** Trade and investment barriers are government restrictions that prevent the flow of goods, services, and financial capital across national boundaries. The lowering of trade barriers makes global business much cheaper and easier. It also allows international firms to move their production facilities to the least-cost location for that activity. A firm might design its product in one country, produce component parts in two or three other countries, assemble the product in yet another country, and then export it around the world. Today, many international companies, such as Ford Motor Company, divide their business across numerous countries.

2. **Technological innovations.** Advances in technology have made it possible to manage the global production and marketing of products. There have been dramatic breakthroughs in communications, transportation, and IT in the last decade. People can communicate and share information more rapidly and cheaply than ever before. For example, using teleconferencing, a business manager in New York can meet with contacts at a firm's European or Asian operations center without ever leaving the office. This has significantly reduced the cost of doing business. Technological advancements are a great equalizer for small companies, enabling them to access customers worldwide through their Web sites at negligible expense, so they can more effectively compete with huge global corporations.

Based on these and other factors, the globalization of markets and the globalization of production has resulted in some international firms becoming so large that they actually generate more revenue than the GDP of many nations. As you can see in ▼ **Figure 4.3**, several American companies rank above many countries in the world in terms of the total revenue they generate.

Global Business Trends

Where will trends in global business take us? Four noteworthy global business trends will impact our future:[8]

1. **A growing role for developing nations.** Over the last several decades, U.S. dominance of world output and world exports has declined in relative terms due to the rapid economic growth of several other countries, most notably

▼ **top**
10 **Countries Where It Is Easy to Do Business 2009**[7]

1. Singapore
2. New Zealand
3. United States
4. Hong Kong, China (tie)
5. Denmark
6. United Kingdom
7. Ireland
8. Canada
9. Australia
10. Norway

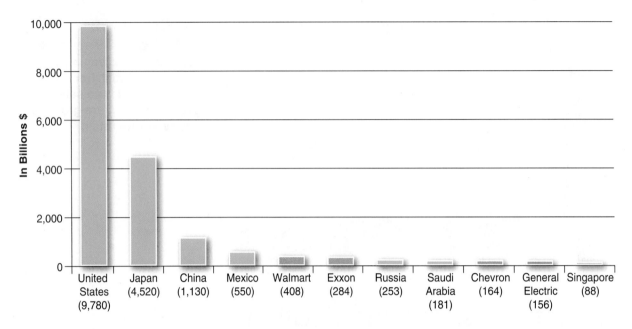

▼ **Figure 4.3
Company Revenue
versus National
Incomes**
Today, many international
businesses are larger than
most countries in terms of the
economic activity generated.

Japan, China, and India. This trend is expected to continue as developing nations, such as China, India, Indonesia, Thailand, and many Latin American nations, continue to increase their presence on the world economic stage.

2. **A rise in non-U.S. foreign direct investment.** Over the previous 30 years, U.S. dominance in **foreign direct investment**, which is the purchasing of property and businesses in foreign nations, has declined. Many other countries have begun to undertake foreign direct investment and have invested much of their money in companies in the United States. Not only is more foreign direct investment flowing into the United States than ever before, but also more and more foreign direct investment is flowing into developing nations.

3. **A rise in non-U.S. multinational enterprises.** Over the last several decades, there has also been a rise in the importance of non-U.S. **multinational enterprises**, businesses that manufacture and market products in two or more countries. Moreover, *mini-multinationals* (small- and medium-sized multinational enterprises) have become prominent on the world stage. Garmin, the maker of global positioning system (GPS) technology, is a good example of a U.S. mini-multinational that has specialized in doing one thing very well. Garmin sells its GPS technology all over the world from its headquarters in Olathe, Kansas, and from its facilities in Oregon, Great Britain, and Taiwan.

4. **Increasing democratization.** With the movement toward democratization and the adoption of free-market economies around the globe, many more nations are becoming involved in the global economy. If this trend continues, the opportunities for international business will be enormous as the global marketplace expands and more locations open as potential production sites.

Remember Devin? Devin has a U.S.-centric worldview that was common a generation ago but is difficult to maintain with the rapid growth of globalization. The Maserati car he would never buy is owned by Fiat, which owns 20 percent of Jeep. And his vacation in New York City? More than one-tenth of all the goods and services produced in New York and 1 in 20 jobs are supplied by companies controlled by foreign investors.[9] And although Devin argues that tariffs will protect U.S. products, most economists believe that in the modern global marketplace, using tariffs to protect a country's trade borders actually reduces domestic jobs and economic health. Devin's view of how the world works has the advantage of being simple, but it no longer reflects the reality that globalization has brought us. ■

International Trade pp. 97–99

Thom McGovern runs a successful textile manufacturing firm. The business was started by his father and has grown every year since Thom took over. He creates high-quality clothing products that his company sells to retail stores. He is a dependable supplier with many satisfied customers who trust his prices and advice on textile products.

Over the past several years, though, there have been increasing business pressures on Thom. Foreign textiles are showing up on the market in greater and greater numbers, selling at prices far below anything Thom can match. His customers have appreciated doing business with him over the years, but Thom could drop their prices and increase their profits if they bought from the foreign suppliers. Thom is angry and frustrated, unsure of how to protect his business and employees. What should he do? ■

Economists argue that international trade flourishes because it is in the best interest of the country as a whole. However, competition in the international market often puts new pressures on domestic businesses like Thom McGovern's firm unless they find ways to keep up with the high-quality and low-cost products that international trade provides. Let's take a closer look at why countries participate in international trade, how trade affects competitiveness, and what costs and benefits are associated with international trade.

International Competition

What is the theory of comparative advantage? Many theories apply to international trade. The most popular theory is the *theory of comparative advantage*, which states that specialization and trade between countries benefit all who are involved. The theory of comparative advantage suggests that a country should sell to other countries the goods that it manufactures most efficiently and effectively and buy from other countries the goods it cannot manufacture as efficiently or effectively. If this method is practiced, each nation will have a greater quantity and variety of higher-quality products to consume at lower prices.

For this mutually beneficial system to work, each country must specialize in the production of those products for which it possesses a comparative advantage. To possess a **comparative advantage** means that a country can produce a good or a service relatively more efficiently compared with other countries. A comparative advantage should not be confused with an **absolute advantage**, which is the ability to produce *more* of a good or a service than any other country. Just because a large country can produce more of a good than a small country doesn't necessarily mean it is relatively more efficient at producing that good. What matters is relative efficiency, or comparative advantage—not absolute advantage.

When all countries focus on producing those products for which they have a comparative advantage, collectively they all have more production to share. This, in turn, creates higher standards of living for these countries. As you've probably guessed, countries export those products for which they have a comparative advantage and import those products for which they do not have a comparative advantage.

Fostering Competitiveness

What can a country do to have an edge in world markets? In many nations, governments focus on improving a nation's resources—natural resources, labor, capital (plant, equipment, and infrastructure), technology, innovation, and entrepreneurialism—to improve competitiveness.

Governments can't do much to improve a nation's natural resources; they have to work with what they have. Nations with abundant natural resources will likely have a comparative advantage in the production of goods that require these raw materials. For example, big-leaf mahogany trees are found in only a few countries, including Mexico and Belize. So these countries have a comparative advantage in the production of mahogany furniture and musical instruments.

However, governments can and do invest in health, education, and training designed to increase the productivity of their labor forces. All international businesses are constantly looking for good workers, and each country wants to attract businesses to enhance employment opportunities for its citizens. For example, officials in Queensland, Australia, have recently budgeted a massive $9.5 billion in education and training, including vocational training and apprenticeships, in the hopes of building a strong employment force for the country.[10]

Many governments try to create incentives for private company investments in capital (plant and equipment). For example, governments may try to keep interest rates low so that private companies will invest in the latest state-of-the art equipment, thereby giving them an edge over foreign competition. Governments also invest in *public capital*, which is sometimes called *infrastructure*. Infrastructure includes roads, bridges, dams, electric grid lines, and telecommunication satellites that enhance productivity.

Governments also try to promote technological advances to give their nations a competitive edge. This can include investments in basic and applied research at state-funded higher education institutions. Finally, governments might also promote innovation and entrepreneurialism. In Norway, 60 percent of university students are women, but men are twice as likely to be owners of entrepreneurial businesses. The government has therefore created an action plan to increase grants accessibility for female entrepreneurs. The objective is to have women representing at least 40 percent of entrepreneurial businesses by 2013.[11] On the flip side, sometimes governments use trade restrictions and added tariffs on goods from other countries to create an artificial competitive advantage. We'll discuss these practices later in the chapter.

What can businesses do to be more competitive? To be competitive, businesses must grapple with many of the same issues as nations do to be more competitive. That is, successful companies try to gain access to cheap raw materials, invest in their workers' training and productivity, and purchase state-of-the-art plants and equipment that will give them an edge. Successful companies also invest in cutting-edge technology in their research and development (R&D) departments. Finally, they promote innovativeness throughout their organizations.

Conversely, if a company, an entire industry, or even a nation has lost its comparative (or competitive) advantage, then it probably failed in one or more of these areas. For example, at one time, the U.S. steel and textile industries had a competitive advantage in the world. Today, however, those industries have fallen behind their international competitors. It is the joint job of government and private business to determine which ways to improve to compete more effectively.

The Benefits and Costs of International Trade

What are the benefits and costs of international trade? The theory of comparative advantage indicates that countries that participate in international trade will experience higher standards of living because of the greater quantity and variety of higher-quality products offered at lower prices. These results stem from the increased competition associated with more open trade. But these benefits are not without their costs.

When foreign imports arrive in the United States, they increase the supply of a product, pushing its price down. Consumers welcome competition and lower prices, but domestic competitors are displeased.

The costs of international trade are borne by those businesses and their workers whose livelihoods are threatened by foreign competition. Some domestic businesses may lose market share to foreign companies, stunting their profitability and ability to create jobs. Other firms may face so much foreign competition that they're driven out of business entirely.

Do the benefits of international trade outweigh the costs? This is a difficult question to answer. The costs of increased international trade—including lost jobs to foreign competitors—are often easy to identify. The benefits are not always easily seen, however, as they are spread out among millions of consumers. For example, a greater quantity and variety of higher-quality products to purchase may not be easily traced to increased international trade because these benefits are often slow and subtle. People benefit from lower-priced products, although price reductions may save people only a nickel here and a dime there. But the sum of these lower prices for the public at large can be dramatic—especially over time. As we'll see in the next section, governments play a large role in determining how much international trade they will support, for example, by choosing to impose restrictions on the quantity and types of goods that can cross their nation's borders.

We started this section by discussing Thom McGovern's textile business, which was struggling in the midst of increased international competition. Did Thom just close up shop or did he adapt to the pressures and take advantages of the opportunities of globalization? As company president, Thom chose to invest in new equipment and training for his workers to try to gain a competitive advantage. He also began to explore acquiring his raw materials from foreign suppliers, a process that is easier to coordinate and arrange than ever before. Finally, he has begun to investigate new markets for his specialty products, expanding into countries like India and Japan. Thom is not sure what his company will look like in five years, but he is sure that the globalization of the world marketplace will bring him both challenges and opportunities. ■

Free Trade and Protectionism pp. 100–106

Farming has changed, and the Miller farm has always changed with the times. As the pressure to produce more from the same size farm has grown, the Millers have begun to use genetically modified organisms (GMOs) to grow crops that are more resistant to frost. Using GMOs has boosted their yield each year, and the farm has never had more output. But, recently, news came out that the EU—the European Union—a block of 27 countries—had released a new health directive: To be eligible for sale in the EU, any product meant for human consumption could not contain any GMOs. The Millers worry this means that the manufacturers they sell to will be dropping their orders because now the entire block of EU business will be closed to them. ■

Countries implement trade barriers for a variety of reasons. Sometimes, as in the case of the Millers, trade barriers may be implemented to protect consumers. Other times, trade barriers are established to protect domestic businesses from international competition that could put them out of business. Many people believe that such protectionist trade barriers are the best way to defend a nation's economy; others are in favor of free trade. **Free trade** refers to the unencumbered flow of goods and services across national borders. That is, free trade is free from government intervention or other impediments that can block the flow of goods across borders. Virtually all economists are free-trade advocates because they argue that, over time, the benefits far outweigh the costs for a nation as a whole. However, some people—especially those who feel their livelihoods are threatened by free trade—are not convinced. In this section, we'll examine both sides of this debate.

"Globalization and free trade do spur economic growth, and they lead to lower prices on many goods."[12]

—Robert Reich, U.S. Secretary of Labor, 1993–1997

Types of Trade Barriers

What trade barriers can governments put in place? There are three types of trade barriers.

1. **Tariffs and subsidies.** The most common trade barrier is the **tariff**, a tax imposed on an imported good or service, such as French wine. Governments prefer to impose tariffs because they raise tax revenues. The opposite of a tariff is a **subsidy**, governments make payments to *domestic* producers, such as California wine growers. A subsidy can take many forms. It can be a direct cash grant or a payment in-kind that could include tax concessions or a low-interest loan.

2. **Quotas and embargoes.** A **quota** is a limitation on the amount of an import allowed to enter a country. For example, a quota on French wine might limit the quantity to 10,000 cases per day. The most heavy-handed government trade barrier is an **embargo**, a total restriction on an import (or an export). Since the 1960s, for example, the United States has imposed an embargo on most goods traded with Cuba. Embargoes are usually tools designed to achieve a political goal. In the case of Cuba, the U.S. embargo began when Fidel Castro moved the country to a one-party communist system. The embargo has been used as a tool to apply pressure for change toward a more democratic system.[13]

3. **Administrative trade barriers.** Several other types of trade barriers can be lumped under the heading of *administrative trade barriers*—government rules designed to limit imports. One example is a **local content requirement**, which is a requirement that some portion of a good be produced domestically. This usually drives up the cost of an import. Administrative trade barriers may also require an import to meet some technical standard or bureaucratic rule, effectively shutting out the import from a domestic market. For example, the EU has banned the importation of all animal meats in which steroids were used to stimulate growth. This decision heavily impacted the U.S. beef and dairy industries. Although administrative trade barriers can be legitimate, they may be designed purely to protect domestic producers from international competition.

Trade Barriers: Winners and Losers

Who benefits and who suffers from trade barriers? Without a doubt, trade barriers benefit domestic producers and their workers but hurt domestic consumers. Trade barriers increase costs to foreign companies or restrict the supply of imports, driving up prices and reducing sales in the domestic market. As a result, higher-priced imports increase the demand for domestically produced substitute goods or services. This higher demand also increases the domestically produced product's price, although it simultaneously increases domestic sales. And this is exactly what trade barriers are designed to do—restrict sales of imports while stimulating sales for domestic firms. Because domestic firms are selling more at higher prices, they are more profitable. This profitability also creates more job security for their employees. The undesirable outcome, however, is that both imports and domestically produced substitute products are now more expensive. Domestic consumers lose while domestic producers and their workers gain. Trade barriers also hurt consumers because the overall quantity, variety, and quality of products are lower as a result of curtailing foreign competition.

What are common arguments in favor of protectionist trade barriers? Four main arguments exist for implementing protectionist trade barriers:

1. **National security.** The *national security argument* states that certain industries critical to national security should be protected from foreign competition. For example, the United States wouldn't want to become dependent on another nation for a critical component of national defense. If all the manufacturers of the targeting systems for Air Force fighter planes were Chinese companies and hostilities increased between the two countries, the interests of the United States might be compromised. However, critics argue that rarely have protected industries used this argument in terms of national defense.

2. **Infant-industry.** The *infant-industry argument* states that an undeveloped domestic industry needs time to grow and develop to acquire a comparative advantage in the global economy. The protected time to grow allows opportunities for an industry to make the needed investments to become innovative. Once comparative advantage is captured, the argument goes, then protection from foreign competition will no longer be necessary. Opponents of this view argue that, in practice, it can be very difficult to determine whether an industry legitimately holds promise of developing a comparative advantage. In addition, they argue that rarely do infant industries ever grow up, thus government protection becomes addictive.

3. **Cheap foreign labor.** The *cheap foreign labor argument* centers on lower wages paid to workers of foreign companies. How can domestic companies compete with these low wages? The issue of balancing wages and worker productivity is complex and has become much more critical with increased globalization. The relevancy for costs of production is not only wages but also productivity

in relation to wages. A company's costs of production can be lower even when it pays its workers twice as much if the productivity of workers is at least twice as high. If a country wants to maintain high wages in a global marketplace, it needs to find a way to increase the productivity of its labor force. Opponents of such protectionist policies argue that trying to protect jobs at the current wage structure might create still higher costs for a nation in the form of higher prices and reduced quantity, quality, and variety of products from which to choose.

4. **Threat of retaliation.** The *threat of retaliation* (or the *bargaining chip*) *argument* says that if a trading partner increases its trade barriers on your exports or fails to reduce trade barriers as you reduce yours, then an uneven, unfair playing field is created. Domestic companies may also be put at a disadvantage if a foreign firm is dumping its product. **Dumping** refers to selling a product at a price below the price charged in the producing country; it is illegal and can be difficult to prove. The intent of dumping is to dominate an industry and then control it. The threat of higher trade barriers can be a bargaining chip in retaliation for dumping or negotiating lower trade barriers for exports. The risk of that policy is that if it fails, the result can be a trade war; nations would implement higher trade barriers and leave everyone at a disadvantage.

How do economists feel about protectionist trade barriers? As noted earlier, most economists are free-trade advocates because they believe that the economic benefits of free trade outweigh the economic costs. Economists insist that the best way to address the concerns of those industries and their workers whose livelihoods are threatened by foreign competition is *not* to impose protectionist trade barriers. Instead, these displaced individuals need to be equipped with the education, training, and skills necessary to smooth their transition into a line of business or work in which the nation has a comparative advantage and demand is rising. Although all governments have protectionist trade barriers in place, they have been working to reduce them because they believe the economic benefits of doing so generally outweigh the costs. This political position explains the recent trend toward reduced trade and investment barriers that have fueled globalization. ▼ **Table 4.1** summarizes the economic benefits and costs of free trade and protectionism for a nation.

International Organizations Promoting Free Trade

What groups are working to promote free trade? Countries realize that unilaterally reducing their trade barriers puts their businesses at an unfair disadvantage. The key for realizing the mutual benefits of international trade is to get all countries to lower their trade barriers simultaneously, which was the reason for creating organizations such as GATT and the WTO.

▼ **Table 4.1**

Economic Benefits and Costs of Free Trade and Protectionism for a Nation		
	Free Trade	**Protectionism**
Economic Benefits	A **greater quantity** and variety of **higher quality** products at **lower prices**	**Increased sales** at **higher prices** improves the profitability of protected domestic companies, creating **greater job security** for their workers
Economic Costs	**Reduced sales** and **lower prices** for domestic firms that find it difficult to compete internationally, which **reduces their profitability** and **lowers job security** for their workers	**Lower quantity** and variety of **lower-quality** products at **higher prices**

The **General Agreement on Tariffs and Trade (GATT)** was created in 1948 with 23 member nations and grew to 123 member nations by 1994. Although GATT was not an organization with any real enforcement powers, its eight rounds of negotiated agreements or treaties were very successful in reducing tariffs and other obstacles to free trade on goods. This, in turn, spurred significant world economic growth.[14] However, GATT was not as successful in reducing trade barriers on services, protecting intellectual property rights, or enforcing agreements among member nations. As a result, the **World Trade Organization (WTO)** replaced GATT in 1995 during the eighth and final round of negotiations (called the Uruguay Round because it was launched in Punta del Este, Uruguay).

The WTO has strengthened the world trading system by extending GATT rules to services and increasing protection for intellectual property rights. But, perhaps most significantly, the WTO has taken on the responsibility for arbitrating trade disputes and monitoring the trade policies of member countries.[15] The WTO operates as GATT did—on the basis of consensus—when settling disputes. However, unlike GATT, the WTO doesn't allow losing parties to ignore the arbitration reports of the WTO. The WTO has the power to enforce decisions, which is something that GATT did not have. ▼ **Figure 4.4** shows which countries are members of the WTO.

Is there more that can be done to promote free trade?

Advocates of free trade argue that much remains to be done to reduce trade barriers in the global economy. The first round of talks under the umbrella of the WTO was launched in Seattle in 1999, but antiglobalization protestors disrupted and derailed these talks. The meetings were relaunched in 2001 in Doha, Qatar, in the Persian Gulf, with an agenda to curtail dumping, reduce protectionist trade barriers, protect intellectual property rights, and reduce government barriers on foreign direct investment.[16] The Doha Round was slated to last three years but had not yet concluded as of the publication of this text.

The 1999 demonstration in Seattle reflects an ongoing concern that free trade may encourage firms to shift their production to countries with low wages and lax labor standards. Critics argue that the exploitation of workers can contribute to the gap

▼ **Figure 4.4**
Countries in the WTO

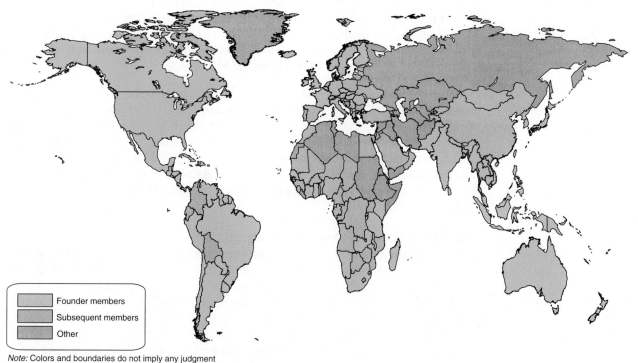

Founder members
Subsequent members
Other

Note: Colors and boundaries do not imply any judgment on the part of WTO as to the legal status or frontier of any territory.

between the rich and the poor. Environmentalists have also expressed a growing concern that expanded international trade encourages companies to move production to countries in which they are freer to pollute and degrade the environment, which contributes to global climate change and all the problems that may stem from global warming. These concerns highlight the fact that the *economic* perspective on the benefits and costs of free trade is not the only perspective. Important social, ethical, political, and environmental concerns also need to be considered.

Regional Free Trade Agreements

What are regional free trade agreements? Many nations have been so eager to achieve the higher standards of living associated with free trade that they have struck out on their own by creating **free trade areas**, or compacts abolishing trade barriers among member countries. Although all current free trade areas still have some obstacles to free trade among their members, many have made considerable headway in reducing these barriers. Let's look at some of the most powerful regional free trade agreements.

The European Union
The greatest free trade area exists among member nations of the EU, which is the oldest and largest free trade area. The EU can trace its roots to 1957 with the creation of the European Economic Community (or Common Market), which consisted of six founding countries: Belgium, France, Germany, Italy, Luxembourg, and the Netherlands. Although many obstacles had to be overcome, such as the concern over the potential loss of national sovereignty, the EU has grown to its current membership of 27 independent states, as shown in ▼ **Figure 4.5**. The EU's success is due in large part to its demonstrated commitment to the free flow of goods, services, capital, and people across borders in Europe.

The EU is currently the world's largest single market, surpassing the United States. It accounts for approximately one-third of the world's total production. The EU is the largest exporter in the world and the second largest importer.[17] In 1999, the EU also surpassed all other free trade areas with respect to economic integration by adopting a common currency—the euro. The euro is currently used by 16 of the 27 member states and has become a major currency in global financial markets.[18] The EU has a population of over 500 million people and is likely to continue to grow as many other countries—such as Croatia, the former Yugoslav Republic of Macedonia, and Turkey—apply to join the EU.

The EU's economic power and political clout has a huge influence on international businesses worldwide. For example, some international businesses have been motivated to invest in production facilities within the EU to hedge against any potential trade barriers. The EU has also established many legal, regulatory, and technical standards for imports to the EU market. In addition, the EU's antitrust rulings have significantly affected U.S. businesses. For example, in 2004, the EU found Microsoft guilty of anticompetitive practices and levied a fine of $613 million on the company.[19]

The North American Free Trade Agreement
The **North American Free Trade Agreement (NAFTA)** is an ongoing agreement to move the United States, Mexico, and Canada closer to true free trade. NAFTA was established on January 1, 1994, after considerable political opposition. The experience of NAFTA so far indicates that earlier claims made by both advocates and critics were exaggerated. One big issue confronting NAFTA is the proposal to expand into a greater Free Trade Area of the Americas (FTAA) that would include most countries in the Western Hemisphere. Although meetings are being held for a

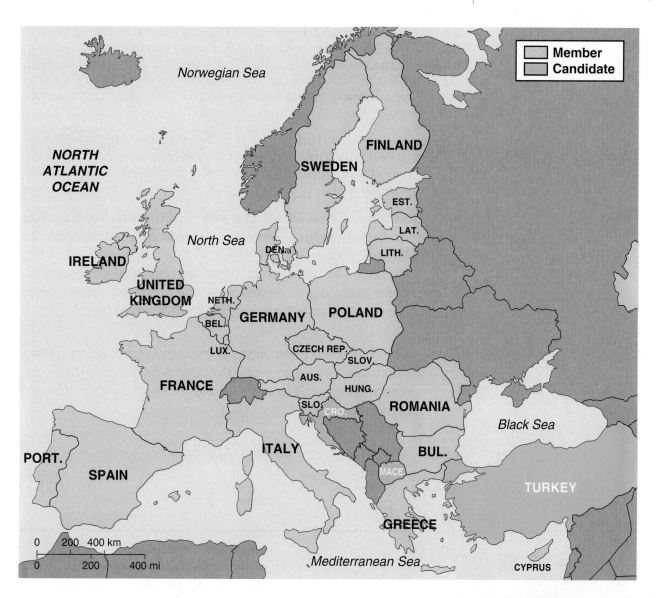

Member
Candidate

▼ Figure 4.5
The European Union
As of 2010, the EU has
27 member countries. It is the
most economically integrated
free trade area in the world.

workable FTAA, some countries, such as Brazil and Venezuela, stand in opposition to this agreement. As a result, significant progress in the near future toward more free trade within the framework of FTAA is unlikely.

Other Noteworthy Free Trade Areas

Many other free trade areas exist in the world. The following are some of the more noteworthy examples:

- The *Andean Group* was formed in 1969 between Bolivia, Chile, Ecuador, Colombia, and Peru. Another free trade pact was formed in 1988 named *MERCOSUR* between Brazil and Argentina and it was expanded in 1990 to include Paraguay and Uruguay. In 1999, these two organizations began negotiating a merger that culminated in 2004 with a signed agreement to move toward integrating all of South America based on the EU model. However, not much progress has been made to date. At the time of this writing, the only full members of MERCOSUR are the original four countries: Brazil, Argentina, Paraguay, and Uruguay.[20]

- The *Association of Southeast Asian Nations (ASEAN)* includes Indonesia, Malaysia, the Philippines, Singapore, Thailand, Brunei, Vietnam, Laos, Myanmar, and Cambodia. Progress toward integration has been limited, but ASEAN has negotiated free trade agreements with China, Korea, Japan, Australia, New Zealand, and India and is working to create a free trade agreement with the EU.

- The *Asia-Pacific Economic Cooperation* (*APEC*) was founded in 1989 at the suggestion of Australia and currently has 21 member countries, including economic powerhouses such as the United States, Japan, and China. The member economies of APEC account for approximately 40 percent of the world's population, approximately 54 percent of world GDP, and about 43 percent of world trade.[21]

Most free trade areas haven't had the kind of success that the EU and NAFTA have had in reducing their trade barriers. However, it is clear that most countries are eager to come together to reduce trade barriers in an attempt to realize the economic benefits of greater free trade.

We started this section with a story about the Miller farm and its struggles to determine what to do in light of a EU decision to disallow GMO products in its member countries. Regional free trade agreements create powerful negotiating bodies, and, as the Millers have found, the EU can make decisions that ripple through many levels of government, all the way to impacting the Miller's farm management.

Now that you have reviewed both sides of the issues concerning protectionism and free trade, what is your opinion? Can a balance be struck between protecting domestic businesses and consumers and opening markets up to more free trade?   ■

Conducting Business Internationally pp. 106–110

Hachimo Isu worked as a professional translator for many years before opening his own consulting business. The company made its mark by offering personalized translation services of spoken languages and written materials with great speed and accuracy. As business grew, Hachimo hired more translators and began to look to expand to more offices. As Hachimo thinks of taking his company to new countries and offering expanded services, he needs to determine which country would be the best starting place. How can he prepare himself for the changes that will come from expanding his business internationally?   ■

All business operations are undertaken within economic, sociocultural, political, and legal environments. When doing purely domestic business, keeping up with environmental forces can be a huge challenge, even for the savviest manager. However, managing an international business is even more complex because additional and different economic, sociocultural, political, and legal environments must be considered. The rest of this chapter will explore some of the numerous important economic, sociocultural, political, and legal differences among nations. An understanding of these differences is critical for successfully conducting global business. First we'll begin by discussing the different strategies of international businesses and how firms enter foreign markets.

Strategies of International Business

What types of strategies can an international business follow?
Every international business needs to determine which strategy it will pursue.

1. **Global strategy.** Companies that pursue a **global strategy** sell a standardized (or homogeneous) product across the globe. Standardized products are basic products that meet universal needs. Examples of standardized products include agricultural products, oil, and raw material commodities. These goods are essentially the same from company to company—they are homogeneous—because they are universally recognized and appeal to consumers across many cultures. When selling standardized products, firms compete aggressively on the basis of price. Firms pursuing a global strategy therefore face strong cost pressures to keep their prices low *because* they are selling a standardized product. The company with the lowest price captures the most market share.

2. **Multidomestic strategy.** Companies that pursue a **multidomestic strategy** customize or differentiate their products to meet unique local needs, tastes, or preferences. Firms pursuing a multidomestic strategy face relatively low pressures for cost reduction because price is often of secondary concern to buyers. Instead, what is important to customers is whether a product meets their needs or is distinct from a competitor's product. Companies that pursue a multidomestic strategy all work to make their respective products appeal to different customers around the globe.

3. **Transnational strategy.** Companies that pursue a **transnational strategy** offer a customized product while simultaneously selling it at the lowest possible price. The strong cost pressures *and* strong pressures for differentiation that motivate this type of strategy are typically at odds. Therefore, a successful pursuit of this type of strategy is difficult in practice.

Entering Foreign Markets

How do international firms enter foreign markets? In addition to determining a business strategy, international businesses must determine how they will serve foreign customers. Companies may undertake one of six strategies:

- Export their product
- Implement a turnkey project
- Undertake franchising
- Enter into a licensing agreement, a joint venture, or a strategic alliance
- Undertake contract manufacturing
- Establish a wholly owned subsidiary

Let's look briefly at each strategy.

Exporting

As noted earlier, *exporting* is the sale of a domestically produced good in a foreign market. Some businesses begin serving a foreign market by exporting and only later switch to another mode to expand sales abroad. Exporting is relatively easy and inexpensive compared with establishing a physical presence in a foreign market. In addition, exporting may help a firm realize lower costs because companies can move production to an inexpensive location and then export its product from that location around the world. Exporting also has a few disadvantages. It is not economical for heavy or bulky products with high transportation costs. Exporting may also become uneconomical if foreign trade barriers are unexpectedly imposed.

Turnkey Projects

When firms export their technological know-how in exchange for a fee, they have implemented a **turnkey project.** Turnkey projects are common in the production of sophisticated and complex manufacturing facilities, such as those involved in petroleum refining, steel, and hydroelectric energy production. Once a facility is up and running and the locals are trained, the keys are turned over to the new foreign owners. Black & Veatch, an engineering firm in Kansas City, has built power plants in China as turnkey projects. Turnkey projects allow firms with specialized know-how, like Black & Veatch, to earn higher profits from their technical expertise. The drawback is that a firm may create a viable competitor if its technological expertise is easily accessible.

Franchising

Franchising involves selling a well-known brand name or a proven method of doing business to an investor in exchange for a fee and a percentage of sales or profits. The seller is the *franchisor*, and the buyer is the *franchisee*. Franchising, which we'll discuss in depth in Chapter 5, is popular both domestically and internationally. Examples of franchising abound in the fast-food and entertainment industries. McDonald's and Kentucky Fried Chicken (KFC) restaurants are now found all over the world. Subway sandwiches can be purchased in over 83 countries.[22] Ruby Tuesday restaurants are found in Saudi Arabia, Dubai, Egypt, Guam, Greece, Honduras, Hong Kong, Iceland, India, Jordan, Kuwait, Romania, and Trinidad.[23] Walt Disney has recently franchised 150 stores in India.[24] Undoubtedly, all of these franchises must be careful to adapt their goods and services to appeal to their different global customers.

The main advantage of franchising is that the franchisor shifts to the franchisee the costs and risks of opening a foreign market. The disadvantages include enforcing franchise contracts that ensure quality control over distant franchisees and ensuring that the product is properly adapted to appeal to customers.

Licensing

Licensing is an agreement in which the licensor's *intangible property*—patents, trademarks, service marks, copyrights, trade secrets, or other intellectual property—may be sold or made available to a licensee in exchange for a royalty fee. The advantage of licensing is the speed with which the *licensor* can enter a foreign market and the assumption of risks and costs by the *licensee*. The disadvantage is the loss of technological expertise to the licensee and the creation of a potential competitor. SRI International is a company that licenses its vast array of intellectual property around the world. Their technological specialty is patents in the biosciences, computing, and chemistry-related materials and structural areas.[25] IBM also licenses its software around the world.[26]

Joint Ventures

Joint ventures involve shared ownership in a subsidiary firm. International joint venture part-

International franchising abounds in the fast-food industry.

ners involve an international business teaming up with a local partner to enter a foreign market. The advantages of a joint venture include gaining local knowledge of the economic, social, and political landscape while sharing the costs and risks of accessing a foreign market. For example, Walmart would love to be a big presence in India. With 1.1 billion people, the market for consumer goods, such as soap, detergent, and shampoos, in India is huge. India, however, has many restrictions on foreign business because the government wants to protect the many small Indian shopkeeper businesses. So Walmart is entering India through a joint venture with the Indian company Bharti Enterprises. It has launched 2 stores and plans 12 more over the next few years.[27]

Entering into a joint venture, like entering into a marriage, requires considerable thought in the selection of a complementary partner. The disadvantage of joint ventures is losing control over a company because compromise with the partner is inevitable. The risk of losing proprietary technology in the event of dissolution or divorce of the joint venture is also a major drawback.

Strategic Alliances

Strategic alliances are cooperative arrangements between actual or potential competitors. Unlike a joint venture, each partner retains its business independence. Strategic alliances are typically agreements for a specific period of time or the duration of a particular project. The advantages of strategic alliances include the pooling of unique talents and expertise and the sharing of the costs and risks of a project for mutual benefit. The disadvantages include a loss of technology and initial difficulty in finding a compatible partner.

The Intel Corporation, an international company based in California, has entered into a long-term strategic alliance with Japanese-owned Nokia Corp. The companies intend to work together to manufacture a new class of computer chips for laptop computers. Together they joined their workforces of talented engineers and their financial clout; now they have the power to define new standards for the industry.[28]

Contract Manufacturing

Contract manufacturing occurs when a firm subcontracts part or all of its goods to an outside firm as an alternative to owning and operating its own production facility. When doing international business, the subcontractor is a foreign firm. Therefore, contract manufacturing is really a form of offshore outsourcing. For example, Hewlett-Packard (HP) uses contract manufacturing in the production of its calculator products. Although the design for its calculators is done in the United States, the manufacturing is done in Taiwan.[29] Contract manufacturing allows international business to enter a foreign market by placing its label on the good and selling it in the foreign market where it was produced. Contract manufacturing also enables a firm to test-market its product in a foreign market with very little expense compared with the high start-up costs of building its own facility. The disadvantage centers on the lack of quality control over the subcontractor.

Wholly Owned Subsidiary

A **wholly owned subsidiary** involves establishing a foreign facility that is owned entirely by the investing firm. For example, Hyundai is a South Korean automotive manufacturer. It entered the Russian market by establishing Hyundai Motor Manufacturing Russia, a wholly owned subsidiary of Hyundai. This is Hyundai's sixth venture into expanding its foreign manufacturing base.[30] The advantages of this entry choice include total control over foreign operations and technological know-how. The disadvantage is that the parent company must bear all the costs and risks of entering a foreign market.

The Advantages and Disadvantages of Each Entry Mode

Which mode of entering foreign markets is optimal? The optimal entry mode depends on many factors, including a firm's strategy. ▼ **Table 4.2** summarizes the advantages and disadvantages of the various entry modes.

We started this section with a story about Hachimo Isu, who was considering expanding his business overseas. After spending more time reviewing the idea of going global, he is thinking of two different target countries: Saudi Arabia or Belgium. For each he needs to consider how he would modify the services he offers to reflect the needs of the local area. For example, Brussels, Belgium, is the headquarters of the EU and has very specific political and legal translation needs. Saudi Arabia is experiencing a construction boom and requires the translation of engineering and legal documents. Hachimo needs to investigate the differences in available networking and computer technology supports because these are so critical to his business. He also needs to review the different entry modes into an international market and decide which mode has the most benefits for his company. It is an exciting time, and there are a lot of frequent flyer miles in his immediate future! ■

▼ **Table 4.2**

Advantages and Disadvantages of the Various Entry Modes

	Advantages	Disadvantages
Exporting	• Speed of entry • Production site in lowest-cost location	• High transportation costs • Threat of trade barriers such as tariffs • Lack of access to local information
Turnkey project	• Increased profits for high-tech firms	• Loss of technical know-how to potential competitors
Franchising	• Costs and risks of opening the foreign market fall on the franchisee	• Difficulty in maintaining quality control over distant franchises
Licensing	• Speed of entry	• Licensee may become competitor • Loss of knowledge to potential competitor
Joint venture	• High potential for learning • Benefit of combined resources	• Shared control of business • Risk of losing specialized technology to partner
Strategic alliance	• Pooled talents and expertise • Shared costs and risks	• Risk of losing specialized technology to partner • Difficulty in finding a compatible partner
Contract manufacturing	• Speed of entry • Low test-marketing costs	• Lack of quality control over distant subcontractor
Wholly owned subsidiary	• Total control over all operations • Preservation of proprietary technology	• Risks and costs of entering a foreign market

International Business: Economic Factors and Challenges pp. 111–115

When Rachel Gao decided to expand her jewelry business to include handbags, she thought importing goods would be cheaper than purchasing them from a domestic company. Her initial thought was to go with a small European designer, but after she saw the exchange rate for the euro, she changed her mind. To make a profit, the retail price would be extremely expensive, and she didn't think her customers would pay such a high price. What other options would still allow her to expand? ■

Businesses are impacted by fluctuating exchange rates every day. Transactions between international companies not only have to specify what each side will be paid but also in which currency. In addition, multinational enterprises use foreign currency to pay foreign workers or invest spare cash in other nations where interest rates may be more attractive. In this section, we'll look at exchange rates and how fluctuations in the value of currency affect the global economy. We'll also explore other economic factors and challenges that affect global business.

The Role of Exchange Rates

What are exchange rates? Foreign exchange markets determine **exchange rates**, the rates at which currencies are converted into another currency. Depending on a firm's perspective, it may prefer a strong dollar or a weak dollar. U.S. exporters prefer a weak dollar because their products will be more affordable to foreigners. However, U.S. importers prefer a strong dollar because the cost of importing foreign goods is cheaper. If goods are imported cheaply, then those savings can be either passed on to the consumer or kept as higher profits.

How do exchange rates affect international business? Changes in exchange rates can have important implications for international businesses. Let's discuss some of these implications.

Export and Import Prices

Suppose that the value of the dollar rises or gets stronger against the yen (the currency of Japan). What impact will this have on U.S. and Japanese businesses? Goods exported from the United States will become more expensive because the Japanese will now need more yen to purchase each dollar. This means, for example, that the cost of a $40 pair of jeans made in the United States will increase in price for the Japanese consumer. Japanese consumers will buy fewer U.S. goods, like jeans, and exports to Japan will fall. U.S. businesses selling to the Japanese will be hurt.

At the same time, this stronger dollar will cause a decline in the relative price of Japanese goods for U.S. consumers because fewer dollars are required to purchase each yen. Thus, due to the currency exchange rate change, the United States will import more Japanese goods, and U.S. businesses will lose market share to Japanese companies.

top 10 U.S. Trading Partners, 2009[31]

Rank	Country	Imports/Exports in Billions of U.S. Dollars
1.	Canada	429
2.	China	365
3.	Mexico	305
4.	Japan	147
5.	Federal Republic of Germany	114
6.	United Kingdom	93
7.	South Korea	67
8.	France	60
9.	Taiwan	46
10.	Brazil	46

This example of Japanese and U.S. trade illustrates that **currency appreciation**, an increase in the exchange rate value of a nation's currency, causes the relative price of imports to fall as the relative price of exports rises. When currency appreciates, the currency becomes stronger. **Currency depreciation**, a decrease in the exchange rate value of a nation's currency, has the opposite effect on the relative prices of exports and imports. A weak currency causes exports to become cheaper and imports to become more expensive.

Changing exchange rates also affect multinational firms in other ways. Many companies, such as GE, feel competitive pressure to shift production to countries with weak or low-valued currencies to take advantage of lower costs of production. For example, a weak Chinese currency reduces labor costs in China. If a firm doesn't shift more of its production to China but its competitors do, then its costs will be higher, and the company will lose global market share.

Trade Deficits and Trade Surpluses

Exchange rate changes can also create *trade deficits* and *trade surpluses* for a country. A **trade deficit** exists when the value of a country's imports exceeds the value of its exports. For example, a stronger dollar will create a trade deficit for the United States because a strong dollar can cause export prices to rise as import prices fall.

The United States has experienced significant trade deficits every year since the early 1980s. The advantage of a trade deficit for a nation is that it enables the United States to consume more than it produces. However, the disadvantage is that domestic assets, such as real estate or stocks and bonds, must be sold to foreigners to pay for the trade deficit. This is similar to an individual who spends more money than he or she makes. The individual will go into debt and eventually have to sell off assets to continue to live beyond his or her means. The U.S.'s experience with trade deficits helps explain the dramatic, news-making purchase of U.S. assets, such as U.S. businesses by foreigners.

A **trade surplus** occurs when the value of a country's exports exceeds the value of its imports. What do countries do when they experience a trade surplus? Often countries that trade in raw materials, such as oil or diamonds, find the price of the commodity fluctuates a great amount from year to year. So, taking the pool of money that exists in the year of a trade surplus and investing it would be a good strategy. **Sovereign wealth funds (SWFs)** are government investment funds that do just that. They are managed separately from the official currency reserves of the country. In 1953, Kuwait established the first SWF, which is now worth over $250 billion. Many countries now have SWFs, including Norway, China, Saudi Arabia, and Singapore. The International Monetary Fund (IMF) estimates that by 2012, the amount held by all SWFs will be over $12 trillion.[32]

SWFs can invest in anything they want, and sometimes the investments of SWFs stabilize and allow foreign companies to expand. But during the recent credit crisis, many SWFs invested in collapsing banks in Europe and the United States. In fact, more than $69 billion was invested in a range of struggling banks and financial institutions.[33] The oil-rich emirate of Abu Dhabi made a $7.5 billion investment in the U.S. banking firm Citigroup in 2007. It is now facing a loss of almost $5 billion, as shares in Citigroup have crashed in value. The political implications of this level of investment make some uneasy about the rapid growth of SWFs. China's fund has made significant investments in major U.S. financial firms. How might that impact the political tensions between the two countries? What if an Arabian SWF invested in a shipping company, giving it control of U.S. ports?

Fixed and Freely Floating Exchange Rate Systems

Exchange rates can be manipulated or fixed by governments. For example, China has fixed its currency to a rate that is weak compared to the dollar. This means Chinese exports to the United States are cheap, and imports from the United States to

China are expensive. As a result, the United States faces a huge trade deficit with China. The U.S. government is now calling on the Chinese to allow their currency to "float," or change in response to changing market conditions. Indeed, most countries operate under a *freely floating* (or *flexible*) *exchange rate system*, a system in which the global supply and demand for currencies determines exchange rates. Many specific factors affect the demand and supply of a nation's currency, such as changing interest rates, tax rates, and inflation rates. Generally, however, changes in exchange rates in a freely floating exchange rate system reflect a country's current economic health and its outlook for growth and investment potential.

The problems with floating exchange rates are that they can create relative price changes outside the control of international businesses and engender risks of losses due to rapid and unexpected changes in exchange rates. For example, in the 1980s, Japan Airlines purchased several 747 airplanes from Boeing and agreed to pay in U.S. dollars. In the interim period between signing the contract and the delivery of the planes for payment, the value of the dollar rose dramatically. The airline company had to pay a lot more money than anticipated for the airplanes, and it almost went bankrupt. This story illustrates that unanticipated exchange rate changes can pose huge risks for international businesses.

Nonconvertible Currency and Countertrade

Governments also reserve the right to restrict the convertibility of their currency. Many developing countries have a *nonconvertible currency*, a currency that can't be converted into another currency in the foreign exchange market. For example, the national currency in Morocco is the dirham. It cannot be converted outside the Kingdom's borders, so visitors want to spend every dirham they have before ending their Moroccan vacations. Governments with nonconvertible currencies often fear that allowing convertibility will result in *capital flight*, the transfer of domestic funds into a foreign currency held outside the country. Capital flight would deprive the nation of much-needed funds for investment and development.

Global companies can still do business with countries that have nonconvertible currencies through the use of countertrade. *Countertrade* is a form of international

---

Biz**Chat**

Which Is Better—A Strong Dollar or a Weak Dollar?

The answer to this question depends on the type of business a firm undertakes. Companies that do a lot of exporting—such as vehicle manufacturers, chemical manufacturers, and farmers—prefer a weak dollar because their product's price is lower in the global marketplace, so their sales and profits will be higher. On the other hand, companies that import components or finished goods for resale in the domestic market prefer a strong dollar because the relative price of their imports is lower.

From a consumer's perspective, a strong dollar is typically preferred because import prices are lower, which has a

tendency to keep domestic competitors' prices low as well. As an employee, if you work for a company that exports much of its product, you would prefer a weak dollar to stimulate sales and ensure your job security.

The benefits of a strong dollar for a nation as a whole are lower-priced imports, such as oil, lower prices, and a lower inflation rate in general. However, a strong dollar creates a trade deficit. A weak dollar, on the other hand, is good for domestic international businesses because it stimulates employment and raises standards of living. The drawback of a weak dollar is the higher costs of energy and other imports that create higher rates of inflation. So, which is better—a strong dollar or a weak dollar? Like most real-world issues, the answer depends on your perspective.

For more information and discussion questions about this topic, check out the BizChat feature on my*biz*lab.com.

barter, the swapping of goods and services for other goods and services. Currently, countertrade may account for as much as 10–15 percent of total world trade. Companies engage in countertrade because of necessity and profitability. Examples of companies that have undertaken countertrade include General Foods, Goodyear, GE, Westinghouse, 3M, General Motors (GM), Ford Motor Company, Coca-Cola, and PepsiCo.[34]

Other Economic Challenges to Conducting International Business

What are some other economic challenges to conducting international business? Changing exchange rates and nonconvertible currencies are not the only economic challenges to conducting international business. Companies must also consider how to adapt their products for sale in developing nations, how certain government policies might affect their business, and how the socioeconomic factors of an area impact the types of products they sell.

Economic Growth and Development

Many developing countries are experiencing more rapid growth than advanced economies are, and they have hundreds of millions of eager new customers ready to put their money into the global market. However, some developing countries still lack the basic infrastructure necessary for the effective transportation of goods and/or lack access to dependable electricity. They may also be lacking in modern communication systems. The implications for companies doing business with these nations are clear. For example, the types of food products offered for sale would have to be altered and packaged differently. The modes of advertising would shift from television to radio, and marketing a product via the Internet wouldn't be effective because few customers would own a computer. It would be important for a business entering India, for example, to know the explosive growth there is not as much toward computer ownership as it is toward mobile phone ownership. In 1999, there were 1.2 million mobile phone subscribers in India; today there are almost 600 million, with 20 million more being added every month.[35] Advertising delivered via mobile phones would be critical in that setting.

Government Economic Policies

The degree to which markets are allowed to operate free from government intervention is another important economic consideration. International businesses prefer free market economies to state-run or socialized economies because the bureaucratic hassles associated with government intervention drive costs up. Other economic factors include the debt load of a nation (the amount of debt a country has), its unemployment and inflation rates, and its fiscal and monetary policies. *Unit labor cost*—a measure that divides a worker's wages by the average productivity of that worker—is also important. Global companies are concerned with labor costs when looking for lowest-cost locations to establish production facilities. In addition, the degree of competition that exists in a nation is important because it's more attractive to relocate to places with fewer competitors.

Socioeconomic Factors

Several socioeconomic factors also need to be taken into account, such as the demographics of population density and age distribution. The birthrates of many developing countries are high and offer exciting opportunities to toy manufacturers such as Mattel. Other socioeconomic factors that firms must consider include income distribution, ethnicity, and the cultural behaviors of a community.

Remember Rachel Gao? She decided to expand her jewelry business to include handbags and thought importing goods would be cheaper than purchasing them from a domestic company. Although she wanted to buy from a small European designer, she quickly realized that based on the exchange rate for the euro, the goods would be too expensive. So, she kept looking and found that many other business owners were importing products from China. She investigated the exchange rate for the Chinese yuan against the dollar and found she would be able to import a variety of handbags at an inexpensive price. Not only would her customers appreciate the price point, she would also be able to make a strong profit on her handbag line. Do you see any risks with her decision? ■

Creating Successful International Businesses pp. 115–118

International sales is the dream job for Joe Stein. He loves travel and is fluent in several languages. He prides himself on being good with people and loves to negotiate. The part of the job that is the most challenging for him is understanding the unwritten rules that are so different from country to country. In Venezuela, he needs to remember that business partners want a firm handshake and a pat on the shoulder when they first meet. In Japan, he needs to be sure to read a new business card carefully on the spot and not just put it in his pocket. Recently, he traveled to India and was given a gift by an Indian business partner. After opening the gift, Joe thanked him profusely, but he sensed that he had done something wrong. Was this going to cost him the deal? What should he have done differently? ■

When a business expands into an international market and lacks cross-cultural awareness, it is destined to fail. Along with cultural norms, political, legal, and ethical ideals vary from country to country. The role of government involvement in business is not universal, so knowing how specific government policies govern business activity is also critical for business success. And because there is no global court to settle differences and disputes, businesses need to thoroughly study what is acceptable legally and ethically. In this section, we'll review the sociocultural, political, legal, and ethical concerns that can make or break a company working in the global marketplace.

Sociocultural Challenges

How does culture affect business? *Culture* is the complex set of values, behaviors, lifestyles, arts, beliefs, and institutions of a population that are passed on from generation to generation. Culture impacts all aspects of business, from managing workers and production techniques to marketing and beyond. Most international businesses fail because they suffer from a lack of cross-cultural awareness.

◉ Off the Mark International Business Blunders

When selling products in the global marketplace, companies must research the cultural norms and language of the location in which they plan to sell. If not, the results could be disastrous, as illustrated by the examples below.[36]

- When American Motors introduced the Matador to the public, the company believed the car's name represented an image of courage and strength—the bullfighter. However, in Puerto Rico, the name means "killer," so the car was not popular on the hazardous roads in the country.

- In many Latin American cultures, women do not order their husbands around, and people are not usually very concerned with punctuality. A popular U.S. telephone company didn't know this. When the company showed a commercial in which a Latino wife tells her husband to call a friend and tell her they would be late for dinner, the commercial bombed.

- P&G could not imagine the backlash it would receive when it used a popular European television commercial in Japan. The ad showed a man entering a bathroom and touching his wife while she bathed. The Japanese disapproved of this ad because the man's behavior did not adhere to the nation's cultural norms.

- When a golf ball manufacturing company tried selling its golf balls in packs of four in Japan, the campaign was unsuccessful. That's because pronunciation of the word for "four" in Japanese sounds like the word for "death," so items packaged in fours are unpopular.

Cross-cultural awareness is an understanding, appreciation, and sensitivity to foreign culture. **Ethnocentrism**, a belief that one's own culture is superior to all other cultures, makes succeeding in international business very difficult. This section will explore some of the most important components of culture that pertain to conducting global business successfully.

Why do aesthetics matter when it comes to international business? *Aesthetics* refers to what is considered beautiful or in good taste. Aesthetics encompasses etiquette, customs, and protocol. Few things are more embarrassing than violating a sense of good taste. For example, a company advertised eyeglasses in Thailand by featuring a variety of cute animals wearing glasses. The ad was a poor choice in Thailand because animals are considered a low form of life there, so no self-respecting Thai would wear anything worn by animals. Likewise, when former president George H. W. Bush went to Japan with the former chairman of Chrysler, Lee Iacocca, and other U.S. business magnates to make explicit and direct demands on Japanese leaders, they violated Japanese etiquette. The Japanese considered this assertiveness rude and a sign of ignorance or desperation. Japanese businessmen don't condone lowering themselves to make direct demands. Some analysts believe this violation of cultural aesthetics severely damaged the negotiations and confirmed to the Japanese that U.S. citizens are barbarians.[37]

What other cultural prejudices must be examined for success in other countries? Attitudes toward time vary considerably across the world. Time is paramount to those in the United States, where people in general expect promptness and directness. Some cultures view this as pushy and impersonal. In addition, the U.S. time horizon differs markedly from, for example, the Japanese perspective. A long-term view to a U.S. citizen may be four to seven years in the future, while the Japanese approach is often to prepare for decades in the future. Attitudes toward work also vary. For example, the Germans argue that people in the United States live to work, while Germans work to live. Germans and other Europeans expect four to six weeks of vacation per year. Compare this to the two weeks on average a person in the United States gets, and it is clear which country values vacation time more.[38]

Religion plays a profound role in shaping a culture. International businesses are well advised to educate themselves on varying religious value systems, customs, and practices if they don't wish to offend customers in marketing campaigns. For example, a soft drink was introduced into Arab countries with an attractive label that had stars on it—six-pointed stars. The Arabs interpreted this as pro-Israeli and refused to buy it. Another label was printed in 10 languages, one of which was Hebrew; again, Arabs largely did not buy the product.[39]

Why is knowing the native language not enough?

Language, both spoken *and* unspoken, is extremely important. Consider a few more examples of international business blunders due to a lack of cross-cultural awareness.[40] A U.S. oil rig supervisor in Indonesia shouted at an employee to take a boat to shore. Because berating a person in public is abhorred in Indonesia, a mob of outraged workers chased the supervisor with axes.

Unspoken language, or body language, also differs significantly around the world. Mountain Bell Company tried to promote its telephone services to Saudi Arabia. Its ad portrayed an executive talking on the phone with his feet propped up on the desk, showing the soles of his shoes—something an Arab would never do.

Although the world is getting smaller and a global culture is emerging, there are still profound and significant cultural differences. Cross-cultural awareness is a prerequisite to successful international business.

Should you bow or shake hands when you visit a Japanese client in Japan?

Political Challenges

What are the political challenges to conducting international business?

International businesses look for nations that have a stable government, a well-established educational system, and a well-maintained infrastructure. Political changes can create disruptive environments that impact business concerns. The political differences among nations can also pose a challenge when conducting international business.

In today's global economy, companies often do business in government-controlled socialist economies, such as China, Cuba, and North Korea. The differences in political systems can cause tensions. One example is the experience of Google in China. China has a questionable record on human rights issues and privacy. When Google wanted to enter China, the government demanded Google comply with Internet censorship laws so the results Google's search engine returned to Chinese citizens were controlled and filtered. Google agreed and became an established presence in mainland China, rising to become the number-two search engine.

Then in 2010 Google experienced a cyber attack originating from China that targeted the gmail accounts of dozens of human rights activists in China. That action, along with an increase in the government blocking of sites such as Facebook, Twitter, and Google Docs, led Google to reverse its decision. It decided to stop censoring results, forcing a standoff with the Chinese government. Ultimately, China did renew Google's license to operate in the country but this is an example of how the pressure from an international business giant can be at odds with political forces in a foreign country.

Government intervention in the process of determining which goods are undesirable and whether goods should be regulated, taxed, or banned also varies from country to country. Many products that pollute the environment are deemed undesirable and have been regulated in one form or another by most governments around the world. The differences in these regulatory standards can impose big differences in costs of production for global businesses. There are also growing pressures on governments to address global climate change issues that will affect international business.

Legal Challenges

What are the legal challenges to conducting international business?

Laws, regulatory standards, and access to unbiased judicial systems based on a rule of law differ considerably around the world. No universal laws, regulatory standards, or global courts exist to settle disputes in the global economy. The different laws governing contracts, product safety and liability standards, and property rights are of particular importance when conducting global business. Property rights violations, including violations of patents and copyrights in the software, music, and publishing businesses, have cost businesses billions of dollars a year. Without adequate protection of intellectual property, technological developments would be too expensive and risky for companies to continue to fund long-term R&D.

Different laws also govern the use of bribery throughout the world. The United States passed the Foreign Corrupt Practice Act in the 1970s in response to questionable or illegal payments to foreign government officials to secure contracts or other favors. The act was designed to restore public confidence in the business community in the United States. But Congress became concerned that U.S. businesses were put at a disadvantage. Many foreign companies routinely paid bribes and were even able to deduct the cost of bribes from their taxes as legitimate business expenses. The United States therefore pushed for the creation of the Organisation of Economic Co-operation and Development (OECD) in 1988, which currently consists of 30 member nations committed to combating bribery. In many places in the world, however, bribes are common and may even be necessary for doing business.[41]

Ethical Challenges

What are some ethical challenges faced by international business?

Bribery is just one of the many ethical dilemmas surrounding global business. Unique differences in economic conditions and cultural values give rise to many ethical dilemmas surrounding global business. For example, should a firm conform to its home country's environmental, workplace, and product safety standards—even though it's not legally required to do so—while operating in another country? Should a company do business with a repressive totalitarian regime? When conducting international business, companies must determine whether they are willing to defy ethical codes to make a larger profit.

We started this section by introducing Joe Stein, who works in international sales and must deal with a variety of cultures. Joe has learned a lot about the world and about himself by working in international sales. When his Indian business supplier offered him that gift, he politely said thank-you and opened it. But he saw Sheshadri's face wince, and others in the group began to look uncomfortable. Joe quickly apologized and asked Sheshadri privately whether he had done something inappropriate. "In India you should never open a gift before the person has left. It shocked a few of us that you would be so rude." Joe thanked him for the insight and made sure to apologize to the people there. As Joe explained later to his wife, "What is truly important is to realize that you can't assume that people will behave in similar ways across various cultures." Understanding and respecting these differences in cultures will help Joe succeed in international business. ■

Chapter Summary

Are you an active learner?

Go to my*biz*lab.com to master Chapter 4's content. Chapter 4's interactive activities include:

- Customizable Study Plan and Chapter 4 practice quizzes
- Chapter 4 Simulation, Going Global, that helps you think critically and prepare to make choices in the business world
- Chapter 4 Video Exercise, Gawker: Business in a Global Economy, which shows you how textbook concepts are put into practice every day
- Flash Cards for mastering the definition of chapter terms
- Interactive Lessons that visually review key chapter concepts

1. What are the implications of the globalization of markets and the globalization of production? (pp. 93–95)

- The **globalization of markets** (p. 94) refers to the movement away from thinking of the market as being the local market or the national market to the market being the entire world. Businesses need to "think globally but act locally," which means that companies must market their products so that they appeal to their local customers.
- The **globalization of production** (p. 94) refers to the trend of individual firms to disperse parts of their productive process to different locations around the world to take advantage of lower costs or enhance quality. The globalization of production often involves **outsourcing** (p. 94), which is contracting with another firm to produce part of a product that formerly was produced in-house. **Offshore outsourcing** (p. 94) has become a significant concern for U.S. workers.

2. Why has globalization accelerated so rapidly? (pp. 95–96)

- The decline in trade and investment barriers, which are government barriers that inhibit the free flow of goods, services, and financial capital across national boundaries, is one factor that has led to increased globalization. This decline has encouraged developing nations to become involved in international trade and allowed companies to base production facilities at the lowest-cost location
- Technological changes that have also contributed to the rise in globalization include the following:
  - Teleconferencing, which allows businesspeople to conduct meetings with contacts around the world
  - IT, such as the Internet and cable and satellite television systems, which allow companies to advertise and sell products on a global scale

3. What are the costs and benefits of international trade? (p. 99)

- The **theory of comparative advantage** (p. 97) states that specialization and trade between countries benefits all who are involved. This is true because countries that participate in international trade experience higher standards of living due to the greater quantity and variety of higher-quality products at lower prices.
- The costs of international trade are borne by those businesses and their workers whose livelihoods are threat-

ened by foreign competition. Businesses may lose their market shares to foreign companies, which in turn force businesses to lay off workers.

4. What are the different types of trade barriers? (pp. 100–106)

- The different types of trade barriers are **tariffs**, **subsidies**, **quotas**, and **administrative trade barriers** (p. 100).
  - Tariffs are taxes imposed on a foreign good or service.
  - Subsidies are government payments to domestic producers in the form of a direct cash grant or a payment in kind.
- Quotas are quantity limitations on the amount of an export allowed to enter a country.
- Administrative trade barriers are government bureaucratic rules designed to limit imports. One example is a **local content requirement** (p. 101), which is a requirement that some portion of a good be produced domestically.

5. What are the three basic strategies of international business? (p. 107)

- The three basic strategies of international business are the **global strategy**, the **multidomestic strategy**, and the **transnational strategy** (p. 107).

6. How can international firms successfully enter foreign markets? (pp. 107–109)

- There are eight common ways for a company to enter foreign markets, as follows:
  - **Exporting** (p. 93), the sale of domestically produced goods in a foreign market
  - **Turnkey projects** (p. 108), firms export their technological know-how in exchange for a fee
  - **Franchising** (p. 108), selling a well-known brand name or business method in exchange for a fee and percentage of the profits
  - **Licensing** (p. 108), an agreement in which the licensor's intangible property may be sold or made available to a licensee for a fee
  - **Joint ventures** (p. 108), the shared ownership in a subsidiary firm
  - **Strategic alliances** (p. 109), cooperative agreements between competitors

Continued on next page

Chapter Summary (cont.)

- **Contract manufacturing** (p. 109), a firm subcontracts part or all of its goods to an outside firm
- **Wholly owned subsidiary** (p. 109), establishing a foreign facility that is owned entirely by the investing firm

7. What are exchange rates, and how do they affect international business? (pp. 111–114)

- An **exchange rate** (p. 111) is the rate at which one currency is converted into another.
- **Currency appreciation** (p. 112), the increase in the exchange rate value of a nation's currency, causes the price of imports to fall and the cost of exports to rise. **Currency depreciation** (p. 112), the decrease in the exchange rate value of a nation's currency, creates the opposite effect.

8. What economic factors and challenges play a role in conducting business on a global scale? (p. 114)

- Economic growth and development present a challenge because some countries lack the infrastructure necessary to transport goods effectively.

9. What are the sociocultural, political, legal, and ethical challenges to conducting business in a global marketplace? (pp. 115–118)

- **Ethnocentrism** (p. 116), the belief that one's own culture is superior to all others, can lead to conflict when conducting business globally. Other sociocultural challenges include differences in aesthetics, religion, and attitudes toward time and work.
- International businesses prefer stable governments with a strong infrastructure. However, many countries do not offer this kind of political and economic environment. Government decisions about taxation, infrastructure investments, and antitrust law enforcement can all affect global business.
- From a legal standpoint, the differences in laws and regulations around the world provide challenges for conducting business. There are no universal laws or policies for governing contracts, product safety and liability standards, or property rights.
- Bribery is an ethical challenge facing international business. Decisions about whether to conform to a home country's environmental, workplace, and product-safety standards while operating in a foreign country are other ethical dilemmas.

Key Terms

absolute advantage (p. 97)

comparative advantage (p. 97)

contract manufacturing (p. 109)

currency appreciation (p. 112)

currency depreciation (p. 112)

dumping (p. 102)

embargo (p. 100)

ethnocentrism (p. 116)

exchange rate (p. 111)

exporting (p. 93)

foreign direct investment (p. 96)

franchising (p. 108)

free trade (p. 100)

free trade areas (p. 104)

General Agreement on Tariffs and Trade (GATT) (p. 103)

global strategy (p. 107)

globalization (p. 93)

globalization of markets (p. 94)

globalization of production (p. 94)

importing (p. 93)

joint venture (p. 108)

licensing (p. 108)

local content requirement (p. 101)

multidomestic strategy (p. 107)

multinational enterprises (p. 96)

North American Free Trade Agreement (NAFTA) (p. 104)

offshoring (offshore outsourcing) (p. 94)

outsourcing (p. 94)

quota (p. 100)

sovereign wealth funds (SWFs) (p. 112)

strategic alliances (p. 109)

subsidy (p. 100)

tariff (p. 100)

trade deficit (p. 112)

trade surplus (p. 112)

transnational strategy (p. 107)

turnkey projects (p. 108)

wholly owned subsidiary (p. 109)

World Trade Organization (WTO) (p. 103)

Self-Test

Multiple Choice You can find the answers on the last page of this book.

1. Globalization involves
   a. making products that protect the environment.
   b. moving toward a more interconnected world economy.
   c. dominating the globe with a single marketing message.
   d. None of the above

2. The globalization of markets and the globalization of production means that
   a. people are no longer in control of their own lives.
   b. we are all connected by the Web.
   c. companies can take one product to international markets without having to adapt it.
   d. companies design products for global markets and can produce them offshore.

3. The theory that states that specialization and trade are mutually beneficial to all economies involved in trade is called the
   a. theory of comparative advantage.
   b. theory of beneficial trade.
   c. theory of absolute advantage.
   d. theory of relative trade.

4. Which of the following are global business trends?
   a. A growing role for developing nations in importing and exporting
   b. A rise in multinational enterprises
   c. Increased adoption of the free-market economy model
   d. All of the above

5. The theory of competitive advantage indicates that
   a. there is an unencumbered flow of goods and services across national borders.
   b. international trade will force domestic businesses to lose market share to foreign competitors.
   c. countries that participate in international trade will have a higher standard of living.
   d. a limit is placed on the amount of goods and services that can be traded.

6. Which of the following international organizations promote free trade?
   a. GATT
   b. The euro
   c. The IMF
   d. All of the above

7. If an international business is selling a standardized product and competing chiefly on price, the business is initiating a
   a. transnational strategy.
   b. multi-domestic strategy.
   c. standard-price strategy.
   d. global strategy.

8. Exchange rates affect international businesses because
   a. nonconvertible currency is worthless.
   b. currency depreciation and appreciation changes the relative price of imports and exports.
   c. U.S. exporters prefer a strong dollar.
   d. exchange rates fluctuate after the G20 meeting each year.

9. Which method of entering foreign markets has the advantage of allowing for test-marketing a product in a foreign market at the lowest cost?
   a. Joint ventures
   b. Wholly owned subsidiaries
   c. Exporting
   d. Contract manufacturing

10. Culture is a complex set of
    a. tariffs and trade agreements.
    b. museums and dance companies.
    c. beliefs that one's own culture is superior to all other cultures.
    d. values, behaviors, lifestyles, and beliefs.

Self-Test

True/False   You can find the answers on the last page of this book.

1. A free-floating exchange rate system uses global supply and demand to set exchange rates.
   ☐ **True** or ☐ **False**

2. Outsourcing sometimes involves moving the production of a product from a domestic location to a foreign location.
   ☐ **True** or ☐ **False**

3. Increasing U.S. dominance of foreign direct investments has helped accelerate globalization.
   ☐ **True** or ☐ **False**

4. As our ability to connect using technology increases, the need for cross-cultural awareness decreases.
   ☐ **True** or ☐ **False**

5. Trade barriers include tools like embargos, quotas, and local content requirements.
   ☐ **True** or ☐ **False**

Critical Thinking Questions

1. Sometimes an international business needs to modify its product to adjust to the specific needs or tastes of the local market. How might a company like Trek modify the design of its line of bicycles for sale in Ghana, China, and England?

2. Modern technology has allowed more connection between people of different cultures than ever before. Does access to Facebook, Xbox Live, and free international calls through Skype mean that a common world culture is being created? Do younger people understand other cultures more easily because of these technologies? Or does it merely create an illusion of understanding?

3. What are the advantages of increased competition in the global market? What are the disadvantages? Is foreign competition *always* good for the consumer? Is foreign competition *always* bad for local businesses?

4. Review the three basic strategies of international business. Discuss the type of companies that would most likely pursue a global strategy, a multidomestic strategy, and a transnational strategy.

5. Organizations to promote free trade, like the EU, have had difficulty creating a common currency. Why do you think not all EU countries use the euro? Why do some countries that are not part of the EU choose to use the euro?

Team Time

The Devil's Advocate

Read the following issues and questions. Which side of the issue do you believe is correct? Form a group with other students in the class who share your belief. As a group, play devil's advocate by creating a case for the opposing side of the issue. Now that you've considered both sides, you're ready to debate the opposition.

1. In the recent wave of globalization, developing countries have become the focus for many international businesses. Is this process of globalization the best way to strengthen developing countries and establish a level playing field or does it keep them under the control of wealthy industries and drive income inequality?

2. Free trade versus protectionism is a heated debate in today's fragile economy. Which is better for the health of the U.S. economy over the next 10 years—free trade or protectionism?

3. Currently, the minimum age for a child to work in Indonesia is 12 years old. The minimum age for a child to work in the United States is 14 years old. If a garment company from the United States decides to outsource production to Indonesia, would it be ethical for the company to hire 12- or 13-year-old workers in the factory?

Process

Step 1. Meet as a group to discuss the issue. Remember that you must build a case for the side you chose. Look for problems with your own personal beliefs to develop a case for your side.

Step 2. Prepare an individual response that supports your side of the issue.

Step 3. Share your response with your group. Think of possible rebuttals for each response. Then alter any responses that can produce a strong rebuttal.

Step 4. Determine who will be the group's primary spokesperson for the debate.

Step 5. Each group will be given five minutes to present its side of the issue. After each group has presented its argument, each team will be given five minutes to prepare a rebuttal and then three minutes to present the rebuttal.

Step 6. Repeat with other groups.

Step 7. After each group has debated, discuss whether anyone's personal views have changed after this assignment.

Ethics and Corporate Social Responsibility

Offshore Outsourcing

Workers in the United States often view offshore outsourcing in a negative light. Many people believe that this practice is a way for companies to make more money by eliminating U.S. jobs. However, offshore outsourcing sometimes seems necessary for the survival of a company. Review the following scenario.

Scenario

You are the owner of a company that makes industrial sewing machines. Currently, your company's profits are decreasing because your competitors have lower prices. You cannot lower the price of your machines without losing a significant amount of money. The majority of your costs come from labor. You have 2,000 employees in your factory, and your company is the primary employer in the region. You could sell your product for a third of the price if you outsourced half your production to a foreign country. However, this would eliminate 1,000 jobs and devastate a community. Also, the country that you would be outsourcing to has a reputation for unsafe working conditions and practices. If you don't outsource some of your production, over time your company may be unable to compete, possibly forcing you to shut down your company.

Questions

1. As a business owner, what are the costs and benefits of moving half your production overseas?

2. Do the benefits of offshore outsourcing outweigh the costs? Why or why not?

3. Are there any possible alternatives to consider? What other decision could you make so that each side (domestic and international) benefits?

Web Exercises

1. **My Ride**
   Select two different luxury cars—one very exclusive and high performance and the other very energy conscious and green. For each car and each manufacturer, investigate where the car is designed, where it is assembled, and where the component parts are produced.

2. **Same Company, Different Products**
   Go to the Web site of the Swedish furniture maker IKEA (ikea.com). Under the "select a location" option, choose the United States. Review the site and note the products and the design of the page. Then go back to the homepage and choose a different country. Look for differences in the appearance of the Web site and the products offered. Why do you think these sites are different for each county?

3. **Go State!**
   Have you ever considered a career with the U.S. State department? At state.gov, under Youth and Education, select Student Career Programs. What aspects of these careers appeal to you? Visit the Fulbright Scholar program. What information in the Fulbright Fellow Orientation Handbook is new to you?

4. **Cultural Guidelines**

Knowing how to behave in a variety of countries is critical with increased globalization. Using the materials at www .kwintessential.co.uk/etiquette/doing-business-in, select three different countries from very different regions of the world. Review the "Doing Business In . . ." guides for each country. Create a pamphlet for business travelers on the business dos and don'ts for each country.

5. **You're the Trader**

Imagine you're in charge of trading goods for a country. Would you focus on building wealth by selling commodities or on developing an industry by purchasing raw materials? Visit www.imf.org/external/np/exr/center/students/trade/index.htm and become the trader. Measure your success on the global economics conditions scale.

Web Case

For more on the business opportunities created by emerging markets, access the Chapter 4 Web case entitled "Focus on GE: Company to Country" located in the End of Chapter Assignments section at my*biz*lab.com.

Video Case

For more on the challenges businesses face during international expansion, access the Chapter 4 Video Case entitled "Lands' End and Yahoo!: Going Global, Acting Local" located in the End of Chapter Assignments section at my*biz*lab.com.

Special Issues in
Online Business

In the past 10 years or so, we've gotten used to seeing *e-* and *i-* before company and product names. E-mail has become so common that we must specify when referring to paper mail (i.e., snail mail). It's not only individual products, such as the iPhone and iPad, that have gone *www*. Entire businesses are now being launched online. Most corporate retailers have online stores, and some, like Zappos .com, are exclusively e-commercial. In this mini chapter, we'll discuss the impact of online life within the business world, particularly the forms e-commerce takes, its impact on banking, how it has changed business marketing and the challenges it creates.

Online Business

You've no doubt realized that the Internet has created markets that didn't exist previously. A random assortment of everything from personal items and collectibles to cars and vacation homes are now available to a global market, thanks to eBay and similar Web sites such as uBid. Now anyone with Internet access can conduct business online, which makes for more consumer choices. Amazon .com, for example, has more books in stock than the biggest bricks-and-mortar bookstore chain in the United States. Online stores can ship items straight from the warehouse to the consumer, bypassing the need to conform to space constraints in retail storerooms. This phenomenon of online markets fostering easy access to hard-to-find items is often called the "long tail" effect.[1]

Perhaps the most dramatic effect that the Internet has had on commerce is allowing businesses to become global. A company no longer requires a location or a partner in another country to conduct business internationally. Thanks to the Internet, business communications move at lightning speed, allowing more opportunities than ever before for companies to establish a worldwide presence. The Internet has also increased outsourcing. This has allowed manufacturers to move production to cheaper locations, including overseas. Many U.S. businesses have moved their back-office tasks, such as their data processing and IT departments, to places such as India and the Philippines. Others have relocated their helpdesk centers overseas as well.

PEARSON
my*biz*lab

E-Commerce

You always thought the cases for the ZBox 400 video game system were dull so you started sketching ideas to improve them. You manufactured those sketches and started selling them to your friends. Soon you've partnered with a friend who finances you, so you can order 50 more cases which you quickly sell to local computer shops. Now it's time to think bigger. Can you start a business and sell 1,000 cases in the first 6 months?

Interaction between business and the consumer has also changed radically since the introduction of the Internet. The most common modes of communication are business-to-business (B2B), business-to-consumer (B2C), and consumer-to-consumer (C2C).

Business-to-Business

Business-to-business (B2B) transactions involve the exchange of products, services, and information between businesses on the Internet. B2B Web sites can be classified as follows:

- *Company Web sites* target other companies and their employees, similar to an exhibit at a trade show. They are designed to sell goods or services to business clients, rather than household consumers. For example, UPS has an interactive and user-friendly B2B site for business owners looking for shipping solutions.

- *Procurement exchange* is a group of companies that act together to purchase goods or services at lower prices. Electronic procurement, known as e-procurement, is the online purchase and sale of products and services between businesses. Procurement exchanges benefit both purchasers and suppliers. For example, the state of Kentucky has an e-procurement Web site. Vendors can register, examine current bidding opportunities and even enter online bidding for contracts through the site.[2]

- *Specialized industry portals* are online gateways to major sources of information, discussion forums, and product listings. To see an example, view the portal page for CEOs at ceoExpress.com. These are also known as *niche portals* or *vertical portals* because they provide expanded information on a specific product or market.

- *Brokering sites* are third-party sites that act as liaisons between providers and potential buyers of goods or services. Brokering sites can be found for a variety of rental goods that businesses may need, from projectors and video equipment to backhoes, excavators, and skid steers.

- *Information sites* provide information about a particular industry. Also called an *infomediary*, an information site gives businesses information about current standards and developments. For example, TheMedica.com is an infomediary that posts news about the health-care and medical industries. It also includes information about trade shows, links to medical publications, and a directory of health-care businesses and products.[3] Infomediaries help facilitate and originate B2B traffic.

"Click and mortar" businesses, such as retailer L.L. Bean, give customers the option of conducting both online and in-store transactions.

Business-to-Consumer

Business-to-consumer (B2C) transactions refer to e-commerce that takes place between businesses and consumers. In fact, it's becoming essential for almost all businesses to sell or at least promote their products to customers online. "Click and mortar" refers to B2C businesses that have both an online presence and a bricks-and-mortar presence. This combination is ideal for customers who like the convenience of online shopping but who also want the convenience of returning products without shipping costs or being able to see a product in person before buying.

To stay in business, B2C companies have gotten savvy with regard to online distribution, advertising, networking, and accessing customers. Some models that have accelerated B2C e-commerce include the following:[4]

- *Online intermediaries* are businesses such as Travelocity and Amazon.com that are not direct producers of products but instead buy goods and/or services and sell them to customers.
- *Advertising-based models* rely on banner ads on other Web sites to attract customers. The two main approaches that advertisers use are *high-traffic* and *niche*. The high-traffic approach is designed to reach a wide audience, with ads placed on popular sites, such as Yahoo! The niche approach best serves companies that target a small, specific audience.
- *Community-based models* allow users with similar interests to interact with each other worldwide. Steam from the Valve Corporation is an example of a community-based gaming Web site where users can purchase and play online games. Steam distributes games from the full range of small independent video game houses as well as major publishers. With over 30 million active accounts[5], Steam members always have someone to play with—and someone to encourage them to buy a new game!
- *Fee-based models* require users to pay a subscription fee to view their content. In these systems, Web site content is restricted until a user registers and pays either a flat monthly rate or a pay-as-you-go fee. Internet dating sites, such as Match and eHarmony, and online journals, such as *Consumer Reports*, are examples of fee-based B2C sites.

Although B2C sites face challenges in keeping regular customers and maintaining a competitive edge, there are advantages to online companies that serve customers directly via the Internet. Many B2C sites have call centers or request forms so customers can ask questions or submit comments to improve the site. Online ads also allow B2C companies to reach a wider audience.

Consumer-to-Consumer

Transactions that take place between consumers are called **consumer-to-consumer (C2C) transactions.** In this e-commerce model, consumers sell goods and services to other consumers, sometimes with the involvement of a third party. A popular C2C marketplace with an intermediary is eBay. File and music sharing are types of C2C exchanges, sometimes referred to as *P2P*, or peer-to-peer. Social-networking sites, including Facebook and MySpace, can fill this role, as well.

The Challenges of E-Commerce

E-commerce is all about convenience, but it can become complicated when tax and jurisdiction issues are taken into consideration.

Taxes
Most Internet sales are tax free, which causes major problems for states that rely on sales taxes to fund their public institutions. The laws regarding e-commerce taxation have been debated since Congress passed the Internet Tax Freedom Act (ITFA) in 1998. This law established a three-year suspension of online sales taxes and was extended for two more years in 2001. It expired in 2003 and was never renewed.[6]

Online sales tax requirements also vary depending on the business. If an e-business also has a physical presence, such as a store or an office, then it must charge sales tax for the states in which it has a physical presence.[7] Target, for example, has some stores in Maryland, so a customer living in Maryland must pay sales tax on a purchase from Target's Web site. On the other hand, if a customer in Georgia orders a bouquet from the 1800Flowers Web site, he or she does not have to pay sales tax because 1800Flowers doesn't have a brick-and-mortar store in Georgia.

Because tax-free shopping is a major appeal to consumers, some large companies have created online stores that are separate legal entities from their brick-and-mortar stores. This allows customers to purchase from their online stores without paying sales tax, although this practice has outraged many retailers that must collect tax from their customers. Businesses that can avoid charging sales tax have a competitive advantage. State governments, however, are losing considerable revenue, and many have now instituted a "use tax." For example, in Pennsylvania you have one month to pay the 6 percent use tax on anything you purchase over the Internet if the seller did not collect state taxes.

Legal Jurisdiction

Jurisdiction is the authority of a government to legislate and enforce its many laws. It is usually territorial, but because the Internet has a geographic territory that is too broad to define, it is difficult to address legal jurisdiction issues for online-only businesses.[8] Disputes over the legal jurisdiction of e-commerce have been occurring since the dawn of the Internet. A large corporation might have offices or stores in several different countries, and it becomes very difficult to comply with the laws of all those countries. In addition, to protect the rights of buyers and sellers and protect copyright material, the Digital Millennium Copyright Act was passed in 1998.[9] In 2000, the World Intellectual Property Organization (WIPO) assured e-businesses that they would have to comply with laws only where they are based.

Marketing Online

The rise of e-commerce has also revolutionized the way goods and services are advertised and promoted. For businesses that have historically relied on traditional forms of advertising, such as television and newspapers, the Internet has become a new source for revenue. For marketing experts, taking advantage of new advertising outlets offers many new opportunities.

Online Advertising

Online advertising refers to any form of advertising that uses the Internet to market its message to customers. This includes everything from banner ads to Facebook campaigns to spam e-mails. More often than not, the online ad is hyperlinked to another Web site and tracks how many "clicks" are registered. The ability to track how many eyes have viewed an ad is, in fact, one of the great allures of Internet advertising.

As the number of households with high-speed broadband Internet access has increased, online advertising has become much more sophisticated.[10] Flash and Java technology allow advertisers to embed animated ads and full-motion video. In addition to the abundance of such rich media ads, programs such as Google's AdWords service and AdSense network employ the process of **pay-per-click (PPC) advertising.** With PPC advertising, advertisers pay only for the number of times a Web surfer clicks on their ad. Google's AdWords and AdSense have been able to translate this simple technique into a successful source of revenue for the company. Mobile platforms are seeing an increase in direct advertising as well. With the release of iPhone OS 4.0, Apple introduced the design of iAds. Instead of redirecting a user out of the application they are in and into a Web browser, iAds will be integrated into the iPhone app so they will fade up, interact with the user, and then fade away—all while the user is still in the original app.[11]

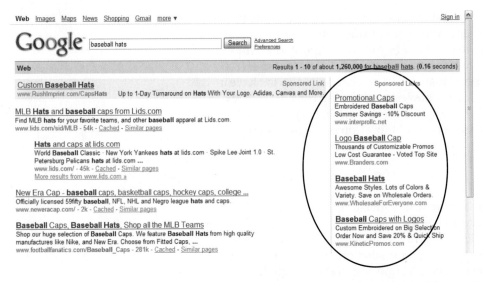

Google employs PPC advertising, like the sponsored links shown here, as an example of online advertising.

PPC ads are effective because they are associated with keywords and are highly relevant to what potential consumers are searching for. The idea was initially conceived by the GoTo search engine before Google began to develop its own AdSense network. Google's popular AdSense network takes PPC ads to the next level. By placing PPC ads on third-party sites, such as blogs and Web forums, they reach readers depending on the content of a particular page instead of search results. Also known as **contextual advertising,** these ads are automatically generated by the content on a specific site. This way, readers of a popular snowboarding blog might see ads with Shaun White promoting Red Bull. Moreover, the AdSense network also allows individual bloggers to generate revenue by hosting these ads on their site. Blogs with a significant readership can earn a great deal of money by giving such ads visibility.

There are drawbacks to online advertising, however. "Click fraud" can occur, in which a competing company clicks on ads to run up the cost of its competitor's advertising. Spam annoys people and fills up their in-boxes. Web surfers also complain about pop-up ads, which open their ads in new browser windows, and interstitials, which are displayed before a viewer can get to the desired content. Also, because the integration of ads on the Internet is so prevalent, many people have grown so used to seeing Web ads that they may not even notice them. ▼ **Table 1** summarizes the pros and cons of online advertising.

Viral Marketing

To get people to notice their advertisements, many marketers are turning to a technique known as **viral marketing.** This practice involves using social networks, e-mail, and Web sites to spread the awareness of a particular brand. Rather than being an overt advertising campaign that relies on airwaves with commercials, a viral campaign is more subtle and dependent on the user to be an active participant in spreading a message. It's designed to appeal to consumers who may be resistant to traditional advertising. Essentially, viral marketing is a Web 2.0 version—that is, a

▼ **Table 1**

Pros and Cons of Online Advertising	
Pros	**Cons**
Reasonable cost: With PPC advertising, the cost of advertising depends on frequency of use.	**Fear of spam:** Web users may avoid clicking ads to avoid receiving spam.
Hitting target markets: Contextual advertising allows for high probability of reaching intended viewers.	**Annoyance factor:** Rather than be drawn in, Web users can become annoyed with flashing ads or pop-ups.
Tracking: Companies are able to keep records of who is clicking ads and where they are located—essential information for designing future campaigns.	**Click fraud:** Companies who invest in PPC advertising may receive unexpectedly large invoices if a competitor purposefully clicks ads in excess.

more consumer-engaged, interactive, and collaborative type—of old-fashioned word of mouth.[12]

Viral marketing gives a company more than the opportunity to promote a product or brand; it allows potential consumers to feel a personal connection to the brand by becoming a part of a communal experience. Hollywood movie studios have been on the forefront of this kind of viral advertising. Consider the marketing campaign for the 2009 science fiction film *District 9*. Before the film's release, public service announcements began to appear in the 15 largest U.S. markets. Bus benches were plastered with signs reading "Bus bench for humans only" followed by a note, "Report nonhumans," and a phone number as well as a Web site address that took visitors to information about the movie.[13] In two weeks there were over 33,000 phone calls as people on the street agreed to play along with the premise that alien beings were residing in their community. The site has language support for both human and nonhuman visitors, as well as games and training simulations. By generating interest about the extensive campaign, the $30 million film took in over $37 million its first weekend.[14]

This dedication to using advertising as a means to develop content and create an entertainment experience is one way the Internet and viral marketing are shifting the paradigm of advertising's capabilities.

Banking Online

The Internet has also transformed the way people interact with their financial institutions. The rise of online banking has allowed people to do banking tasks online, from shopping for interest rates to paying bills. Convenience is a big advantage of online banking, but it also offers great organization of all your financial records.

In England, *District 9* marketers placed posters like these on phone booths to generate interest in the movie.

Most traditional banks and credit unions have some sort of presence online. Whether it's a large national bank like Wachovia or a smaller local one, many of these "click and mortar" banks offer their customers the same services online. Additionally, these banks allow their patrons to interact with their accounts using money-managing software, such as Quicken. Even those who aren't capable of initiating transactions online may still allow people to view their account balances through the computer or by a texting system to their phone.

Online banking may prove challenging when it comes to making cash deposits. If you are using direct deposit, making deposits is automatic and invisible, but placing a cash deposit still involves traveling to your local branch, or, in the case of Internet-only virtual banks, sending the money through the mail.

To maintain the security of your online financial records, avoid accessing them from public computers.

Another security challenge people might encounter is dealing with financial records over the Internet. Although most banks' Web sites have secure connections for doing online banking, you might still be uncomfortable sending such sensitive information via the Internet. Moreover, while the connection to your bank may be secure, it is still wise to handle any online transactions from a home computer or your own mobile device. Accessing your financial records on a public computer—at a library or in an airport lobby—has the potential to leave your personal information accessible to the next person who uses that particular computer, and if it's an unsecured wireless connection, it can be vulnerable to hackers. The best way to ensure that your transactions are secure and your records are safe is to deal with reputable institutions that are FDIC insured.[15]

The **Future** of **E-Business:** **Growth** and **Challenges**

Although online businesses or other businesses with an online component have the most potential for growth and expansion, they are also the most vulnerable to threats, such as security breaches and viruses. If you've ever clicked on a banner ad or downloaded a program, you've run the risk of allowing adware or spyware onto your computer. **Adware** is any software application that displays banner ads or pop-up ads while a program is running. At best, this is annoying. At worst, it installs **spyware,** which tracks your personal information and passes it on to a third party without your knowledge.[16]

Spyware operates in the backchannel of an Internet connection, collecting data and relaying that data to interested parties for fraud or identify theft.[17] This can cripple businesses, as hackers can use spyware to steal money, erase valuable information, or even crash an entire company's system. The most insidious spyware can capture keystrokes, thereby stealing passwords and other confidential information, which can grant hackers unlimited access to company networks.[18]

Any business that processes transactions online is at risk of having their customers' credit card information stolen by hackers. Spyware is not the only method that hackers use to obtain private information. **Phishing** is a common way to trick online users into sending their credit card numbers straight to hackers.[19] Suppose you have an account with Bank of America and you receive an e-mail from them informing you that your online banking account is about to expire. This e-mail requests that you fill out a secure form with your personal information so Bank of America can reactivate your account. The e-mail has the Bank of America logo and background, and it includes a link to the secure form to be filled out. You click on the link, which takes you to an online form on the Bank of America Web site. After completing the form, which asks for your name, address, password, credit card number, and credit card expiration date, you click the Submit button and send all of that information to Bank of America.

Surprise! You've just been phished. That e-mail was not from Bank of America but from hackers who had broken into the Bank of America network and copied their logo and e-mail design. The link you clicked took you to a fake Web site that was designed to look like an authentic registration form. You just sent your banking information to phishers, who can now use your credit card to make fraudulent purchases in your name. This identity theft can destroy your credit rating. It also hurts Bank of America because the bank will have to track and cancel any illegal transactions and issue you a new credit card account. If you find yourself in this situation, be sure to report it to the company's fraud or abuse center.

Banks are not the only businesses that suffer from phishing. Online retailers, such as eBay, or payment services, such as PayPal, have been the victims of spyware and phishing.[20] This can cost them dearly because customers may no longer trust these Web sites after they have been scammed. Businesses that have been hacked often spend thousands of dollars on reclaiming lost information and updating their antivirus programs and security systems to prevent future break-ins. Although these security breaches

Hackers "phish" for private banking information, which they can use to make fraudulent purchases.

remind us of the risks of online transactions, they also force online businesses to remain current in their network protection and take extra precautions to protect consumers.

The rise of the Internet and, in turn, e-commerce has brought about revolutionary changes in the business world. E-commerce has played a key role in the advancement of globalization and has opened up a vast array of opportunities and possibilities in the B2B, B2C, and C2C worlds. Although online security and privacy remain challenging issues within the realm of e-commerce, they are unlikely to hamper this burgeoning area's continued growth in the future.

Small Business: The Mainstream of the American Economy

Joleen Wilson left a secure position in a good company to start her own business. For Joleen, the financial risk of leaving a set salary and retirement plan was offset by independence and flexibility. What exactly is a small business? And why are they so important to the American economy?

Objective 1 What is the role and structure of the small business within the U.S. economy? (pp. 135–136)

Entrepreneurs and the American Dream

The Wahoo brothers took the concept of a fish taco and created a multimillion dollar business with several locations. Their success is not just based on their delicious food. What else about these brothers, and their business, makes them successful entrepreneurs? Do you have what it takes to be an entrepreneur?

Objective 2 What are the traits of an effective entrepreneur, and what are the different types of entrepreneurs? (pp. 141–146)

Buying Franchises and Existing Businesses

Have you ever thought of owning your own business but didn't know where to start? Aisha Lawrence had always dreamed of running a restaurant. Should she start her own from scratch? Or would buying a franchise or an established restaurant be the right move for her?

Objective 3 What are the advantages and disadvantages of franchising within the context of entrepreneurship? (pp. 147–150)

The Risks of Small Businesses and Where to Get Help

There's a good reason why entrepreneurs are known for being risk takers: Starting a

small business is risky! Roger Sherman knew the pressures and risks of business as he left a failing company to start his own. After making a good start, Roger needed some assistance. Where can Roger go for advice and some minor short-term financial assistance?

Objective 4 Why is a business plan crucial to small business success, and what factors lead to small business failure? (pp. 153–154)

Objective 5 How do resources, including the Small Business Administration (SBA), mentoring sources such as the Service Corp of Retired Executives (SCORE), business incubators, and advisory boards, provide assistance and guidance to small business owners? (pp. 154–156)

Financing Considerations

All that stands between many would-be entrepreneurs and their pot of gold at the end of the rainbow is a way to finance their dream business. Although operating a sandwich shop was not Fred DeLuca's dream, it did become his pot of gold as it turned into one of the world's top franchise opportunities and largest privately held businesses. And it all started with a $1,000 investment from a friend. How do small businesses obtain financing? What are the considerations between all the options?

Objective 6 What are the potential benefits and drawbacks of each major source of small business financing? (pp. 157–159)

PEARSON
my*biz*lab

Conducting a SWOT Analysis

Recently, you and a fellow engineer friend have been working to boost the performance of hybrid car batteries. As you've learned more about the hybrid car industry, you've discovered a potential unmet need for the service and replacement of these batteries. Some dealerships offer these services, but there may be an opportunity for you to open a specialty shop in your area that focuses solely on these batteries. Can you become the Donald Trump of hybrid car batteries?

Objective 7 Test yourself using my*biz*lab.com to show that you understand the chapter objectives.

Small Business: The Mainstream of the **American Economy** pp. **135–140**

Joleen Wilson thought she had landed the job of a lifetime when the offer came a month before graduation. She worked for a large, secure company; she received a regular paycheck, had a 401k plan, and had already been promoted twice. By other's standards, life was good.

But now, Joleen felt something was missing. She fantasized about owning her own business, of making her own decisions, having some flexibility in her schedule, and hopefully not having someone else set her earning potential. But she never could gather enough courage to leave the stable paycheck. Finally, with the threat of a potential downsizing ahead of her, Joleen jumped the corporate ship and started her own professional organizing business. She had helped to organize many garages, basements, and offices for friends and family, but she had never considered charging for her time. It was just fun for her. Now, she was actively seeking clients, marketing her services, and enjoying the results. Business has been steady but not overwhelming, so Joleen is glad that she has a nest egg to rely on during slow times, but she has not regretted her decision one bit. ■

Although starting your own small business might not be the answer to all your problems, it can mean independence, control, and flexibility, as it did for Joleen. For many people seeking a new opportunity, it's a promising and attractive option. Many new small businesses today are founded to solve a unique problem with an innovative solution. Many provide a specialized product to other corporations. Small businesses often fill a niche that large companies do not. As a whole, small businesses in the United States play a major role in the economy.

Small Business and the Economy

What is a small business? The **Small Business Administration (SBA)**, an independent agency of the federal government that was formed to aid, counsel, assist, and protect the interests of small businesses, defines a **small business** as one that is independently owned and operated and not dominant in its field of operation.[1] To qualify for governmental programs and benefits specifically targeted for small businesses, a small business must also meet employee and sales standards established by the SBA. In general, most small businesses must have fewer than 500 employees, though, as shown in ▼ **Figure 5.1**, the majority

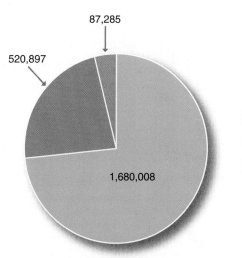

87,285

520,897

1,680,008

▼ **Figure 5.1 Small Business Breakdowns in the United States**

■ Firms with **5-19** employees
■ Firms with **20-99** employees
■ Firms with **100-499** employees

of all small businesses have 20 or fewer employees.[2] Also, to qualify as a small business, the SBA places restrictions on how much annual revenue a small business can earn. The limits on average annual revenue vary significantly by industry, but in the retail and service industries, which account for the majority of small businesses, the standard annual revenue for a small business is $7.5 million.[3]

Why are small businesses important to the economy?

Because there are so many small businesses, they are very important to the economy and the job market. In fact, small businesses provide 52.6 percent of all retail sales in the country[4] and account for more than one-half of America's economic output.[5] In addition, they comprise 99.7 percent of all U.S. private employers and create more than one-half of the U.S. gross domestic product.[6] This makes U.S. small businesses the world's third largest economy, preceded only by the European Union and the entire U.S. economy, putting them ahead of Japan, China, and Germany, as shown in ▼ **Figure 5.2**.[7,8] Small businesses also export an average of $375 billion in goods and services every year.[9]

How do small businesses foster innovation?

Small companies often introduce new products or procedures that many large businesses do not have the flexibility, the time, the resources, or the inclination to offer. Smaller companies are also often better poised to take risks, more flexible to explore innovative techniques, and better equipped to push through inventions than larger firms. In fact, small businesses create 13 times more patents per employee than large firms do.[11]

The impact of small business innovations is well known in the computer, IT, and communications industries. For example, Michael Dell shook up the computer retail industry by being the first to market computers directly to customers via the Internet, rather than through retail stores. By taking direct orders from customers, Dell was able to order parts directly from suppliers on an as-needed basis, freeing his company from carrying large inventories of parts that could become outdated by the next technological innovation. Michael Dell's process improvement gave Dell an advantage over its competitors and helped Dell Computers, then a fledgling start-up company, take the lead in the PC retail market. The market responded favorably, and the competition responded in kind. Today, Dell's competitors—Hewlett-Packard, Toshiba, and Sony—all have online, customized shopping options.

Other industries have also benefited from the innovative contributions of small businesses. For example, in the biotechnology industry, many small businesses have found innovative solutions to medical issues. One such company is the Insulet Corporation, which received an innovation award from the Smaller Business Asso-

PEARSON
my*biz*lab

For an interactive, real-world example of this topic, access this chapter's **BizSkill** entitled Conducting a SWOT Analysis, located at **my*biz*lab**.com.

▼ **Figure 5.2
U.S. Small Businesses versus World Economies**[10]

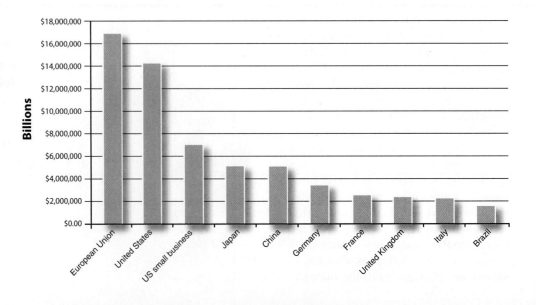

ciation of New England for developing the OmniPod. This tiny instrument, weighing a little more than an ounce, sticks to the skin and delivers insulin at a constant rate based on instructions programmed into its wireless companion.[12] The flexibility inherent in small businesses such as the Insulet Corporation allows them to react more quickly than larger companies to changing market trends and needs. As such, small businesses play an important role in maintaining a healthy economy.

How do small businesses help bigger companies? Small businesses often operate in cooperative relationships with bigger businesses. In the automotive industry, for example, small businesses are important because they make and supply parts that are required in large manufacturing processes. In fact, 70 percent of the 15,000 parts that go into a single automobile, such as seats, engine blocks, and bumpers, are provided by independent suppliers.[13] Using small businesses to provide the small and specialized parts not only helps large manufacturers, such as Ford Motor Company, reduce their costs, but also helps with product design and innovation. Many of the features in cars, such as heated seats and intermittent windshield wipers, were first developed by small companies and later sold to large automotive manufacturers. It is estimated that small business suppliers now provide two-thirds of the value added in the production of a vehicle through their increase in R&D.[14]

How do small businesses help consumers? Small businesses directly provide us with many of the specialized products and services we use every day. Service businesses, such as hair salons, landscapers, and dry cleaners, as well as local restaurants, auto repair, and many other "mom and pop" stores, provide the services and products larger businesses can't or don't want to provide.

Small Business and the Workforce

What kind of workers do small businesses employ? Almost all new businesses are small; therefore, they account for a substantial portion of the newly created jobs in the United States. In fact, small businesses create over 60 percent of net new jobs every year.[15] In addition, small businesses hire a larger proportion of younger workers, older workers, and part-time workers, so they help employ millions who do not fit into a traditionally corporate structure.[16]

Do small businesses provide opportunities for minorities? Many individuals see owning and operating their own business as a means of achieving the American dream. To that end, women, minorities, and immigrants are becoming more important players in the small business arena. According to a 2009 SBA report, approximately one-fifth of all U.S. small businesses in 2007 were owned by minorities. African-American- and Asian/American Indian-owned businesses account for approximately 5 percent each of all U.S. firms, and Hispanic-owned businesses accounted for 10 percent of all U.S. firms (see ▼ **Figure 5.3**). Women owned 5.3 million businesses, representing approximately one-third of all small businesses. The number of minority-owned businesses is increasing. Between 2000 and 2007, the number of businesses owned by African Americans grew by 36 percent. The number of Hispanic-owned businesses grew an amazing 109 percent during this period, and firms owned by women increased by nearly 10 percent.[17] (Note: The SBA's 2009 report reflects the most recent data available.)

The infusion of foreign nationals and ethnic cultures in America has spawned more small business opportunities to provide services and products that cater to new needs and tastes. For example, Rajbhog Foods, Inc., which started as a small, family-owned Indian sweets shop in Queens, New York, provides the Indian community there with authentic Indian sweets and snacks. As the Indian population increased in the area, so did the volume of items made and sold by Rajbhog Foods. The company eventually

▼ **Figure 5.3**
Small Business
Ethnic Ownership[18]

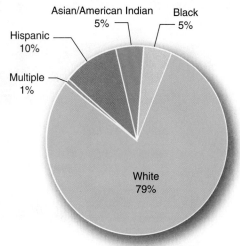

expanded its operations to sell to 41 states and Canada and also caters to large weddings and conventions. In 2001, the company began to franchise its operations in other New York locations where large populations of Indians have settled.

The Impact of Technology on Small Businesses

How has technology affected new small businesses? Entrepreneurial success stories, such as YouTube, Facebook, and Google, illustrate the vast opportunities that technology creates for new business start-ups.

The Internet

In addition to creating entirely new business opportunities, the PC and the Internet have made starting a new business much easier. Small businesses can flourish with an Internet connection; a modest Web site for marketing and communication; and a computer for financial, database, and research needs. Entrepreneur Nick Swinmurn, for example, went on a search for a new pair of his favorite boots one fateful day in 1999 and had a complete lack of success. He decided to form an Internet shoe store. The site started small, but after Swinmurn realized the potential for advancement, he expanded the selection and shipping capacity of the site, and Zappos.com was born. Over 80 percent of small businesses have a homepage, and nearly 25 percent take sales and orders online. Almost 45 percent of small businesses promote their products on a company Web site, and one-third of small businesses promote their products through e-mail marketing.[19]

In addition, sites such as Alibaba.com and Elance.com help with locating product designers, manufacturers, and freelance professionals. Knowing about these sites helped Bill McNeely create a new product and build a business from Kunduz, a northern Afghanistan city in which he was working as the manager of logistics operations at a training camp for the Afghan National Police.[20]

Social Media and Beyond

Technology advances and innovations are also creating new ways for small businesses to interact with, market to, and keep abreast of their customers through services, such as blogs, social networks, smartphone apps, and podcasts. These new advancements can be beneficial to small businesses because they are generally low-cost means of marketing. For example, Sprinkles Cupcakes, a cupcake bakery based in Beverly Hills, California, has used Facebook to its advantage (see ▼ Figure 5.4). Each day a secret word is posted on Sprinkles' Facebook page. Customers who retrieve the word and mention it at any one of the locations get a free cupcake. This strategy has caused many to "become a fan" of the company on Facebook. In fact, Sprinkles launched a contest for a trip to the Sprinkles Hollywood store for a randomly chosen "BFF" (Best Friend Forever) when they reached 100,000 Facebook fans. In addition, the company also uses

▼ **Figure 5.4 Many companies are using Facebook to connect more directly to their customers.**

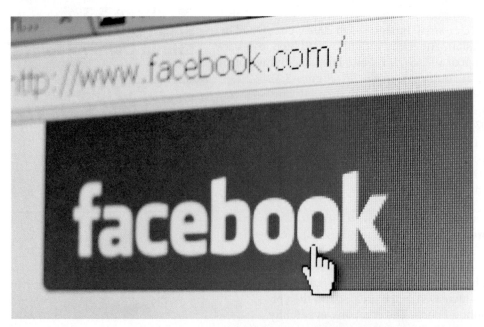

Facebook to pretest flavor ideas and upcoming promotions in an effort to increase interaction with customers.

However social media can also become problematic if not managed well. Creating a fan page on Facebook without monitoring what people are saying about your business may not be useful. Similarly, writing a blog may help get out your message, but if no one reads the blog, it's not effective. A well-thought-out technology plan is an important aspect of a new business's overall strategy.

Reasons for Starting a Small Business

Why would I want to start my own business? Bill McNeely, a logistics operations manager at a training camp for the Afghan National Police, hopes starting a business will enable him to leave his current job that keeps him so far away from his family in Texas. But people start small businesses for many different reasons:

1. **Opportunity Knocks.** An idea for a new company often starts when someone envisions a product or a service that isn't being offered yet. Other people create opportunities from their own obstacles. For example, a father frustrated at watching his autistic child try to communicate with others founded the Animated Speech Corporation, a company that develops software-based conversational language learning systems to help autistic children communicate.[21]

2. **Financial Independence.** Many people begin a small business because they want financial independence. Still, most small businesses don't start out as profitable ventures. Traditionally, it takes three to five years for new businesses to become profitable.

3. **Control.** Many people starting their own business state that they want to take more control of business decisions than their current position allows. Others know that they aren't satisfied working for someone else.

4. **Flexibility.** Many small business owners appreciate the work/life balance that owning their own business affords. Many also view working in a small business as more rewarding than working for a larger company. Small business owners believe their companies offer less bureaucracy and more flexibility than larger firms. With fewer channels to go through when decisions need to be made, small business owners can react more quickly to take advantage of immediate opportunities. In addition, small business owners say running their own business allows them the flexibility to adjust their work to their particular situations.

5. **Unemployment.** Whereas most individuals start their own businesses for the reasons mentioned previously, some are pushed into starting their own businesses because they have no other employment opportunities. "Life begins when you get fired," muses Bruce Freeman, owner of ProLine Communications Inc. Three months after being fired, he couldn't think of what to do next. Then, encouraged by a friend, Bruce started his own business. His first client was a company he worked with in his previous job. Now, over 10 years later, he's making more money than he ever could have in his old job.[23]

Small Business Structures

What kind of structure should I choose for my small business? Many small businesses start out initially as a one-person, individual business called a *sole proprietorship*. This is

Off the Mark iSmell

The dot-com era produced many businesses that just couldn't get off the ground. One example was the iSmell, a product that plugged into a computer's USB port and promised to enhance a user's Web surfing experience by generating different scents. Using the iSmell, you could smell a new perfume before buying it or conjure up the smell of a ballpark while playing a baseball videogame. Unfortunately, iSmell never made it beyond the prototype stage. Its parent company, DigiScents, shut its doors in 2001.[22]

because sole proprietorships are the quickest and easiest way to start a business. However, there are five common legal structures businesses, including small businesses, can take:

- Sole proprietorship
- General partnership
- Limited partnership
- Corporation
- LLC

We'll discuss these different legal structures in more detail in Chapter 6. As we'll see, the decision as to which business structure to choose is centered primarily on two issues: legal liability and tax considerations. Depending on the nature of the business, owners may need to protect their personal assets should something go wrong with the business. Certain corporate structures protect owners' personal assets from claims against the company. Similarly, different corporate structures have tax advantages and disadvantages that are important for small business owners to consider.

Starting a small business is a sizable challenge, as Joleen can attest to. It didn't solve all her problems; in fact, it might have created a few more, but she is glad to be in control of her own situation. It is a challenge to which many entrepreneurs, looking for their piece of the American dream, enthusiastically rise. For Joleen, having a flexible schedule, doing what she loves to do, and making money doing it made the risks of starting her home organizing business worth taking. ■

Entrepreneurs and the American Dream pp. 140–146

Who would ever have thought that blending Mexican, Brazilian, and Asian cuisines and $30,000 would lead to 50 restaurants in 4 states 20 years later? Certainly not the Wahoo brothers. If you ask them, it just kind of happened. The Wahoo brothers—Wing, Ed, and Mingo—were raised above their parents' Chinese restaurant. They took the concept of a fish taco—a staple they had grown to love while surfing in Mexico—and enhanced it with their favorite Brazilian and Asian dishes. Combined with a casual, surf-inspired decor, their concept was well received by the local southern California crowd. The brothers brought in another partner to help manage their second location, and the business quickly took off from there.[24] So, what qualities do the Wahoo brothers have to take their small fish taco eatery and turn it into a multimillion-dollar business? What makes them entrepreneurs? ■

We've all heard of Starbucks, Nike, and Microsoft, but you probably don't associate these big-name companies with small business. At one point, however, each of these companies originated as a small business. They were all started by **entrepreneurs**—people who assume the risk of creating, organizing, and operating a business. Not all small businesses are entrepreneurial. What makes a new venture entrepreneurial is that the idea behind the business is innovative or change oriented. Entrepreneurs most often start a business to satisfy a need in the market that is not being adequately fulfilled. This area of need is called an **opportunity niche.**

Like the Wahoo brothers, the brothers who started McDonald's spotted an opportunity niche. Realizing that the hamburger was the best seller in their California restaurant, they created an assembly line that allowed them to produce burgers quickly and inexpensively, and business boomed. It expanded even more when businessman, and entrepreneur, Ray Kroc, who was selling milkshake machines in California, convinced the brothers not only to use his milkshake machines but also to let him open another McDonald's restaurant in Chicago. Seeing the opportunity niche in fast food, Kroc later bought the McDonald's restaurants from the McDonald brothers. The company now operates over 32,000 restaurants in 117 countries, generating more than $20 billion in revenue annually.[25]

The Traits of Successful Entrepreneurs

What are the traits of successful entrepreneurs? Businessman Wayne Huizenga started Waste Management Inc., a leader in the waste and environmental services industry, by buying a single garbage truck in 1968. He expanded the company by buying other trash collection services, and by 1983 the company had grown into the largest of its kind in the United States. But Huizenga didn't stop there. He also started Blockbuster Video, the video rental company, as well as AutoNation, the behemoth automotive dealer.[26] How can some entrepreneurs like Wayne Huizenga begin successful businesses, while others have a difficult time getting their ideas off the ground? How do successful entrepreneurs see an opportunity niche and know exactly what they need to do to seize the opportunity and succeed?

Although luck and timing play a large role in entrepreneurial success, research has also shown that successful entrepreneurs have the following characteristics:

- Are innovative
- Take risks
- Are motivated to succeed
- Are flexible and self-directed
- Work well with others and possess good leadership skills
- Are "system thinkers," seeing the whole process rather than just individual pieces of it

How are entrepreneurs innovative? Successful entrepreneurs see problems to be solved or opportunities that aren't being addressed in the marketplace; they recognize opportunity niches. They also make improvements to existing products or systems, or they introduce something new and make profitable solutions out of problems. Renowned management and business thinker Peter Drucker noted that successful entrepreneurs "exploit change as an opportunity for a different business or a different service."[27] For example, Henry Ford turned his knowledge of engines into the first "horseless carriage," which he later improved to become the Model T.[28] His improvement was not only in creating a new machine but also in developing an assembly line process by which his company could make multiple automobiles more efficiently. Ford's innovative assembly process became the standard for efficient manufacturing.

Think about other entrepreneurs and the innovation behind their success. Ben Cohen and Jerry Greenfield of Ben & Jerry's Ice Cream didn't invent ice cream; rather, they capitalized on people's growing desire for high-quality food products and

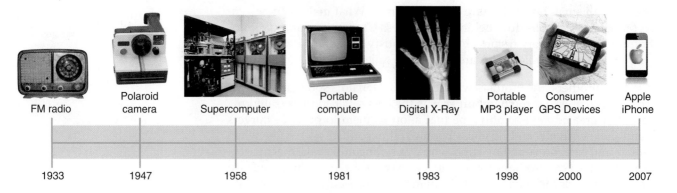

FM radio	Polaroid camera	Supercomputer	Portable computer	Digital X-Ray	Portable MP3 player	Consumer GPS Devices	Apple iPhone
1933	1947	1958	1981	1983	1998	2000	2007

▼ **Figure 5.5
Entrepreneurial
Innovations**

used the best and biggest chunks of nuts, fruits, candy, and cookies in their ice cream.[29] The McDonald brothers learned how to produce good hamburgers quickly and cost-effectively. ▼ **Figure 5.5** lists some other important innovations by entrepreneurs in the twentieth century.[30]

How do entrepreneurs take risks ❓

Being an entrepreneur involves risk, encompassing the risk of failure, the risk of losing one's career, and, of course, financial risks. Because entrepreneurs are often creating new and innovative products, the processes they develop are also often untried and therefore involve risk. Successful entrepreneurs are aware of these risks, recognize that they can influence events but do not have complete control over them, and are willing to accept the knowledge that they may fail. Successful entrepreneurs therefore take calculated risks—that is, they consider the likelihood of success before deciding whether to take a particular risk.

What makes entrepreneurs motivated to succeed ❓

Entrepreneurs are motivated by many different factors. Some entrepreneurs are motivated to provide for themselves or their families. These individuals may be driven to pursue multiple ventures before uncovering a successful idea. Other entrepreneurs are motivated to succeed by the personal fulfillment they feel after successfully launching a business.

"If you take risks, you may still fail; but if you do not take risks, you will surely fail. The greatest risk of all is to do nothing."[31]

—Roberto Goizueta, *CEO of Coca-Cola* (1980–1997)

The entrepreneur's keen desire to tackle challenges and succeed has led one entrepreneur, Ted Kennedy (not the former Massachusetts senator), to start a company rooted in this notion. Kennedy noticed that many participants in the Ironman Triathlon Challenge were corporate executives. He also noticed that these executive triathletes sought above-average accommodations, as well as enjoyed meeting and socializing with other CEOs prior to and during their competition. So Kennedy formed CEO Challenges, providing sporting competitions specifically for the CEO. Although Kennedy began his company focusing on triathlons, he has since expanded it to offer cycling, hockey, fishing, golf, sailing, tennis, and other competitive adventures to executives. The company has also expanded to hold challenges in Canada and Europe. He estimates that his company will have made over $5 million in revenue by 2010.[32]

Why do successful entrepreneurs need to be flexible and self-directed ❓

Because entrepreneurial ventures are subject to uncertainty and risk, entrepreneurs need to be able to react quickly to new and unexpected situations, such as the sudden and unexpected downturn in the financial markets in 2009. Jason Hogg, founder and CEO of Revolution Money, Inc., now a part of American Express, credits his company's success during this unsettled time to being "flexible and creative." He had to quickly reevaluate his business plan and develop new partnerships. "It's an evolution that startups go through and the ones that are good at those adaptations survive; the ones that are too rigid go under," he says.[33] And because entrepreneurs are their own bosses, they need to be able to make their own decisions. An entrepreneur must be able to wear many hats, acting not only as executive but also sales manager, financial director, secretary, and mail-room person.

Why are people skills and leadership skills important to entrepreneurs? They may come up with the initial idea behind their businesses, but entrepreneurs rarely work by themselves. As much as they have the capacity to wear many hats, at some point most entrepreneurs need other people with complementary skills to join them in their ventures. If their businesses expand, they must hire employees and other managers to help them run it. Leadership and communication skills are therefore important traits of successful entrepreneurs who must motivate others to feel as passionately about the entrepreneurial enterprise as they do.

What does it mean for entrepreneurs to be "system" thinkers? Although entrepreneurs develop companies from an idea, they must focus on the entire process of turning their idea into a business to succeed. Successful entrepreneurs are able to see the whole picture when they establish their businesses. They determine how to resolve a problem or capitalize on an opportunity by developing a solid plan, including producing, financing, marketing, and distributing the service or the product. For example, Pete Slosberg, founder of Pete's Brewing Company, recognized the rise in popularity of microbreweries and brewpubs around the country. Slosberg saw the opportunity and began the process of creating his company with not only an idea but also a system: create a "great beer, a great name, and an interesting label. Have the name and the label to get people to try it for the first time, and a great beer so they keep coming back."[34] In 1998, Pete's Brewing Company had $19 million in sales before being sold to the Gambrinus Company.

Types of Entrepreneurs

Are there different types of entrepreneurs? Beyond traditional entrepreneurs described in the previous sections, other entrepreneurial categories have begun to crop up:

- Lifestyle entrepreneurs
- Micropreneurs
- Home-based entrepreneurs
- Internet entrepreneurs
- Growth entrepreneurs
- Intrapreneurs
- Social entrepreneurs and social intrapreneurs

Let's take a look at each of these types.

What are lifestyle entrepreneurs? **Lifestyle entrepreneurs** look for more than profit potential when they begin their businesses. Some lifestyle entrepreneurs are looking for freedom from corporate bureaucracy or the opportunity to work at home or in a location other than an office. Others are looking for more flexibility in work hours or travel schedules. Take Richard Dahl, for example. He is traveling around the country in a travel trailer selling more than 300 items, including his flagship water filter system at trailer parks, campgrounds, and motor home shows.[35] His business, the RV Water Filter Store, allows him to fulfill his passion of traveling around the country with this wife.

What are micropreneurs? **Micropreneurs** start their own businesses but are satisfied with keeping their businesses small in an effort to achieve a balanced lifestyle. For example, a micropreneur might open a single restaurant and be satisfied with running only that one restaurant, instead of expanding as Ray Kroc did with the McDonald brothers' restaurant. Micropreneurs, or small-business people, have no aspirations of growing large and/or hiring hundreds or thousands of employees. Businesses such as dog-walking services, painters, and special-occasion cake bakers would all be considered micropreneurial opportunities.

What are home-based entrepreneurs? As the name suggests, **home-based entrepreneurs** are entrepreneurs who run their businesses out of their homes. Home-based entrepreneurs are often parents who like being able to stay home with their children and run a business. Sheena Edwards was a stay-at-home mom who was looking for a creative outlet. Sheena decided to start making crystal-embellished women's flip-flops and now runs Lizzie Lou Shoes from her home.

Production of the shoes is managed by Sheena's cousin in New Delhi, India. "I love owning my own business, as it gives me the creative outlet I crave while still allowing me to be home with my kids and not miss a thing (with the exception of sleep!)," says Sheena.[36] In addition to offering lifestyle advantages, such as being able to stay at home with children, home-based businesses offer several financial advantages. Staying at home eliminates commuting time and costs, as well as office rent and other overhead costs. Also home-based entrepreneurs can take advantage of deducting from their taxes a part of their rent or mortgage payment, depreciation, property taxes, insurance, utilities, household maintenance, and home repairs and improvements.

What are Internet entrepreneurs? Advances in technology have spawned another type of entrepreneur, the **Internet entrepreneur,** who creates businesses that operate solely online. The early 1990s saw the first group of Internet entrepreneurs, but most did not survive the dot-com era. Now, however, with the advent of Web 2.0 technologies (such as blogging and social networking), smartphone apps, contextual Web-based advertising (such as Google Ads) that help to provide revenue, along with faster broadband connections, a greater number of successful online businesses are being established.

Youth may have an advantage in this entrepreneurial genre because success requires little investment, some spare time, and a good understanding of what their peers are looking for. For example, David and Catherine Cook and their older brother Geoff started myYearbook.com over spring break in 2005. The social-networking site invites members to meet new people through playing games, chatting, and sending virtual gifts purchased with Lunch Money, the site's virtual currency. Members are also given the opportunity to donate Lunch Money to their favorite charity through their charity application. myYearbook had a revenue of $20 million in 2009.[37] Some of the most famous Internet entrepreneurs include Mark Zuckerberg (Facebook), Jeff Bezos (Amazon), Pierre Omidyar and John Donahoe (eBay), Sergey Brin and Larry Page (Google), and Jimmy Wales (Wikipedia).

What are growth entrepreneurs? **Growth entrepreneurs** strive to create fast-growing businesses and look forward to expansion. The companies that these types of entrepreneurs create are known as *gazelles*. Typically, a gazelle business has at least 20 percent sales growth every year for 5 years, starting with a base of at least $100,000.[38] It is hard to recognize a gazelle business during its rapidly growing period, though companies such as eBay and Google can clearly be identified in retrospect as having been gazelles in their early years.

What are intrapreneurs? You don't necessarily have to leave your company to have an entrepreneurial experience. Some companies are fostering **intrapreneurs**—employees who work in an entrepreneurial way within an organizational environment. At the home appliance company Whirlpool, for example, developing intrapreneurs is an important part of corporate success. The company's success depends on producing creative solutions to household problems. Instead of relying solely on the traditional research and development (R&D process, Whirlpool management is tapping the creative juices of their employees by encouraging them to generate ideas that will enhance the company's existing products. Although employees are not separately compensated for their ideas, they are pleased that the company asks for their ideas and have responded enthusiastically. By the end of the first year of the program, 60 ideas were in the prototype stage, and 190 were close to entering the marketplace.[39,40] Other examples of products generated from employee innovation include Post-it Notes, the Sony PlayStation, the Java programming language, and ELIXIR guitar strings.[41]

What are social entrepreneurs and social intrapreneurs? Just as a business entrepreneur seeks to create innovative solutions that satisfy an unfulfilled corporate or consumer need, the idea can be extended to society at large. **Social entrepreneurs** set out to create innovative solutions in the social sector; they are entrepreneurs with a social mission.[42] For example, Mimi Silbert founded Delancy Street Foundation, a residential education center that teaches substance abusers, former felons, and the homeless the necessary skills to enable them to lead productive lives. The foundation runs on income generated by businesses created by the foundation that act as the training ground for program participants. It has been called the most successful rehabilitation project in the United States.[43]

Similarly, **social intrapreneurs** build and develop ventures within a company that are designed to identify and solve large-scale social problems."[44] In an effort to create a "social corporate enterprise," eBay, for example, gathered 40 employees to discuss ways to make eBay a more environmentally conscious company. What resulted was a myriad of projects, ranging from rideshare programs and community gardens to the largest solar installation in San Jose, California, at their corporate headquarters.[45]

Entrepreneurial Teams

How do I know if I'd be a good entrepreneur? Look at the list of entrepreneurial traits described earlier in this section. In addition to being innovative, motivated, and self-directed, an entrepreneur initially may need to fill the role of executive, sales manager, financial director, secretary, and mailroom person. If you don't possess all of these traits, it doesn't preclude you from starting your own business and becoming a successful entrepreneur. If you have an idea and really want to make it happen, you might want to reach out to others who can do what you can't or don't want to do and assemble an entrepreneurial team.

What is an entrepreneurial team? An **entrepreneurial team** is a group of qualified individuals with varied experiences and skills that come together to form a new venture. The skills of the entrepreneurial team members complement one another so that as a group, the team has the necessary skills and traits to manage a successful project. For example, Lin Miao, Andrew Bachman, Lucas Brown, and Lee Brown came together to form Tatto Media, an Internet marketing company that would "fundamentally change the way advertisers pay for display advertising." The company's success is in part due to the "genius of Lin, and the design and engineering skills of Luc and Lee." Andrew Bachman, the president, confesses, "I never would have had a product to sell because I can't see it like Lin sees it, and I can't build it like Luc and Lee build it."[46]

Entrepreneurial teams are also great for those who want to run their own businesses but perhaps lack the personal experience. For example, many college and business school students form entrepreneurial teams to get their first project launched. There

On Target
Facebook

When Mark Zuckerberg, a Harvard student, came up with the idea for Facebook, he didn't realize that he was spearheading a multibillion dollar organization. The idea behind "The Facebook," as it was originally called, was to provide a forum for Harvard University students to network and display pictures of themselves and their friends. The site was launched on February 4, 2004, and within a month, half of the undergraduates on the Harvard campus were users of the site. Expansion came quickly, as Dustin Moskovitz and Chris Hughes joined Zuckerberg to help promote the site. Within two months, the entire Ivy League was included in the Facebook network. In September 2005, these entrepreneurs decided to allow high schools and other colleges to join the network. Finally, on September 11, 2006, the general public was allowed to join Facebook, so long as all potential members had a valid e-mail address and were at least 13 years old.

Mark Zuckerberg's brainchild has become so successful that he reportedly turned down a $750 million offer to purchase Facebook. Media giants such as Google and Yahoo! have been attempting to outbid each other for ownership of Facebook, but Zuckerberg claims that he is not interested in parting with his creation. And why should he be? The site has over 400 million active users worldwide and is constantly expanding![47]

are several examples of students who met in college and began to work on projects together that turned out to be successful businesses. Students from Stanford University have come together to create well-known companies such as Google, HP, Cisco, Imagen, and Yahoo! Many schools run entrepreneurial challenges, such as the Big Bang competition at the University of California at Davis. In this year-long program, UC Davis students, alumni, staff, and faculty join forces to construct and test their business plans, which serve as the springboards for new companies, such as Advanced Enological Closures, which designed a "breathing screw cap" for wine that eliminates the product variability because of the amount of oxygen traditional or synthetic corks allow into a wine bottle.[48]

Perhaps you're part of an entrepreneurial team, an employee in an intrapreneurial company, or prefer to go it alone. Maybe you want to keep your business small or expand it like the Wahoo brothers or McDonald's. Whatever the case, being an entrepreneur is more than just being in business for yourself. Taking advantage of an opportunity niche, riding the bumps along the way with creative solutions, and being system thinkers all describe successful entrepreneurs. Do you have what it takes to be an entrepreneur? Entrepreneurial opportunities exist if you're up to the challenge. ■

Buying Franchises and Existing Businesses pp. 147–152

I t was a desired change in lifestyle that prompted Aisha Lawrence to think about starting her own business. She had always dreamed of running her own restaurant, but she didn't have much business background or restaurant experience. What she did have was a lot of tenacity and knowledge of marketing. Additionally, she was a people person—a necessity for restaurant owners. Still, she was unsure of where to begin.

Aisha knew that the risks were way too high to start a restaurant on her own or buy an existing restaurant. On the other hand, she felt that she could run a small, single-product food business, such as a coffee bar or an ice cream shop, to give her the experience she would need to run her own restaurant some day. But Aisha was still uncomfortable starting from scratch. She felt that she needed the support of someone who had been through the process before, so she looked into buying a franchise. The main question was: Which franchise would be best for her? ■

Franchises have been around a long time. In the United States, Singer Sewing Machines was one of the first franchises, started in 1851. Today, they are a popular way for people like Aisha to enter the world of small business. In this section, we'll look at what it means to buy a franchise. We'll also discuss another small business option: buying an existing business and molding it into your own.

Franchising Basics

What is a franchise? A **franchise** is a method of doing business whereby the business (the **franchisor**) sells a company's products or services under the company's name to independent third-party operators (the **franchisees**).[49] Aisha would be a franchisee using a franchisor's marketing methods and trademarked goods under the name of the business. In exchange, she would make monthly payments to the franchise.

What kinds of business opportunities are available as franchises? Franchises play an important part in our economy. Over 880,000 franchised businesses are in operation, employing approximately 9.5 million people, with an output of nearly $845 billion.[50] Franchises in the business services, fast-food restaurants, and personal services are projected to have the largest percentage increase in sales, and fast-food restaurants are projected to have the largest percent increase in the number of establishments in 2010.[51] But franchise opportunities exist in nearly every industry, and many can be run from your home, which lowers the start-up costs because there is no need to purchase or rent real estate. Most can be purchased for less than $50,000.[52] Home-based franchises, such as Jani-King, ServPro, Jazzercise, and Matco Tools are among the top home-based franchises. Additionally, as we discussed in Chapter 4, franchising provides a great opportunity for doing business internationally. For example, the European Franchise

▼ **Table 5.1**

Web-based Resources for Potential Franchisees

The **SBA** and **FranNet** sponsor a site that features a video that explains what franchising is, how to determine if franchising is right for you, and how to select the right franchise.

The **American Franchisee Association** offers advice on buying a franchise, legal resources, and opportunities to network with other franchisees.

The **Federal Trade Commission** provides consumer information on franchise and business opportunities. The publication *Buying a Franchise: A Consumer Guide* outlines the steps to take before selecting a particular franchise, how to shop at a franchise exhibition, and what you should know before signing the franchisor's disclosure document.

Entrepreneur.com's **Franchise Zone** allows users to search a directory of franchising opportunities and provides tips on buying a franchise. This site also ranks the top franchises in terms of growth, cost, global appeal, and other aspects.

The **International Franchise Association** provides answers to frequently asked questions about franchising and resources for potential and current franchisees. This Web site also hosts a directory of franchising opportunities in various industries.

Source: "SBDCNet.org http://sbdcnet.org/SBIC/franchise.php and "Buy a Franchise," Small Business Association. www.sba.gov/smallbusinessplanner/start/buyafranchise/index.html.

Federation estimates that there are over 8,500 distinct franchise brands operating in the EU compared to about 2,500 U.S. brands, and about one-third of U.S. franchisors would consider expanding into the EU.[53]

If you are thinking of purchasing a franchise, you will need to do your homework. There are several sources of helpful information about franchises that you should study before taking the leap. ▼ **Table 5.1** lists several helpful Web-based resources that you can begin with.

Pros and Cons of Franchising

What are the advantages of franchising? For many, franchising is an easier, less risky means of starting a business. Because the franchisor provides much of the marketing and financial tools needed to run a business, all the franchisee is expected to bring to the table is management and marketing skills, time, and money. In addition to a recognized brand name, there are many other advantages of owning a franchise.

- **It is a proven system of operation.** Instead of wading through the muddy waters of new business ownership by themselves, franchisees benefit from the *collective experience* of the franchise company. The franchisor has determined, through trial and error, the best system of daily operations for the established business. New franchisees can therefore avoid many of the common start-up mistakes made by new business owners because they will be working with standardized products, systems, and financial and accounting systems.

- **There is strength in numbers.** You are not alone when you buy a franchise. Because you belong to a group, you might benefit from economies of scale achieved by purchasing materials, supplies, and services at discounted group rates. In addition, it is often easier to get approved for business loans when running a franchise, as lending institutions often view that there is less risk associated with a franchise.

- **Initial training is part of the deal.** The beauty of franchising is that you're in business *for* yourself but not *by* yourself. The franchisor offers initial training to ensure you have a successful opening and might offer ongoing training if new products or services are being incorporated into the franchise line.

- **Marketing support is provided.** As a franchisee, you are often given marketing materials generated at the corporate level and have the benefit of any national advertising programs that are created. Although you are expected to run your own local marketing efforts, you have the support of other franchisees in the area to help you in your efforts.

- **Market research is often provided.** Good franchisors do considerable market research and can generally conclude whether there is demand for the product or service in the area before selling the franchisee a franchise. The franchisor should also help to identify the competition and offer strategies to differentiate the franchise from them.

Costs & Fees	Subway	McDonalds	Jazzercise
Total Investment:	$78,600–$238,300	$950,200–$1,800,000	$3,000–$75,500
Initial Franchise Fee:	$15,000	$45,000	$500–$1,000
Royalty Fee:	8%	12.5%	Up to 20%
Term of Agreement:	20 years	20 years	5 years
Renewal Fee:		$45K	

What are the disadvantages of franchising? Although buying a franchise provides the franchisee with many benefits, there are some disadvantages too.

▼ **Figure 5.6
Start-up Costs
and Franchise Facts**

- **Lack of control.** There is not much opportunity to contribute creatively to the franchise because the franchisor often controls the look of the store and the product or the service. The franchisee, however, is expected to bring the necessary drive and spirit to make the franchise a success.

- **Start-up and ongoing costs.** Most franchises require more than $50,000 to start, although there are some that require less (see ▼ **Figure 5.6**). For example, the franchise fee for the very popular Subway is $15,000. Jan-Pro, a commercial cleaning franchise company and the fastest growing franchise in the United States, requires just $3,000 to start a unit franchise. Other franchises, such as H&R Block, Jani-King, and Jazzercise, can also be purchased with less than $50,000.[54] Other start-up costs the franchisee might incur include real estate purchase or rental, equipment purchase or rental, extra signage, and opening inventory. In addition, franchisees must pay a monthly royalty fee to the franchisor, which is typically 6–10 percent. The royalty fees are usually reinvested into the growth of the franchise corporation and are due regardless of how the business is doing. Royalty fees can be a huge overhead expense.

- **Workload.** As with any new business owner, new franchisees shouldn't expect easy hours. Aisha Lawrence admits that she spends a lot more time running her franchise than she thought she would. However, because she can hire employees to run the day-to-day operations, her time is spent more on the business development and management end of the business.

- **Competition.** Some franchises do not restrict the location or number of their franchise locations. In those instances, franchisees could experience serious competition not only from another company but also from other franchisees in the same franchise organization. In addition, some franchises do not offer geographic or demographic studies of the best location to open a new store and instead may expect the franchisee to have completed a good market analysis and be familiar with the surrounding competition.

- **Share common problems.** If the franchisor or another franchisee is having problems, all franchisees will feel its pain. For example, when a Wendy's restaurant was falsely accused of serving chili with a human thumb mixed in, business in all Wendy's restaurants plummeted.

Franchising Considerations

What are things to watch out for when considering buying a franchise? The most common piece of advice offered to anyone interested in buying a franchise is to do homework up front. Although much of the start-up process is done for you, you are still buying a business that will require your time and money and is not guaranteed to succeed. ▼ **Table 5.2** shows suggested questions to ask the company that you are buying the franchise from and other people who have bought franchises from the company before you take the plunge.

▼ **Table 5.2**

Questions to Ask Before Buying a Franchise		
	Questions to Ask the Franchisor	**Questions to Ask Other Franchisees**
Competition	• What is the competitive advantage of the product/service? • What makes the business more attractive to an owner and more attractive to a customer?	• How is your system better than competitors'? • How does your business match up? • Who are your competitors?
Franchise System	• How time tested and standardized is the franchise system? • What franchise system is used and how does it work? • How long has the franchise been in business and what improvements has the franchise company made recently?	• How long have you been in business? • Does your location meet your customers' needs? • Who selected the site?
Support and Training	• How much support does the franchisor give the franchisee? • What is the initial and ongoing training? • Are there toll-free help lines, field support, annual meetings, local meetings, purchasing programs, and marketing promotion?	• How is the relationship with the franchisor? • How were the initial training and ongoing training and ongoing support? • How are the marketing, advertising, and promotional programs handled?
Financial Strength	• What is the financial strength of the company and the experience of management? • How much revenue comes from franchise fees and how much revenue comes from royalties? • How has the stock performed?	• Are you pleased with earnings? • Is volume growing?
Franchise Relationships	• How important is the franchisee to the franchise? • How can they describe the relationship with the franchisor?	• Have there been lawsuits and/or arbitration? • If so, how have they been resolved? • Do you have second thoughts (would you do this again)? • Would you own more units?

Source: Based on "A Checklist of Questions to Answer Before You Buy a Franchise," PowerHomeBiz.com. www.powerhomebiz.com/vol2/ franchisechecklist.htm.

Buying an Existing Business

Are there other ways to start a business besides starting new or buying a franchise? Although buying a franchise is a popular way to begin a business without starting from scratch, another way is to buy a preexisting business. Just like buying a franchise or starting from scratch, the decision must be well thought-out.

What are the advantages of buying an existing business? Just as with buying a franchise, buying an existing business has certain advantages:

- **Ease of start-up.** It's often simpler to buy an existing business than to start one from scratch. For example, there is a reduction in start-up time and energy if you are purchasing a business that is operational and without serious problems. This means that suppliers, existing staff and management, and equipment and inventory are all in place to help facilitate the transition.

- **Existing customer base.** An existing business may have a satisfied customer base already in place. If no significant changes are made to drive away current customers, the business can continue to run and provide immediate cash flow.

- **Financing opportunities.** If the business has had a positive track record, it might be easier to obtain financing to purchase the existing business.

What are the disadvantages of buying an existing business?

There are also disadvantages to buying an existing business:

- **High purchase price.** Because you may need to buy the owner out of the business, the initial purchase price may be high. This can be more than the immediate up-front costs associated with a start-up but not necessarily any different from a franchise. Although you can easily determine the value of the physical business and its assets, it is more difficult to determine the true value of the previous owner's **goodwill**—the intangible assets represented by a business's name, customer service, employee morale, and other factors—that might be lost with a change in ownership. Often the intangible assets are overvalued, making the business cost more than it is worth.

- **Inheriting the previous owner's mistakes.** In addition, with a preexisting business, you are sometimes stuck with the previous owner's mistakes. This means you might inherit dissatisfied customers, bad debt, and unhappy distributors or purchasing agents. You'll need to work to change the minds of people who have had a bad experience with the previous ownership.

- **Unknowns in transition.** There is no guarantee that existing employees, management, customers, suppliers, or distributors will continue to work with the business once new ownership takes over. If the staff does stay, you might be inheriting unanticipated problems.

What do I need to check before I buy a business?

Existing businesses are sold for many reasons. Before buying an existing business, make sure you perform **due diligence**—research and analyze the business to uncover any hidden problems associated with it. You want to avoid buying a company with a dissatisfied customer base or with a large amount of unpaid bills. ▼ **Table 5.3** provides a brief checklist of things you should look into before buying a business.

Not all businesses for sale have problems. For example, some family-run businesses run out of family members to whom to pass the business. This was the situation that Dan Ratto, a business consultant in Texas, and Chris, his godson in California, came across. Chris knew of a restaurant near his home that was on the market. The restaurant had been part of a family business for many years, but no one in the family wanted to continue the business, so it was put up for sale. Dan and Chris did their due diligence and came up with their estimate of the restaurant's value. The owner's price was much less than Dan and Chris's estimate, so they scooped up the business. With only a few minor improvements, Dan and his godson exceeded initial sales expectations within the first year of ownership. They have since opened a few other locations and are considering the possibility of franchising the operation in other states.

We started this section with a story about Aisha Lawrence, who had a dream of owning a restaurant. What did she decide? Ultimately, Aisha decided that she wanted to open an ice cream franchise. There were many to choose from, so she spent months doing product research, visiting and tasting the various frozen treats offered

▼ **Table 5.3**

Things to Consider Before Buying a Business
Initial Questions to Ask
• Why is the business for sale?
• What do current customers say?
• Are there opportunities for growth? How much time does the current owner put into the business?
• Who is the competition?
Due Diligence Checklist
• Get an independent valuation of inventory and equipment.
• Have an accountant review the financial statements for the past three years.
• Have a lawyer analyze pertinent business documents—property leases, employment contracts, and so on.
• Talk to suppliers to see if they will continue to supply the business when ownership changes hands.
• Check for lingering or festering hazardous waste problems. They'll become your responsibility as the new owner.

Biz**Chat**

What's in a Name?

Naming a business should be fun, but it can be stressful, especially if you make some of the more common mistakes:

Mistake 1 │ Involving friends, family, employees, or clients in the naming decision. The name should communicate the key elements of your business, not the combined efforts of your friends and family.

Mistake 2 │ Description + Product = Name. Although it might seem catchy at the time, the result of company names that try to marry description with product is forced and often trite. A service franchise named QualiServe or a day spa named TranquiSpa ultimately aren't the right choices.

Mistake 3 │ Using generic names. Gone are the days when GE or ACME Foods work as corporate names. In such highly competitive times, when new products or services are fighting for attention, it is best to choose a more unique name.

Mistake 4 │ Making up a name. Although using generic names may not be good, be careful to avoid names that are obscure, hard to pronounce, or hard to spell unless there is solid market research behind it.

Mistake 5 │ Using geographic names. Unless you plan to stay local, including a specific geographic name may imply that you won't go beyond that regional territory.

TIP: You might need to hire a company to create a name for you. Acura, Flixx, and Compaq are all names that were created by experts.

For more information and discussion questions about this topic, check out the BizChat feature on my**biz**lab.com.

by most of the ice cream franchises. Ultimately, Aisha decided to buy a Cold Stone Creamery franchise because she thinks its product is superior. Whether you buy an existing business or franchise or begin a business of your own, you'll be joining a large group of small business owners who make a significant contribution to the U.S. economy. ■

The Risks of Small Businesses
and **Where** to **Get Help** pp. 152–157

When Roger Sherman heard rumors that the company he was working for was trying to keep from filing bankruptcy, he felt he would be better off on his own. Roger took advantage of an early retirement package and, together with his life savings, began to fiddle around with energy-efficient, solar-powered scooters and bicycles. But even Roger's well-thought out business plan couldn't predict the sudden and massive downturn in the economy that has kept his business slow. Roger was concerned he might not be able to make payroll or keep all his employees. What should he do? ■

In this section, we'll talk about the risks facing small businesses and where owners can go for help.

Why So Many Small Businesses Fail

What are the risks of owning my own business?

Starting a business is a lot of hard work and comes with no guarantee for success. As shown in ▼ **Figure 5.7,** nearly one-fourth of all start-ups fail in the first year, and two-thirds survive only two years, with just over one-half surviving after five years of operation.[55]

While many feel the benefits of owning their own businesses are worth the risks, it is important to be aware of why so many businesses fail. Reasons for failure include the following:

- Accumulating too much debt
- Inadequate management
- Poor planning
- Unanticipated personal sacrifices

Let's examine each risk in more detail.

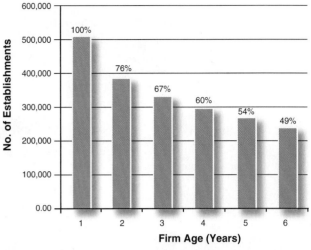

▼ **Figure 5.7 Average Survival Rate of Small Business Start-ups**

What causes excessive debt accumulation? One reason many new
businesses fail is that they accumulate too much debt. Most begin a new business by borrowing funds. Regardless of whether the loan comes from a bank, an outside investor, or a credit-card company, if the new business does not generate returns quickly enough to begin to pay back the initial loan, there is a temptation to take on more loan debt to keep the business running. Interest on loans can accumulate too, causing an owner to become further entrenched in a potentially unrecoverable situation. What's worse is that some business owners borrow against their personal assets, putting them at risk of personal bankruptcy.

How does poor fiscal management lead to failure? Although entre-
preneurs and small business owners are good at coming up with ideas, they may not be great at managing the books. The fact that so many businesses fail due to high levels of debt can be a sign of poor financial and business management. It is important that financial statements and budgets are created and adhered to honestly and accurately each month, accounts receivable are religiously collected, and accounts payable are aggressively managed. Take Jodi Gallagher, for example. Jodi owns a business designing and creating lingerie. In an effort to get her product into as many stores as possible, Jodi was lenient on the terms of collection. Rather than insisting on immediate payment, she extended stores at least 30 days credit, and, as a result, it took her months to collect. Realizing that her mistake almost cost her business, Jodi no longer extends credit.[56]

What other types of improper management lead to failure? For
some the challenge of managing growth has driven them under when they find that they cannot handle the increase in sales. This was a large part of many dot-com busts in the late 1990s. Many successful e-commerce businesses did not plan for rapid growth and therefore did not have sufficient inventory to fulfill orders when they came in. They also didn't take into consideration the subsequent impact this would have on dealers and retailers who were a part of their distribution channels.

Many business owners ignore the signs of a business beginning to fail or attribute the failure to the wrong reasons. Good management stays on top of all aspects of

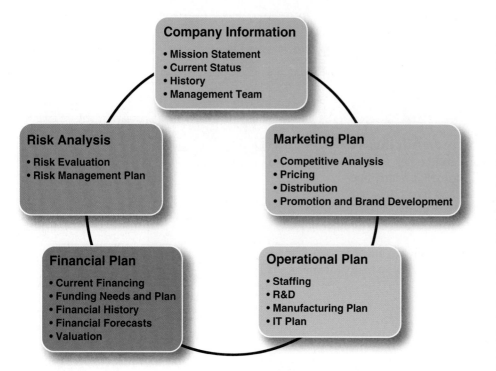

Company Information

- Mission Statement
- Current Status
- History
- Management Team

Risk Analysis

- Risk Evaluation
- Risk Management Plan

Marketing Plan

- Competitive Analysis
- Pricing
- Distribution
- Promotion and Brand Development

Financial Plan

- Current Financing
- Funding Needs and Plan
- Financial History
- Financial Forecasts
- Valuation

Operational Plan

- Staffing
- R&D
- Manufacturing Plan
- IT Plan

▼ **Figure 5.8
A Business Plan
Outlines a Company's
Goals and Strategies**

For an interactive, real-world example of this topic, access this chapter's **BizSkill** entitled Are You an Entrepreneur? Getting Your Bsuiness Off the Ground, located at **my***biz***lab**.com.

the business and makes the tough decisions, when necessary. As Nina Riley, CEO and founder of Water Sensations, a company that makes clear-liquid flavor enhancers for water says, "When things go bad—at the first indication—you gotta nip it in the bud, wrestle it to the ground to fix it. You just can't let it go. If this is your own company, you have to strive to be perfect."[57]

How important is planning to business success or failure? Accumulating debt and poor business management happen after the business has developed. One of the biggest reasons businesses fail is that there was no formal plan in place to begin with. The old adage "failing to plan is planning to fail" certainly applies to starting a business.

Many budding business owners, in the excitement of starting something new, neglect to take the boring but necessary steps of building an effective business plan. A **business plan** is a formal document that states the goals of the business as well as the plan for reaching those goals.

As shown in ▼ **Figure 5.8,** the plan includes the company's mission statement, history, and the qualifications of the owners and management team and any resources they might have to contribute to the business. It also includes a marketing plan, an operational plan, a financial plan, a risk analysis; it identifies the competition and highlights opportunities for success. (You'll learn more about creating successful business plans in Mini Chapter 2.)

Neglecting to consider any of these factors can doom a business from the start; writing a business plan forces you to think through some of the more difficult aspects of the business up front. Poor planning can lead to unnecessary spending. Equally, a well-written and thought-out business plan can lead to greater financing options. Success is a lot more difficult without adequate funding.

New businesses also may fail when owners do not adequately anticipate the many personal sacrifices—financial and otherwise—that new business owners are forced to make. For example, the cost of health insurance and retirement accounts falls solely on the shoulders of the new business owner. Often, profits are put right back into the business, and the expense of health insurance and long-term retirement funding often gets postponed. Additionally, the amount of time and effort owners must invest in the business, as well as the necessity to take on multiple responsibilities, makes running your own business not for the faint of heart.

Getting Help

Where do small business owners go for advice? Most new business owners are just that—new. Because they haven't experienced much of what they will encounter, knowing when and where to go for help, a second opinion, or just advice can make all the difference. There are several sources of help and advice that a small business owner can turn to (▼ **Figure 5.9**).

- **The Small Business Administration.** As noted earlier, the SBA is an independent agency of the U.S. government. Its sole purpose is to cater to the needs of small businesses. The SBA offers assistance in the legalities associated with beginning and operating a business as well as education and training, financial assistance, disaster assistance, and counseling. The SBA holds events in major cities in all states, such as workshops in financial analysis, creating a business plan, and launching a business. It also offers free online courses and coordinates links to academic institutions that offer private online training. The SBA also acts as an advocate for small business owners to national and state policymakers. It works to reduce regulatory requirements and maximize benefits that small businesses receive from the government.

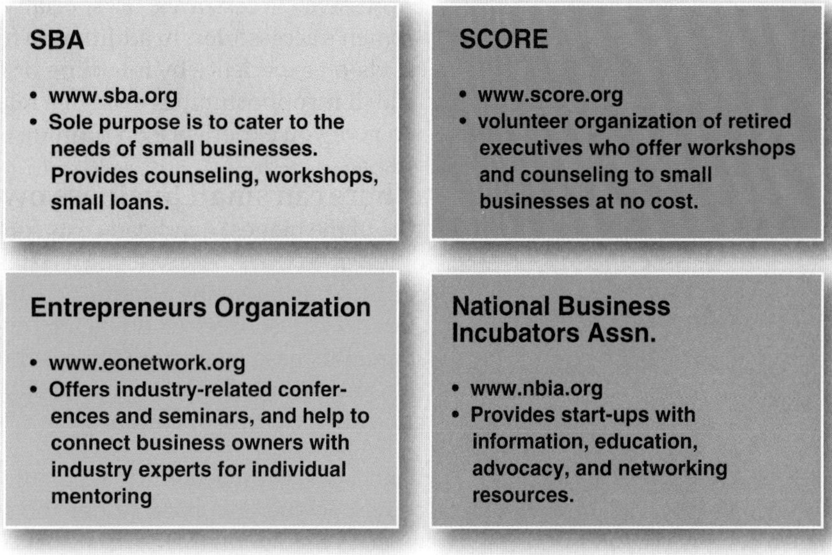

SBA
- www.sba.org
- Sole purpose is to cater to the needs of small businesses. Provides counseling, workshops, small loans.

SCORE
- www.score.org
- volunteer organization of retired executives who offer workshops and counseling to small businesses at no cost.

Entrepreneurs Organization
- www.eonetwork.org
- Offers industry-related conferences and seminars, and help to connect business owners with industry experts for individual mentoring

National Business Incubators Assn.
- www.nbia.org
- Provides start-ups with information, education, advocacy, and networking resources.

▼ **Figure 5.9 Small Business Support Websites**

- **SCORE.** The nearly 11,000 volunteers who compose the SBA's Service Corp of Retired Executives (SCORE) offer workshops and counseling to small businesses at no cost. The volunteers are currently working in or have been in the field and can therefore provide advice to new or existing small business owners. They review business plans, help with tax planning, and offer new ideas and fresh insights. SCORE lists as some of its success stories such companies as Vermont Teddy Bear, Vera Bradley Designs, and Jelly Belly Candy.

- **Other Mentoring Sources.** SCORE is not the only resource new business owners can turn to for mentors. Industry-related conferences or seminars often present new business owners with opportunities to find others who can serve as sounding boards and mentors. In addition, other organizations, such as the Entrepreneurs Organization (EO), connect business owners with experts in their industry for individual mentoring. Although EO is for those who are currently in a viable operation (its requirements are that you must be a founder, cofounder, owner, or controlling shareholder of a business with a minimum of $1 million in annual gross sales and younger than 50 years old), such mentoring services can be helpful to second-stage small business owners.

What kind of training is appropriate for small business owners?

Before jumping into any endeavor, it's always good to have some experience or training. Although many entrepreneurs have advanced degrees in business, that level of formal education is often not necessary. If you are currently in college, look for internship opportunities in your industry of interest. Some internships are with big, well-known companies, but smaller companies are beginning to realize that hiring interns can be a cost-effective way to get some help. Internships can be seen as an extended "dating period" between employer and candidate, reducing the risk on both sides of making the wrong long-term decision. Internsforyou.com is a small recruiting company that focuses on finding the right interns for businesses with fewer than 20 employees.

Most community colleges offer business classes for credit, or noncredit community education classes that are taught by industry professionals. Trisha Wosny had been an elementary education teacher for many years but had always wanted to own her own business. Because she didn't know where to start, a friend told her about programs offered at her local community college for women business owners, small business start-ups, and management. A year later, she opened Adornment

Expressive Accessories, a specialty retail shop offering unique purses and women's accessories. In addition to formal classroom training, you can also obtain hands-on experience by interning or working part-time for a company in a related field; if no opportunities exist in a related field, working for any start-up company can give you experience on running a small company.

Where can small business owners go for other support services?

One of the biggest overhead costs for many new businesses is the support services required to run the business. **Business incubators** are organizations that support start-up businesses by offering administrative services, technical support, business networking, sources of financing, and more that a group of start-up companies share. Business incubators are often run by two- and four-year colleges, universities, and technical schools, and many are sponsored by economic development organizations, cities, or counties.

There are several benefits to incubation beyond sharing a receptionist and a photocopy machine. Incubators offer the support and advice that many start-ups lack when operating on their own. Eventually, incubator participants must run on their own, but participation in an incubation program increases the success rate of a start-up company by as much as 90 percent.[58] The primary goal of a business incubator is to produce successful businesses that are able to operate independently and become financially viable in the early years when they are most vulnerable to failure. Incubators create a synergistic environment where companies can act as peer-to-peer mentors, sharing both success and failures. Incubators also lend legitimacy to a beginning company as well as a more professional atmosphere than someone's home office. And the success rate suggests that incubators are meeting their goal.

Incubators can be either private organizations or public services. Over the past few decades, many cities as well as developed and developing countries have started public business incubators, often in conjunction with universities and research institutions, to promote new business development. Rensselaer Polytechnic Institute runs one of the oldest incubator programs in the country.

What other options exist for small business advice and assistance?

As noted earlier, starting up a small business requires owners to take on multiple roles, acting not only as the CEO but also the COO, the CFO, and any other position that may need to be filled. Many owners quickly realize that their strengths lie in only one or a few of these areas and therefore seek assistance from others. One option is to team up with *partners* who offer the company strengths that the new owner does not possess, who in turn share in its profits and liabilities. Forming an advisory board is another option. An **advisory board** is a group of individuals who offer guidance to the new business owner. Such boards are similar to boards of directors in publicly held companies except that they generally do not have the authority to make decisions.

Does where I locate my business make a difference in the type of help I can get?

In most cases, new business owners look for a location that is suitable for a new business, has good traffic flow, is safe, and so on. However, in an effort to build up and even resuscitate communities throughout the United States, federal and state governments have established **enterprise zones,** geographic areas targeted for economic revitalizing. Almost every state has some form of enterprise zone program. In addition, the federal government has designated a total of 172 enterprise communities and empowerment zones across the United States. These designations are based on various criteria, including population, poverty rates, and economic distress. Businesses receive generous tax benefits for locating and hiring in these enterprise zones. Given the success of many businesses established in enterprise zones, the economic benefits companies receive when they locate in an enterprise zone outweigh the risk of locating in a distressed area. And the state also wins with the creation of new jobs and new businesses.

Remember Roger Sherman? When he found he had troubles with his small business, Roger decided to consult with a SCORE volunteer and took advantage of SBA services. Many new business owners think they can't afford professional advice, so they rely on their own efforts, advice from friends and family, and trial and error. Often, they find that it takes more than a good idea and hard work to make a business successful. Knowing all the resources available to fledgling businesses can help entrepreneurs avoid making the mistakes that eventually lead to the demise of their businesses. Careful financial decision making, savvy management, meticulous planning, and the willingness to make significant personal sacrifices all play key roles in creating a successful business. Knowing when, where, and how to ask for help is also a factor critical to success. ■

Financing Considerations pp. 157–159

Fred DeLuca began his sandwich shop in 1965. He had just graduated from high school and was worried about how he was going to pay for college with his $1.25 per hour minimum wage job at a local hardware store. A family friend, Dr. Peter Buck, suggested that Fred open a sandwich shop. All he needed to do was to rent a shop, build a counter, buy some food, and make the sandwiches. Customers would come in and pay; then Fred could pay his suppliers and still have enough money to pay for college. Dr. Buck was so sure this would work, he gave Fred $1,000 to begin. Four decades later, Subway is one of the largest privately held businesses, with restaurants around the world.[59] ■

Although Fred started with a loan from a family friend, there are other means for entrepreneurs to finance their new ventures before going to more formal financing arrangements. In this section, we'll present the many sources of funding available to small business owners, and we'll discuss the problems associated with some of them.

Cash and Credit

Where can I get the money to start a business? Most new ventures need some capital to purchase inventory, secure a physical location, and begin some modest marketing efforts. Often, the new business owner must make do with whatever sources of financing are available, often just what is in his or her own pocket. When entrepreneurs start a business with little capital, they are said to be using **bootstrap financing.** This type of financing, such as using your own money, borrowing funds from friends or family, or trading services or products with vendors or clients, may be the only way a new venture can begin if the business is too small or uncertain for more formal funding options.

Beyond tapping into personal savings, friends and family are generally secondary sources of cash, which was the case for Fred DeLuca, the founder of Subway. Friends and family are often good sources for financing because, unlike banks, they often do not require a high rate of return or generally do not demand that the business turn a quick profit. However, it is important when borrowing from friends and family that you treat them as professionally as possible. Make sure you give them a document with an indication of how you intend to pay them back and some sort of a contingency plan if things go wrong. In addition, they should be kept informed of any risks of the venture—up front and ongoing. Other means of bootstrap financing include using *trade credit*, *factoring*, and *leasing*, which we will discuss in Chapter 15.

Should I use credit cards to finance my business? Credit cards offer a convenient way to obtain funds quickly, especially with some of the zero percent financing options available. If used wisely, credit cards are a convenient means of financing short-term needs. However, credit cards should be used only if you can pay the balance *completely* every month. The risk associated with using credit cards for your initial business financing is the high rate of interest charged on unpaid balances.

Small Business Loans and Grants

What if I need more money than what I can provide myself? For larger amounts, new business owners sometimes borrow against their own assets, such as the equity in their homes or against their retirement accounts, but the consequences of the business failing are very severe. Bailing out a failing business with your life savings or home equity has caused some to file personal bankruptcy and even completely lose their homes.

If you're purchasing an existing business or a franchise, banks and savings and loan institutions often are willing to provide funding. These institutions offer start-up loans and lines of credit (sources of credit that can be drawn on at the borrower's discretion) that help businesses make payroll during slower periods as well as capital loans to buy equipment or machinery. In fact, roughly half of all small businesses use bank loans and lines of credit as part of their financing strategy.

Can I apply for grants to help start my business? Grants are financial awards that are usually offered by federal and state governments and some private organizations. Although grants do not need to be repaid, the application process is quite substantial and includes considerable amounts of paperwork. The biggest hurdle in applying for a grant is writing the proposal. Make sure you understand the grant writing procedure, as many a good application has not been funded because of an oversight in the grant application. Depending on the nature of your business, federal grants are usually not available, but state governments typically offer grants to small businesses that are in an industry that the state is nurturing to expand in their state economy. Make sure, however, you read through the entire grant application and understand any requirements that may be expected of a grant recipient. Failure to comply with grant requirements will generally result in the grant proceeds being converted to a loan, with interest.

Venture Capital and Other Forms of Financing

What if I need additional sources of funds through investors? There are other sources of funding if you choose not to finance your business with loans or if loans are not an option. For example, businesses can be financed by outside investors such as angel investors, venture capital, or small business investment companies (SBICs).

- **Venture Capitalists.** Venture capitalists are one source of funding. Unlike banks, where there is a contractual agreement to pay back the money, **venture capitalists** contribute money to a business in return for some form of equity—a piece of ownership. Venture capitalists are very picky about the projects in which they invest. They look for the potential of a public stock offering; therefore, such financing is generally available only to those businesses that have been operating for several years and have the potential to become larger regional or national companies. To protect their investments, venture capitalists sometimes require that they play an active role in the management of the company, so business owners must be open to the idea of relinquishing control when they seek venture capital funding.

- **Angel Investors. Angel investors** are wealthy individuals who are willing to put up their own money in hopes of a profit return later on. Angel investors fund approximately 30,000 small companies each year, with investments that range between 25,000 to $1 million.[60] Palmer "Pam" Reynolds, founder of Phoenix Textile Corp. in St. Louis, Missouri, owes her success to an angel investor. Out of work with 13 years of experience in the textile business, Pam decided to start her own company. If not for an angel investor who put up $250,000, Pam would not be running a $43 million textile company today. Angel investors often provide funding in the earlier stages of a business, when more money is needed than friends and family can or are willing to contribute, but before bringing in the venture capitalists. Angel investors typically have industry experience in the area in which they are investing and can provide guidance and advice. Unlike venture capitalists, angel investors usually do not seek a management position or control of the business.

- **The SBIC Program.** If venture capital is not available or suitable, an alternative is a **small business investment company (SBIC) program.** SBICs are private venture capital firms licensed by the SBA to make equity capital or long-term loans available to small companies. The size of the financing provided by SBICs is generally in the $250,000 to $5 million range.

The downside of using outside investors is that, to protect their investments, these investors often are looking for some controlling or managerial role in the business. Usually these investors come in at the second stage of financing needs, after the company has been established and has shown some potential.

Funding a business is a task fraught with challenges and difficult decisions, as Fred DeLuca would attest. Beginning with just the money offered by a family friend and his own savings, Fred turned a simple sandwich shop into a global franchise operation. But whether the money comes from your own pocket, a friend, or an outside investor, the stakes—personal, professional, and financial—are quite high. Thorough research and careful planning are essential to navigating these tricky issues. By understanding the available options and being prepared to deal with financial predicaments, business owners give themselves the best chance at success. ■

Chapter Summary

Are you an active learner?

Go to my*biz*lab.com to master Chapter 5's content. Chapter 5's interactive activities include:

- Customizable Study Plan and Chapter 5 practice quizzes
- Chapter 5 Simulations, Conducting a SWOT Analysis and Are You an Entrepreneur?: Getting Your Business Off the Ground, that help you think critically and prepare to make choices in the business world
- Chapter 5 Video Exercise, Joie de Vivre: Small Business and Entrepreneurship, which shows you how textbook concepts are put into practice every day
- Flash Cards for mastering the definition of chapter terms
- Interactive Lessons that visually review key chapter concepts

1. What is the role and structure of the small business within the U.S. economy? (pp. 135–136)

- A **small business** (p. 135) is a business that is independently owned and operated, is not dominant in its field, and has fewer than 500 employees and less than $6.5 million in annual revenue.
- Small businesses are important to the economy for several reasons. They account for more than one-half of America's economic output, help foster innovation, supply larger companies with products and services that larger companies do not or cannot supply themselves, supply products and services to consumers that large companies cannot or will not provide, and employ approximately 50 percent of the private workforce.

2. What are the traits of an effective entrepreneur, and what are the different types of entrepreneurs?? (pp. 141–146)

- An **entrepreneur** (p. 140) is someone who assumes the risk of creating, organizing, and operating a business.
- Entrepreneurs are innovative, risk-taking individuals who are motivated to succeed and who are flexible and self-directed. They work well with people, possess good leadership skills, and are "system thinkers."
- Not all entrepreneurs are the same: **lifestyle entrepreneurs** (p. 143) look for a business that matches their desired lifestyle, **micropreneurs** (p. 144) are satisfied with keeping the business small to achieve a balanced lifestyle, **home-based entrepreneurs** (p. 144) run their businesses out of their homes, and **Internet entrepreneurs** (p. 144) run their businesses strictly online. **Growth entrepreneurs** (p. 144) strive to create fast-growing businesses and look forward to expansion, and **social entrepreneurs** (p. 145) start businesses with a social mission in mind. Lastly, **intrapreneurs** (p. 145) are entrepreneurs who work in an entrepreneurial way within an organizational environment.

3. What are the advantages and disadvantages of franchising within the context of entrepreneurship? (pp. 147–150)

- A **franchise** (p. 147) is a method of doing business whereby the business sells a company's products or services under the company's name to independent third-party operators.

- The advantages of franchising include that the business is a proven system of operation, franchises benefit from economies of scale, and the franchisor often offers training and marketing support as well as market research.
- The disadvantages of franchising include a lack of control over the look of the store and the product or service being offered, start-up costs and monthly fees that must be paid to the franchisor, operating a franchise often includes a heavy workload, and that franchises will be affected by negative news involving the franchisor or another franchisee of the same company.

4. Why is a business plan crucial to small business success, and what factors lead to small business failure? (pp. 153–154)

- A **business plan** (p. 154) outlines the goals and strategies of a company, including company information, marketing plans, financial forecasts, a risk analysis, and an operational plan. Neglecting to consider any of these options can doom a business from the start.
- The reasons new businesses fail include accumulating too much debt, inadequate management, poor planning, and unanticipated personal sacrifices.

5. How do resources, including the SBA, mentoring sources such as SCORE, business incubators, and advisory boards, provide assistance and guidance to small business owners? (pp. 154–156)

- The **Small Business Administration** (p. 135) offers assistance in the legalities associated with starting and operating a business as well as education and training, financial assistance, disaster assistance, and counseling.
- **SCORE** (p. 155) volunteers provide free assistance by reviewing business plans, helping with tax planning, and offering new ideas and fresh insights. Other mentoring sources include industry-related conferences and other organizations, such as the EO.
- Business owners can receive formal classroom training at two- and four-year colleges and participate in internships with companies in similar industries for hands-on training.
- **Business incubators** (p. 155) support start-up businesses by offering resources such as administrative services,

technical support, business networking, and sources of financing that a group of start-up companies share.

- **Advisory boards** (p. 156) offer guidance to new business owners but they generally do not have authority to make decisions.

- **Enterprise zones** (p. 156) are geographic areas targeted for economic revitalizing by state and federal governments. Businesses receive generous tax benefits for locating and hiring in these enterprise zones.

6. **What are the potential benefits and drawbacks of each major source of small business financing?** (pp. 157–159)

- The benefit of using cash borrowed from friends and family members is that unlike banks or other lending institutions, these contacts often do not require a high rate of return or demand to see the business turn a quick profit. However, the potential drawback is that these types of personal loans can sometimes be handled unprofessionally.

- The benefit of credit cards is that they are a convenient means of acquiring short-term cash. However, the risk associated with using credit cards for initial business financing is the high rate of interest charged on unpaid balances.

- When more money is needed than credit cards, friends, or family can provide, another source of financing are small business loans from banks and savings and loan institutions. Lines of credit or start-up loans are also available and can be used to bridge short-term capital needs. Federal and state **grants** (p. 158) may also be available, depending on the nature of the business.

- The advantage of obtaining funding from outside investors is that these individuals contribute money to a business in return for some form of equity instead of a contractual agreement to pay back the money. However, outside investors sometimes require playing an active role in the management of the company, so this funding option may not be attractive to business owners who aren't open to the idea of relinquishing control.

Key Terms

advisory board   (p. 156)

angel investors   (p. 159)

bootstrap financing   (p. 157)

business incubator   (p. 156)

business plan   (p. 154)

due diligence   (p. 151)

enterprise zones   (p. 156)

entrepreneur   (p. 140)

entrepreneurial team   (p. 145)

franchise   (p. 147)

franchisee   (p. 147)

franchisor   (p. 147)

goodwill   (p. 151)

grants   (p. 158)

growth entrepreneur   (p. 144)

home-based entrepreneur   (p. 144)

Internet entrepreneur   (p. 144)

intrapreneurs   (p. 144)

lifestyle entrepreneurs   (p. 143)

micropreneurs   (p. 144)

opportunity niche   (p. 141)

Service Corp of Retired Executives (SCORE)   (p. 155)

small business   (p. 135)

Small Business Administration (SBA)   (p. 135)

small business investment company (SBIC) program   (p. 159)

social entrepreneur   (p. 145)

social intrapreneur   (p. 145)

venture capitalists   (p. 159)

Self-Test

Multiple Choice
You can find the answers on the last page of this book.

1. Which is a key trait of an entrepreneur?

   a. Flexibility

   b. Risk taking

   c. Creative thinking

   d. All of the above

2. Sally started her new business venture five years ago. The business now operates in three locations and has good prospects for future expansion, which is exactly what Sally had in mind. Which type of entrepreneur best describes Sally?

   a. Social entrepreneur

   b. Lifestyle entrepreneur

   c. Growth entrepreneur

   d. Gazelle

3. One of the first things someone needs to do before starting a business is to write which of the following?

   a. A business plan

   b. A loan application

   c. A partnership statement

   d. A franchise agreement

4. Which of the following is not a characteristic of a small business?

   a. They generally have between 500 and 1,000 employees.

   b. On average, the annual revenue is $6.5 million.

   c. It is independently owned and operated.

   d. It is not considered a dominant player in its industry.

5. Steven Ye wants to start a company. He has a rough draft of his business plan and some tentative funding but needs some additional advice and guidance to help him through the start-up. The best source for Steve is

   a. an angel investor.

   b. a SCORE volunteer.

   c. his parents.

   d. a bank loan officer.

6. Kazuto is interested in starting a new business. Which is a reason Kazuto should consider a franchise over starting a business from scratch?

   a. He will get more market research.

   b. He will be able to make all the decisions.

   c. He will need less capital up front.

   d. He will need to work fewer hours.

7. Wayland just opened a Rita's Italian Ice franchise. Which is *not* a benefit Wayland receives as a franchisee?

   a. Supplies to make Rita's Italian water ice

   b. Signage and posters to help with advertising

   c. Retirement benefits from Rita's

   d. Training and ongoing advice and assistance from Rita's

8. Rebecca has been operating a pet grooming business for several years and has already maxed out her personal credit and savings. She has designed a device that will make the pet grooming process more efficient but needs about $500,000 to take the idea further and perhaps sell it to other pet groomers. Which is the most likely source of financing that Rebecca could use?

   a. Credit cards

   b. Line of credit

   c. Funds from an angel investor

   d. Venture capital financing

9. Which of the following factors commonly leads to small business failure?

   a. Too much planning

   b. A small advertising budget

   c. Unanticipated personal sacrifices

   d. All of the above

10. Rashid is starting a consulting business. He doesn't want to rent an office right now, but he needs a receptionist, a place to meet clients, and other aspects of an office. A good solution for Rashid to consider would be a(n)

    a. mentoring group.

    b. advisory board.

    c. business incubator.

    d. entrepreneurial team.

Self-Test

True/False
You can find the answers on the last page of this book.

1. Being part of a franchise allows you to have some of the marketing program created for you.
   ☐ True or ☐ False

2. A social intrapreneur is someone who provides funding for those in third-world countries who want to begin their own businesses but have no capital with which to do so.
   ☐ True or ☐ False

3. According to the SBA, to be considered a small business, a company can have only one location.
   ☐ True or ☐ False

4. A growth entrepreneur is best described as one who starts a business in the agricultural industry.
   ☐ True or ☐ False

5. Credit cards are a convenient way to help finance business expenses as long as the balances are paid in full every month.
   ☐ True or ☐ False

Critical Thinking Questions

1. Sam Walton (Walmart), Debbi Fields (Mrs. Fields [cookies]), and Sean Combs (Sean John [clothing]) are some well-known successful entrepreneurs. What common traits do these individuals possess that have led to their success?

2. Why would someone want to start a franchise rather than start a business from scratch? What are the drawbacks of starting a franchise?

3. Discuss the benefits of using an incubator when beginning a small business. Are there drawbacks to using an incubator?

4. How has technology affected small businesses?

5. Compare the different sources of funding available to small business owners. What types of funding are better at the beginning stages of a business? What types of funding may be better once the business is better established and is looking to expand?

Team Time

Starting a Business: Brainstorming

Assemble into groups of four or five.

1. Before meeting as a group, think about what you are passionate about and whether there is a potential market involving your interests. Develop one or two ideas for potential businesses based on your passions. Do not consider any idea impossible at this stage.

    a. Consider if there is something missing in the current market. For example, are you passionate about locally grown organic vegetables but are frustrated that there isn't a place nearby to purchase these items? If so, you've developed an idea for a local farmers market.

    b. Consider combining two ideas together. When school has a half-day or full-day off, consider having high school students form a daytime child care service for elementary students.

    c. Consider business ideas that have potential but aren't doing very well now. Are there ways to make them better?

2. Gather your group and go over each other's ideas. Refine the list to two or three ideas.

3. Have each group member refine an idea even further, identifying the target market and outlining the business goals and objectives.

4. Meet as a team one more time to pick one business idea.

5. If time permits, the group can develop this idea further by using the Business Plan project template. See the Mini Chapter 2 for more information.

Ethics and Corporate Social Responsibility

Social Entrepreneurship: Pepsi Refresh Project

The soft drink company PepsiCo now runs the Pepsi Refresh Project, a program in which the company awards millions of dollars to fund consumer-generated ideas that will have a positive impact on their communities. Grants range from $5,000 to $250,000.

Step 1. Visit refresheverything.com to see the types of projects that are being proposed and the recipients of awards. Download the toolkit to learn more about how to submit an idea and the Pepsi Refresh Project.

Step 2. In groups, discuss the needs your school or community has and create a list of ideas that your group feels would be good candidates for the Pepsi Refresh Project.

Step 3. Each group should present their idea to the class; as a class, vote on the best idea to send to the Pepsi Refresh Project.

Web Exercises

1. **A Closer Look at Franchising**
Using the Internet, research a franchise that you think would be a viable investment opportunity for you. Write a brief report that outlines the following information about your chosen franchise: fees (initial and ongoing), location/ site assistance, training and ongoing support, marketing assistance, competition (both from other businesses and additional franchises within the organization), and the pros and cons of starting a business with this franchise.

2. **Micro-Financing: A Little Money Can Go a Long Way**
Visit www.kiva.org and click on the "Lend" tab to view the list of entrepreneurs. Use the drop-down menus in the "Find Loans" search bar to locate an entrepreneur or entrepreneurial team to whom you would consider lending. In a brief report, discuss the entrepreneur or group you chose, including information on the loan amount requested, the percentage of funds raised, the entrepreneur's country of origin, and a summary of the entrepreneur's business venture. In your report, explain your reasons for choosing to loan to this particular entrepreneur.

3. **Do You Have What It Takes to Be an Entrepreneur?**
In this chapter, you learned that there are several personality traits common to successful entrepreneurs. Do you possess any of these traits? Using a search engine, find an entrepreneurial quiz that will help you determine if you have what it takes to be an entrepreneur. What aspects of your personality make you a good candidate to be an entrepreneur? What is holding you back?

4. **Build a Business with a Conscience**
What does it take to create a socially conscious business? Play the game on the New Heroes from PBS to see if you have what it takes: www.pbs.org/opb/thenewheroes/ engage/business.html.

5. **Small Business Owners: Where to Go for Help**
If you were a new small business owner, where would you go for help? Many colleges have a small business development center (SBDC). These centers, which are affiliated with the SBA, provide information and guidance to current and prospective small business owners. Use the SBDC Locator (www.sba.gov/aboutsba/sbaprograms/sbdc/sbdclocator/ SBDC_LOCATOR.html) to identify the nearest SBDC in your area; then research the services it can provide.

Web Case

For more on leveraging collective knowledge and experience to discover a niche, access the Chapter 5 Web case entitled "Focus on Global Warming Solutions, Inc.: Saving the World" located in the End of Chapter Assignments section at my*biz*lab.com.

Video Case

For more on proven methods niche businesses use to grow brand awareness and gain customers, access the Chapter 5 Video Case entitled "Student Advantage: Paying Less, Getting More" located in the End of Chapter Assignments section at my*biz*lab.com.

Forms of Business Ownership

Sole Proprietorships

When an entrepreneur starts a business, choosing the proper business structure is vital to the company's success. When Jennifer Perez decided to start her own cleaning business, she became a sole proprietor. Her business began growing so fast, and she couldn't figure out if that was right for her. Do you know what business structure would be best for your company?

Objective 1 What are the strengths and weaknesses of a sole proprietorship? (pp. 167–170)

Partnerships

Trying to do a job alone can sometimes be overwhelming. Because of this, businesses may partner together to share information and resources for the benefit of everyone involved. Partners Hang Win and Stefan Brown brought their skills and finances together to begin a new venture. Why might a partnership be a good business structure for their venture? What difficulties should the two new partners prepare for?

Objective 2 What are the advantages and disadvantages of a partnership and a partnership agreement? (pp. 171–175)

Corporations

When some people hear the word *corporate*, they think of corruption, greed, and big businesses. Lehman Brothers Holding Inc. was a global financial services corporation that was forced to declare bankruptcy in 2008 following the exposure of their use of misleading accounting practices. People use the word *corporation* frequently, but what *is* a corporation? What are the advantages of a corporation versus a sole proprietorship or a partnership?

Objective 3 How is a corporation formed, and how does it compare with sole proprietorships and partnerships? (pp. 176–180)

Objective 4 What are the major differences between a C corporation, an S corporation, and a limited liability company? (pp. 180–183)

Alternative Business Arrangements

Darrell Hammond knew he could make a difference in the life of inner-city children by giving them safe places to play. He quickly outgrew his modest volunteer activities and knew he wanted to expand to help more children. He needed a corporate structure that would allow him to take his profits and put them back into communities nationwide. What type of alternative business structure would work best for him?

Objective 5 What are the characteristics of not-for-profit corporations and cooperatives? (pp. 184–186)

Mergers and Acquisitions

Companies constantly search for opportunities to expand by adding to their product lines, spreading into different geographic areas, or gaining a competitive advantage. Because R&D can take years for results, mergers and acquisitions are two ways that companies can expand quickly. What is the difference between a merger and an acquisition? When do they occur?

Objective 6 What are the different types of mergers and acquisitions, and why do they occur? (pp. 186–190)

PEARSON

my*biz*lab

Are You an Entrepreneur? Small Business and the Entrepreneur

For the past seven years, you've been buying lottery tickets with a group of friends from work. One evening, your number hits. After taxes and dividing it amongst you, you have won $3.5 million. What are you going to do with all of the money? Perhaps starting a business would be right for you. Do you have what it takes to be an entrepreneur?

Objective 7 Test yourself using my*biz*lab.com to show that you understand the chapter objectives.

Sole Proprietorships pp. 167–170

Jennifer Perez runs a small cleaning business from her home. She has no employees, and she reports the business's income and expenses on her personal income taxes. However, the business has grown so fast that she needs to add employees, so she is concerned something could go wrong unexpectedly. As a sole proprietor, she knows that she is held responsible for any and all damages her company commits. In addition, now that Jennifer's small business has become so successful, it may make more sense to report its earnings on a separate tax return, rather than running them through her personal tax return. She realizes that being the owner of a growing company requires more decisions than she had anticipated. ◼

Jennifer Perez chose to begin her company as a sole proprietorship because it was quick and easy to establish. No legal paperwork is required to begin a sole proprietorship, and all the financial information can be reported on the owner's personal tax returns. Because of these advantages, a sole proprietorship is a common form of business ownership for start-up businesses. Many businesses also start out as a sole proprietorship because the owner is unfamiliar with other forms of business ownership.

Choosing the right legal structure for Jennifer's business may have initially seemed simple, but her business quickly outgrew its form. Should she have chosen a different form of ownership in the beginning? Could she have anticipated her immediate success? How difficult is it to change ownership forms? Although Jennifer's rapid growth and success is not the norm for every start-up business, not having the right form of ownership can have significant consequences. So how do you know which form is best for your company? Choosing a form of ownership depends on many factors:

- Legal liability
- Tax implications
- Future capital needs
- Cost of formation and ongoing administration

Your decision on business ownership can affect the personal liability you face, how much you pay in taxes, your ability to borrow money, and the amount of paperwork your business is required to file.

The U.S. economy—as well as the global economy—is based on a variety of enterprises, including not only sole proprietorships (businesses owned by one person) but also, partnerships (where two or more people legally share ownership of a business) and corporations (businesses that are formed as separate legal entities). ▼ **Figure 6.1** shows these common forms of business ownership. In this chapter, we'll explore each of these forms of business ownership in greater detail.

Why is sole proprietorship a popular form of business ownership? A **sole proprietorship** is a business owned, and usually operated, by a single individual. Because no legal paperwork is necessary to establish a business as a sole proprietorship, many small business owners are sole proprietors without

PEARSON
mybizlab

For an interactive, real-world example of this topic, access this chapter's **BizSkill** entitled Are You an Entrepreneur? Small Business and the Entrepreneur, located at **my**bizlab.com.

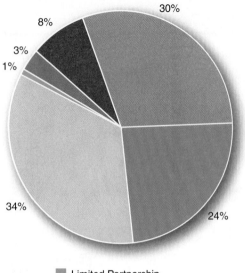

Limited Partnership
General Partnership
C Corp.
Sole Proprietorship
S Corp.
LLC

▼ **Figure 6.1**
Businesses by Type of Ownership
Sole proprietorships and LLCs are popular forms of business ownership. Why might business owners be inclined to establish these types of businesses?

even knowing it. Although a sole proprietorship has only one owner, it can have any number of employees. For example, you can be the owner of a plumbing business with several other plumbers working for you and still operate as a sole proprietorship. Other characteristics of a sole proprietorship are listed in ▼ **Table 6.1.**

Starting a Sole Proprietorship

How do I start a sole proprietorship? The minute you begin doing business by yourself—that is, collecting income as a result of performing a service or selling a product—you are operating as a sole proprietor. There are no special forms to fill out, and there are no special filing requirements with state and federal governments. At a minimum, you might need to obtain local licensing or permits, or you might have to ensure that you're operating in an area zoned for such business activity. You might also need to register your company name and obtain an EIN if you're hiring employees.

Advantages and Disadvantages

Are there advantages to being a sole proprietor? There are several advantages in forming your business as a sole proprietorship—one of which we have already discussed: ease of formation. With only one person making all the decisions and no need to consult other owners or interested parties, sole proprietors also have greater control and more flexibility to act quickly. Another advantage is that there are no specific corporate records to keep or reports to file, including tax reporting. Because there is no legal distinction between the owner and the business, no separate tax return is required. As a result, the income and expenses of a sole proprietorship flow through the owner's personal tax return.

For example, imagine you run a landscaping business during the summer in addition to your regular job. If the lawn mower breaks down and needs to be replaced, that expense could be more than all the earnings you collected, generating a loss for your lawn mowing business. You can subtract that loss from the income earned from your regular job, reducing your income tax obligation. ▼ **Table 6.2**

▼ **Table 6.1**

Characteristics of a Sole Proprietorship	
Characteristics	**Sole Proprietorship**
Preliminary paperwork	There are no special forms or state or federal filing requirements.
Period of existence	Proprietorship is terminated when sole proprietor dies or ends business.
Liability	Sole proprietor has unlimited liability.
Operational requirements	There are minimal legal requirements.
Management	The sole proprietor has full control of management and operations.
Taxation	Not a separate taxable entity; taxes are paid through sole proprietor's personal returns.
Reporting of income/loss	Income/loss is reported on owner's personal income taxes.
Raising capital	Outside sources of income are difficult to raise; funding usually comes from owner contributions.

▼ Table 6.2

Personal Income with and Without a Business Loss from a Sole Proprietorship		
	With Business Loss	**Without Business Loss**
Wage income	$14,500	$14,500
Business loss	−$3,000	
Net income	$11,500	$14,500
Tax due	$2,437	$2,887
	Difference: $450	

and ▼ **Figure 6.2** show how a business loss can reduce your tax payment. A business loss of $3,000 reduces the overall federal tax due by $450. In the beginning years of a business, this can be advantageous because business losses can offset other sources of income, thus reducing your overall tax burden.

Why wouldn't I want to begin my business as a sole proprietorship? One of the biggest disadvantages of a sole proprietorship is exposure to personal liability. If the type of business you're running has the potential for someone to sue you because of errors on your part, you may not want to operate as a sole proprietorship. A sole proprietor is personally responsible for all the debts and

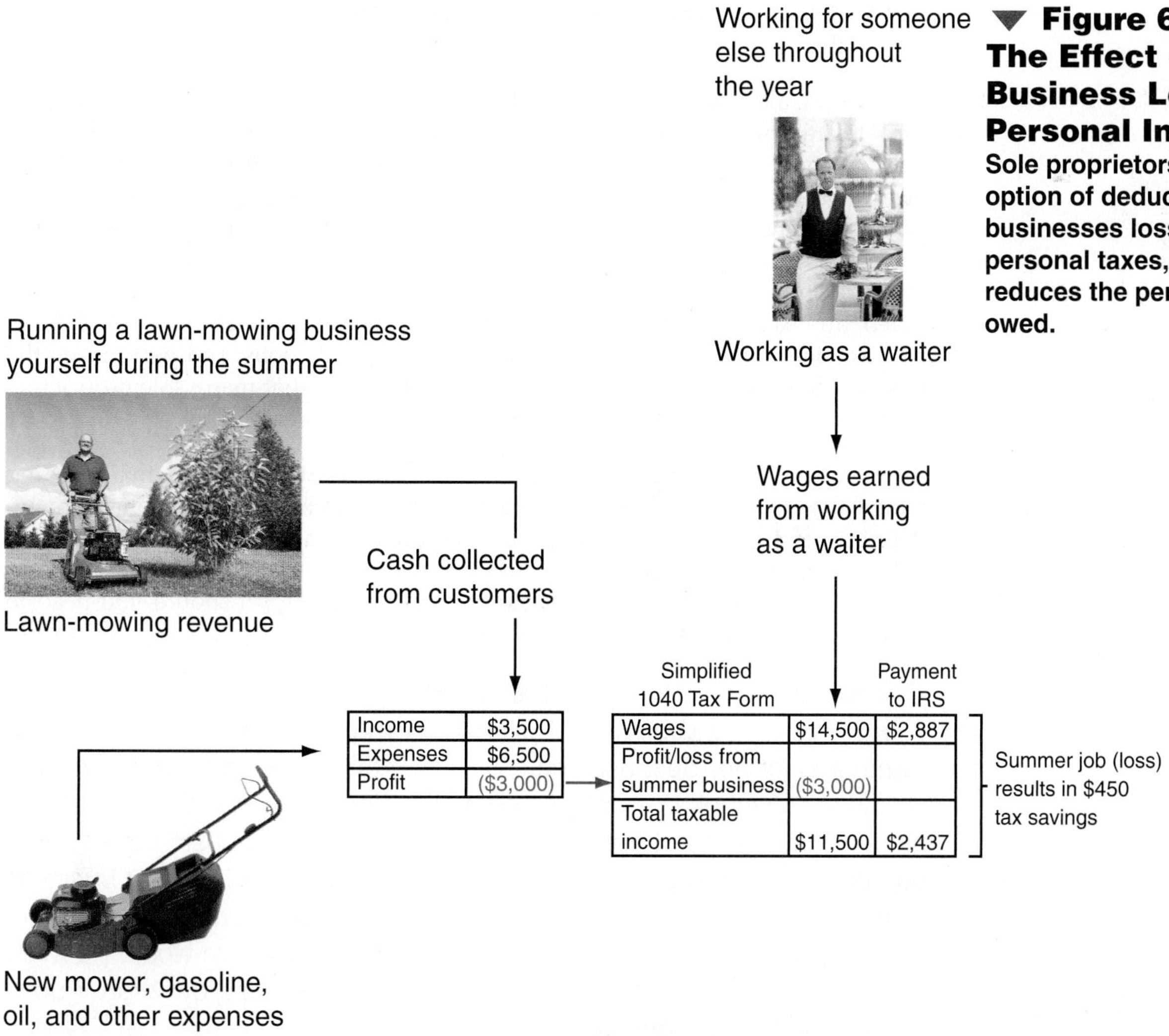

Working for someone else throughout the year

Working as a waiter

▼ Figure 6.2
The Effect of a Business Loss on Personal Income
Sole proprietors have the option of deducting businesses losses from their personal taxes, which reduces the personal taxes owed.

Running a lawn-mowing business yourself during the summer

Lawn-mowing revenue

Cash collected from customers

Wages earned from working as a waiter

New mower, gasoline, oil, and other expenses

Income	$3,500
Expenses	$6,500
Profit	($3,000)

Simplified 1040 Tax Form — Payment to IRS

Wages	$14,500	$2,887
Profit/loss from summer business	($3,000)	
Total taxable income	$11,500	$2,437

Summer job (loss) results in $450 tax savings

liabilities of the business. A **liability** is the obligation to pay a debt, such as an account payable or a loan. A sole proprietor may also incur a liability if he or she becomes responsible for paying for any damages or personal injuries the owner or the employees cause. Although there is no limit on the number of employees in a sole proprietorship, there is also unlimited liability for their actions. **Unlimited liability** means that if business assets aren't enough to pay business debts, then personal assets, such as the sole proprietor's house, personal investments, or retirement funds, can be used to pay the balance. In other words, the proprietor can lose an unlimited amount of personal assets.

Imagine that you own a catering business. While you're preparing food in someone's house, the oven catches fire because you forgot to take the egg rolls off the paper tray. You are personally responsible, or liable, for paying for any damages if your business assets are not sufficient to cover the damages. If the damages are severe enough—perhaps your client's entire house burns down—you could lose all your assets, including your own home and savings. If you decide that a sole proprietorship is the right business form for you for other reasons, buying insurance—such as errors or omissions insurance, disability insurance, and insurance to protect your assets—will help protect you against unforeseen situations.

Are there other things to consider with running a sole proprietorship? Although running your own business certainly has its advantages—flexibility, independence, and financial control—there are some things that you need to consider. Financial control is great, but it can come with a price. Generally, the owner is the last person to get paid and often doesn't have enough left over to put into a retirement account. It's often helpful to run a sole proprietorship as a part-time business and still work for someone else until the business is running well so that you have the security of another salary as well as health-care benefits.

In addition, although it can be beneficial to flow the business through your personal tax return, owners still must contribute toward Social Security and Medicare by paying self-employment taxes. Most importantly, running a sole proprietorship means that all the management is on one person—you! Many owners of sole proprietorships neglect to consider that there are other responsibilities to running a business besides performing the service or making the product. There is a lot of paperwork and time involved to ensure that invoices are created, payments are collected, and salaries and benefits are paid (if there are other employees). This, as well as generating new business, following up on prior jobs, and performing the tasks of the business, makes for a commitment of time that many sole proprietors do not anticipate and that can undo many new businesses quickly.

Another drawback of a sole proprietorship is the potential difficulty in borrowing money to help your business grow. Banks will be lending to you personally, not to your business, so they will be more reluctant to lend large amounts, and the loan will be limited to the amount of your personal assets. Other business structures, which we will discuss later in the chapter, are more helpful should you need to raise large amounts of money.

Remember Jennifer Perez? Soon after starting her business, Jennifer realized that a sole proprietorship wasn't the best form of ownership for her because she didn't want to risk losing her personal assets in the event of an employee error. Jennifer, like many other small business owners, learned that making decisions about choosing the correct corporate structure is complex. After getting advice from other business owners, Jennifer decided that her business needed to undergo some corporate restructuring so that the company's business form would be more conducive to her needs. What other forms of business ownership does Jennifer have to choose from? ■

Partnerships pp. 171–175

Hang Win had his eye on a piece of property for a storefront in an up-and-coming neighborhood. Because of the recent economic and real-estate market downturns, it was more affordable but still slightly out of his reach. It also needed some renovations and modest reconstruction—skills that Hang did not have. Stephan Brown, a friend of Hang's college roommate, had some construction and carpentry experience and was also looking for a business opportunity but didn't have as much capital. After much thought and conversation, Hang and Stephan agreed to form a partnership, buy the property, and embark on the renovations. What contributions did Hang and Stephan each bring to the partnership? What might be some difficulties the two new partners should prepare for? ■

Starting a new venture can be a difficult task, so sometimes a partner is needed to share the burden. Even large companies such as Target find partnerships useful in keeping their businesses up-to-date and running at its best. In this section, we'll look at partnerships in more detail.

Advantages and Disadvantages

When is it good to bring in a partner? Sometimes, running a business by oneself can be a daunting task, so adding one or more owners can help share the responsibilities. A **partnership** is a type of business entity in which two or more entities (or partners) share the ownership and the profits and losses of the business. There are several reasons why joining with someone else makes sense. More owners help contribute to both the starting and ongoing capital of the business. Multiple people are involved in partnerships, so there is more time available to increase sales, market the business, and generate income. Sharing the financial responsibility brings on more people who are interested in the company's overall profitability and are as highly motivated as you are to make the business succeed. Therefore, additional owners, unlike employees, are more likely to be willing to work long hours and go the extra mile.

Adding partners to help share the workload also allows for coverage for vacations or when a partner is out due to illness or personal issues. Moreover, if partners have complementary skills, they create a collaboration that can be quite advantageous. Partners can help discuss ideas and projects as well as make the big decisions. For example, if you're great at numbers but hate making sales calls, bringing in a partner who loves to knock on doors would be beneficial for your business.

Are there disadvantages to adding partners? For every advantage a partner can bring, adding the wrong partner can be equally problematic. Obviously, adding partners means sharing profits and control. A potential partner may have different work habits and styles from you, and if the partner's style isn't complementary, the differences can be challenging. In addition, as the business begins to grow and change, your partner might want to take the business in a different direction than you do. Like entering into marriage, you want to consider carefully the person(s) with whom you will be sharing your business.

BizChat

How Do You Find the Right Business Partner?

Business partners are like spouses; finding each other is often through circumstance and happenstance. Because of the high financial stakes, many look to partner with those whom they trust most: spouses, friends, or relatives. Hiring friends or relatives can have its benefits, but what do you do if your best friend doesn't do the job right?[1] You might instead want to turn to your casual acquaintance network—your gym buddy, a parent of your child's friend, a classmate—to find a business partner. If your network isn't turning up any promising leads, turn to others' networks. Similar to finding a job, write a description of the "perfect partner" and send it to as many people as you can. Make sure you interview the candidates and look for those who have similar goals but complementary skills. By all means, "date" the prospective partner before jumping into a business marriage; there is too much at risk to proceed too quickly.

For more information and discussion questions about this topic, check out the BizChat feature on my*biz*lab.com.

As a business form, how does a partnership compare to a sole proprietorship? Partnerships and sole proprietorships are very similar; in fact, the biggest difference between the two is the number of people contributing resources and sharing the profits and the liabilities. It's just as easy to form a partnership as a sole proprietorship. The government does not require any special forms or reports, although some local restrictions may apply for licenses and permits. For example, you and your brother-in-law form a small partnership called "All in the Family Electricians." Before you are able to do business, you might have to apply for a license, but you do not need any special papers to create the partnership itself. Also, like a sole proprietorship, partnerships do not file a separate tax return. All profits and losses of the partnership flow directly through each partner's individual tax return. ▼ **Table 6.3** outlines other characteristics of a partnership.

Elements of a Partnership Agreement

What goes into a partnership agreement? Although no formal documentation is required to create a partnership, it's a good idea to draw up an agreement. A partnership can begin with a handshake, and many of them do, but it is best for all involved parties that a written document, called a **partnership agreement**, formalizes the relationship between the business partners. Think of a partnership agreement as a business prenuptial agreement. It helps settle conflicts when they arise and may discourage small misunderstandings from erupting into larger disagreements. Many points can be included in a partnership agreement; however, the following items should always be included:

1. **Capital Contributions.** The amount of **capital**, or investments in the form of money, equipment, supplies, computers, and other tangible things of value, that each partner contributes to begin the business should be noted in the partnership agreement. In addition, the agreement should also address how additional capital can be added to the business—who will contribute it and whether there will be a limit to a partner's overall capital contribution.

2. **Responsibilities of Each Partner.** To avoid the possibility of one partner doing more or less work than others, or a conflict arising over one partner assuming a more controlling role, it is best to outline the responsibilities of each partner from the beginning. Unless otherwise specified, any partner can bind the partnership to any debt or contract without the consent of the other part-

▼ **Table 6.3**

Characteristics of a Partnership	
Characteristics	**General Partnership**
Preliminary paperwork	No special forms are required for state or federal filings; a partnership agreement is recommended.
Period of existence	Partnership is terminated on death or withdrawal of a partner unless otherwise provided for in the partnership agreement.
Liability	Partners have unlimited liability.
Operational requirements	There are minimal legal requirements.
Management	The partnership agreement should specify management roles, although each partner generally has an equal voice.
Taxation	Not a taxable entity; income flows through individual partner's tax returns, and each partner pays tax on his or her share of income; losses can be deducted against other sources of income.
Reporting of income/loss	Income/loss is reported on partners' personal income taxes.
Raising capital	Capital is primarily raised through partner contributions; additional capital is raised as partners are added.

ners. Therefore, it is especially important to spell out the policy regarding who assumes responsibility for entering into key financial or contractual arrangements.

3. **Decision-Making Process.** It is important to consider how decisions will be made. Knowing whether decisions will be the result of mutual consent of all or several partners or whether just one or two partners will make the key decisions is essential to help partners avoid disagreements. What constitutes a key decision should also be defined in the agreement. In a partnership of two, where the possibility of a deadlock is likely, some partnerships provide for a trusted associate to act as a third partner whose sole responsibility is to act as the tiebreaker.

4. **Shares of Profits or Losses.** Not only should the agreement specify how to divide profits and losses between the partners, but it should also specify how frequently this will be done. One partnership agreement might stipulate that the profits and losses will be proportional to each partner's initial contribution to the partnership, as reflected in ▼ **Figure 6.3,** whereas another partnership agreement might split the profits evenly. It is also important to detail how adjustments to the distributions will be made—if any at all—as the partnership matures and changes.

5. **Departure of Partners.** Eventually, the composition of partners may change as original partners leave and new partners come onboard. The partnership agreement should have rules for a partner's exit, whether voluntary, involuntary, or due to death or divorce. Provisions to remove a partner's ownership interest are necessary so the business does not need to end (i.e., liquidate). The agreement should include how to determine the amount of ownership interest and to whom the departing partner is permitted to transfer his or her interest. It is important to consider whether a partner can transfer his or her ownership solely to the remaining partners or whether individuals outside the existing partnership can buy the departing partner's share.

6. **Addition of Partners.** The partnership agreement also helps spell out the requirements for new partners entering the partnership. How the profits will be allocated and whether there will be a "junior partner" period during which the new partner can prove himself or herself before obtaining full partner status should also be included.

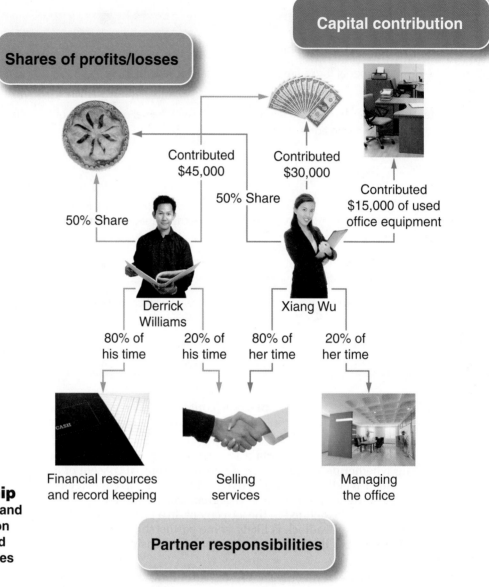

Capital contribution

Shares of profits/losses

Contributed
$45,000

Contributed
$30,000

Contributed
$15,000 of used
office equipment

50% Share

50% Share

Derrick
Williams

Xiang Wu

80% of
his time

20% of
his time

80% of
her time

20% of
her time

Financial resources
and record keeping

Selling
services

Managing
the office

Partner responsibilities

▼ **Figure 6.3**
Share of Profit and
Loss in a Partnership
Partners' shares of profits and
losses can be dependent on
the capital contribution and
the assumed responsibilities
of each partner.

Types of Partnerships

Are there different types of partnerships? There are several types of partnerships. The distinction between the different types usually involves who accepts most or all of the business liability. The two most common partnership forms are *general partnerships* and *limited partnerships*.

What is a general partnership? A **general partnership** is the default arrangement for a partnership and is, therefore, the simplest of all partnerships to form. For instance, if two friends, Juan and Franklin, set up an ice cream stand at the local park, sell ice cream cones, and split the profits at the end of the day, they have created a general partnership. For Juan and Franklin, this is a logical arrangement because they share the profits equally, and there is little worry about liability. In a general partnership, each partner has unlimited liability for the debts and obligations of the partnership, meaning every partner is liable for his or her own actions, as well as the actions of the other partners and the actions of any employees.

What is a limited partnership?

Sometimes, a business can bring on additional "limited" partners, mostly to provide capital and earn a share in the profits but not operate the business. To encourage investors to contribute capital to a business without risking more capital than they have contributed, a **limited partnership** is created. In a limited partnership, there are two distinctions of partners. **General partners** are full owners of the business, are responsible for all the day-to-day business decisions, and remain liable for all the debts and obligations of the business. **Limited partners** are involved as investors and, as such, are personally liable only up to the amount of their investment in the business and must not actively participate in any decisions of the business. Limited partnerships can be very complex to form, so it may be worth exploring other business structures before deciding on this strategy. Another kind of limited partnership is a *master limited partnership* (*MLP*). This business structure combines the tax benefits of a limited partnership, but it is similar to a corporation (which we discuss next) in that it is publicly traded on a securities exchange. MLPs are mostly restricted to certain businesses pertaining to the use of natural resources (such as petroleum or natural gas) and real estate.

What business structure is best when liability is a concern?

Although forming a general partnership for Juan and Franklin's ice cream business makes sense for them, it's not right for every business. In some situations, especially if liability is a concern, neither a sole proprietorship nor a partnership will protect the owner(s) from unlimited risk. For instance, if Sarah and Hannah decide to form Personal Training Partners, a personal training and fitness motivation company, they know that each partner is liable—not only for her own business debts and actions but also for each other's business debts and actions. Therefore, they need a type of structure that would protect their homes and savings and other personal assets from being lost in case of a business disaster. If a client claims that Sarah mistreated him or her and the client sues the business, not only are the business assets at risk but Sarah's and Hannah's personal assets are also at risk. To avoid this situation, a different type of ownership should be considered. Both partners want to be protected so only the business assets, like the building they bought for their gym, the exercise machines, and the computers they use, are at risk, not any of their personal assets. In this case, a partnership is not the best business structure because a partnership has unlimited liability and does not protect against losses of personal property. There are some options available for Personal Training Partners that are like partnerships in many ways but also help insulate an owner's personal liability from the business. We'll discuss these next.

Hang and Stefan's partnership benefitted from complementary skills and resources that each partner brought to the table. Because Hang had more financial exposure, it was important to him that he and Stefan sign a partnership agreement. After the renovations were complete and the space was ready for commercial use, Hang and Stefan brought in one more partner, Lily Ye, who had considerable retail and marketing experience—just what they needed to move forward in their venture. But Lily was concerned about the personal exposure she would have. She suggested the partnership look into a different kind of corporate structure. What other options do the partners have? ■

Corporations pp. 176–183

In 2009, Lehman Brothers Holding Inc. went from being one of the premier investment banks on Wall Street to being responsible for nearly crippling the U.S. economy. Lehman Brothers was caught taking bad debt (called "toxic loans") off its books by temporarily transferring the debt to another company in exchange for cash. Although this practice is not uncommon, what made this fraudulent was that Lehman Brothers disclosed these transactions as sales rather than loans, which wildly inflated the financial health of the corporation in its quarterly and annual reports. Although no criminal charges have yet to be made against Lehman Brothers, the stockholders (the owners of the corporation) would not be held accountable if charges were filed, nor would their personal assets be used to pay corporate debts. ■

The U.S. writer Ambrose Bierce once defined a corporation as "an ingenious device for obtaining profit without individual responsibility."[2] Unlike partnerships and sole proprietorships, corporations provide business owners with better protection of their personal assets. What is a corporation? Why might a business owner choose to form a corporation? What are the different types of corporations? In this section, you'll find the answers to these questions and more.

What is a corporation?
A **corporation** is a specific form of business organization that is legally formed under state laws. A corporation is considered a separate entity apart from its owners; therefore, a corporation has legal rights like an individual, so a corporation can own property, assume liability, pay taxes, enter into contracts, and can sue and be sued—just like any other individual. Most corporations are run as **C corporations**, which refers to Subchapter C of the Internal Revenue Code by which it is governed, though sometimes a corporation can be run as a S corporation (which we discuss next). Other characteristics of a C corporation are listed in ▼ **Table 6.4.**

▼ **Table 6.4**

Characteristics of a C Corporation	
Characteristics	**C Corporation**
Preliminary paperwork	Paperwork must be filed with both state and federal agencies.
Period of existence	Corporations are separate entities; existence is not dependent on founders, owners, or partners; shares of stock are easily transferred.
Liability	Shareholders are usually not personally liable for the debts of the corporation.
Operational requirements	Must have a board of directors, corporate officers, annual meetings, and annual reporting.
Management	Shareholders elect the board of directors, which provides the global management of the corporation.
Taxation	Taxed at the entity level; if dividends are distributed to shareholders, dividends are also taxed at the individual level (double taxation).
Reporting of income/loss	Corporations are separate entities; no income or loss is reported on shareholder's tax statements.
Raising capital	Capital is raised through the sale of stock shares.

Advantages of Incorporation

When does it make sense to form a business as a corporation?
Some business owners incorporate just to be able to end a company's name with "Company," "Co.," "Incorporated," or "Inc." Having "Co." or "Inc." at the end of the business name can give a start-up business an air of legitimacy, which can be a perceived benefit to prospective clients and lenders and potentially a greater threat to the competition. More importantly, forming under a corporate structure provides many advantages not found with other business structures.

How can a business owner protect his or her personal assets?
Because a corporation is a separate legal entity and is responsible for its own debts and obligations, it has separated liability from an owner's personal assets. This is one of the main reasons owners incorporate their business. When a corporation runs into problems, only the corporate assets can be used to remedy the situation; the owners are not personally liable for business debts.

What happens to a corporation when an owner leaves? Sole proprietorships and partnerships, by their nature, are dependent on their founding owners. When an owner dies or otherwise leaves, the partnership or sole proprietorship is usually terminated. On the other hand, corporations enjoy extended life and ownership transfer because shareholders own a corporation, so its existence doesn't depend on its founding members. Shares of ownership are easily exchanged, so the corporation will continue to exist should an owner die or wish to sell his or her interest in the business. Theoretically, a corporation is capable of continuing forever.

It is easier for corporations to raise capital? Incorporating offers a business greater flexibility when raising capital. Banks and venture capitalists are more likely to lend money to an incorporated business. In times when greater sources of funds are needed than what venture capital or bank loans can raise, a corporation can extend its ownership by "going public"—selling shares of ownership in the corporation to the general public on the stock exchange. A stock certificate is the tangible evidence of investment and ownership.

Are corporations taxed the same as other types of businesses? A corporation is taxed at 15 percent for its first $50,000 in annual profits, whereas the same amount of profits from a sole proprietorship or partnership would be taxed at a rate of 25 percent through individual taxes.[3] Although most large businesses will have more than $50,000 in annual profits—in which case this tax advantage is not applicable—it may be helpful to those smaller businesses that have incorporated. Small business owners might run the numbers to see which makes more financial sense.

Are there any other benefits from incorporating? Structuring a small business as a corporation allows the corporation to provide benefits to its employees. In a corporation, you can be the owner and the employee, and as the employee you can receive benefits. For example, if you started a computer repair and consulting business and structured it as a corporation, the corporation could hire you, pay you a salary, and provide benefits, such as medical insurance and life insurance. The corporation considers these legally deductible expenses—thus reducing the income of the company and consequently lowering the company's tax obligation—putting more money in your pocket as the owner.

Structure of a Corporation

How is a corporation structured? A corporation's organizational structure is composed of three basic groups: shareholders, a board of directors, and corporate officers, as shown in ▼ **Figure 6.4.** Each group has different responsibilities.

▼ Figure 6.4 Organizational Structure of a C Corporation

In a C corporation, the shareholders have the power to elect a board of directors. The board, in turn, has the ability to hire (or fire) the company's corporate officers.

Shareholders

Shareholders (or stockholders) have an ownership interest in the company. For their investment, they receive a stock certificate from the corporation, identifying the number of shares (called *apportioned ownership interest*) they own. A **publicly owned corporation** is a corporation that is regulated by the Securities and Exchange Commission. Although shareholders serve as the owners of the corporation, they have no involvement in the direct management of the corporation. Instead, they influence corporate decisions by electing directors, overseeing the laws and rules that govern the organization, and voting on major corporate issues.

In **privately held** (or **closed**) **corporations**, corporations are owned, in most cases, by the company's founders, a management team, or a group of private investors. The owners are generally involved in the management and daily operations of the business, assuming more decision-making responsibilities than do shareholders of publicly owned corporations. The owners of privately held corporations are generally the sole shareholders. Any shares of privately held corporations are not traded on public stock exchanges.

Directors

In an effort to separate ownership and management, the directors—or the **board of directors**—usually set policy for the corporation and make the major business and financing decisions. Directors authorize the issuance of stock, approve loans to or from the corporation, and decide on major real estate transactions. Although the shareholders elect the board of directors, the board of directors elects the management team of corporate officers and, by doing so, can influence the very nature of a business.

The board is also responsible for ensuring that the corporate managers are doing their jobs. Not all boards are effective in doing so, however, as has been demonstrated by corporate scandals, including those most recently in the financial sector. For example, the board of directors of Lehman Brothers were apparently unaware of the scandalous financial transactions chairman Richard Fuld Jr. and his team were conducting. In essence, the firm borrowed billions of dollars to repay debt it had on its books, but managers didn't show the new borrowings anywhere in Lehman's financial statements. The firm had substantially understated its financial leverage and liquidity problem to its shareholders and the SEC. As a result, in 2008, the firm filed for bankruptcy, which sparked a financial crisis that rippled globally. The firm has since been investigated for fraudulent behavior. The Lehman board should have been aware of what was going on, but in this case, it was not.

In a reaction to similar incidences of board negligence at the beginning of the century, the Sarbanes-Oxley Act of 2002, a U.S. federal law, was enacted to provide a new set of standards of accountability for the board of directors. If the members of a board of directors ignore their responsibilities of managing the internal controls of a company, they incur the risk of long prison sentences and huge fines.

Officers

Officers are elected by the board of directors and are responsible for the daily operation and management of the company. The typical lineup of officers includes the CEO, the CFO, and the COO. The **chief executive officer (CEO)** is typically responsible for the entire operations of the corporation and reports directly to the board of directors. The **chief financial officer (CFO)** reports directly to the CEO and is responsible for analyzing and reviewing the financial data, reporting financial performance, preparing budgets, and monitoring expenditures and costs. The **chief operating officer (COO)** is responsible for the day-to-day operations of the organization and reports directly to the CEO. Often there is a chief legal officer or general council, and, depending on the needs of the company, there might also be a chief information officer (CIO). In actuality, any "officer" position can be formed if it makes sense for the company.

In large companies, the responsibilities of each officer are demanding enough that separate positions are necessary. In smaller companies, only one or two persons might perform the role of several different officers. After having worked as a yoga instructor for local gyms, Maureen Priest opened Moyo, her own yoga studio in a Philadelphia suburb. "I wanted to be an instructor, but found in my first year that I needed to be the marketing manager, finance director, and chief operating officer, as well. I had to learn quickly how to get my name and my new studio to many people; and I had to learn how to price my services and figure out my expenses so I could come close to breaking even, if not making a profit. Lastly, I had to locate a studio, negotiate a rental contract, and renovate the space to accommodate my specific business needs. I wore many hats that first year."[4]

Disadvantages of Incorporation

Are there any disadvantages of structuring a business as a corporation? Forming a corporation is a much more cumbersome process than forming a sole proprietorship or a partnership. ▼ **Figure 6.5** shows the steps involved in forming a corporation.

Because a corporation is a separate legal entity, there are many requirements that must be fulfilled to maintain corporate status. For example, all companies must file an annual report and maintain written minutes of annual and other periodic board of director and shareholder meetings. Resolutions or consents of major decisions must be recorded, including decisions involving the issuance of stock; the purchase of real property; the approval of leases, loans, or lines of credit; the adoption of or changes to stock options; and retirement plans. A corporation must also record financial transactions in a double-entry bookkeeping system and file taxes on a regular basis (quarterly or annually).

Another disadvantage of the corporate structure is the idea of double taxation. **Double taxation** is the situation that occurs when taxes are paid on the same asset twice. The classic business example of double taxation is the distribution of dividends. Double taxation occurs because a corporation is first taxed on its net income, or profit, and then distributes that net income to its shareholders in the form of dividends. The individual shareholder must then pay taxes on the dividends (which have already been taxed at the corporate level). Therefore, the same pool of money—corporate profits—has been taxed twice: once in the form of corporate

▼ **Figure 6.5 Steps in Forming a Corporation**
Corporations provide owners with more protection than other business structures, although forming a corporation is a more complex process.

Choose a Name → Appoint Directors → File Articles of Incorporation → Draft Bylaws → Hold a Meeting of the Board → Issue Stock → Obtain Licenses and Permits

profits and again as dividends received by the shareholders. Although this is a commonly mentioned disadvantage of corporations, it does not affect all corporations.

Can a business have the protection of a corporation but not pay corporate taxes ? When choosing a legal structure for their businesses, most entrepreneurs will site two goals: protecting personal liability and flowing taxes through their individual tax returns. As has already been discussed, operating as a sole proprietorship or a partnership allows business profits and losses to flow through an owner's individual tax return, but an owner of a sole proprietorship or members in a partnership assume the risk of personal liability exposure. A corporate structure offers the reverse; it protects an owner's personal assets from being touched if the corporation is in difficulty, but the corporation is taxed as a separate entity without flow-through to the owner's returns. Fortunately, there are two forms of business ownership in which both goals can be met: the *S corporation* and the *LLC*.

S Corporations

What is an S corporation ? An **S corporation** is a regular corporation (a C corporation) that has elected to be taxed under a special section of the Internal Revenue Code called Subchapter S. Like C corporations, S corporations have shareholders, and they must comply with all the other regulations involving traditional C corporations.

How is an S corporation different from a C corporation ? Unlike C corporations, S corporations do not pay corporate income taxes. Instead, as with a partnership or a sole proprietorship, the shareholders in an S corporation owe income taxes based on their proportionate share of the business profits they receive and pay taxes through their own individual tax returns. Passing taxes through personal tax returns is one of the primary advantages of forming a business as an S corporation. However, even though S corporations do not *pay* taxes like C corporations, they still must *file* a tax return every year. In addition, S corporations must comply with the meeting and reporting requirements established for C corporations. Other characteristics of an S corporation are shown in ▼ **Table 6.5.**

▼ **Table 6.5**

Characteristics	S Corporation
Characteristics	**S Corporation**
Preliminary paperwork	Forms must be filed at the state and federal levels.
Period of existence	Corporations are separate entities; existence is not dependent on founders, owners, or partners; must observe Internal Revenue Service (IRS) regulations on who can own shares of stock.
Liability	Shareholders are typically not personally liable for the debts of the corporation.
Operational requirements	Must have a board of directors, corporate officers, annual meetings, and annual reporting.
Management	Shareholders elect a board of directors, who provide the global management of the corporation.
Taxation	There is no tax at the entity level.
Reporting of income/loss	Income/loss is reported on the shareholders' taxes.
Raising capital	Capital is raised through the sale of stock shares.

How does an S corporation handle personal liability? The beauty of an S corporation is that it offers the best of both worlds: profits and losses pass through to the shareholders, *and* the corporate structure provides some limitations on personal liability. Although an owner's personal assets will be protected in case of a large claim against the corporation, the S corporation does not assume liability for an owner's personal wrongdoings. This is true for any corporate structure—whether it is a C corporation, an S corporation, or an LLC (discussed later). So, if an owner directly injures someone or intentionally does something fraudulent, illegal, or reckless that causes harm to the company or someone else, he or she will be held personally responsible and is not protected under the corporate umbrella.

For example, suppose William is the owner of a boating business that offers day cruises in the San Francisco Bay. Unfortunately, one foggy day, William collided with another boat, causing his boat to capsize. Before leaving the dock that morning, William failed to provide sufficient life jackets for all his passengers and overloaded the boat. As a result, William would be held personally liable for his negligent actions, even though he had structured his company as an S corporation. William would not only be in danger of losing the business but also may be forced into personal bankruptcy.

Can any business elect to be an S corporation? There are certain qualification requirements a business must meet to elect S corporation status. According to the Internal Revenue Code,[5] an S corporation must have the following characteristics:

- The company must not have more than 100 shareholders.
- Shareholders must be U.S. citizens or residents.
- The company must issue only one class of stock.
- The company must distribute proportionately all profits and losses to each shareholder based on each one's interest in the business.

S corporations are the most appropriate business structure for small business owners who want the legal protection of a corporation but also want to be taxed as if they are the sole proprietor or a partner of a business. If a business does not meet these standards but personal liability protection with pass-through tax benefits is still desired, an LLC would be a suitable alternative corporate structure.

Limited Liability Companies

What is an LLC? A **limited liability company (LLC)** is a distinct type of business that, like an S corporation, combines the corporate advantages of limited liability with the tax advantages inherent in partnerships. LLCs are the relatively new kid on the block, and they are receiving quite a bit of interest in the business community because of their many benefits and flexibility that suit a start-up business. Similar to creating an S corporation or a C corporation, an LLC requires articles of organization, so it is a separate legal entity. But an LLC is free of many of the annual meetings and reporting requirements imposed on C and S corporations, so it is simpler to maintain. Because of fewer corporate formalities, limited liability provisions, and the treatment of taxes, it is a popular business structure choice for many new businesses.

It is important to note that some states may have restrictions on the types of businesses that can form as an LLC. Other characteristics of an LLC are outlined in ▼ **Table 6.6.**

What's the difference between an LLC and an S corporation? Although LLCs and S corporations share certain similarities, there are several

▼ **Table 6.6**

Characteristics	LLC
Preliminary paperwork	Paperwork must be filed with both state and federal agencies.
Period of existence	Ongoing existence is determined by requirements imposed by the state of formation; transferability is determined by the operating agreement.
Liability	Members are not typically liable for the debts of an LLC.
Operational requirements	There are fewer formal requirements than for corporations.
Management	Management details are described in an operating agreement.
Taxation	By default, it is taxed as a partnership, although it can elect to be taxed as a corporation.
Reporting of income/loss	Income/loss is reported on members' taxes.
Raising capital	Members may sell interests to raise capital; there may be operating agreement restrictions.

distinctions between LLCs and S corporations that should be considered before choosing either form:

- **Ownership.** S corporations are restricted to the number of owners the company can have, but LLCs can have an unlimited number of owners (called *members*). In addition, LLC members are not limited to just U.S. residents and are not subject to other ownership restrictions imposed on S corporations.

- **Perpetual life.** When a member leaves an LLC, the LLC must dissolve. In addition, some states also require that a dissolution date be listed in the articles of organization, so an LLC has a limited life span.

- **Stock transfer.** Stock in an S corporation, like a C corporation, is freely transferable, whereas the ownership interest in an LLC is not and generally requires the approval of other members.

- **Profit and loss distributions.** LLCs may allocate profits in whatever manner best suits the owners, but the profits of an S corporation are allocated in proportion to a shareholder's interest. So, if two members own a business, and one contributes 75 percent of the capital but only does 25 percent of the work while the other member contributes 25 percent of the capital but does 75 percent of the work, the two members can decide that a fair allocation of profits is 50/50. This arrangement would be possible with an LLC, but with an S corporation, the profits would need to be distributed based on the 75/25 ownership interest.

- **Owner and employee benefits.** An S corporation may offer fringe benefits to its owners, such as health insurance and direct reimbursement of medical expenses, life insurance, and a company car. Because S corporations have stock, they can also offer their employees' stock options and other stock bonus incentives. LLCs are limited in the benefits their members can be offered, and because LLCs do not have stock, they cannot offer stock benefits to their employees.

What kinds of businesses are best suited as an LLC? There are many types of businesses in which an LLC structure is appropriate, but in particular, LLCs are often used by professional corporations formed by accountants, attorneys, doctors, and other similar professionals who want to separate themselves from partner liability but still reap the other benefits of a partnership. LLCs may be a good choice for start-up businesses, not only for the tax benefits but also because it is easier to obtain financing because the number of investors (owners) is not limited.

Comparing Forms of Ownership

Which form of ownership is best? See ▼ **Table 6.7** to see how the most common forms of ownership stack up to one another.

Acorporation is different from sole proprietorships and partnerships because it is considered its own legal entity. It has its own tax return, and it can sue and be sued. Although some businesses starting out become corporations to appear more stable and legitimate, which in turn helps them gain clients and lenders, a significant advantage is that the owners' personal assets are protected should claims be made against the corporation. Reviewing the Lehman Brothers scandal shows the complexities of large corporations. Although many stockholders and employees lost much of their investment as the stock value plummeted to nothing, the shareholders—Lehman's "owners"—were not held personally liable for the illegal behaviors of the management team. And, although the corporate structure protected innocent managers and owners, it will not protect the guilty managers and owners from their illegal actions should action be taken against them. ▪

▼ **Table 6.7**

Comparing the Forms of Business Ownership

Type of Business	Sole Proprietorship	General Partnership	C Corporation	S Corporation	LLC
Ownership	Business owned and operated by one person.	Two or more partners jointly own and operate the business.	Formed under state and federal law; separate entity from owners.	Structured like a C corporation but taxed like a partnership.	Created by statute; owned by members.
Start-up requirements	Easiest form to set up; no required state or federal filings.	Easy to form and operate; no required paperwork; written partnership agreement is recommended.	File articles of incorporation with the state in which it is incorporated; specific paperwork required.	Meet S corporation requirements; articles of incorporation are required.	Articles of organization are required; specific paperwork required by the state.
Taxes	Profits taxed once; profits and losses reported on individual's tax return.	Profits taxed once; each partner's share of profits and losses reported on individual return.	Subject to double taxation; profits and losses reported on corporate tax return.	Each shareholder reports share of profits and losses on individual return. S corporation does not pay taxes.	Taxed like a general partnership or an S corporation.
Liability	The owners' personal assets are at risk.	Each partner's personal assets are at risk.	Owners' personal assets are not at risk, unless personal negligence or fault is involved.	Same as a C corporation.	Same as a C corporation.
Termination	Terminates by desire or death of owner.	Terminates by agreement of partners, or death or withdrawal of partner, depending on the partnership agreement.	Formal dissolution required; not affected by death or departure of owner.	Same as a C corporation.	Same as a general partnership.

Alternative Business Arrangements pp. 184–185

Darrell Hammond had volunteered to make playgrounds while he was in college. Then, several years later, he read about two inner-city children who had suffocated while playing in an abandoned car and realized that if the children had a safe place to play, the tragedy could have been avoided. Shortly afterward, Darrell and his friend, Dawn Hutchinson, built a community playground for a day of service they led, and a year later they founded KaBOOM![6] How could he structure KaBOOM! to protect himself financially, gain credibility, and continue to serve the community? ■

In some business ventures, the goal is not to generate a profit but rather make a difference in the lives of community members. When forms of business ownership, such as sole proprietorships, partnerships, and corporations, don't fit, business owners use alternative business arrangements. What are some of these alternative business arrangements? What are the benefits and drawbacks of using these forms of ownership? We'll answer these questions next.

Not-for-Profit Corporations

What is a not-for-profit organization? Legally, a **not-for-profit organization** (or nonprofit organization) is a business that does not seek a net profit. Instead, after paying normal operating expenses—such as salaries; rent; and purchases of inventory, supplies, materials, and equipment—a not-for-profit organization uses the remaining revenue for the business's declared social or educational goals. Not-for-profit organizations must apply for tax-exempt status with the federal government and sometimes with the state in which they are operating.

Can not-for-profit organizations act like corporations? Not-for-profit corporations are not-for-profit organizations that are incorporated and, as such, are subject to most of the laws that govern for-profit corporations. Not-for-profit corporations receive limited liability protection when they become incorporated and are established as a separate legal entity. Similar to a for-profit corporation, a not-for-profit corporation is required to hold board meetings and keep complete books and records. The greatest distinction between a for-profit corporation and a not-for-profit corporation is that a not-for-profit corporation cannot be organized for any person's private gain—that is, no profits are retained, and any excess revenue is distributed back to the organization. Not-for-profit corporations do not issue shares of stock, and their members (or owners) may not receive personal financial benefit from the organization's profits (other than salary as an employee). However, some not-for-profit corporations do provide employee benefits, such as health insurance. In addition, should the not-for-profit organization dissolve, the organization's assets must go to a similar not-for-profit group.

Do not-for-profit corporations generate *any* profits? Not-for-profit organizations are not in the business to generate a profit, unlike for-profit organizations; however, they still need to generate even a modest profit to survive. Not-

top **10** Largest U.S. Charities, 2009[7]

1. United Way
2. Goodwill Industries International
3. Salvation Army
4. Food for the Poor
5. Feed the Children
6. Brother's Brother Foundation
7. AmeriCares Foundation
8. American Cancer Society
9. YMCA National Council of the USA
10. World Vision

for-profit organizations generate their revenues primarily through fund-raising and donations. To maintain their tax-exempt status, not-for-profit organizations must demonstrate that a substantial portion of their income or revenue is spent on services to achieve their goals.

What are the benefits of being tax-exempt? As a corporation that has received 501(c)(3) status, the donations that are the corporation's primary source of revenue are tax deductible to the donor, which encourages funding. Other benefits of tax-exempt status are that the not-for-profit corporation is exempt from paying most federal and/or state corporate income taxes and may also be exempt from state sales and property taxes. Such not-for-profit corporations are able to apply for grants and other public or private distributions, as well as discounts on postal rates and other services.

Cooperatives

What structure would be best for groups of businesses with common goals? Cooperatives are businesses that are owned and governed by members who use its products or services, not by outside investors. Cooperative members can be individuals, such as individual farmers in an agricultural cooperative, or businesses, such as individual hardware stores, florists, or hotels that have come together to create cooperatives. You might be surprised to learn that Ace Hardware, Land O'Lakes, and Florida's Natural Growers are all cooperative ventures.[8] Cooperatives are motivated to provide services to people with common interests and/or needs and are not motivated by profits. Any profits made by a cooperative are returned to members in proportion to their use, not their investment or their ownership share.

How are cooperatives structured? Members are the most important part of a cooperative. They buy shares to help finance the cooperative, elect directors to manage the cooperative, and create and amend the bylaws that govern the cooperative. Cooperatives depend on their members to volunteer for projects supported by the cooperative and serve on boards and committees. The board of directors in a cooperative appoints committees for specific purposes, such as member relations and special audits. The board of directors also hires the cooperative manager who handles the daily affairs.

What is the benefit of cooperatives? Cooperatives form because a group of individuals or businesses become dissatisfied with how the marketplace is providing the needed goods or services at affordable prices or acceptable quality. Cooperatives use the benefit of group power, individuals (people or companies) coming together for a single cause, to negotiate within their marketplace. Therefore, members enjoy reduced costs due to greater bargaining power and marketplace strength associated with a large member group.[9]

For example, Florida's Natural Growers is a cooperative of citrus growers who own their own groves in Florida. A group of growers formed the cooperative in 1933 to market their crops. Today, the Florida's Natural Growers Cooperative processes 129,000 boxes of fruit per day—an improvement from the original 3,000 boxes of fruit the cooperative originally handled.[10]

Some businesses don't fit the mold of sole proprietorship, partnership, or corporation. When this occurs, business owners might form not-for-profit organizations or cooperatives. Darrell Hammond did not care about personal profit; he just wanted to create an organization that would help improve communities, so he found that forming a not-for-profit organization was best for him. ■

Mergers and Acquisitions pp. 186–190

I n 2008, Delta Airlines began the process to acquire Northwest Airlines to create the world's largest airline.[11] By coming together, the two companies hoped to gain financial and operational efficiencies to counter rising fuel prices and the effects of an economic downturn. Two years later, United Airlines and Continental Airlines begin merger talks to gain a competitive advantage over the larger Delta and become the world's largest airline. Were the airline companies making the right move? ■

Sometimes, in the evolution of a business or in response to market forces, companies seek opportunities to expand by adding new product lines, spreading out into different geographic areas, or growing the company to increase their competitive advantage. Often product or market expansion is done gradually by slowly adding new product lines or penetrating new areas. However, it takes time and investment to research and develop new products or to locate and build in new areas. Sometimes, especially to remain competitive, expansion needs to happen more quickly. In that case, it is easier to integrate another established business through the process of mergers or acquisitions. Mergers and acquisitions are two quick ways that companies can increase their competitive advantage and gain synergy. Are these the only reasons companies decide to merge with another? Why do companies try to acquire other companies? What are advantages and disadvantages of mergers and acquisitions? We'll answer these and other questions in this section.

Mergers versus Acquisitions

What are mergers? When two companies come together to form one company, a **merger** takes place. Generally, a merger implies that the two companies involved are about the same size and have mutually agreed to form a new combined company. In some instances, both merging companies cease to exist, and one new company takes over. For example, in 2005, Sprint Corporation, a global Internet carrier, acquired Nextel Communications, a U.S. telecommunications company, to form Sprint Nextel. In other situations, only one corporate name survives, such as when Delta merged with Northwest; the combined airline operates under the Delta name.

What are acquisitions? An **acquisition**, on the other hand, occurs when one company completely buys out another company. The purchased company ceases to exist, and it operates and trades under the buying company's name. Often, acquisitions are friendly, as was the case when the data-processing equipment and services provider Jack Henry & Associates Inc. purchased iPay Technologies. iPay had been working with Jack Henry and similar companies to provide online bill payment services to financial institutions. The acquisition of iPay will enable Jack Henry to expand into the electronic payments industry more easily and successfully than had it tried to develop the capabilities from the ground up.[12]

Are all mergers and acquisitions mutually desired by both companies? Although many mergers and acquisitions are "friendly" and mutually agreed on between companies, such as those between Delta and Northwest Airlines and Jack Henry and iPay, some acquisitions are "unfriendly." An unfriendly acquisition occurs when one company tries to take control over another company against its wishes. Unfriendly acquisitions are referred to as *hostile takeovers*. An unfriendly or hostile acquisition attempt occurs through a *tender offer*, where the acquiring firm offers to buy the target company's stock at a price higher than its current value, which is meant to induce shareholders into selling.

For example, in 2010, billionaire investor Carl Icahn mounted a hostile takeover of Lionsgate Entertainment Corp. by proposing a tender offer of $6 per share when the closing price was $5.45. If successful, Icahn would increase his ownership in the company from 18.9 percent to 29.9 percent. That would make him the company's largest shareholder and give him more control over the financial and strategic decisions of the company. Lionsgate rejected the offer and not enough shares were tendered; several months later, Icahn increased his offer to $7 per share.[13]

Another method of acquiring a company against its wishes is through a *proxy fight* in which the acquiring company tries to persuade the target company shareholders to vote out existing management and introduce management that is sympathetic to the goals of the acquiring company. This is the strategy Microsoft pursued when it unsuccessfully tried to take over Yahoo! in 2008.[14]

Some takeovers initiated by an outside group of investors, employees, or management are financed with debt. The acquiring group borrows the funds necessary for the acquisition, using the assets of the acquired company as collateral. This type of transaction is called a *leveraged buyout (LBO)*. LBOs can be either friendly or hostile, and companies of all sizes have been the targets of LBO transactions. Some of the more recent and largest LBOs involved the Hertz Corporation, Metro-Goldwyn-Mayer, and Toys"R"Us.

Advantages of Mergers and Acquisitions

Why do mergers and acquisitions occur?

Synergy is the business buzzword often used to justify a merger or an acquisition. **Synergy** is the effect achieved when two companies combine, in which the result is better than each company could achieve individually. Synergistic value is created when the new company can realize operating or financial economies of scale. Combined firms often lower costs by trimming redundancies in staff, sharing resources, and obtaining discounts accessible only to a larger firm. In other instances, synergy is achieved by combining resources that could not have been created independently by either party. Such was the case with the merger of satellite radio providers Sirius and XM. Each satellite radio provider had exclusive contracts with different sports programmers. Customers were having a hard time choosing between one and the other. The merger gives customers the benefit of both.

"Are you thinking what I'm thinking?"

Off the Mark
AOL-Time Warner Merger

In 2000, America Online (AOL), an Internet services company, merged with Time Warner, a media and communications company, in what was (and still is) the largest merger in the United States, valued at $111 billion. At the time, it was believed that the combination of an Internet giant and a media behemoth would, in the words of Gerald Levin, CEO of Time Warner, "create unprecedented and instantaneous access to every form of media and to unleash immense possibilities for economic growth, human understanding and creative expression."[15] According to AOL cofounder Stephen Case, the merger was "a historic moment in which new media has truly come of age."[17] However, the deal began to sour almost immediately, as it was soon quite apparent that the two companies had very different cultures. In addition, AOL, "the crown jewel of the transaction," ran into great financial difficulties as the dot-com bubble began to burst only months after the merger. Moreover, investigations by the SEC and the Department of Justice revealed that AOL had been improperly inflating its advertising revenue. In 2009, Time Warner revealed plans to spin off AOL as an independent company,[18] and the deal goes down as one of the worst mergers in history.

Is competition a driving force for mergers and acquisitions? Achieving a greater competitive advantage is one reason mergers and acquisitions take place. Often, companies join to become a more dominant force in their market. For example, in 2009, Pfizer, the world's largest drug maker, acquired rival Wyeth and claimed that the newly combined company would be "one of the most diversified in the industry."[16] One of the compelling reasons Pfizer pursued the acquisition was to become more competitive by gaining access to Wyeth's portfolio of new vaccines and biotechnology medicines.

Do companies add value to their product line by mergers? Many times, larger companies acquire smaller companies for their innovativeness, and a smaller company will agree to merge or be acquired if it feels it wouldn't have the opportunity to go public and couldn't survive alone otherwise. IBM has long used the strategy of adding to its product line through acquisitions. For example, IBM acquired iPhrase, a privately held company that specializes in making software, so IBM could "establish a new level of customer value for discovering and delivering actionable information."[19] IBM also acquired PureEdge Solutions Inc., one of the leading developers of electronic forms, so IBM could offer a seamless integration of electronic forms to IBM's customers. Both iPhrase and PureEdge Solutions Inc. have helped IBM in its quest to provide software that enables businesses to make sense of the consumer data they receive from online sales.

"Nothing focuses the mind better than the constant sight of a competitor who wants to wipe you off the map."[20]

—Wayne Calloway, CEO of PepsiCo (1986–1996)

Types of Mergers

Are there different types of mergers? The rationale and strategy behind every merger is different, but, as illustrated in ▼ **Figure 6.6**, there are some consistencies, distinguished by the relationship between the two companies that are merging:

- **Horizontal merger.** Two companies that share the same product lines and markets and are in direct competition with each other, such as Exxon and Mobil and Daimler-Benz and Chrysler.

- **Vertical merger.** Two companies that have a company/customer relationship or a company/supplier relationship, such as Walt Disney and Pixar or eBay and PayPal.

- **Product extension merger.** Two companies selling different but related products in the same market, such as the 2005 merger between Adobe and Macromedia.

- **Market extension merger.** Two companies that sell the same products in different markets, such as when NationsBank, which had operations primarily on the East Coast and in southern areas of the United States, merged with Bank of America, whose prime business was on the West Coast.

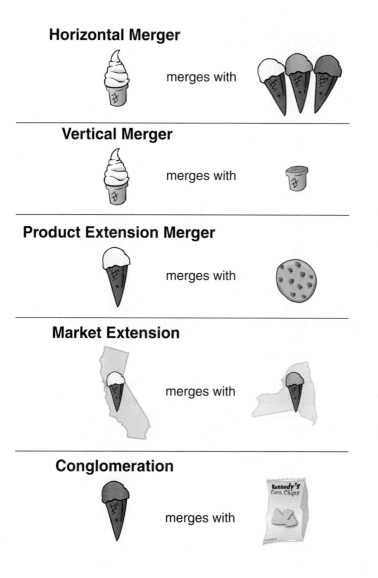

Horizontal Merger

merges with

Vertical Merger

merges with

Product Extension Merger

merges with

Market Extension

merges with

Conglomeration

merges with

▼ **Figure 6.6
Different Types
of Mergers**
Companies merge for
different strategic reasons.
Sometimes, companies merge
to enter new markets,
whereas others want to
expand into new fields and
save costs.

- **Conglomeration.** Two companies that have no common business areas merge to obtain diversification. For example, Citicorp, a banking services firm, and Travelers Group Inc., an insurance underwriting company, combined to form one of the world's largest financial services group, Citigroup Inc.

Disadvantages of Mergers

Are there disadvantages with mergers? Despite the perceived advantages of mergers, more than one-half of all mergers fail completely or don't live up to financial expectations.[21] The primary culprit of a failed merger is poor integration following the transaction. After an exhausting process, which may cause top executives to take their eyes off business, little energy or motivation may be left to plan and manage how the two companies will come together to work as one. Although cost-cutting may be the initial primary focus of some mergers, revenues and profits may ultimately suffer if day-to-day activities are neglected. Additionally, corporate cultures may clash, and communications may break down if the new division of responsibilities is vague. Conflicts may also arise due to divided loyalties, hidden agendas, or power struggles within the newly combined management team. Employees may be nervous because most mergers result in the elimination of jobs, and more turnover may be created as those employees whose jobs may not be threatened by the merger seek employment in a more stable environment.

Social Media: Merger and Acquisition Mania

Google, Facebook, and Twitter have all risen to the top of their industries on their own. Unlike these start-ups-turned-behemoths, many Internet start-ups, once they begin to experience success, are acquired by a larger company. As with most mergers, the motive for these deals is for the larger company to squelch competitive threats or acquire a new technology or product line.

Many companies operating in traditional media (newsprint, television, radio) are interested in Internet start-ups, thinking the acquisition will enhance the company's digital, or computer-based, media operations.[22] For example, Rupert Murdoch's media conglomerate News Corp. (the parent company of Fox Broadcasting and other media enterprises) acquired Intermix Media, and with it, MySpace, in July 2005. Although MySpace has lagged behind Facebook and Twitter since the acquisition, Murdoch is still supporting the social-networking site and has no plans to sell.[23] On a smaller but similar note, Gannett, a media and marketing solutions company, purchased Ripple6, a provider of social media services. Ripple6 will continue to power some of Gannett's social media–enriched Web sites such as MomsLikeMe.com and MixingBowl.com.

But social media acquisitions are not limited to the media industry. The three largest interactive deals were Apple's acquisition of mobile ad network Quattro Wireless for $275 million, Monster's acquisition of online recruiter HotJobs from Yahoo! for $225 million, and Dentsu's acquisition of digital agency Innovation Interactive from ABS Capital Partners for $220 million.[24] Unlike many other industries that are not in the position to make big merger or acquisition plays, digital media transactions are anticipated to continue to be very active.

Although mergers and acquisitions historically have been unsuccessful, why do you think companies like Delta and Northwest and United and Continental continue to pursue such strategies? Are there other motives behind the merger or acquisition that prompts such corporate restructuring? Are there other ways companies can come together to achieve synergies? ▪

Chapter Summary

Are you an active learner?

Go to my**biz**lab.com to master Chapter 6's content. Chapter 6's interactive activities include:

- Customizable Study Plan and Chapter 6 practice quizzes
- Chapter 6 Simulation, Are You an Entrepreneur? Small Business and the Entrepreneur, that helps you think critically and prepare to make choices in the business world
- Chapter 6 Video Exercise, Forms of Business Ownership, which shows you how textbook concepts are put into practice every day
- Flash Cards for mastering the definition of chapter terms
- Interactive Lessons that visually review key chapter concepts

1. **What are the strengths and weaknesses of a sole proprietorship? (pp. 167–170)**

   - A **sole proprietorship** (p. 167) is a business owned and usually operated by a single individual.
   - The sole proprietorship is a common form of business ownership because it is the easiest to establish, but there are both strengths and weaknesses inherent to this business form.
     - The advantage of establishing a business as a sole proprietorship is that there are no formal, legal requirements for starting the business, and the revenues and expenses are reported directly on the business owner's personal income tax return.
     - The primary disadvantage of a sole proprietorship is that personal and business assets are at risk in the event of a business catastrophe.

2. **What are the advantages and disadvantages of a partnership and a partnership agreement? (pp. 171–175)**

   - A **partnership** (p. 171) is a business structure that is easy to establish and has no formal, legal requirements.
   - Partnerships offer the benefit of two or more individuals sharing aspects of the business, including financial management and sales and marketing responsibilities. Income and expenses flow directly through each partner's individual tax return.
   - Partnerships are recommended to have a **partnership agreement** (p. 172), which is a formal document that outlines the responsibilities for each partner and includes provisions when there are disputes among partners.
   - Problems can occur when partners do not agree on the nature of the business or have different work ethics.
   - Partners' personal and business assets are at risk, with each partner being solely liable for any part of the business. Responsibility is not limited to each partner's financial contribution to the business.

3. **How is a corporation formed, and how does it compare with sole proprietorships and partnerships? (pp. 176–180)**

   - **Corporations** (p. 176) are businesses structured as separate legal entities. Corporations are structured with different levels of management, including shareholders, board of directors, and corporate officers, such as the chief executive officer (**CEO**; p. 179), the **chief financial officer** (**CFO;** p. 179), and the **chief operating officer** (**COO;** p. 179).
   - Corporations differ from sole proprietorships and partnerships for the following reasons:
     - Corporations are difficult to set up.
     - Corporations require much ongoing paperwork, including annual reports, corporate minutes, and formal financial records.
     - Corporations must file separate tax returns.
     - Corporations can sue and be sued.
     - Corporations protect an owner's personal assets.

4. **What are the major differences between a C corporation, an S corporation, and an LLC? (pp. 180–183)**

   - **S corporations** (p. 180) are like **C corporations** (p. 176) that offer the protection of limited liability, but S corporations allow the shareholders to flow the corporate revenues and expenses through their personal tax returns.
   - S corporations have certain restrictions, which include having no more than 100 shareholders, requiring shareholders to be residents of the United States, allowing for the issuance of only one class of stock, and basing profits and losses on the proportional interest of each shareholder.
   - The corporate structure of a **limited liability company** (**LLC;** p. 181) is similar to an S corporation that offers the protection of limited liability of a corporation. LLCs differ from S corporations because they can have unlimited members, must dissolve when any member leaves, and do not base distribution of profits on the direct proportion of a member's financial contribution.

5. **What are the characteristics of not-for-profit corporations and cooperatives? (pp. 184–186)**

   - **Not-for-profit corporations** (p. 184) are corporations whose purpose is to serve the public interest rather than to seek to make a profit. Not-for-profit corporations are tax exempt, and donations to the organization are deemed tax deductible.
   - **Cooperatives** (p. 185) are businesses that are owned and governed by members who use its products and services, not by outside investors.

Continued on next page

Chapter Summary (cont.)

- Cooperatives are motivated to provide services or goods to people with common interests or needs.
- All profits generated by the cooperative are returned to the members in direct proportion to their share of ownership.
- Cooperatives use the benefit of group power to negotiate within their marketplace.

6. **What are the different types of mergers and acquisitions, and why do they occur?** (pp. 186–190)
   - Mergers and acquisitions are business practices that bring companies together (in two distinct manners) for the purpose of achieving better **synergy** (p. 187).
   - A **merger** (p. 186) occurs when two companies of similar size mutually agree to combine to form a new company. Some types of mergers are as follows:
     - **Horizontal mergers** (p. 188): Two companies that share the same product lines and are in direct competition with each other merge.

- **Vertical merger** (p. 188): Two companies that have a company/customer relationship or a company/supplier relationship merge.
- **Product extension merger** (p. 188): Two companies selling different but related products in the same market merge.
- **Market extension merger** (p. 188): Two companies that sell the same products in different markets merge.
- **Conglomeration** (p. 189): Two companies that have no common business areas merge to obtain diversification.
  - An **acquisition** (p. 186) occurs when one company buys another company outright. The purchased company ceases to exist and starts to operate under the buying company's name and management. Acquisitions can be friendly (mutually agreed on) or unfriendly (one company buys the other against the wishes of the management and/or owner).

Key Terms

acquisition (p. 186)

board of directors (p. 178)

C corporation (p. 176)

capital (p. 172)

chief executive officer (CEO) (p. 179)

chief financial officer (CFO) (p. 179)

chief operating officer (COO) (p. 179)

closed corporation (p. 178)

cooperatives (p. 185)

corporation (p. 176)

double taxation (p. 179)

general partners (p. 175)

general partnership (p. 174)

horizontal merger (p. 188)

liability (p. 170)

limited liability company (LLC) (p. 181)

limited partner (p. 175)

limited partnership (p. 175)

merger (p. 186)

not-for-profit corporation (p. 184)

not-for-profit organization (p. 184)

partnership (p. 171)

partnership agreement (p. 172)

privately held corporation (p. 178)

publicly owned corporation (p. 178)

S corporation (p. 180)

shareholder (p. 178)

sole proprietorship (p. 167)

synergy (p. 187)

unlimited liability (p. 170)

vertical merger (p. 188)

Multiple Choice You can find the answers on the last page of this book.

1. Mustafa and Sam are physical therapists who work together. Their office is on the first floor of an apartment building Mustafa owns. They need protection of their personal assets. Which business structure would best suit their company?

   a. A general partnership

   b. A sole proprietorship

   c. A not-for-profit corporation

   d. An LLC

2. Why might a potential business owner want to establish a business as a sole proprietorship?

   a. The owner can use personal assets to satisfy any business liabilities.

   b. The owner can take into consideration the opinions of other business owners.

   c. The owner can generate a separate tax return for business expenses.

   d. The owner is not required to file legal paperwork to start up the business.

3. Trudy and Usha have come together to run Salford Children's Center, a place where parents on welfare can drop their children off to be cared for while the parents are looking for work. The center receives income from state and federal grants, and whatever is left over is put back into the center for additional resources. Salford Children's Center would best be described as a(n)

   a. partnership.

   b. LLC.

   c. not-for-profit corporation.

   d. sole proprietorship.

4. Jackson Eats is a partnership owned by Jesse and Robert Jackson. They need additional capital to expand to a new location, so they have decided to bring in Sean, who will not only contribute some capital but will also manage the new restaurant. Sean would best be considered as a(n)

   a. general partner.

   b. limited partner.

   c. owner.

   d. None of the above

5. Which of the following is a reason for creating a new business as a C corporation?

   a. The owner's personal assets would be protected.

   b. The owner could raise greater sources of funds by selling shares of ownership.

   c. The corporation would continue to exist even if the owner left the business.

   d. All of the above

6. Which of the following types of business structures would require that all excess revenues be put back into the corporation?

   a. An LLC

   b. An S corporation

   c. A not-for-profit corporation

   d. A sole proprietorship

7. If you were concerned about protecting personal liability but still wanted to flow income and losses through to your personal taxes, which form of corporate structure would be best?

   a. A C corporation

   b. A sole proprietorship

   c. A general partnership

   d. An LLC

8. Which is a benefit of cooperatives?

   a. The group power enables them to negotiate for goods and services at a favorable price.

   b. They are exempt from paying federal and state taxes.

   c. They are established to serve the public interest rather than make a profit.

   d. They provide services to people with differing interests and needs.

9. If Mom's outdoor clothing store combined with Dad's camping equipment store to form Mom & Dad's Outdoor Store, which of the following best describes the type of transaction that occurred between the two companies?

   a. A vertical merger

   b. A product extension merger

   c. A horizontal merger

   d. A conglomeration

10. The management team of Company A decides to offer to buy the stock from all the shareholders of Company B at a higher price than current market value. Company A is launching a

   a. proxy fight.

   b. tender offer.

   c. friendly acquisition.

   d. friendly takeover.

Self-Test

1. Any business can elect to be an S corporation.
   ☐ **True** or ☐ **False**

2. A company's officers are responsible for electing the board of directors.
   ☐ **True** or ☐ **False**

3. Cooperatives are organizations that raise money for the common good and not for any company's individual gain.
   ☐ **True** or ☐ **False**

4. A significant disadvantage of forming a corporation is the amount of paperwork and reporting that is required.
   ☐ **True** or ☐ **False**

5. A partnership agreement should include procedures that handle a partner's departure from the business as well as how any new partners are to be brought in.
   ☐ **True** or ☐ **False**

Critical Thinking Questions

1. Why might it be important to structure your business as a C corporation, even if you are the only person running the business?

2. Discuss the various types of mergers and give examples of each.

3. Describe a corporation's organizational structure. What are the three basic groups, and what are their roles?

4. Investigate a nonprofit organization in your area. What cause is it serving? What is the primary source of its income? What are its main expenses?

5. Research a merger or acquisition that occurred at least five years ago. What is the state of the company today? Was the merger successful? What do you think has led to the success or failure of this merger?

Team Time

What's the Plan?

Imagine that you work for the SBA and have the opportunity to advise new business owners on the form of ownership their businesses should take. Form groups of three to five people and choose one of the business ideas below. Work as a group to create a business plan for each business idea. What kind of business forms would you suggest for each idea and why? Be sure to consider the potential risks and liabilities, the potential income tax situations, and the current and future investment needs of each business. Assume in five years, the business needed additional capital to expand by adding a new building in a different location. Would your business structure support raising the necessary capital? Why or why not?

Business Ideas:

- Roofing and siding company
- Ice cream parlor
- Yoga instruction
- Lawn mowing company
- Clothing donation company

Process

Meet as a group to discuss your business idea. Remember that you must prepare a business plan. Use what you know about the forms of business ownership to create the business plan.

Step 1. Prepare an individual report that explains the form of ownership your business should take and outline why it should take this form.

Step 2. Determine who will be the group's primary spokesperson for your business plan.

Step 3. Your group will have five minutes to present your recommendations.

Step 4. After each group has presented, discuss any differences of opinion about the proposed business structures.

Ethics and Corporate Social Responsibility

Sarbanes-Oxley

Sarbanes-Oxley has been called the "most sweeping corporate regulation measure in decades," and yet, as has been evidenced by the ethical and legal violations incurred by some large banks and investment banks since the passing of Sarbanes-Oxley, it seems as though the measure was not enough. The surge of scandals continues to be fueled, in part, by trying to improve stock value to meet shareholder expectations. Often this results in companies avoiding actions that might result in short-term losses but that would be overall beneficial in the long run. Instead, companies favor transactions that improve share value for a short period of time but which may not be in the long-term best interest of the company. Moreover, because top-level executives are compensated by stock performance, they, too, are driven by such transactions.

Questions for Discussion

1. How do you think executive pay is tied into corporate integrity? Do you think executives' compensation should be tied to corporate performance? Why or why not?

2. How do you think managing a company for stock market performance might lead to risky behavior from the corporate officers and board of directors?

Web Exercises

1. **Business Combinations**
   Look on the Internet for a current example of a business merger, takeover, or acquisition. Explain the circumstances of the event. What companies are involved? Was the event friendly or unfriendly? What are the reasons given for the combination? What is your opinion of this business combination? Do you think it is a good business decision? Why or why not?

2. **Don't Forget the Domain Name**
   You have decided to start your own business and have just the right name in mind. It's important for your business that you also have a Web site. But you can't assume that your business name (or something close) will be available between the www. and the .com (known as the *domain name*). Research how you pick a good domain name and how you can determine whether it is still available.

3. **The Perfect Partner**
   Go to www.inc.com/guides/leadership_strat/23041.html and read the advice for how to pick the perfect business partner. Using information you learned from this chapter and the Web site, write a list of rules for picking the perfect business partner. What factors should be taken into account? What can you do to avoid trouble in the future?

4. **Plan with the End in Mind**
   Beginning a business requires a lot of planning, but even still, the business often fails. However, most business owners do not have an "exit plan" in mind when they start the venture. Research the main causes of business failures and what kind of exit strategies can be set in place at the beginning to ease the pain if the business needs to close.

5. **Preparing for Business**
   Think of a business idea you might like to pursue some day. Imagine that "some day" is today. Visit the Score.org Web site, search for the business quizzes, and then and take the quizzes there to see if you're prepared to start your business. Are you really ready to begin your business venture?

Web Case

For more on restructuring a business to attract investors, access the Chapter 6 Web case entitled "Focus on Global Warming Solutions, Inc.: Restructuring for Success" located in the End of Chapter Assignments section at my*biz*lab.com.

Video Case

For more on the advantages and disadvantages of different forms of business ownership, access the Chapter 6 Video Case entitled "Amy's Ice Creams: Churning Success One Scoop at a Time" located in the End of Chapter Assignments section at my*biz*lab.com.

Constructing an Effective
Business Plan

From the moment you received money for mowing your neighbor's lawn or babysitting your neighbor's child, you've been interested in starting your own business. But where do you begin? Do you purchase business cards? Do you create and distribute flyers? Although these might be good ways to get your business moving, they are not the first things you should do when starting a business. The SBA suggests that the very first step in starting a business is *planning*. Writing a business plan is usually the first step in that planning process. A business plan is a written document that details a proposed or existing venture, describing the vision, current status, the markets in which it operates, and the current and projected results of a business.

Traditionally, a potential business owner writes a business plan *before* a business is launched, but it can be written well after a business has been established. In some instances, and especially in industries in which change occurs rapidly, a business opportunity might be lost if you do not start operations immediately; you may not have time to take the weeks or months often required to write a business plan. In this situation, you should still begin by answering a few discrete and pointed questions, such as those shown in ▼ **Figure 1.** This will help you determine whether the business you're pursuing will be worth the effort. Eventually, a formal business plan should be written to more thoroughly define the goals and objectives of the business and the means to achieve them.

PEARSON
my*biz*lab

Are You an Entrepreneur?: Getting Your Business Off the Ground

You won $3.5 million in the lottery and decided to start a new fishing bait business. You've found a partner and a great location to set up shop in Montana. But suddenly, troubles are creeping up. Can you manage them and make your entrepreneurial dreams come true?

Planning—It's Never Too Late

In 1958, college-aged brothers Dan and Frank Carney borrowed $600 from their mother to open a pizza parlor in Wichita, Kansas. This venture marked the inception of the Pizza Hut empire. The brothers had neither a formal business plan nor

Although Pizza Hut owners Dan and Frank Carney launched a successful business without a formal business plan, they soon found that planning was necessary for continued success.

Step One: Write a mission statement. To help explain the purpose of your business answer the following questions:
- Why should this business exist?
- Who will be the target customer?
- How will the customer benefit from the business?

Step Two: Find the key to your success. To help figure out how your business will be successful, answer the following questions:
- Where will your operations take place?
- What three or four critical factors will be essential to your business s survival?
- What obstacles will you have to overcome?

Step Three: Perform a simple market analysis. To help determine how many potential customers your business will have, answer the following questions:
- At which businesses are your customers current patrons?
- Who are your main competitors?
- Are there enough potential customers?

Step Four: Perform a simple breakeven analysis. To help figure out how much money your business must produce to cover your costs, answer the following questions:
- What is the total cost of your operations?
- How many units of sales will you need to cover your costs?
- Are your sales goals realistic?

Step Five: Really think about it. To help decide if you are prepared to start a business, answer the following questions:
- Do you feel ready to start a business?
- Are you willing to commit long hours to making your business work?
- Have you discussed your idea with a business counselor or coach?

Considering your answers to these questions, do you still feel prepared to start a business? If so, get started, but find time to create a thorough business plan to use as a guide as your business develops.

▼ **Figure 1**
The Simplified Start-up Plan

a clear vision of the path their business would take. In fact, the Carneys simply gave away pizza on their opening night to garner the public's interest. Although it was impulsive, their gimmick worked. Less than a year later, the boys incorporated and opened their first franchise unit in Topeka, Kansas. Within the next 10 years, more than 150 franchises opened nationwide, and one international franchise opened in Canada. However, in 1970, the company's growth became explosive. Pizza Hut went public, and the brothers quickly became overwhelmed. "We about lost control of the operations," Frank Carney said in 1972. "Then we figured out that we had to learn how to plan."[1] Ultimately, Frank and Dan developed a plan that kept operations constant and under control. They also created a corporate strategy that enticed PepsiCo to purchase Pizza Hut in 1977. At that time, Pizza Hut sales had reached $436 million a year.[2] The Carneys' story is a success; however, if they had developed a clear business plan from the beginning, they may have been better prepared to handle their company's incredible growth.

The **Purpose** of a **Plan**

A business plan is your "business story"—a story that you will tell to a wide variety of people, from personal friends and casual acquaintances to potential partners, suppliers, customers, and investors. There are three purposes to writing a business plan: development, management, and communication.

- **Development.** Writing down your business plan solidifies and defines your intentions. It forces you to think through many aspects of a business that might otherwise be overlooked, identify roadblocks and obstacles, and determine ways to resolve or avoid them. Business plans can be used to get the entire management team, and perhaps the employees of the company, to understand where the company is and where it is heading.

- **Management.** Of course, the goal of most businesses is to make money, so a business plan should summarize how a business opportunity will translate into profits. A business plan also helps in the management of a company. Because it is a living document, it should be modified as the business changes and reaches certain milestones. It can be used to track and monitor the progress of the company, as well as evaluate projections with respect to the actual performance.

- **Communication.** A business plan is often used to attract investors or obtain loans. It can also be used to attract strategic business partners, additions to the management team, or high-quality employees. As such, the plan needs to communicate that you have taken an objective and realistic view of your company and thought through all the potential problems and determined reasonable alternatives.

While some business plans are lengthy, formal documents that can take weeks or months to prepare, others are short, informal outlines. Regardless of when or how it is written, a business plan is a crucial part of a successful business operation.

Business Plan Competitions

A business plan can help you determine whether your idea is feasible, to pitch your idea to others, and, in some cases, help you win a bit of necessary start-up cash. Many top business schools and colleges in the United States offer business plan competitions, with cash prizes that range from $10,000 to $100,000.

Business plan contests, once deemed as the culmination of an academic exercise, are now sources of serious money. In 2010, Rice University hosted the first business plan competition that offered over $1 million in prizes. The winner, BiologicsMD, a start-up with a new treatment for osteoporosis, walked away with $300,000 in investments, $39,250 in cash grants, and $80,100 in business services and gift cards from the competition. Not too long after taking the top prize at Rice University, BiologicsMD won $12,000 cash at the Arkansas Governor's Cup, $15,500 cash at the University of Louisville Cardinal Challenge, and $10,250 cash at the University of Cincinnati Business Plan Competition.[3]

One notable winner of the MIT 100K Entrepreneurship's Business Plan Competition was Harmonix, the video game development company responsible for creating Guitar Hero and Rock Band.

Business plan competitions have given life to hundreds of business ideas. The venerable MIT (Massachusetts Institute of Technology) 100K Entrepreneurship's Business Plan Competition is the final step of a trio of contests, including the Elevator Pitch and the Executive Summary Contest. The MIT competition has been giving away prizes since 1990 and has sparked the formation of approximately 130 companies. One of the more notable winners is Harmonix, the company that created Guitar Hero and Rock Band. Harmonix was acquired by MTV Networks in 2006 for $175 million. In 2008, the founders, Alex Rigopulos and Eran Egozy, were named as 2 of the 100 most influential people in the world in *Time Magazine*.[4]

Before the Business Plan: Finding the Right Fit

Before you begin to think about writing a business plan, you should do some soul searching to determine your own goals and objectives and whether they match those of the business that you've imagined. You might want to visit the SBA's Web site. There you'll find questionnaires and quizzes that might help you focus your ideas.

Not everyone wants to be (or can be) the next Bill Gates. Some individuals are quite content running a successful business that consists of a few employees and never sees figures in the millions. However, some ambitious entrepreneurs would like to have their ideas realized on a much larger scale. Regardless of the size of business you would like to own, it is important to try to articulate your own personal business plan by answering questions like the following:

- Do you want to be able to have a balance between your business life and your personal life? Or is it okay for your business to be your life?
- How do you define "success"? Is it a monetary goal, a production goal, or a lifestyle goal?
- What is your timeline for "success"? Do you want to achieve it quickly or is it acceptable to work slowly toward graduated markers of success?

Determining the answers to these questions will help to crystallize your focus, realize what your priorities are, and clarify your business goals and objectives. Once this preparation is complete, you're poised to begin writing your business plan.

Components of a Business Plan

There is no one right way to write a business plan. Each business is unique, so business plans can be drawn up in a variety of ways. Still, most business plans share a few basic components. A typical business plan for a start-up company is about 35–60 pages in length and contains eight key elements, as illustrated in ▼ **Figure 2.** The order in which the key elements are included is not random; they should be in the order of importance to the person reading the document. Therefore, although a complete description of your product may be of utmost importance to you, your investors and key contributors first need to know about the market before the specifics of your product. Let's look at each of the basic components of a business plan in more detail.

▼ **Figure 2**
Basic Components of a Business Plan

| Cover Sheet and Table of Contents | Executive Summary | The Company and Management Team | Market Analysis | Product Service | Sales and Promotion | Financials | Appendices |

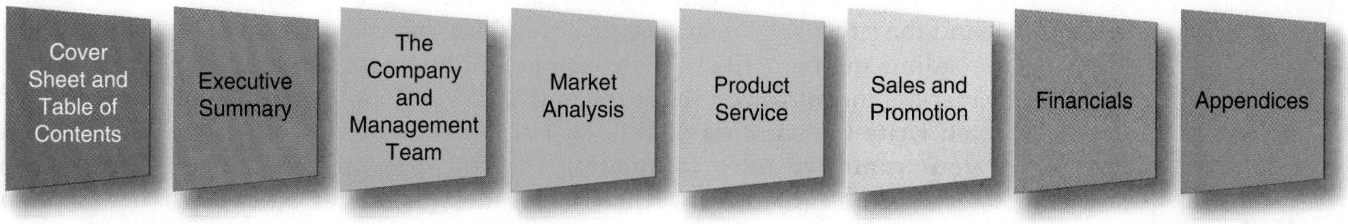

AB Environmental Consulting
21 N. LaSalle Street
Chicago, IL 60611
(312) 555-6439
www.abenvironmentalconsulting.com

Business Plan

Prepared by:

Adam Bernard
President & Owner
(312) 555-6438
abernard@abenvironmentalconsulting.com

January 2011

#AB5336

▼ **Figure 3**
Sample Business
Plan Cover Sheet

The Cover Sheet and Table of Contents

The *cover sheet* of a business plan is like the cover of a book; it provides the first impression of your plan and your business. This component is crucial, but many business planners don't include the right information on the cover sheet, which may turn off potential investors. As shown in ▼ **Figure 3,** the cover sheet should include the following:

- Basic company information (name, address, phone number, and Web address)
- The company logo (if applicable)
- Contact information of the owner(s) and any officers (name, titles, addresses, phone numbers, and e-mail addresses)
- The month and year the business plan was created
- The name(s) of those who prepared the plan
- A unique record number so that you can track who received which copy so you can easily follow up with him or her

The *table of contents* follows the cover sheet. It should be well organized so that the reader can quickly find information on any aspect of the business. It should also include the page number of the first page of each section, and all pages in the document should be numbered.

The Executive Summary

An **executive summary** is a clear and concise (abbreviated) form of the entire business plan, generally no more than two or three pages long. After reading the executive summary, a person should understand the business's purpose, value, operating methods, and profitability outlook. An executive summary should contain information about the company's unique competitive advantage and projections for future sales, growth, and profits. If the business plan is to be presented to potential investors, the executive summary should also include a statement regarding the amount of and uses for capital, as well as plans and a timetable for repaying investors.

Ultimately, the executive summary should convey excitement and entice the reader to want to read more. Because this is often the only part of a business plan that is read completely, it is the most critical and, as a result, requires more of your time, thought, and attention than the rest of the business plan. Executive summaries are especially important when presenting your business plan to potential investors. If investors don't get excited about your business and the prospects of success after reading the executive summary, they'll stop reading and most likely file your plan in the trash. Because the executive summary is meant to condense the entire plan into a few pages, many people often write the summary as the last step in the business plan process. Writing your summary after completing the rest of your plan ensures that you've worked out all the kinks and made sure the other sections of the plan are sound.

The Company and Management Team

The next section of the business plan presents the "big picture" and defines the company and its purpose. The company section should include the following elements:

- **The mission and vision statements.** As we discussed in Chapter 7, the *mission and vision statement*s should spell out what the founder ultimately envisions the business to be with respect to growth, values, and contributions to society. They may also offer the company's business strategy that defines the business, identifies the intended customer, and explains how the business will benefit them.

- **Industry profile.** The *industry profile* describes the context in which the business will operate. This section discusses economic trends that affect the business and provides background on the industry, the current outlook for the industry, and a brief discussion of future growth potential.

- **Company profile and strategy.** The *company profile* provides details regarding how the business works and why it has a unique chance to impact the industry. The *company strategy* summarizes the company's plans for growth and profits. It is important to be optimistic while also being realistic in discussing goals and strategy. It is even more important to back up the strategy with details of the company's past and present conditions so that the strategy is convincing.

- **Anticipated challenges and planned responses.** This section discusses potential vulnerabilities from competition, suppliers, resources, industry, or economic situations. It also discusses legal factors that might affect the business—either positively or negatively—including changes to legal restrictions, pending lawsuits, expiring patents, copyrights, and the like. This section should also state possible resources the company could make available should the need arise. Finally, the section should mention any protection from copyrights, trademarks, or patents.

- **The management team.** This section should list the members of the management team—finance, marketing, and production specialists—and the pertinent experience, knowledge, or creative ability that each member brings to the team. If your company is large enough to have a board of directors, those members should be listed in this section as well. Because résumés of key personnel will be attached to the back of the business plan, keep this section brief and dedicate only a paragraph or two to each individual.

A successful business plan weighs both the positive and negative aspects of a business.

Market Analysis

The **market analysis** section identifies who your customers are and explains how you will reach them. The main purpose of this section is to explain the *benefits* of your product. It should answer the question, "What is it about your product that creates a competitive advantage?" For example, your product might be homemade pasta. Your customers might benefit from an authentic Italian taste at a price that is lower than the competition's price. Or, your product could be made with all organic ingredients, which benefits health-conscious consumers. Consumer benefits are those things that do something better for the customer. They affect a person's feelings, pocketbook, or both. The market analysis section should include an assessment of the general market and, more specifically, the competition:

- **Market research.** This section should contain an analysis of the market to determine whether enough customers exist and will continue to exist to make your business profitable now and in the future. First, you need to describe exactly what you see as the target market for your product—that is, identify your customer. For example, is your ideal customer teenagers heading off to college, owners of pets with little time to walk them, or those needing a great meal in a relaxing location? Once you've identified and described your customer, you need to determine whether the market is growing or shrinking. Your analysis should reach the conclusion that the market is big enough for your business to enter with adequate growth potential to make your time and investment worthwhile.

- **Assess the competition.** It is important to show that you have a clear understanding of your competition. Therefore, you should list your main competitors and their perceived strengths and weaknesses. You should then clearly articulate your plan to take advantage of their weaknesses and respond to their strengths.

The Product

In the next section of the business plan, you describe your product and list its important details. Your product's description should include any testing you've conducted and approvals you've received, as well as trademarks, copyrights, or patents to protect your product. It is also important to discuss ongoing service aspects that are provided with the product, such as warranties and repairs. Your business plan should articulate how the product will be produced. If part of your product is dependent on outside suppliers, you should list those suppliers and verify their reliability. If your business is a service, you should discuss how you intend to find and train personnel who will deliver your service.

How will you promote your business? A business plan will help you decide whether to post a flyer on a busy street corner or place an ad in a popular magazine.

Most importantly, whether for a good or a service, this section should cover your pricing strategy. In your pricing discussion, detail any aspects of the product that require a higher price, such as using premium materials. Additionally, you must conduct a thorough analysis of what the competition is charging for a similar product, noting the differences in their product or your product that justify a price differential. Lastly, the section should list what you expect customers will be willing to pay for your product.

Sales and Promotion

The sales and promotion section of the business plan explains how you intend to implement the marketing plan. It should describe the approaches you'll take to promote the product. This should include promotional avenues beyond basic advertising. Include your social media strategy, such as using blogs, Facebook, Twitter, Foursquare, or YouTube, and also how you are monitoring the feedback derived from your social media strategy.

This section should also describe your selling approach. For example, are you selling the product with a sales force, over the Internet, through direct mail, via retail outlets, or simply by word of mouth? By all means, include evidence of promotional success, such as current newspaper articles, customer referrals, or letters of satisfaction.

Financials

This section includes several pages of financial statements: the income statement, the balance sheet, and the cash flow statement. In addition, you should cover the financial history of the company to date and have several different forecasts and scenarios projecting the anticipated performance of the business in the next several years. You should put your financials through a stress test by showing how you expect the business to perform under worst-case, expected-case, and best-case scenarios. If one of the primary purposes of this business plan is to seek outside financing assistance, then another component of this section is a statement of funding requirements indicating information such as the amount of capital needed, the type of funding, the term of loan, and how funds will be used. Investors will also want to see how you intend to pay them back—the timing, the return on investment, and an exit strategy that you might want to suggest to investors.

Don't underestimate the importance of preparing the financial information or be misled into thinking that developing the financial information will or should be easy. This exercise forces you, as a new business owner, to face up to the reality of your business's finances beyond daily cash flow. The numbers need to show that you can be successful in the short term as well as over the long term.

Oddly, more is not better in presenting the financials of a company. More importantly, if you use a software program to generate financials, make sure you understand and can defend and explain every number in every line. It's not uncommon for someone who is reviewing the financials of a business plan to ask very specific questions, such as "What does the figure on line 24 in the income statement mean?" If your answer is, "I'm not sure, the software program generated that number," you are not creating investor confidence in your ability to understand and manage the financial aspects of the business. If necessary, consult an accountant to help you prepare and/or interpret the financial statements and projections included in the business plan.

Including the actual financial statements, forecasts, and scenarios in the business plan is not enough. You need to explain and summarize the key information from those statements and specifically state how they relate to the marketing, sales, and production plans already discussed.

Appendices

The final pages of a business plan should be devoted to appendices. Any additional information that adds to the credibility of your business, the management team, or the industry that is not included in the body of the business plan is included in the appendices. Appendices will include information such as the following:

- Résumés of key managers
- Pictures of the product, facilities, production, and so on
- Letters of recommendations, professional references
- Published information
- Contracts and agreements; copies of patents, copyrights, trademarks
- Media, articles

Writing a business plan can seem like a formidable task. But if you have a clear idea and vision of your business venture, your task will become a little easier. It is also important to know that you're not alone. The SBA and SCORE provide a wealth of information and resources for the potential small business owner.

Remember, your business plan should be exciting, dynamic, and compelling. The plan's purpose is to make others as excited about your business idea as you are. If you carefully follow the steps for writing a business plan and strongly believe in your idea, you may soon have investors beating down your door to be a part of your project.

CHAPTER 7

Business Management and Organization

The Foundations of Management

Xerox Corporation CEO Ursula Burns started her career at Xerox in 1980 as a mechanical engineering intern. What kind of management skills did she display over the years to rise to the top of a multibillion dollar corporation?

Objective 1 What are the levels of management, and what skills do managers need to be successful? (pp. 207–211)

The Functions of Management: Planning

Planning is critical as a business gets off the ground, and every day after that. How does a tattoo artist take his skills forward into a real business? What sequence of planning stages and what tools can he use to accomplish his ultimate goals?

Objective 2 How are the strategic plan, the corporate vision, and the mission statement defined for a business? (pp. 212–214)

Objective 3 Why do managers need tactical plans, operational plans, and contingency plans? (pp. 215–217)

The Functions of Management: Organization

Carrie and Mark have the same position at competing firms, but their day-to-day experiences differ greatly. Why is this?

Objective 4 What is the significance of organizing, and how are most companies organized? (pp. 217–221)

The Functions of Management: Controlling

It all sounded so good. The planned reorganization was going to push the company to the next level of competition. So why was everything such a mess now?

Objective 5 How do managers ensure the business is on track and moving forward? (pp. 222–226)

PEARSON **my**biz**l**ab

Plan for Success

You've recently been hired as a store manager for a retail clothing store. Anxious to prove yourself to your new boss, you dive into the challenges facing the underperforming store. The holiday season is coming, a detailed inventory count is needed, employees are dropping like flies, and you need to market and sell your products. You want to exceed your boss's goals and get your bonus. Are you up to the challenge?

Objective 6 Test yourself using my*biz*lab.com to show that you understand the chapter objectives.

The Foundations of Management pp. 207–211

Ursula Burns, the current CEO of Xerox Corporation, didn't start at the top. Instead, she rose from a position as a mechanical engineering summer intern at Xerox in 1980 to assume the role of chairperson and CEO in 2010. This was a historic event: It was the first time that a female CEO of a major U.S. company, Anne Mulcahy, handed the reins of a company over to another woman. Burns' personal story is dramatically American; she was raised by a single mother in a New York City housing project and now heads a $17 billion company.

It hasn't been all smooth sailing for Burns, however. Xerox Corporation faces serious challenges as business moves increasingly into electronic communication, therefore printing and copying less. But Burns has a track record for pushing forward new products with vision. In 1997, she helped direct Xerox into the field of color copying. Her vision moved Xerox out of manufacturing and diversified the set of products it offers. She is also willing to take the company in entirely new directions. An early move in her reign was the $6.4 billion acquisition of Affiliated Computer Services, leading Xerox into the arena of providing full solutions to business data processing and document management problems. In addition, many note her talent at being able to communicate her understanding of technology to the board of directors and other key members of the management team, an important trait. ■

What makes Ursula Burns such a talented and effective manager? What skills does she possess, and how does she apply them? In this chapter, we'll study what management is and discuss the skills integral to successful management.

Business Management

What exactly is management? Have you ever been in a team situation in which one person has been instrumental in making the group work more effectively? That person could have been a peer or a superior, but somehow he or she knew exactly what had to be accomplished, assessed the resources that were available to achieve the goal, and organized and led other group members to accomplish that goal. If so, you've seen management in action.

Management is the process of working with people and resources to accomplish the goals of an organization. An organization can be a simple working group, a corporate department, or a multibillion-dollar company. The size of the group doesn't matter, but the skills of a manager and the process a manager goes through are similar across all management levels.

What are the four functions of management? As illustrated in ▼ **Figure 7.1**, management involves four primary functions: planning, organizing, leading, and controlling/monitoring. These functions integrate all of a company's resources, including human, financial, and technological. In the remainder of this chapter, we'll examine three of these functions in more detail: planning, organizing,

▼ **Figure 7.1
The Four Functions
of Management**

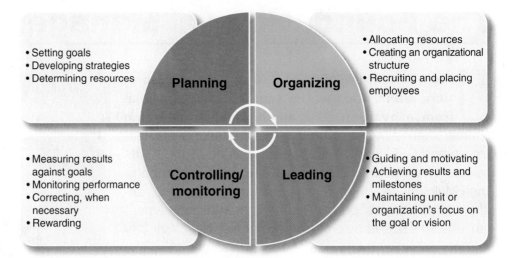

- Setting goals
- Developing strategies
- Determining resources

Planning

Organizing

- Allocating resources
- Creating an organizational structure
- Recruiting and placing employees

- Measuring results against goals
- Monitoring performance
- Correcting, when necessary
- Rewarding

Controlling/ monitoring

Leading

- Guiding and motivating
- Achieving results and milestones
- Maintaining unit or organization's focus on the goal or vision

and controlling/monitoring. In Chapter 8, we'll examine leadership as a function of management.

Levels of Management

What are the different levels of management? The term *manager* is used in common English to describe any position that has employees reporting back to a supervisor. In the study of management, the company's management team has many different levels of managers, with increasing levels of responsibility. ▼ **Figure 7.2** shows a traditional managerial pyramid with examples of jobs held by managers at each level and the tasks they perform.

What do top managers do? At the peak of the pyramid, **top managers** are the corporate officers who are responsible for an organization as a whole. Most established corporations determine the corporate offices, especially the chief executive officer (CEO), or president. Depending on the size and organizational complexity of a company, top management can also include the chief financial of-

---

Are Successful Managers Effective Managers?

Although most people would agree that a manager's responsibilities center on planning, organizing, leading, and monitoring/controlling, what do managers really do? According to a study by Fred Luthans at the University of Nebraska–Lincoln, there are two types of managers: successful managers and effective managers. Successful managers are those who are rapidly and consistently promoted, whereas effective managers are those who "get the job done and do it right." It might seem that to be suc-

cessful, you must be effective, but according to the study, the two types have little in common.

After four years of observation, Luthans determined that "successful" managers—those who were promoted relatively quickly—spent most of their time networking, whereas "effective" managers—those who have satisfied subordinates and high-performing units—spent most of their time using interpersonal skills to communicate with and motivate employees. Interestingly, of the nearly 400 managers tracked, about 10 percent fell into both "successful" and "effective" categories. What does this mean for management today?

For more information and discussion questions about this topic, check out the BizChat feature on my***biz***lab.com

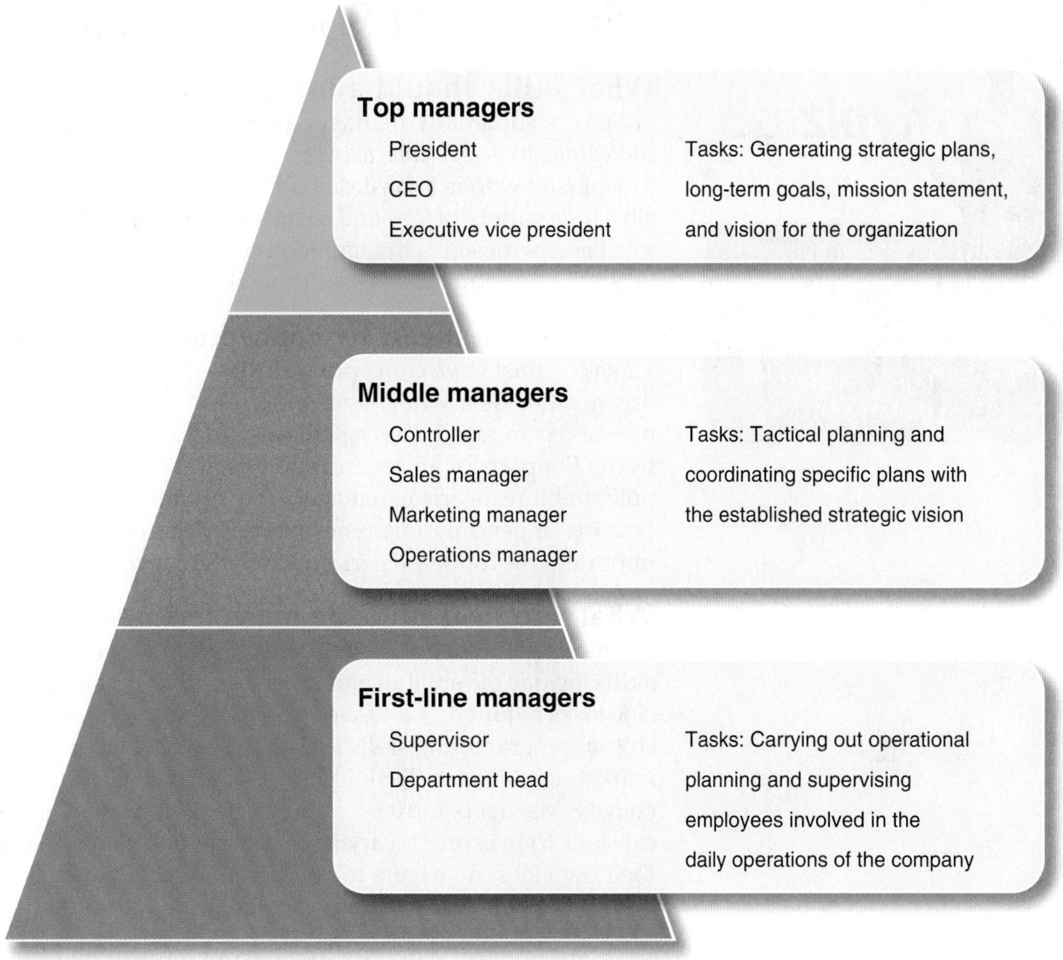

Top managers

President
CEO
Executive vice president

Tasks: Generating strategic plans, long-term goals, mission statement, and vision for the organization

Middle managers

Controller
Sales manager
Marketing manager
Operations manager

Tasks: Tactical planning and coordinating specific plans with the established strategic vision

First-line managers

Supervisor
Department head

Tasks: Carrying out operational planning and supervising employees involved in the daily operations of the company

▼ **Figure 7.2
The Managerial
Pyramid**

ficer (CFO), the chief operations officer (COO), and the chief information officer (CIO). Top managers generate the "big picture" for a company, defining its long-term goals and its vision. Then they create plans that will take a company in that direction. They establish the culture of an organization and inspire employees to adopt senior management's vision of the organization. In smaller corporations, especially small start-up companies, top managers may also be responsible for planning and carrying out the day-to-day tasks of a company. But as the business grows, such companies will need to add more employees and divide the work into smaller tasks and areas of specialty, requiring a new layer of management.

What do middle managers do? Middle managers can be thought of as top managers for one division or a segment of an organization. As such, they are responsible for creating specific plans that coordinate with the strategic vision set by the top managers. Included in this management layer are positions such as division managers (finance, marketing, sales, operations, and IT) or team leaders who are not arranged by function but are responsible for a group of employees who must carry out specific tasks for an organization.

Are the people who supervise the day-to-day operations also managers? The bottom of the managerial pyramid includes **first-line managers.** These managers fill a supervisory role over those employees who carry out the day-to-day operations of a company.

Does every company have all these different managers? Not all companies have all three layers of management; some have more, and some have fewer. Typically you'll find the extra layers are middle managers. However, many businesses are organized along the lines of the managerial pyramid.

The Skills of Successful Managers

What skills should a manager have? Because managerial tasks are so varied, a successful manager needs to possess a variety of skills, including *conceptual, technical, time management, interpersonal,* and *decision-making skills.* It is a rare person who is a master of all these skills. Moreover, because they are responsible for a variety of jobs and because these jobs can change quite rapidly, managers must assess the skills that are required in any given situation. Managers must also be willing to acquire these skills quickly if necessary.

What do we mean by conceptual skills? To make good decisions, a manager must have **conceptual skills**—the ability to think abstractly to picture an organization as a whole and understand its relationship to the remainder of the business community. Such skills also include understanding the relationships between the parts of an organization itself. Whenever new market opportunities or potential threats arise, managers rely on their conceptual skills to help them analyze the impending outcomes of their decisions. Conceptual skills are extremely important for top managers and are often developed with time and experience.

What technical skills do managers need? Every job has a specific set of technical skills that are important for that business's managers to possess. **Technical skills** include the abilities and knowledge that enable employees to carry out the specific tasks required of a discipline or a department, such as drafting skills for an architect, programming skills for a software developer, or market analysis skills for a marketing manager. Technical skills may also include how to operate certain machinery. Managers must be comfortable with technology and possess good analytical skills to interpret a variety of data. In addition to having the skills pertinent to their own jobs, managers must also know how to perform, or at least have a good understanding of, the skills required of the employees they supervise.

What time management skills does it take to succeed as a manager? Managers who possess **time management skills** are able to be effective and productive with their available time. As a manager, how do you do this? Eliminating time wasters, such constant interruptions, setting aside time each day to return phone calls and e-mail, ensuring that meetings have a clear agenda, and successfully delegating work to others, can increase the productive use of your available time. Analyzing your day to track carefully how your time is spent can also be an important key to improving time management.

Why do some people consistently make better decisions than other people? It is critical that managers have good **decision-making skills**—the ability to identify and analyze a challenge, examine the alternatives, choose and implement the best plan of action, and evaluate the results. When making important decisions, managers often go through a formal decision-making process similar to that shown in ▼ **Figure 7.3.** Analyzing data and looking for trends allows a manager to *identify unseen problems or opportunities.* Examples may include poor growth in sales, an increase in customer dissatisfaction, or an opportunity to expand into a new market. Next, managers work with their teams to *generate possible solutions.* They can then *evaluate each potential solution* based on various criteria, such as cost, feasibility, and time and resources needed. Once they have evaluated the potential solutions, managers *select the best plan of action.* At this point, managers

▼ **Figure 7.3 Stages of Decision Making**

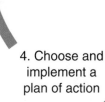

1. Identify problems or opportunities

2. Generate possible solution

3. Evaluate the potential solution

4. Choose and implement a plan of action

5. Evaluate the decision

BizChat

Social Media: How Do Web-Based Tools Make Time Management Easier?

Calendars have traditionally been a tool used by individual people. But with modern social media tools, Web-based calendars can provide for an easy exchange of information and synchronization of schedules. Various Web-based tools are available that allow multiple viewers to add new content to the calendar, thus making the scheduling of meetings more effective. For example, Meeting Wizard is a product that sends out e-mail invitations with a poll of suggested meeting times. It then creates a report for you with the group responses and will send a confirmation e-mail of the final time chosen to all participants. NeedtoMeet is another application that allows you to have the entire group enter their available times on a Web-based calendar. Doodle for iPhone is a mobile version of scheduling software that lets you check out the yes/no votes for suggested meeting times on your phone.

Such tools have proven useful to many managers, but some people argue that Web-based tools can make simple tasks more complicated and can make us actually less productive. What do you think? Do we rely too much on fancy tools to manage our lives and our time?

For more information and discussion questions about this topic, check out the BizChat feature on my**biz**lab.com.

---

may seek customer or market opinion on the chosen plan of action before completely committing to this choice. If market or customer feedback is not positive, management may look to pursue another alternative. When the final choice has been made, plans are established to *implement the plan of action*. Finally, managers *evaluate the results of their decisions*. If changes need to be made, the entire process begins again.

Why are interpersonal skills important for managers? Managers

achieve their goals by working with people both inside and outside an organization, so it is critical that they have strong interpersonal skills. **Interpersonal skills** enable managers to interact with other people to motivate them. It is important that managers develop trust and loyalty with the people they interact with, so they can motivate and encourage employees to work together.

Interpersonal skills are important skills at any management level. Top managers must be able to communicate with the board of directors, investors, and other leaders in the business community. They must also communicate with middle managers to clearly understand the goals and strategies of an organization. Middle managers must communicate with all levels of management and act as liaisons among groups. Lower-level managers must be able to motivate employees, build morale, and train and support those who perform the daily tasks of an organization. As workforce and business relationships continue to become more diverse, it is becoming increasingly important for managers to take into consideration the needs, backgrounds, and experiences of many different people when communicating with individuals and groups in an organization.

Think back to Ursula Burns, the CEO of Xerox Corporation. How did her education equip her with the technical skills she uses to achieve success? Do you think her success reflects strong interpersonal skills? What does the direction she is taking Xerox in say about her decision-making and conceptual skills? How might time management skills come into play in her ability to manage a giant corporation? Clearly, Burns' prominence and success in business demonstrate that a combination of management skills is vital. ■

The Functions of Management: Planning pp. 212–217

William Lee knew his skills as a tattoo artist could lead into his own business if he did the right things. But where does he start? First, he sat down and wrote a vision of why he wanted to start the business and what he hoped to see it add to the world: "To inspire self-expression and creativity through fine arts tattoos." Seeing it written on a page helped solidify some ideas in his mind, even though it seemed like a grandiose statement. Next was the "how"—how could he create a business from this idea? What were his goals for the future? How would he find a space to rent, the money to set up shop, and the expertise to help him run it? What was his competitive advantage over other tattoo artists and how would he communicate it? There was a lot of work ahead. ■

In today's busy world, it is easy to become distracted. Just as William Lee felt when beginning to plan for his business, goals and plans focus our intentions in a way that leads to results. **Planning** is the process of establishing goals and objectives and determining the best ways to accomplish them. **Goals** are broad, long-term accomplishments an organization wants to achieve within a certain time frame—in most companies, this is about five years. **Objectives** are the short-term targets that are designed to help achieve these goals. Planning happens at all levels of an organization. In this section, we'll discuss the different levels of planning that occur in an organization. We'll start by looking at strategic planning.

Strategic Planning

What is the highest level of planning in an organization? A **strategic plan** is the main course of action created by top-level managers that sets the approach for achieving the long-term goals and objectives of an organization. Simply put, a strategic plan points an organization to where it wants to be in the future and identifies how it will get there. It helps to answer three questions: "Where are we going?"; "What do we want to focus on?"; and "What is the best means to get there?" To be effective, a strategic plan should be realistic and obtainable and look at the big picture. Although individual goals sometimes contribute to the plan, the overall strategic plan is focused on an entire organization or an entire department.

Consider the strategic plan development in 2010 for the Wikimedia Foundation (WMF). WMF supports the online collaborative encyclopedia Wikipedia, as well as nine other projects with a common goal (Wikibooks, Wikiquotes, Wikiversity, etc.). The long-term goal of the organization is as follows: "Imagine a world in which every single human being can freely share in the sum of all knowledge. That's our commitment."[1]

In 2009, WMF began to modify its strategic plan for the period 2010 to 2015. It began by assessing where WMF stood in achieving its vision. The organization found

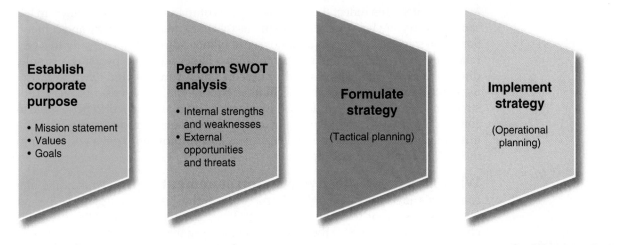

▼ **Figure 7.4**
The Strategic
Planning Process

that only about 15 percent of the world was using Wikimedia products. For example, even in the United States, only about one-third of online users had ever accessed a Wikimedia product. Next the organization examined the challenges in achieving its vision. One problem was that participation and contributions to WMF projects had begun to decline—in fact, over 50 percent of the content was coming from about 1 percent of the contributors. In addition, the organization wanted to enhance the ability of the WMF community to think strategically, with long-term focus on achieving WMF's vision.

To develop a plan that could address these problems and challenges, WMF relied on engagement from their community of contributors and asked for proposals. Every submission was available for the entire WMF community to view and comment on. Together the community created goals and decided how to achieve these through specific actions. The process is ongoing but has the unique feature of being conducted primarily online, appropriate for the tech-savvy WMF community.

How is a strategic plan developed? A good strategic plan reflects what is going on inside and outside an organization and how those conditions and changes will affect an organization in the future. Those making strategic plans must pay attention to the capabilities and resources of an organization, as well as changes in the environment. There are several steps to the process of developing a strategic plan, as shown in ▼ **Figure 7.4.**

Vision and Mission Statement

What helps define the direction of a business? The first step in creating a strategic plan is to establish a corporate purpose through a clearly defined *vision*. A **vision** identifies what the business wants to be in the future. For example, the vision statement for GE under the former CEO Jack Welch read as follows: "To become the most competitive enterprise in the world by being number one or number two in every business in which we compete."[2] The vision should be made clear to all employees and people investing in a company.

What is the difference between a vision and a mission statement? People often confuse the vision of a company with its mission statement. The vision statement sets the long-term objective of a company and tells where the company is headed. A **mission statement** is a more current description of an organization's purpose, basic goals, and philosophies. A mission statement not only helps management remain focused but also lets employees understand the core values of the company for which they work.

Mission statements reflect the personality of a company, so even companies in the same industry can have mission statements that vary greatly in design and content. Some use scientific jargon in a no-nonsense manner directed specifically to a certain target audience. Others may try to reach a larger audience by using a simple, direct statement that inspires the average consumer. You may find that a company uses its mission statement to highlight its environmental awareness or to set an abstract goal for the firm's employees, like working to make the world better able to communicate. Other companies may only discuss their own business goals. The mission statement is a chance for consumers and employees to get a window into the central values of the company.

What makes an effective mission statement? An understanding of a company's mission can help fuel employee enthusiasm. If employees feel an owner's passion for the business through the mission statement, their goals and objectives as employees of the business are incorporated into their daily work and passed onto customers and suppliers through their words and actions. This clarity tends to strengthen a company's position. Even simple mission statements have the power to say a lot about a company and can be very effective if they are written clearly and convincingly.

What are some benefits of well-defined vision and mission statements? The vision and mission statements are important to help keep management on track, help inspire employees working for an organization, and indicate to investors or consumers what type of organization they are investing in. They also provide a guide for management as they evaluate alternative plans and strategies to ensure they are consistent with an organization's current and future direction.

Are mission statements tied to profits? Mission statements are not only for for-profit companies. The mission statement of not-for-profit organizations are focused on outreach to the community or a specific public service rather than on investor return. For example, the American Cancer Society's mission statement is as follows: "The American Cancer Society is the nationwide, community-based, voluntary health organization dedicated to eliminating cancer as a major health problem by preventing cancer, saving lives, and diminishing suffering from cancer, through research, education, advocacy, and service."[3] This statement reflects the organization's commitment to serving the community.

How can I find a company's vision and mission statements? Both the vision and mission statements are usually found on an organization's Web site. However, because the mission statement is directed toward customers—unlike the vision, which is directed toward employees—the mission statement is often used alone on advertising materials or on the actual product.

SWOT Analysis

How does the management team begin to move a company toward achieving its vision? Once a company's vision and mission statements have been articulated, management must assess the company's own strengths and weaknesses as well as its position among its competitors. In addition, management must assess what changes are anticipated to occur and determine whether the company is poised appropriately to respond to such changes. This analysis of strengths, weaknesses, and anticipated changes is called a **SWOT analysis** and helps determine the strategic fit between an organization's internal, distinctive capabilities and external possibilities relative to the business and economic environments.

What does SWOT stand for? SWOT stands for **S**trengths, **W**eaknesses, **O**pportunities, and **T**hreats. ▼ **Figure 7.5** gives a brief explanation of each quadrants of the SWOT analysis. In evaluating a company's internal *strengths* and

SWOT Analysis

Internal Strengths
Potential internal assets that give a company a competitive advantage
Examples for Walmart:
- Powerful brand
- Reputation for value, convenience
- Wide range of products in one store

Internal Weaknesses
Lack of internal capability or expertise compared to the competition
Examples for Walmart:
- Not as flexible as competitors who sell just one type of product (clothing)
- Global but still in only a few countries

External Opportunities
Foreseeable external changes that could favorably affect a company's competitive capability
Examples for Walmart:
- Expand to new locations and new types of stores
- Take over or form alliances with other global retailers in Europe or China

External Threats
External conditions that could negatively affect a company's competitive capability
Examples for Walmart:
- Intense price competition increasing
- Global retail exposes Walmart to political problems in the countries where it operates
- Being Number 1 makes Walmart the target of competition

▼ **Figure 7.5**
SWOT Analysis

weaknesses, management must analyze a company's internal resources, including such elements as its financial health; the strengths of its employees; and its marketing, operations, and technological resources. For example, a company's strength might be its strong marketing department, but its weakness could be an unfavorable location.

To evaluate a company's external *threats* and *opportunities*, management should assess various external elements, such as economic, political, and regulatory environments as well as social, demographic, macroeconomic, and technological factors that could affect the company and industry. It also must perform analyses on the state of the industry and market as well as the company's competitors. For example, a recession could threaten an alternative energy company, whereas increasing awareness of global warming may provide greater opportunity for market growth.

What happens after a SWOT analysis? After conducting a complete SWOT analysis, managers establish a set of goals and objectives. In defining exactly what a specific goal is, it is best to make sure clear deadlines are specified and measureable outcomes are included. The acronym SMARTER is helpful when designing and wording goals and objectives. Goals should be **S**pecific, **M**easurable, **A**cceptable (to those working to achieve the goals), **R**ealistic, **T**imely, **E**xtending (the capabilities of those working to achieve the goals), and **R**ewarding to the employees as well.[4]

Tactical and Operational Planning

How does management decide how to execute a strategic plan?
The next part of the process of creating a strategic plan is to have middle management generate *tactical plans* to carry out the goals of a company. **Tactical plans** specifically determine the resources and the actions required to implement particular aspects of a strategic plan. Whereas strategic plans have a long-term focus, tactical plans are made with a one- to three-year horizon in mind. Determining a company's annual budget, for example, is one function of a tactical plan. Let's say one goal of the strategic plan of a paper supply company is to sell more products to large offices on the East Coast. One part of this company's tactical plan might be to determine how much money should be allocated to advertising in that area.

How is a tactical plan translated into instructions for employees?
The specifics of carrying out tactical plans are *operational plans*. In an **operational plan,** first-line managers precisely determine the process by which tactical plans can be achieved. Operational plans depend on daily or weekly schedules and focus on specific departments or employees. For example, once the paper supply company determines how much of its budget can be allocated to advertising, specific department managers might have to determine which employees will travel to advertise the product.

Contingency Planning

What if unforeseen events occur? Tactical and operational planning are two methods that companies use to carry out plans. Sometimes, however, extreme circumstances occur that force a company to find alternative means to survive. We have seen all too frequently the effects that natural disasters can have on businesses. For example, two months after Hurricane Katrina, the Bureau of Labor Statistics reported the overall job loss in New Orleans and adjacent areas to be approximately 35,000; many businesses were devastated.[5]

We have also seen companies quickly fall into disfavor due to unexpected failures in product quality, such as the lead paint found on Mattel toys that resulted in millions of toys being recalled. All the best corporate strategies can be negated quickly if an unexpected crisis occurs and a plan is not in place to deal with it adequately. What happens if a company suddenly has more sales than production can handle, or if the best-selling product is recalled due to a defect? Who would run the company if the CEO or the company owner unexpectedly died? How should a company fight off an unpredictable takeover threat from a competitor or a rapidly spreading computer virus that threatens to shut down all internal and external lines of communication?

How can planning help companies weather unexpected events?
Contingency planning is a set of plans that ensures that an organization will run as smoothly as possible during an unexpected disruption. Such planning encompasses how management will communicate, both internally and externally. Internally, management must inform its employees how they should continue to do their jobs. Externally, an organization must have a plan in place to deal with requests for information either from employees, the families of employees, or even the media. Contingency planning involves determining what departments within a company are vital to the immediate needs of the organization when an unexpected crisis occurs. The particulars of each plan differ depending on the size and function of a company and the magnitude of crisis for which the plan is needed.

For example, the Vanguard Group, an investment management company, has in place specific, formal business contingency plans to respond to a range of incidents—from worst-case scenarios, such as the loss of a data center, buildings, or staff, to more common occurrences, such as power outages.[6] As important as it is to have plans in place, it is just as important to ensure the plans are tested and that key individuals know exactly what is expected of them. Similar to fire drills in school, companies should periodically review and rehearse their plans. Vanguard officials put their contingency plans through rigorous testing, including full-scale practice drills in which the company closes a building and works from a remote location. The company also conducts mock disaster drills together with local, state, and federal authorities. Because Vanguard's business would be impacted significantly should a disruption in any of its technical systems occur, it also conducts tests to determine how quickly its IT systems can become operational in the event of a disruption. ▼ **Figure 7.6** summarizes the types of plans that companies such as Vanguard use to carry out their goals.

The Four Types of Management Plans

Strategic Plan
- **Generated by top management**
- Sets the approach for achieving an organization's long-term goals and objectives
- Acts as a framework for decisions
- Assists in setting corporate benchmarks

Tactical Plan
- **Generated by middle management**
- Determines resources and actions necessary to implement strategic plan
- Made with a one- to three-year horizon in mind

Operational Plan
- **Generated by first-line managers**
- Involves planning the execution of the tactical plan
- Depends on daily or weekly schedules
- Focuses on specific departments or employees

Contingency Plan
- **Generated by middle management**
- Keeps an organization running in the event of a disruption
- Details internal and external communication procedures for such an event
- Determines which departments are most vital to an organization during a crisis

▼ **Figure 7.6
The Four Types of
Management Plans**

Now that a few years have passed, William Lee smiles when he thinks of the early planning of his business. There have been hundreds of decisions along the way to opening the tattoo shop he now owns. At many points, he needed to think tactically and conduct a full SWOT analysis to determine where his strengths and weaknesses were so he could set the long-term and short-term goals. He also has contingency plans in place if he runs into problems in the future. "You never know what the future will bring," he says, "but you know if you don't plan you won't win." ■

The Functions of Management: Organizing pp. 217–222

Carrie Witt and Mark Healy have a lot in common: They both graduated with degrees in business, and they both acquired jobs as marketing associates at medium-sized firms that design solar energy panels for commercial use. Nevertheless, their professional experiences have been markedly different. At her firm, Carrie is part of the marketing department. She is training to become an expert in getting new clients within a specific region of the state. She reports directly to the department head, but her work is also overseen by several middle managers, including the marketing department supervisor and the marketing manager. They, in turn, take their orders from top managers: the executive vice president, the CEO, and the president. At his firm, Mark works on a team with individuals from a variety of areas, including marketing, R&D, finance, and operations. They work on a variety of projects as a comprehensive unit. One manager supervises his team and coordinates the team's efforts directly with the goals and instructions from the firm's CEO and president. ■

Carrie and Mark's jobs seem similar, yet their everyday experiences contrast significantly. Why is this? It's all about organization. Which organizational structure does Carrie's firm implement? Which one does Mark's firm use? Why are these structures necessary, and what are the benefits of each? Every company, regardless of its size or specialty, needs a solid organizational structure. Without one, employees may have trouble making decisions and assigning responsibility. But this doesn't mean there's just one way to organize a company. In this section, we'll explore different aspects of organization.

Organizational Structures

How do managers put their plans into action? Once goals have been finalized and plans have been made, the next step in the management process is to put those plans into action. **Organizing** is the process of structuring the capital, personnel, raw materials, and other resources to carry out a company's plans in a way that best matches the nature of the work. Part of organizing is to establish an organizational structure. Organizational structure depends on a variety of factors, such as the number of employees in the organization, the speed at which decisions need to be made, the subjectivity of the business to rapid change, and the collaborative nature of the work.

How do companies document the structure of an organization? Smaller companies with relatively few employees tend to be organized differently than large corporations. Small companies tend to have much simpler structures compared with large companies. Regardless, to accomplish many tasks at the same time, organizations must have some division of labor and allocate work into smaller units. An **organizational chart,** like that shown in ▼ **Figure 7.7,** shows how groups of employees fit into the larger organizational structure.

How is power distributed in an organization? There are two common approaches: either (1) the power belongs to a few, and most people are in positions where they obey a supervisor, or (2) power is distributed among many. The first approach is called a **vertical organization** (or a *tall organization*) with few people in power and many following. In a vertical organization, power is centralized with a small controlling group. The organizational chart tends to have long vertical columns showing which positions report to which managers.

▼ **Figure 7.7**
Organizational Chart
An organizational chart is used to display the division of labor and the organizational structure within a company.

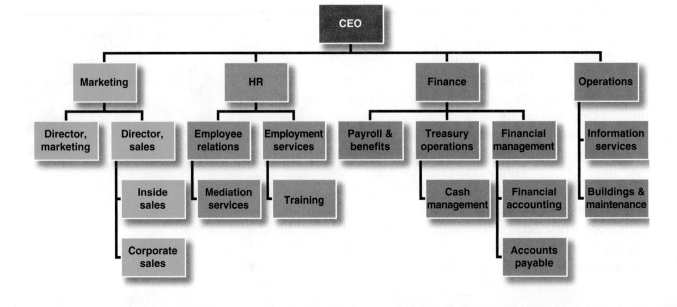

The second approach is called a **horizontal organization** (or a *flat organization*). In a horizontal organization, the traditional managerial pyramid is flattened, and the management layers are collapsed. Decision control is decentralized and spread out across many more people than in a traditional hierarchical structure. A horizontally structured organization still has some of the pyramidal aspects, including a CEO and perhaps another layer of middle management, but then the organization concentrates the majority of the remaining employees into working teams or groups. Here the organization chart would be flat and wide because there are many people with authority and fewer people in positions of direct control. ▼ **Figure 7.8** illustrates the basic differences in organizational charts of a vertically structured organization and a horizontally structured organization.

What are the pros and cons of vertical organization? In a vertical organization, a company is organized by specific functions, such as marketing, finance, purchasing, IT, and human resources. In such structures, levels of expertise within functions are developed, and managers have direct authority and reporting responsibility for their area. Potential problems may arise, however, because integration between functions and divisions is not always easy. Vertical organization usually calls for long lines of communication and "reporting up." This makes it difficult for a company to respond quickly to changes in a market or provide new innovation because keeping each division updated means spending time doing so.

Vertical organization has been the primary structure of business since the Industrial Revolution. This traditional pyramidal management has its benefits because there is ultimately one person in charge and a clear point of authority for decisions. However, in the early 1990s, vertical organizational structures were criticized as being overspecialized, fragmented, and inflexible. Some businesses, such as Ford Motor Company, Xerox Corporation, and Barclay's Bank, found that they were more successful when they organized differently and formed management groups around areas of specific production.[7]

▼ **Figure 7.8
Vertically and
Horizontally
Structured
Organizations**

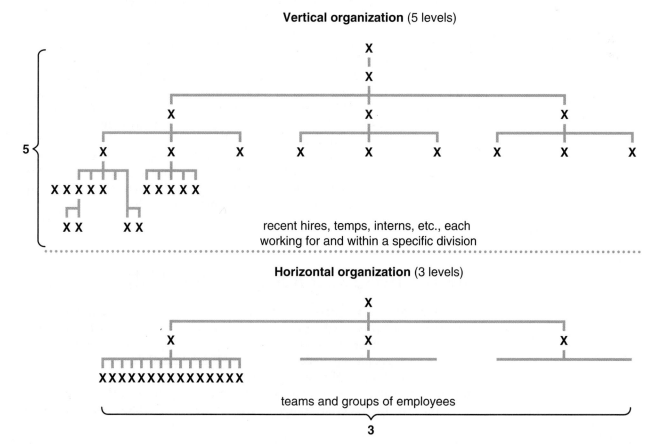

Vertical organization (5 levels)

recent hires, temps, interns, etc., each working for and within a specific division

Horizontal organization (3 levels)

teams and groups of employees

What are the pros and cons of horizontal organization? The benefit of a horizontal organization is that each team has more responsibility for the outcome of its work. There is less of a sense of competition for power and more of a push toward collaborative work. Each employee is empowered to have more responsibility and contribute more directly to the company. There are fewer layers of management, so fewer reporting issues arise, and, if needed, the bosses' approval can be sought and received much faster. The company can be more responsive because individuals in a horizontal organization are more empowered to make decisions. Horizontal structures have been deemed the "model for the knowledge age." Now everyone has equal access to information, which many argue makes the horizontal structure more effective. They are suitable for industries that require rapid responses to quick changes.

Changing Structures

Does a company's organizational structure ever change? Occasionally, when companies have grown so large that there are a variety of product lines, geographic regions, or manufacturing processes that can be difficult to manage, they restructure from a vertical organization to a horizontal one. In these situations, managers often try to streamline functions to make management easier. For example, they might structure the organization into divisions of employees who work on just one product line. Or they might divide a company into teams to specialize in one geographic region or work through one manufacturing process.

In essence, these divisions work like separate mini-companies. Each division has its own set of functional expertise, so separate managers are in charge of finance, marketing, human resources, IT, and so on. The groups work autonomously and are highly differentiated—so much so that they create barriers to coordination across functions. In today's business environment, there are fewer and fewer organizations structured vertically by function.

One company that made the shift from being a vertical organization to a horizontal one is the Xerox Corporation. It was once arranged in a traditional vertical structure, organized by function, such as R&D, manufacturing, and sales. To allow the business to become closer to the customer, the company realigned itself in the early 1990s around individual business markets, such as small businesses, office document systems, and engineering systems. Each individual group had its own set of financial reports, and factories were focused on individual product lines. "We've given everyone in the company a direct line of sight to the customer," says Paul Allaire, the CEO at the time of the restructuring.[8] Today, the company continues to maintain a flat organizational structure organized by product category, as well as by region, to take into account the company's global presence.

Alternative Organizational Structures

What is a matrix organization? In vertical organizations, employees are grouped together based on their function—all accountants are in one department, all engineers in another, and so on. A **matrix organization** is type of management system in which people are pooled into groups by skills and then assigned to projects as needed. So an employee might answer to the engineering supervisor but suddenly be assigned to a critical project and become accountable to a project manager as well. The matrix organization is useful when the business is project based because it promotes resource sharing. The shared authority and responsibility can mean better coordination between management and lead to better project results. However, having two bosses can create conflicts, so the matrix style is useful only in specific settings.

What is an inverted organization? The traditional vertical hierarchy can

be mated with another structure that is quite different, the **inverted organization.** In this structure, management is answerable to employees. The role of management in an inverted organization is to enable, encourage, and empower employees to do what they do best. Empowered employees can make decisions on the ground without the delay of forwarding requests upward through layers of management. Most firms end up implementing inverted structure along with the traditional vertical structure. So although employees still have supervisors and supervisors answer to managers, managers are equally accountable to their employees. The rationale for this approach is that the core business of the company is to create value. The value creators in the company are the front line employees. So management contributes to the company's success by empowering the employees, putting employees first.[9]

One company that has grown with this philosophy is HTC Technologies, a provider of IT services. Founded by Vineet Nayar, HTC introduced inverted organization in 2005 and saw growth of over 20 percent per year between 2005 and 2010, during a worldwide recession. HTC tripled annual revenues and is ranked as India's best employer. "How did I do this?" asks Nayar. "I didn't. The people of our company accomplished the transformation. How did I persuade them to do it? I spoke the truth as I saw it, offered ideas, told stories, asked questions, and even danced." Nayar wrote a book documenting the experience, entitled *Employees First, Customers Second* (Harvard Business Press, 2010). The result of taking care of employees was that customers were more satisfied and received better services and products.[10] Many other companies, such as Southwest Airlines, have employed elements of the inverted organization.

What organization works across multiple companies? Although

the majority of companies are structured with the more traditional vertical structure or the group-oriented horizontal structure, another new business structure is emerging. Instead of the customary means of producing a product or a service in which one company is responsible for all functions, **network organizations** are collections of **independent,** mostly single-function firms that collaborate on a product or a service. For example, Boeing recently completed production of its latest airplane, the Boeing 787. In the past, airplanes were assembled in one hangar. This time, however, Boeing relied on the expertise of hundreds of manufacturers worldwide to independently manufacture the components of the plane and ship the individual pieces for assembly in its main plant. The wings and landing gear are assembled in Italy, and the nose and cockpit are assembled in Wichita, Kansas. Individual or combined elements are then shipped to Everett, Washington, where they are finally assembled into a single 787 plane.

In addition to Boeing, other companies are using a network arrangement, including Nike, which owns only one manufacturing plant, and Reebok, which designs and markets but does not produce any of its products. A network structure is not suitable for every company, but it may be successful for those companies that require the following characteristics:

- To be as flexible and innovative as possible
- To respond quickly to threats and opportunities
- To save time
- To reduce costs and risk

Reflect back on Carrie and Mark. Carrie works under the supervision of the marketing department head and several middle managers in the same department, who in turn report to top management. Mark works on a team with people from various departments at his company. Is it clearer now why their experiences were so different despite the seeming similarity between their jobs? Carrie's company is a vertical, or tall, organization. The company is organized around specific business functions, and there are several levels of first-line and middle managers. Mark, on the other hand, works at a horizontal, or flat, organization. There are fewer middle managers, and employees work in groups. How would their work lives change if their companies reorganized to a matrix organizational style? To an inverted organization? ■

The Functions of Management: Controlling pp. 222–226

It wasn't supposed to end like this. Over many months, company executives had worked together to make plans for the reorganization of the company. Matt Finley remembered the excitement of it; everyone knew moving toward a horizontal organizational structure would benefit managers, employees, and customers alike. It felt like great times were ahead. But six months later, sales are down, morale is low, and no one knows quite why. Matt believed in the goals the management team had established. What went wrong? ■

The best-laid plans are meaningless if they aren't put into place effectively. As managers form plans and carry out strategies to meet the goals of an organization, they must also determine whether their plans and strategies are generating the desired results. In this section, we'll look at how managers *control* (or *monitor*) their organizations, and why doing so is so important.

Controlling to Stay on Course

Why does a company need to adapt to stay on course? Controlling (also called **monitoring**) is the process by which managers measure performance and make sure the company's plans and strategies are being or have been properly carried out. Through the control process, managers ensure that the direction a company is moving toward aligns with its short- and long-term plans. The controlling process also can detect errors in systems, so if a plan is not meeting its goals, it can be modified. Chapter 3 discussed the importance of running an ethical organization. Making sure that people are doing what they should and acting appropriately is a primary rationale for instituting control functions in an organization.

Control Strategies

How is performance in moving toward the corporate vision measured? Most companies have control systems that help measure the plans they set in place to carry out the goals and objectives of an organization. In general, the control system forms a cycle, as shown in ▼ **Figure 7.9:** Performance standards are set, and performance is measured and compared against the standard. To measure performance, reporting tools, such as financial statements and sales reports, are used. These reports help determine whether the products are competitive, using capital wisely, and being produced as efficiently as possible. Based on the results, adjustments are made, and the cycle begins again.

Are financial measures the only tools for assessing performance? In addition to meeting financial, production, and sales measures, another measure of performance is quality—the products or services a company provides must meet and exceed customer expectations. Many managers use **total quality management (TQM),** an integrated approach that focuses on quality from the beginning of the production process up through managerial involvement to detect and correct problems.

There are seven basic tools managers use to monitor quality-related goals (an example of each is shown in ▼ **Figure 7.10**):

1. **Check sheet.** A simple sheet recording the number of times certain product defects occur.
2. **Control chart.** A graph that shows the average and fluctuations of a process being monitored to determine whether it is behaving within the limits of proper functioning.
3. **Histogram.** A graph that displays the number of times a specific event occurs (e.g., the number of times the smoothness of a tube produced was in the range 1.2 to 1.3).
4. **Pareto chart.** A combination bar and line graph that shows different categories of problems and the total (cumulative) number of problems.

◉ On Target Pest Control Company Controls Their Fleet

Anchor Pest Control is a small pest control service with a fleet of 15 vans and trucks. When a van is down for repairs, the company experiences a serious loss of income. So keeping the entire fleet in top operating condition, with a minimum of cost and downtime, is an important business goal.[11] Another key goal is customer satisfaction. This includes drivers arriving on time, driving to and from sites carefully, and completing their work in a timely manner. Initially, Anchor owner Don Wolf tried using GPS devices in each van to monitor whether these business goals were being met. But he soon realized these systems would track the vehicles but were not helping him answer the business questions he had: When did each van need to go in for maintenance? How hard was the engine working? Which driver was making the most stops in a day?

Wolf found a monitoring device called CarChip that he could afford to install in each vehicle. By downloading the information from CarChip to a software program, each vehicle can be sent in for maintenance at just the right moment, before it breaks down but not before it is required. CarChip can set a top speed for each vehicle so he knows drivers are being careful on the road. Drivers can also be ranked by safety rating or total miles driven, letting him reward top performers.

As a good manager, Wolf had to know what his goals were for Anchor and then investigate the right products and tools to monitor performance. Using data to check the business's progress toward meeting those goals has helped the company be the most efficient and profitable it can be.

▼ **Figure 7.9
The Monitoring/
Control Cycle**

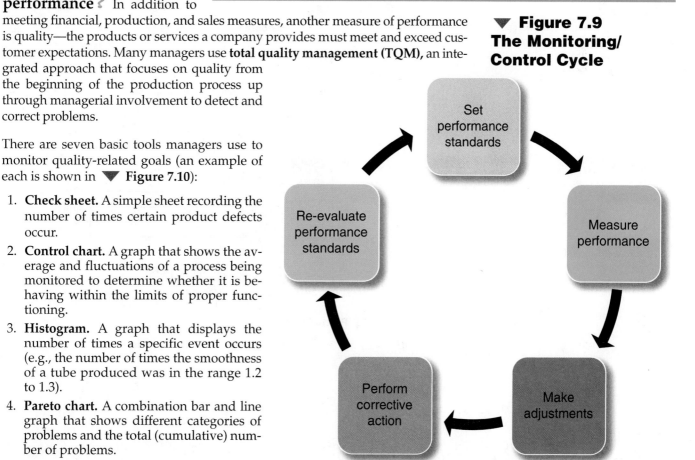

▼ **Figure 7.10**
The Seven Basic
Tools of TQM

Name of Data Recorder: Jigme Patel
Location: Bowie, AZ
Data Collection Dates: 10/1–10/15

Defect Types/ Event Occurrence	Sunday	Monday	Tuesday	Wednesday	Thursday	Friday	Saturday	TOTAL
Overheated		‖‖‖‖	‖‖‖‖	‖‖‖	‖			20
Cooled too long			‖	‖		‖		5
Weak welds								0
Misaligned			‖	‖				3
Broken								0
Discolored		‖		‖‖				6
Spotting					‖			2
Paint defect								0
Irregular shape				‖				1
Inaccurate measurements						‖‖‖		5
TOTAL		10	10	12	4	7		

Check Sheet

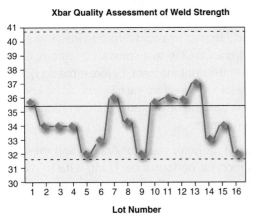

Xbar Quality Assessment of Weld Strength

Control Chart

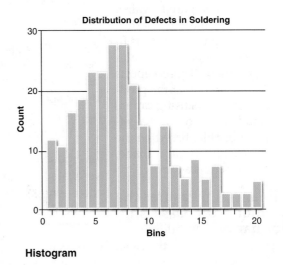

Distribution of Defects in Soldering

Histogram

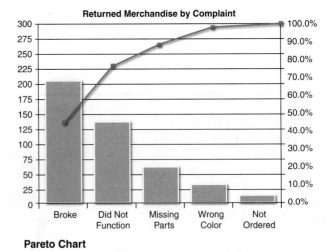

Returned Merchandise by Complaint

Pareto Chart

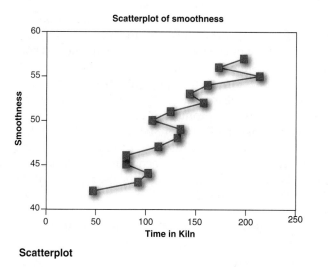

Scatterplot

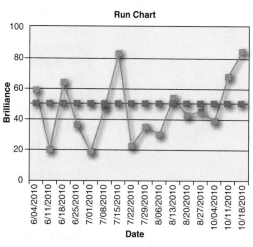

Run Chart

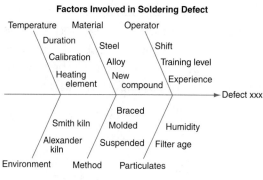

Cause-and-Effect Diagram

5. **Scatter plot.** A graph that displays the values of two variables to see if there is a relationship between the variables. For example, in producing a ballpoint pen, how does the temperature of the plastic injected into the mold affect the amount of time required for the pen to cool before the next step in production?

6. **Run chart.** A graph that displays the value of some data across a specific set of dates. Managers can then identify problems that occur in a certain cycle, for example, once a month the number of defects increases dramatically.

7. **Cause-and-effect diagram.** Also called a *fishbone diagram*, this illustrates all of the contributing factors in the product design that might lead to faulty production. For example, if the defect being analyzed is cracks in the glazing of a vase, the cause and effect diagram would show that contributing factors could be from personnel, materials, or methods. Personnel could be a problem because of differences in training of employees, or perhaps a specific operator is causing defects.

There are many more advanced statistical tools available, but managers often begin their drive toward TQM with these seven basic tools.

Another well-known quality initiative is **Six Sigma,** a statistically based, proactive, long-term process designed to examine the overall business process and prevent problems. To achieve the "Six Sigma standard," a business must not allow more than 3.4 defects per million opportunities. To achieve such levels, it can take years to train and implement a staff that understands the approach. The techniques of Six Sigma produce results that are consistent and repeatable, which translates into very few defects and very consistent high levels of customer satisfaction.

Jack Welch, CEO of General Electric (GE) from 1981 to 2001, was a huge proponent of the Six Sigma method and pushed it into every corner of the company. In those 20 years, he increased revenues at GE by over $100 billion. However, there is controversy around the proper use of Six Sigma monitoring in the business community.[12] For example, Robert Nardelli worked under Jack Welch and left GE to become CEO of Home Depot, where he applied Six Sigma practices with great fervor. Home Depot initially saw great growth in profits, but the huge amount of paperwork and data collection began to take a toll on store workers. It left them less time for customer interaction, causing customer satisfaction to plummet, falling from first to last place in the American Customer Satisfaction Index. The current CEO of Home Depot, Frank Blake, is modifying Six Sigma's approach to allow store managers to make more decisions independently.

The missing piece for Matt Finley's company, which was struggling despite a promising reorganization plan, turned out to be a lack of adequate control. The company began its reorganization with well-designed goals but never chose which tools it would use to monitor the results. Matt recognized this and established a set of procedures so managers could measure both financial progress as well as product quality. He had to bring himself up to speed on some new tools for quality reporting—Pareto charts and cause-and-effect diagrams—but once the processes for collecting and reporting data were in place, the picture became clear. The new organizational structure began working once these important adjustments were made. ■

Chapter Summary

1. What are the levels of management, and what skills do managers need to be successful? (pp. 207–211)

- **Management** (p. 207) is the process of working with people and resources to accomplish the goals of an organization. Management involves four primary functions: **planning** (p. 212), **organizing** (p. 218), **leading**, and **controlling/ monitoring** (p. 222).

- **Top managers** (p. 208) are the corporate officers who are responsible for the organization as a whole. **Middle managers** (p. 209) can be thought of as top managers for one division or a segment of an organization. **First-line managers** (p. 209) fill a supervisory role over those employees who carry out the day-to-day operations of the company.

- Because managerial tasks are so varied, a successful manager needs to possess a variety of skills, including **conceptual** (p. 210), **technical** (p. 210), **time management** (p. 210), **interpersonal** (p. 211), and **decision-making skills** (p. 210).

2. How are the strategic plan, the corporate vision, and the mission statement defined for a business? (pp. 212–214)

- Managers use planning, goals, and objectives to help achieve the corporate vision and stay on task. **Planning** (p. 212) is the process of establishing goals and objectives and determining the best ways to accomplish them. **Goals** (p. 212) are broad, long-term accomplishments an organization wants to achieve in about a five-year time frame. **Objectives** (p. 212) are the short-term targets that are designed to help achieve goals.

- Top managers put together a **strategic plan** (p. 212), or a main course of action, that maps out the means by which the corporation will achieve its goals.

  - Before the strategic plan is in place, management must define the organization's purpose, basic goals, and philosophies through **vision** (p. 213) and **mission statements** (p. 213). The corporate vision is what the business wants to be in the future. A mission statement is a more current description of the organization's purpose, basic goals, and philosophies.

  - Part of the strategic planning process is conducting a **SWOT analysis** (p. 214) to help management determine the strategic fit between an organization's internal capabilities and external possibilities. The SWOT analysis stands for strengths, weaknesses, opportunities, and threats.

3. Why do managers need tactical plans, operational plans, and contingency plans? (pp. 215–217)

- **Tactical plans** (p. 215) specifically determine the resources and the actions required to implement particular aspects of a strategic plan. Tactical plans are made with a one- to three-year horizon in mind and are determined by middle management.

- **Operational plans** (p. 216) determine the process by which tactical plans can be achieved. Operational plans depend on daily or weekly schedules and focus more on specific departments or employees. Operational plans are determined by first-line managers.

- **Contingency planning** (p. 216) is a set of plans that ensures that an organization will run as smoothly as possible during a disruption and determines how management will communicate, both internally and externally.

4. What is the significance of organizing, and how are most companies organized? (pp. 217–221)

- **Organizing** (p. 218) is the process of structuring the capital, personnel, raw materials, and other resources to carry out a company's plans in a way that best matches the nature of the work. An **organizational chart** (p. 218) shows how groups of employees fit into the larger organizational structure.

- A **vertical organization** (p. 218) is organized by specific functions, such as marketing, finance, purchasing, IT, and human resources. Managers can better keep track of economic and environmental conditions that affect their functional area. However, potential problems may arise because integration between functions and divisions is not always easy. Vertical organization usually calls for long lines of communication and "reporting up."

Continued on next page

- A **horizontal organization** (p. 219) is flattened, and the management layer is collapsed. This type of organization concentrates the majority of employees into working teams or groups. Teams have more responsibility for the outcome of their work. Bosses' approval can be sought and received much faster.

- **Matrix organization** is type of management system in which people are pooled into groups by skills and then assigned to projects as needed.

- **Network organizations** (p. 221) are collections of independent, mostly single-function firms that collaborate on a product or a service.

- In an **inverted organization** (p. 221), management is answerable to employees, and management's role is to empower and encourage employees to do what they do best.

5. How do managers ensure the business is on track and moving forward? (pp. 222–226)

- **Controlling** (also called **monitoring**; p. 222) is the process by which managers measure performance and make sure a company's plans and strategies are being or have been properly carried out.

- Performance standards are measured with reporting tools, such as financial statements and sales reports. Quality measures are also in place to ensure that products or services meet customer requirements. **Total Quality Management** (TQM; p. 223) focuses on quality control throughout the entire production process. Basic mathematical and graphical tools, such as scatterplots and Pareto charts, are used to monitor quality goals.

Key Terms

conceptual skills   (p. 210)

contingency planning   (p. 216)

controlling (or monitoring)   (p. 222)

decision-making skills   (p. 210)

first-line manager   (p. 209)

goal   (p. 212)

horizontal organization   (p. 219)

independent   (p. 221)

interpersonal skills   (p. 211)

inverted organization   (p. 221)

management   (p. 207)

management skills   (p. 210)

matrix organization   (p. 220)

middle managers   (p. 209)

mission statement   (p. 213)

network organization   (p. 221)

objective   (p. 212)

operational plan   (p. 216)

organizational chart   (p. 218)

organizing   (p. 218)

planning   (p. 212)

Six Sigma   (p. 225)

strategic plan   (p. 212)

SWOT analysis   (p. 214)

tactical plans   (p. 215)

technical skills   (p. 210)

time management skills   (p. 210)

top managers   (p. 208)

total quality management (TQM)   (p. 223)

vertical organization   (p. 218)

vision   (p. 213)

Self-Test

Multiple Choice   You can find the answers on the last page of this book.

1. The four primary processes of management are

   a. planning, optimizing, leading, and controlling.

   b. organizing, controlling, planning, and leading.

   c. prioritizing, leading, controlling, and organizing.

   d. planning, leading, organizing, and deciding.

2. In business terms, a(n) _____ is a broad, long-range accomplishment, and a(n) _____ is a specific, short-term target.

   a. Goal; objective

   b. Objective; goal

   c. Objective; task

   d. Task; goal

3. Julius knows how to identify the key problems on a project, examine alternatives, and implement a plan of action. His last performance review mentioned this when it read as follows:

   a. "Julius shows very polished interpersonal skills."

   b. "Julius has demonstrated excellent decision-making skills."

   c. "Julius exhibits advanced conceptual skills."

   d. "Julius has marketable skills that contribute to a project's success."

4. The organization you work for just hired a new CEO. Within the first week in her new position, the CEO drafted a memo for the board and members of senior management that defined the purpose of the business, as well as the basic goals and philosophies of the business. This document serves as a draft of a new

   a. vision.

   b. mission statement.

   c. goals and objectives statement.

   d. tactical plan.

5. A good strategic plan

   a. determines the best ways to accomplish goals of an organization.

   b. is specific and tactical.

   c. concentrates only on what is going on inside an organization, not outside an organization.

   d. is wide ranging.

6. Which organizational structure describes a business in which management is responsible to the employees?

   a. Horizontal organization

   b. Vertical organization

   c. Network organization

   d. Inverted organization

7. A horizontal organization requires

   a. more use of collaborative teams.

   b. a strict chain of command.

   c. a tall organization chart.

   d. None of the above

8. The seven basic tools for monitoring a business include all of the following except

   a. Pareto analysis.

   b. Monte Carlo statistical simulations.

   c. scatterplots.

   d. cause-and-effect diagrams.

9. Shauna is the sales manager for a regional chain of bookstores. Shauna reports to the executive vice president of sales and marketing, and each sales manager reports to Shauna. Shauna would be considered a

   a. top manager.

   b. middle manager.

   c. first-line manager.

   d. Both b and c

10. Which would *not* be something that might describe a company's organizational structure?

    a. Vertical

    b. Inverted

    c. Network

    d. Spiral

Self-Test

1. A company with a vertical organization cannot use an inverted organization.
   ☐ **True** or ☐ **False**

2. A SWOT analysis is used to determine the strategic fit between an organization and its internal and external environments.
   ☐ **True** or ☐ **False**

3. When a company is organized primarily in teams or groups, it is considered a vertical organization.
   ☐ **True** or ☐ **False**

4. Every manager has responsibility for planning, organizing, leading, and controlling.
   ☐ **True** or ☐ **False**

5. A mission statement is different from the statement of corporate vision because it sets the long-term objectives of the company.
   ☐ **True** or ☐ **False**

Critical Thinking Questions

1. Recall your own personal working experiences and the managers with whom you have had interaction. Discuss the skills that define the best manager with whom you have worked and discuss the skills that define the worst manager with whom you have worked.

2. Contingency plans are important in any business. Discuss what kinds of plans your school might have in place. How would these plans differ, if at all, from those of a local business in your area? What are a few possible scenarios that would require contingency plans in your school or at a local business?

3. How do you rank leadership qualities? Rank the following qualities and compare your results with your classmates: honest, loyal, competent, caring, determined, ambitious, inspiring, forward looking, self-confident, and imaginative. What are the top three qualities?

4. Analyze your own ability to be a manager. What skills do you have now that are already polished? What skills would you need to improve? What skills would you still need to acquire? How could you go about acquiring or improving those skills you do not have?

5. How does the complexity of a project impact quality control? As software projects grow to have many millions of lines of code, can that industry still achieve Six Sigma quality? What kind of tools and processes would it require?

Team Time

On a Mission

Research and print out several mission statements. Be sure to choose statements from both not-for-profit organizations and for-profit organizations. Bring these mission statements to class.

Process

Step 1. Assemble into groups of four or five.

Step 2. As a group, evaluate the mission statements you've chosen for similar components, such as a statement of the product, the service, or the primary market; an indication of commitment to quality; an indication of a commitment to social responsibility; and a declaration of corporate philosophy.

Step 3. Make notes of the components that are included in the majority of mission statements and those that are included in only a few mission statements.

Step 4. As a group, decide which mission statement is the most inspiring. Why? Which is the least inspiring? Why?

Step 5. As a class, compare the statements deemed most inspiring from each group and determine which is the most effective. Finally, openly discuss with your classmates how the winning statement would affect their inclination to work for this organization.

Ethics and Corporate Social Responsibility

Assessing Social Responsibility

One of the functions of management is control, which includes measuring financial performance. But how often and with what tools does a manager assess an organization's social responsibility?

Process

Step 1. As a class, in small discussion groups, discuss the following:

→ the planning and organizational changes that might need to be implemented

→ the controls that a manager might use to measure and monitor the results of his or her social responsibility initiatives

Step 2. After this discussion, research companies that are known for their social responsibility efforts. Then discuss what impact their efforts have had on management.

Web Exercises

1. **Employees First**
Research on the Internet for a company that has implemented an inverted organization by emphasizing "Employees First." Is this reflected in the company's mission statement? Does it seem to be improving the company's performance? How has this message changed customer relationships?

2. **Organizational Charts: The Big Picture**
Look on the Internet for a company's organization chart, an organization chart for the company you work for, or the organizational chart for your school. Analyze the chart and determine whether the company or school is structured vertically or horizontally. Can you find an organizational chart for a competitor? Critique both organizational charts. Are the two company's organizational charts similar? Do you think your company or school could be structured in any other way? Why or why not?

3. **How Well Do You Manage Your Time?**
Time management skills are important for a manager to have to work efficiently and accomplish all the tasks a manager is expected to handle on any given day. How are your time management skills? Even as a student, you are your own manager and can benefit from being more in control of your time. Find a quiz online that assesses your ability to manage your time. Write a brief report answering the following questions:

- What online assessment did you find?
- What were the results?
- How can you improve your time management skills?

4. **Predictably Irrational**
Visit the Ted.com Web site and search for the 20-minute video "Are We in Control of Our Own Decisions" by Dan Ariely, a behavioral economist. Watch the video. Concentrate on the example of the doctor and the patient. Are there business decisions that managers make where factors outside their decision-making process influence the outcome?

5. **Get SMARTER**
The acronym SMARTER reminds us that goals should be specific, measurable, acceptable, realistic, timely, extending, and rewarding. Using the resources at rapidbi.com/created/WriteSMARTobjectives.html, create two goals for yourself for next semester. Document how they are SMARTER goals.

Web Case

For more on the correlation between corporate culture and business success, access the Chapter 7 Web case entitled "Focus on Toyota: The Toyota Way of Management" located in the End of Chapter Assignments section at *mybiz*lab.com.

Video Case

For more on the organizational changes necessary for successful expansion, access the Chapter 7 Video Case entitled "Nantucket Nectars: The Juice Guys on Organizing" located in the End of Chapter Assignments section at *mybiz*lab.com.

Motivation, Leadership, and Teamwork

Motivation

At Ana Gutierrez's public relations firm, employees were suffering from a severe case of demotivation. Translating motivational theories into practical applications is a challenge many business managers face. How can Ana use abstract concepts about human behavior to inspire her workforce and turn around her struggling company?

Objective 1 How do motivation and work environment encourage "flow"? (p. 235)

Objective 2 What are the main theories of motivation, and how are they applied to the workforce? (pp. 237–241)

Objective 3 How have motivational theories and industrial psychology changed the work environment since the early twentieth century? (pp. 241–243)

Leadership

Sausage had been the family business for generations. Ralph Stayer, CEO of Johnsonville Sausage, knew the company could be doing better. What kind of leader did he need to be to take the company to new levels of success?

Objective 4 What are the various identifiable leadership styles and traits, and how do they affect business leadership? (pp. 243–249)

Teamwork

Teamwork can bring about great success in business. This was the case with the development of the Motorola Razr. But effective teams must be created and managed thoughtfully for businesses to reap the benefits. How can managers accomplish this?

Objective 5 What are the best ways to create, manage, and participate in teams? (pp. 250–256)

PEARSON
mybizlab

Team Management

You're a quality manager at Wurley Bikes, a bike manufacturing company. Over the past two months, the front wheels on your BMX bikes have been defective at a high rate. Management wants the failure rate to drop by 90% within 30 days. Can you meet the quality improvement challenge?

Objective 6 Test yourself using mybizlab.com to show that you understand the chapter objectives.

Motivation _{pp.} 235–243

" **A**ll of my employees were so . . . *uninspired*," Ana Gutierrez laments. "People seemed to be just 'showing up'; the sense of apathy in the office was almost palpable. The quality of our work was suffering. I wasn't sure what to do."

Ana, the founder and CEO of a small public relations firm, was facing a crisis of motivation within her workforce. The sales team hadn't scored a new account in months, and existing clients were complaining about their representation. "You're not delivering on your promises," one client, the leader of a local not-for-profit organization, blurted during a particularly tense conference call. "A recent event was poorly advertised and poorly attended. There were errors in the latest press release. And your associates take two days to respond to my e-mails."

Ana had already tried a variety of tactics to motivate her employees. She dangled the possibility of additional bonuses and free dinners to the sales teams—to no avail. She instituted a new policy requiring all employees to work nine hours a day, plus two weekends a month. It didn't work. She told her associates she was prepared to promote at least three of the highest-performing employees among them to more lucrative positions within six months. No one was interested.

How could Ana apply what she knows about motivational theories to light a fire under her employees and save her business? ■

We hear the word *motivation* often. When players stay on the field an extra 30 minutes after practice to keep working on a skill, we say they are motivated athletes. When students seek out extra learning opportunities to go beyond a course's general requirements, they are described as motivated learners. But what does motivation have to do with working in a business? Are all of a business owner's actions motivated solely by profit? Does an employer who pays well always have strongly motivated employees? In this section, we'll examine motivation in detail and look at techniques used in the past and the present to motivate employees.

Personal Motivation

What drives you to do your personal best? Even when pursuing personal goals, everyone retains and loses motivation for very singular reasons. Think of times you have pushed to be your best, whether at school, in sports, or in other activities. Is it easier for you to build enthusiasm for tasks you're sure you can accomplish? Or do you set difficult goals and draw energy from the challenge of attaining them? Some people need immediate gratification or success to stay motivated. Others are able to postpone short-term success in pursuit of long-term gains. Do you need to be rewarded immediately for what you do or are you more motivated by long-term benefits?

Now think about how hard you work when you receive positive feedback (either financial or emotional). Is getting praise or money for a job important to you? Or are you driven more by the values of the place where you work, your beliefs, or in doing a job well? For some people, being part of the accomplishments of a team is what motivates them. Are you one of those people?

What does it feel like to be optimally motivated? Have you ever been working on a project in which you were so immersed in what you were doing that, when you looked at your watch, four hours had gone by? Psychologist Mihaly Csikszentmihalyi refers to this state of rapt attention as **flow**.[1] A flow state happens when you are completely involved and focused on what you are doing. Often people produce their best work, make the best use of their skills, and feel the most pleasure when they are in such a flow state. They feel a strong match between their own abilities and the challenge of a task—it is neither too difficult, which can lead to frustration, nor too simple, which can lead to boredom. They report a sense of control over what is happening and a feeling of effortlessness in their work. How do you create this sense of flow? This is the subject of **organizational psychology**— the study of how to create a workplace that fosters motivation and productivity among employees.

Motivating Employees

How does a work environment encourage "flow"? The *Q12* is a 12-question survey of employee engagement administered by the Gallup Organization. Based on respondents' answers to a series of questions, it classifies employees as "engaged," "not engaged," or "actively disengaged" (see ▼ **Table 8.1**). According to Q12 survey results, 73 percent of U.S. employees are not engaged or are actively disengaged in their work.[2] Imagine a workplace in which three out of four employees are complaining about the company all day long, disrupting activities during the day, and constantly trying to sabotage—or at least ridicule—the employees who are trying to do a good job. This statistic makes it clear that encouraging flow in the workplace is an important challenge.

One company that has succeeded in creating an environment that engages workers and supports the creative experience of flow is SAS, a business software company in North Carolina. With an incredibly low employee turnover rate of just 2–5 percent and annual revenues of over $2.3 billion,[3] the company has created such an atmosphere in part thanks to the policies of CEO Jim Goodnight. Goodnight lists the following as ways in which SAS works to foster a creative environment:

- It keeps employees intellectually engaged.
- It removes distractions so employees can do their best work.
- It makes managers responsible for sparking creativity.

▼ **Table 8.1**

Types of Employees		
Engaged	**Not Engaged**	**Actively Disengaged**
• Work with passion	• Work with minimal effort	• Work in a disruptive manner
• Feel connected and obligated to the company	• Are indifferent to the company	• Are unhappy with the company
• Add to the success of the company	• Make little or no contribution to the company	• Combat the efforts of engaged workers

- It has managers eliminate the arbitrary distinctions between administrative "suits" and more abstract "creatives."
- It engages customers as creative partners.

In addition to fostering strong professional lives, SAS supports its employees in their private lives as well. On the SAS campus, you'll find medical facilities for employees and their families, a Montessori day care center, and a cafeteria where families can eat lunch together. "The corporate philosophy is, if your fifth grader is in his first school play, you should be there to see it," says Goodnight. Such a philosophy has led to SAS earning a spot on *Fortune* magazine's Best Company to Work For list[4] and a spot on *Working Mother* magazine's list of best companies.[5]

What are the benefits of keeping employees motivated? Both employer and employee benefit from a motivated workforce. Employers find workers are more productive, more creative, and have much better retention levels when care is taken to provide a motivating environment and motivating tasks. Employees often spend the majority of their waking day at their jobs, and their quality of life and overall happiness are enhanced when they feel excited about the work they contribute. In fact, according to Gallup's calculations, the cost to the U.S. economy from disengaged employees is up to $350 billion a year in reduced productivity.[6] The results of a study commissioned by Sears, Roebuck and Co. supports the idea that employee motivation significantly influences company revenue. It found that increased employee-satisfaction scores at stores led to increased customer-satisfaction scores. This, in turn, led to a growth in revenue.[7]

Theories of Motivation

What are the different theories for what motivates people?
Several theories explain how and why people are motivated:

1. Maslow's hierarchy of needs
2. McClelland's "three needs" theory
3. Herzberg's motivator-hygiene theory

Let's take a look at each one.

What is Maslow's hierarchy of needs?
One early researcher in the area of human motivation was Abraham Maslow (1908–1970), who published the book *Motivation and Personality* in 1954. In his theory of motivation, Maslow suggests that humans have a **hierarchy of needs,** and that primary needs are met first before higher-level needs are addressed (see ▼ **Figure 8.1**). The first needs to be met are inborn, basic needs—termed **physiological needs**—such as the need for water, food, sleep, and reproduction. This means that before we as humans can think about anything else in our lives, we must ensure that these basic physiological needs are met.

Once our physiological needs have been met, Maslow's theory holds that people strive to satisfy **safety needs.** This includes establishing safe and stable places to live

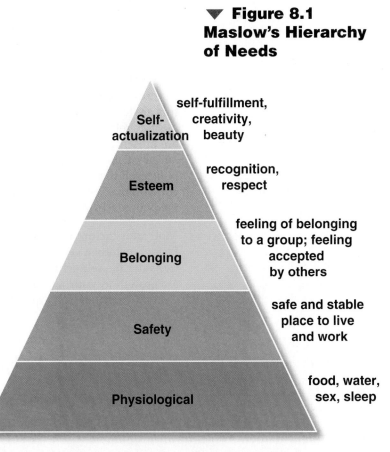

▼ **Figure 8.1 Maslow's Hierarchy of Needs**

- Self-actualization: self-fulfillment, creativity, beauty
- Esteem: recognition, respect
- Belonging: feeling of belonging to a group; feeling accepted by others
- Safety: safe and stable place to live and work
- Physiological: food, water, sex, sleep

and work. Once both physiological and safety needs have been met, we can consider social or **belonging needs.** This includes the need to belong to a group and feel accepted by others. The next level in Maslow's hierarchy includes **esteem needs.** These are satisfied by the mastery of a skill and the attention and recognition of others. Finally, **self-actualization needs** are at the top of the hierarchy. These needs include the desire to maximize your own potential through education and self-fulfillment as well as experiences of beauty and spirituality. These higher-level self-actualization needs cannot be addressed unless and until the lower level needs have been adequately met.

Maslow suggested that different people find themselves at different places in the hierarchy, and so their motivations may be different. Although an offer of overtime pay may be a successful motivator for a person concerned with safety needs, it might be the opposite of what someone working to satisfy their need for self-actualization finds motivating.

What is McClelland's "three needs" theory? Other researchers have proposed different models to map human needs to motivation. Psychologist David McClelland's (1917–1998) **three needs theory** suggests there are three main motivators:

1. *the need for achievement*—to accomplish something difficult on your own
2. *the need for affiliation*—to form close personal relationships
3. *the need for power*—to be able to control the behavior of others

According to McClelland, which need we try to satisfy depends on a variety of complex factors, including our cultural background. Although an individual may have multiple needs, McClelland suggests that one tends to be dominant over the others. In a workplace, this theory could account for differences in motivation among coworkers. For example, a person whose main need is for affiliation may have little motivation to perform a solitary task, whereas a person with a high need for achievement may be highly motivated to perform a difficult task alone.

How does Herzberg's motivator-hygiene theory explain motivation? In 1959, psychologist Frederick Herzberg (1923–2000) proposed a theory for job satisfaction called the **motivator-hygiene theory** (or the **two-factor theory**). According to the theory, two factors influence a person's motivation. **Hygiene factors** are factors such as a safe working environment, proper pay and benefits, and positive relationships with coworkers. People rarely notice hygiene factors if they are present. However, if hygiene factors are absent or inadequate, people tend to be dissatisfied. Consider basic working conditions, benefits, or other company policies. If there suddenly is no heat in the place where you work or if your pay is cut, you may be motivated to find a way to meet these needs. But if these are already in place, they are taken for granted and may not serve to motivate you.

Motivator factors represent the second set of factors in Herzberg's theory. These factors include a sense of responsibility, recognition, promotion, and job growth. Consider the self-actualization needs from Maslow's hierarchy. If there is no path for growth in your job or little recognition of your achievements, you probably would not immediately quit, but it would create a set of conditions that would fail to motivate you.

Applying Motivational Theories

Do managers actually use theories of motivation? Theories of motivation can be very abstract. How can a manager of an assembly line at an automotive plant or a team leader of a software development company take what

researchers know about human behavior and use it to increase productivity and the satisfaction of employees? The theories of human motivation you have just read about have given rise to several different approaches for organizing and motivating people in the workplace.

What can a manager do to enhance employee motivation? In the workplace, there are some external motivating factors that managers can control. These motivators, called **extrinsic motivators**, include such things as pay, promotion, and verbal praise. Other factors, called **intrinsic motivators,** are beyond a manager's control because they are internal to each individual employee. These motivating influences are based on a person's actual interest in his or her work and stem from the sense of purpose or value a person derives from the work being done.

A recent educational study in England showed the differences between these two types of motivators.[8] Children from an all boys' school and an all girls' school were asked to make a poster about their lives. One group was told its poster would decorate a local hospital for sick children. The other group was told it would be paid for its work. Which group of children would produce the better work—those who perceived the task as being worthwhile or those who were promised payment? In this case, much more sophisticated and detailed work came from the group that was working for free. The children were motivated more by the knowledge that they would be helping sick children than by financial reward.

Different people have different balances between intrinsic and extrinsic motivators. So how can business managers best motivate all their employees? An individual motivated intrinsically is working for his or her own satisfaction and may value challenging work that he or she perceives as meaningful to the company more than extrinsic factors like pay. Intrinsic motivators also tend to be higher on Maslow's hierarchy. So, for example, a boss who offers unsatisfying work, even though he or she offers bonuses and promotions, will have difficulty motivating an intrinsically motivated worker.

What other motivational models exist? In addition to the theories proposed by Maslow, McClelland, and Herzberg, several models have been developed that provide theoretical explanations of what motivates employees specifically in a business or workplace context:

1. Theories X, Y, and Z
2. The Vroom model
3. Strength-based management

▼ **Figure 8.2 Comparison of Theory X and Theory Y**

What are the Theory X and Theory Y models? In 1960, the social psychologist Douglas McGregor proposed the Theory X and Theory Y models (see ▼ **Figure 8.2**). The **Theory X** model suggests a view of people as inherently disliking work and wanting to avoid it. Because of this view, Theory X management suggests employees must be coerced and controlled by management to be productive. This leads to an authoritarian, hard-line management style. In contrast, the **Theory Y** model suggests that people view work as being as natural as playing and

Theory X		Theory Y
Not motivated: People naturally dislike working and avoid it when given the opportunity.	**Motivation**	**Naturally motivated:** People see work as a natural part of life.
Authoritarian: Managers must use heavy controls to get people to work efficiently.	**Management**	**Democratic:** Managers need not use heavy controls. Managers allow employees to create their own motivation.
Followers: Employees would prefer to follow the direction of management than solve problems on their own.	**Leadership**	**Leaders:** People are creative problem-solvers whose ideas can be used in the workplace.
Avoiders: People do not want responsibility and avoid it when possible.	**Responsibility**	**Seekers:** People inherently seek responsibility and are willing to accept it when asked.
Security: People are not complex and mainly want security in their jobs.	**Needs**	**Creativity:** People need to be intellectually stimulated and feel that their ideas are used.

resting. People are naturally motivated and will direct themselves to work for the aims of the organization if they are satisfied with their jobs. Theory Y managers believe that, on average, people will accept and seek out responsibility. Such managers have a softer style of management that involves the participation of many.

Clearly, Theories X and Y would not work equally well in any given situation. Theory X style management—which is authoritarian and hard line—is often seen in large-scale operations such as mass manufacturing. In the knowledge industry, in which there is a mix of professionals working together to solve complex problems, Theory Y is more likely to be seen with a participative, gentler management style.

How is the Theory Z model different? In 1981, William Ouchi, a professor at UCLA, put forward a **Theory Z** model based on a Japanese management style that relied heavily on collaborative decision making. In many corporations in Japan in the 1980s, one person might be responsible for many different aspects of a single project. Employees tended to become generalists rather than specialists who were trained in a very narrow set of tasks. Theory Z management offers long-term employment with an emphasis on individual responsibility. Workers tend to show a desire to cooperate and be loyal to an organization. As a result, companies that apply Theory Z management often reap the benefits of low turnover, high productivity, and strong morale among the workforce. Morale, a sense of purpose and enthusiasm toward one's work, is an important factor in an employee's level of motivation.

Do any motivational models describe an individual person's motivation? Although Maslow's hierarchy and other theories describe human motivation, they do so in terms of an overall model for all employees. In 1964, Victor Vroom proposed a theory named **expectancy theory,** which has been developed by other researchers since. The expectancy theory suggests an individual's motivation can be described by the relationship among three psychological forces. He put forward the following formula to describe the motivation a person feels in any given situation:

Motivation = Expectancy * Instrumentality * Valence

Expectancy is the idea that a person's effort has an appreciable effect on a situation's result—whether it is a success or failure. Does working harder lead to a more positive outcome for an employee and/or a company? Or does it not make a difference? This is what expectancy measures. **Instrumentality** refers to the idea that the outcome of a situation is related to rewards or punishment. For those who are extrinsically motivated, instrumentality answers the question, "What are the chances I'm going to be rewarded if I do a good job?" For those who are intrinsically motivated, instrumentality answers the question, "How good will I feel if I can accomplish this task?" **Valence** is the importance that the individual places on the expected outcome of a situation. It answers questions such as "How great a reward will there be if my performance is exemplary?" and "How serious a punishment do I expect if I under-perform?" In common terms, Vroom's formulas for high and low motivations read as follows:

> **High Motivation** = (My work actually affects the outcome.) * (There's a good chance I'll get a reward if this works out.) * (If it works out, it'll be a really big reward!)

> **Low Motivation** = (Nothing I do is going to impact this situation.) * (Even if it does go well, I probably won't see any benefit.) * (The only reward from this is incredibly small.)

The Vroom formula can be used to analyze factors such as how satisfied employees are at their jobs, how likely it is they will remain at their jobs, and how hard they will work at their jobs. In addition, unlike Maslow's and McClelland's models, which address typical needs across large groups of people, Vroom's model, with its three independent variables measuring the specific levels of expectancy, instrumentality, and valence, can generate a much more specialized result, attuned to the mental state of a specific individual.

What is the approach of strength-based management?

Management often works to help employees improve skills in areas in which they are weak. But is this the best investment of resources for a corporation? **Strength-based management** is a system based on the belief that, rather than improve weak skills, the best way to help employees develop is to determine their strengths and build on them.[9] This system is supported by research that shows that people can learn the most about areas in which they already have a strong foundation. Strength-based programs identify employees' current talents and skills and then provide additional training and support to develop them into areas of excellence.[10] By designing a match between an employee's strengths and his or her daily activities, and working around his or her weaknesses, each employee becomes more motivated and engaged in his or her work.

"We reward top executives at the agency with a unique incentive program. Money."

Evolution of Motivational Theories

How have motivational theories changed?

In the early twentieth century, as the Industrial Age saw the creation of large corporations, issues of efficiency and labor costs became critical. Researchers like Frederick Taylor (1856–1950) began to study how to manage people optimally. In 1911, Taylor published his findings in *The Principles of Scientific Management*. Based on his research and experimentation, he proposed ways that managers could increase productivity. He encouraged managers to use scientific study to determine the best methods to complete tasks and then train employees in these methods. Many of his ideas were implemented in factories. By the 1920s and 1930s, a field of academic study called **industrial psychology** was created to further address these issues. The objective of industrial psychology is to understand scientifically how to manage employees and work optimally.

Other researchers, such as Frank and Lillian Gilbreath, used photography to study employee work patterns and then analyzed these patterns to increase productivity. For example, they used time-motion studies to analyze factory jobs and then train workers in the precise sequence of steps that would make them most productive.

Another famous study of the period was work of Elton Mayo, a professor at Harvard University, at the Hawthorne plant of the Western Electric Company in Illinois. The study ran from 1927 to 1932 and examined physical influences on the workplace (such as lighting and humidity) as well as psychological aspects (such as group pressure and working hours). The major finding, known as the **Hawthorne effect,** was that *regardless of the experimental changes made,* the production of the workers improved. Researchers concluded that the increase in productivity was based on the attention the workers were receiving. Because they knew they were being studied, the employees felt special and produced more, regardless of the conditions Hawthorne studied. The Hawthorne effect is used now as a term to describe the increase in productivity caused by workers being given special attention. After World War II, the direction of research in management theory shifted

What motivates people to take on time-consuming, difficult tasks for no pay during their free time? Can answering this question tell us how to motivate people in business?

from management of an individual worker toward management of the entire organization, its structure, and policies.

What motivational theories fit the modern workplace? The fields of organizational psychology and industrial psychology are still very active, and new theories of management practices continue to appear. These theories aim to better describe and understand the challenges in managing a modern, globalized, knowledge-based economy. One recent theory is the **uncertainty management theory**, which suggests that when people face increased uncertainty, fairness becomes more important to them. They have very strong reactions to actions and situations they judge to be unfair, which in turn influences their job satisfaction and performance.[11]

Another motivational theory that is important for the modern workplace comes from examining the open-source movement (software projects that are developed, tested, and maintained for free by worldwide volunteers). Projects like Wikipedia, Linux, and other open-source projects are hugely successful and were created by professional people working many hours for free—outside their regular jobs. What incentive is causing people to behave that way?

Four academic economists explored this by running an experiment where people were recruited to perform a range of tasks—some that required motor skills, some creative, and some needing concentration. Monetary rewards were promised for three levels of performance with the top performers receiving the equivalent of five months pay! The result was that the higher the incentives, the *worse* the performance. In 2009, similar results were seen when the London School of Economics reviewed corporate pay-for-performance plans.[12] Using economic rewards to motivate employees can actually lead to poorer performance when the work is a creative, cognitive task. Additional study has shown that modern information workers value three commodities much more highly than money: autonomy, mastery, and purpose. People value having some control over their work lives, having a sense of skill and time to develop and improve their skills (mastery), and wanting their lives and work to have a higher purpose. Companies that can adjust their incentive structure to recognize this will see great benefits.

Another theory for motivating and organizing a modern workplace is based on the idea of **sociocracy.** Sociocracy is a system of organization and management in which the interests of everyone are served equally. In a sociocracy, all members of the organization are involved in decision making, and the final decision must be acceptable to all.[13] This doesn't mean everyone must love the decision; the goal is that no one finds the decision impossible to live with.

Companies adopting a system of sociocracy find that workers feel they are treated fairly, appreciated, and respected. Proponents of sociocracy claim the system naturally fosters innovation, creativity, and a sense of belongingness among employees. One company using the concept of sociocracy is Ternary Software. The Philadelphia-based company has been named one of the best places to work in the Philadelphia region and has won awards for being one of the most democratic places to work.[14]

Its founder, Brian Robertson, believes the model of "decision making by consent" has helped his company more efficiently develop software and has created a culture in which very highly motivated employees flourish. The system has paid off: revenue at Ternary increased an average of 50 percent a year. "We could never have achieved this under a traditional management system,"[15] Robertson says.

Remember Ana Gutierrez and her team of uninspired public relations professionals? "I realized that extrinsic motivators didn't have much of an effect on my employees, nor did a hard-line management style based on the Theory X model," she says. "So I changed my approach, and I soon saw positive results." In an attempt to increase the level of intrinsic motivation among her employees, Ana met with her associates and asked them which accounts they found most meaningful and satisfying to work on. She modified her staff appropriately and found that levels of motivation increased when employees worked with clients with whom they felt a personal connection. Ana also eliminated the nine-hour day mandate, but soon found that many of her newly motivated employees voluntarily worked at least that many hours—if not more! The company, once struggling, now flourishes: Sales are up, and clients are thrilled. With experimentation and careful thought, Ana achieved the goal of all business managers: translating motivational theory into business success. ■

Leadership pp. 243–250

Johnsonville Sausage CEO Ralph Stayer was running a successful family business. Sales were good in the business' home state of Wisconsin and were rising in nearby Minnesota, Michigan, and Indiana. Competition from national sausage makers was always a problem, but Johnsonville had the potential to improve its performance. Even though the company was making enough money, Stayer knew they could do better. Employees were bored and making thoughtless mistakes; entire batches of sausage were thrown out because of improper handling or wrong seasoning. How could he lead the company out of this doldrum and into a new chapter of success? ■

An organization is often successful when employees have a strong leader to demonstrate what it takes for a company to achieve its goals. **Leading** is the process of influencing, motivating, and enabling others to contribute to the success and effectiveness of an organization by achieving its goals. As we discussed in Chapter 7, leading is one of the four functions of management (other functions include planning, organizing, and controlling/monitoring). In this section, we'll look at what it takes to be a leader and what leaders bring to a company.

Are all managers leaders? Famed management researcher and author Peter Drucker once noted that "management is doing things right; leadership is doing the right things."[16] Both leaders and managers strive to motivate people, but they have different scopes. Typically, managers spend their time making sure that specific tasks are done well and completed on time. The leadership of a company, on the other hand, is focused on setting the long-term vision and strategies a company will need to survive and flourish. Truly great leaders are able to be both managers and leaders: They define a vision, foster agreement across the company, and then implement the strategy.

What styles of leadership exist? Many different leadership styles exist, and leaders often employ different styles in a given situation depending on a complex mix of their own personality, the corporate culture, the type of company, and the employees they manage. ▼ **Table 8.2** lists four of the most common: *democratic, autocratic, affiliative (laissez-faire),* and *visionary*.

What are democratic and autocratic leaders like? Consider Henry Chang, who runs the kitchen of a large restaurant. Henry allows his staff to offer opinions as he develops the menu. He also lets them experiment with different recipes and food presentations and features their work on the main menu when possible. The kitchen staff members love working with Henry because he allows them to be creative and innovative. He also encourages them to cultivate the skills they need to run their own restaurant someday. However, Henry's restaurant often attracts important political dignitaries and famous entertainers. Sometimes, the restaurant becomes unexpectedly busy. In these circumstances, Henry doesn't leave anything to chance and dictates exactly what needs to be done and who should do it. Henry knows he might hurt someone's feelings, but, ultimately, his staff trusts him to make the right decisions to obtain the best results for the restaurant.

For the most part, Henry is a **democratic leader,** delegating authority and involving employees in the decision making. Because Henry knows that by involving his employees they become more invested in the process, he feels the ultimate output is better. The trade-off, Henry recognizes, is that his democratic style of leadership requires more time and advanced planning. When such time is not available, Henry must take complete charge. In those instances, he becomes an **autocratic leader,** making decisions without consulting others. A good leader knows that

▼ **Table 8.2**

Styles of Leadership				
	Democratic	**Autocratic**	**Affiliative (Laissez-Faire)**	**Visionary**
Leader characteristics	Is a • superb listener • team worker • collaborator • influencer	• Commands—"do it because I say so" • Threatens • Has tight control • Monitors studiously • Creates dissonance • Contaminates everyone's mood • Drives away talent	• Promotes harmony • Empathizes with others • Boosts morale • Solves conflicts	• Inspires • Believes in own vision • Is empathetic • Explains how and why people's efforts contribute to the "dream"
Benefits to style	Values people's input and gets commitment through participation	Soothes fear by giving clear direction in an emergency	Creates harmony by connecting people to one another	Moves people toward shared dreams
When style is appropriate	To build buy-in or consensus or get valuable input from employees	In a crisis, to kick-start an urgent turnaround, or with problem employees; traditional military	To heal rifts in a team, motivate during stressful times or strengthen connections	When changes require a new vision or when a clear direction is needed; radical change

such commanding leadership can be an effective style in certain circumstances when quick decisions need to be made or when it seems as if the group cannot come to a consensus.

What are affiliative leaders?

Some leaders take a more hands-off approach to management and act more as consultants rather than participants. **Affiliative (or laissez-faire) leaders** are more advisory in style, encouraging employees to contribute ideas rather than specifically directing their tasks. This style of leadership is often best used with groups and teams. Affiliative leadership implemented properly can give employees a sense of challenge,

French chef Alain Ducasse, left, cooks with his aides in the kitchen of his restaurant Le Louis XV in Monaco. Chefs like Ducasse may use a variety of leadership styles, depending on the situation.

commitment, and renewed energy as they are left to handle tasks on their own. As businesses continue to reduce the layers of management, affiliative and democratic styles are becoming the leadership styles of choice. However, it is possible for affiliative leaders to lose too much involvement in the group's processes. If the group or team members feel that management is virtually absent, team members may choose actions and strategies that are easy and not in line with the goals of a company.

What makes a leader a visionary?

Visionary leaders are able to inspire others, believe in their own vision, and move people toward a shared dream. John Lasseter was an animator in Disney's computer animation department when George Lucas' company Lucasfilm opened a computer animation division. Lasseter was drawn to the vision of what might be possible with the advances in technology he saw in use at Lucasfilm, so he left Disney in 1984 to spend a month at ILM. He has been there ever since. In 1986 that division was purchased by Steve Jobs and became its own company, Pixar. Lasseter is currently Pixar's chief creative officer. He has assembled a uniquely creative collection of employees and led them to producing a series of new classics in animated film—including *Toy Story*, *A Bug's Life*, and *Cars*.

As a visionary leader, Lasseter had to create the special environment that would allow creative people the freedom to be inventive but also the structure to meet the deadlines required on a multimillion-dollar film schedule. One example of his leadership is in the production of *Toy Story*. At that time, Pixar had never produced anything longer more than a short, five-minute-long film; it was not clear whether the company could actually produce a full-length film. *Toy Story* was being produced and distributed by Disney (in a partnership with Pixar), and Disney executives called a meeting to see a segment. Disney wanted to make sure the film had the quality it wanted from its new partner. Lasseter remembers the meeting: "I was pretty much embarrassed by what was on the screen. I had made it. I directed everybody to do this . . . but it was a story filled with the most unhappy, mean people." Disney wanted to shut down production and fire staff. But Lasseter negotiated a two-week reprieve and returned to lead his team of cowriters and animators. "Let's make the movie we wanted to make," he told them, and the story took on a gentler, sweeter tone. The team had to work nonstop for the two-week reprieve, with the threat of massive layoffs over their heads. The ending of the story is well known: *Toy Story* went on to achieve $190 million in domestic box office receipts, and Lasseter earned an Honorary Oscar for the achievement. Lasseter has since used visionary leadership to guide the studio to successes with many movies.[17]

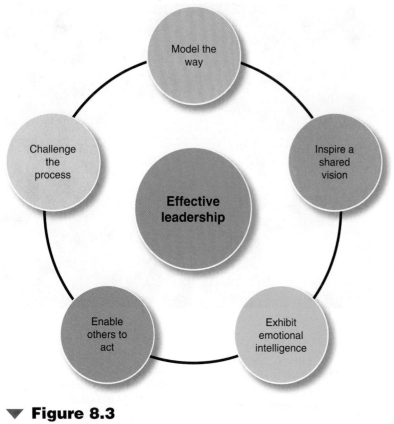

**▼ Figure 8.3
Traits of Effective
Leadership**

Traits of Leadership

What are the traits of great leaders?
As illustrated in ▼ **Figure 8.3,** the best leaders share some common traits.

- Great leaders *challenge the process* by not always accepting conventional beliefs and practices as the only way to accomplish tasks. Leaders set goals and have a vision of the future that may be different from the norm. Leaders are not afraid to alter their methods, plans, or even thinking if the situation calls for change. Also, leaders exemplify resourcefulness as they continually brainstorm for solutions to problems and more effective ways of reaching goals.

- Great leaders *inspire a shared vision* and motivate people to care about the corporate goals or an important mission. Leaders influence in a positive and moral way (rather than in a selfish and destructive way) and garner trust, respect, and commitment to their vision. They can communicate a vision throughout the organization and inspire others to adopt the same vision and work toward common goals.

- Great leaders *model the way* by serving as a living example of the ideals in which they are asking their employees to share. Leaders have a good handle on their business and industry. They are willing to admit mistakes and constantly seek more information to make informed and reasoned decisions. Good leaders base their decisions on facts. They are well organized and detail oriented. Strong leaders often model the ethical tone they want to set for their businesses through their choices in speech and action.

- Great leaders *exhibit emotional intelligence*. Most successful leaders possess a high degree of **emotional intelligence**—the ability to understand both one's own and others' emotions. It is a term for the set of skills including self-awareness, self-management, social awareness, and relationship management. Leaders can use their awareness of others' emotional states to inspire people to feel more positive and connect with others by being honest and open about their own ideals, concerns, and goals. In working with these types of leaders, people tend to feel secure and free to explore and share their creative ideas.

- Great leaders *enable others to act* by giving people the access to information and empowering them to perform to their fullest potential.[22] Leaders need to achieve and are constantly striving for improvement. They have a high energy level and are ambitious and persistent in the face of obstacles. True leadership drive, however, does not come at the expense of others; therefore, leaders delegate authority and responsibility to others to promote their success also. They are the catalysts for positive action.

These traits are essential to effective leadership and are common to most good leaders.

Are there systems for measuring leadership potential? There are
many personality tests that can provide information that people can then use to assess their leadership potential and improve their leadership skills. Popular person-

◎ Off the Mark Robert L. Nardelli

Robert L. Nardelli, who was named CEO of Home Depot in 2000, is known for his autocratic leadership style. As CEO, he implemented a policy that required that all aspects of store performance be carefully measured, and he held executives responsible for meeting strict goals. (Nardelli applied the six-sigma quality assessment system, discussed in Chapter 7.) He also implemented major cost-cutting measures, replacing thousands of full-time workers with part-time employees. Financially, Nardelli's style seemed a boon for the company; Home Depot sales rose from $46 billion in 2000 to $81.5 billion in 2005, an average annual growth

Robert L. Nardelli

rate of 12 percent. However, the strong numbers could not make up for an autocratic leadership style that many experts say alienated both employees and customers. In January 2007, facing pressure from the board of directors, Nardelli resigned from the company. Controversy continued as it was revealed he had negotiated a "golden parachute" compensation package that paid him almost $210 million on his departure.[18]

His next position was as CEO of Chrysler. Chrysler was one of the U.S. automotive companies that was forced to turn to the federal government for bailout funds as their last ditch attempt to avoid bankruptcy. In 2009, the government offered Chrysler a $750 million loan, but Nardelli instead led Chrysler to take more expensive financing from private banks. Reports from the Treasury's office later indicated that Nardelli and other Chrysler executives had refused to accept the cheaper bailout money because one condition of accepting the money was that it forced a limit—or placed a cap—on executive compensation. (Chrysler had earlier accepted a government loan of $1.5 billion when easier rules were in place regarding executive pay.) Chrysler eventually went bankrupt, and Nardelli left as CEO.[19]

---

ality assessments include the *Big Five*, the *Cattell 16 PF*, and the *Thematic Apperception Test*. Although no one personality test is recognized as the perfect tool, all of them strive to provide us with a better understanding of the traits that are the foundation of successful leadership.

Leadership and Corporate Culture

How does the management's leadership style influence the work environment? The **corporate culture** is a collection of values, norms, and behavior shared by management and workers that defines the character of an organization. Google, for example, has a unique culture, established by a corporate philosophy that includes statements such as "You can make money without doing

Biz**Chat**

Do You Have to Be Tall to Be a Leader?

What does height have to do with successful leadership in business? A lot, according to many industry experts and observers. Lara Tiedens, an organizational behavior professor at the Stanford University Graduate School of Business, cites height—or in some cases, the illusion of height—as a tool business leaders use to appear powerful. Several studies have also found positive correlations between height and salary.[23] What do you think? How much does appearance affect success in business and, more specifically, as a leader? Do top CEOs tend to be taller than average? Or is the idea that DNA, rather than skills and talents, seals one's leadership fate a myth?

For more information and discussion questions about this topic, check out the BizChat feature on my**biz**lab.com.

evil" and "Work should be challenging and fun."[24] ▼ **Figure 8.4** shows the company's top 10 reasons it feels people should work there, and its unique corporate culture shines through. Corporate culture will dictate what style of dress is appropriate at work, the work environment itself, rules for getting ahead and being promoted, what is valued, who is valued, and even what kind of work/life balance is expected. Typically this is done without written rules and open guidance; it is an attitude of "this is how we do things here" and a consistent pressure to make employees fall in line with that model. This is why it is important that your personal goals and style match the corporate culture of the organization you choose to work for.

In a corporation in which the culture is not well defined—or even worse, one that supports questionable behavior—problems result. This was the case for the natural gas giant Enron, which eventually went bankrupt because of a significant lack of control and the poor ethical behavior of top management. On the other hand, when the corporate culture is strong and all employees accept the culture as their own, they are motivated to maintain it and monitor their own behavior.

How does a leader establish corporate culture?
Tony Hsieh of Zappos .com, the online shoe giant, is a powerful example of how a leader can establish corporate culture. Hsieh started Zappos at a time when selling a product like shoes online was thought to be impossible. He was sure that top notch customer service would be the difference. In his book *Delivering Happiness: A Path to Profits, Passion and Purpose* (Business Plus, 2010), he explains how first establishing a corporate culture naturally led to the customer service levels he wanted, the profits he wanted, and the purpose he wanted in his life and for his employees.

It began with hiring. Hsieh and the two other founders developed a set of 10 core values and interviewed candidates around those.[25] For example, value 10 is "Be Humble." Candidates are picked up from the airport with a Zappos shuttle bus. Later, the bus driver is

▼ **Figure 8.4 Reasons to be a Googler**
The corporate culture at Google shines through on its Jobs site.

Google US jobs   Search US openings [   ] (Search)

Jobs > Life at Google > Top ten reasons to work at Google

Jobs
Life at Google
Office locations
Joining Google
Student jobs

Top 10 Reasons to Work at Google

1. **Lend a helping hand.** With millions of visitors every month, Google has become an essential part of everyday life – like a good friend – connecting people with the information they need to live great lives.

2. **Life is beautiful.** Being a part of something that matters and working on products in which you can believe is remarkably fulfilling.

3. **Appreciation is the best motivation,** so we've created a fun and inspiring workspace you'll be glad to be a part of, including on-site doctor; massage and yoga; professional development opportunities; shoreline running trails; and plenty of snacks to get you through the day.

4. **Work and play are not mutually exclusive.** It is possible to code and pass the puck at the same time.

5. **We love our employees, and we want them to know it.** Google offers a variety of benefits, including a choice of medical programs, company-matched 401(k), stock options, maternity and paternity leave, and much more.

6. **Innovation is our bloodline.** Even the best technology can be improved. We see endless opportunity to create even more relevant, more useful, and faster products for our users. Google is the technology leader in organizing the world's information.

7. **Good company everywhere you look.** Googlers range from former neurosurgeons, CEOs, and U.S. puzzle champions to alligator wrestlers and Marines. No matter what their backgrounds, Googlers make for interesting cube mates.

8. **Uniting the world, one user at a time.** People in every country and every language use our products. As such we think, act, and work globally – just our little contribution to making the world a better place.

9. **Boldly go where no one has gone before.** There are hundreds of challenges yet to solve. Your creative ideas matter here and are worth exploring. You'll have the opportunity to develop innovative new products that millions of people will find useful.

10. **There is such a thing as a free lunch after all.** In fact we have them every day: healthy, yummy, and made with love.

interviewed to see how the candidates treated the driver; in this way, the interview started before the candidates realized it. Another key interview question relates to value 3, "Create Fun and a Little Weirdness." Candidates are asked "How weird are you on a scale of 1 to 10?" Zappos is looking for employees who are willing to bring their personality to the office, not hide behind what they think is expected. (You can see evidence on blogs.zappos.com, where the video from the Zappos Prom is posted as are several videos of office pranksters at work.) And one week after they have been hired, every employee is offered $2,000 to leave Zappos if they don't think it is for them.

The leadership team also designed the work environment to support the core values. To boost interaction, Zappos offers free lunch to keep folks in the building talking instead of racing off to restaurants. Managers are encouraged to spend 10–20 percent of their time outside the office with employees to build personal relationships, not just professional relationships.

What did all this focus on building a specific corporate culture do for the company? Zappos has become a company with a "higher purpose of vision that is more than just about money or profits or being No. 1 in the market," describes Hsieh.[26] Along the way, the staff has become renowned for outstanding customer service, being friendly, accommodating, and spending hours on the phone with a single caller if needed. That has translated into over $1 billion in annual sales; the company was acquired by Amazon.com for $1.2 billion in 2009.

On Target Jon Huntsman

Jon Huntsman, of Huntsman International LLC, is an example of a leader who uses an affiliative style of leadership. Huntsman started his petrochemical and plastics company in 1970, and by 2000, it had worldwide revenue of $8.5 billion. But in January 2001, the market saw some dramatic changes, and every advisor advocated that the company file Chapter 11 bankruptcy. Huntsman refused, and the company rebounded. By early 2005, when the company went public, its annual revenues were more than $12 billion. Huntsman outlines the pillars of his innovative leadership style in his book *Winners Never Cheat* (Wharton School Publishing, 2008):

- Compete fiercely and fairly but do not cut in line.
- Set the example for handling risk, handling responsibility, and demonstrating reliability.
- Revenge is unproductive—learn to move on.
- Operate businesses and organizations as if they are family owned.[20]

Huntsman also emphasizes the importance of being ethical, respectful, and charitable in both business dealings and life. And Huntsman practices what he preaches: He and his wife have raised and donated more than $350 million for the Huntsman Cancer Institute in Salt Lake City.[21]

How did Ralph Stayer, CEO of Johnsonville Sausage, lead the company to new profitability? Stayer understood that for the company to fulfill its potential, he had to get employees motivated and make them care. So, over time, Stayer gave employees more and more responsibilities. Until then, product quality was evaluated by senior management, not the people actually making the sausage. Stayer transferred quality control to the line workers, the employees actually manning the production line making the product, telling them it was their responsibility to ensure good

"I don't know how it started, either. All I know is that it's part of our corporate culture."

products left the plant. Line workers took control and created teams to handle problems related to taste and packaging. This one small change produced unexpected results; product rejects went from 5 percent to 0.5 percent. Line workers also took responsibility to ensure that everyone in their department met performance standards. This was so successful that more personnel responsibilities, such as employee selection and training, were left up to line workers. Because people were taking on additional tasks, Stayer changed the company's policy for pay rates and bonuses. Additional responsibilities added additional pay to their income. Performance profits, similar to bonuses, were given every six months; calculations were based on an appraisal system and overseen by volunteers.

The true turnaround came when Stayer stopped owning problems and let his team members work them out on their own. He stopped attending meetings and reviewing product problems. He realized every word and action had meaning, whether symbolic or literal, so before reacting, he questioned whether what he was about to do or say would reinforce his vision for the company. His proudest moment came when an opportunity for extensive expansion was offered to the company. His executive board would have declined the offer because it was too risky, but Stayer posed the question to the entire company. Small groups discussed the deal, and over the course of a few days a decision was made: Expansion was a go! Since then, Johnsonville Foods has expanded into over 30 countries[27] and has over 1,400 employees.[28] Stayer maximized the company's success by reevaluating his own leadership and adapting to the needs of the company.[29] ■

Teamwork pp. 250–256

ave you ever seen a Motorola Razr cell phone? If so, you've seen the product of true teamwork in action. At the start of the project, Motorola began with a modest goal: to design a phone that celebrities would be happy to show off during the Academy Awards, generating a lot of publicity and buzz for Motorola products. A special team of 20 engineers was formed and given the task of creating the thinnest phone ever released. How did they do it? ■

It's challenging to develop effective teams, but the benefits can be extraordinary. Although different personalities have the potential to create conflict within a team, they can also create unique ideas. In this section, we'll discuss teamwork and how it affects organizations.

The Advantages of Teams in the Workplace

What is the value of using teams in the workplace? In good, working teams, there's agreement on the objectives at hand and the best approach to solve a problem.[30] Teammates depend on one another's ideas and efforts to successfully complete tasks. There is a sense of accountability, and members are committed to one another's success.

One company that makes use of teams is MasterCard. From 1987 to 1997, the company implemented five different advertising campaigns, yet it was still eclipsed by rival company Visa.[31] In an attempt to change this pattern, MasterCard commissioned McCann Erikson, an advertising agency, to come up with a new campaign. The agency enlisted a seasoned creative team to tackle the project. After much brainstorming, the team came up with a new tagline: "There are some things money can't buy. For everything else, there's MasterCard." The team then worked on developing ideas for commercials based on the tagline. By combining their creative talents, the team members came up with a "priceless" idea. Their commercials started by listing the prices of ordinary items, such as popcorn or soda. They ended by mentioning an item that is priceless, such as spending time with your family. Since then, commercials based on this theme have been shown in 105 countries and translated into 48 languages. Most importantly for Master-Card, it has issued U.S. credit cards at nearly twice the rate Visa has since the campaign began.

For an interactive, real-world example of this topic, access this chapter's **BizSkill** entitled Team Management, located at **my*biz*lab**.com.

The Challenges of Teams in the Workplace

Do teams always improve the development process? Although teams have been shown to be effective in many situations, some people suggest that teamwork does not always bring more creative output. Research conducted by Barry Staw at the University of California at Berkeley found that when college students were asked to think of business ideas either individually or in teams, the individuals came up with more ideas than did the teams. In addition, the individual's ideas were voted as more creative than were the teams' concepts. Staw concluded that collective thinking does not lead to increased creativity and can, in fact, hamper it. One possible reason, Staw proposes, is that team members often want to "fit in" rather than "stand out," and true creativity and original thinking is largely dependent on one's willingness to stand out and take risks.[32]

Not every team performs at its best.

If a team is not carefully selected, this behavior of "wanting to fit in" can lead to narrow-mindedness. This is a phenomenon referred to as **groupthink.** People who are from similar backgrounds and sectors of a company tend to have a set of familiar ideas and work with the same set of unspoken assumptions. These may lead to rejecting different ideas without fair examination. The impact of groupthink can be chilling to the creative output of a team, although this challenge can be minimized with thoughtful design in team membership.

In the twenty-first century, another challenge to successful workplace teams is the fact that

▼ Table 8.3

Four Generations in the Workplace

Generation	Birth Years	Famous Man	Famous Woman
Silent	1925–1942	Colin Powell	Barbara Walters
Boomer	1943–1960	Steven Spielberg	Oprah Winfrey
Gen-X	1961–1981	Matt Damon	Jennifer Lopez
Millennial	1982–2002	LeBron James	Miley Cyrus

Source: Neil Howe and William Strauss, Millennials Rising: The Next Great Generation *(Vintage, 2000).*

there is now a wide mix of generations in the workforce (see ▼ **Table 8.3**). In fact, it is possible for there to be three or even four generations assigned to a single team. People from separate generations have grown up with social and educational experiences that are so different that they take on distinct styles in the workplace.

Are generational differences really that significant❓

In their book *Millennials Rising: The Next Great Generation* (Vintage, 2000), researchers Neil Howe and William Strauss discuss the three dominant generations in the workplace today: the baby boomers, those born between 1943 and 1960; the Gen-Xers, those born between 1961 and 1981; and the Millennials, those born between 1982 and 2002. The baby boomers are the veterans in the workforce, and many have been with the same company for more than 30 years. Gen-Xers, who are known for their independent thinking and hankering for change, are the first generation of workers to value family life over work life.

Like Gen-Xers, Millennials want their jobs to accommodate their personal lives, but they also have very high expectations for achievement in their careers. Millennials, who are now entering college campuses and the workforce, believe in their self-worth and value—whether deserved or not.[33] They feel they have the capability to change the companies they work for and the world. According to Howe and Strauss, members of this generation expect to make their greatest marks in society by using technology to empower the community. Also important to note is that this generation is the focus of marketing efforts because they are the biggest youth spenders in history, most often in "copurchases" with their parents. Teamwork, good behavior, and citizenship are much more important to Millennials than to earlier generations, and they see equality between different races and genders.

⊚On Target Red Teamers in the Military

Teamwork is a critical part of business, but one place you might not think of team decision making is in the military. Military organization is based on unquestioning obedience to orders. But the military is sensitive to how this conditioning could contribute to groupthink in team decision making. So a program of study was developed to produce "Red Teamers," officers trained in analyzing problems from a wide range of points of view—how the decision will impact military allies, how the decision will impact allied countries' military forces, how the different cultural perspectives of the occupied country will respond. Red Team students study military theory but also Eastern philosophy, for example. "We want them to understand that their view of the world is very narrow," says Bob Topping, who develops the curriculum for the program. "We look at the world through a straw. We're shielded."[35] In Iraq, Red Team officers were used, for example, on teams making decisions regarding the use of military dogs because Iraqi citizens generally consider dogs unclean and even evil. A Red Teamer is responsible for raising issues that the group might not have considered, but then stepping out of the way and not obstructing the decision making. The same idea of injecting a skeptic to a group to promote a variety of points of view is used in other government agencies. For example, the Federal Aviation Administration (FAA) uses Red Teams to conduct airport testing to find and resolve security weaknesses. Is there a Red Teamer in your group . . . or do you need one?

How will this affect business? Strauss predicts, "Young workers will demand that employers adjust to the needs of workers who wish to build careers and families at the same time and lead lower-stress lives than their parents did. Older employees will admire their skills, confidence, and team spirit, but will question their creativity and toughness."[34]

Best Practices for Teams

What kinds of practices set the stage for the best team performance❓

Psychologist Mihaly Csikszentmihalyi has extended his idea of flow into the team setting. **Group flow** occurs when a group knows how to work together so that each individual member can achieve flow. The characteristics of such a setting are as follows:

1. Creative spatial arrangements: Pinning ideas on the walls and using large charts to combine ideas from the entire group tend to lead to the open consideration of ideas. Tables are used less because working while standing and moving promotes more discussion and interaction.

2. Playground design: This begins with creating a "safe space," agreeing it is safe to bring out ideas that normally one might just keep to himself or herself. Often a large number of charts display information inputs, graphs, and the project summary. Wall space can be used to collect results and lists of open topics.

3. Constant focus on the target group for the product.

4. Heavy use of visualization and prototyping to construct early models. These are then refined to make the models more efficient.

The environment itself can also be fine-tuned to help promote the success of the team. Management must also be sure to praise team accomplishments. The Razr team, for example, was asked to come to company headquarters for a meeting of top executives. What was the purpose of the meeting? The company's top executives wanted to thank the team members; they did so by giving them a standing ovation as well as stock options.[36]

How do managers form the best teams? Some important aspects a manager should consider in forming a team include the following:

- **Size:** A team that is too large may struggle with cohesiveness. At the same time, a large group can offer the benefit of diverse perspectives.

- **Time Frame:** Some teams may be formulated to work on a specific problem or project within a short time frame, while others may work together for longer time periods on everyday tasks.

- **Status:** A team that is formally created by a company may be required to provide progress reports and updates, and it often has access to company resources. Less formal teams may need to take initiative in maintaining lines of communication.

According to business writer and theorist R. M. Belbin, effective teams are composed of people with diverse skills, talents, and points of view. Team members' respective skills and talents should complement one another so the team can perform at an optimum level. For example, what might happen if everyone on a team was extremely creative yet inexperienced in effective time management? What if five of six team members were all aggressive leaders? Clearly, a balance of people who embody different team roles is key in the success of a team.

Belbin's model of nine team roles is outlined in ▼ **Table 8.4**. Considering both these roles and the personality traits of potential members can be helpful when designing teams.

What are cross-functional teams? Traditionally team members were often chosen from the same department, all reporting to a common supervisor. But today's markets demand such quick response and adapting to conditions that a new model is emerging: cross-functional teams. In a **cross-functional team,** members are selected across a range of critical functional divisions of a business. For example, in 2004 the LEGO Group was near bankruptcy.[37] Investments in the LEGO theme parks had failed,

▼ **Table 8.4**

Belbin's Nine Team Roles

Role	Personality Traits
Plant	Creative and imaginative
Resource investigator	Extroverted and communicative
Coordinator	Mature and confident
Shaper	Challenging and dynamic
Monitor evaluator	Serious and strategic
Teamworker	Cooperative and diplomatic
Implementer	Disciplined and reliable
Completer finisher	Painstaking and conscientious
Specialist	Dedicated and self-starting

Source: R. M. Belbin, "Team Role Descriptions," Belbin Associates. www.belbin.com/content/ page/731/Belbin_Team_Role_ Descriptions.pdf. Adapted with permission from Belbin Associates, www.belbin.com

and some products like Clikits had struggled in the marketplace. The management created a cross-functional team named the Executive Innovation Governance Group. It consisted of employees who could contribute in product innovation, pricing, business processes, marketing, and community building. The group ushered through modifications to existing product lines as well as new products, such as the series of LEGO board games, a new product category for LEGO. In 2010, during a declining toy market overall, LEGO saw a 30 percent increase in revenues.

What effect does technology have on team design ?
Modern telecommunications allows team members to live far from each other. In a **virtual team**, members are located in different physical locations but work together to achieve a goal. The need for virtual teams has grown out of the increased globalization of business. Familiar tools like conference calls and e-mail have evolved to include video conferencing and live broadcasting of key meetings and events over the Web. Webcasts can now support interactive participation of the viewing audience. In real time, audience members can ask questions, exchange electronic files with the group, and record the presentation for repeated viewing. Web conferencing software like WebEx and Microsoft Office Live allow participants in any geographic location to brainstorm together in real time on a common "virtual whiteboard," watch demos and presentations live, and record and annotate these discussions for later playback.

How can social media tools like wikis help modern teams ?
Modern tools for collaboration are now often replacing endless streams of e-mails with files attached. Wikis are one example. *Wikis* are Web sites that support editing by multiple authors. Team members can work on one common document all at the same time, watching each other make editing changes, having a live chat window open at the same time. Changes are archived and can be recalled; if a member of the team later reads the document and wants to revert back to an earlier version, he or she can do so with just one click. The problem of having multiple versions of a document is eliminated, so there are no concerns about synchronizing the different versions between all team members; the most current version is always available on the wiki.

Through the use of Web conferencing software, teams with people in various countries can work together seamlessly.

One of the best known public wikis is the encyclopedia project Wikipedia. Wikipedia is not the only use of wikis however. Wikis can be run and maintained by individuals or within a specific corporation. Sites like wikimatrix.org can help identify the type of wiki software best suited to a specific virtual team. Products like Blackboard and Microsoft Windows SharePoint contain wiki tools as part of the main product.

Is designing a strong virtual team the same as creating a strong face-to-face team ?
The best practices for creating strong virtual teams are emerging as virtual teams become a more accepted and useful teaming solution.[38] Most successful virtual teams include some periodic face-to-face meetings. Very few virtual teams are 100 percent virtual. Although technology allows teams to communicate without ever meeting face-to-face, it is still important to have the group occasionally

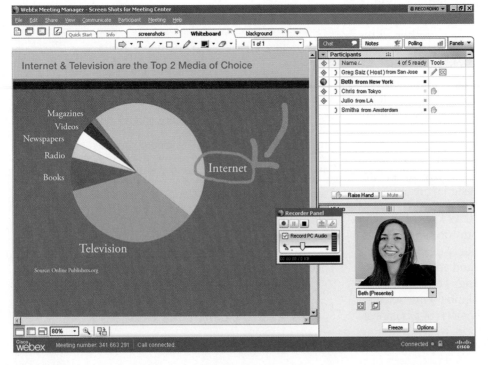

meet with each other in the same space to build social connections. Keeping the team connected is a key priority for a virtual team, and it can be difficult to keep contacts strong from a distance. There can be communication delays from working across time zones or using e-mail as a primary mode of communication. Establishing team rules, such as agreeing to respond to e-mail messages within a certain window of time or initiating global office hours, can minimize these problems. (For more on communicating with teams, see the Business Communications Mini Chapter.)

Your Role on a Team

How can I be a valued team player? It is important to begin now to build the skills that will make you successful in team settings. As we have seen, the best teams are carefully planned and selected and can be the place where some of the most exciting and innovative work in the company is happening. Preparing yourself to contribute in a team setting may be the most important thing you can do to increase your value to an organization, no matter what position you hold.

What habits will give me the best chance to contribute to a team? There are many skills that you can build to enhance your success as a member of a team. One model that organizes these skills is the **Seven Habits model** developed by famed management author Stephen Covey.[39] He has found that there are seven habits of behavior exhibited by successful people:

1. **Be proactive.** This is the ability to control your environment rather than have it control you. Proactive team members are constantly looking "down the road" in terms of their time management, work, and obstacles coming that may impede the success of a project.

2. **Begin with the end in mind.** This means that you are able to see the desired outcome and concentrate on activities that help in achieving it. Staying focused on the ultimate goal allows you to avoid taking the team in directions that will cause divisiveness and waste resources and energy.

3. **Put first things first.** This skill works together with the second habit in pushing you toward success in your team role. Manage your time and energy so that the required tasks are prioritized. Covey thinks of the second habit as a mental creation and the third habit as a physical creation.

4. **Think win-win.** This is the most important aspect of interpersonal leadership because most achievements are based on cooperative effort; therefore, the aim needs to be win-win solutions for all.

5. **Seek first to understand and then to be understood.** In communicating with other members of the team, it is critical to develop and maintain positive relationships. This style of communication recommends listening and working to give your teammates the feeling they have been heard as key to your own success in being understood and contributing.

6. **Synergize.** This is the habit of creative cooperation—the principle that collaboration often achieves more than could be achieved by individuals working independently toward attaining a purpose.

7. **Sharpen the saw.** This catch phrase comes from the metaphor of chopping down a tree. If you are constantly sawing and never take time to stop and sharpen the saw, you'll feel as if you're investing tremendous energy, but the results will not be what they could be if you just stopped to sharpen the saw first. Strong team contributors avoid the work mode of continually reacting to crises. Instead, they take time to step back and develop skills and analyze the task at hand so that they can work more efficiently.

If you work to develop and use these habits in your role on teams, you will find that your teams become more successful—and that you are in demand for the next team.

Effective teamwork involves a complex blend of personalities, skills, and actions. Achieving this blend in the business environment can be a great challenge. As the Motorola Razr team demonstrated, however, it can be done. For almost a year, the team met daily, often for hours at a time, to work on the top-secret project. The team struggled to come up with a practical yet innovative design, often engaging in spirited debate over such matters. Despite the many challenges, the hard work paid off. The team that created the Razr not only created one of the best-selling technology products of all time but also contributed to creating a new Motorola. In fact, Motorola reported that in 2006, its Razr cell phone even outsold the popular Apple iPod. Its success is the kind to which all managers and team members aspire. ■

Chapter Summary

Are you an active learner?

Go to my**biz**lab.com to master Chapter 8's content. Chapter 8's interactive activities include:

- Customizable Study Plan and Chapter 8 practice quizzes

- Chapter 8 Simulation, Team Management, that helps you think critically and prepare to make choices in the business world
- Chapter 8 Video Exercise, Teamwork, Motivation, and Communications, which shows you how textbook concepts are put into practice every day
- Flash Cards for mastering the definition of chapter terms
- Interactive Lessons that visually review key chapter concepts

1. How do motivation and work environment encourage "flow"? (p. 235)

- **Flow** (p. 236) is a state of feeling completely involved and focused on a task. Managers can increase motivation and foster flow by keeping employees intellectually engaged, removing distractions, encouraging creativity and flexibility, and supporting employees in all aspects of their lives.

2. What are the main theories of motivation and how are they appled to the workforce? (pp. 237–241)

- Maslow's hierarchy describes motivation as a response to a progressive set of needs for **physiology** (p. 237), **safety** (p. 237), **belonging** (p. 238), **esteem** (p. 238), and **self-actualization** (p. 238).
- McClelland's **three needs theory** (p. 238) states the main motivators are the need for achievement, affiliation, and power.
- Herzberg broke the idea of motivation into two categories: **hygiene factors** (p. 238) and **motivators** (p. 238).
- **Extrinsic motivators** (p. 239) are external factors that generate engagement with the work, such as pay or promotion.
- **Intrinsic motivators** (p. 239) are internal drives that come from the actual interest of the work or from a sense of purpose and value in the work being done.
- **Theory X** (p. 239) posits that humans inherently dislike work and will try to avoid it if they can. As a result, managers should adopt a hard-line, authoritarian style.
- **Theory Y** (p. 239) proposes that people view work as natural and will be motivated to work as long as they are satisfied with their jobs. Thus, managers should implement a softer style that involves ample employee participation.
- **Theory Z** (p. 240) suggests workers want to cooperate and be loyal to an organization. It emphasizes collaborative decision making.
- **The Vroom model** (**expectancy theory;** p. 240) states that an individual's motivation can be described by the relationship between expectancy, instrumentality, and valence.

3. How have motivational theories and industrial psychology changed the work environment since the early twentieth century? (pp. 241–243)

- **Industrial psychology** (p. 241) is a field of academic study developed to scientifically understand how to optimally manage people and work.
- A 1932 study by Elton May concluded that when workers feel important, productivity increases. This is called the **Hawthorne effect** (p. 241). After World War II, research began to focus on the management of entire organizations rather than individual workers.
- Modern workplaces are influenced by new ideas, including the **uncertainty management theory** (p. 242) and **sociocracy** (p. 242). Studies of people engaged in creative work are showing they are demotivated by traditional financial incentives and highly motivated by offers of autonomy, mastery, and purpose.

4. What are the various identifiable leadership styles and traits, and how do they affect business leadership? (pp. 243–249)

- Leaders may exhibit a **democratic** (p. 244), **autocratic** (p. 244), **affiliative** (**laissez-faire;** p. 245), and/or **visionary** (p. 245) style. Many top executives demonstrate one or more of these styles in their business dealings.
- Certain traits are common among effective leaders. They challenge conventional beliefs, inspire a shared vision, model by example, use emotional intelligence, and enable others to perform to their fullest potential.

5. What are the best ways to create, manage, and participate in teams? (pp. 250–256)

- Teams can benefit the workplace, allowing creative exchanges, organization, and positive competition.
- Effective teams must be designed and managed thoughtfully. The modern workplace includes workers spanning many generations, and it takes care and insight to make them mesh well on a single team.

Continued on next page

Chapter Summary (cont.)

- **Group flow** (p. 252) is achieved when a group knows how to work together so that each individual member can achieve flow. Best practices for creating strong teams include considering the size, the life span, and the status of the team.

- R. M. Belbin outlined a model of nine team roles. An effective team requires a variety of roles, and the members must be matched carefully to the team needs.

- Technology allows for virtual teams in which members are in different locations around the country or the world. Webcasts, electronic file exchange, and Web conferencing software make this more effective each year.

- Stephen Covey's **Seven Habits model** (p. 255) can help employees enhance their success as members of a team.

Key Terms

affiliative (or laissez-faire) leader (p. 245)

autocratic leader (p. 244)

belonging needs (p. 238)

corporate culture (p. 247)

cross-functional team (p. 253)

democratic leader (p. 244)

emotional intelligence (p. 246)

esteem needs (p. 238)

expectancy (p. 240)

expectancy theory (p. 240)

extrinsic motivators (p. 239)

flow (p. 236)

group flow (p. 252)

groupthink (p. 251)

Hawthorne effect (p. 241)

hierarchy of needs (p. 237)

hygiene factors (p. 238)

industrial psychology (p. 241)

instrumentality (p. 240)

intrinsic motivators (p. 239)

leading (p. 243)

motivator factors (p. 238)

motivator-hygiene theory (two-factor theory) (p. 238)

organizational psychology (p. 236)

physiological needs (p. 237)

safety needs (p. 237)

self-actualization needs (p. 238)

Seven Habits model (p. 255)

sociocracy (p. 242)

strength-based management (p. 241)

Theory X (p. 239)

Theory Y (p. 239)

Theory Z (p. 240)

three needs theory (p. 238)

valence (p. 240)

virtual team (p. 254)

visionary leaders (p. 245)

uncertainty management theory (p. 242)

Self-Test

Multiple Choice   You can find the answers on the last page of this book.

1. **Flow is a psychological state characterized by**

   a. a lack of interest in the world as it "flows" by.

   b. anxiety and sometimes depression.

   c. an intense desire to compete and win.

   d. being so involved and focused in an activity you may not realize time has passed.

2. **When employees are motivated,**

   a. they often take more time to be with their families.

   b. they often move on to other companies.

   c. net profits tend to decline.

   d. they are more productive and creative.

3. **Maslow's hierarchy of needs**

   a. is a theory of why people are motivated.

   b. uses three factors to compute the motivation of a person in a situation.

   c. was developed to address the Hawthorne effect.

   d. was displaced when Theory Z was introduced.

4. **With creative and abstract work, studies find that the principle motivators are**

   a. financial incentives.

   b. autonomy, mastery, and purpose.

   c. competitive push for advancement.

   d. reduction in hours involved at work.

5. **Teams improve creativity**

   a. when the phenomenon of groupthink sets in.

   b. no matter what the makeup of the team.

   c. when best practices for selecting the team members and roles are followed.

   d. when individuals work with others who are just like them.

6. **An example of Herzberg's hygiene factors is**

   a. open-mindedness.

   b. groupthink.

   c. cleanliness.

   d. a safe working environment.

7. **Theory Z is different than Theory X or Theory Y because**

   a. it relies heavily on collaborative decision making.

   b. it is authoritarian and hard line.

   c. it is often seen in mass manufacturing settings.

   d. managers believe people will seek out responsibility.

8. **Virtual teams are teams that**

   a. are incomplete and need to be established.

   b. only communicate through face-to-face meetings.

   c. primarily focus on technology-based projects.

   d. work in different physical locations.

9. **The Vroom model of motivational theory uses**

   a. expectancy, instrumentality, and valence.

   b. Rorschach ink blot testing.

   c. openness, conscientiousness, extraversion, and neuroticism.

   d. visualization that leads to daydreaming and lost time.

10. **Extrinsic motivators include such things as**

   a. knowing your supervisor cares about you.

   b. believing your opinion matters.

   c. knowing there is a large financial bonus for good work.

   d. working for a company whose mission is meaningful to you.

Self-Test

True/False You can find the answers on the last page of this book.

1. Organizational psychology studies how people organize labor movements.
   ☐ **True** or ☐ **False**

2. The Gallup Q12 survey is a study of the economies of the top 12 countries.
   ☐ **True** or ☐ **False**

3. Intrinsic motivators come from a sense of purpose and value in the work employees are doing.
   ☐ **True** or ☐ **False**

4. Strength-based management believes the best way to develop talent is to help employees add skills and knowledge that build on their existing strengths.
   ☐ **True** or ☐ **False**

5. Groupthink is the convergence of the group on the best idea.
   ☐ **True** or ☐ **False**

Critical Thinking Questions

1. There are several different theories of motivation. How does an abstract theory impact the day-to-day management tasks of a manager? Is there one theory that is correct? Or is there a need for a set of different theories?

2. Is it better for a business to respond to a changing climate by hiring a different style of leader or expect the current leadership to adapt its style to new conditions?

3. What factors are the most important for creating a team that works efficiently together? What problems have you seen in your own academic career when working in group settings, and how could they be prevented?

4. Consider the traits of effective leaders presented on page 246 in the chapter. Then consider your own personality traits. How could you strengthen the leadership traits you do not currently see in yourself?

5. Stephen Covey's Seven Habits model is focused on making you a more successful, efficient person. What impact would these seven habits have on your relationships with your friends and family?

Team Time

Forming a Successful Team

A shoe retailer's sales and earnings have a history of lagging during the spring and summer months. The company wants to reverse this trend by appealing to young people, a rapidly growing consumer base with increasing amounts of disposable income. The company has decided to give one team almost unlimited resources and freedom to develop a flip-flop sandal for modern, gadget-loving youth. You need to apply the best-practices principles in team formation to determine the personalities and strengths of each member and assign roles in which the members will be motivated and contribute.

Process

Step 1. Break up into teams of three or four individuals.

Step 2. Begin by deciding what tool you will use to evaluate each member for personality traits, strengths, and weaknesses.

Step 3. Develop a strategy for assessing what work needs to be done and then how your team will assign appropriate responsibilities to each member.

Step 4. How will you evaluate the level of motivation and creativity for the team? What changes can be made if the team's performance is not adequate?

Step 5. Present your findings to the class for discussion.

Ethics and Corporate Social Responsibility

Ethics in Teamwork

Being a member of a team means you are accountable for your actions and the actions of your fellow teammates. Review the following scenario.

Scenario

Imagine you work at an advertising firm. You're on a team that is developing an advertising campaign proposal for a chain of fitness centers. The firm has been struggling and needs your team to land this account. At a meeting, one of your teammates reveals that he has hacked into a competing firm's network and has a draft of its proposal for the same account. Your teammate wants to steal the idea and use it in your team's proposal. Most of your teammates agree with this idea, but you think it is unethical.

Questions

1. How would you handle this situation? Would you voice your objection or go along with the team?

2. If you decide to voice your objection, do you address the entire team or speak to members individually? Why?

3. How would you reconcile your role as a loyal employee and team player with your need to uphold ethical standards?

Web Exercises

1. **Testing 1, 2, 3 . . .**
   Find three online leadership, team roles, and/or personality assessment tools. See http://testyourself.psychtests.com for examples. How consistent are the results in describing your personality or tendencies? How accurate would you rate the results?

2. **Great American Leaders**
   Visit www.hbs.edu/leadership/database/index.html, the twentieth century great American leaders database, maintained by the Harvard University Business School. Select one leader from your state, one of your gender, one leader of the same ethnicity, and two additional people profiled from different industries. What similarities and differences do you see in this group of five great leaders?

3. **Drive**
   Visit the Web site of the Royal Society for the encouragement of Arts, Manufactures, and Commerce (theRSA.org) and view the talk given by Dan Pink on intrinsic motivation entitled Drive. You can see a wonderful animated version of the talk at www.youtube.com/watch?v=u6XAPnuFjJc. Describe his presentation in terms of what motivates you in school and in your free time.

4. **More Motivation**
   Review the set of motivational theories described on http://changingminds.org/explanations/theories/a_motivation.htm. Select three theories that were not discussed in this chapter and compare them to the motivational theories presented. How are they similar and how are they different? How would using these theories change how employees were treated in a workplace?

5. **Evaluating Team Dynamics**
   Consider a team that you are part of and complete the Team Dynamics Analysis form at Metarasa.biz. Submit the form and examine the report presented. Do you agree with the analysis of team dynamics? The Questions button on the report returned to you provides a set of questions to discuss within the group to examine problems and improve relationships. How do they work to spark useful discussion in your team?

Web Case

For more on the significant role of teamwork in innovation, access the Chapter 8 Web case entitled "Focus on Toyota: Teamwork and the Prius" located in the End-of-Chapter Assignments section at my*biz*lab.com.

Video Case

For more on building a corporate culture that maximizes organizational performance, access the Chapter 8 Video Case entitled "Kingston Technology: Big Company, Family Environment" located in the End-of-Chapter Assignments section at my*biz*lab.com.

Human Resource Management

H and R—two simple letters that, when taken together, represent a vital component of any successful business. Indeed, a well-managed human resources (HR) department is essential to the smooth operation of all organizations. HR managers like Leslie Booth are responsible for many tasks, from hiring to firing and everything in between. Why is HRM so important?

Objective 1 What processes are involved in human resource management (HRM)? (pp. 265–270)

Training and Evaluating Employees

Training allows a business to leverage the talents of its employees across a whole company. George Hensel knows how to run the perfect meeting. How can his company use him most efficiently to train others?

Objective 2 How are employees trained and evaluated? (pp. 271–276)

Compensating, Scheduling, Promoting, and Terminating Employees

To attract high-caliber applicants, companies need compensation packages that are comparable with their competitors or better. Kathy Sanchez is a full-time graphic designer but is struggling to afford health insurance. What other types of benefits are important in a good compensation package?

Objective 3 What are the main components of compensating and scheduling employees? (pp. 276–281)

Objective 4 How does employee status change through promotions, termination, and retirement? (pp. 281–282)

Managing Workplace Diversity

Diversity is encouraged because it benefits a company, but it has been a challenge for Chandraki Patel to manage the widely diverse group she is responsible for. What issues do companies and managers face when establishing more diversity in the workplace?

Objective 5 How does incorporating diversity affect the workforce? (pp. 283–285)

Labor and Union Issues

Workers form unions in an effort to protect their interests. If management makes a decision to reduce health care or salaries, union leaders are there to fight for the rights of workers. In 2007, the writers of television and movies went on strike, ending new episodes of popular shows for months. Did the union decision to strike help or hurt the writers?

Objective 6 What are the objectives, structures, and future of labor unions in the global business environment? (pp. 286–288)

PEARSON
my*biz*lab™

Hiring a New Employee

You're an employee at a medical products company named QueStar, with a staff of 150 and a sales force of 20. Management has asked you to increase sales revenue by 15 percent—no easy task in a competitive market. Can you do it?

Objective 7 Test yourself using my*biz*lab.com to show that you understand the chapter objectives.

Human Resource Management pp. 265–270

When HR manager Leslie Booth was assigned to find a new senior account executive, she weighed her options carefully. To fill such a senior position required patience. She hired a recruiter to find outside candidates to interview for the position, and, to keep her options open, she also placed job postings online and in newspapers. When no one with the right qualifications had shown up in four weeks, she began to feel serious pressure from her boss to get the position filled. What should she do? ■

When you think about the resources required to run a business, you probably think about things like money, space, equipment, and supplies. Although financial and material resources are key aspects of a business, the resource often taken for granted, but that is arguably the most important, is the "human" resource—people. People provide ideas, creativity, knowledge, and ingenuity that make a business run. An organization can have all the money and materials in the world, but without the right people doing the right things, it will not be successful.

Human resources—the people in an organization—need to be managed just as carefully as the material and financial resources of a business. **Human resource management (HRM)** is the organizational function that deals with the people in the business: executives and managers plus frontline production, sales, and administrative staff. HRM encompasses every aspect of the "human" in a business, including hiring, training, motivating, evaluating, and compensating personnel, as shown in ▼ **Figure 9.1.** In addition to the traditional functions, HRM also works through the many challenges in today's workplace, such as diversity issues, work/life preferences, and global business considerations. In this section, you'll learn the ins and outs of HRM.

▼ **Figure 9.1 The Functions of HRM**

Managing Staffing Needs

How does planning for staffing needs change as a company evolve? A small business start-up may initially have one person serving as the company's CEO and financial manager, as well as the sales executive and the marketing director. As a business expands, new people are brought into the organization. At that point, the owner may still serve as the HR director, hiring, firing, and realigning employees to fill the growing needs of the expanding business. Although keeping track of HR needs at small businesses can be fairly simple, companies that add employees and continue to grow require more specific HR planning.

Poor staff planning can be costly. Being overstaffed burdens a company with the unnecessary expense of maintaining salaries, benefits, and training for surplus employees. An understaffed organization can lead to a loss of sales and competitiveness if customer needs are not met. Planning staffing needs consists, therefore, of two components: (1) assessing the supply of and the demand for current and future employee resources and (2) evaluating job requirements.

How does a company determine whether it has the right amount of employees?

The first component of HR planning is to assess the current supply of and the demand for employees. The current supply of employees is determined by developing a workforce profile. A **workforce profile** is a personnel inventory that includes information about each employee, such as age, education, training, experience, specialized skills, and current and previous positions held within the company.

The future demand for employees is determined in a process called **forecasting.** Forecasting is based on several factors, such as the predicted sales of a company's goods or services, the current workforce skill level, the effect of technology changes on staff needs, and changes in employment practices (such as using more or less temporary staff). In addition, staffing changes that are expected to occur through normal turnover, retirement, and any planned reassignments are also taken into consideration. If forecasting indicates an imbalance between the supply of and the demand for employees, further action must be taken. Such actions may include recruitment, training, retraining, labor reductions, or changes in workforce utilization.

How do companies identify the exact jobs they need to staff?

Before making shifts in staffing levels, the HR department completes a study of the tasks to be performed within the organization. A **job analysis** defines in detail the particular duties and requirements of the tasks and responsibilities an employee is required to perform. A job analysis includes a **job description,** a formal statement that summarizes what the employee will do in that role. It includes the responsibilities of that position, the conditions under which the job will be performed, and its relationship to other functions in the organization. Job descriptions are important because they define job objectives that are used later in performance appraisals. They also can become a part of the legal contract between the employee and the employer.

To assist in recruiting the right person to fulfill a job's requirements, **job specifications** are also defined in the job analysis. Job specifications are the skills, education, experience, and personal attributes that candidates need to possess to successfully fulfill the role. ▼ **Figure 9.2** shows a job analysis with a sample job description and the job specifications.

Once a job is well defined, how does HR find the best candidates to interview?

Matching the right person for each job depends on a well-devised recruiting plan. **Recruitment** is the process of finding, screening, and selecting people for a specific job. The recruitment process uses a variety of methods and resources. **Internal recruiting,** or filling job vacancies with existing employees from within a business, is the first choice of many companies. Often, companies post job openings on the company intranet, on staff notice boards, in in-house newsletters, and in staff meetings. Internal recruitment has several advantages. It tends to be a morale booster for employees because they know that the

Company: Nelson Wireless	
Position title: Marketing manager	
(a) Job description	**(b) Job specifications**
Join a team of marketing professionals focused on mobile technologies in the consumer market segment. The marketing manager is responsible for coordinating and/or implementing marketing projects designed for the consumer market segment. Working in cooperation with the sales team, product offers, and other headquarters marketing teams, the marketing manager will coordinate public relations projects and other promotional activities to drive Nelson Wireless brand awareness and product demand and generate consumer purchases. The marketing manager will provide strategic oversight for regional-level industry events, and be responsible for planning and executing customer events. The marketing manager will be responsible for coordinating budgets and timelines, maintaining accurate records of expenditures, and compiling reports of activity results. Additionally, he/she will be responsible for managing a team of 8–10 marketing associates. The marketing manager role will also include administrative elements such as invoice processing, event scheduling, and maintenance of a promotional calendar.	• College degree required with emphasis in marketing, business administration, or communications preferred • 3+ years marketing/communications experience required • Excellent demonstrated verbal and written communication skills • Demonstrated experience in event execution • Demonstrated ability to coordinate cooperative working relationships across multiple parties • Ability to work well under pressure • Extremely well organized, strong project management and time management skills and strong ability to multi-task • Proven ability to operate in a fast-paced, high-growth professional environment

▼ **Figure 9.2 A Sample Job Analysis Including a (a) Job Description and the (b) Job Specifications**

company has an interest in promoting their own employees. In addition, because employer and employee have established a working relationship, there is a reduced risk of selecting an inappropriate candidate for a desired position. Additionally, choosing from within is potentially quicker and less costly because it reduces the costs associated with outside recruiting and often shortens the length of training time.

However, there are disadvantages to solely looking internally and not considering outside sources. This includes the possibility of not getting the best candidate due to a limited search process. In addition, another internal vacancy is created that must be subsequently filled. Moreover, relying on internal employees may discourage new perspectives and ideas and eventually make a business resistant to change. As a result, businesses also rely on external recruiting to meet staffing needs. **External recruiting** looks outside a business to fill job vacancies.

▼ **Figure 9.3** lists various resources HR staff use when recruiting externally. Depending on the type of position, employment agencies or consultant firms may used. Employment agencies often specialize in specific sectors, such as accounting, sales, or clerical services. Employment agencies provide a screened pool of candidates, which reduces the hiring company's administrative burden of recruitment. However, these agencies can be costly. Recruitment consultants, often referred to as "headhunters," conduct more specialized searches, usually for senior management or key employees. Recruitment consultants are often expensive, but the costs

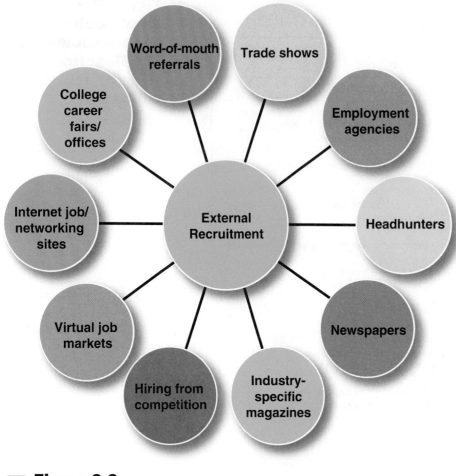

▼ **Figure 9.3 External Recruitment Resources**

of finding the wrong candidate can be even higher. Posting ads in local newspapers, on Internet job sites, or in specialized trade magazines can be advantageous methods because they are not expensive and reach a wide audience.

How do social-networking sites impact recruiting?

You're familiar with social-networking sites like Facebook and Twitter. The same concept is applied to the professional community through sites such as LinkedIn (linkedin.com), Jigsaw (jigsaw.com), and Spoke (spoke.com). LinkedIn is an online network of more than 70 million[1] experienced professionals from around the world whose connections are made through college, graduate school, or professional affiliations. Most people would like to hire or work with someone they know, and LinkedIn can provide helpful colleague and customer recommendations. Using applications such as SlideShare and Google Presentations, LinkedIn members can post presentations they have given as well as showcase their portfolios of work. This helps recruiters quickly evaluate and sort prospective candidates. With versions supporting most mobile devices, such as the Blackberry and the iPhone, LinkedIn is always available when an HR recruiter wants to follow a lead. Additionally, LinkedIn may assist job seekers by providing them with "insider" information on companies and employees. For example, before an interview, LinkedIn might be able to provide background information on the person with whom you are meeting. Knowing more about the interviewer and the company can provide good conversation during the interview.

What are some challenges in recruiting?

One of the newer challenges facing recruiting specialists is the use of technology. People looking for a job and companies looking to hire use online job and résumé posting sites, Web and video blogs, virtual job fairs, and podcasts to find job prospects and job candidates. When the use of technology was new, these methods were often highly successful and cost-effective. The dramatic growth of job and résumé postings has made the efficient and effective use of technology in recruitment more challenging. Online job postings yield many responses and thus a large pool of candidates, so sifting through these responses to find the right person for the job can be a time-consuming process for HR professionals. In fact, one of the greatest recruiting challenges cited is the difficulty of finding qualified candidates for critical positions.[2] Therefore, HR managers must know how to skillfully use technology. At a basic recruiting level, this means learning how to make a posted job description appeal to the most qualified candidates as well as stand out from competitors in the online environment so the right person can find the open position more readily. It also means becoming familiar with the new social-networking technologies and techniques to post jobs and find recruits.

BizChat

HR and Social Media Risks

Social media force us to consider new questions about the boundaries between work and personal life.

What are the risks of posting information on social media sites? Consider corporate hiring practices. As a job applicant, should you expect that the HR department will review any public information posted—such as reading your Facebook Wall and checking out the Facebook pages of your friends? What if during an interview an employer asks that you "friend" them into other areas of your Facebook site as part of the interview process? Should employee evaluations include an examination of public postings to see what kind of comments the employee is making about the company's products and services? What if confidential information that is sensitive to the company appears on your Twitter feed—can the company take action against you? What if the company feels that by posting your current location you have given away information important to the company? Already policies are appearing to examine some of these issues. For example, the FTC has indicated employees must disclose employment relationships when commenting on their employer's products/services on social media.

On a positive side, social media can be used as your own personal marketing agency, creating a "brand" for you as a prospective employee. More and more HR directors are using LinkedIn and Facebook as places to find talent for the positions they need to fill. Does your Facebook page attract a second look from a professional recruiter? Does it include presentations and videos that show your abilities and potential?

For more information and discussion questions about this topic, check out the BizChat feature on my*biz*lab.com.

Hiring

What happens in the hiring process? As shown in ▼ **Figure 9.4,** hiring is a multistep process. The first step is to narrow down the group of applicants to form a select pool of candidates. To do this, HR managers compare the candidates' qualifications to the job specifications. In addition, many companies use special applicant-tracking system software to quickly sort through résumés and job applications. HR managers also use systems that build assessments into the application process to help prescreen for certain personality traits. For example, Kay Straky, senior vice president of human resources at Universal Studios Hollywood, needed a system to manage the recruiting efforts required to fill high-turnover positions at the studio. In addition, rampant theft from employees demanded that Straky find a way to hire more responsible and honest employees. Her solution was to use Unicru, an applicant-tracking and workforce-optimizer system developed by Kronos. This system allows an employer to build a job application that includes a dependability assessment to screen candidates who are inclined to steal or skip work. The changes in the application and screening process improved the turnover rate for Universal Studios Hollywood from a high of 40 percent down to 10 percent.[3] Other companies, such as Lowes and Target, also use Unicru to evaluate an applicant's personality as part of the interview process. This practice is not

▼ **Figure 9.4**
The Hiring Process

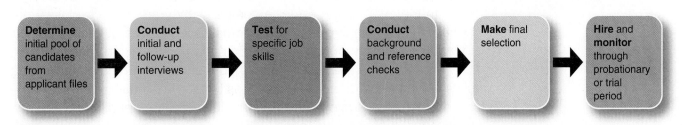

| **Determine** initial pool of candidates from applicant files | **Conduct** initial and follow-up interviews | **Test** for specific job skills | **Conduct** background and reference checks | **Make** final selection | **Hire** and **monitor** through probationary or trial period |

without controversy, however. Some groups feel such tests discriminate against those who are "different" in any way, for example, people who are more socially withdrawn.

After identifying a small pool of appropriate candidates, department and HR managers interview them to gauge a candidate's personality, clarify information in the candidate's résumé, and determine whether he or she is the best match for the position. The candidate might also need to complete some skills-related tests. If necessary, a candidate will be brought back for follow-up interviews.

Before offering a candidate a position, it is important that the company completes thorough background and reference checks. It's not uncommon to hear stories about companies that failed to conduct background checks and hired someone who falsified his or her educational or professional experiences or who had been in trouble with the law. For example, the Treaty Group Inc. relied on a large global personnel and training firm to help with its hiring needs. Unfortunately, the person whom Treaty hired to assist with bookkeeping functions defrauded the company of over $250,000. It was discovered later that the hired bookkeeper had been convicted of defrauding a former employer prior to joining Treaty.[4]

What legalities must be considered when hiring Several federal laws must be observed during the hiring process:

1. **Federal Equal Employment Opportunity.** Established in 1965, the Federal Equal Employment Opportunity Commission (EEOC) works to "ensure equality of opportunity by vigorously enforcing federal legislation prohibiting discrimination in employment." This legislation consists of a number of different acts and laws, known as equal employment opportunity (EEO) laws. As part of this mission, the EEOC investigates claims of discrimination and files lawsuits against companies when necessary.[5]

2. **The Civil Rights Act of 1964.** The Civil Rights Act of 1964 prohibits discrimination based on race, color, gender, religion, and national origin. Title VII of the act also established the EEOC to enforce antidiscrimination laws.

3. **Americans with Disabilities Act.** The Americans with Disabilities Act of 1990 (ADA) prohibits discrimination based on disabilities (or perceived disabilities). It also requires employers to make reasonable accommodations to the known disability of a qualified applicant or employee as long as it does not impose an "undue hardship" on the operation of an employer's business. Reasonable accommodations might include providing wheelchair accessibility, modified equipment, or interpreters.[6]

4. **Age Discrimination in Employment Act.** The Age Discrimination in Employment Act (ADEA) of 1967 makes it unlawful to discriminate against a person because of his or her age with respect to employment. It also prohibits the inclusion of age preferences in job notices or advertisements, except in specific circumstances where age is considered necessary to the job's function.[7]

HR departments take care of a company's biggest resource—its employees. HR managers like Leslie Booth must possess a variety of skills to capably oversee a wide array of complex tasks. Although these tasks—planning, recruiting, and hiring—may not seem directly related to the overall success of a company, they are, in fact, closely entwined. After not finding a strong candidate for four weeks, Leslie decided to rewrite the job description to more carefully match the job specifications. She expanded the search into virtual job markets and Internet networking sites and offered a bonus to employees for word-of-mouth referrals. Applications began to arrive that were from higher-caliber candidates, and she is confident that she'll hire soon. ∎

Training and Evaluating Employees pp. 271–276

George Hensel is an expert at running meetings—and everybody knows it. A meeting with George in charge will be just the right length, everybody will have their voice heard, and creative results often emerge. Employees throughout the national company would love to run a meeting like George does, but there is no time or budget to send him around the country to train them on how to do so. How can George's skills be leveraged to help the entire company? ■

Employee training is important for many reasons because it often contributes to many employee characteristics:[8]

- Increased job satisfaction, motivation, and morale among employees
- Greater efficiency in work, resulting in financial gain
- More effective use of new technologies and methods
- The development of new strategies and products
- Lower employee turnover
- Fewer interpersonal conflicts and better communication

Companies that emphasize training and development experience greater employee productivity, loyalty, and retention—all of which are good for the bottom line. In this section, you'll learn about how training and evaluating employees can enhance the success of a business and ensure that employees stay in top form.

Training Methods and Requirements

What kind of training do new employees receive?

Initially, when an employee is hired, an organization uses an **orientation program** to integrate a new employee into the company. Orientation can be as simple as an overview of an organization and the distribution of basic information, such as company procedures and expectations. Today, however, many companies are going beyond the traditional orientation program of explaining rules and regulations, as reflected in the orientation checklist in ▼ **Table 9.1.** Orientation is more

▼ **Table 9.1**

New Employee Orientation
Action
Your First Day
• You will be introduced to the current staff and your appointed mentor. • You will see your new workspace and have a tour of the facilities. • You will review the job description, including the job's responsibilities and expectations. • You will receive a copy of the company handbook. • You will review any health or financial benefits that are available. • You will be introduced to general administrative practices used by the department. • You will have an opportunity to ask questions.
Your First Week
• You can expect to have brief, daily meetings with your direct manager so that you understand your responsibilities for the day. • You will meet with your appointed mentor to discuss issues or problems. • At the end of the week, you will have a meeting with your employer to discuss any professional questions or personal concerns you may have.

effective if it becomes a means of familiarizing the employee with a company's mission, discussing how a new employee's contribution can add to a company's success. In addition, employees should be introduced to associates in their department so they feel at ease and can quickly become as productive as possible. A failure to adequately integrate new hires into a company leads to low retention rates.

What other training is required of new and present employees?

Training begins where orientation ends. Training should teach employees skills or ways to improve on existing skills. For example, a salesperson might know how to sell a product but may not know all the intricacies of selling a new product. Often, other employees in the department or the recent hire's mentor can conduct **on-the-job training.** With on-the-job training, employees learn skills by performing them. For example, there are many training and certification programs to become a pharmacy technician. But the specialty of nuclear pharmacy technician, a position that requires dispensing radiopharmaceuticals for use as therapies or for diagnostic testing in hospital settings, requires 500 additional hours of on-the-job training in a nuclear pharmacy.[9]

Some trades require an apprentice training program. An **apprentice training program** trains individuals through classroom or formal instruction and on-the-job training. For example, there is a growing need for underwater welders to repair the infrastructure of bridges and other structures where the key components are underwater. The training to be an underwater welder requires completing a surface welder program and a commercial diving program. Next you would apply to a commercial diving company that offers underwater welding as a service. You would begin your career as a diver tender (apprentice diver) to build experience in the trade. Once you have proven sufficient skills, you can advance to welder-diver status.

Some jobs are more readily learned through a **programmed learning approach** in which an employee is asked to perform step-by-step instructions or respond to questions. These often come in the form of computerized multiple-choice tests that provide immediate feedback. The benefit of programmed learning is that an employee can progress at his or her own pace, picking up information piece by piece. For some settings though this kind of training may not match the type of complex decision making needed to teach employees. It also requires a commitment in providing computer access to employees and in acquiring and maintaining the automated training software.

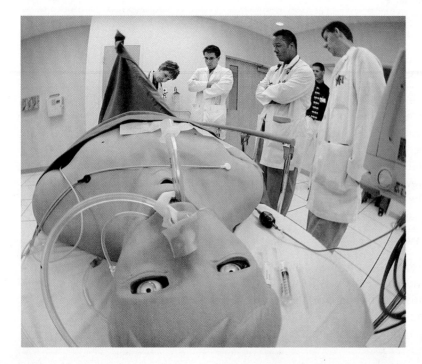
Robots are used in simulation training for medical students.

What kind of impact does technology have on training?

Improvements in technology provide companies with other training options, such as simulated training and interactive multimedia training. Some companies, such as Cold Stone Creamery, are turning once-dull training into a good time by taking advantage of "serious games" to train their employees. Stone City[10] is a training game used by new Cold Stone Creamery frontline employees that focuses on portion control and customer service.

Other companies are offering simulation training that allows their employees to really get a taste for their jobs. **Simulation training** (or **vestibule training**) provides realistic job-task training in a manner that is challenging but does not create the threat of failure. It is most suitable for airline pilots, astronauts, and surgeons for whom making mistakes during training is not an option or is too costly. However, other organizations take advantage of simulation training as well. For example, at the Institute for Simulation & Training at the University of Central Florida, students interact with virtual students in a classroom simulation program.

Online training, or distance learning, allows employees to take college classes on the Internet at their convenience, enabling them to obtain specific job-related education or pursue a degree. Other forms of Internet-based distance learning training involve instructors in a centralized location teaching groups of employees at remote locations via television hookups (*teletraining*) or through a combination of audiovisual equipment (*videoconferencing*). Pulse is a Kansas-based company that creates patient relationship management software for hospitals and medical facilities. Physicians, front office staff, and billing staff use the product to streamline patient care. When Pulse began to expand with offices in other states, it needed a quick way to train its own helpdesk staff when product feature upgrades came out. It also wanted to be able to quickly reach out to customers if they needed additional training. Pulse found Web and videoconferencing to be the solution. Using videoconferencing, the company can hold meetings and training using audio and video broadcasting and can also share documents, applications, and even use remote control of an attendee's desktop to illustrate a point.[11]

For employees who are accustomed to playing video games, learning through computer simulation programs is an attractive option. Would you want to try it?

Electronic Performance Support Systems (*EPSSs*) are another form of training technology. These systems provide employees with information, advice, and training when they need it, automatically, so they can accomplish specific tasks quickly. EPSSs are especially useful to train and support helpdesk and on-call operators as well as to act as an in-house helpdesk alternative. When Pitney Bowes, a provider of mail and messaging management equipment, previously upgraded its information management system, few employees took advantage of the half-day, instructor-led training programs the company offered. Instead, employees inundated the company's helpdesk with their questions, which turned out to be a very inefficient and costly result. With their next software upgrade, Pitney Bowes implemented an EPSS mentor program and found that the volume of helpdesk call requests declined by over 2,000 calls per week, saving the company an estimated $50,000 per week.[12]

Do managers need training? Because of their roles in the organization, managers require different training than their frontline workers. Managerial training therefore often focuses on leadership, communication, teamwork, and relationship-building skills. In addition, managers need to keep abreast of changes in employment laws, such as discrimination and harassment, as well as updates in using new tools for electronic communication.

In addition to training for current managers, many companies offer **management development programs** that prepare management-trainees to become managers within an organization. These programs may have trainees participate in an on-the-job training program, which might include *job rotation*, in which an employee rotates through different departments to learn firsthand the various aspects of the business, or a *coaching/understudy program*, in which an employee works directly with senior management in planning and other managerial functions. *Action learning*, another management development training approach, focuses on solving real problems on actual work projects. Action learning allows trainees to work together on teams to analyze real-time corporate problems that extend beyond their areas of expertise. Companies such as GE and Johnson & Johnson (J&J) have successfully implemented action-learning teams as part of their management development programs.[13]

Some companies use **off-the-job training and development** techniques that require employees to participate in outside seminars, university-conducted programs, and corporate universities. Hamburger University, McDonald's corporate training facility, trains restaurant managers and midlevel managers. Management hopefuls enroll in extensive classroom and field instruction and can earn credit that can even be applied toward a two-year or four-year degree.[14]

What about mentors? Senior managers often use *executive coaches* to further develop their effectiveness. Executive coaches identify a manager's strengths and weaknesses by interviewing those who work closely with the manager. They then meet with the manager to work on eliminating weaknesses and further developing strengths. Mentoring is another option that companies use to enable their experienced employees to work closely with inexperienced employees. **Mentors** are experienced individuals who help a less experienced person by explaining how to perform specific tasks, creating opportunities to learn new skills, and counseling about the consequences of particular actions and decisions. Like other forms of training and management development, mentoring increases employee performance, satisfaction, and loyalty.

Performance Appraisals and Alternatives

Why are performance appraisals necessary? A **performance appraisal** is an evaluation of an employee's performance that gives feedback about how well an employee is doing, as well as where changes and improvements are needed. A sample appraisal form is shown in ▼ **Figure 9.5.** Managers use the results of performance appraisals in decisions about promotion, raises, additional training, or reassignments. The performance appraisal process is important for both employees and the organization as a whole and includes three aspects:

1. Determining standards that employees should aim for in their work.

▼ **Figure 9.5 A Sample Performance Appraisal**

Annual Employee Performance Evaluation

Employee's Name:		Supervisor:	
Job Title:		Date Hired:	
Department:		Date of Review:	

Evaluation

This form is designed to assess your current performance and to help in setting goals for the future. This form is considered confidential and will only be reviewed by you and your supervisor(s).

Overall Job Knowledge/Experience Level

	Consistently meets requirements
	Generally meets requirements
	Does not meet requirements

Comments:

Quality of Work

	Exceeds expectations
	Meets expectations
	Does not meet expectations

Comments:

Attendance

	Rarely tardy or absent
	Sometimes tardy or absent
	Frequently tardy or absent

Comments:

Cooperation

	Consistently participates and contributes to the team
	Generally participates and contributes to the team
	Does not participate or contribute to the team

Comments:

Future Goals:

2. Evaluating an employee's performance in comparison with these standards.
3. Providing feedback to reduce and eliminate poor performance and improve or enhance positive performance.

When employees are hired, they should have a good understanding of what is expected of them. These expectations become the performance standards on which they'll be measured. Appraisals act as a confirmation of these standards and help employees establish quantifiable and measurable goals for improvement in the upcoming year.

Are there problems with performance appraisals? Performance appraisals, when conducted properly, are very helpful to an employee and ultimately an organization; however, they are often not effective. Because appraisals often lead to criticism, many managers shy away from them because they are uncomfortable handing out bad or harsh comments. Additionally, some managers have a difficult time quantifying performance and fear not being able to defend their ratings if questioned. Although performance appraisals often suggest means to improve weak performance or enhance solid performance, the process does not always offer the opportunity to follow up and ensure that such means have been acted on. Often, it's not until the next performance appraisal that it is recognized that such training and development did not occur. And when the next appraisal can be a year away, more immediate crises can take time away from the focus on an appraisal's recommendations.

What alternatives exist for performance appraisals? An alternative to a performance appraisal is performance management. **Performance management** is an approach that combines goal setting, performance appraisals, and training and development into a unified and ongoing process. As such, it is more of a cyclical and fluid process than the single occurrence of a performance appraisal. Employees are constantly receiving feedback and given opportunities for training and development to ensure that they have the right tools with which to perform their jobs. ▼ **Table 9.2**

▼ Table 9.2

Aspects of Performance Management	
Direction sharing	Communicating an organization's higher-level goals, such as vision, mission, values, and strategy
Role clarifying	Defining roles in terms of daily work tasks
Goal setting and planning	Redefining organizational or departmental goals into specific employee goals, which includes an employee's development of the steps necessary to achieve goals
Ongoing performance monitoring and feedback	Periodic performance reports regarding progress on meeting goals as well as feedback regarding progress toward goals
Coaching and support	Ongoing as a part of the feedback process
Performance assessment (appraisal)	An element in the performance management process that offers specific, defined knowledge on how an employee's performance is improving company results
Rewards, recognition, and compensation	Given as appropriate to motivate an employee toward achieving current and future goals
Workflow, process control, and return on investment management	Making sure an employee's measurable performance is linked to measurable goals of company

summarizes several aspects of the performance management process. The concept, while often applied to employees, is also applicable to other components of an organization, including an entire department, a product or a service, or an organization as a whole.

Performance management, appraisals, and training can play a significant role in keeping a business productive and efficient. At George Hensel's company, management decided that knowing how to run and participate in a productive meeting was a skill that all employees should have. They therefore created online learning modules that featured videos in which George explained how people often allow meetings to go off track. The company then created a simulation game that allowed players to conduct a virtual meeting and be "scored" for how efficient they were. Employees who logged a certain number of attempts at the online training and simulation received special credit in their performance appraisal. The company commitment to training is having benefits, though meetings still aren't anyone's favorite activity. ■

Compensating, Scheduling, Promoting, and Terminating Employees pp. 276–282

Kathy Sanchez loves what she does. Since graduating from college two years ago, she has worked for a small start-up company as a graphic designer, creating brochures and other materials for a wide variety of clients. Because the company is so small, she gets to work on projects she would never have a chance to work on in a bigger company. She also loves the relaxed atmosphere of the office and feels like her coworkers are actually her friends. So what's the problem? Because the company is just getting on its feet, it isn't able to offer her much in the way of pay or benefits. Although she loves her work, she is tired of reaching the end of each pay period with no money left. And don't even ask her about her retirement plan or health insurance! What should she do? ■

Having the right pay system in place is very important for a company to become and remain competitive. A good compensation package attracts high-quality employees and keeps them from leaving. But compensation is not just about monetary rewards. In today's workplace, employees frequently receive compensation in a variety of forms, including work/life benefits, health insurance, and retirement plans. Because there are many ways to structure compensation, the decision is not an easy one. It's often a delicate balance between paying to attract and keep the best and not jeopardizing the financial security of a company. In this section, you'll learn about payment structures, as well as two more functions of the HR department: promotions and terminations.

Compensation Strategies

Are all employees paid in the same way? There are many ways to pay workers for their time and effort. **Compensation,** payment for work performed, is generally offered through direct financial payments in the form of fixed **salaries** (annual pay for a specific job) or **wages** (payments for hourly work). Usually, on an annual basis, an employee's compensation level has the potential to increase based on the results of employee evaluations. Some positions, such as those in sales, are better compensated with an **incentive-based payment** structure that has a lower base salary enhanced with **commissions,** compensation based directly on an employee's performance. Incentive-based compensation motivates employees to perform at their best. **Bonuses,** compensation based on total corporate profits, help tie employees' efforts to the company's bottom line. Higher corporate profits mean higher bonuses.

What types of retirement plans do companies offer employees?

The most popular retirement plan offered today is the 401(k) plan. A **401(k) plan** is a defined contribution plan in which pretax dollars are invested in a bundle of investments that are generally managed by an outside investment company, such as the Vanguard Group or Fidelity Investments. The amount of the annual contribution is determined by the employee as a percentage of salary up to a specified legal limit. In some cases, a company will match a portion of the employee's contribution to the account.

Some companies offer their full-time employees the opportunity to participate in a pension plan. **Pension plans** are programs that provide income to individuals in their retirement. There are two types of pension plans:

- With *defined benefit plans*, employees know ahead of time how much pension they will receive when they retire. Defined benefit plans are not popular with employers, as a company takes on the financial risk if the fund's investments do not perform as expected.

- *Defined contribution plans* specify the annual amount employees will contribute to their pension plan through payroll deductions. With defined contribution plans, the actual amount received at retirement depends on the amount contributed and the fund's investment earnings. The burden of risk falls on employees with defined contribution plans, and there is no way they can determine how much will ultimately be available until they actually retire.

A **profit sharing plan** is a term used for a range of different types of compensation options. At many businesses, profit sharing means that if the company hits certain profit targets, then there is a bonus structure for employees. Sometimes the term *profit sharing* is used for company contributions to an employee retirement plan. Profit sharing plans are often offered as a part of executive compensation in larger companies, but in many small companies, they are a way to motivate employees, especially during the start-up phase when cash is tight and salaries may be low.

What other financial incentives do companies offer employees?

Stock option agreements allow an employee to purchase a specific number of shares of stock at a specific price but only at a specific point in time. If the stock value increases beyond that point, the employee can reap a huge financial reward. If not, however, the employee gains little. For example, when Bonnie Brown joined Google in 1999 as an in-house masseuse, Google had only 40 employees. She was offered a small salary and a stock option package that would allow her to buy a huge number of shares of stock for just a few dollars a share. She never imagined the stock would be worth more than that. A few years later when she left Google she could "exercise" her option, or cash in by buying Google stock, now at $85 a share for her agreed-on price of just a few dollars. She became a multimillionaire in that transaction, but her best decision was to keep a certain percentage of her options. A few years later, when Google stock rose to over $740 a share, she cashed in those shares and now has her own in-house masseuse business.[15]

Employee stock purchase plans allow employees to buy company stock at a discount (usually at 85 percent of market value). Companies typically limit the amount of stock an employee can purchase this way to 10 percent of their total salary. **Employee stock ownership plans (ESOPs)** use a company's pension plan for employees to invest in company stock, effectively giving employees significant ownership in a company. For example, in 1994, United Airlines was failing and needed to negotiate dramatic wage reductions with its unions (pilots, flight attendants, etc.). The employees formed the United Airlines ESOP and then agreed to 8–15 percent wage cuts for the next five years. In return, the ESOP acquired 55 percent ownership of United Airlines. An advantage of providing employees with ownership in a company via stock transactions is that employees feel more connected to the business and are motivated to ensure that the business succeeds. For United Airlines, the next several years saw the value of the company rise by $4 billion.[16]

Benefits

What are noncash forms of compensation?

An important part of the business planning and management process is determining the type and amount of **employee benefits,** or indirect financial and nonfinancial payments an employer offers that supplement cash compensation. Benefit compensation often enables a company to attract, motivate, and retain the best employees. Benefits come in many forms, including health and disability insurance, vacation and sick pay, and retirement plans. Vacation time, holidays, and pensions, once referred to as "fringe benefits," constitute a significant percentage of total compensation.

The Googleplex, Google's Mountain View, California, campus, has several pools, 11 free gourmet cafeterias, volleyball courts, and massage services.

Some companies offer **flexible benefit plans** (or **cafeteria plans)** that permit an employee to pick from a menu of several choices of taxable and nontaxable forms of compensation. Flexible benefit plans allow employees to choose the benefits that are most important to them, while reducing the cost of offering all benefits to all employees.

What are work/life benefits?

Work/life benefits are benefits that help an employee achieve a balance between the demands of life both inside and outside the workplace. Work/life benefits include flexible schedules, relaxed atmospheres, and child care and fitness/gym programs. For example, the SAS Institute, the largest privately held software developer in the United States, offers employees an on-site fitness club with indoor pool, on-site car detailing, massages, and a hair salon. Although seemingly expensive, this strategy of keeping its employees happy saves the company approximately $70 million per year because it experiences low turnover. In fact, compared with an industry average of 20 percent turnover, SAS has kept its turnover rate at about 2 percent.[17]

What are some other trends in employee benefits?

In the early 80s, the *Village Voice,* a free alternative weekly newspaper in New York City, began offering *domestic-partner benefits.* These benefits provide for an employee's unmarried partner of the same or opposite sex. Since then, domestic-partner benefits have become increasingly common components of compensation packages. In fact, almost 60 percent of Fortune 500 companies offer domestic benefits to their employees.[18] Benefits such as health care and family leave policies are extended to domestic partners. Recently, companies have also begun to address taxation inequities for domestic partner benefits. Same-sex couples pay a tax on the health benefits for their partners that married couples do not. In 2010, Google began a policy to reimburse same-sex couples the $1,069 they pay in federal taxes for their domestic-partner benefits.[19] Other Silicon Valley companies are expected to follow suit as they compete for the same talent.

The Phoenix Companies Inc., a life insurance and wealth management corporation, recently enhanced its employee benefits package with *paternity and adoption benefits* that allow time off for new fathers and reimbursement and paid leave for adoption. The company is following a trend that, according to the Families and Work Institute and the Society for Human Resource Management, is represented by approximately 15 percent of companies in the United States that offer paternity benefits.[20]

In addition to these voluntary benefits, the Family and Medical Leave Act states that companies with more than 50 employees must allow all eligible employees to take up to 12 weeks of unpaid time off to be with family because of medical issues, births, or adoptions. Upon the employee's return, the act guarantees that the employee can return to his or her job or a comparable job.

Alternative Scheduling and Work Arrangements

What work arrangements are possible for those who choose not to work a traditional workweek? An increasing number of employees are finding that managing the demands of work and personal life results in doing neither well. The added stresses that employees today face from child care, elder care, commuting, and other work/life conflicts have led to a decrease in productivity and an increase in employee absenteeism and tardiness. As a result, more and more employers are offering alternatives to the traditional 9 AM to 5 PM, Monday to Friday workweek. In fact, a study looking at the behavior of over 24,000 IBM employees found that employees with flexible schedules and the ability to work from home worked an additional 19 hours per week.[21]

The most popular flexible work arrangements include the following:

1. **Alternative scheduling plans (flextime).** In *alternative scheduling plans* or **flextime,** management defines a total number of required hours as a core workday and is flexible with the starting and ending times. Managers must rise to the challenge of ensuring that required hours are met and monitoring employee performance. However, overall, flexible arrangements allow for increased productivity due to reductions in absenteeism and tardiness.

2. **Permanent part-time. Permanent part-time employees** are hired on a permanent basis to work a part-time week. Unlike temporary part-time workers who are employed to fill short-term needs, permanent part-time employees enjoy the same benefits that full-time employees receive.

3. **Job sharing. Job sharing** is an arrangement in which two employees work part-time to share one full-time job. Those who share a job have been found to be very motivated to make this

UPS offers a permanent part-time package handler position in which employees work 3.5 to 4 hours per day, Monday through Friday, with no weekend or evening work required. In addition to traditional health insurance, vacations, and a stock purchase plan, UPS offers tuition assistance as an additional benefit, which makes this type of position perfect for the working student.

flexible situation work, so productivity and employee satisfaction increase. On the other hand, conflicts may arise if the job sharers don't have a clear understanding of who is in charge of what or if there is confusion from other employees about whom to contact and when. Therefore, job sharers must carefully coordinate and communicate both with one another and their employer to ensure that all responsibilities are met.

4. **Compressed workweek.** A **compressed workweek** allows employees to work four 10-hour days instead of five 8-hour days each week, or 9 days instead of 10 in a two-week schedule for 80 hours. Such arrangements can reduce worker overtime, make more efficient use of facilities, and provide employees with longer blocks of personal time and less commuting time. The disadvantages are a potential increase in employee fatigue and conflicts with state labor laws that cite overtime requirements for hours worked in excess of 8 per day.

What if employees want to work from home? Telecommuting allows employees to work in the office part-time and work from home part-time or work completely from home, making only occasional visits to the office. Telecommuting reduces commuting costs and allows employees to take care of home needs while also fulfilling work responsibilities. For example, Cisco now has a workforce that telecommutes an average of two days per week and estimates it has saved the company $277 million.[22] Telecommuting arrangements are also necessary for those employees dealing with clients, colleagues, or suppliers who are on the other side of the globe. Taking calls at 2 AM is much easier at home than at the office. The disadvantages of telecommuting include monitoring employees' performance at a distance, servicing equipment for off-site employees, and communication issues. Additionally, employees who telecommute may become isolated from other employees.

Despite the costs associated with designing and implementing flexible working arrangements, employers can expect positive bottom-line results due to increases in employee satisfaction, decreases in absenteeism, and increases in worker productivity. Similarly, reductions in employee turnover lead to a decrease in time and costs associated with employee recruiting and replacement training.

Contingent Workers

Why does a company hire contingent workers? Contingent workers are people who are hired on an as-needed basis and lack status as regular, full-time employees. These workers often fulfill important and specific functions. Contingent workers are most likely hired by companies in business and professional services, education and health-care services, and construction industries. Companies hire such temporary workers to fill in for absent employees or augment the staff during busy periods. Long-term temporary staff is often hired for indefinite periods of time to work on specific projects. In many cases, temporary staffing is part of a company's HR "temp to perm" strategy in which temporary employees are evaluated and then moved to a permanent position if they are found to be reliable and skilled.

Independent contractors and **consultants** are another form of contingent workers who are generally self-employed. Companies hire them on a temporary basis to perform specific tasks. Often, contractors are hired for those jobs that involve state-of-the-art skills in construction, financial activities, and professional and business services. For example, it might be most cost-efficient to hire a Web-page developer as an independent contractor rather than keeping one on staff permanently. Consultants are hired to assist with long-term projects, often at a strategic level, but also with a specific end in sight. For example, a company that is reviewing its executive management compensation arrangements might hire a compensation consultant.

Why would someone want to be a temporary worker? Temporary staffing is a $70 billion industry, represented by companies such as Kelly Services, Manpower, Accountemps, and Spherion. Many people cite flexibility and variety as a benefit of working for a temporary agency. Because their assignments are short-term, temporary workers are able to experience working in many different companies, doing different jobs, and meeting numerous people. In many instances, temporary workers are hired permanently. Recent college graduates and college students find temporary work as a means to gain real-world experience in an industry they are interested in pursuing on a full-time basis. Other temporary workers are retired professionals who want to do something productive in their free time but still maintain some flexibility. Also, parents who need to earn income but also require a flexible schedule find that temporary work enables them to accomplish both. The U.S. Bureau of Labor Statistics estimates that the temporary workforce accounts for between 2 percent and 4 percent of the U.S. workforce.[23]

Promotions

How can employees increase their level of responsibility in a company? After performing successfully in a position, many employees look to increase their level of responsibility and stature in a company or a department through a promotion. Usually, a promotion means more pay and responsibility. Employers like to promote from within because they can reward exceptional behavior and fill positions with tested employees. However, promotion may not always result in a positive situation if it is seen as being draped in secrecy, unfairness, or arbitrariness. Therefore, management must ensure that promotions are based on a distinct set of criteria, such as seniority or competency.

Do promotions always move you into management positions? Consider an engineer who succeeds on the job but has no desire to manage. Some companies provide two career paths: one toward management and the other for "individual contributors" with no management aspirations. Therefore, engineers, for example, with a desire to manage can pursue one track, and other engineers without managerial aspirations or capabilities can be promoted to a position such as "senior engineer." Alternatively, it's always possible to keep employees in their same job but give them more responsibility, thus enriching their experience while continuing to prepare them for further advancement.

Terminating Employees

Why do companies lay off workers? At times, it becomes necessary to reevaluate an employee's contribution or tenure at a company or reevaluate the composition and size of the workforce altogether. Downsizing and restructuring, the growth of outsourcing and offshoring, the pressures of global competition, and the increased uses of technology are also reasons companies look to reduce the number of employees. **Termination** refers to the act of permanently laying off workers due to poor performance or a discontinued need for their services. Companies often offer a set of benefits for terminated employees, including the continuation of health-care coverage, severance pay, and outplacement services like résumé writing and career counseling.

Terminating employees due to poor performance or illegal activities is a complex process. Most states support **employment at will,** a legal doctrine that states that an employer can fire an employee for any reason at any time. Likewise, an employee is equally free to resign at any time for any reason. Exceptions to the

PEARSON **my*biz*lab**

For an interactive, real-world example of this topic, access this chapter's **BizSkill** entitled Firing an Employee, located at **my*biz*lab**.com.

employment-at-will doctrine include the inability for employers to discriminate and fire someone because of legally protected characteristics or activities, such as race, religion, age, gender, national origin, or disability. In addition, companies cannot terminate employees because of whistle-blowing (revealing company wrongdoing to authorities), filing a worker's compensation claim, jury service, or testifying against a company in a legal proceeding.

Before firing an employee for wrongful acts or incompetence, managers must take steps to avoid a wrongful discharge lawsuit. These steps include maintaining solid records so that they can build a case for dismissal with sufficient documentation and evidence. Courts have sided with the terminated employee, especially when not enough evidence of poor behavior is brought forth. Written evidence is the only material evidence accepted, which makes building an employee's personnel file with documented proof of poor performance critical. Hearsay and rumors do not stand up in legal proceedings. For example, Riam Dean was a 22-year-old law student when she began working at Abercrombie & Fitch in London. She explained she had a prosthetic arm because she was born without a left forearm. The company agreed she could wear a cardigan to cover the prosthesis and work on the store floor. But she later was removed when higher management learned of her situation and felt she was breaking the company "look policy" that all employees "represent Abercrombie & Fitch with natural, classic American style." She sued for wrongful dismissal and won compensation for her lost wages and damages.[24]

Retirement

Is there a set age when employees retire? It used to be that employees retired when they became 65 years old. **Retirement** is the point in one's life where one stops participating full-time in a career. Although nearly three-fourths of all workers would like to retire before the age of 60, a survey by the John J. Heldrich Center for Workforce Development at Rutgers University[25] indicates that nearly 7 in 10 workers plan to keep working past retirement age. Although some survey respondents indicated that the reason for staying on the job was to remain active, the major factor contributing to this shift is financial need.

One impact of this shift in workforce demographics is more competition for younger employees to be promoted into certain jobs. For employers, an aging workforce may present other challenges, such as age-discrimination lawsuits if they aggressively lay off older workers. Therefore, to encourage older workers to retire, companies have offered financial incentives, known as **worker buyouts** (or *golden parachutes*). This was the case at Toyota in 2009. A global recession resulted in a 32 percent U.S. sales drop, so wages were frozen, and temporary workers were cut. An additional step was to offer assembly line workers a buyout if they would leave voluntarily. Under the terms of the buyout, workers would receive 10 weeks of pay plus 2 weeks of pay for every year of service as well as a $20,000 lump sum payment.[26]

Remember Kathy Sanchez, who loved her job but was struggling with deciding what to do because of her low pay and benefits? After some serious soul-searching, Kathy decided to stay on at the small company, but she has set a limit of two more years before she starts looking for a job elsewhere. She is hoping that within that timeframe, the start-up company will get a solid footing and be able to offer its employees not only a positive work environment but also an attractive and competitive compensation package as well. ■

Managing Workplace Diversity pp. 283–285

Chandraki Patel always thought of herself as someone who was familiar with a range of types of people and cultures. Though she was born in Wisconsin, her parents came from India, and she has often traveled abroad for vacations. But now that she is a manager at an international marketing firm, she is faced with issues she never anticipated. She has a staff that includes men and women from six different nationalities with five different religions (each with different holiday calendars). In addition, she is responsible for remotely managing a site in Dublin, Ireland, and one in Beijing, China. The language and cultural differences there have caused misunderstandings more than once. How could anyone manage so many different types of people and locations? ■

Most likely, you work, study, and socialize with people who are of different gender, age, religion, race, sexual orientation, mental and physical ability, and educational background than you. In this section, you'll learn about what makes the modern workplace so diverse and how diversity introduces both challenges and benefits to organizations.

Benefits and Challenges of Diversity

Why has the modern workplace become so diverse? Several changes have led to increased diversity in the workforce. For example, advancements in technology have made it possible for businesses to operate with relative ease on a global basis. It's not unusual for companies to offshore work to other countries to decrease labor costs or establish operations in other countries to broaden their market reach. Moreover, U.S.-based companies are hiring workers who have emigrated from other countries to the United States. European and Middle Eastern companies are experiencing similar increases in immigration.

Meanwhile, more women are entering the workforce than ever before, and baby boomers, those born between 1946 and 1964, now compose about one-third of the U.S. workforce. Many baby boomers are indicating that they would like to and need to work beyond the traditional retirement age, meaning increased age-diversity in the workforce. For all these reasons, the modern workplace is now very diverse in age, gender, and ethnicity.

How is a diverse workforce beneficial? Diversity is an important component of the modern workplace. For many companies, hiring to diversify the workforce initially meant fulfilling an **affirmative action** requirement by filling positions with a certain number of women, Hispanics, or African Americans. Some criticized this strategy as unfair and bad for a company if the best candidate was not hired in favor of meeting such a requirement. Over time, however, many companies have come to embrace the idea of diversity beyond just satisfying a requirement. It's now becoming clear that companies should embrace diversity as a strategy and resource to become more competitive in the global market.

Harley-Davidson realized that to remain competitive, it needed to understand the needs and wants of customers beyond the traditional stereotype of the white male. Since then, the motorcycle manufacturer has made a significant effort to hire and retain women and minority managers.[27]

Promoting diversity in the workplace is more than affirmative action that prescribes a company employ a certain number of minorities and women. Instead, diversity should be aggressively pursued as a means to improve a company's competitiveness and its bottom line. A diverse workforce helps companies offer a broad range of viewpoints that are necessary to compete in a world that is more globalized. Such variety in viewpoints promotes creativity in problem solving with improved results.

In addition, products and services need to cater to customers and clients with diverse backgrounds, so it's vital to have a workforce that understands the nuances of different cultural needs. Additionally, a diverse staff helps strategize ways to handle markets that have become segmented, both culturally and demographically.[28] For example, PepsiCo's Frito-Lay division launched a Doritos guacamole-flavored tortilla chip to appeal especially to Latino consumers. The Latino Employee Network provided valuable feedback on taste and packaging to ensure that the Latino community would consider these chips as authentic. The product generated more than $100 million in sales in its first year, making it the most successful product launch in the company's history.

What issues do companies face while managing diversity?

Despite its many benefits, a diverse workforce can pose challenges. For example, a more culturally diverse population naturally brings about a wider variety of religious beliefs and practices, with more employees trying to integrate their religious practices into their workday. As employers struggle to accommodate workers' religious needs, they must also try to avoid the potential friction that open demonstrations of religious practices might provoke. Many employers strike a balance by allowing employees to take prayer breaks, enabling employees to take time off to observe religious holidays, catering to dietary requirements, and permitting differences in dress. Value City Department Stores, for example, have created quiet prayer rooms for Muslims. Some employers encourage workers to form religious-based support groups, such as Bible study groups.

Although the number of women in the workforce is growing, women are still battling some of the same issues that their mothers and grandmothers faced: sexism, salary inequities, and sexual harassment. Historically, women in similar positions as their male counterparts were paid less and have experienced fewer promotions, despite documented higher performance ratings. Many gender-discrimination and sexual harassment lawsuits continue to receive national press and indicate that gender-related challenges have not gone away.

The aging workforce also creates several challenges. Compared with younger workers in the same position, older workers often expect higher salaries and better benefits. Health-care costs, for example, are higher with an older workforce. However, many employers find that hiring and retaining older employees has several benefits, including less turnover and absenteeism, lower training costs, and a willingness to learn new skills and help and train younger coworkers. These ben-

Off the Mark Only One Diversity Training Does Not Fit All

Because promoting diversity is a priority for most companies in today's global marketplace, so too is the implementation of diversity training programs. These often-costly programs typically involve workshops and seminars that teach managers about the benefits of a diverse workforce. And yet, according to a recent study, most of them simply don't work.[29] After analyzing years of national employment statistics, the study concluded that standard diversity training rarely had an effect on the number of women or minority managers employed at companies where it was used. Why not? Some theorize that mandatory training inevitably leads to backlash; others say altering people's inner biases is a nearly impossible task.

Hope for promoting diversity in the workplace is not lost, however; the study also found that two techniques had significant, beneficial effects on workplace diversity: (1) the appointment of a specific person or committee who is specifically accountable for addressing diversity issues within the company led to 10 percent increases in the number of women and minorities in management positions. (2) Mentorships increased the number of African-American women in leadership positions by 23.5 percent.

efits offer enough savings to a company to negate the higher costs in retaining more senior workers.

How can employees improve their understanding of each other's differences? Differences can create misunderstandings and conflict, even over the most well-intentioned behaviors. Therefore, it is important that employers provide effective **diversity training** for their employees. It is also important for coworkers to learn to look at situations from a perspective that is different from their own. While implementing a diversity plan, it is important to ensure that Caucasian men who have been instrumental in the company do not feel tossed out or undervalued if they are passed up for promotion in lieu of someone from a more diverse background. Ultimately, managing diversity is developing a workforce that has a capacity to accept, incorporate, and empower the diversity of human talents and perspectives.

Recall Chandraki Patel who was responsible for a staff with different cultural backgrounds, languages, and beliefs in her position at an international marketing firm? She decided to take on diversity management as an area where her performance could improve. She began by researching all the ways that the diversity of the group she managed had led to innovative solutions to problems. As she counted the many benefits of working with such a varied range of people in the group, she felt more motivated to manage some of the challenges. She began a training program to help employees become more adept at examining issues from a variety of perspectives. Not only did that help within the group she headed up, but it also led to better cooperation with the Chinese and Irish divisions. ■

Labor and Union Issues pp. 286–288

It was a really exciting day in early 2006 when Gavin Smith joined the Writer's Guild of America (WGA). It meant he really did have a career as a writer. Before you can even apply for membership, the WGA requires that you have written material for television, movies, or radio. Now that he was part of the WGA, he had a credit union, a health plan, and a pension plan. He could connect with other screenplay writers and really boost his career.

But in November, the WGA declared a strike. Picketing began at CBS, NBC, Disney, Fox, Sony, Warner Bros—just about every entertainment company Gavin had ever hoped to work for! He received a memo from the WGA telling him that he was required to picket at Paramount Studios. It was Paramount that had given him his big break, cowriting part of a screenplay that was going into production soon. This would kill his relationship with the executives who hired him and paid him so well if they now drove past him as he carried a picket sign every day![30] ■

Have you ever passed a picket line and wondered why the workers were on strike? A **strike** occurs when workers agree to stop work until certain demands are met. In this section, you'll learn about the role of organized labor in the workplace and how this role is changing in today's global economy.

Organized Labor

What is a labor union? A **labor union** is a legally recognized group dedicated to protecting the interests of workers. Unions represent many types of workers in public-sector industries, such as teachers, nurses, and firefighters; in manufacturing industries such as the automotive industry; and in construction specialty "craft" groups such as engineers, plumbers, and roofers. Entertainers and supporting industries, such as actors and writers, also have unions. Labor unions negotiate various employment issues, such as salary, benefits, and working hours.

What are the objectives of organized labor? Labor unions began as a means to protect workers from the terrible injustices employers inflicted on their workers in the nineteenth century during the U.S. Industrial Revolution. During that time, employers took advantage of workers, subjecting them to long hours, low pay, and health risks. Women and children were often treated even worse and paid less. Labor unions formed to fight for better working conditions and employee rights. These individual labor unions, by joining together, proved to be more effective in bettering working conditions. Two of the more influential unions are the **American Federation of Labor (AFL),** founded in 1886 to protect skilled workers, and the Industrial Workers of the World, founded in 1905 to represent mainly unskilled workers.

The **Congress of Industrial Organizations (CIO)** was formed in 1935 to represent entire industries rather than specific workers' groups. The CIO was initially a separate organization within the AFL but soon split to form its own organization. In

1955, the two were reunited to form the AFL-CIO, which is still in effect today as a federation composed of 56 member unions. The Change to Win Federation, formed in 2005 as an alternative to the AFL-CIO, is the newest member to organized labor. Other prominent unions include the United Auto Workers (UAW), the International Brotherhood of Teamsters, and the Service Employees International Union.

How are labor unions structured? To form a union, a group of workers must either have their employer voluntarily recognize them as a group or have a majority of workers form a **bargaining unit** for union representation. A bargaining unit is a group of employees that negotiates with an employer for better working conditions or pay. When a union forms, workers join and pay membership dues. Most unions have paid, full-time staff that is often supplemented with substantial volunteer workers. In addition to dues, some unions create strike funds that help support workers should they strike. Union members elect officers and shop stewards who make decisions for the entire body and represent the members in dealings with management. So that unions can better represent specific interests, union **locals** are created by workers of the same industry, company, region, or business sector.

Collective Bargaining

What is the collective bargaining process? One of the primary roles of a union is to negotiate with an employer for better work conditions and terms of employment. This generally is done through a **collective bargaining** process. Negotiation is between union representatives and employers usually over concerns related to wages, benefits, working hours, insurance benefits, and grievance procedures. A collective bargaining agreement is the result of such negotiations, and it forces an employer to abide by the conditions specified in the agreement. Change can only be made through subsequent negotiations.

What happens if an agreement cannot be reached through collective bargaining? If negotiating does not produce a collective bargaining agreement, and both parties seem to be at an impasse, then other means to settle the dispute are used before workers go on strike. **Mediation** is a process that involves a neutral third party that assists the two parties both privately and collectively to identify issues and develop proposals for resolution. The mediator works with both sides to understand their genuine interests and helps each side generate proposals that address those interests. In **arbitration,** a dispute is sent to an arbitrator for a decision. Arbitrators hear both sides of a dispute, and the parties involved agree in advance that the arbitrator's decision is final. Sometimes, arbitration is nonbinding, meaning that neither party is required to accept the arbitrator's decision.

What happens when negotiations break down? When negotiation reaches an impasse, union workers can take several actions to prompt management to accept union demands. Union members and those who are sympathetic to their cause can stage a **boycott,** in which supporters refuse to buy or handle a company's products or services. On the other hand, companies can use a **lockout** in which management refuses to allow union members to enter the premises. Lockouts are legal only if negotiations have come to an impasse and the company is defending a legitimate position.

As a last resort, union workers may vote to go on strike and agree to stop working. Strikes jeopardize the productivity of an organization, so they are used to force management into making concessions that they might not have made otherwise. Strikes also gain considerable media publicity, especially when workers **picket** a workplace by walking outside a company's entrances with signs that reflect the employees' grievances. Workers do not easily make the decision to strike, as they risk losing income throughout the strike period. For example, a six-week strike would cost a worker earning $700 per week a total of $4,200 in lost wages. If the new contract negotiated a weekly wage increase of $1, it would take about two years to recover the lost wages. Additionally, strikers might be fired or replaced as management has the authority to hire replacement personnel, known as **strikebreakers,** or scabs. Some states prohibit public safety workers, such as police officers and hospital workers, from going on strike. In these cases, workers often have "sick-outs," during which union members are not officially on strike but instead call in sick, refusing to come to work.

The State of Labor Unions

Are labor unions still effective today? In the United States, the role of labor unions is declining. As of 2009, 15.3 million people representing 12.3 percent of employed workers[31] were union members (see ▼ **Table 9.3**). Many private-sector unions, such as the automobile workers and construction trade unions, have experienced dramatic reductions in membership. This decline is the result of several factors, but arguably, the most prominent reason is a reaction to their own success by fighting for better working conditions, higher wages, and more benefits. Additionally, the introduction of technology has resulted in a shift from blue-collar–based industries to professional white-collar service-based industries, for which unions are less common. Despite declining numbers, labor unions continue to be influential in many industries, as well as in other countries.

What is the future of unions and labor-management relations? In response to a more globalized working community, unions have begun to build alliances with unions in other countries. They recognize that when multinational corporations decide to move production abroad, for example, there might be a negative impact on local and international workers. Consequently, in an effort to protect their interests, unions must broaden their reach and make a commitment to international labor solidarity. Immigration is another issue affecting unions. Immigrant workers are crossing borders and threaten to take jobs traditionally supported by labor unions. Unions, especially in California and Florida, continue to grapple with integrating and embracing these potential new members into the organization. Lastly, and perhaps most importantly, unions, will need to transform themselves to survive the effects of globalization.

Remember Gavin Smith, the WGA member faced with a strike action? In 2007 more than 12,000 writers joined the WGA strike, which lasted 100 days. Estimates were that the strike cost the Los Angeles economy between $1 and $2 billion.[32] But the agreement reached addressed the key area of concern—royalties for new media such as DVD sales, Internet downloads, and streaming video. Before the strike, writers had no compensation for these, and the three-year agreement reached in 2008 meant that writers felt protected as television and movies migrated toward the Internet. For Gavin, it meant he saw income from the DVD and Pay-Per-View distributions of his screenplay. Although it was a scary and difficult time, he feels the solidarity of the union helped the industry move forward in the right direction. ■

▼ Table 9.3

Union Membership in the United States, 2000–2009	
Year	Union Membership as Percentage of Employed Workers
2000	13.4
2001	13.3
2002	13.3
2003	12.9
2004	12.5
2005	12.5
2006	12.0
2007	12.1
2008	12.4
2009	12.3

Source: "Data Retrieval: Labor Force Statistics," U.S. Bureau of Labor Statistics. *www.bls.gov/webapps/legacy/cpslutab1 .htm and "Economic News Release,"* U.S. Bureau of Labor Statistics, *January 22, 2010. www.bls.gov/news.release/ union2.nr0.htm.*

Chapter Summary

1. What processes are involved in HRM?
(pp. 265–270)

- **Human resource management** (**HRM;** p. 265) is the organizational function that encompasses every aspect of the "human" in a business, including hiring, training, motivating, evaluating, and compensating personnel.
- Staff planning involves determining how many employees a company needs. A **workforce profile** (p. 266) is compiled as a form of "personnel inventory" and includes information about each employee. The future demand for employees is determined in a process called **forecasting** (p. 266).
- **Recruitment** (p. 266) is the process of finding, screening, and selecting people for a job.
- Hiring begins by narrowing down candidates who have been identified in the recruiting process to a select group of applicants.

2. How are employees trained and evaluated?
(pp. 271–276)

- An **orientation program** (p. 271) integrates new employees into an organization. Other forms of training include **on-the-job training** (p. 272), **apprentice training programs** (p. 272), and **simulation training** (p. 272).
- **Management development programs** (p. 273) prepare management-trainees to become managers within an organization by having them participate in on-the-job training programs.
- **Off-the-job training and development** (p. 274) require the employee to participate in outside seminars, university-conducted programs, and corporate universities.
- A **performance appraisal** (p. 274) is an evaluation of an employee's performance that gives feedback and suggestions for improvement. They are useful when done properly, but many managers avoid performance appraisals because they do not feel comfortable critiquing employees harshly.
- **Performance management** (p. 275) is an alternative to performance appraisals. It approaches employee evaluations as ongoing and systematic.

3. What are the main components of compensating and scheduling employees?
(pp. 276–281)

- **Compensation** (p. 277), or payment for work performed, consists of financial and nonfinancial payments.
- **Salaries** (p. 277) and hourly **wages** (p. 277), **bonuses** (p. 277), **commissions** (p. 277), and retirement **pension plans** (p. 277) constitute financial compensation.
- Defined benefit plans define the amount of retirement benefit the employee will receive, and defined contribution plans define the contribution the employee must make to the plan. **401(k) plans** (p. 277) allow employees to contribute pretax dollars to their retirement plans.
- Noncash **employee benefits** (p. 278) come in many forms, including health and disability insurance, vacation and sick pay, and retirement plans.
- **Work/life benefits** (p. 278), such as gym memberships, are important for those employees who are trying to balance busy lives both in and out of work.
- Alternative scheduling arrangements enable employees to have more flexibility in their workday times. **Flextime** (p. 279), **job sharing** (p. 279), **permanent part-time** (p. 279), **telecommuting** (p. 280), and **compressed workweeks** (p. 280) are alternative scheduling methods.

4. How does employee status change through promotions, termination, and retirement?
(pp. 281–282)

- Employees increase their level of responsibility through promotion—taking on a job that has more responsibility and stature in a company or a department.
- **Termination** (p. 281) is when companies permanently lay off workers due to poor performance or a discontinued use for their services. Downsizing and restructuring, outsourcing and offshoring, pressures of global competition, and increased uses of technology are reasons companies look to reduce the number of employees through termination.
- **Retirement** (p. 282) occurs when employees decide to stop working on a full-time basis or stop working altogether. Financial security, staying active and engaged, and learning something new are reasons seniors cite for deferring retirement.

Continued on next page

Chapter Summary (cont.)

5. How does incorporating diversity affect the workforce? (pp. 283–285)

- The workforce today consists of employees from many different cultures and religions, which can lead to challenges in helping employees understand one another.
- More women are entering the workforce, but few are reaching executive management levels. Sexism, salary inequity, and sexual harassment remain prominent issues.
- The workforce is getting older as more baby boomers work beyond typical retirement age. An aging workforce increases health-care costs but also increases productivity and decreases training costs.
- A diverse workforce has proven to be more creative and innovative. Diversity keeps companies competitive in a global business community.

6. What are the objectives, structures, and future of labor unions in the global business environment? (pp. 286–288)

- A **labor union** (p. 286) is a legally recognized group dedicated to protecting the interests of workers. Labor unions typically negotiate various employment issues, such as salary, health benefits, and work hours.
- Representatives of the labor union form a **bargaining unit** (p. 287) that negotiates with employers in a **collective bargaining** process (p. 287) in hopes of reaching an agreement that is satisfactory to both sides.
- If satisfactory terms cannot be agreed on by both sides, the process is often turned over for **mediation** (p. 287), in which a neutral third party assists both sides and generates a proposal that addresses each party's interests.
- In the **arbitration** (p. 287) process, a third party settles the dispute after hearing all the issues.
- If negotiations break down, unions may choose to **boycott** (p. 287) a company.
- As a last resort, union members may vote to go on **strike** (p. 286) and agree to stop working altogether.
- As the business community continues to expand globally, unions will need to change their definition of membership to handle the increase in immigration workers.

Key Terms

401(k) plan   (p. 277)

affirmative action   (p. 283)

American Federation of Labor (AFL)   (p. 286)

apprentice training program   (p. 272)

arbitration   (p. 287)

bargaining unit   (p. 287)

bonus   (p. 277)

boycott   (p. 287)

collective bargaining   (p. 287)

commissions   (p. 277)

compensation   (p. 277)

compressed workweek   (p. 280)

Congress of Industrial Organizations (CIO)   (p. 286)

consultants   (p. 280)

contingent workers   (p. 280)

diversity training   (p. 285)

employee benefits   (p. 278)

employee stock ownership plan (ESOP)   (p. 278)

employee stock purchase plan   (p. 278)

employment at will   (p. 281)

external recruiting   (p. 267)

flexible benefit plan (cafeteria plan)   (p. 278)

flextime   (p. 279)

forecasting   (p. 266)

human resource management (HRM)   (p. 265)

incentive-based payment   (p. 277)

independent contractors   (p. 280)

internal recruiting   (p. 266)

job analysis   (p. 266)

job description   (p. 266)

job sharing   (p. 279)

job specifications   (p. 266)

Self-Test

Multiple Choice   You can find the answers on the last page of this book.

1. Sally McGowan, the HR director for her company, is assessing whether her company has adequate staff. To do so, Sally needs to compile a

   a. job analysis.

   b. workforce profile.

   c. job description.

   d. job specification.

2. Walter Thompson will be interviewing candidates for an administrative assistant's job. Which of the following interview questions is legally inadvisable for him to ask?

   a. What church do you attend?

   b. What are your strengths and weaknesses?

   c. What are your hobbies?

   d. Who do you think will win the Super Bowl?

3. In training some professionals, such as airline pilots or physicians, the risks of poor judgment are so high that training programs often use

   a. online training.

   b. programmed learning.

   c. vestibule training.

   d. teletraining.

4. The performance review process often includes all of the following except a(n)

   a. evaluation of the employee's social standing in the work environment.

   b. assessment of performance as compared to defined standards.

   c. specific feedback on how to enhance positive performance.

   d. clear definition of expectations from the employee.

5. Amit Patel, as part of his compensation package, was offered an opportunity to purchase company stock at a later date but valued at the current, lower price. Which of the following is Amit given?

   a. Stock option

   b. Stock ownership plan

   c. Stock purchase plan

   d. None of the above

6. James Rodriguez wants to spend more time at home with his two-year-old granddaughter and is considering leaving the company. He could receive three months pay and the same retirement package he will be eligible for in three years time if he leaves now. This type of offer is called a(n)

   a. independent consultant status.

   b. worker buyout.

   c. retirement.

   d. compressed workweek.

7. Which one of the following is NOT a reason to hire a contingent worker?

   a. To fill in for absent employees

   b. Not enough office space for a full-time employee

   c. To supplement staff during particularly busy times

   d. To evaluate how a person performs on the job before hiring permanently

8. Which of the following are benefits companies have experienced from employing a diverse workforce?

   a. Cultural differences add more perspectives and promote better problem solving.

   b. They fulfill expected affirmative action standards.

   c. Companies become more competitive in the global marketplace.

   d. All of the above

9. The AFL-CIO, the UAW, and the Teamsters are examples of

   a. illegal organizations.

   b. labor unions.

   c. labor relations.

   d. union locals.

10. Which of the following are actions that management can take when threatened with disgruntled employees walking out on their jobs?

   a. Hiring strikebreakers

   b. Boycotting employees

   c. Imposing a lockout

   d. Both a and c

Self-Test

True/False
You can find the answers on the last page of this book.

1. Frontline employees are the only employees who require training.
   ☐ **True** or ☐ **False**

2. Affirmative action plans are recommended but not required in the United States.
   ☐ **True** or ☐ **False**

3. Some managers use an alternative to performance appraisals called performance management.
   ☐ **True** or ☐ **False**

4. Free gourmet lunches, on-site child care, and on-site health facilities are benefits provided by some U.S. companies.
   ☐ **True** or ☐ **False**

5. A diversified workforce adds creativity and a variety of viewpoints to the workforce, which often helps improve a company's competitiveness and its bottom line.
   ☐ **True** or ☐ **False**

Critical Thinking Questions

1. Human resources is a separate function in most large companies. Explain how HR concepts and techniques can be useful to all employees in a company.

2. Performance management is one alternative to a traditional performance appraisal. Which style of evaluation would you prefer as an employee? Which would be more useful to you as a manager?

3. Discuss the various types of training you have had as an employee. What suggestions would you make to improve the training? What parts of the training did you find the most effective? How important is training employees to a company's overall goals and strategies?

4. Labor unions were born at a time when working conditions were quite exploitive and even dangerous in many parts of the United States. Do labor unions serve a purpose in today's workplace environment? Discuss what functions unions provide that benefit a company as a whole.

5. Describe the "perfect" benefits package that would be most important to you when applying for a job. What kinds of questions could you ask to determine how and when those benefits will be offered to you? How does salary/pay level affect your decision? Would you accept a lower salary/pay level for better benefits?

Team Time

Seeing Both Sides

Walmart has been both praised and criticized for many of its HR policies. Assemble into teams of four students. Divide each team into two subgroups.

a. Subgroup 1—Good HR Practices: Going back no more than five years, research articles about the positive HR policies and practices Walmart has implemented. Prepare a summary paper outlining your findings.

b. Subgroup 2—Bad HR Practices: Going back no more than five years, research articles about the negative HR policies and practices Walmart has implemented. Prepare a summary paper outlining your findings.

Process

Step 1. As a group, compile your findings, comparing the positive and negative policies. Were there instances where a policy started out as a positive and ended up as a negative or vice versa? How did their policies work with Walmart's strategic goals? How have their policies affected Walmart's stock price and bottom line?

Step 2. If you were employed as an HR consultant for Walmart, what kind of advice would you give the company based on your findings?

Ethics and Corporate Social Responsibility

The Ethics of Interviewing

The interview and hiring process is fraught with ethical concerns. Form a small group and discuss the ethical implications of the following scenario.

Scenario

Where does a candidate's right to privacy end and a company's right to know begin? As you learned in this chapter, federal laws protect potential employees from discrimination. Hiring managers must observe these laws by refraining from asking certain questions during the interview process, such as direct questions about age and physical disabilities. However, to find out about these topics while still staying within the bounds of legality, managers have devised alternative questions.[33] For example:

Instead of asking . . .	They ask this legal alternative . . .
Which religious holidays do you observe?	Can you work our required schedule?
Do you have children?	What is your experience with "X" age group?
Do you have any disabilities?	Are you able to perform this position's specific duties?

Process

With your group, discuss your opinions on the use of these "legal alternatives" as an HR strategy. They are legal, but are they ethical? Do managers undermine the laws by finding ways around them? Or does a company have a right to know about these topics to make the best hiring decision?

Web Exercises

1. **Analyzing Annual Reports**
   Using the Internet, access the annual reports of three companies in different industries. How are human resources handled in the annual report? What kind of issues do these companies discuss that relate to human resources? What is similar and different among the companies?

2. **Online Training**
   There are several free online training sites. Can you find training modules on the following topics?
   - Driving a forklift
   - Using Microsoft Excel
   - Project management

   What kinds of training would you want to have face to face rather than in an online environment?

3. **Organized Labor**
   Explore the AFL-CIO Web site (www.aflcio.org). What are its current concerns and causes? How does one become involved in this organization? What is its history? Which historical, political, and social forces propelled the organized labor movement?

4. **Benefits Packages**
   Many companies have determined that their biggest asset is their employees, so taking care of employees is a mission critical objective. Research companies that use benefits packages as a way to make their employees feel cared for and retain a high percentage of employees. Consider both small and large businesses.

5. **Legal Matters**
   Visit the ACLU Action Center Web site (http://action.aclu.org/site/PageServer?pagename=AP_action_homepage) to find information about current issues concerning employee rights, antidiscrimination laws, or other HR concerns. What are the circumstances of these cases? What is your opinion on them?

Web Case

For more on the impact of labor relations on customer service, access the Chapter 9 Web case entitled "Focus on Toyota: The T-Ten Program" located in the End of Chapter Assignments section at my*biz*lab.com.

Video Case

For more on centralizing human resources, increasing employee effectiveness, and addressing high employee turnover rates, access the Chapter 9 Video Case entitled "Park Place Entertainment: Getting Everyone on Board" located in the End of Chapter Assignments section at my*biz*lab.com.

10 Business Technology

Information Technology Basics

When Melissa McGregor started working for a hardware store, she was amazed that the technology it used was so outdated. There was no Web site or e-mail account, and the cash registers weren't even connected to an information system. How could advancements in technology benefit the store?

Objective 1 What are the functions of a company's chief information officer (CIO) and information technology (IT) department? (pp. 297–298)

Objective 2 How are information technology, information systems, information, and data interrelated within a business? (pp. 298–300)

Computer Systems in Business

Frank Ordoqui is an IT specialist and an expert when it comes to advising businesses on how to use technology. He has seen the costs of failing to use technology, as well as the costs of using technology in ways that don't benefit a business. How can companies best take advantage of technology while avoiding its pitfalls?

Objective 3 How are major types of hardware, software, and networks used in business? (pp. 301–307)

The Benefits and Challenges of Technology

Mark Dagostino has worked as an IT specialist at an insurance firm for 15 years. Now, more than ever, he is on-call around the clock and even monitored by his boss electronically. How has business technology affected employees? How has it affected the bottom lines of businesses?

Objective 4 What are the benefits and risks of technology in the workplace, taking into account safety, creativity, communication, productivity, privacy, and ethics? (pp. 307–311)

The Global Impact of Business Technology

Peggy Best left the business world 12 years ago to raise her children. She's reentering the pharmaceutical industry and finding the differences between now and when she left shocking. Not only does she spend most of her day at her office in Pennsylvania using teleconference programs to communicate with her clients in China, but she also has to make sure that her work can be picked up seamlessly at the end of the day by the pharmaceutical team in India. How is the new global landscape affecting employees, businesses, and countries?

Objective 5 What is the impact of technology on the international business environment based on offshoring, outsourcing, and alternative methods of communication? (pp. 311–316)

PEARSON **mybizlab**

Technology Direction

For the last four years, you've been Director of Information Technology of East Coast Operations at Magnificent Tees. A position for Chief Information Officer has opened up, and two people are competing for the job. Can you make the right decisions over the next few days to show that you're the best person to be the new CIO?

Objective 6 Test yourself using mybizlab.com to show that you understand the chapter objectives.

Information Technology Basics pp. 297–300

When Melissa McGregor began working for a hardware store, she thought all she'd be doing was updating their Web site and maintaining the computer system. But when she saw the outdated technology they were using, she was amazed the place was still in business. There was no online ordering from the Web site, no e-mail accounts for internal communication, and the cash register was simply a calculator. The store owner told her that he wanted to give the store a makeover and update the technology so he could increase his profits. Melissa didn't know where to begin. What role does IT play in business? ■

Try to imagine a type of business that doesn't use computer systems for at least some primary functions—it's hard to do! Any modern business must be able to reach consumers via electronic communication media such as e-mail, Facebook, and Web sites. Accounting information can be managed electronically so that taxes are filed easily, and word processors and databases are vital to any business. In retail, point-of-sale terminals collect information that is fed into inventory and sales computer systems so that stock can be reordered, fast-moving products can be identified, and accounting information can be kept current and accurate. At Apple's retail stores, employees roam the store with mobile "cash registers" in hand. They complete credit card transactions, e-mail sales receipts, and have customers in and out of the store in no time. Many grocery stores, as well as Home Depot warehouses, provide self-service automated checkout systems, reducing the need for cashiers. It's clear that technology is changing fundamental aspects of how business is conducted.

In this chapter we'll examine how IT is changing the way we do business. Whether it's a small family-owned business getting its first electronic accounting system or a huge corporate conglomerate launching a new interactive Web site, the business world is getting more technologically advanced every day.

PEARSON **mybizlab**

For an interactive, real-world example of this topic, access this chapter's **BizSkill** entitled Technology Direction, located at **my*biz*lab**.com.

IT Professionals and the IT Organization

Who is in charge of business technology? Information technology **(IT)** is the design and implementation of computer-based information systems. In many organizational structures, the person responsible for such technology is the **chief information officer (CIO).** This is typically a position at the same level as the CFO of a firm, for example. As ▼ **Figure 10.1** shows, the CIO is in charge of information processing, including systems design and development and data center operations. He or she is responsible for updating or replacing the computer systems and the software the company uses. The CIO must also manage a budget that balances the benefits of technology against the ever-rising costs of upgrading to the latest systems. In addition, CIOs are involved in creating business and e-business opportunities as well as defining governing policies for the company in areas such as privacy and security.

▼ **Figure 10.1
The Many Functions
of a CIO**
Because technology is spread
across all divisions and major
functions of a modern
business, a CIO requires
excellent leadership and
organizational skills.

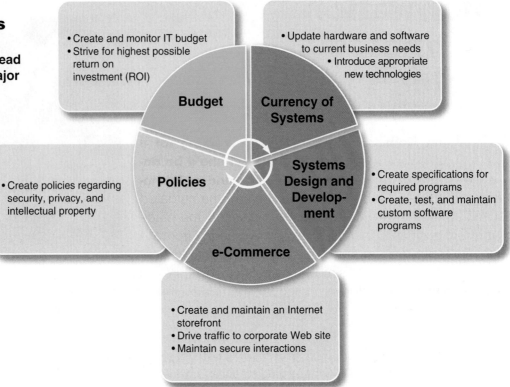

- Create and monitor IT budget
- Strive for highest possible return on investment (ROI)

- Update hardware and software to current business needs
- Introduce appropriate new technologies

Budget

Currency of Systems

Policies

Systems Design and Development

- Create policies regarding security, privacy, and intellectual property

- Create specifications for required programs
- Create, test, and maintain custom software programs

e-Commerce

- Create and maintain an Internet storefront
- Drive traffic to corporate Web site
- Maintain secure interactions

What happens in an IT department? The IT department is composed of several professionals responsible for everything from hardware components and software programs to networking strategies. Members of this department are also responsible for security, both in response to computer virus attacks and emergency recovery from power outages and system failures. In addition, the department keeps all the computers, printers, and other equipment operational and current. The IT department manages the design of a company's networks and databases where information is stored. The department is also responsible for selecting the appropriate software programs and providing training to employees. Sometimes, IT professionals must also create custom software to bridge the gaps between the products available and the needs of a firm. The IT department also maintains and manages the use of mobile computing throughout the company. Equipment includes notebook computers, Internet tablets like the iPad, smartphones, and other devices. Finally, the IT department is responsible for implementing remote access to computing resources, such as employees' access to work files or e-mail when they are working outside the office.

Information Systems

What's an information system? The main difference between an IT system and an **information system (IS)**, also called a **management information system (MIS)**, is that an MIS is focused on applying IT to solve business and economic problems. For example, the payroll department may need to upgrade to a new accounting system or software package. It is the role of the MIS to investigate the impact of that change on the other technology systems in the company and rate the amount of gain against the cost required for the new software. So, MIS professionals bridge the gap between purely technical knowledge and how it will impact a business.

What is the difference between data and information? In common usage, the terms *data* and *information* are often used interchangeably, but they have different meanings. **Data** are the representations of a fact or idea. Data may be a number, a word, an image, or a sound. **Information,** however, is data that have been organized or arranged in a way that makes the data useful (see ▼ **Figure 10.2**). The extraction of information from raw data is critical to the success of many business enterprises. Businesses try to use all the resources at their disposal to gather raw data. For example, media, credit bureaus, and information brokers often purchase data made public in court proceedings. These data are processed into useful information for that business or later resold to other companies. So, a health club in Massachusetts may request a list of recently divorced women from the family court. The health club's plan is to process that raw data into a mailing list of a specific target audience for its membership services.[1]

How can collecting data help an organization?

Businesses can easily collect and store large amounts of data, but turning them into useful information is a challenging task. Several software systems help in this regard. A **decision support system (DSS)** is a software system that enables companies to analyze collected data so they can predict the impact of business decisions. A DSS can also retrieve data from external sources and display results tied to business decision making. An **executive information system (EIS)** is a software system that is specially designed for the needs of management. This system can consolidate and summarize the transactions within an organization by using both internal and external sources. The terms DSS and EIS are sometimes used interchangeably, but usually an EIS has a more graphical interface compared to a DSS, which often uses spreadsheets and can show only one department or product at a time.

Business intelligence software can also assist managers in reporting, planning, and forecasting workforce performance. Business intelligence packages allow managers to analyze financial states, customer satisfaction, sales analysis, and supply chain status. Managers can quickly display the answers to several questions:[2]

- Who are my top 10 revenue-generating customers?
- What factors (e.g., regions, products, or customers) are the greatest contributors to bad debt?
- Which vendors have unpaid invoices, and how much money do these vendors owe?
- How many days' worth of inventory is in each warehouse?
- Which plants have completed the highest number of work orders on time?

How can companies make sense of all their data?

Data are stored in **database management systems (DBMSs).** DBMSs are collections of tables of data that organize the data and allow simple analysis and reporting. As companies begin to store vast amounts of data in database systems separate from their production databases, **data warehouses** are created. These can hold terabytes (thousands of gigabytes) of transaction data. Sometimes, subsets are created to isolate one product or one department. These smaller data sets are called **data marts.** The process of exploring and analyzing the data mart to uncover data relationships and data patterns that will help a business is referred to as **data mining.** Data mining can be used in many ways. For example, suppose a supermarket uses data mining

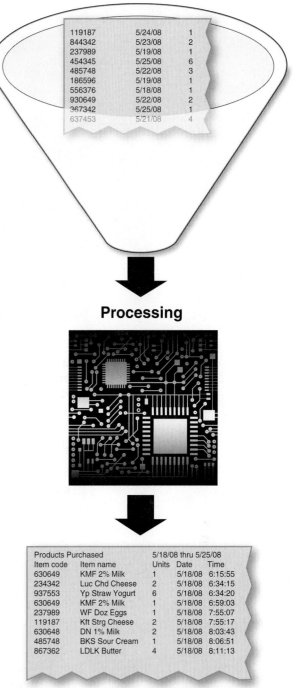

Processing

Information

▼ Figure 10.2 The Processing of Data into Useful Information

The raw data from a grocery store's sales log can be processed into information that will help the storeowner know when to schedule the store's milk shipments.

Many businesses use software programs to organize and analyze the data they collect.

to help decide whether to restock a product that isn't selling well. If data mining reveals that the few people who typically buy the product are among the supermarket's most profitable customers, it will most likely be worth keeping the product on the shelves to retain their business. Although data mining has not yet lived up to its full potential, new advances in hardware and software are making it a larger part of business decision making.

Even small businesses, like the hardware store where Melissa McGregor works, need someone with IT experience to bring their businesses into the modern age. Melissa's boss recognized that the success of his business was dependent on upgrading the technology used at his store, but he wasn't sure where to begin. Melissa began by developing a social media strategy, giving the company a Facebook and a Twitter presence, tying that to the online store at the company Web site and marketing materials sent out via e-mail. Melissa showed her boss that he would better be able to stay in touch with his customers by using this technology. She also recommended that the store upgrade to computerized cash registers, which would help employees process the sale and exchange of goods more efficiently. As the store's business improves, and they begin to realize benefits and profits from these initial changes, Melissa hopes to have the opportunity to make additional IT changes. ■

The IT department is responsible for everything from hardware to software to networking.

Computer Systems in Business pp. 301–307

A marketing firm contracted **Frank Ordoqui to act as an IT advisor to help upgrade the company's systems. The firm's CIO wanted the company** to have up-to-date technology, so he proposed issuing all members of the sales staff mobile devices. He wanted each salesperson to be issued a smartphone, a global positioning system (GPS) monitor, a mobile projector, and a portable printer. Frank advised that issuing all these devices to every salesperson would be wasteful. The excessive devices would cost the company a lot of money and require complicated maintenance and updates—and not necessarily increase company profits.

The previous year, Frank had served as an advisor for a company that wanted to incorporate only minimal technology. He gave that company the opposite advice, encouraging it to make a big investment in mobile devices. For that situation, Frank determined that such an investment was not going to waste the company's money—in fact, not doing so was wasting potential for the company. Its growth was limited because customers could not access salespeople and support staff quickly and easily. How does Frank determine what to recommend at each different consulting assignment? ■

With advancements in technology happening daily, what role do modern technologies, such as mobile devices, play in business? Is there such a thing as too much technology? In this section, you'll learn about the various types of business technology and what these different technologies accomplish in the workplace.

Hardware

Is business computing the same as personal computing? You're probably familiar with the hardware basics of a home computing system. A well-designed PC has a balance between the amount of (slow and inexpensive) hard disk storage, the amount of (faster and more expensive) volatile memory called random access memory (RAM), and the speed of the central processing unit (CPU). In a business setting, these measurements are still critical to the design of a system, but there is a different emphasis. Entertainment features, such as powerful video graphics processing for video games or 7.1 channel sound cards, are typically not part of a business system.

Hard disk storage, however, becomes incredibly important in a business environment. If a hard drive with critical information fails, it can impact an entire organization. For this reason, business systems often use a number of backup strategies, including storage to online servers and storage to local networked server computers. In addition, a hard disk backup design called *RAID (redundant array of independent drives)* can be employed. RAID systems use two disk drives instead of one and copy each piece of information stored onto both drives at the same time, making a perfect backup on a completely separate drive. There are other types of RAID that are more efficient, but the idea of using multiple drives to increase data security is the same. RAID technology is seen on some high-end home user systems, but it is more popular and more commonly used in the business setting.

▼ **Table 10.1**

Component	Range	Unit
Common Ranges for Business Computing Components		
CPU speed	2.5–3.6	GHz (gigahertz)
RAM	4–12	GB (gigabytes)
Hard Disk Storage	500–2,000	GB (gigabytes); 1,000 GB = 1 Terabyte

Depending on the type of analysis being done on a particular business workstation, the processing power and speed of the CPU may need to be more advanced than that of the typical home computer. Because the amount of RAM is also related to the overall processing speed of the system, business workstations often have more memory. The exact speed of the processor and the amount and speed of memory vary dramatically each year as new systems are introduced. To be able to understand and compare specifications, it is useful to be familiar with the ranges of values for these components, shown in ▼ **Table 10.1.**

What role do mobile devices play in a modern business strategy? Although the availability of Internet access enables workers to make decisions and conduct meetings virtually, business travel is still in huge demand. Business travelers, whether they are salespeople or field engineers, no longer need to be out of touch with their workplace when spending time in cars, airports, and hotels. Cell phones and more fully featured **smartphones,** such as the BlackBerry Bold or the iPhone, allow employees to access their e-mail and the Internet from virtually anywhere. Furthermore, smartphones running the Windows Mobile operating system enable users to read Microsoft Word, Excel, and Access files as well. Tablet computers, such as the Apple iPad, present business travelers with online connectivity, additional processing power, and a 9.7-inch screen, while many netbooks offer larger screen sizes, at two pounds or less. Navigation devices, such as the Garmin Nüvi, use a GPS to provide turn-by-turn directions to travelers and can locate the nearest restaurant, hospital, or gas station.

Projectors and printers are available in mobile sizes as well. Projectors as light as one pound make it easy to bring a complete presentation that is ready to play at any location. Mobile printers are small enough to tuck into a carry-on bag and allow users on the go to print documents.

Mobile devices, such as smartphones, GPS devices, and portable printers and projectors, enable business travelers to stay in touch when they are out of the office.

As more and more devices appear on the market and as prices continue to drop, CIOs find they need to have a consistent policy for managing mobile devices. The requests for IT support can quickly cause a quagmire of technical support demands. In a corporate setting, support for a mobile device costs an average of about twice as much as the cost of purchasing the device itself.[3] It is critical to select the type of devices that will be easy to manage when more and more are rolled out into a company.

Software

What analytical software is common in business? Managers need to make decisions driven by data. A variety of analytical software packages are used to support numerical analysis:

1. **Spreadsheet Programs. Spreadsheet programs,** such as Microsoft Excel or OpenOffice.org's Calc, can run hundreds of different statistical and financial functions with no programming required. They support "what if?" calculations, allowing managers to change one or two variables and easily interpret the results. They also provide a rich graphing environment for charting data in a variety of visual presentations.

2. **Database Programs.** Database programs allow businesses to quickly enter data, filter and sort information, and generate reports. Forms can be easily designed so that data can be entered and validated for accuracy. These forms—such as weekly time cards or customer surveys—can be delivered through e-mail, and the responses automatically added into tables in the database. The collected data can be queried to create reports that describe specific conditions, such as the addresses of all employees who worked overtime in the past week.

3. **Online Analysis Packages.** An **online analysis package (OLAP)** is a software application that enables very quick analysis of combinations of different business factors. OLAPs are designed to help analysts combine multiple pieces of information into a clear picture of the state of the business. These software applications are used for tasks such as reporting sales figures and budgeting and forecasting. OLAP products in the marketplace include MS Analysis Studio, the open-source product Openi (pronounced "open eye"), and Jedox Palo software.

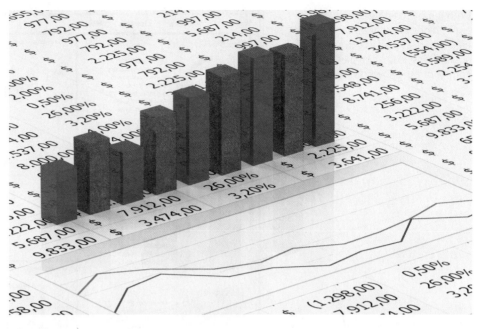

Spreadsheets allow for quick calculation of formulas to evaluate "what if . . ." scenarios.

What software applications help manage the details of a business effectively?
Software packages can help businesses make strategic decisions about the use of resources, the direction of new marketing campaigns, or daily operations. Software can also help with the mechanics of the business world—such as payroll, accounting, and tracking benefits for individual employees. For example, many companies use software that allows employees to monitor their benefits package—tracking the number of remaining personal leave days they have available, the insurance options they have selected, the amount of money they have placed into retirement, and other aspects.

QuickBooks is a very popular accounting package used by small businesses worldwide to handle accounting and budgeting needs. It can also handle many other common business tasks, such as processing UPS and FedEx shipments or paying income taxes from payroll. In addition, QuickBooks can help a business become more tech-savvy with the package's full service Web storefront program that allows businesses to create an online store, take credit card payments, and automatically record all transactions into the accounting system.

HRM systems are software tools that organize people-related management tasks, such as employee reviews, compensation calculations, and applicant management. Packages such as PeopleTrak and eAppraisal make it easier to execute and document the management of employees—from the hiring process through performance evaluations. These tools help employers know when to offer additional training and how to assist employees in achieving their future career goals.

What communications technology is commonly used in businesses?
E-mail and instant messaging aren't the only forms of business communication. The following are other communications technologies frequently used by businesses today:

1. **VoIP.** Telephone communications have taken an important step forward through the use of the *Voice over Internet Protocol* (*VoIP*). VoIP technology lets

With remote conferencing applications, presenters can see and hear others as well as run software applications, exchange files, and take control of others' workstations.

users check their voicemail messages from any Internet browser. Products such as Skype use VoIP to allow national and international calls to be made for free over the Internet instead of over traditional phone networks.

2. **Remote Conferencing. Remote conferencing** allows many people to join a common discussion regardless of their physical locations. Conferences can be conducted with or without video cameras at each workstation, and participants can each work collaboratively on a single document using a common virtual whiteboard. Some products even allow a participant to take control of another's desktop to demonstrate software to the group or make a presentation. As participation in virtual meetings increases, the environmental impact of such a shift in business practices is significant. For example, one businessperson moving her sales presentation online in place of flying from New York to London saves 2,690 pounds of carbon dioxide emissions. This shift across large sections of the business world could have a powerful, positive impact on the environment.

What specialized software applications are needed for marketing? Marketing is an aspect of business that has responded to changes in business technology by redefining itself. In today's world, a marketing department must consider the Internet as a tool both for collecting information on its customers and distributing information about its products and services. Companies such as Lyris, Topica, and Constant Contact can organize and control mass e-mail campaigns by providing templates for e-mail newsletters or advice on how to create e-mail surveys. They also provide services that generate reports to track the number of people who read the e-mail message, how many followed the links inside, and how many forwarded the e-mail to another contact.

Networks

Why are business networks created? In many homes, a family may have more than one computer but only one printer or Internet connection. Each computer user in the household can share peripheral devices or connections by im-

plementing a **network**—a set of computers and other devices joined together using cables, wireless connections, or fiber optic links. Networked computer systems can easily exchange information. For example, this means a printer can receive printing jobs from multiple computers. This sharing capability helps households save on expensive resources that are needed for only brief periods of time. In business, companies also want to use resources efficiently. Expensive devices such as color laser printers or important collections of secure, protected data may need to be accessed by numerous employees in an organization. The most efficient way to provide needed resources to everyone is to create a network.

But only techies need to know about networks, right? Some employees may be interested enough in networking to follow that as a career path, but even those who do not work in the IT department need to have a basic understanding of networks. In most workplaces, employees use networks to access shared files and documents, to access their private personnel data, and to communicate with others in the firm. Understanding the basic structure and operation of networks helps employees do their jobs more efficiently. Managers need to know about networking because the use and maintenance of networks as a company resource are important in their decision making.

What types of networks are in the workplace? There are two types of networks commonly used. An **intranet** is a network that is accessible only to employees or others with authorization. An intranet's Web site looks just like any other Web site. However, specialized firewall software surrounding an intranet keeps unauthorized users from gaining access to the site. An **extranet** is an intranet that is partially accessible to authorized outsiders. Customers or vendors with a valid username and password are able to see certain parts of the network. Extranets are becoming a very popular means for business partners to exchange information.

Do networks come in different sizes? Some networks include only machines in close physical proximity to one another, such as the computers in one office building. These are known as **local area networks (LANs).** The different computers on the network may be joined by physical cables, run through the walls and floors of a building, or by using a Wi-Fi (wireless fidelity) signal. If the LAN is connected wirelessly instead of with cables, it is referred to as a **wireless LAN (WLAN).** Often, **Wi-Fi hotspots,** places where access to a wireless LAN is available, are advertised in airport terminals, coffee houses, and hotels trying to appeal to business travelers who need to reach server files, access e-mail, or use the Internet while traveling. A collection of LANs can be joined into one network, forming a **wide-area network (WAN).**

As networks grow and begin to link sites very far apart geographically, **virtual private networks (VPNs)** are often used. A VPN may connect some of its systems by cables that the company owns, but other sections of the network will be joined using the public Internet. This requires the encryption of information so that a company's private information is kept secure as it travels across public sections of the network. For example, if a company merged offices in two different cities into one network, a VPN would ensure the secure flow of information.

Consider the medical practice of four physicians, Associated Gastroenterologists. They had three offices but no system to easily and securely move files electronically between their offices. The staff of 55 took time to either carry paper charts from location to location or fax them between offices. Their IT solution provider revamped their workflow by installing a small business server network with security devices and site-to-site VPN. Now a physician can dictate exam notes into an electronic patient chart, and it is immediately available to the staff at all three sites over the VPN. The system also sends prescriptions electronically to a patient's pharmacy, does a backup of patient records every 15 minutes, and eliminates the old practice of transcribing medical records.[4]

Is the Internet a network? The **Internet** is a large network that connects millions of computers internationally. The **Internet2**, a network of networks that can communicate at speeds a hundred to a thousand times faster than the original Internet, is a collaboration of over 200 universities and 120 companies. Internet2 has been running since 1996, exploring projects that require incredibly high-speed data transfer, such as real-time high-definition video applications. The showcase archive of Internet2 projects includes international communities in biomedical research, fully immersed virtual reality medical simulators, and a global Internet telescope.[5]

The Internet and the World Wide Web are not the same thing. The **World Wide Web (WWW)** is a way of accessing information available on the Internet. The Web uses a specific protocol, the hypertext transfer protocol (HTTP), to send data between systems. **Protocols** are the different languages that are used to transfer information across the Internet. Some examples of other protocols include file transfer protocol (FTP), a protocol for moving files, and simple mail transfer protocol (SMTP), which handles outgoing e-mail.

New Technology Trends

How is social networking changing businesses? Several new technologies are changing the face of business today. *Enterprise social networking* refers to the application of products like Facebook in a corporate setting. In fact, enterprise versions of products like Facebook, Twitter, and workplace wikis are already beginning to appear in the office. Imagine using the collaborative power of Facebook and wikis within a company to increase collaboration and unify the entire business. It is hoped that such tools will speed up decision making and ensure a smoother customer experience.

What is cloud computing? **Cloud computing** refers to the sharing of information, resources, and software over the Internet and is another new trend in business technology. Using cloud computing, online backup systems can work through a "cloud" so that files are automatically backed up and made available to a whole set of users instantly. As more services beyond just storage begin to take advantage of cloud computing, businesses will become more agile and efficient.

How will the drive to reduce energy usage impact technology? Several technological advances are also making for a greener business landscape. **Green computing**, the careful monitoring of power consumption and other environmental impacts of computing devices, is becoming more popular and more vital to business success. For example, more devices are offering smart power management, such as Western Digital Caviar Green hard disk drives. These devices detect their load and usage patterns and adjust to use the minimum amount of electricity.

In addition, businesses are looking to use *green supply chains*—those that are more automated—reducing the need for paper and allowing businesses to choose green-aware partners who have set specific carbon reduction goals.

Telecommuting is also reducing business traffic and office energy needs and is contributing to a more environment friendly, greener business landscape. The increase in video meeting quality and the ability to use two-way audio-video communications and the on-demand transfer of video content will continue the demand for such virtual meetings in the future.

As you read at the beginning of this section, Frank Ordoqui has seen both ends of the spectrum when it comes to advising companies on the types of computer systems and mobile devices that would be most beneficial to their businesses. New technology can be both exciting and overwhelming to business managers. Some executives are tempted to incorporate every piece of new technology into their business operations, regardless of actual need, while others resist new technology, even though it could prove helpful, because they fear it could overcomplicate their business. Frank advises all of his clients to incorporate new technology at a pace that follows the individual needs of the company. ■

The Benefits and Challenges of Technology pp. 307–311

Mark Dagostino has been a successful IT specialist at an insurance firm for 15 years. He was excited by the prospect of being able to access his work files from home because he figured it would allow him to spend more time with his family. However, Mark now finds that the office is in constant contact with him. The insurance agents work shifts around the clock, processing claims from clients, and Mark is frequently asked to work at all hours to solve technological problems. He even had to work on a computer crisis on Christmas Day one year, much to the chagrin of his family. Mark has reached a new level of frustration with his job, and he is strongly considering taking a pay cut and a different job in a different industry in exchange for a less chaotic schedule. ■

Is the ability to work from home beneficial to employees? Is it beneficial to employers? Does constant connection to the workplace increase employee productivity or employee frustration? In this section, we'll discuss the benefits and risks of IT.

IT Benefits and Challenges for Employees

What are the benefits and challenges of IT for employees? There are aspects of technology that clearly benefit employees. In rescue operations, robots and robotic assistance have relieved human rescue personnel of dangerous tasks. In automotive plants, robots have taken over most of the very monotonous, unfulfilling work, freeing humans for more creative positions. But some uses of technology in the workplace have brought about difficult changes. The increasing volume of e-mail can contribute to a breakdown in communication as fewer personal exchanges take place. Communication experts agree that in face-to-face discussions, up to 93 percent of the meaning of the messages exchanged is communicated in nonverbal ways—through gestures, glances, body position, and facial expression.[6] As more office discussions take place via e-mail, the chance of misunderstandings and errors continues to rise.

The boundary between work and home has also blurred dramatically because of the increase of technology. Once a worker has access to office files from home, and the office has access to employees via smartphones or live videoconferencing, the workday can extend dramatically.

Has technology increased productivity?

What is the business value of IT? Many studies have been conducted to answer this question, and their findings differ widely. Some conclude that corporate investment in IT has led to increased productivity from employees, whereas others find that the investment has actually led to a drop in productivity. It's a complex question, and some of the discrepancies depend on the actual definition of productivity. Are they looking at knowledge workers only or blue-collar workers as well? How was the impact of the overall strength of the economy factored into the measurement of productivity? Other researchers question whether profitability, consumer benefit, and productivity are actually related. Although employees certainly have more access to information through technology, it is up to the individual to use that information appropriately. There is no guarantee that new technology will make a workforce more productive, so the task of selecting IT solutions and tools is very difficult. IT managers try to find solutions that will yield enough benefit to outweigh the investment of purchase, training, and maintenance.

How do intellectual property laws affect knowledge workers?

With increasing levels of technology in place at businesses, more employees are becoming knowledge-based workers. Their contribution to the company is measured by their creativity and originality. But who owns the idea that an employee has while at work? In most businesses, the idea is the property of the company, even if it is a brainstorm that occurred during lunch instead of during an afternoon meeting.

For example, a software engineer working at a health information management center is struggling to come up with a way to store large files of hospital records on one drive. Suddenly, an idea for the design of a microchip comes to her while she is driving to work. Even though the idea was formed outside the work environment, the idea belongs to the company because it was based on previous work. Intellectual property and copyright law are constantly evolving. As technology creates a higher percentage of knowledge workers, the issue of ownership of ideas will affect more and more employees.

How does technology affect employee privacy?

At home, U.S. citizens are guaranteed specific levels of privacy and freedoms. In the workplace, however, the expectation of privacy is quite different. **Electronic monitoring** is commonly used to track employees' keystrokes and e-mails, examine their Internet browsing histories, and even monitor their cell phone and instant messaging usage.[7] Camera surveillance can be conducted with recording devices so small that employees do not realize they are being recorded. Used appropriately, these technical tools can help a company eliminate a drain of business resources for personal use. But to some employees, the work environment then begins to feel so monitored that they no longer produce their best work. In a study conducted at Bell Canada, a telecommunications company, researchers found that 50 percent of employees in the customer service department reported an increase in stress and anxiety when their calls were being monitored. Employee stress can lead to job dissatisfaction and prompt health problems.[8] Finding the balance between an appropriate level of monitoring and an optimal work environment is a continuous challenge.

Can technology support ethical conduct?

Part of the Sarbanes-Oxley Act of 2002 mandates that all public companies have procedures for handling the concerns of whistle-blowers—persons who report on illicit activities. Several corporations now use their intranet to allow whistle-blowers to make anonymous reports. Organizations such as the Occupational Safety and Health Administration (OSHA) and the American Civil Liberties Union (ACLU) also have designed their Web sites to allow people to file reports easily and safely, shielding them from possible retaliation.

This type of reporting system is common in hospitals and medical centers. Staff members can report "near misses"—mistakes that could have occurred but were caught and corrected—through the organization's intranet. This allows an organization to learn from possible mistakes but safeguards the employee from embarrassment or disciplinary action. Without the benefit of anonymity, many mistakes and unethical actions might go undetected.

⊙ Off the Mark Spying Scandal at HP

HP crossed the ethical lines of employee privacy in 2006 in an attempt to discover the source of an anonymous article that leaked private company information. Chairwoman Patricia Dunn hired private investigators and allegedly authorized them to use illegal tactics to uncover the source of the leak. The private investigators used pretexting, or lying about one's identity, to gain access to phone records, tracer e-mails containing spyware, and the surveillance of journalists. Placing physical spies in a newsroom was even discussed. Dunn resigned from HP in 2006, as well as board member George Keyworth, who was discovered to be behind the information leak. The scandal ended up costing the company several board members, millions of dollars, and bad press.

Employee privacy concerns are a big issue today, as technology makes it easier to spy on employees. Although HP engaged in illegal methods of observation, companies can legally screen the e-mail and Internet histories of employees, raising ethical concerns about the right of companies to do so.

Other Web sites are more controversial in how they support similar activities. The site WikiLeaks (wikileaks.org) describes itself as "a multi-jurisdictional public service designed to protect whistleblowers, journalists and activists who have sensitive materials to communicate to the public."[9] But it has sparked several controversies as they have made public confidential documents from the U.S. military, the Central Intelligence Agency (CIA), the U.S. Embassy, and a variety of private corporate reports and e-mails. For example, WikiLeaks made public a video of a 2007 U.S. Army helicopter strike in Iraq against a group that included children and two Reuters journalists.[10]

IT Benefits and Challenges for Management

What risks does technology pose for management? Although the increase in IT has allowed many advances for businesses, it has also added risks. The stability of a business can be jeopardized if technology is not implemented reliably. Even a short blackout of vital services, such as internal e-mail or customer access to the corporate Web site, can damage a company's reputation and value. For example, recently, the Hawaiian airline Go! attempted to sell 1,000 tickets for $1. The promotion caused so many people to access the company's Web site that it crashed, and customers could not get tickets. The company was forced to double the number of $1 tickets it was offering to assuage upset customers.[11] One survey of managers in the United Kingdom found that 70 percent said IT failure was the top threat to their organizations, whereas only 2 percent cited a concern over terrorism disrupting their business.[12]

Another challenge IT brings to management is security. With so much of the value of a modern business stored in electronic material—whether as documents, software programs, or e-mail files—a company can be vulnerable to hackers. **Hackers** are individuals who gain unauthorized entry into a computer system. Their goal may be to disrupt the operation of the system or gain access to protected data. For example, in May 2008 agents raided a set of homes in Miami-Dade County and retrieved a dozen computers and $422,000 cash. On those computer hard drives, they found evidence of a hacking ring that had stolen more than 170 million credit card

BizChat

How a Simple Mistake Can Lead to a Major Data Breach

In May 2006, the U.S. government experienced the second largest data breach to date. This occurrence wasn't attributed to savvy hackers though. Rather, an employee for the Department of Veterans Affairs (VA) went against policy and took a laptop home, and it was stolen during a burglary. The laptop contained the names and Social Security numbers of over 26 million veterans. According to Bill Conner, CEO of Entrust, a digital security company, lost or stolen laptops are the primary way to compromise a company's security. Web sites like breachalerts.trustedid are dedicated to detailing security breaches that affect millions of people. The VA breach prompted the U.S. House of Representatives and the U.S. Senate to speed up bills waiting to be passed. These bills mandated criminal penalties for data breaches and disclosure agreements for consumers. The VA laptop was eventually recovered in July 2006. Fortunately for the VA and the vets involved, sensitive information on the computer had not been accessed.

For more information and discussion questions about this topic, check out the BizChat feature on my*biz*lab.com.

---

numbers worth hundreds of millions of dollars. The hackers had committed online thefts from a wide range of stores, such as 7-Eleven, Dave & Buster's, and T.J. Maxx.[13]

The risk of a security breach becomes even greater if unprotected wireless networks are in use. If no encryption scheme is used, then the data traveling through a wireless network are available to anyone in range.

Does keeping pace with technology put a financial burden on businesses? Another challenge IT poses for business is the financial burden placed on companies trying to stay up-to-date. The full cost of any new piece of technology includes not only the purchase of the software and hardware itself but also potential hardware upgrades required to make the new product useful.

For example, suppose management decides it wants to upgrade the operating system that runs on the company's computers. This requires that the firm buy not only licenses for the operating system software but also memory upgrades for computer systems. In addition, the IT department will need to take time to test the software prior to deployment, establish a support staff, install the software, and train users on how to interact with the programs. Before adopting new technology, business managers must evaluate whether the benefits of new technology will exceed the costs.

Sometimes, management may feel pressure to upgrade software or hardware because the entire market has switched to a new product or because customers or vendors have already moved to a new version of a program or device. In such circumstances, the CIO must evaluate the available workforce and determine whether there are sufficient people trained with the new software or hardware to make the return on investment significant and worthwhile. Occasionally, software products are released and working, but they are not yet supported by other companies' software products. For example, when Microsoft released the Windows Vista operating system, many midsize companies found they would be required to upgrade their hardware, adding hard disk drives, more memory, or possibly even buying entirely new computers because their existing processors were too slow for Vista.[14] However, Microsoft predicted a savings of $340 a year per machine in IT labor and support costs. In these cases, the CIO must evaluate whether adopting a new piece of technology is in the best interests of a company.

What are the pros and cons of conducting business online? Taking advantage of cyberspace storefronts is a major benefit of increased technology in business. But it brings with it a set of concerns that managers must be prepared to face. Because customers are justifiably worried about possible online threats to their privacy, every aspect of an online store must be secure and inspire consumer trust. This can create some complicated decisions for management.

For example, some companies use **cookies**, small text files written to a user's hard disk that track customer preferences and Web clicks, or they store previous responses to online forms. This allows a company to customize its Web storefront for each customer. For example, an estimated 35.6 million U.S. visitors hit the Yahoo! homepage each day.[15] By using cookies, Yahoo! collects a significant amount of data about its users—almost 12 terabytes of data a day. Sophisticated analysis programs try to predict consumer behavior when processing these data. This valuable information can then be sold to marketing firms or used to justify high prices for Yahoo! ad space. Some people feel this practice compromises their security. Just that perception, whether it is truthful or not, can cost a company business. So, should a company use cookies or not? Some companies, such as Yahoo!, say yes. Others, such as Google, refuse to collect such information about their users.[16]

"**Good news! According to our personal finance program, we can afford the system upgrade.**"

▼ **Figure 10.3**

The rapid advancement of technology has brought about many changes in the workplace. As with Mark Dagostino, those changes can have both positive and negative effects. Finding an appropriate balance between the benefits and challenges of new technology can be a daunting task for business owners, CIOs, and employees alike. ■

The Global Impact of Business Technology pp. 311–316

When Peggy Best worked at a pharmaceutical company 12 years ago, her main clients were located within 100 miles of her company's main office in Pennsylvania, and all of her coworkers worked on-site. When Peggy returned, she found the company, and business in general, had changed dramatically. Now most of the company's clients are located in foreign countries, and many of her coworkers work outside the office. She even has coworkers in India. Peggy has found adapting to the new technology the most difficult part of the transition. She has to be trained in a variety of virtual communication programs so she can speak to her international clients, and she needs to become familiar with the company's information network so she can share information with her counterpart in India. Peggy is enjoying learning about new technology and other cultures, but at times she feels overwhelmed. ■

Earlier in this chapter, you learned how business technology can impact companies. But how does technology affect business on a global scale? In this section, you'll read about the ways in which technology is changing where businesses are located, what goods are produced, how goods and services are marketed, and what will be expected of employees in the new global marketplace.

Offshoring

How has technology impacted international business? One impact of technology has been the increase in **offshoring**, the relocation by a company of a business process from the U.S. to another nation. In the past, this practice was employed primarily for production and manufacturing. The North American Free Trade Agreement (NAFTA, enacted in) 1994, made it easier for companies to shift work from the United States to Mexico and opened the door to expanding offshoring. As technology provided secure and simple means to transmit data files, white-collar offshoring began to take off. Workers in many sectors of the economy who had been insulated from foreign competition began to see changes. For example, in 2001 and 2002, the unemployment rate for computer programmers rose significantly above the national average, despite remaining well below it for the previous 20 years. The financial services industry—retail banking, investment banking, and insurance—has also been very aggressive in moving call center jobs and clerical jobs offshore.

Location has become much less important, and countries that have educated, English-speaking citizens can bid for work that has previously taken place in the United States. With a population of more than 1 billion, India graduates 350,000[17] engineers each year, compared to 60,000 in the United States.[18] This has fueled 10 years of double-digit increases in salary in India for many technology workers, as U.S. firms send a variety of programming and support positions to Indian companies. Although the income of Indian workers has risen, the economic advantage of offshoring to India is fading. Now China is beginning to show it has the necessary infrastructure and pool of talent to become an offshoring destination for knowledge work.

Although Asian countries are seeing the most offshoring activity, some U.S. companies prefer to keep their business a little closer to home. **Near-shoring** is a form of offshoring in which a company moves jobs to a foreign location that is geographically close or linguistically and culturally similar to the domestic country. Sending work from the United States to countries such as Canada, the United Kingdom, and Australia could be considered near-shoring. Google, Yahoo!, and HP all have offices in Dublin, which is where they send a portion of their IT work. Although labor in these countries may not be as low-cost as labor in some Asian countries, similarities in geography, language, and culture make it easier to integrate foreign workers into the daily operations of the original location.

What changes might offshoring bring for U.S. companies and employees? The drastic difference in wages between offshore countries and the United States is the key ingredient that makes offshoring profitable for a business. A U.S. technology factory worker averages $2,000 a month income. In China, Foxconn Technology, an electronics manufacturer that produces parts for iPhones and Dell computers, recently doubled worker salaries to about $3,600 a *year*.[19]

Offshoring is not just impacting manufacturing jobs, however. As design projects between U.S. and foreign companies become more common, design and engineering positions will be split among a wider international pool of labor. For example, GM is working with its partner Shanghai Automotive Industry Group to develop the EN-V (Electric Networked Vehicle), a two-seat electric vehicle intended to address transportation problems with the increasing density of urban populations.[20]

Engineers and designers from both countries are involved in developing the project. As the international pool of technical talent becomes the new marketplace, U.S. workers can expect to see a slowing of wage growth. It will be important for U.S. workers to have increased language skills and shift their view of their careers and opportunities toward the reality of a global economy.

It is also important to point out that U.S. workers will see benefits from offshoring. As middle-class jobs appear in India and other developing countries, the middle class in those countries will expand. Companies and workers in the United States will benefit in the long run when more countries are politically stable and the demand for U.S. products increases. Another benefit comes from time zone differences. For example, there is almost an 11-hour time difference between India and the United States. As the workday ends in New York, people are beginning to wake up and head to work in Bangalore and Hyderabad. By using teams of workers that are divided between both locations, companies can conduct business nearly 24 hours a day. If a well-designed and well-managed team can exploit the time zone difference, it holds the possibility of great success for the team and the business overall.

The EN-V is a project whose design and development is using engineering talent from both the United States and China.

What is the difference between outsourcing and offshoring?

Outsourcing takes place when a company contracts with an outside firm to handle a specific part of its daily business activities. *Offshoring* is the relocation of part of a business to a lower-cost location, typically a foreign country. Sometimes, the terms *outsourcing* and *offshoring* are mistakenly used interchangeably. Outsourcing, for example, includes a real estate company hiring a graphic design firm to create a special layout for a sales brochure. Most companies outsource work to outside firms that can do a job or project better, faster, or cheaper than the company could do on its own.

Companies such as GE Capital employ people in New Delhi, Bangalore, and other cities in India to answer calls from credit card customers, perform accounting tasks, and manage computer systems.[21]

The International Business Environment

How does technology change marketing in a global marketplace?

Internet technology allows every company with a Web site to advertise to anyone in the world with Internet access. The site must support multiple languages as seen in ▼ **Figure 10.4,** but more importantly, it must also make sure the content for different countries is culturally customized. Every marketing campaign is now global.

Budweiser launched a campaign during the 2010 World Cup that demonstrated how these pieces can be woven into a single campaign.[22] The "Bud United" campaign followed 32 soccer fans living in a single house, one representing each nation in the World

**▼ Figure 10.4
The Global Web**

Thanks to Internet technology, every company with a Web site is now capable of advertising globally. This page markets Pearson publishing products to a Japanese audience.

Cup. As each country was eliminated, that person left the house. Daily video content from the house was published on YouTube, and daily updates were posted to Facebook and Twitter. A worldwide television and online advertising campaign accompanied the "reality ad" video content. Coordinated television ads were run in 20 countries, and online ads in a range of sports-related sites in local markets all worked to drive users to the Bud United site. Each house member had his or her own Facebook and Twitter page in his or her native language, reaching out to fans around the world. Offline, the campaign extended to include display ads in stadiums in South Africa and video content aired in New York's Times Square. For the first time ever, Bud worked with FIFA (the Fédération Internationale de Football Association) so that fans could vote for the most valuable player (MVP) of each match online and through mobile text messaging. Social media technologies, Web, and video technologies were combined with traditional marketing tools and expanded across a global scale for one unified campaign.

How can technology redefine boundaries of business cooperation?

Business technology has helped fuel the collapse of fixed boundaries between international divisions of a business. Time and distance are no longer barriers between the collaboration of two parts of a business. Instead, different countries can bring the energy needed to foster breakthrough, high-impact innovation. It can be challenging to take the necessary risk to create new ideas, especially once executives and business units have a record of proven success. International, high-stakes competitions have ignited new designs. The 2010 Progressive Automotive XPrize is one example. That competition awards a $10 million prize to the team that can develop a car that delivers 100 miles per gallon. International teams have entered and are a combination of high school students, professional engineers, academic researchers, and corporate developers. To coordinate all these members, modern networking and electronic communication tools are required. For example, the WikiSpeed team has one group in Seattle developing a prototype, a second team in Michigan, and the team members are distributed across the United States and Ireland. Technology allows them to communicate easily, and the XPrize blogs and wikis allow them to keep an eye on what the other teams are doing, leading to a healthy competitive setting that hopefully will produce revolutionary results.

How is technology affecting the world's production and design centers?

For several decades, China has grown as a production center for the world. "Made in China" is stamped on products from clothing to machinery. But the design centers drafting the products have been traditionally located in the United States and Western Europe. As business technology and education continue to blossom in China, design is shifting there as well. Political forces can act to accelerate this as well. The Chinese government has put forth a proposal for "indigenous innovation," which would encourage government agencies to purchase high-tech goods from companies that did development in China.[23] This would give an advantage to Chinese firms or force foreign firms to find ways to begin design/development work in China. The impact of indigenous innovation is not yet certain. The additional financial support that China is providing to universities and venture capital investments to assist joint research projects between Chinese universities and foreign companies could mean benefits for U.S. companies.

Design projects can also benefit from the multinational teams technology makes possible. Consider GM, which owns a plant in a suburb of Shanghai. The design of the latest model Buick LaCrosse was left to an open internal competition between U.S. and Chinese designers in design studios 6,000 miles apart. Both teams excelled in the competitive environment. Ultimately, the Chinese GM design team was given the redesign for the LaCrosse interior and overall flow, and the U.S. team worked on the exterior. The teams reported in for reviews with the Chinese employees in Shanghai and GM management in Detroit by using a virtual reality suites.[24]

Technology Creates a Global Village

Where will the next generation of workers live? On one hand, employees with skills that stand out in the global talent pool will be able to live anywhere. With employees relocating often and internationally, the demand for workers with language and communication skills will increase. On the other hand, the introduction of millions of talented knowledge workers worldwide may cause workers who have only average or marginal skills to be displaced.

What skills will be expected in the global workplace? Flexibility on the part of employees will be expected in the global workplace. Communication skills and social understanding of a range of cultures will be invaluable, as will mathematical skills, which transcend language boundaries. Demonstrated fluency in learning new technologies will let employers know a prospective employee can be counted on to handle a multitude of projects.

Knowledge of English is incredibly important, as it is becoming the language of international problem solving. Globally, over 2 billion people are working to learn English.[25] In 2009, China became the country in the world with the largest number of English-speaking people. But knowledge of other languages in addition to English will be a key asset to business technology employees. Considering the fact that the population of China is 1.3 billion and growing, the demand for Chinese-language speakers is increasing. As other developing countries continue to grow, so will the demand for foreign language skills.

How does an understanding of digital culture help in business? Those raised with Internet access, digital media, and easily available computer-processing power have developed a different set of skills, strengths, and demands than the generations that preceded them. In today's workplace, three different generations are often working on the same project; being able to understand and adapt between the different styles of each generation is key to having a successful team. It is also critical for understanding the marketplace, which is composed of both "digital natives" and "digital immigrants."[26] Digital natives are those who have never known a time without the Internet (those born after 1980 or so). Studies show that the typical 8- to 18-year-old spends more than 50 hours *per week* with digital media.[27] Researchers agree that this contributes to physiological changes in the structure and functioning of the brain that make digital natives different from digital immigrants (those who were born before the Internet). The cognitive structures of digital natives support very quickly linking from one topic to another. They show very long attention spans for materials presented in a densely hyperlinked style and short attention spans for traditionally organized reading materials.

These differences mean many changes in how businesses are organized so that they can make the best use of digital natives as employees. In part because of the richness of social media that digital natives grew up on, they are very skilled at collaborative and social methods of accomplishing global tasks. Teamwork and smooth handoffs throughout the development process are the hallmark of many high school and college students, but these are not yet the standard at most corporations. In marketing and designing products for this generation, businesses need to recognize the immediate interconnectedness of digital natives. Bad initial reviews of a product or a service will be circulated at incredible speed through consumer ratings and comments available on mobile devices and the Web. Digital natives are perhaps the best people to understand and design for digital natives.

Improvements in business technology have allowed for greater co-ordination between countries in business. Peggy Best, who is re-turning from a 12-year absence from the workforce, is seeing this firsthand. Companies like Peggy's employer commonly use practices such as off-shoring and outsourcing to lower costs. These practices allow companies to pay lower wages for work and choose from a greater pool of skilled employees. Workers within the United Sates, like Peggy, are challenged to compete in an international skills market. Advances in business computing allow for global marketing campaigns, and consumers expect interactive Web media. Telecommuting has become increasingly popular, as employees can complete tasks from home while being able to care for their children or aging parents. The spread of work to foreign countries will force employees to develop greater communication skills and cultural awareness. ■

Chapter Summary

1. What are the functions of a company's CIO and IT department? (pp. 297–298)

- A company's **chief information officer** (**CIO;** p. 297) is the executive in charge of information processing, including systems design and development and data center operations. He or she is also responsible for the following:
  - Updating or replacing computer systems and software a company uses
  - Managing a budget that balances the benefits of technology against the ever-rising costs of having the latest systems
  - Setting policy for privacy and security concerns
  - Creating business and e-business opportunities
  - system design and development of required software programs

- The IT department consists of a number of professionals responsible for everything from hardware components to software programs to networking strategies. The IT department also has the following tasks:
  - Maintain security both in response to computer virus attacks and emergency recovery from power outages and system failures.
  - Keep all of an organization's computers, printers, scanners, and other equipment operational and current.
  - Design networks used within a company and databases where information is stored.
  - Select or create software programs used by the business and provide software training to employees.
  - Maintain and manage the use of mobile computing throughout a company.
  - Implement remote access to computing resources, such as employees' access to work files or e-mail when they are working from home.

2. How are IT, information systems, information, and data interrelated within a business? (pp. 298–300)

- **Information technology** (**IT;** p. 297) is the design and implementation of computer-based information systems.

- **Information systems** (**ISs;** p. 298) focus on applying IT to the solution of business and economic problems. IS professionals bridge the gap between purely technical knowledge and how it will impact business.

- Raw **data** (p. 298) must be organized and arranged into useful **information** (p. 299). IS professionals and other decision makers can then use this information to determine which IT solutions to implement.

3. How are major types of hardware, software, and networks used in business? (pp. 301–307)

- Types of hardware, such as hard drives, are used for data storage. CPU speed is also important in business, depending on the type of analysis being done on a particular computer workstation.

- Software packages are used to drive decision making for executives, HR personnel, and accounting functions. Communications software allows remote conferencing, instant messaging, and mass e-mail marketing campaigns.

- Business **networks** (p. 305) allow multiple users to work with limited resources. Networks can be organized to allow access to internal employees only or a mix of internal and external people. They can be joined locally or across distance using encryption schemes to ensure data security.

4. What are the benefits and risks of technology in the workplace, taking into account safety, creativity, communication, productivity, privacy, and ethics? (pp. 307–311)

- Among the risks of technology in the workplace is an increased chance of IT failures and loss of vital services and issues related to maintaining security.

- One of the benefits of technology in the workplace is that it frees up employees to spend more time on creative tasks.

- Although technology allows employees to stay connected even when they aren't physically in the office, it also introduces risks related to communication.
  - The increasing volume of e-mail can contribute to a breakdown in communication because fewer personal (face-to-face) exchanges take place.

Continued on next page

Chapter Summary (cont.)

- With remote access to work files and features such as live videoconferencing, the workday for employees can extend round the clock.

- In terms of productivity, the risks and benefits of technology are unclear. Some studies conclude that corporate investment in IT has led to increased productivity from employees, whereas others find that the investment has actually led to a drop in productivity.

- Electronic monitoring and other advances can help companies eliminate a drain of business resources for personal use. However, these practices also carry the risk of invading employees' privacy.

- One of the benefits of technology is that it can support ethical conduct within the workplace. Several federal organizations have Web sites that allow people with complaints or allegations of misconduct to file reports easily and safely, shielding them from possible retaliation.

5. **What is the impact of technology on the international business environment based on offshoring, outsourcing, and alternative methods of communication? (pp. 311–316)**

- **Offshoring** (p. 312) and outsourcing allow many types of work to be located outside the United States. This shift in production and design centers requires employees to develop communication skills and social understanding of different cultures as well as demonstrating fluency in new technologies.

- Technology has allowed more people from around the world to interact, therefore increasing the demand for foreign language skills.

Key Terms

business intelligence software   (p. 299)

chief information officer (CIO)   (p. 297)

cloud computing   (p. 306)

cookies   (p. 311)

data   (p. 298)

database management system (DBMS)   (p. 299)

data mart   (p. 299)

data mining   (p. 299)

data warehouse   (p. 299)

decision support system (DSS)   (p. 299)

electronic monitoring   (p. 308)

executive information system (EIS)   (p. 299)

extranet   (p. 305)

green computing   (p. 306)

hackers   (p. 309)

information   (p. 299)

information system (IS)/management information system (MIS)   (p. 298)

information technology (IT)   (p. 297)

Internet   (p. 306)

Internet2   (p. 306)

intranet   (p. 305)

local area network (LAN)   (p. 305)

near-shoring   (p. 312)

network   (p. 305)

online analysis package (OLAP)   (p. 303)

offshoring   (p. 312)

outsourcing   (p. 313)

protocols   (p. 306)

remote conferencing   (p. 304)

smartphone   (p. 302)

spreadsheet program   (p. 302)

telecommuting   (p. 306)

virtual private network (VPN)   (p. 305)

Wi-Fi hotspot   (p. 305)

World Wide Web (WWW)   (p. 306)

wireless local area network (WLAN)   (p. 305)

wide-area network (WAN)   (p. 305)

Multiple Choice   You can find the answers on the last page of this book.

1. **IT is**

    a. internship technology opportunities.

    b. company-wide investigations of office conduct.

    c. building a networking plan for the flow and use of information.

    d. the design and implementation of computer-based systems.

2. **MIS is different from IT because**

    a. MIS focuses on applying IT to solve business problems.

    b. MIS is the branch of IT focused on Internet usage.

    c. IT focuses on hardware, and MIS focuses on software.

    d. MIS is applied, and IT is theoretical.

3. **DSSs are used most often by**

    a. managers who make decisions based on current data.

    b. employees who decide how to solve technical problems.

    c. clerical staff that organize and format documents and reports.

    d. trainers who teach staff and employees new software products.

4. **Data warehousing is**

    a. the storing of terabytes of transaction data.

    b. not used when DBMSs are in place.

    c. is not used now because data marts have replaced it.

    d. is the management of large quantities of paper records.

5. **OLAP**

    a. is illegal in the United States.

    b. allows a company to monitor employees' usage of its technology resources.

    c. is a spreadsheet that supports a number of financial functions.

    d. helps analysts compile multiple pieces of information into one clear picture.

6. **Hackers can infiltrate systems**

    a. only if they use cookie files to store information.

    b. if the systems are isolated as a single corporate extranet.

    c. All of the above

    d. None of the above

7. **Which of the following is related to using encryption to keep information safe as it travels?**

    a. WWW

    b. WLAN

    c. OLAP

    d. VPN

8. **The speed of Internet2 is *most* useful for**

    a. e-mailing.

    b. the real time exchange of immersive virtual reality medical simulator images.

    c. downloading music files.

    d. saving files to your desktop.

9. **Outsourcing of knowledge work is**

    a. dangerous to national security.

    b. different from offshoring.

    c. difficult because of different levels of commitment to the protection of intellectual property in different countries.

    d. Both b and c

10. **Social media technologies have impacted**

    a. marketing campaigns.

    b. the time between updates to new hardware systems.

    c. the number of required reports filed with tax authorities.

    d. All of the above

Self-Test

True/False You can find the answers on the last page of this book.

1. The CIO is the director of IT and reports to the CFO.
   ☐ **True** or ☐ **False**

2. Business intelligence software supports decision making by presenting visual, interactive views of the state of a business.
   ☐ **True** or ☐ **False**

3. A Wi-Fi hotspot is a location where access to a WLAN is available.
   ☐ **True** or ☐ **False**

4. Information is data that has been arranged in a way to make it more useful.
   ☐ **True** or ☐ **False**

5. Near-shoring is the process of sending work to a foreign country that is geographically far and culturally different.
   ☐ **True** or ☐ **False**

Critical Thinking Questions

1. There is much concern over the "Digital Divide," the gap in IT resources among industrialized countries and developing countries. The explosive growth of smartphones may be a path that allows developing countries to move quickly into the digital age. What advantages would there be to supporting the growth of smartphone usage over computer usage in a developing country? What infrastructure would be required to take the most advantage? What other devices might be useful to minimize the Digital Divide?

2. There are many differences between "digital natives" and "digital immigrants." From your experiences, how would you define each term? What experiences have you had, at school or in the workplace, with the different attitudes of the two groups? Different skills? Different approaches to problem solving?

3. What responsibilities accompany the new amount of information we can collect through modern information technologies? If airlines can cross-reference travel data with bank records and identify suspicious patterns, do they have a responsibility to alert authorities? Or should they be forbidden from looking for patterns as "profiling" (the extrapolation of certain psychological and physical characteristics)? What if a college IT department finds a threatening message that has been sent from a student e-mail account? What if it is not "threatening" but in very bad taste? Where is the boundary of the college's responsibility?

4. Discuss the impact of offshoring of knowledge-based work. Is it in the interests of the nation to try to stop the export of certain types of work? Is it possible to do that? What benefits might arise from a more global structure for a business?

5. Think about how a CIO can determine whether a business will benefit enough from a specific hardware/software upgrade to justify its purchase. What information would he or she need? How might past experience benefit the decision that needs to be made today?

Team Time

The Winds of Change

Assemble into groups of three. Each member of the group should select one of the following areas:

a. Business hardware/software/networking

b. Ethical impact of business technology

c. Global impact of business technology

Process

Step 1. As a group, determine what innovation in business technology will have the most impact over the next year, 5 years, and 10 years. After the group has selected a specific innovation, each group member should prepare a short presentation on why that particular technology change will be significant in his or her area.

Step 2. Evaluate the innovation by asking the following:
→ How many businesses will be impacted?
→ How many aspects of business activity will be impacted?
→ How many consumers and/or vendors will be impacted?
→ Will the innovation lead to additional changes in the business in the future?

Step 3. Optional: As a class, compare the group results. Determine which innovation has the most likelihood of coming to fruition. How will it change your career and the world you will be part of in the future?

Ethics and Corporate Social Responsibility

Computer Hacking: A High Price to Pay

Read the following case study. Then, as a class, discuss the questions that follow.

One night, 21-year-olds Brian Salcedo and Adam Botbyl were driving around in Adam's car with a couple of antennas hanging out the window and a laptop powered up looking for open wireless networks they could access. As they drove past the Lowe's home improvement store, they found one. Lowe's had set up its wireless network so that scanners and other devices could connect to its network without cabling. Six months later the pair decided to place a modified program onto Lowe's computer system. Now, when credit card transactions were processed, a copy of the number would be sent to a special file they could use later. The FBI investigated and arrested them before they ever saw a single credit card number. They pleaded guilty and worked with Lowe's to boost its security. Even so, Brian Salcedo was sentenced to nine years in prison, one of the longest sentences in U.S. history for computer hacking, and Adam Botbyl was sentenced to 26 months.

Questions

1. Who holds responsibility for Lowe's customers?

2. How can consumers know that their purchases are safe?

3. Were the sentences given to the pair appropriate? Why or why not?

Web Exercises

1. **WikiLeaks**
   Visit the WikiLeaks Web site and select two of the most current leaks posted. Evaluate the value of these pieces of information being made public. Does it violate the privacy rights of the individuals involved? Does it make available the means to expose a criminal act? Would you argue the benefits outweigh the violation of confidentiality or not?

2. **To Censor or Not to Censor**
   In 2010, Google reversed its previous position and stopped enforcing censorship of its search engine results to Chinese users. Instead Google began to redirect users to an uncensored search engine based in Hong Kong. What led to the change in Google's corporate position? What response did Google receive from the Chinese government? How do other U.S. companies, such as Microsoft (which distributes the Bing search engine), work with the censorship restrictions of the Chinese government?

3. **Global Marketing**
   Visit the BMW Web site. This international portal redirects customers to one of many hundred of country-specific sites. Select three different countries and investigate the

Web site presented. What elements are kept the same? How does BMW maintain a unified international marketing message? Which components are different? How does your Web browser handle the differences in character sets for different languages?

4. **Data Breach!**
   Visit the homepage of Breachalerts (http://breachalerts.trustedid.com/) and review the recent data breach reports posted there. Select one of these reports and note relevant information about the breaches, such as the source(s) of data loss, the date(s) of the occurrence, the sizes of losses, and the individuals or geographic area(s) affected. How did the losses occur? How might they have been prevented?

5. **Meeting Online**
   Visit three or four remote conferencing sites (search Google for a selection to choose from). Does the software support cross-platform meetings (Windows, Mac, Linux)? Which sites offer free meetings? How many participants may be included in each meeting? What features make each product unique?

Web Case

For more on how technology improves efficiency and predicts the needs of consumers, access the Chapter 10 Web case entitled "Focus on Toyota: A Data Debacle: MIS to the Rescue" located in the End of Chapter Assignments section at my*biz*lab.com.

Video Case

For more on using information technology to increase market share and employee productivity, access the Chapter 10 Video Case entitled "Boeing Satellite Systems: Orbiting the Information Superhighway" located in the End of Chapter Assignments section at my*biz*lab.com.

The Production of Goods and Services

Steve Schmidt loved his job of welding together custom-made bicycles. His partner, Ralph Brinsdorfer, loved providing the customer service in ensuring the bikes were delivered on time, offering financing, and providing friendly and efficient repair service. Their goal, like the goal of all businesses, is to deliver a quality good or service to customers. What is involved in the production of goods and services? How important is production to the U.S. economy and also world economies?

Objective 1 How is manufacturing and production important to the U.S. economy and global economies? (pp. 325–327)

Operations Management

Arthur Riddle's furniture company has had great success in northern California, and he's considering expanding operations to a new location. What factors does Arthur need to consider before choosing a new location? How should the facility be arranged, and how does he determine the best suppliers to use?

Objective 2 What is operations management, and what is important in determining a facility's location and layout? (pp. 327–333)

Production Management

Sylvia Ackerman loves the simple lines and clean design of IKEA products and can't wait to furnish her new apartment with IKEA merchandise. Moreover, she knows she'll be able to afford what she needs and can assemble the furniture on her own, with minimal help from others. How does IKEA produce inexpensive, high-quality goods for its franchised stores around the world?

Objective 3 What is production management, and what production processes are used by businesses? (pp. 333–336)

Objective 4 How does technology influence the production process? (pp. 336–339)

Objective 5 How is a production plan developed and controlled? (pp. 339–342)

Quality Control

Jeanette Pae's excitement of getting a new iPhone4 was dampened slightly with rumors of a recall to replace or repair faulty antennas. Jeanette had grown to trust Apple and was disappointed that a quality issue was affecting this otherwise reliable company. Similar situations happened to her friends and family members, who had experienced the recall of toys, medicine, computer batteries, and cars. What can companies do to ensure the production of a high-quality product?

Objective 6 What is quality control, and how do ISO (International Organization for Standardization) standards help companies produce high-quality goods and services? (pp. 342–345)

PEARSON
mybizlab

Improving a Business

You've inherited a family-run pizza restaurant and delivery business that is plagued by excessive inventory costs, late deliveries, ordering mistakes, no computerized system, and customer complaints. But you still have a secret family recipe for pizza dough and sauce that customers rave about. Armed with common sense, pizza genes, and operations management expertise, can you turn your restaurant around?

Objective 7 Test yourself using mybizlab.com to show that you understand the chapter objectives.

The Production of Goods and Services pp. 325–327

Steve Schmidt covered his face with the protective shield and began to weld together the seat tube. This was his third and last bicycle today. Steve loves his job building custom bicycles, and this particular bike was no exception. Although many bicycles are mass-produced, his shop builds bicycles by hand only, and he has a growing list of customers, mostly professional athletes and triathletes who appreciate the attention to quality each bike receives during the production process. Moreover, Ralph Brinsdorfer, Steve's co-owner of the shop, provides an incredible amount of service. Ralph makes sure bikes are delivered damage free and on time, and he runs a quick and reliable repair service. He also offers financing to local bike teams and sponsors an annual bike race to support the community's Boys & Girls Club. Both Steve and Ralph agree that it just couldn't be done any other way. ■

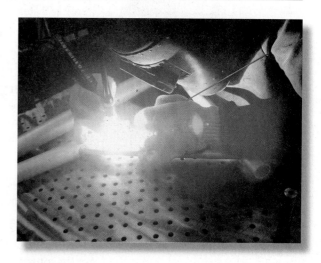

The goal of business is to deliver a good or a service to customers. **Production** is the process of getting a good or a service to the customer; it is a series of related activities, with value being added at each stage. Many people think that businesses that produce manufactured goods ("things"), such as bicycles, automobiles, and computers, are the only businesses that require some form of production process. But even businesses that offer services, such as restaurants, repair shops, and retail stores, require some form of production. How a company handles the production process can either help or hinder the overall success of the business and the competitiveness of the good or the service in the marketplace. In this chapter, you'll learn about the various concerns for both the production of goods and the production of services.

The Importance of Production

Why is the production of goods and services a critical component of any business? Companies strive to make a profit by providing goods or services to consumers. To increase their profits and decrease production costs, businesses must find the most efficient production process possible. Increasing competition, global manufacturing pressures, changing customer needs, increasing prices on resources and labor, and the sagging economy are just some of the issues that require companies to scrutinize the efficiencies of their production process. To remain competitive, companies must be cost-effective, efficient, innovative, and flexible.

How important is manufacturing in the United States? Manufacturing, although it has been hit hard in the past decade—and certainly in the past couple of years—by significant increases in imported goods and related job losses, remains a fundamental component of the U.S. economy. In fact, despite jobs being moved offshore, and many terminated with the closing of several manufacturing facilities during the most recent recession, the U.S. manufacturing sector accounted for one-tenth of all U.S. jobs in 2009.[1] The manufacturing sector is

For an interactive, real-world example of this topic, access this chapter's **BizSkill** entitled Improving a Business, located at **my*biz*lab**.com.

also responsible for a significant share of U.S. economic production, generating 23 percent of the total GDP in 2009.[2] Moreover, because manufacturing firms use a substantial amount of commodities and services as inputs, the manufacturing sector is actually responsible for a bigger share of total output. Some believe that it is the manufacturing sector that will help stimulate the economy and help bring about a faster recovery.

Moving to a Service-Based Economy

How are services important to the U.S. economy? Despite the ongoing importance of the manufacturing sector, the United States, like most developed nations, has transitioned itself from an industrial-based, manufacturing economy to a service-based economy. Services make up nearly three-fourths of the U.S. GDP, and about 80 percent of jobs are in the service sector.[3] The primary reason for this is that service businesses are easier to start because they require less capital for real estate, factories, and equipment. Small home, Internet, and Web-based businesses are popping up all the time. They offer consulting, repair and support services, bookkeeping, child care, and even retail services.

Of course, not all service businesses are small. One-third of the 30 firms that currently compose the Dow Jones Industrial Average (DJIA) are in the service sector. These include American Express (which in 1982 became the first services firm to be added), AT&T, Bank of America, Cisco, McDonald's, JP Morgan Chase, Travelers, Verizon Communications, Walmart, and Walt Disney.

Some companies are considered to be both manufacturing and service based. GE and IBM, also on the DJIA, are considered manufacturing companies, and both are also considered as the largest and most competitive service operations in the world. McDonald's is a service organization, but it also produces the menu items that are served in its restaurants. And, because there are also indexes specifically for transportation companies and utilities, those types of service-based industries are not included on the DJIA but are obviously very important to the U.S. economy.[4]

The Global Production Landscape

How is U.S. manufacturing competing globally? When seemingly all product labels indicate that the goods we use are made somewhere other than in the United States, it is hard to imagine that the United States is still a globally important manufacturing country. However, according to the authoritative *CIA World Factbook*, the United States is still "the leading industrial power in the world."[5] Even in the midst of a global recession, the United States is the fourth largest exporter, having exported nearly $1 billion worth of goods in 2009.[6] Nearly one-half of U.S. exports are goods, such as transistors, aircraft, motor vehicle parts, computers, and telecommunications equipment; industrial supplies such as organic chemicals account for another one-fourth of U.S. total exports; and consumer goods, such as automobiles and medicines, make up another 15 percent.[7]

How does manufacturing affect the global economy? Although manufacturing is important in the United States, as stated earlier, it has become a more service-oriented economy. This is also true of the majority of developed economies, such as those in Europe. Developing economies, such as those in Asia and Africa, have become more manufacturing oriented, which has helped the world economy by creating a higher standard of living for millions of people. This new trend is due largely to the reduction of barriers to trade that were predominant in the pre-Internet days. Now the world can almost be thought of as a single global market with increased trade and better utilization of capital and labor. However, when the pace of manufacturing slows in China, India, and Japan, it affects the rest of the world's economies, as was experienced in the global economic slow-down in 2009 and 2010. This is because manufacturing generates other service-based economic activities, such as transporting goods, generating software that is needed to assist with processes, and marketing and selling the goods.

In many respects, small bike shops, like the one run by Steve Schmidt and Ralph Brinsdorfer, are significantly different from their larger competitors, such as Trek, Cannondale, and Schwinn. But all the companies share similar concerns with regard to producing a quality product. Where to locate the business or plant, determining which suppliers to work with, ensuring the right inventory is on hand, and achieving and maintaining high quality are all concerns of every business—whether it is big or small or produces a good or a service. ■

Operations Management pp. 327–333

Arthur Ridder owns a furniture company in northern California. His company has enjoyed a great deal of success; its close proximity to natural resources and dependable suppliers, as well as a large employee base, has allowed it to produce large quantities of high-quality furniture. Shipping has been efficient, as the factory is located 3 miles from a major highway and 20 miles from a port for international delivery. Due to the success of his first location, he is considering opening a new location in Europe to expand the business internationally. The European factory is in a remote area of Switzerland near the Alps. Natural resources are amazingly abundant—they are what drew Arthur to the area—but the area is not densely populated, and finding an adequate quantity of skilled employees may be difficult. Shipping is also a concern, as the area is not centrally located. Weighing the pros and cons, what should Arthur do? ■

Picking the right location for your business can be a complex issue, but it is only one component of **operations management.** Operations management consists of managing the activities and processes to produce and distribute goods and services. These activities and processes, usually overseen by an operations manager, generally include how the facility should be organized, what supplies to purchase, what materials and inventory to keep on hand, how the product is produced, and how quality is measured and controlled—all of which are all important in ensuring that a good or a service is created and delivered successfully to the customer. In this section, we'll look at some of the more important factors that a company must consider when looking for the ideal location and determining how the facility will be organized. In later sections, we'll look at production management and quality control.

Determining Facility Location

What factors must businesses consider when determining where to locate their facilities? Some businesses, such as restaurants, supermarkets, and service businesses, must choose their locations based on their

The Karl Strauss Brewing Company has brewery locations close to its targeted customers.

proximity to market; they need to be close to their potential customer base. A restaurant that is easily visible to passing cars and pedestrians has more of an advantage in attracting business than a restaurant tucked away in a remote part of town where few people visit. For example, when Tony Calamunci and his brother John wanted to expand their family's hot dog joint, they took great care in selecting the right locations for their additional stores. Because college students and budget-conscious families were most attracted to their low-cost hot dogs and burgers as a lunch item, the Calamunci brothers considered locations only with high daytime traffic and populations with these demographic characteristics.[8] Johnny's Lunch is currently operating in seven locations with plans to double in the near future.[9]

For some businesses, the costs and logistics of transporting raw materials is a bigger issue than proximity to the market. Transportation costs are one of the major expenses that many manufacturing companies must consider. In fact, transportation costs for supplies coming in and goods going out can be as much as five times the cost of operating a production facility.[10] Therefore, locating a facility with easy access to natural resources or suppliers helps a business keep transportation costs low.

Transportation systems become more complex and costly when a company's supply chain is global, so global companies that learn how to reduce transportation costs and manage transportation processes more efficiently are more likely to have a competitive edge over other large-scale companies that have less efficient and more costly transportation operations. For example, Tata Steel is one of the world's leaders in steelmaking. One of Tata's success factors is its proximity to raw-material sources.[11] Although the company is headquartered in India, Tata Steel operates in 24 countries. Tata secured the iron ore mines in India, and its overseas operations in Southeast Asia, Australia, and parts of Africa are focused on securing raw-material sources at these locations. Similarly, Arthur Ridder in the opening story became acutely aware of how transportation affected his location decision. His initial U.S. location for his business was ideal, but finding a location in Europe was proving to be more difficult.

Why is it important to consider utility supply when determining location? The **utility supply** refers to the availability of public infrastructure services, such as electricity, natural gas, water, and communications. For example, a company that is establishing a large facility, such as a bottling plant or a warehouse, wouldn't want to situate it in a remote location with little public in-

frastructure, even if the land is cheap. Because such a large facility requires ample amounts of electricity or running water to operate properly, the cost to establish this infrastructure could be enormous. Moreover, locating manufacturing operations in an area where easy access to these utilities and resources is inexpensive greatly reduces costs. Waste management, another common public utility is also essential for business operations. Just as being "off the grid" wouldn't make much sense in terms of selecting a business location, a remote location would also render waste disposal and treatment difficult.

Why is hazardous-waste disposal important?
Many businesses, as part of their day-to-day operations, create large amounts of hazardous waste that must be dealt with correctly. Even everyday materials, such as paint and cleaning fluids, are considered hazardous waste and must be disposed of properly.[12] The proper disposal of this waste has ramifications on a business's location. Each state, county, municipality, or other local government will have its own guidelines and procedures for dealing with hazardous waste. Businesses that generate large amounts of hazardous waste should locate in an area that has reliable hazardous waste removal or treatment facilities nearby. Small businesses will benefit from locating in a community that offers disposal services for hazardous wastes. For example, Pinellas County, Florida, offers EnviroBusiness Days and Mobile Collection services to make it more convenient for small businesses to dispose of small hazardous waste items, such as toner cartridges, fluorescent light bulbs, computers, and cleaners.[13] Responsible organizations must be aware of the disposal options that are available in their areas.

What else impacts location selection?
Another consideration when choosing a production location is the human factor, which refers to how the location decision affects the people in a surrounding community and vice versa. Companies need to hire employees to maintain their operations, but they also need to be aware of how their presence affects the community overall. The human factor has three separate, though interrelated, components:

- Labor availability
- Living conditions
- Laws and regulations

What labor factors must a company consider?
One component of the human factor is the availability of labor. After all, labor is a necessary factor of production for a company to operate successfully. Choosing a location for virtually any business requires finding an area with an abundance of workers who possess the necessary skills. California's famed Silicon Valley became a top hub for the tech industry's software and hardware manufacturing businesses because of its proximity to Stanford University, its abundance of local engineers, and the area's history in developing technology.[14]

However, seeking skilled workers is only part of the decision-making process. Health care, education, costs of living, and the general business environment are some of the other factors that can determine a company's ideal location. Many businesses need to find a workforce that they can afford financially as well. One of the reasons some corporations send their manufacturing operations outside the United States is because those countries contain highly skilled workers who require lower wages than their U.S. counterparts. India is the primary destination for outsourced high-tech labor because it offers an experienced, skilled, and affordable labor pool.[15]

How is an organization mindful of impacting living conditions in a community?
Another way the human factor figures into selecting a manufacturing location is through its impact on living conditions. Manufacturing can alter these conditions either positively or negatively. On the one hand, a business brings opportunities to citizens of a community by creating jobs and a higher

Solar-panel manufacturer SunPower provides green collar jobs. Here, a 150-acre solar installation uses panels that follow the sun's path across the sky to generate more electricity than conventional systems. The solar system delivers electric power to approximately 8,000 homes.

standard of living. Similarly, many businesses seek out areas where the quality of life is already high (good schools, pleasant weather, low crime rates, etc.) before finalizing a location. Some social entrepreneurs might take it upon themselves to locate their businesses in an impoverished area to revitalize the local economy. Environmentally aware politicians advocate green collar jobs precisely for their ability to rejuvenate economically depressed communities.

Conversely, a business could also have negative effects on the surrounding area. Some corporations have been accused of lowering a community's living conditions by exploiting workers or increasing local traffic. For example, Teva Pharmaceuticals is proposing to build a new North American headquarters facility in Warrington, Pennsylvania. However, concerns over the increased traffic to an already congested area have brought much opposition from local residents, despite company promises to improve local roads.[16]

Does the government have a say in location? To try to maintain a balance between business and community interests, governments have created many laws and regulations to protect individuals and the environment. The U.S. Department of Labor is one federal agency that monitors many laws and regulations affecting workers. Each state also has its own labor department responsible for enforcing local labor laws and regulations. Florida, for example, has embarked on a plan to create a biotech hub similar to that of Silicon Valley in California, in an effort to create wealth, high-paying jobs, and increased economic development in a state that traditionally has been thought of for tourism and good weather only.[17]

Determining Facility Layout

Why is facility layout important? Facility layout refers to the physical arrangement of resources and people in the production process and how they interact. The design of a facility's layout is important to maximize efficiency and satisfy employees' needs. It involves everything from the arrangement of cubicles in an office space to the position of robotic arms in an automobile manufacturing plant.

When determining or renovating a facility layout for maximum effectiveness, business owners must also consider many operational factors. For example, facilities should be designed so that they can be easily adjusted to meet changing production needs. Having to undergo extensive renovations or completely relocate as a company's operations change or expand can be a costly endeavor; therefore, operations managers must be prepared to factor possible growth at the planning stage. Additionally, the facility layout should be in accordance with Occupational Safety and Health Administration guidelines to ensure worker safety.

How does facility layout affect production? A facility layout should be able to handle materials orderly and efficiently to ensure a smooth flow of production. To do so, designers need to use available space effectively. Warehouses, for instance, need to have enough space to stack goods, and products need to be easily accessible for workers using equipment such as forklifts and conveyor belts.

The distance that a work-in-progress must travel within a facility must also be taken into account. This is true not only for the production of goods but also in the production of services. For example, the layout of a fast-food restaurant can help the employees involved in the different parts of the process—preparing food and serving customers—to work in a more integrated fashion.

Are there different types of facility layouts? Different manufacturing processes require different types of facility layouts. There are four common types: process layout, product layout, cellular layout, and fixed position layout.

Many new office layouts take into consideration a more horizontal management structure where there are open work areas. Some offices also give employees spaces where they can meet to share ideas and work together as teams.

- **Process layout** groups together similar tasks, and the partially assembled product moves from one station to the next as workers perform a particular step in the production process. Process layout is used mostly to produce low-volume, customized products. For example, Vermont Teddy Bears are produced in a process layout: Each bear is assembled and dressed according to specific customer orders.

- **Product layout** is used mostly for high-volume, standardized products that can be produced in a sequential fashion, such as Crayola Crayons. Batches of crayons go through parallel processes of melting and coloring wax, shaping into molds, wrapping, and then finally coming together and assembled into boxes.

Crayola Crayons are produced using a product layout, which is suitable for high-volume, standardized products.

Both of these layouts are organized by function. However, these arrangements are not always efficient as production can stall if a problem occurs at one station, and workers can get bored with repetitive tasks.

- To overcome the shortcomings of process and product layouts, some manufacturers have adopted **cellular layout.** Cellular layout places small teams of workers who handle all aspects of assembly, so each station is equipped with the parts and tools necessary to produce a product from start to finish, and the worker moves through the workstation as he or she conducts the assembly process.

- Lastly, **fixed position layouts** are used for manufacturing large items, such as ships, airplanes, and modular homes. With a fixed position layout, the product stays in one place, and the workers move around the product to complete its assembly.

Does facility layout affect employees? Facility layout may even affect the productivity of individual employees. Spacious cubicles and window views, for example, can greatly improve the morale and, therefore, the productivity of office workers. Other layout options that could improve employee productivity include providing a break room, a cafeteria, or on-site child-care services. However, a company might need to decide whether an increase in productivity outweighs the cost of including such features.

Working with Suppliers

What is a make-or-buy decision? When starting the production process, one of the first decisions that operations managers make is what needs to be manufactured and what needs to be purchased from outside suppliers. This is commonly called a **make-or-buy decision.** If a company plans to manufacture a product that will carry both the company's name and reputation, it has to decide if it will make the entire product in-house or if the product will be assembled from a combination of parts manufactured in-house and parts purchased from suppliers. It is not always necessary for a company to make everything in-house, so how does a company decide what to make and what to buy? A company must consider factors such as cost and quality. If it is less expensive to outsource the production of certain parts elsewhere, that may be the best decision. However, it is important that a company can trust the quality of any parts that are produced elsewhere and that appropriate quantities are delivered in a timely manner.

How does a company decide which suppliers to use? Selecting suppliers is an important part of the make-or-buy decision. After all, establishing a business relationship with a supplier is like entering into a partnership. Customers don't see a product that is supplied by one company with parts provided by different suppliers; they see a total product. Customers will hold the company responsible even if an individual supplier is to blame for making a faulty part or missing a deadline and causing a delay. For example, recently Mattel had to recall close to one million toys because its supplier in China had coated the toys in lead paint. Mattel was later fined $2.3 million by the Consumer Product Safety Commission.[18] Such recalls not only can be financially costly but also damaging to a company's reputation. So having a good supplier that meets a company's needs and cares about a company's customers as if they were its own is an invaluable asset.

A company's first step in finding suppliers involves clearly defining and understanding its needs so that it can find suppliers that truly fit its requirements. Cost is always a factor, but it should never be the sole factor. For example, if several potential suppliers offer similar products with similar prices, other factors will come into play: For example, a company may need a supplier that is reliable or one that is fast. Likewise, one supplier may offer a part for significantly less but of such poor quality that later repairs or recalls would end up costing a company more than the cost of quality parts; its reputation would also be affected. Understanding these needs before choosing a supplier will make the process easier and more beneficial in the end.

There's a vast collection of resources designed to help businesses connect with suppliers. These resources include the Better Business Bureau, the local chamber of commerce, exhibitions, trade magazines, the Internet, and old-fashioned recommendations from friends and business acquaintances. The challenge for operations managers is in finding the best people for the job and determining which of those suppliers offer optimal solutions for production needs.

Operations Management for Service Providers

Does operations management differ in the service sector? Operations management has been traditionally associated with manufacturing goods, but many of the concepts apply to the service industry, too. There are some inherent differences between the industrial sector and the service sector. Service providers have more contact with their customers than do manufacturers. Also, services are usually customized to satisfy the specific needs of a customer. For example, a house painter applies the colors chosen by the customer, and a doctor treats his or her patient's specific symptoms. However, despite these differences, the ultimate goal of providing a quality product in a cost-efficient manner is similar to manufacturers and service providers. Service providers have implemented much efficiency in their processes. For example, banks and fast-food restaurants have installed drive-up windows. As noted earlier, the location for a manufacturer is dependent on the proximity of resources and suppliers, whereas the location for a service provider needs to be near the customer. The size of a manufacturing facility is dictated by the extent of the production process, whereas the size of a service business must take into consideration fluctuating demands and capacity.

Taking transportation, human, and physical factors into consideration, businesses ultimately choose a location that will allow them to be competitive. In addition, determining the correct facility layout and choosing the right suppliers can further enhance a company's operations management. Creating a proper facility for operations is only the first step for a successful business owner. The next step involves determining and developing a proper production-management plan. Think back to the furniture company example that starts this section. Given what you know now about choosing a manufacturing location and operations management, is Switzerland the best location for Arthur Ridder's furniture company? ■

Production Management pp. 333–342

The ink was barely dry on the lease, as Sylvia Ackerman drove to IKEA to pick out furniture for her new apartment. Sylvia loves the Swedish furniture manufacturer because of the simple lines and clean designs of its products. In addition, because she has only herself to rely on, she can easily move her purchases into her apartment by herself because the products are packaged in flat packs. Sylvia also loves the challenge of assembling the products herself. More importantly, Sylvia knows that it is hard to beat IKEA pricing; she will always get quality products at a low cost. ■

What sets IKEA apart from other furniture companies is the packaging and storage of its products. Most of the furniture it produces is shipped in flat packs to be assembled at the consumer's home. These condensed packages minimize shipping and storage costs, which, in turn, lower the retail cost of IKEA products. The company has many factories worldwide and is constantly opening new locations to supply its growing number of franchised stores. IKEA is a great example of a company that uses intelligent production management to enhance its business.[19]

Goods and services don't exist in a vacuum; therefore, the whole point of production is to provide the process through which products are created and given value. **Production management** refers to the planning, implementation, and control measures used to convert resources into finished products. These activities are similar to those in operations management but are more focused on the product. The scope of production management includes determining what to produce, what processes and machinery to use to minimize costs, the number of products that need to be produced each month, and how to meet the needs of all employees while maintaining quality standards. The act of production gives these finished products value, or **utility,** by satisfying consumers' wants or needs.

To ensure that a product provides utility, production managers must successfully develop and carry out a production plan. A **production plan** is a description of how resources are to be used to develop a product in a specific way. A well-thought-out plan will ensure a smoothly run production process. Production managers are in charge of setting schedules, choosing what parts and supplies to buy for the assembly process, overseeing quality control, and managing other important issues. Production managers who plan effectively are able to increase productivity, reduce costs, and improve customer satisfaction.

The Production Process

What production processes are used by businesses? There are several types of production processes that businesses can use. The type that is chosen depends on the company and what types of goods or services it produces. Common production processes and techniques include the following:

- Mass production
- Mass customization
- Flexible manufacturing
- Lean production

Let's examine each in detail.

How do large quantities of goods get produced? The method of producing large quantities of goods at a low cost is called **mass production.** This method relies on machines and automated assembly lines to produce goods that are identical and adhere to certain standards of quality. Mass-produced goods are usually manufactured along an **assembly line** (or production line), in which partially complete products are moved from one worker to the next on a conveyor belt.

The cost to run an assembly line is kept low because machines do the majority of the work, and the laborers don't need to be especially skilled to perform their repetitive tasks. This method also cuts down on production time, allowing a large quantity of goods to be produced very quickly. Because machinery is the main component, the risk of human error is virtually eliminated. A major disadvantage, however, is that mass production is inflexible. After a production line is established, it is very difficult to change or alter the process if an unexpected problem occurs.

Can product customization be done with mass production? When mass production was implemented, if any customization, or individualization, of product design was desired, the process had to be stopped or slowed down to customize small batches. Now, due to advances in digital and production technologies, the once difficult, time-consuming, and more costly customization process has become accessible to a wide variety of markets. **Mass customization** is the production of goods or services tailored to meet customers' individual needs cost-effectively. It ranges from the bulk customization of industrial supplies, such as valves, switches, and instruments, to individual customization that is most often seen with clothing, shoes, glasses, and bicycles. For example, Blank Label allows customers to design their own shirts online for nearly the same price as a store-bought shirt. The benefit of this process is that Blank Label does not need to produce shirts of every size and style, thus incurring additional warehousing and shipping expenses. This is the same model that Dell Computers employed in the

Countries with the Largest Car Production, 2009

Rank	Country	Millions of Cars Produced
1.	China	10,383,831
2.	Japan	6,862,161
3.	Germany	4,964,523
4.	South Korea	3,158,417
5.	Brazil	2,576,628
6.	United States	2,246,470
7.	India	2,166,238
8.	France	1,819,462
9.	Spain	1,812,688
10.	Iran	1,359,520

1990s. Rather than warehouse potentially unused parts that soon would be obsolete, Dell allowed customers to design their computers to the specifications that best met their needs. Now, most PC manufacturers offer online customization for their products.

How is mass customization achieved?

A solution to the rigid system of mass production is a method of production called *flexible manufacturing*, or a **flexible manufacturing system (FMS)**. In this system, several machines are linked together by one central computer. All the machines in the system can process different part types simultaneously. Unlike a mass-production system, an FMS can adapt to changes in schedules and product specifications. There are four components to an FMS: processing machines, a material-handling system, a central computer, and human labor.[20] For example, Victory Motorcycles, a division of Polaris, the off-road vehicle manufacturer, uses an FMS to create motorcycles that customers design online to their specific needs and tastes.

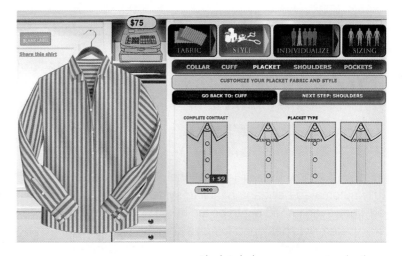

Blank Label uses mass customization to produce customer-designed men's shirts.

Can mass customization be used in service industries? The technologies of mass customization have also enabled many service-based organizations to meet the individual needs of their customers. Burger King, for example, introduced its "Have It Your Way" campaign, which took the mass production of standardized fast food to a more personalized delivery and allowed customers to "tweak" what went on their hamburgers to meet their specific tastes. The Ritz Carlton Hotel takes overnight visits to a new level. Most hotel chains offer a preference of bed size and perhaps room location, but the rest is pretty standard no matter which city or country you are in. But the Ritz trains its staff to record unique habits, preferences, and dislikes of each guest, which it enters into a database that is used to further customize a guest's current stay and also make the next stay filled with personal touches. Each guest is greeted by name, the hotel knows whether there is a preference for feather or nonallergenic pillows, and has the guest's favorite newspaper placed at the door every morning. They anticipate a customer's every need, without having to ask. The results of this customized program have been a 23 percent increase in guest retention.[21]

Victory Motorcycles uses an FMS to produce their customer-designed, made-to-order motorcycles.

What type of production focuses on efficiency?

One of the most important aspects of the production process is making sure that work gets done as efficiently as possible. Increased efficiency helps work get done faster, cheaper, and sometimes with better quality. Although efficiency has always been a concern, the success of lean production has made efficiency a primary focus for many companies. **Lean production** is a set of principles concerned with reducing waste and improving flow. The basic tenet of lean production is to do more with less through the elimination of wasteful overproduction, unnecessary wait time, needless

Biz**Chat**

Technology: Too Much of a Good Thing?

In 1995, the new Denver International Airport boasted a fully automated baggage-handling system. The technology, however, turned out to be too much of a good thing. The system was designed to move luggage along an automated track between airport terminals and baggage-claim areas, some of which were as far as a mile apart in the large airport. A centralized computer system would control the entire operation, eliminating the need for human baggage handlers to physically move baggage from one point to another. But after 10 years of misplaced luggage, glitches in the system, and soaring maintenance costs, the error-prone system was finally shut down. In 2005, the only airline to ever use the system, United Airlines, went back to using baggage handlers to complete the tasks previously handled by the automated system. In a test run before the switch was made, human baggage handlers beat the automated system's error rate hands down. With the help of mobile devices, such as handheld scanners, United Airlines is now able to track luggage better than the automated system ever could. In some cases, a little technology goes a long way.

For more information and discussion questions about this topic, check out the BizChat feature on my**biz**lab.com.

transportation, excess inventory, superfluous motion, redundant over-processing, and careless defective units. This system was first defined and employed by Toyota in the 1980s with great success. Although lean production originally was used for manufacturing, the principles behind it are highly flexible and can be used in every step of the production process.

Technology in the Production Process

What is the role of technology in the production process? With thousands of goods to produce at a given time, you might guess that technology plays an integral role in facilitating the flow of any production process. When managed efficiently, the technological aspect of a production process should lead to increases in productivity and reductions in costs. Technology may also improve the quality and increase the variety of products, which influences a customer's buying decisions. Customers are more likely to buy a product that is not only low-priced compared to other similar products but also of high quality and readily available in many varieties. It is essential for businesses in today's globally competitive environment to be up-to-date on new technologies that can improve any or all aspects of the production process.

What has helped automate the production process? Humans are sometimes at a disadvantage when it comes to performing a task repetitively for many hours and with great precision and accuracy. This is where robots come in; an *industrial robot* is any device that performs automatically, typically completing repetitive tasks.[22] Not only can robots work around the clock tirelessly, and with accuracy, but they can also work in potentially hazardous conditions, thereby protecting human workers from dangerous environments. The two biggest industries employing robot applications are the automotive industry—which uses robots for welding, painting, assembly, and handling various materials—and the household appliances industry—which requires sealing, painting, and installing appliances such as microwave ovens.

What is the advantage of robots?

Robots offer consistency in reducing production costs, raising productivity, and producing high-quality products. Industrial robots may take away some production-related jobs, but the technology has also created many new jobs for technicians and engineers. Companies that can effectively apply robotic technology in their production processes are more likely to gain an economic advantage in the global marketplace.

How has technology improved the design process?

Computer-aided design (CAD) refers to using a computer and software to create two-dimensional or three-dimensional models of phys-

ical parts. With CAD systems, the models displayed on-screen can be modified in size or shape, viewed internally, and rotated on any axis. CAD also enables part testing by simulating real-world environments. CAD, however, cannot design a model of a product on its own. A designer must first translate the design into a geometrical model for the CAD system to display. Once the model data are received, the CAD system provides the designer with tools and a flexible environment. By programming a simple design change into the CAD system, a manufacturer can produce custom-designed products, such as clothing and cars, without incurring extra costs. CAD is not only used to design smaller products; it can also be used to design houses, machinery, tools, and commercial structures.

Robots play a big part in automobile manufacturing, but they are also used to weld, paint, assemble, package, inspect, and test many other types of products.

How is CAD used on bigger projects?

Some manufacturing processes that are more complicated, such as those for motor vehicles, airplanes, and ships, need more than one CAD program to design and incorporate all the different model parts. For instance, the design of a ship may require one CAD application for the steel

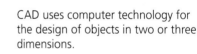

CAD uses computer technology for the design of objects in two or three dimensions.

structure and another CAD program for the propeller. A disadvantage of this method is that it requires knowledge of all the different software applications used as well as how to integrate them in the end. On the other hand, the Boeing Company's 757 model is a good example of how integration can be achieved. The 757 model is composed of parts from 50 different firms, so Boeing's CAD system effectively integrates all the parts, ensuring a precise fit. This system then effectively reduces the number of prototypes needed and the working hours for assembly.[23]

How does CAD information get incorporated into the manufacturing process? Once a design is approved, **computer-aided manufacturing (CAM)** uses the design data to control the machinery used in the manufacturing process. The integration of CAD and CAM systems with the various aspects of a firm's production process is referred to as *simultaneous engineering*. Ford Motor Company's engine division, for example, successfully integrated all its production and design systems into one database that could be accessed by PCs and workstations of employees and suppliers involved with design and production.[24] This type of facilitated communication is a huge benefit for firms with complex systems. One of the main disadvantages of using CAD/CAM systems is that they require considerable time and investment to set up and learn the necessary software, hardware, communications, and integration.

Can an entire facility be automated? **Computer-integrated manufacturing (CIM)** systems combine design and manufacturing functions with other automated functions, such as order taking, shipment, and billing for the complete automation of a manufacturing plant. For example, the printing company VistaPrint uses CIM not only to manufacture its products but also help customers create and place orders for custom-designed business cards, brochures, and even T-shirts. Through the use of CIM, the company has expanded its business and is able to serve more customers while continuing to offer affordable prices.[25]

What effect has automation had on the production process? CAD, CAM, and CIM have dramatically improved the process of producing goods by reducing the time between design and manufacturing, thus making a significant impact on productivity. These systems have also increased the scope of automated machinery in the production process. Through the rapid pace of technological advancement, CAD, CAM, and CIM systems are not limited to large mass-production facilities; they are entering smaller companies as well.

How has social networking impacted production? The social-networking structure of the Internet, along with hardware and software tools, has created a ready-made distribution system for more creative consumers who want to "have it their way." Using social media tools, such as blogs, web videos, and podcasts, as well as social-networking sites like Facebook and Twitter, consumers can not only design their own products but also have direct influence on what companies develop and produce.

In 2006, the Trendwatching Web site coined the phrase *customer-made*, defining it as the "phenomenon of corporations creating goods, services, and experiences in close cooperation with experienced and creative consumers, tapping into their intellectual capital, and in exchange giving them a direct say in (and rewarding them for) what actually gets produced, manufactured, developed, designed, serviced, or processed."[26] Since then, the trend has taken off, and it is now an established business practice. The previously mentioned Blank Label is a relative newcomer to this growing genre, and Adidas with their mi Adidas campaign and Converse's Make One Yours are proven examples that this design-your-own trend has caught on.

Beyond design, social media capabilities enable consumers to directly influence what companies develop and produce, as well as give instant feedback on whether their initiatives are worthwhile. Nokia was one of the earliest manufacturers, with its Nokia Experience Lounge site, to invite consumers to "join in" and collaborate, converse, and connect. Starbucks and Dell have similar sites with MyStarbucks-Ideas and Dell's IdeaStorm, respectively, that invite their customers to share product development ideas. And third-party sites, such as Engadget, have been running "How Would You Change or Improve" topics that give users a place to voice their insights and suggestions about products such as the Xbox360, Skype, TiVo, and the Electrolux Roomba. The Internet and social media have created a virtually new world of opportunities for anyone to innovate, produce, and process an idea.

Controlling the Production Process

How does scheduling shape the production process? When it comes to production, **scheduling** refers to the efficient organization of equipment, facilities, labor, and materials. There are two different types of scheduling: *forward* and *backward*. With *forward scheduling*, you start with the date that materials are available, create the most efficient schedule, and then determine a shipping date based on that schedule. *Backward scheduling* is the exact opposite: You are given a shipping or due date, and you have to determine the start date and the most efficient schedule based on when everything must be finished.

There are two major components that go into making an effective schedule: loading and sequencing. *Loading* is assigning a job to a specific machine or an entire work center. *Sequencing* is assigning the order in which jobs are processed.

What tools are available to help with scheduling? There are numerous pieces of software and systems that are designed to put together a cohesive schedule of loading and sequencing to ensure that all the right tools are working on the right jobs at the right times, such as *Gantt charts* and *PERT charts*. But no matter how complex the system, all configurations are just estimates based on the data input into the system and the rules it uses. Having a person oversee scheduling is still invaluable because that individual can bring experience and judgment that cannot be programmed into a computer.

What is a Gantt chart? One method for keeping tabs on the progress of a given project is a **Gantt chart,** a tool developed by Henry Gantt in the 1920s. A Gantt chart is formatted similarly to a horizontal bar graph. It is used to lay out each task in a project, the order in which these tasks must be completed, and how long each task should take. ▼ **Figure 11.1** shows an example of a Gantt chart for a remodeling project. Originally used for large-scale construction projects, such as building the Hoover Dam in the 1930s, Gantt charts are still used today to manage a variety of both large-scale and small-scale projects. At any point in the process, project managers and manufacturers can see at a glance which tasks have

▼ **Figure 11.1
Sample Gantt Chart**

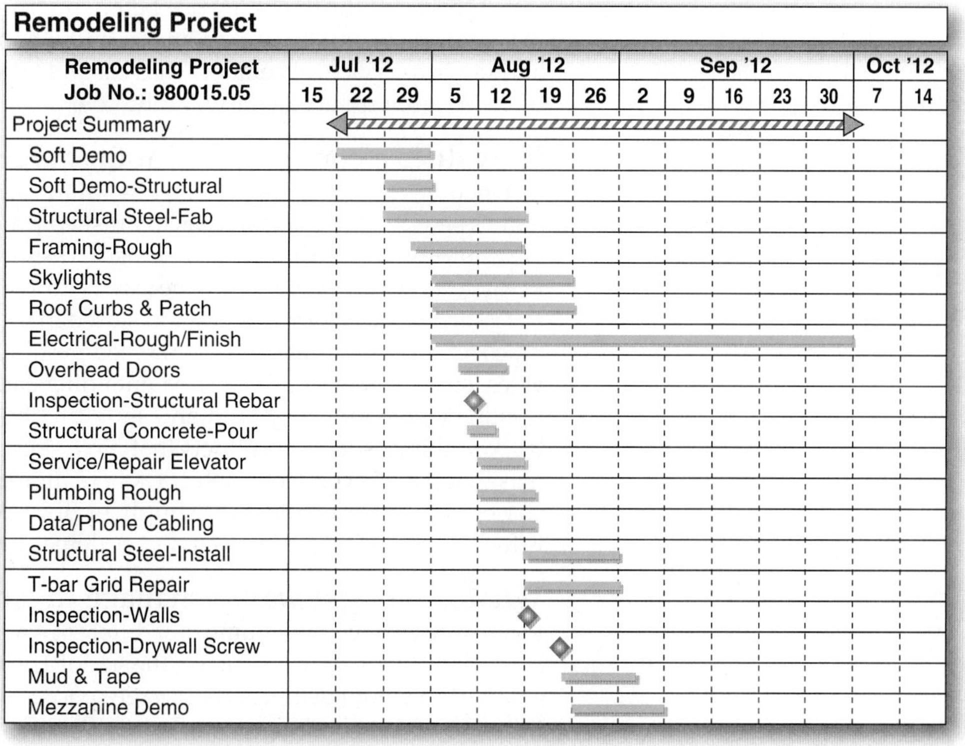

Remodeling Project														
Remodeling Project Job No.: 980015.05	Jul '12			Aug '12				Sep '12					Oct '12	
	15	22	29	5	12	19	26	2	9	16	23	30	7	14
Project Summary														
Soft Demo														
Soft Demo-Structural														
Structural Steel-Fab														
Framing-Rough														
Skylights														
Roof Curbs & Patch														
Electrical-Rough/Finish														
Overhead Doors														
Inspection-Structural Rebar														
Structural Concrete-Pour														
Service/Repair Elevator														
Plumbing Rough														
Data/Phone Cabling														
Structural Steel-Install														
T-bar Grid Repair														
Inspection-Walls														
Inspection-Drywall Screw														
Mud & Tape														
Mezzanine Demo														

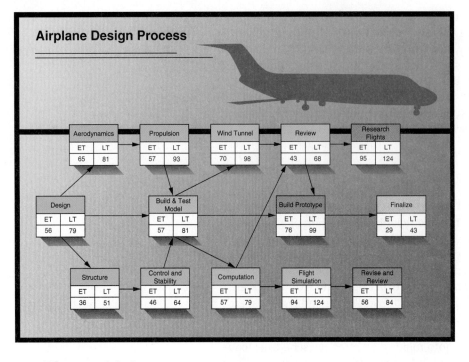

Airplane Design Process

Aerodynamics		Propulsion		Wind Tunnel		Review		Research Flights	
ET	LT	ET	LT	ET	LT	ET	LT	ET	LT
65	81	57	93	70	98	43	68	95	124

Design		Build & Test Model		Build Prototype		Finalize	
ET	LT	ET	LT	ET	LT	ET	LT
56	79	57	81	76	99	29	43

Structure		Control and Stability		Computation		Flight Simulation		Revise and Review	
ET	LT	ET	LT	ET	LT	ET	LT	ET	LT
36	51	46	64	57	79	94	124	56	84

▼ **Figure 11.2**
Sample PERT Chart

been completed and whether these tasks were completed on schedule.

What is a PERT chart? The **program evaluation and review technique (PERT)** was first used in the development of submarines in the 1950s. This method maps out the various steps involved in a project, differentiating tasks that must be completed in a certain order from tasks that may be completed simultaneously. The result is a Weblike diagram similar to the example shown in ▼ **Figure 11.2.**

In creating a PERT chart, time estimates are assigned to each task. Creating the chart helps identify the *critical path*, or the path of sequential tasks that will take the most time to complete. This helps managers determine an overall timeline for completing a project or, from a manufacturing standpoint, producing a particular good or service. However, because delays can cause the critical path in a project to change, PERT charts are limited in their ability to predict project completion times.

Purchasing and Inventory Control

How are materials used in the production process acquired? **Purchasing** is the task of acquiring the materials and services needed in the production process. As noted earlier, production managers need to find reliable suppliers who can provide high-quality resources at the best price. The Internet has made purchasing a much more competitive process. Just like you might use the Internet to search for the best price before buying a particular product, purchasing managers can compare prices and services between suppliers online before embarking in a service agreement. The cost and time associated with purchasing have therefore been reduced considerably.

How does a company maintain inventory control? **Inventory control** includes the receiving, storing, handling, and tracking of everything in a company's stock, from raw materials to finished products. Inventory often makes up a large portion of a business's expenses. Therefore, proper management is not only a way to stay informed but also necessary to keep costs low while ensuring that all necessary materials are in stock and stored in the proper place. There are four main types of stock: raw materials, unfinished products, finished products, and consumables (such as pens and paper). Maintaining each of these kinds of stock helps determine where money should and shouldn't be spent. Proper maintenance keeps track of things such as products that have shelf lives that could deteriorate, products that have become obsolete, or where more stock than necessary is being purchased. Ensuring an adequate supply of finished products or other types of stock is further complicated when customer demand is variable.

What is the best way to manage inventory? Managing stock or inventory can be achieved in a number of different ways, and no single method works best for every business. Factors such as the size of a business, the amount of inventory necessary, the amount of inventory storage space, and the proximity to suppliers all contribute to which inventory control method will work best for an individual company.

The least involved way to manage inventory is to simply eyeball it. This method works really well for smaller companies or companies that don't maintain large amounts of stock. When accuracy is a necessity, a *stock book solution*, where stock on hand is tallied in a book along with stock on order and stock that has been sold, would probably work best. Another less complicated management system is called the *reserve stock system*. This is where stock is set aside in reserve so that it cannot be used. The company goes through its inventory as it regularly would, and when it has to dip into the reserve stock, it knows it is time to reorder that item. It is important for managers to keep in mind when using this system that however much stock is in reserve should be enough to last the amount of time it takes to resupply.[27]

Whereas these systems can work well with smaller businesses, larger businesses generally require a more complicated inventory-management system. A **just-in-time (JIT) inventory control** system keeps the smallest amount of inventory on hand as possible, and everything else that is needed is ordered so that it arrives when it is needed. Storing fewer items and using items right away can reduce storage costs. Dell Computers made its mark in the PC manufacturing industry by embracing JIT inventory control. The company adopted a build-to-order system, making PCs directly to customer specifications, and needed to order the specific parts only as required by each order. This reduced the huge expense of carrying components that may not be used and subsequently become obsolete and useless. Over a four-year period after adopting this system, Dell's revenues grew from $2 billion to $16 billion.[28]

This system, however, is not without its drawbacks. To work properly, a company must have a very good relationship with its suppliers to ensure that appropriate quantities arrive on time and are delivered to where they are needed. Even then, unexpected shipping delays due to weather can occur, and the shipping costs may become quite high.

How is technology used to streamline inventory control?

Many organizations rely on a computerized inventory system that uses a barcode or **radio frequency identification (RFID)** tag on each item, allowing a computer to keep track of the status and quantity of each item. Each item is logged and classified when it is stocked and an identifying barcode or RFID tag is attached to the item. Both barcodes and RFID tags store all the specific information for each item, such as cost, stock number, and storage location. Using these systems, items in inventory can be scanned when they are used or sold, and the computer can continuously update the information for each item. Depending on the system used, computerized inventory makes it easier to analyze the quantitative factors of managing stock, such as how quickly each item is sold, how much really needs to be held in inventory at once, and when it is time to restock items.

With barcodes and RFID tags, items can be scanned and inventory can be monitored electronically.

What is materials requirement planning?

More appropriate to the production side of inventory management is **materials requirement planning (MRP),** a computer-based program used for inventory control and production planning. When an order is made, the specifics of that order are input into the MRP system. The MRP system then determines which parts will be needed to finish the job and compares these findings to the current inventory. Based on this information, it highlights what needs to be obtained, either through production or a supplier, as well as when the parts will be needed. It uses previous manufacturing data to break the job into parts. A process is input into the system, and the MRP portion of the system determines which components are needed to meet customers' order quantities and due dates. The end result should be the best estimate based on previous data. Knowing these estimates helps determine both part and labor shortages before a project even starts.

There are many limitations to MRP, the biggest being that it is only as effective as its data. So if the data are not well maintained, the estimates that it provides will become increasingly useless. Another limitation to MRP is its scope: It focuses only on the management of needed component parts in the *manufacturing* processes of a company.

What is enterprise resource planning? One way around the limitations of MRP is to use **enterprise resource planning (ERP)**[29] instead of MRP. ERP systems can do the same inventory control and process scheduling that MRP systems can do, but they can integrate these functions with other aspects that business management would like to tie together, such as finance and human resources. Through various types of computer software and hardware, the usual ERP system consolidates information into a central database that is accessible to various system modules. Companies that specialize in ERP systems include Oracle, SAP, and Microsoft.

ERP systems allow companies the ability to streamline the various workflows and share information across departments. This allows for improved productivity from all employees. With an ERP system in place, the various aspects of an organization can work together without worrying about compatible software. Unfortunately, there are disadvantages for a business that fails to fully invest in an ERP system. These problems can range from inadequate tech support to limited customization of the system.

Innovations in the production process have been the key to producing more goods at a lower cost. These innovations have helped many businesses achieve success. IKEA has demonstrated its ability to produce standardized goods in mass quantities while maintaining quality and efficiencies. Other companies have found ways to customize their products to meet specific customer needs or demands. In either situation, technology plays a big part in the management of today's production process, from automating production with robots to facilitating the design and manufacturing of products with CAD and CAM programs. Inventory controls, MRP systems, and ERP tools also help to make the entire production process most efficient. ■

Quality Control pp. 342–345

Jeanette Pae nearly shook with excitement as she took her new iPhone 4 out of its packaging. She had wanted an iPhone for a long time but had to wait for her former cell-phone contract to end. As the contract expiration neared, leaks of a new Apple iPhone appeared everywhere. Then, finally, confirmation! She preordered the newest device as soon as she could, and now the day was here when she could finally use it. But her excitement was slightly marred by rumors of a recall—something about calls dropping and antenna issues. Jeanette and her family were no strangers to recalls. Jeanette had owned one of those Dell laptop batteries that were overheating and causing fires, her mother had to return some Mattel toys that she had purchased for Jeanette's little sister because of fears of lead paint, and her father had been taking Vioxx to control his arthritis when Merck recalled the product due to it elevating the chances of heart attack or stroke. Even the cherished family Toyota was recalled. What was going on? Why were even the most reliable products having quality issues? ■

The use of techniques, activities, and processes to guarantee that a certain good or service meets a specified level of quality is referred to as **quality control.** Quality control has evolved from the formation of craftsmen's guilds in medieval Europe to improving methods of total quality management in the twentieth century.[30] In this section, we'll look at some important areas of quality control, starting with quality management.

Quality Management

Has quality control always been part of the production process?
The old method in the United States was to delegate quality control to a separate department that would inspect and test products for flaws after a product had been manufactured. This inspection method of quality control involves checking work at the *end* of the process before products are delivered. Unfortunately, several problems arise with this method. For one, it is expensive in terms of time and labor. Because inspection is performed by outside people instead of by the workers making the product, each inspector can pass or fail a product using his or her own standards and procedures. Moreover, inspecting finished products and discovering defects means some of these defects have to be scrapped or reworked, which can be costly.

What methods are used to improve quality?
Merely controlling for quality through inspection and monitoring employees is like visiting a doctor to treat the symptoms as opposed to remedying the source of an illness. So, since the 1980s, firms have been focusing on building quality into every step of the production process instead of merely taking action to scrap or fix defects. This concept of "total quality" at every stage of a production process was fully embraced by U.S. companies only after Japanese manufacturers implemented company-wide quality-improvement methods and strengthened their presence in the global market.[31] The Japanese produced exports not only at lower prices but also at higher levels of quality. Finally, by the 1980s, companies in the United States began to implement the **total quality management (TQM)** approach in their production processes. As you learned in Chapter 7, unlike the old inspection method of quality control, in which products are reviewed at certain points of the process (usually the end), TQM involves every factor in producing high-quality goods—management, customers, employees, and suppliers. At any point, employees and leaders are aiming to produce high quality.

> "Quality is not something you install like a new carpet or a set of bookshelves. You implant it. Quality is something you work at. It is a learning process."[32]
>
> —W. Edwards Deming, American statistician

TQM involves ongoing improvement of products, services, and processes. This can be accomplished by undertaking a plan-do-check-act (PDCA) cycle, created by American statistician W. Edwards Deming.[33] Using the PDCA cycle, organizations first formulate a plan to reduce potential errors, carry out the plan on a small scale, check the outcome and effectiveness of the change, and then implement the plan on a larger scale while monitoring results continually.

One popular tool used to check or measure if quality goals are being met is **statistical quality control (SQC),** or the continual monitoring of each stage of the entire production process to ensure that quality standards are being met at every stage. **Statistical process control (SPC)** uses statistical sampling of products at every phase of production and displays the results on a graph to show potential variations that need to be corrected. A common SPC tool is **Six Sigma,** a method that seeks to eliminate defects by removing variation in outcomes and measuring and analyzing manufacturing processes to see if standards are being met. A company with Six Sigma quality produces at a low defect rate of just 3.4 defects per 1,000,000 opportunities.

On Target Six Sigma Takes Organizations to the Top

Bill Smith, an engineer at Motorola, developed Six Sigma in the 1980s. It involves using SPC and also builds in TQM ideas of finding assignable causes for variations and always striving for *continuous improvement*. Motorola managed to achieve Six Sigma quality in 1992 after adopting continuous quality-improvement methods in the 1980s.[34] Other large corporations, such as GE and Honeywell, have followed suit. Over the past several years, Motorola has taken the concept of Six Sigma even further by adapting it to the innovation involved in creating new products. At Motorola, designers are free to develop new products, and "project hoppers" are on hand to ensure that new projects meet quality standards.[35] As a result, innovation is encouraged, and, at the same time, projects are monitored at every step to uphold quality and increase profitability. But, as has been discussed in earlier chapters, Six Sigma is not best in all situations, and corporate specifics should be considered before employing.

How does TQM cater to the customer? It's not enough to simply implement quality-management tools. A significant aspect of TQM is catering to a customer's needs and desires. SGL Carbon, a manufacturer of graphite specialties, emphasizes adherence to a TQM approach by giving its customers the final say in determining whether a product meets the requirements of high-quality standards. Although firms may define in the beginning what makes their products high quality or low quality, those companies that learn how to simultaneously emphasize quality throughout the production process and incorporate the desires of customers will make a greater presence in the global marketplace.

ISO Standards

What is the ISO? The International Organization for Standardization (ISO) is an organization dedicated to creating worldwide standards of quality for goods and services. ISO was created in 1947 and is headquartered in Geneva, Switzerland. The organization has published more than 18,000 standards, and over 1,000 new standards are published every year.[36] ISO's objective is to develop production processes that are equal in quality and capability in all participating countries.[37] More than 161 countries have adopted these standards, and thousands of companies require their products to be ISO certified. Some industries have even developed their own industry-specific set of ISO standards.

The ISO standards apply not to the products themselves but to the production methods and systems used to manufacture them, as well as other areas, such as communication within the company and leadership. Such a standardized system is necessary to avoid trying to comply with various conflicting systems. Most of the standards generated by the ISO are product specific, but there are two "generic" standards that can be applied to any organization regardless of size, product/service, sector, or type of business enterprise. These standards are ISO 9001 and ISO 14001. **ISO 9001** implements a quality management system, and **ISO 14001** implements an environmental management system.

What is the ISO certification process? Certification is usually done by a third-party registrar. This registrar conducts an assessment of a company's quality-assurance manuals and practices. First, a preliminary assessment is conducted, during which the registrar reviews the documents that outline a company's standards and processes. If the manual and other printed documents pass the review, a company can proceed with the rest of the assessment. If the registrar finds errors in these documents, further review is delayed until the mistakes are corrected.

During the formal assessment, the registrar reviews the corrected documents and interviews employees and administrators in the company. The goal of this part of the assessment is to ensure that written policies and procedures are being implemented in the company's production methods. Finally, the registrar issues an audit report that summarizes the results of the assessment and lists any areas that need improvement. If corrections are required at this stage, the company can make them and document them in a report to the registrar. After satisfactory corrections have been made, the registrar can then award certification to the company. Once it has earned certification, the company can put the ISO seal on its promotional materials and its letterhead.

After certification, the registrar returns to the company twice a year to make sure the company is still in compliance with ISO standards. These spot-checks are conducted without advance warning, and the registrar focuses on areas that were notably weak during the initial assessment. Every three years, the registrar will complete another assessment and issue a new audit report. The company must also establish an internal auditing program that is responsible for keeping ISO standards in practice.

What are the benefits of ISO certification?

Companies that have successfully gone through the ISO certification process have indicated significant benefits, including improved customer satisfaction and international recognition. More tangible benefits include increased efficiency, procedural consistency, and a factual approach to decision making that are all due to the guidelines and training that need to be established to obtain certification. Companies with ISO certification also enjoy marketing advantages because they can now easily publicize that their company has reached this quality standard to attract new and maintain existing customers. As a result, companies have reported increased revenue, due to improved financial performance and increased productivity, and a boost in customer satisfaction. For example, after implementing ISO 14001 environmental standards, Ford Motor Company reduced its water consumption by nearly 1 million gallons per day and saved over $65,000 in electricity costs by no longer using fluorescent light bulbs. The company also began to recycle paint waste, thus reducing disposed paint sludge, and began to use reusable plastic or metal containers instead of cardboard and plywood boxes.[38]

It's no surprise that Jeanette Pae's confidence in the quality of her new iPhone was shaken. The loss of consumer confidence in a company to produce quality products is costly: Sales are lost, and the process needed to repair a company's reputation and earn back the customer's respect can be even more expensive. Mattel, Merck, and Dell each experienced the repercussions of poor quality management, even though some of the problems were due to supplier error. Putting the focus on quality management at the beginning of the production process and adopting a quality-orientation throughout the company can ensure that a consistent product is produced. ■

Chapter Summary

1. How is manufacturing and production important to the U.S. economy and global economies? (pp. 325–327)

- **Production** (p. 325) is the process of getting a good or a service to the customer; it is a series of related activities, with value being added at each stage. Companies are in business to provide a service or a good to consumers. The more efficient they can produce and deliver the product or the service, the greater the profit a company will generate.

- Although the manufacturing industry has been declining over the years, it still accounts for almost one-fourth of the U.S. GDP and one-tenth of all U.S. jobs. Moreover, manufacturing uses services and commodities as inputs, so manufacturing is actually responsible for a bigger share of total output.

- The service industry is very important to the U.S. economy, and accounts for nearly 75 percent of the U.S. GDP and about 80 percent of jobs. Service businesses range from small start-ups and home-based businesses, to large corporations that are represented on the DJIA.

- Despite the push to outsource and offshore jobs and manufacturing to low-cost locations, the U.S. manufacturing industry is still globally important. The United States is still the leading industrial power in the world.

2. What is operations management, and what is important in determining a facility's location and layout? (pp. 327–333)

- **Operations management** (p. 327) consists of managing the activities and processes to produce and distribute products and services. Operations management includes how the facility should be organized, what supplies to purchase, what materials and inventory to keep on hand, and how quality is measured and controlled.

- When determining a location for a facility, companies consider their proximity to market, the cost of transporting raw materials, the presence of highways and other transportation systems, **utility supply** (p. 328), hazardous waste disposal, labor availability, living conditions, and laws and regulations.

- **Facility layout** (p. 330) refers to the physical arrangement of resources and people in the production process and how they interact. The design of a facility's layout is important to maximize efficiency and satisfy employees' needs.

- When starting the production process, one of the first decisions that operations managers make is what needs to be manufactured and what needs to be purchased from outside suppliers. This is commonly called a **make-or-buy decision** (p. 332).

- Although operations management has been traditionally associated with manufacturing goods, many of the concepts also apply to the service industry.

3. What is production management, and what production processes are used by businesses? (pp. 333–336)

- **Production management** (p. 333) refers to the planning, implementation, and control measures used to convert resources into finished products. These activities are similar to those in operations management but are more focused on the product.

- **Mass production** (p. 334) is the method of producing large quantities of goods at a low cost. The benefits of mass production include low cost, decreased production time, and virtually no human error, due to the reliance on machinery. A major disadvantage is that mass production is inflexible, making it difficult to alter the process if an unexpected problem occurs.

- **Mass customization** (p. 334) is the production of goods or services tailored to cost-effectively meet customers' individual needs. Mass customization is achieved with a **flexible manufacturing system** (**FMS;** p. 335)—a system in which machines are programmed to process different part types simultaneously—allowing a manufacturer to mass-produce customized products. The primary benefit of an FMS is that it provides the flexibility to make products with many slight variations. A challenge of an FMS is that it is not well suited for goods that are in high demand.

- **Lean production** (p. 335) is a set of principles concerned with reducing waste and improving flow. The basic tenet of lean production is to do more with less through the elimination of wasteful overproduction, unnecessary wait time, needless transportation, excess inventory, superfluous motion, redundant over-processing, and careless defective units.

4. How does technology influence the production process? (pp. 336–339)

- Robots offer consistency in reducing production costs, raising productivity, and producing high-quality products.

- **Computer-aided design (CAD)**, **computer-aided manufacturing (CAM)**, and **computer-integrated manufacturing (CIM**; pp. 337–338) have dramatically improved the process of producing goods by reducing the time between design and manufacturing, thus making a significant impact on productivity. These systems have also increased the scope of automated machinery in the production process.

- The social networking structure of the Internet, along with hardware and software tools, has created a ready-made distribution system for more creative consumers who want to "have it their way." Beyond design, social media capabilities enable consumers to directly influence what companies develop and produce, as well as to give instant feedback on whether their initiatives are worthwhile.

5. How is a production plan developed and controlled? (pp. 339–342)

- Effective **scheduling** (p. 339) can help managers control the production process. Gantt and PERT charts are scheduling tools to ensure that all the right tools are working on the right jobs are the right times.

- **Purchasing** is the task of acquiring the materials and services needed in the production process. In doing so, production managers must find reliable suppliers who can provide high-quality resources at the best price.

- **Inventory control** includes the receiving, storing, handling, and tracking of everything in a company's stock, from raw materials to finished products. A **just-in-time (JIT) inventory control** (p. 341) system keeps the smallest amount of inventory on hand as possible, and everything else that is needed is ordered so that it arrives when it is needed.

6. What is quality control, and how do ISO standards help companies produce high-quality goods and services? (pp. 342–345)

- **Quality control** (p. 343) is the use of techniques, activities, and processes to guarantee that a certain good or service meets a specified level of quality.

- **Total quality management (TQM;** p. 343) involves every factor in producing high-quality goods—management, customers, employees, and suppliers. At any point, employees and leaders are aiming to produce high quality.

- The ISO has created worldwide standards of quality for goods and services. ISO standards apply not to the products themselves but to the production methods and systems used to manufacture them, as well as other areas, such as communication within a company and leadership.

Key Terms

assembly line (p. 334)

cellular layout (p. 331)

computer-aided design (CAD) (p. 337)

computer-aided manufacturing (CAM) (p. 338)

computer-integrated manufacturing (CIM) (p. 338)

enterprise resource planning (ERP) (p. 342)

facility layout (p. 330)

fixed position layout (p. 331)

flexible manufacturing system (FMS) (p. 335)

Gantt chart (p. 339)

inventory control (p. 340)

ISO 9001 (p. 344)

ISO 14001 (p. 344)

just-in-time (JIT) inventory control (p. 341)

lean production (p. 335)

make-or-buy decision (p. 332)

mass customization (p. 334)

mass production (p. 334)

materials requirement planning (MRP) (p. 341)

operations management (p. 327)

process layout (p. 331)

product layout (p. 331)

production (p. 325)

production management (p. 333)

production plan (p. 334)

program evaluation and review technique (PERT) (p. 340)

purchasing (p. 340)

quality control (p. 343)

radio frequency identification (RFID) (p. 341)

scheduling (p. 339)

Six Sigma (p. 343)

statistical process control (SPC) (p. 343)

statistical quality control (SQC) (p. 343)

total quality management (TQM) (p. 343)

utility (p. 334)

utility supply (p. 328)

Self-Test

Multiple Choice   You can find the answers on the last page of this book.

1. The advantages of mass production include which of the following?

    a. Large quantities of goods produced at a low cost

    b. Standardization of goods

    c. Low consumer costs due to low production costs

    d. All of the above

2. Mass customization is achieved by using which type of system?

    a. FMS

    b. Lean production

    c. Forward processing

    d. Backward processing

3. Which production process strives to reduce waste and improve production flow?

    a. Mass customization

    b. Mass production

    c. Lean production

    d. Assembly line production

4. If the Ford Motor Company wants to understand the aerodynamics of a new auto body, which of the following would be used to create a virtual three-dimensional model of the auto body?

    a. CAD

    b. Simultaneous engineering

    c. CIM

    d. Robotics

5. Which of the following is a set of generic quality standards that can be applied to any organization?

    a. ISO 14001

    b. Six Sigma

    c. ISO 9001

    d. TQM

6. An effective plan by a production manager should lead to

    a. increased productivity.

    b. reduced costs.

    c. improved customer service.

    d. All of the above

7. Which is a good use for a PERT chart?

    a. Creating a timeline of production tasks

    b. Creating a workflow for production equipment

    c. Predicting the completion time of a project

    d. All of the above

8. Radio frequency identification is used to

    a. keep track of the status and quantity of each item.

    b. keep track of the customer base for an item.

    c. stay in touch with other workers in a factory.

    d. manufacture stereo systems.

9. Which type of facility layout would be best used for the production of potato chips?

    a. Product layout

    b. Process layout

    c. Cellular layout

    d. Fixed position layout

10. TQM is geared toward

    a. producing the largest quantity of goods in the time allotted.

    b. reducing errors throughout the production process.

    c. eliminating humans from the workplace.

    d. meeting government standards for emissions.

Self-Test

True/False   You can find the answers on the last page of this book.

1. Robots can work around the clock with good accuracy and in potentially hazardous conditions.
☐ **True** or ☐ **False**

2. CAD and CAM have dramatically reduced the time between the design and manufacturing stages of production.
☐ **True** or ☐ **False**

3. Manufacturing is more important to the U.S. economy than services are.
☐ **True** or ☐ **False**

4. The make-or-buy decision comes at the end of the production process if a product has not turned out as planned.
☐ **True** or ☐ **False**

5. The JIT method of inventory control consists of keeping a large amount of inventory in the warehouse to be sure that all deliveries will be made on time.
☐ **True** or ☐ **False**

Critical Thinking Questions

1. When the United States was facing one of the worst recessions in its history, the Stimulus Act was passed to help ailing companies. Did the Stimulus Act help the manufacturing sector, the service industry, or both? Do you think the Stimulus Act worked as the government intended? Why or why not?

2. You have decided to open a company that produces wooden furniture, and you must select a suitable location for production. The first option is in a remote region of Montana with easy access to abundant raw materials but far away from a skilled worker base. The second option is in Southern California in close proximity to many skilled workers as well as several major highways for distribution. Which location would you choose for your business and why?

3. A sports equipment company is known for a special grip on its tennis rackets that is imported from South America. The cost of shipping these grips has grown steadily more expensive, and the business would like to produce the grips in-house. What factors does the business need to consider before adding another step to the production process?

4. Mass customization is a new trend in production. What technological changes have enabled this trend to take place? What are the advantages and disadvantages of this type of production process compared to mass production?

5. Give an example of what the TQM process would involve in a restaurant. What steps can restaurants take to ensure that a high level of quality is maintained consistently in their food delivery process?

Team Time

To Outsource or Not to Outsource . . . That Is the Question

Divide into two teams to represent both sides of the issue:

a. One group that thinks the company should make the component.

b. One group that thinks the company should outsource the component.

Scenario

The Grindstone Supply Company of New Jersey is attempting to expand its manufacturing of large wall clocks. In years past, the company has outsourced the manufacturing of clock springs to a company in Nebraska. This has been cost-effective in the past, but now that demand for the springs has increased, Grindstone is considering manufacturing the springs in-house. Although the cost of producing the springs in-house is lower, it is unclear whether it will be profitable in the long run, as the manufacturing process will change greatly. New machines for the production of springs will be needed, as the factory works exclusively in wood and plastic. With the new machines comes the need for new technicians to monitor and service them. Should the Grindstone Supply Company alter its manufacturing process to include the production of clock springs or should it continue outsourcing to Nebraska as it has in the past? What factors contribute to this decision? Will this be more profitable in the long run? How will it affect employee morale and relations?

Process

Step 1. Record your ideas and opinions about the issue presented in the scenario. Be sure to consider the issue from your assigned perspective.

Step 2. Meet as a team and review the issue from both perspectives. Discuss why the position of your group is the best decision.

Ethics and Corporate Social Responsibility

Environmental Shipping Concerns

You have just been promoted as the head of the shipping department for your office supply company, and it is now your responsibility to determine routing. The company is located on the eastern seaboard, near major highways as well as the ocean. In the past, trucking has been the preferred method of shipping, as it was deemed the most cost-effective. Shipping by boat, however, would greatly reduce the negative effects on the environment caused by truck emissions. After calculating the cost on paper, you realize that shipping by sea would have a negative effect on the overall profit margin, but the company would still generate solid profits.

Questions

1. What decision would you make in this situation—land or sea?

2. If you were told that you would take a personal pay cut from switching to the more environmentally friendly route, how would that affect your decision?

3. What kind of impact do you think one company switching to less environmentally damaging practices could have on the general atmosphere of the shipping world?

Web Exercises

1. **Have It Your Way**
   Burger King introduced mass customization to its fast-food offerings in the mid-1970s, thus revolutionizing how fast food could be delivered. Today, mass customization is aided by the Internet and other technologies. Search the Internet and find five companies that use mass customization. Is customizing a product to your specific needs important to you? Why or why not?

2. **Greening America**
   Although the United States has become more of a service-based economy, many feel that the focus on creating new, environmentally friendly technologies may bring manufacturing back to the country and help power an economic recovery. Others feel that this is not the right time to invest in speculative undertakings and should be delayed until we have fully emerged from the recession. Research what kinds of environmental technologies are being manufactured in the United States today. Do you think a greater investment in these technologies could help fuel an economic recovery? Why or why not?

3. **Radio Frequency Identification**
   The use of chips to track goods during the shipping process is becoming more widespread. Use the Internet to research options for RFID. What are some of the options for tracking goods? What kind of range can these products cover?

4. **Efficiency in Production**
   Research the Toyota production system on the Internet. Why do you think this system has been so effective for Toyota? What are the major concepts that set the Toyota system apart from the competition? How have the 2009–2010 recalls of several Toyota models affected their production system, if at all? Write a short paragraph considering the system and these questions.

5. **Quality Control**
   Quality control is a major issue in the mass production of goods. Many systems have been used to assure quality control in manufacturing. Find two different systems of quality control on the Internet. What are the merits and downfalls of each? If you were in charge of the production of a product, which system of quality control would you choose? Write a paragraph comparing and contrasting these two quality control systems.

Web Case

For more on managing operations to minimize error and increase revenue, access the Chapter 11 Web case entitled "Focus on Toyota: Eliminating Waste, Just in Time for Production" located in the End of Chapter Assignments section at my*biz*lab.com.

Video Case

For more on production management issues created by licensing agreements and brand extensions, access the Chapter 11 Video Case entitled "Body Glove: Surfing the Production Tidal Wave" located in the End of Chapter Assignments section at my*biz*lab.com.

Business Communications

We communicate and interact with others all day, every day. In fact, people in organizations spend at least 75 percent of their time in interpersonal situations—one-on-one; in groups; intra-organizational; or with customers, suppliers, investors, and advisors.[1] Communicating effectively is critical in the business world, yet it can present significant challenges. When you consider the impact poor communication can have on business—such as a loss of customers from poor customer service, a lack of focus on business objectives, and stifled innovation—it becomes clear why effective communication is an important business goal. In this mini chapter, we'll discuss how you can improve your communication skills in the workplace.

Improving Your Presentation Skills

In business, you often need to persuade, educate, or inform a group about your ideas. If you don't have strong presentation skills, your audience won't be receptive. Good presentation skills begin with good oral communication skills, so you need to make sure you speak loudly and clearly. Change your vocal intonation to add emphasis or interest when appropriate. It is important to engage audience members by looking directly at them, often changing your focus to different individuals around the room. Relax and smile, just as you would if you were talking to your friends.

Presentation software, such as Microsoft's PowerPoint, can be a great addition to a presentation if it is used correctly. We have all sat through boring presentations where the speaker reads directly from the slides or used too many distracting graphics, animations, and blinding color schemes. When used to its best capabilities, PowerPoint can be a very effective tool. On the next page, you'll find some tips to make your next PowerPoint presentation successful.

The complement to good oral communication skills is active listening skills. To ensure that you're being attentive when listening,

PEARSON
my*biz*lab

Business Communications

You're the Program Manager for TeleCellTronics, a company that produces components for cell phone manufacturers. You act as the face of the company to clients, and you're responsible for the work done by your team. Today begins with a crisis call that could send ripples through the entire company. Can you manage it well enough to keep your job?

repeat back or summarize the points that you believe were made. Good listening also means asking good questions but avoid becoming distracted by trying to think of what you're going to say next. If you need clarification, try to respond with statements such as "Tell me more." Finally, keep an open mind to others' ideas and suggestions. You do not necessarily want to have a solution or outcome defined in your mind before you hear what everyone else has to say.

PowerPoint **Tips**

1. **Keep it simple.** Just because the software is capable of doing amazing things, don't feel as if you have to use all the bells and whistles. Keep the design clean and charts simple and easy to understand. Limit the number of animations and special effects. In addition, use graphics to illustrate or highlight what you're saying—not serve as the focus.

2. **Follow the 6 × 6 × 24 rule.** Remember, PowerPoint slides should represent only an outline of key points you are making. Don't include everything you plan to say on the slides. Place only those key words or thoughts you want your audience to remember. As you speak, fill in the other details. To help keep the content of your slides to a minimum, presentation experts suggest you use no more than six words in a bullet point, six bullet points on a slide, and a font size that is at least 24 points. Also try to keep the total number of slides to a minimum.

Delivering effective presentations requires planning and practice.

3. **Use graphics and media to convey ideas.** Combining a strong oral presentation with visual cues on slides can make PowerPoint a very effective part of your delivery. We can better remember what someone is saying if we see key words at the same time that we hear them. We remember even better when the right graphic or image is used to convey an entire idea. Consider incorporating short video pieces into your presentation to add a bit of humor, bring in a different "speaker," or convey a message in a different way. YouTube and Google Video are useful storehouses of video, as are Vimeo, Ustream, and Ted.com.

4. **Use color sparingly but effectively.** A light background with dark text is the best color combination for most light conditions. Adding color sparingly will help add visual interest and bring special attention to key areas of the presentation. Too much color can be distracting.

5. **Edit and proofread.** Typographical and spelling errors as well as grammatical mistakes make it appear as if you didn't review your presentation slides and leave a bad impression with your audience. If you know that grammar is a weak area for you, ask a friend who is a good editor to review the slides for you.

6. **Practice.** Practice giving your presentation several times aloud before giving it live in front of an audience. If you find yourself stumbling through a part, think more about the exact idea you need to communicate—additional examples you could use, analogies that might explain it better to your audience, and so on. When you practice your presentation, use the Rehearse Timings mode to record how many seconds you are staying on each slide. Review these numbers and make sure you are spending the most time on the sections that are most critical to your message.

Improving Your Writing Skills

In business, written communication is often in the form of a business letter or memo. Let's look at each of these forms of writing.

Business Letters

There is still a place in the business world for nonelectronic communication. For example, when a company offers you a position, they will often mail a business letter documenting the responsibilities and benefits of the offer. Communications sent via U.S. Mail are also often used when a formal, documented series of actions is being conducted between two people. As shown in ▼ **Figure 1**, a traditional business letter has a specific format that includes the date at the top, the address of the person receiving the letter, and a formal salutation. Businesses typically have a stock supply of letterhead paper, imprinted with their logo and design, on hand for mailings.

If you are on a first-name basis with the intended recipient, then your salutation can use the first name, such as "Dear Rebecca." In other cases, use a title and last name such as "Dear Mr. Consuelas." Letters can be more descriptive and include

▼ **Figure 1**
A Traditional Business Letter

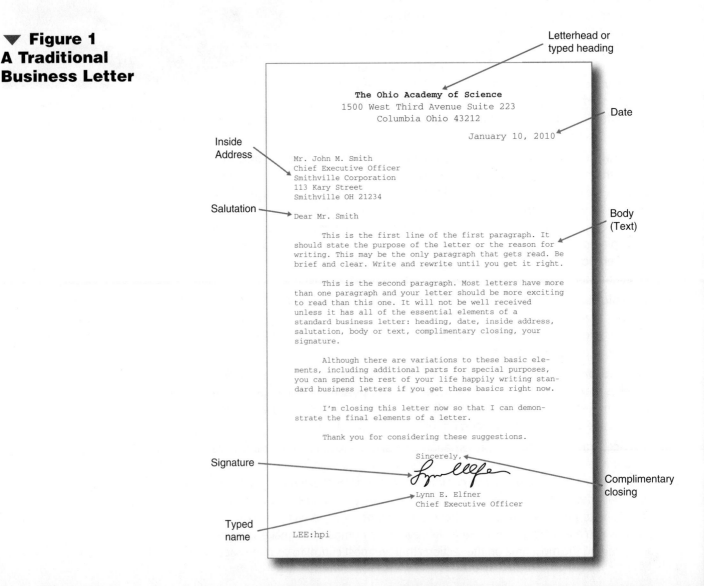

more detail than other summary types of communications, but they still need to be clear and to the point. Assume that the recipient doesn't have time to read through flowery prose. As with any other piece of writing, a business letter should have a beginning, a middle, and an ending. State the purpose of the letter in the first paragraph: "As you requested, I am providing more information . . .," "I regret to inform you that . . .," "I am enclosing. . . ." The paragraphs that follow should add supportive details. The final paragraph should offer information about what action will follow or what is expected from the recipient. Business letters should end with a formal closing, such as "Sincerely," with your full name and title. You may include your contact information after your title if it's not included in the letterhead information. It is important that information in a business letter be written precisely. Make sure the language is clear and simple.

Memos

Memos are used to make announcements, summarize facts from a conversation or a meeting, or request or exchange information. They are either formal or informal, depending on the content. Typically, they're used for communications within an office or a company, not between companies and external contacts or clients. As shown in ▼ **Figure 2**, memos have a standard heading format that contains the date, the person(s) to whom the memo is addressed (the To: line), the name of anyone else receiving a copy (the Cc: line), the name of the sender (the From: line), and a concise statement of the memo's topic (Subject: or Re). You can find a large number of predesigned memo templates for Microsoft Word on the Microsoft Office Web site. The box below has some points to remember when writing memos.

Memo Writing **Tips**

- Be concise.
- Use headings, bullets, and/or numbered lists to highlight key points.
- Keep each paragraph short and focused on one main idea.
- Always proofread carefully. Check all facts for accuracy.
- Identify any attachments so they don't go unnoticed.

▼ **Figure 2**
A Standard Memo

TO:	Angela Erkle
FROM:	Christina Helios
DATE:	August 29, 2010
RE:	Report on proposed acquisition of Megabots, LLC

As you asked, my team and I have prepared the enclosed report on the proposed purchase of Megabots, LLC, by Gigabots, LLC.

The contents of the report summarize Megabots' current market and financial position and analyze the potential risk and benefits of purchasing the company. The report also contains our final conclusions on the proposed sale and our recommendations for moving forward.

I would like to thank my full team for their time and effort, and would be happy to answer any questions that you may have about the report.

- Closings are unnecessary. The "From" line eliminates the need.
- Remember that memos should be professional in tone and appearance.

What Form of Communication Should You Use?

There are many options when it comes to getting your message across. Should you send an e-mail? Write a letter? Visit your client face-to-face? Let's investigate the specific strengths and weaknesses of each type of communication so you can better match your delivery choice to the situation.

Oral communication allows participants to assess the meanings of the speaker's words and voice intonations. When speaking in person, participants also use "unspoken" messages sent by body language and facial expressions when interpreting the message. The speaker can adapt his or her message by assessing a listener's attentiveness. However, oral communication is not perfect. To deliver your message accurately, especially to those with whom you're not very familiar, it is important to offer clear, unbiased language and avoid clichés, negative metaphors, and culturally specific references. For example, using the expression "down to the last out" is meaningful to an American baseball fan but perhaps not to someone from another country.

Written communication has more permanency than oral communication. You can revise it before sending or review it at a later date. In addition, the receiver has more time to analyze the content before responding. On the other hand, the sender has no control over when the recipient chooses to read the message and does not benefit from immediate feedback; the sender is not always given the opportunity for further clarification. Finally, written communication can lead to misunderstandings due to the lack of face-to-face interaction. Albert Mehrabian from UCLA found that 55 percent of meaning in an interaction comes from facial and body language and 38 percent comes from vocal inflection. The words convey only 7 percent of meaning.[2] Therefore, if the nature of a written communication contains anything sensitive or complicated, it might be wise to follow up with a quick phone call or an in-person meeting.

E-Mail

E-mail is perhaps the most used form of digital written communication, although social networks, wikis, podcasts, and blogs are becoming increasingly popular in the business world. E-mail is quick and convenient, and the sender and receiver don't need to be available at the same time to communicate. Popular mobile devices, such as smartphones, and Internet tablets, such as the iPad, enable people to read and reply to e-mail any time they have a phone signal or Wi-Fi connection.

In the business world, your e-mail is all that many people see of you. It is important to take time to understand the audience to whom the e-mail is being sent and structure it accordingly. Obviously, an e-mail to a friend will be different from one to your boss or a client. A friend may expect a loosely formatted e-mail—full of slang and spelling errors. However, in a business context, such an e-mail will give people a negative impression of you. Your e-mails represent you and your organization; therefore, sending clear, organized, and thoughtful messages is critical. The following box has some pertinent tips for e-mail writing.

Tips on Writing Effective Business E-Mail

1. **Use a meaningful subject line.** Subject lines help the reader prioritize and organize e-mail messages. Instead of "Here's what you're asking for," try to be more specific, such as "3/3/10 Client X Update." Create agreed-on acronyms for use in subject lines that help to better identify messages and/or actions required, such as AR (Action Required) or MSR (Monthly Status Report). Using consistent identifications can help with filtering/sorting functions as well as help prioritize actions that are required. If possible, condense the entire message into several words that fit in the subject line, such as "2 P.M. meeting on 2/15/10 confirmed."

2. **Watch slang and offensive or potentially damaging content.** E-mails are business documents. Err on the side of being utterly conservative in your language and content. You don't want to offend anyone by using the wrong words or including something deemed inappropriate. Do not use texting abbreviations.

3. **Proofread and edit.** Quickly firing off an e-mail without proofreading can lead to big mistakes or misunderstandings. Make sure the message is free of grammatical and spelling errors.

4. **Keep it brief and focused.** Your e-mail may be one of 200 (or more!) read by the recipient that day, so keep the content brief and focused. Organize with bullets or short sentences so the reader can clearly understand key points. Be specific. If you send a 20-page attachment, tell the recipient that the important information is on pages 2 and 17.

5. **Be considerate of file format.** When it is questionable if the recipient has the right software to view an attachment, use a universal format, such as a PDF.

6. **Include previous messages in a reply.** Even if you only copy a phrase from a previous e-mail, including messages in a reply helps when responses are not immediate. You wouldn't pick up a phone and say "I agree," and expect the person on the other end to understand what you're agreeing with if you hadn't spoken in a day or two. However, be careful when including an entire message if you're adding someone new to the e-mail. Long threads of e-mail exchanges may contain information that is not appropriate for a new person to see.

7. **Use a signature line.** The line should include your title and full contact information.

E-mail has other limitations, so users need to be aware of them to avoid problems. Be considerate of the size for attachments. Most e-mail servers have a limit and will not allow an e-mail through if it has exceptionally large attachments. If large files need to be exchanged, consider placing the information on an intraoffice Web site. There are also free web services like YouSendIt that allow you to easily send files up to 2GB in size.

Also, apply caution when using e-mail because it is not as private as a regular letter. E-mail is more like a postcard that can be read, copied, saved, shared, and exchanged by anyone. Work e-mails can be legally monitored by your boss and may be subject to review if a lawsuit is filed against your company.[3] In addition, serious mistakes have occurred when users have mistakenly "replied to all" with comments about one of the people on the distribution list or have forwarded the message to the wrong person. Because of its ease of use and access, many users have gotten into troubling circumstances after shooting off an e-mail in frustration or anger rather than waiting to cool off and respond in a calmer and more professional state of mind. The bottom line: E-mail really should be used with care and should not be used to communicate secure, private, or potentially damaging information.

Companies are beginning to recognize the problems erupting from the high volume of e-mail. The tool that offers us an easier way to communicate is, in some instances, actually making it harder for us to communicate. Companies in all industries are adopting "e-mail–free" days to reduce the e-mail overload and encourage employees to get out from behind their digital devices and actually talk to their colleagues and customers, whether in person or on the telephone. The results have been astonishing. For example, when U.S. Cellular enforced a no–e-mail Friday, two coworkers who had been communicating with each other exclusively by e-mail found out that instead of being across the country from each other, they were only across the hall. Now, their working relationship is much stronger due to their in-person interactions. When people were forced to call public affairs manager Tyler Caroll on no–e-mail Fridays, many were surprised to find out that the person they assumed was "Mr. Caroll" was a woman.[4]

E-mail–free workdays have been highly successful in increasing teamwork, providing better customer service, and helping companies solve problems quickly. As a result, many companies are looking for other ways to reduce the stresses caused by electronic overload and an "always-on" environment, such as "no-meeting Fridays" or "quiet time" to allow employees time to work uninterrupted in an offline mode.

Instant Messaging

In many settings, texting has become a part of business.

Instant messaging (IM) is quickly catching on in the business community as a means for conducting personal chats. Because of its immediacy and streamlined efficiency, many business users prefer IM to phone calls and e-mail. However, like e-mail, IM should not be used to communicate confrontational, sensitive, or confidential information. IM messages can be copied and saved to a Word document or archived in their entirety, so discretion is important. Instant messaging is great when used to convey simple messages, clarify a point, confirm a meeting, and the like.

Texting

Texting is another popular form of digital communication. As a means of exchanging quick messages via a cell phone, texting can be as useful as IM. When texting is done with devices that do not have a full keyboard, the sender has to communicate solely with the 9-digit text/number pad found on phones. Texting users have responded by developing a shorthand-type language that uses abbreviations for traditional words or phrases. Texting is finding more and more uses in business meetings and during business travel; however, avoid using texting abbreviations, which are very informal, in more formal business texting. Many businesses also use text messaging as a means to "push" information to users via their cell phone. For example, airlines use texting to confirm flight information, and real estate agents use it to inform buyers when new listings that fit their specifications come on the market. Advertisers are also finding text messaging a convenient way to alert users to new product information.

Using Collaborative Communication Tools

In addition to presentations, memos, e-mail, and so on, there are a variety of tools to aid collaborative business communications.

Videoconferencing

Videoconferencing uses two-way audio and video technology to allow people in two or more locations to interact simultaneously. This means that people in different parts of the country or the world can have virtual meetings in which they can see each other and interact face-to-face. In addition to reducing travel costs, companies that use videoconferencing have found that increasing face-to-face time between employees is beneficial. Videoconferencing has also been implemented as a means of following up with clients and as a mode of effectively training workers in multiple locations.

Popular devices, such as the iPhone 4, now support videoconferencing. Each iPhone 4 has two cameras, one pointing to the speaker's face and one pointing out the back of the camera. An iPhone 4 user can videoconference with another iPhone 4 user, sending the video of them speaking or switching to a video of something else in the room.

Videoconferencing unites attendees in different locations with a real-time audio and video connection.

There are other technologies that offer efficient and effective collaborations in a virtual workplace. Online meeting software, such as WebEx, allows users to run and archive meetings with users from any location. Each person can stream in video from a webcam or just join in through voice. Users can participate whether they are at a computer workstation, on a laptop, or using a smartphone. Meeting participants can present slideshows, take live questions, run software applications, and share documents. Remote desktop control allows anyone in the meeting to take control of each user's desktop to make a point or illustrate a feature. Tools like WebEx are used for conferencing but also for interactive customer training, sales presentations, and customer support.

Wikis

A wiki is a collaborative Web site that allows users to create, add, edit, or remove Web content using any Web browser (see ▼ **Figure 3**). It's like a shared workspace where everyone has full and equal access to the same project, only better. Because all versions of the Web content are saved, users can revert back to a previous version of a document, as well as track all edits and who made the edits. Wikis provide an excellent means of collaborative writing and allow multiple authors to edit and produce a single document.

Unlike exchanging e-mails and attachments, there are no timing and version issues. Moreover, all users can see and comment on the document at any time, thus making the process more collaborative and accessible to all. The cost of using wikis is virtually negligible because the software for wikis is free, and little—if any—additional hardware or IT support is required. Beyond team collaboration, businesses are using wikis to ask questions, offer help, correct and add information

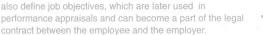

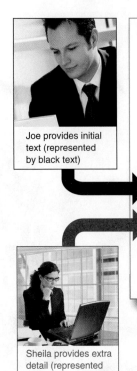

Joe provides initial text (represented by black text)

Before hiring additional employees, an analytical study of the tasks to be performed within the organization should be completed. With small businesses, this might be a simple process conducted by the business owner, as small business owners usually have a good idea of the tasks that need to be done and even who is the most qualified person to perform those tasks. As an organization grows, and more employees are required to ensure that the goals of the organization are met, this analysis becomes a function of human resources. A job analysis identifies and defines in detail the particular duties and responsibilities an employee is required to conduct. In a job analysis, each task is defined by a job description, a formal statement that summarizes the job objectives, responsibilities, and conditions under which the job will be performed. Job descriptions are important as they define the job's relation to the rest of the organizational structure. They also define job objectives, which are later used in performance appraisals and can become a part of the legal contract between the employee and the employer.

Steve adds more text (represented by green text)

Sheila provides extra detail (represented by red text)

▼ **Figure 3**
Professional
Collaboration
Wikis are great collaboration tools.

to documents and presentations, brainstorm, and keep everyone informed about projects. Although some wikis, such as Wikipedia, the wiki-based online encyclopedia, are available and accessible to the general public, you can make wikis private and available to only a select group of individuals, thus reducing privacy and confidentiality issues. Wikis can contain a variety of formats, such as documents, spreadsheets, and presentations, and they can be arranged into different pages for better content organization.

Blogs

A blog is a Web log that is usually authored by an individual and cannot be changed or edited by visitors. Visitors can, however, add comments to the original content. In some instances, blogging and business have not mixed well, such as when bloggers have written unflattering tales about their employers or when their blogosphere persona is radically different from their corporate persona. For example, Google fired Mark Jen after postings on his blog criticized Google and allegedly revealed sensitive financial information.[5] The PittGirl, a popular blogger in Pittsburgh who used comedy and commentary to jibe the mayor, ran into conflict between the anonymity of cyberspace and the demands of the business world. The PittGirl blog became a popular site and, eventually author Virginia Montanez revealed her identity. The next day she was fired from her job for the Negro Educational Emergency Drive.[6] It is still unclear how anonymous you are as a blogger and when legal action can be taken to force your identity to be revealed.

Many companies recognize that blogs afford them an opportunity to reach a wide audience and elicit feedback via commenting sections. Blogs offer companies the opportunity to interact with their customers in ways that other forms of communication do not. Because companies can sift through blogs to determine the "pulse" of the public—what they are talking about, what is important to them, and what they like and dislike about current trends or products—blogs are a valuable marketing research tool. In fact, more than 22 percent of *Fortune* 500 companies have active business blogs with content about the company and/or its products.[7] For example, Dr. Laundry is a blog created by the Clorox Company about bleaching tips. Marriott on the Move is a blog written by Bill Marriott, chairman and CEO of Marriott International, one of the world's largest hotel chains. When Bob Lutz, vice chairman of GM, began his FastLane Blog, readers bombarded it with their critiques and suggestions.

Podcasts

A podcast is another form of digital communication that the business community is embracing—in fact, 19 percent of *Fortune* 500 companies provide podcasts.[8] A podcast is an audio (or video) file stored on the Internet that customers can download to their computers or MP3 players and listen to whenever they want. Podcasts are unique in that customers can subscribe to programs they are interested in and have them automatically downloaded to their computers every time new content is available. Because the downloading process is quick and automatic, podcasts are simple and convenient for businesses and customers alike. Best of all, most podcasts, as well as the necessary software, are free.

Podcasts are audio or video broadcasts pushed automatically to your computer or mobile device.

Effective, efficient communication is key in today's dynamic global economy. Fortunately, there are many options from which to choose when it comes to business communications, from traditional phone conversations and letters to high-tech videoconferencing and wikis. Remember to choose the best form for a given situation, and, most importantly, use it wisely.

PEARSON
mybizlab

Apply these key concepts by revising a new document. Go to Mini Chapter 3 in my*biz*lab.com and select Document Makeovers.

12 Marketing and Consumer Behavior

Marketing Fundamentals

Ford Motor Company started production of the first Model T in 1913. Nearly 100 years later, the automobile manufacturer is still producing vehicles. Part of the company's success is that it has changed its marketing concepts to meet the times. How has marketing evolved? How does marketing benefit the customer, the seller, and even society?

Objective 1 How has marketing evolved over the production concept era, the sales concept era, the marketing concept era, and the customer relationship era? (pp. 364–366)

Objective 2 What are the benefits of marketing to customers, sellers, investors, employees, and society at large, and what are the criticisms of marketing? (pp. 367–369)

Marketing Tactics

Aaron Hoffman has a business idea to start a mobile pet-grooming service. An advisor told him that he needs to create a "marketing strategy." What is a marketing strategy? Why is it necessary?

Objective 3 What are the two basic elements of a marketing strategy and the 4 Ps of the marketing mix? (pp. 369–372)

Objective 4 How do firms implement a marketing strategy by applying the marketing process? (pp. 372–373)

The Marketing Environment

Amelia Russo runs a store selling inexpensive dress shoes that she imports from overseas. The value of the U.S. dollar has gotten so low that she needs to raise her prices. Her marketing environment is forcing her to change the way she does business. What is a marketing environment? How can it pose constraints on a business?

Objective 5 How do the various factors in the marketing environment influence a firm's ability to manipulate its marketing mix? (pp. 373–377)

Marketing Research and Planning

Tiara Watson has decided to start a salon supply business. She knows that there is a demand for her products, but she wants to draw up a carefully organized marketing plan to ensure the success of her business. There are over 30 salons in her city, and Tiara has the connections to offer them products at a lower cost. What steps must she take to get her name known in the salon supply world? What can she do to ensure success in her new business?

Objective 6 What is the marketing research process, and what are the elements of a good marketing plan? (pp. 377–384)

Consumer Behavior

Will Giusto needs to buy a computer and is overwhelmed at the selection in front of him at the store. His girlfriend has a Mac, and his best friend has a top-notch gaming machine. Will isn't looking for a name brand or a computer with lots of features. What factors will help him choose one computer over another?

Objective 7 How do the buying decisions and marketing processes in business-to-business markets compare to those in the consumer market? (pp. 385–389)

PEARSON **mybizlab**

Market Research Matters

You've recently been promoted to regional vice president of a thriving medical center. Several opportunities for growth exist in your area, your company has the financial resources to pursue them, and shifting competitive forces are rewarding only the savviest organizations in the market. Can you successfully expand your medical center?

Objective 8 Test yourself using mybizlab.com to show that you understand the chapter objectives.

Marketing Fundamentals pp. 363–369

The innovation of the assembly line enabled Ford Motor Company to mass-produce millions of Model Ts when production began in 1913. When times changed, and the Model T did not, customers wanted something different. Production of the Model T stopped in 1927, and six months later a new Model A rolled off the line. The Model A responded to a more affluent consumer market, offering both style and comfort. The Great Depression four years later caused production to halt on the Model A. Nearly two decades later, economic fortunes had changed again, this time for the better, and so had customers' tastes. The '49 Ford was all the rage, with elegance meeting performance. It was offered in a wide range of body styles so that there was "something for everyone," while the Ford Thunderbird, produced in 1955, captured the free spirit of the time. Ford continued along the "road to postwar prosperity"[1] over the next several decades despite stiff competition from other domestic and foreign automobile manufacturers, as well as economic and gas crises. Now, in the early years of the twenty-first century, and after a near collapse of the company, Ford Motor Company is back—some say better than ever. As this brief history of the company indicates, the company's marketing strategies have evolved over time. Will it be able to continue its marketing success in the future? ■

In its broadest sense, *marketing* can be thought of as identifying and meeting human needs and wants. However, the degree to which marketers have identified and met people's needs and wants has changed over time, as has the American Marketing Association's (AMA's) official definition of marketing. In 2004, the AMA revised the definition to reflect a new focus on value for customers and recognize the importance of managing customer relationships. The AMA now defines **marketing** as "an organizational function and a set of processes for creating, communicating, and delivering value to customers and for managing customer relationships in ways that benefit the organization and its stakeholders."[2]

What does a marketing department do? Marketing departments serve a variety of functions. First and foremost, marketers are responsible for keeping an eye on what people need and want and then communicating these desires to the rest of the organization. Marketing departments help establish desirable pricing strategies and promote an organization by persuading customers that their products are the best. As you've learned, a **product** is any tangible good, service, or idea available for purchase in a market, as well as any intangible benefits derived from its consumption, such as the brand. Marketing departments are also responsible for distributing products to customers at a place and time most suitable to the customer. But perhaps the most important aspect of marketing, as reflected in the

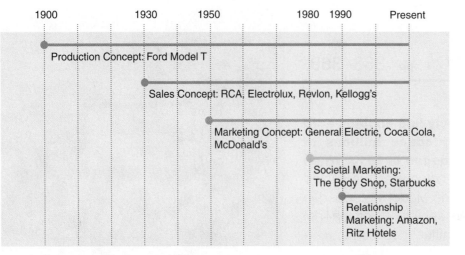

AMA's most recent definition of marketing, is to successfully establish meaningful relationships with customers, to instill loyalty, and to ensure repeat business. Marketing is one of the most visible functions of any organization; however, the public sees only the tip of the iceberg. In this chapter, we'll present some basic aspects of marketing, including marketing strategies, the four Ps of marketing, and consumer behavior. We'll start by looking at how marketing has changed over time.

▼ **Figure 12.1
The Evolution of
Marketing**

The Evolution of Marketing

How has marketing evolved over time? The nature of marketing has evolved over four general eras (see ▼ **Figure 12.1**):

1. The production concept era
2. The sales concept era
3. The marketing concept era
4. The societal marketing era
5. The customer relationship era

Although each concept experienced a peak in popularity during a specific time period, some companies still employ marketing concepts from an earlier era. Today's most successful marketing campaigns are a sophisticated combination of the best of each of these concepts.

What was the marketing philosophy of the early 1900s? From the Industrial Revolution until the 1920s, most companies focused solely on production—thus the *production concept era* evolved. The prevailing mind-set was that a good quality product would simply sell itself. This approach worked for many organizations during this era because of strong demand and a limited supply of products. Whenever demand outstrips supply, it creates a seller's market. This may have motivated Henry Ford to remark in relation to his Model T cars that customers could have "any color [they wanted], so long as it's black."[3] At the time, black was the only color available.

What was the sales concept era? From the mid-1920s through the early 1950s, technological advances accelerated production. In the first part of the era, however, the United States was in the middle of the Great Depression, during which unemployment was nearing 30 percent, and people bought only what they absolutely needed. Supply far exceeded demand for most products; therefore, competition for customers became more intense. Businesses began to undertake aggressive sales tactics to sell or "push" their products, and the use of heavy public advertising in all available forms of media became prevalent. Thus began the *sales concept era*. During this era, marketing generally took place after a product was developed and produced. Heavy emphasis was placed on selling existing products. Even today, many people associate marketing with selling or advertising; however, it has become much more than that.

What was the marketing concept era? By the 1950s, production continued to expand more quickly than the growth in demand for goods and services, creating a buyer's market and the start of the *marketing concept era*. Soldiers returning from World War II were getting married, starting families, and willing to spend their money on goods and services. Consumers were beginning to tire of the "hard sell" tactics that companies were using to force them to buy products they didn't necessarily want or need. Eventually, businesses began to realize that simply producing quality products and pushing them onto customers through clever advertising and promotional campaigns didn't guarantee sales.

Companies needed to determine what customers wanted and then produce products that met those wants and needs, as opposed to producing products and then trying to convince customers to buy them. The **marketing concept** changed the focus from finding the right customer for a product to producing the right product for a customer and doing it better than the competition. As you can see in ▼ **Figure 12.2**, the marketing concept also focuses on aligning all functions of organization to meet or exceed these customer needs through superior products and customer service, as well as realizing a profit (not just sales) by satisfying customers over the long term.

▼ **Figure 12.2 The Marketing Concept**

GE was one of the first companies to implement this new marketing strategy that focused more on meeting the needs of the customer. GE's 1952 annual report outlined the philosophy: "Thus marketing, through its studies and research, will establish . . . what the customer wants in a particular product, what price he is willing to pay, and where and when it will be wanted. Marketing will have authority in product planning, production scheduling, and inventory control, as well as sales, distribution, and servicing of the product."[4]

This requires constantly taking the pulse of changing customer needs and wants and then quickly adapting to meet them. Moreover, it may mean anticipating customers' changing preferences—before they are expressed or even known by the customer—and satisfying these preferences before competitors. Even today, companies such as Apple have had great success following this philosophy. Apple has become a master of anticipating customers' desires and fulfilling them with its range of iPods, iPod accessories, iPhones, iPhone apps, and now the iPad.

Does marketing also take into consideration what's best for society?
In addition to considering a customer's wants and needs, companies began to realize that they must also take into consideration the long-term interests of society. *Societal marketing*, an offshoot of the marketing concept and corporate social responsibility, began in the late 1960s and early 1970s. It challenges companies to work for the benefit of both consumers and society while still attaining a profit. For example, The Body Shop, a skin and cosmetics company, sells products that are made with only 100 percent natural ingredients. The company also actively supports and pursues community trade—using highly skilled but small-scale farmers, craftsmen, and rural cooperatives—"not because it's fashionable, but based on the belief that it's the only way to do business."[5] Other examples of the societal marketing approach in action include companies that are going green, such as the automotive industry manufacturing more fuel-efficient vehicles, or industries that are influencing healthy behavior and discouraging unhealthy practices, such as the new diet-conscious menu additions at fast-food restaurants.

PEARSON **my*biz*lab**

For an interactive, real-world example of this topic, access this chapter's **BizSkill** entitled Market Research Matters, located at **my*biz*lab**.com.

What marketing philosophy encourages customer loyalty? The late 1990s saw the beginning of the *customer relationship era*, in which organizations try to intensify their focus on customer satisfaction over time. The result has been the creation of **customer relationship management (CRM)**, the process of establishing long-term relationships with individual customers to foster loyalty and repeat business. The marketing concept is good for *acquiring* customers by offering customized products, among other things, but customer relationship management goes one step further by trying to please customers *after the sale*. It combines IT with customer service and marketing communications to *retain* customers to stimulate future sales of similar or supplementary products. For example, several popular clothing stores, including the Gap, Banana Republic, and Old Navy, offer coupons to customers who join their mailing lists. Customers on the list also receive information about sales and promotions to keep them up-to-date on the latest deals at the store. Amazon.com uses its massive database and IT to offer suggestions for future purchases to customers based on their prior purchases or browsing interests.

The idea is to learn as much as possible about customers and their shopping behaviors and create a meaningful one-on-one interaction with each of them. In practice, CRM often involves the sales force gathering information about specific customers to create a customer database. Other companies use CRM software to personalize e-mail or other communications. It enables a company to offer products tailored to specific customers' needs and desires. CRM databases also mean that customers visiting an organization's Web site or phoning the customer service call center can be quickly and easily recognized so that offerings can be adapted to their preferences. CRM is part of why airlines offer frequent flyer programs and why credit card companies offer customized services and low-interest balance transfer to certain targeted customers.

Marketing for Not-for-Profits and Others

How do not-for-profit organizations market their products?
Although the objective of traditional marketing is for businesses to encourage customers to purchase their products and ultimately generate a profit, many not-for-profit organizations also have an interest in marketing. Rather than a product or a service, these organizations look to market an event, a cause, a place, or a person. For example, environmental organizations, such as the Sierra Club, the National Wildlife Federation, and the Nature Conservancy, and other not-for-profits, such as the Red Cross, the American Cancer Society, and the Peace Corps, rely on marketing to raise awareness of and increase donations to their causes. Likewise, some churches and other civic organizations market their missions to attract new membership and garner contributions. Countries, states, and cities also run marketing campaigns to attract tourists and businesses to their locations. Museums and zoos also undertake "place marketing" by emphasizing the value of visiting their locations.

You may be familiar with the public service advertising campaigns run by the Ad Council, such as Smokey the Bear reminding us that "Only You Can Prevent Forest Fires," "A Mind Is a Terrible Thing to Waste" for the United Negro College Fund, the "You Could Learn a Lot from a Dummy" that promotes the use of seat belts with crash test dummies, and the "Friends Don't Let Friends Drive Drunk" drunk driving prevention campaign.[6]

Is it possible to market a person? Politicians and political parties market candidates for elected office. Agents for athletes, movie stars, television personalities, and musicians market their clients. We market ourselves when we interview for a job. You may have marketed yourself for acceptance to your college or university. To a certain extent, we market ourselves at both work and play. Regardless of what is being marketed—an event, a cause, a place, a person, a good, or a service—the essence of marketing remains the same. The only differences between marketing practices by for-profit and not-for-profit organizations are the stakeholders involved and their objectives.

Drunk Driving   Buzzed Driving

Buzzed driving is drunk driving.

Ad campaigns from the Ad Council have been effective tools in marketing public service interests.

Benefits of Marketing

How does marketing benefit consumers? As consumers, we have many needs—food, clothing, housing, medical care, and transportation, among others. Marketers don't really *create* needs; instead, they *respond* to them in an effort to *satisfy* needs. Indeed, many businesses have become extremely profitable by finding a need and convincing you to choose their specific product over competing products. Subway and Quiznos go to great lengths to convince you to buy their sandwiches to satisfy your need for food, just as Toyota and Ford try to convince you to purchase their vehicles to fulfill your transportation needs. When needs are satisfied, *utility* is created.

What do we mean by utility? There are five kinds of utility that marketing provides to customers:

1. When a company produces a product from raw materials, such as a designer swimsuit from fabric and raw materials, it creates **form utility**. The product takes on a form that pleases the customer.

2. When a store sells the swimsuit, it transfers ownership from the store to the customer, creating **ownership utility**. The buyer derives satisfaction from owning the latest swimwear.

3. When a business makes the swimsuit available in time for summer, it creates **time utility** because the swimwear is available for sale at a time when it is most needed.

4. When the swimsuit is stocked and placed on display at your local department store, it creates **place utility** by making the product available for purchase at a place that's convenient for buyers.

5. When someone performs a service for someone else, such as when a seamstress alters a swimsuit, they create **task utility**.

How is product value measured? Whenever a business satisfies a need or a want, it creates value for a customer. But how do customers measure value? The **value** of a product equals the ratio of a product's benefits to its costs (value = benefits ÷ costs). With a high-value product, its benefits far exceed its costs. A low-value product has few benefits in relation to its costs. Successful marketing finds ways to increase value to customers—to increase the real or perceived benefits of a product or minimize customers' costs by reducing the price or maximizing convenience. Organizations that offer the highest-valued products win the most customers and thrive. Those organizations that offer low-value goods and services lose market share or go out of business entirely.

How do investors and employees benefit from marketing? Investors receive profits to reward them for devoting their financial resources to successful organizations. Indeed, more and more investment flows to those businesses that are most successful in satisfying customers because investors are rewarded with higher profits. Employees benefit from successful marketing as well because their jobs and livelihoods are more secure. In addition, new job opportunities are created as production expands to satisfy the growing demand for high-value products.

How does society benefit from marketing?

Society at large benefits from successful marketing because scarce resources are more efficiently allocated or channeled into the production of those goods and services most desired by society. Resources, such as raw materials and labor, flow into the production of those goods and services in greatest demand and away from low-value products with falling demand. The market mechanism ensures it. For example, if the public demands more of Research in Motion's (RIM's) BlackBerrys, then RIM's profits rise, and RIM has a huge incentive to produce more BlackBerrys. Because more resources are required to produce more BlackBerrys, the demand for resources and labor used in BlackBerry production rises, raising prices and wages, and more resources flow into the production of BlackBerrys.

Profitable businesses that satisfy public needs and wants, like RIM, attract more resources. Unsuccessful businesses and their unsuccessful products use fewer resources. The market mechanism benefits society by shifting scarce resources away from less desired products into more desired products. When resources are used more efficiently, society is able to consume more products, increasing the average standard of living.

How do sellers benefit from marketing?

Of course, if marketing is successful, a company also benefits because it sells more product. As long as the costs of the marketing campaign and the production of a product are less than the revenue generated by the sales of a product, a company generates a profit. Hence, sellers benefit from successful marketing because their profits enable the organization to not only sustain itself but also prosper and continue to provide value to customers—ideally, it's a win-win arrangement.

Was it ignorance of the harm their product could have on society or a conscious effort to deceive the public for selfish gain that motivated tobacco companies to undertake promotions like this one in the 1950s? Many believe that ad campaigns such as this one fall under the heading of unscrupulous marketing.

Criticisms of Marketing

What are the criticisms of marketing?

Over time, certain social shortcomings have emerged from marketing techniques. Some of the questionable tactics criticized include price gouging (setting a price that is widely considered unfair), high-pressure selling, the production of shoddy or unsafe products, planned obsolescence (the product becomes obsolete after a period of time planned by the manufacturer), poor customer service, the misuse of customer information, confusing and deceptive labeling, and other deceptive practices such as hidden fees and charges.

Let's consider some examples of the costs to society of questionable marketing:

- **Misuse of personal information:** Marketing often involves the collection of personal information about customers. Companies conduct marketing surveys to find out the marital status, annual income, age, sex, race, and other characteristics of their primary customers. Many of us feel violated when this personal information is not adequately protected or resold without our permission, especially in the age of identity theft.
- **Hidden fees:** Many of us feel taken advantage of when we must pay hidden fees and charges not included in the advertised price. Products that require additional parts or shipping and service fees often make customers upset.

- **Consequences of purchase:** Unscrupulous marketing may take advantage of less sophisticated members of society. To what extent is it reasonable to hold buyers responsible for being aware of the consequences of their purchases? This is especially important when purchasing expensive or sophisticated goods and services, such as a car or a mortgage on a home. Similar concerns emerge when marketing is directed at children.

The many criticisms of marketing should not be taken lightly. These concerns may help explain the strong support for consumer protection laws and other regulations governing business behavior. Too often the social costs of marketing stem from unethical business behavior. As we discussed in Chapter 3, all companies should have a code of ethics and policies in place to curb unethical behavior within their organizations. However, not all companies do, which allows for questionable products to be marketed. The AMA has a statement of ethics that contains guidelines on ethical norms and values for marketers. (Visit www.marketingpower.com/AboutAMA/Pages/Statement%20of%20Ethics.aspx to review this code.)

As you can see, the marketing landscape has changed drastically over the past 100 years or so. Companies that have managed to stay in business—such as Ford Motor Company—have changed their products and marketing strategies to match changes in consumers' wants and needs. For Ford, those transitions ranged from mass-producing one model of a car to producing dozens of models and styles today that each strive to meet individual customer preferences, tastes, and budgets. ■

Marketing Tactics pp. 369–373

Aaron Hoffman is determined to work for himself, and he knows he can do that with his own mobile pet-grooming service. Because he worked as a pet groomer for seven years, he has enough experience to branch out on his own. Aaron has already found a van to hold all his equipment, and he knows a few of his previous customers are interested, but he isn't sure what the next step should be. Someone suggested he come up with a marketing strategy. What does a marketing strategy do? And how should Aaron apply it to his new business? ■

All organizations can benefit from a well-developed marketing strategy. In this section, we'll discuss the factors that are involved in the marketing process.

Marketing Strategy: The 4 Ps of Marketing

What is a marketing strategy? A marketing strategy consists of two major elements: An organization must determine its *target market* and then develop a *marketing mix* to meet the needs of that market. The **target market** is a specific group of potential customers on which a firm focuses its marketing efforts. (We'll discuss target marketing in more detail later in the chapter.) The **marketing mix** is the combination of four factors—called the 4 Ps of marketing—designed to serve the target market:

- Product
- Price
- Promotion
- Place

The idea is to provide the *product* that customers need and want at an appropriate *price* and *promote* its sale and *place* or distribute the good or the service in a convenient location for the customer to purchase. The 4 Ps of the marketing mix need to be blended in the most appropriate manner to best meet the needs of the target market. As you can see in ▼ **Figure 12.3**, finding the best blend of the 4 Ps is constrained by environmental factors beyond a firm's control. We'll discuss these constraints found within the broader market environment later in this chapter. Let's first look at each of the 4 Ps in a bit more detail.

Product

Distinguishing your product from that of your competitors is critical. If you don't do something that's different from or superior to the competition, why should customers buy from you? *Product differentiation* is the creation of a real or perceived difference in a product designed to attract customers. Product differentiation is one of the most critical success ingredients for most businesses and will be discussed in greater detail in Chapter 13. Product differentiation can take the form of functionality, styling, quality, safey, packaging, warranty, accessories, or brand

"We read advertisements to discover and enlarge our desires. We are always ready—even eager—to discover, from the announcement of a new product, what we have all along wanted without really knowing it."[8]

—Daniel J. Boorstin, U.S. historian (1914–2004)

▼ **Figure 12.3**
The Marketing Mix
Effective marketing requires the appropriate blend of the 4 Ps directed at targeted customers. This blend is constrained by forces beyond a firm's control and found within the broader market environment.

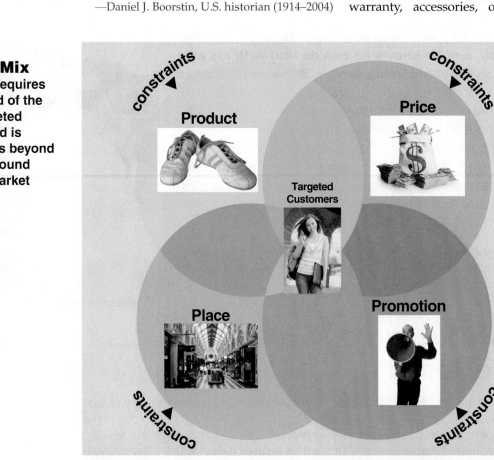

Biz**Chat**

Is There a Fifth P?

Although the 4 Ps of marketing are the accepted criteria for the marketing mix, there has been some discussion of adding a fifth P to the mix. In today's competitive business world, some say it is necessary to have a "purple cow" factor—something that makes your business or product stand apart from the competition. A company that has attained success using a purple cow is the Geek Squad. An affiliate of Best Buy, the Geek Squad provides a wide range of technical and computer services to customers. What makes it stand apart is its image. Geek Squad employees make house calls, driving PT cruisers with Geek Squad logos. The IT world is considered a nerdy field, and the Geek Squad embraces that image and runs with it. As a result of its unique marketing approach, the Geek Squad is one of the most recognizable technical service businesses.[7]

For more information and discussion questions about this topic, check out the BizChat feature on my**biz**lab.com.

name image. A **brand** is a name, term, symbol, or design that distinguishes a company and its products from all others.

Price

There's a lot to consider when deciding on the price for a product. Of course, the price will have to be sufficient to cover costs if you wish to make a profit. However, the product must be competitively priced to appeal to customers. We'll investigate the price component of the marketing mix in more detail in Chapter 13.

Promotion

The **promotion** part of the marketing mix consists of all the methods to inform and persuade targeted customers to buy a product and build positive customer relationships. Communicating the benefits of your good or service to customers includes advertising, sales promotions, personal selling, public relations, direct marketing, and publicity. We'll explore promotion more fully in Chapter 14.

Place

The **place** (or **distribution**) component of the marketing mix refers to all the methods involved in getting a product into the hands of customers. A product isn't beneficial to a customer if it can't be purchased when and where it is needed. When a business is providing a good instead of a service, the delivery component is often more complicated. Many goods, such as grocery store items, go through a *distribution channel*, which is a series of firms or individuals that participate in the flow of a product from the manufacturer to the consumer. The middlemen in a distribution channel are sometimes called *distributors* or *wholesalers*. Some goods, such as food products, go through many wholesalers before reaching a retail outlet (e.g., a grocery store) and, finally, the

Costco offers its warehouse members a more direct distribution channel and, therefore, saves them money.

▼ Figure 12.4
The Five Steps in the
Marketing Process

consumer. Other goods, such as automobiles, typically move from the manufacturer to just one wholesaler, the car dealership, and then the consumer. Still other goods bypass wholesalers altogether and move from the manufacturer directly to the consumer, such as L.L.Bean clothing products, which are ordered from a catalog and shipped directly to consumers.[9] In Chapter 14, we'll examine finding the appropriate distribution channel and managing it efficiently to get the product to the right place at the right time, in the proper quantity, and at the lowest cost.

The Marketing Process

What are the steps in the marketing process? There are five steps in the marketing process, as outlined in ▼ **Figure 12.4**.

1. **Identify a market need.** Think back to Aaron Hoffman's mobile pet-grooming service. Aaron has his own pets, and before he became a groomer himself, he formerly took his dogs to the pet-grooming service at which he was later employed. Transporting his dogs was a huge hassle, and he felt horrible about leaving them in a cage for part of the day. He didn't know it at the time, but Aaron had identified an unfilled market need: a *mobile* pet-grooming service that eliminates the hassle and guilt that trouble pet owners have when they take their pets to a grooming service. This is the first step in the marketing process.

2. **Conduct market research and develop a marketing plan.** The next step is to conduct research on the profitability of a potential business. By analyzing the marketing environment, Aaron can determine if any political, economic, societal, and/or technological factors could affect his business. In addition, Aaron conducts an internal analysis that includes evaluating his potential customers, competitors, and collaborators. These analyses form the foundation for his marketing plan. As Aaron researches, he discovers that many other people share his desire for a more convenient pet-grooming service. It appears sufficient demand already exists for the services of his potential business. We'll discuss how to analyze the marketing environment, as well as how to conduct market research and develop a marketing plan in more detail later in the chapter.

3. **Identify target customers.** The third step is to determine a target market. Without this focus, Aaron will waste effort and money promoting a service to individuals who are not interested in his service. When selecting a target market, Aaron must visualize his ideal customer. Aaron thinks about what his ideal customer does, thinks, and wants and then uses that image to form his marketing decisions. We'll discuss target marketing in more detail later in the chapter.

4. **Implement the marketing mix.** Once Aaron selects a target market, the fourth step is to implement the marketing mix—product, price, promotion, and place. Once an unfilled customer need has been identified, it is important to develop a *product* that not only meets that need but also fulfills it better than the competition. For Aaron's product (i.e., service), he should start by creating a memorable brand name to distinguish his business and services from all others. Having a memorable brand name will make it easier to attract customers.

   Having developed a set of goods and services and a brand that distinguishes his business from all others, Aaron will want to contemplate his *pricing* strategy. What price are people willing to pay, and how sensitive are customers to price changes? Will different hourly rates be charged for grooming on weekdays compared to Saturdays or Sundays? Will seasonal differences influence prices? Will Aaron charge more for larger pets?

   Promotion is the most visible part of the marketing mix. It can be very expensive yet very fruitful. How should a mobile pet-grooming service be promoted?

   The *place* component of the marketing mix often involves deciding how his product will be distributed to customers. The initial size and mobility of

Aaron's business affords him great flexibility; he will be delivering his product to his customers, within a reasonable distance, with little or no inventory management required.

5. **Nurture good customer relationships.** The final step in the marketing process is to manage customer relationships. As we noted earlier, the goal of CRM is to establish long-term, trusting relationships with individual customers to foster loyalty and repeat business. Aaron must develop a rapport with his customers and their pets. He should know which customers are returning clients and note any particular grooming preferences. He might even offer discounts for select customers. Aaron should not only solicit but also respond to suggestions by customers on how to improve his services. To build customer trust, he should also offer customers their money back if they are unsatisfied. To maintain and foster interest in his services, he may want to create a mailing list for select customers. Aaron may also want to establish relationships with veterinary clinics and dog breeders. Above all, it's critical to personalize and maintain good customer relationships.

Marketing is an ongoing process of tweaking a business to satisfy customers to ensure quality, value, and repeat business. The marketing process may seem simple when it is written on paper, but it's as much an art as it is a science. Aaron Hoffman's mobile pet-grooming service would have a completely different marketing strategy than a non-mobile stand-alone business producing a good. Each product needs to be looked at individually to tailor an appropriate marketing mix. ■

The Marketing Environment pp. 373–377

Amelia Russo runs a successful shop selling inexpensive dress shoes for women. She gets most of her stock from France, so the value of the U.S. dollar makes a big difference in her total costs. However, the value of the dollar has fallen so low that Amelia is considering limiting her overseas orders and using domestic distributors. This would save money on purchasing shoes as well as delivery; however, the quality and style would be different than what her customers expect. If she keeps the same stock, she'll be forced to raise her prices, and her sales may fall significantly. What other types of environmental influences might affect Amelia's business? ■

The 4 Ps in the marketing mix are variables under the direct control of an organization. However, the **marketing environment** includes environmental influences beyond a firm's control that constrain the organization's ability to manipulate its marketing mix. These environmental influences include the competitive, economic, technological, and sociocultural environments as well as the political, legal, and regulatory environments, as shown in ▼ **Figure 12.5**.

Marketers must be keenly aware of the marketing environment when selecting their marketing mix. In fact, one of the key responsibilities of managers in any organization is to undertake **environmental scanning**, the process of surveying the marketing environment to assess external threats and opportunities. A successful business detects changes in the marketing environment and adjusts its

▼ **Figure 12.5
The Marketing Mix
and the Marketing
Environment**
The marketing mix (the blend
of the 4 Ps) can be controlled
by marketing managers. The
marketing environment
represents external forces
that can't be controlled by
marketing managers and
impose constraints on their
ability to blend the 4 Ps.

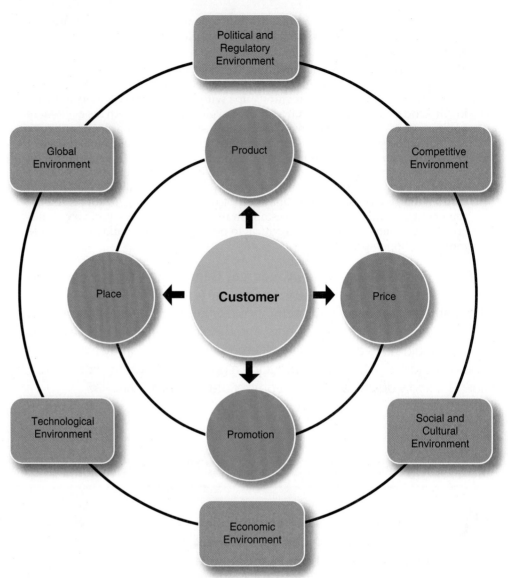

marketing mix (4 Ps) quickly and appropriately, inasmuch as the overall marketing environment will allow it to do so. Let's study each element of the marketing environment in a bit more detail.

The Competitive Environment

Why is analyzing the competition important? Assessing the competitive environment, or the degree of competition facing a firm, is critical to creating an effective marketing mix. You may recall from Chapter 2 the basic market environments with respect to the varying degrees of competition facing firms: perfect competition, monopolistic competition, oligopoly, duopoly, and monopoly. The degree of competition impacts a firm's production, pricing, promotion, and place (distribution) strategies in many ways. A successful business must be aware of competition and always try to stay one step ahead. Amelia Russo's shoe store had an edge on the competition due to her low prices. As a result of the dollar's weakness, however, Amelia is going to lose her competitive pricing advantage and be forced to create new marketing ideas.

The Economic Environment

Why is the economy important for marketing? The economic environment can affect customers' willingness and ability to spend their money on a firm's product. Therefore, marketers must keep abreast of changes in inflation, interest rates, unemployment, and economic growth rates over the course of the business cycle. Part of this is keeping up with changes in consumer confidence levels and government fiscal and monetary policies. Moreover, because of globalization, prudent firms follow global economic trends as well. This is especially important if a firm is involved in international business.

How does the economic environment affect a marketing strategy? The economic environment impacts a firm's marketing strategy in many ways. For example, a rising inflation rate reduces the purchasing power of money, and sales may fall. A recession will reduce the demand for most products. Even the best-laid marketing plans will fail when customers can no longer afford to buy a company's product. If interest rates are high, then the cost of borrowing is up, and consumers who buy on credit will purchase less and sales may fall. As a final example, suppose the value of the dollar falls (gets weaker) in foreign exchange markets. This will cause imported goods to become more expensive, like Amelia Russo's French dress shoes. Importing firms may need to raise their prices, which could significantly reduce sales. Savvy marketers try to keep their fingers on the changing pulse of the economy to forecast looming problems or potential opportunities and make the necessary adjustments.

The Technological Environment

How does technology affect marketing? The technological environment can also influence the marketing mix. Indeed, advances in communications and transportation technologies may be one of the most influential factors affecting modern business, especially with the onset of social media and Web-based communications. The Internet alone has enabled many small businesses to compete with large corporations around the world by marketing and selling their products online. Moreover, modern, sophisticated manufacturing innovations have enabled many firms to more easily customize their products and offer them at dramatically reduced prices to satisfy the varying tastes of targeted customers. The availability of mass-produced, inexpensive dress shoes and expedient shipping allowed Amelia Russo to make her shoe store a profitable venture. Successful marketing requires using the latest technologies to reach and satisfy target customers wherever they may be. This also includes using computer databases to enhance CRM.

The Social and Cultural Environment

How do cultural and social trends affect marketing? In Chapter 4, we examined the critical role that the sociocultural environment has on international business. We saw that most international business blunders have resulted from a lack of sensitivity or understanding of cultural differences. Domestic businesses must also realize that culture is dynamic, and effective marketers must be able to adapt to different attitudes and keep up with changing social trends. Demographic shifts—such as age, gender, ethnicity, and marital status—and changing values can signal opportunities for businesses. For example, we can expect the demand for medical care, pharmaceuticals, and nursing homes to increase as the

◉Off the Mark Aqua Teen Hunger ◯Force Campaign Blunder

In an effort to raise curiosity and promote a new movie based on the Aqua Teen Hunger Force animated television series, Turner Broadcasting System, Inc., placed blinking electronic characters on public structures near major roads, subways, and bridges throughout Boston and nine other cities in January 2007. The animated series is targeted at 18- to 30-year-old males and has a particular cult following. Unfortunately, what was conceived as a clever advertising campaign was horribly misperceived in the post-9/11 era as a potential terrorist bomb threat and resulted in the closure of the major transit arteries throughout Boston. The devices, measuring approximately one square foot, were battery-powered, printed circuit boards, with LED lights that displayed a "Mooninite"—an outer-space delinquent who makes frequent appearances on the cartoon. But the discovery of nine of the light boards around Boston sent bomb squads scrambling. As a result, Turner was required to pay $2 million to cover the costs incurred by the Boston police department and U.S. Department of Homeland Security.

average age of the population increases. We've also observed greater demand for convenience foods and restaurant services over the years as lifestyles have changed. Amelia Russo recognized the demand for inexpensive, high-quality dress shoes from a younger crowd and took advantage of the opportunity.

The Political, Legal, and Regulatory Environments

How does politics and legislation affect marketing?

It has been said that in a democracy, the squeaky wheel gets the grease. Special interest groups try to influence the political process in various ways. Businesses are no exception. They try to wield political influence through contributions to political parties, individual candidates, and political action committees (PACs) because government laws and regulations

▼ top 10 Corporate Contributors to Political Parties

LEGEND: 🐘 Republican 🐴 Democrat ▌ On the fence

▌ = Between 40 percent and 59 percent to both parties

🐴 or 🐘 = Leans Democratic or Republican (60–69 percent)

🐴🐴 or 🐘🐘 = Strongly Democratic or Republican (70–89 percent)

Rank	Organization Name	Total	Contribution Tilt 1989–2008	Contribution Tilt 2005–2006 Only
1.	AT&T Inc.	$38,473,085	▌	🐘
2.	Goldman Sachs	$27,172,482	🐴	🐴
3.	Citigroup Inc.	$23,033,490	▌	▌
4.	Altria Group	$22,923,875	🐘🐘	🐘
5.	UPS	$21,508,040	🐘	🐘
6.	FedEx Corp.	$21,288,684	▌	🐘
7.	Time Warner	$17,483,375	🐴	🐴🐴
8.	JP Morgan Chase & Co	$16,970,798	▌	▌
9.	Microsoft Corp.	$16,653,584	▌	▌
10.	Verizon Communications	$15,975,908	🐘	🐘

significantly impact business interests. In addition, a variety of regulatory agencies enforce laws and regulations constraining marketing efforts. These include the Environmental Protection Agency (EPA), the Consumer Product Safety Commission (CPSC), the Food and Drug Administration (FDA), and the Federal Trade Commission (FTC). Businesses are forced to consider the political and legal environment in making marketing decisions, as these factors can play a major role in overall success.

The Global Environment

How does the global environment affect marketing? Thanks in part to the Internet, world trade has increased significantly. Customers can search globally for products at attractive prices, and businesses can search globally for suppliers. In addition, in efforts to tap new markets, companies have expanded internationally. Therefore, marketers have needed a global perspective in many of their campaigns. However, global trade and the marketing efforts that accompany such increases in global trade and consumerism are not without difficulties. Marketers need to be aware of cultural and social differences before launching their products and their marketing campaigns. Political landscapes with differing policies and regulations can also affect how a company does business in another country. Lastly, businesses must also be aware of the complications involved in shipping products to foreign countries.

So what did store owner Amelia Russo decide to do when her stock from France became more expensive due to a weakened dollar? She judged her options and decided to buy domestically until the dollar gets stronger. Her customers were generally satisfied with the domestically produced substitute dress shoes, so Amelia was able to stay in business. Successful businesses like Amelia's are constantly on the lookout for changes in the market environment and are prepared to adjust accordingly. ■

Marketing Research and Planning pp. 377–384

Tiara Watson decided that opening a salon supply business in her city would be a great investment. The next closest supplier is over 70 miles away, so salons have to pay unnecessarily high shipping costs. If her business is in the city, the shipping costs for salons will be nominal compared to the other company. Tiara started researching and found over 30 salons around the city, so she has a strong target market. She's already met with some of the owners to see if they'd be willing to switch suppliers, and they seem interested. She knows she can't start out selling supplies to every salon in the city, but she isn't sure where to start. How can she determine which salons to target for her start-up business? ■

Look back at the five-step marketing process shown in Figure 12.4. You'll notice that after a market need is identified, a firm needs to conduct *market research* to

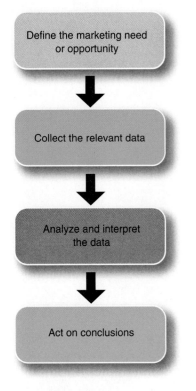

**▼ Figure 12.6
The Market
Research Process**

determine the profitability of a venture, develop a marketing plan, and determine its target market. In this section, we'll explore each of these processes in more detail.

The Market Research Process

What is market research, and what are the steps involved in the process? **Market research** is the process of gathering and analyzing market information for making marketing decisions. Market research can be as simple as including a brief survey with an invoice or via e-mail, or it can be as complex as conducting a full-blown analysis that is necessary before launching a new product. Although there are dozens of intermediate steps in conducting marketing research, they all fit into these basic steps (shown in ▼ **Figure 12.6**):

1. Define the marketing need or opportunity.
2. Collect the relevant data.
3. Analyze and interpret the data.
4. Act on conclusions.

Why is it important to identify the marketing research objective? Perhaps you want to launch a new product or service or feel that your product is not as visible as it could be. Perhaps a problem has created a poor company image or reputation, so you need to find a way to recover. Generally, at least one member or group in an organization already recognizes a need or an opportunity. For example, Tiara has defined the need for a salon supply company that is in close proximity to city salons. In this phase of the process, marketing managers and researchers need to work together to clearly define the objective of the research from all perspectives. They should determine the exact nature of the business need or opportunity and the information desired. They should also determine why that information will be helpful. This step will help the researcher determine the approach, establish a budget, and collect relevant and appropriate data for analysis.

What kind of data should be collected? Determining which types of data will be collected and how the information will be collected is the next step. Two general types of data exist: primary and secondary.

- **Primary data** are raw data collected by a researcher. The data are frequently collected through observation, questionnaires, surveys (via mail, e-mail, or telephone), focus groups, interviews, customer feedback, samples, and controlled experiments. A **focus group** is typically a group of 8–10 potential customers who are asked for feedback on a good or a service, an advertisement, an idea, or packaging style. They are often used in test-marketing an idea or a new product. For example, when Ford Motor Company began developing the new MyFord Touch system, they wanted to know from the customers what it was about certain technology that made them "must haves." Could the company successfully get customers "lining up around the block"?[10] Using a multitude of focus groups, they came up with a next-generation in-car entertainment system that the company hopes will be a winner.[11]

- **Secondary data** are data that have already been collected and processed. An example of secondary data are census data. This information is usually much cheaper to obtain.

Tiara Watson has collected primary data about the interest of salon owners in changing to a closer, cheaper supplier and secondary data about the location of the closest salon supply companies. Examples of primary and secondary data sources are summarized in ▼ **Table 12.1**.

▼ **Table 12.1**

Examples of Primary and Secondary Data Sources	
Primary Sources of Data	**Secondary Sources of Data**
• Observations • Questionnaires • Surveys • Focus groups • Interviews • Customer feedback • Sampling • Controlled experiments	**Government Sources** • U.S. Bureau of Economic Analysis, Survey of Current Business • U.S. Bureau of Labor Statistics • U.S. Census Bureau • U.S. CIA—*World Fact Book* and *Handbook of International Economics* • U.S. Department of Commerce (links to national and international governmental databases) • U.S. Federal Reserve • U.S. government materials • U.S. Office of Trade and Economic Development • U.S. Statistical Data International and National Stat-USA
	Commercial Sources • Nielsen Company • Information Resources, Inc. • Gallup
	Organizational Sources • Chamber of Commerce • Pew Research Center
	Magazines • *BusinessWeek* • *Time* • *Fortune* • *Forbes* • *Fast Company* • *Advertising Age* • *Entrepreneur*
	Newspapers • *Wall Street Journal* • *Washington Post* • *New York Times* • *Barrons* • Local newspapers
	Internal Sources • Accounting records • Annual report • Tax records • Financial statements
	Other sources • Social media • Internet databases and search engines • Commercial databases

How is social media used in market research?

Social media sites, such as Facebook and Twitter, are becoming invaluable tools for businesses to get in touch with the public at large. Not only can companies find out what is being said about their products, but they can also find out what is being said about the competition. Both types of information are invaluable—regardless of whether the opinions are good or bad. The value social media has over focus groups is twofold: size and immediacy. Focus groups are limited in size, and you are never sure whether you've picked the right people. Because of the formality of a focus group, they often require much planning and can be quite expensive to implement. On the other hand, social media networks gather quick results from substantial numbers of consumers. For example, when the design of the Tropicana orange juice container was changed from the traditional orange with a straw image to a more "updated" image of a glass of orange juice wrapped around the corner of the carton, consumers complained so much that the old container was quickly brought back. Social media gives honest and candid feedback from audiences who are eager to voice their opinions. Not every company or marketing research project will lend itself to social media tools. But, if a fit is determined, social media gives marketers another valuable tool for obtaining consumer insights.

> "Twitter is the ultimate focus group. I can post something and in a minute get feedback from 700 people around the world, giving me their real opinions."
>
> —Peter Shankman, public relations executive[12]

How are the data analyzed and interpreted?

Once the data have been collected, they must be assembled into a format that can be easily analyzed and interpreted. The analysis of data requires a knowledge of appropriate statistical techniques that are beyond the scope of this text; however, the ultimate goal is to conduct careful analyses that will lead to conclusions about what marketing strategies to implement. Honest analysis is necessary, and you should never adjust your data to get the results you want. Tiara's research showed over 30 salons in the area in which she was planning on locating her business, indicating she had a strong potential target market.

What happens when the research is completed?

The whole purpose of marketing research is to point managers toward better marketing decisions. Once the information is collected and analyzed, it is usually presented in an organized manner to decision makers. A formal presentation may be given to the sales and marketing teams or a plan outlining a new advertising strategy may require hiring an advertising agency.

Marketing research should be ongoing. Changing market conditions require businesses to continually adapt and constantly search for better ways to provide value to customers. Part of acting on the conclusions of marketing research is creating a marketing plan, which we'll discuss next.

The Marketing Plan

What is a marketing plan?

A **marketing plan** is a written document that specifies the marketing activities that will take place to achieve organizational objectives. It is the roadmap that will help carry out the strategies as determined by marketing research. A marketing plan is typically a *written* document because details about tasks to be performed by employees can be easily lost or forgotten if communicated orally. Moreover, written objectives can be compared with actual measurements to see whether objectives are being met.

▼ top 10 Best Social Media Tools for Small Businesses[13]

1. *Google Apps for Domains*: Web-based productivity software suite

2. *LinkedIn*: Social-networking site geared toward hiring and job networking

3. *Basecamp*: Project management and collaboration tool designed for small businesses

4. *Facebook*: Social-networking site useful in building relationships, raising visibility, and targeting customer niches

5. *Twitter*: Microblogging service for broadcasting small posts as well as listening to the pulse of the market

6. *Get Satisfaction*: Forum where customers can get answers, solutions, and submit suggestions

7. *MailChimp*: Web-based mailing list manager

8. *UserVoice*: Site that tracks and manages customer feedback; includes customer polling, ranking of suggestions, and feedback

9. *YouTube*: Site that can be used to post video walk-throughs of products or implement a viral video strategy

10. *Monitter*: Site that monitors Twitter feeds for keywords to monitor what people are saying about a company or a product

What are the elements of a good marketing plan? Four elements emerge from all good marketing plans:

- A clearly written marketing objective
- Performance of situational analysis
- Selection of a target market
- Implementation, evaluation, and control of the marketing mix (the four Ps)

Why is a marketing objective necessary? A **marketing objective** is a clearly stated goal to be achieved through marketing activities. It should be realistic, quantifiable, and time specific.[14] A marketing objective of having every home in the United States purchase a specific product is unrealistic. Selling 100,000 units in a year is a more realistic, quantifiable, and time-specific marketing objective. When objectives are realistic, they are attainable and can motivate employees toward the goal. When they are measurable, a firm can determine whether they are being achieved. If deadlines are also imposed, then firms know whether they are reaching their goals in a timely manner.

What is situational analysis? Creating clearly stated objectives is the first step in any good marketing plan. The next step is conducting a *situational analysis*. There are several methods that can be used to conduct a situational analysis, which is similar to the SWOT analysis discussed in Chapter 7 because it includes an evaluation of internal *strengths* and *weaknesses*, as well as the *opportunities* and *threats* found in the external environment; however, it focuses on marketing only, rather than the entire organization.

What do we mean by internal strengths? In terms of marketing, a company's internal strengths refer to the competitive advantages or core competencies that a company has at its disposal to meet a specified marketing objective. Core competencies provide customer benefits and are not easily imitated by other companies, setting a company apart from its competition. For example, John Deere has been very successful in expanding its business by transferring the strength of its brand-name reputation of superior-quality agricultural products into lawn tractors and mowers for urban dwellers and earth-moving equipment for the construction industry. Indeed, a significant portion of John Deere's revenues now come from its nonagricultural sales.[15]

How does a company assess its weaknesses? Assessing internal weaknesses means that a company must perform an audit of current managerial expertise, manufacturing and financing capabilities, and an organization's execution of the 4 Ps in the marketing mix. By honestly assessing its weaknesses, a company can determine a realistic marketing objective. For example, a company that makes handmade watches and has only three employees cannot expect to produce 75,000 watches a week.

Why look to the external environment? The dynamic and ever-changing external environment offers many opportunities and creates many threats. Changes in the degree of competition facing firms, the economy, technology, and sociocultural forces, as well as changes in the political, legal, and regulatory environments have caused some firms to thrive while damaging others. This is especially true for international businesses because the number of market environments compounds the analysis. Rapid changes in technology create new opportunities, such as expanding sales over the Internet, but also pose new threats, such as requiring additional technological expertise to protect against hackers. Successful companies continually evaluate environmental factors as part of their situational analysis to match their strengths with opportunities and address their weaknesses to avoid threats.

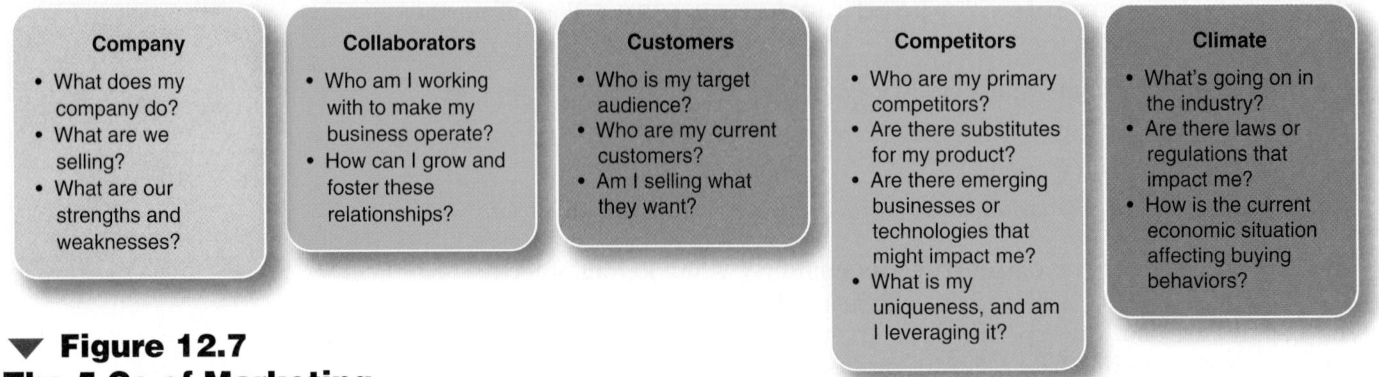

Company	Collaborators	Customers	Competitors	Climate
• What does my company do? • What are we selling? • What are our strengths and weaknesses?	• Who am I working with to make my business operate? • How can I grow and foster these relationships?	• Who is my target audience? • Who are my current customers? • Am I selling what they want?	• Who are my primary competitors? • Are there substitutes for my product? • Are there emerging businesses or technologies that might impact me? • What is my uniqueness, and am I leveraging it?	• What's going on in the industry? • Are there laws or regulations that impact me? • How is the current economic situation affecting buying behaviors?

▼ **Figure 12.7**
The 5 Cs of Marketing

Are there other ways to perform a situational analysis? Another useful tool for conducting a situational analysis is by analyzing the 5 Cs of marketing. This type of situational analysis looks at a company, its collaborators, its customers, its competitors, and the climate. It can be used separately, or in conjunction with analyzing the strengths, weaknesses, opportunities, and threats of its market environment. Looking carefully at ▼ **Figure 12.7** and the type of questions a 5 C analysis invokes, you will notice, especially in the company and climate areas, that there is some overlap with a marketing situational analysis. In combination with the marketing situational analysis, managers should be able to formulate a sound marketing plan.

Target Markets

How are target markets determined? Once an organization has evaluated its internal strengths and weaknesses, as well as the external opportunities and threats of the market environment, it is ready to determine its target market. If a business doesn't focus its marketing efforts, it will likely waste time and money promoting its product to individuals who are not interested.

How do you determine a target market? Determining a target market begins with **market segmentation**, the process of separating the broader market into smaller markets (or market segments) that consist of similar groups of customers. A **market segment** is a subgroup of potential customers who share similar characteristics and therefore have similar product needs and preferences. So, for example, rather than selling to all the salons in the county, Tiara, from the opening story, decided to focus on a smaller market segment of just those salons in the city. Some markets, called **niche markets** are even more narrowly defined. For example, a company that sells specialized gear shifters for racing bicycles is operating in a niche market.

Marketers choose those market segments that offer the greatest profit potential for their products, and these become the target markets. But, for the segments to be practical, they should be identifiable, accessible, substantial, stable, and have unique needs. For each target market, a company tries to blend the four Ps of the marketing mix to best satisfy their targeted customers. The process of developing a unique marketing mix that best satisfies a target market is known as **positioning**.

How are consumer markets segmented? Consumer markets can be segmented based on many variables or characteristics of customers. Four of the most common market segmentation classifications are geographic, demographic, psychographic, and behavioral. These types of market segmentations are summarized in ▼ **Table 12.2**.

▼ **Table 12.2**

Consumer Market Segmentation			
Geographic	**Demographic**	**Psychographic**	**Behavioral**
• Region • Suburban • Rural • City • County • Population density • Climate • Terrain	• Age • Race • Religion • Family size • Ethnicity • Gender • Income • Education	• Lifestyle • Personality traits • Motives • Values	• Benefit sought • Volume usage • Brand loyalty • Price sensitivity • Product end use

How are markets defined by location or region? Segmenting markets according to geographic characteristics is called **geographic segmentation**. For example, clothing apparel, skis, snowblowers, four-wheel drive vehicles, air conditioning, and heating needs differ according to regional climate differences. Taste in food products also varies by region. For example, McDonald's offers special menu items to cater to the tastes and preferences of a particular region or country. McLobster Rolls are served in Canada and the northeastern region of the United States; Saimin (a noodle soup) is sold at McDonald's in Hawaii; and because people in India do not eat beef, the Maharaja Mac, made of lamb or chicken meat, is the big seller. For Tiara Watson's salon supply company, the prominent hairstyles in some parts of the city may require specialized products that are not as popular in other locations.

How are markets defined by different population characteristics? Often, products are best received by men, or athletes, or seniors. **Demographic segmentation** is market segmentation according to age, race, religion, gender, ethnic background, and other demographics. For example, it's estimated that by the year 2020, one in five Americans will be of Hispanic origin.[16] Few businesses want to miss out on this growing market segment. It's now common to find labels or instructions written in both English and Spanish. There are also Spanish language television stations and newspapers, as well as companies marketing their products to this growing community in the United States.

Automobile companies also use demographic segmentation. They are keenly aware of how important it is to position their models to appeal to different age groups, income levels, and differences in gender. The salon supply company that Tiara is starting focuses primarily on African-American women's hair product needs.

Can a market be segmented based on opinions or interests? Harley-Davidson offers a wide variety of motorcycles, and each model attempts to cater to a particular lifestyle.[17] Cat food ads cleverly focus on "cat lover" personalities, whereas many beer commercials target specific personality types. Market segmentation based on lifestyles, personality traits, motives, and values is called **psychographic segmentation**. When motives are used to determine the appropriate market, marketers focus on why consumers make a purchase. For example, Whole Foods Market and Trader Joe's focus on consumers interested in healthier, organic foods, and Planet Fitness sells memberships to customers concerned with their health but who are also price conscious. Salons that will purchase Tiara's products are motivated by the need to supply customers with high-quality beauty products.

Sophisticated marketers closely examine their customers' lifestyles, personality traits, motives, and values because, unlike geographic and demographic variables, these psychographic variables can be manipulated by marketing efforts. Whatever

What market segments best fit an organic food store?

consumers may value, whether it be quality, social status or affiliation, safety, health, privacy, technology, or appearance, you can bet that businesses will offer a good or service to satisfy that real or perceived need. They will be rewarded with profits for doing so.

How can consumer behaviors define a market segment? Do you buy only one particular brand of, for example, laundry soap, soda, or toothpaste, regardless of price? Do you buy cranberry sauce only at Thanksgiving? These types of behaviors define **behavioral segmentation**, the market segmentation based on certain consumer behavior characteristics, such as brand loyalty, price sensitivity, the benefits sought by a product, occasions that stimulate purchases, and the ways in which a product is used. For example, a company that produces herbal supplements is appealing to the specific benefits sought by its consumers.

Brand loyalty is another kind of behavioral segmentation. It can impact price sensitivity: The more loyal the customer, the less sensitive he or she is to a price increase. If a customer has been using the same brand of toothpaste for 12 years and has had no cavities in that time period, a small price increase will most likely not be an issue to that customer. Finally, knowing how a product is actually used can help companies develop packages that appeal to customers. For example, having vitamins for adults packaged with lids that are easily turned by arthritic hands can be useful for some consumers.

The marketing process may involve only a few steps, but each of these takes some time and plenty of focused effort. Tiara Watson has given much thought to whom she wants to target as customers. However, without performing a marketing situational analysis, she wasn't sure where to start. Once she stepped back and took time to go through the research process, she knew where to begin. Tiara is off to a good start, but she still has some work ahead of her in implementing her marketing mix and nurturing good customer relationships. The next two chapters explore the implementation of the marketing mix in more detail to nurture good customer relationships. ■

Consumer Behavior pp. 385–389

Will Giusto is standing in front of a shelf of laptop computers. He has to buy one for school but has left the task to the last minute, and he really can't leave without one. Not knowing much about computers, they all look pretty much the same to him, so how is he to decide? His girlfriend has a MacBook Pro and loves it, but she loves everything Apple makes. His best friend has a Dell and raves about how awesome it is, but he's a gamer, and Will knows that his friend's Dell is top of the line. Will isn't looking for a fancy label or a "tricked out" machine; he just needs something to type his papers on and access Facebook. But staring at the row of similar looking laptops is just plain intimidating. How can Will make the best purchasing decision? What factors will influence his decision? ■

The term **consumer behavior** refers to the ways individuals or organizations search for, evaluate, purchase, use, and dispose of goods and services. Notice that consumer behavior involves the study of individual consumers or business organizations as buyers in the market. Most of us intuitively think of a market as being a consumer market. Consumer markets are the markets we, as consumers, are most familiar with. In a **consumer market**, individuals purchase goods and services for personal consumption. But there are also business-to-business markets. In **business-to-business (B2B) markets**, businesses purchase goods and services from other businesses. In this section, we'll explore both markets and examine the buying behavior differences between consumer markets and B2B markets.

Consumer Markets

Why study consumer behavior? A knowledge of consumer behavior helps marketers select the most profitable target markets and guides the implementation, evaluation, and control of the marketing mix (the 4 Ps) for selected targeted markets. For example, consumers are becoming increasingly concerned about gas mileage. Automobile manufacturers that realize this can create more gas-efficient vehicles or drop the prices on less-efficient models to compensate for poor gas mileage.

How does a consumer make a buying decision? The consumer buying process involves five steps:

1. Need recognition
2. Information search
3. Evaluation of alternatives
4. Purchase or no purchase decision
5. Postpurchase evaluation

Not all consumers go through each step in the process, and the steps do not need to be completed in the same order. The process can be interrupted at any time with a "no purchase" decision.

Consider your decision to purchase the educational services of your college or university. You first recognized the need for higher education. You likely obtained information about colleges from many sources, including your friends, family,

PEARSON
mybizlab

For an interactive, real-world example of this topic, access this chapter's **BizSkill** entitled Product Development, located at **mybizlab**.com.

Sociocultural Influences: Culture, Subculture, Social class, Family, Peers

Personal Influences: Age, Economic situation, Lifestyle, Personality

Psychological Influences: Motivation, Perception, Attitudes, Learning

Buyer
Purchase Decision Process:
1) need recognition
2) information search
3) evaluation of alternatives
4) purchase or no purchase decision
5) postpurchase evaluation

Marketing Mix Influences: Product, Price, Promotion, Place

Situational Influences: Physical & social surroundings, Type of product purchased

▼ Figure 12.8 Major Influences Impacting a Consumer's Buying Decision

Many factors influence consumer buying decisions. Effective marketing attempts to help consumers with their information search and the evaluation of alternatives.

counselors, and perhaps even the annual college rankings of the *U.S. News & World Report*.[18] You may have also visited a few college campuses to gather firsthand information. You then evaluated your choices based on a variety of factors, including tuition (price), geographic location, or perhaps where your friends were going to college. Your final choice may have been based on rational analysis or the result of an emotional decision (based on some gut feelings). After making a purchase, we also evaluate our decision in terms of how well our expectations are being met. You'll likely continue to evaluate your college choice long after you graduate.

What influences consumer decision making?

The consumer decision-making process is part of a broader environmental context that influences each step. Marketers should be aware of these factors when developing an appropriate marketing mix for the target market. These environmental forces are shown in ▼ **Figure 12.8**.[19]

How does culture affect a person's buying behavior?

Culture is the set of learned attitudes, beliefs, and ways of life that are unique to a society and are handed down from generation to generation. Subcultures are specific groups within a culture that share attitudes and life experiences. Some examples of subcultures include churches, community organizations, and online communities like Facebook and MySpace. Together, a buyer's culture, subculture, social class, family, and peers compose the *sociocultural influences* that affect buying decisions. Cultural values change over time. For example, as the obesity epidemic becomes more pronounced, many people today value healthier lifestyles, which has begun to change their buying patterns. Social class refers to a combination of factors, such as education, income, wealth, and occupation common to a group of people. Social class can have an impact on purchasing decisions, as some possessions are considered status symbols, like the MacBook Pro that Will's girlfriend owns. Apple computers are often viewed as just being "cooler" than other types of computers.

What unique personal influences shape buying behaviors?

Personal influences on a buyer's consumption choice are often shaped by his or her age, gender, economic situation, lifestyle, and personality. For example, knowing that there is a difference between how men shop and how women shop can help influence a sales strategy. Women often like to browse, linger, and socialize, whereas men often prefer to get in and get out of a store. The owner of a Canadian women's clothing boutique recognized these patterns. To cater to her female customers, she hosts "trunk shows," during which her customers get together with their friends to have a glass of wine while reviewing a designer's new line. Similarly, she caters to her male customers more efficient buying preferences by keeping a database of their personal information and preferences. Prior to special occasions, she'll contact her male customers and let them know she has the perfect gift for their spouse or partner.[20]

How do personal attitudes affect buying decisions?

One goal of marketing is to shape the perception of a product in the minds of consumers. Attitudes toward a product put customers in a frame of mind that either predisposes them to favorably view a product or not. *Psychological influences* include differences in a buyer's motivation, perception, attitudes, and learning. Equally important is an effort to create positive product experiences. Good experiences with brands result in repeat business; bad experiences stunt future sales. It is more expensive to find new customers than to keep existing customers, so investing in methods to ensure that existing customers' needs are met and that they remain loyal to the brand is very important.

Can temporary conditions affect how buyers behave? *Situational influences* include the physical surroundings, the social surroundings, and the type of product purchased, and these all can influence how a buyer behaves. Some factors, such as where products are placed or how a store is organized, can be easily controlled. However, other factors, such as adverse weather conditions or a consumer's negative mood, are not as easily managed, such as the hurried purchase Will Giusto was about to make because he had left his purchase to the last minute. He may not feel able to make a calm and informed decision due to the immediate pressure of the moment.

How does the marketing mix influence purchases? *Marketing mix influences* include the product, price, promotion, and place (distribution) aspects (the 4 Ps) of purchases. As stressed throughout this chapter, marketing is interested in producing a product that buyers want at an affordable price, promoting awareness of the attributes of that product, and placing the good or the service in a timely and convenient location for consumers to buy.

A knowledge of consumer buying behavior and the influences on the buying decision is critical to effective marketing. Some of these influences, like personal influences, are beyond the control of marketers, while other influences, like psychological influences, can be impacted by businesses. All of these influences should be kept in mind when selecting a target market; implementing, evaluating, and controlling the marketing mix; and building customer relationships.

B2B Markets

What is the difference between consumer markets and B2B markets? The difference between consumer and B2B markets hinges on who's doing the buying. If a good or a service is purchased in a B2B market, it is purchased by a business for further processing, for resale, or to facilitate general business activity. The B2B market is significantly larger compared to consumer markets because virtually all consumer products go through a number of distributors or wholesalers before reaching the final consumer at a retail outlet. In fact, each time an unfinished product is bought and sold through the many stages of a product's development, a separate B2B market exists. Think of all the transactions involved in producing a car. Most of the components are produced by separate firms. Moreover, each of these firms derives its inputs from different businesses.

What are the characteristics of a B2B market? The first step in selling to a business market and the consumer market is the same: identify the customer and determine why the customer needs your product. However, the rest of the process is distinct for each end market because of the inherent differences among the markets. If marketing to a business, it is important to understand the characteristics that distinguish it from a consumer market. B2B markets are generally more relationship driven than product driven; however, the quality of a product is very important to them, as the profitability of their businesses hinge on their suppliers. Therefore, they are sophisticated and will want to know specific information about

a product that a typical consumer would not need. In addition, some other important characteristics of B2B markets are as follows:

1. **A few buyers that purchase in large quantities.** B2B markets typically involve a few buyers that purchase very large quantities. For example, only a few airline companies buy most of Boeing's jets.

2. **Highly trained buyers.** Most business purchasing agents are highly skilled at their jobs. They often weigh the benefits and the costs in a more systematic fashion and are less influenced by emotional factors than buyers in consumer markets. This requires sellers to pitch their products at a much more sophisticated level.

3. **Group purchasing decision.** A team of individuals within purchasing departments usually collaborates in making a purchasing decision in B2B markets. This means marketers must be prepared to be patient and mindful of the concerns of all decision makers to seal a deal.

4. **Close customer relationship.** Because there are only a few sophisticated buyers that purchase large quantities, marketers find it necessary to establish a much closer relationship with customers compared to the relationship with buyers in consumer markets. As a result, B2B marketing is more focused on personal selling compared to the mass advertising campaigns that typify consumer markets.

5. **Geographically concentrated buyers.** Most buyers in B2B markets are concentrated in a few of the most industrialized states where most large businesses are located. This reduces the costs of reaching buyers.

6. **Direct purchasing.** Buyers in B2B markets often purchase directly from sellers, as opposed to consumer markets, where products typically go through many wholesalers before a product arrives at the end user.

These key differences between consumer and B2B markets are summarized in ▼ **Table 12.3**. These differences can be organized by differences in market structure, the nature of the buying unit, and the purchasing process.

How does a business make a buying decision, and what influences that decision? The consumer decision-making process discussed earlier is equally applicable to business purchasing decisions. Businesses begin by recognizing a need; they seek out information to aid them in the purchase de-

▼ **Table 12.3**

Differences Between B2B and Consumer Markets		
	B2B Market	**Consumer Market**
Market Structure	• Few customers • Large-volume purchases • Geographically concentrated	• Many customers • Small-volume purchases • Geographically dispersed
Nature of the Buying Unit	• More professional and rational purchase decision	• Less sophisticated and more emotional purchase decision
Purchasing Process	• Highly trained buyers • Group purchasing decision • Complex buying decisions • Formalized buying procedures • Close and personal selling relationship between marketer and buyer • Personal selling • Geographically concentrated	• Untrained buyers • Individual purchasing decision • Relatively simple buying decisions • Informal buying decision • Impersonal relationship between marketer and buyer • Mass advertising • Geographically dispersed

cision; evaluate alternatives; decide to either purchase or not to purchase; and undertake a postpurchase evaluation. However, business purchases are generally more rational, reasoned, objective decisions based on various influences, such as the state of the economy; technological factors; the degree of competition; political and regulatory concerns; and organizational objectives, policies, and procedures.

Is the marketing process different for B2B markets? The marketing process remains the same for all markets: identify a need, undertake research to come up with a marketing plan, select a target market, implement and control the marketing mix, and nurture customer relationships.

Will Giusto finally made his purchase. After consulting with a sales clerk about each of the brands, he chose a Mac. Was it the marketing power of Apple that swayed his decision? The influence of his girlfriend? Or something else? ■

Chapter Summary

Are you an active learner?

Go to my*biz*lab.com to master Chapter 12's content. Chapter 12's interactive activities include:

- Customizable Study Plan and Chapter 12 practice quizzes
- Chapter 12 Simulations, Market Research Matters and Product Development, that help you think critically and prepare to make choices in the business world
- Chapter 12 Video Exercise, Jones Soda: Marketing and Consumer Behavior, which shows you how textbook concepts are put into practice every day
- Flash Cards for mastering the definition of chapter terms
- Interactive Lessons that visually review key chapter concepts

1. How has marketing evolved over the production concept era, the sales concept era, the marketing concept era, and the customer relationship era? (pp. 364–366)

- During the production concept era (from the Industrial Revolution until the 1920s), most companies focused solely on production. Demand was often greater than supply, and the prevailing mind-set was that a good-quality product would simply sell itself.

- During the sales concept era (from the mid-1920s through the early 1950s), technological advances meant that production increased more sharply than demand for goods and services. The use of heavy public advertising in all available forms of media became prevalent.

- During the marketing concept era (from the 1950s through the 1990s), production continued to expand more quickly than the growth in demand for goods and services. The **marketing concept** (p. 365) changed the focus from finding the right customer for a product to producing the right product for a customer and doing it better than the competition.

- During the societal marketing era (1960s to the present), companies began to realize that they must also take into consideration the long-term interests of society. Companies began to work for the benefit of both consumers and society.

- During the customer relationship era (from the late 1990s to the present), organizations have worked to establish long-term relationships with individual customers to foster loyalty and repeat business.

2. What are the benefits of marketing to customers, sellers, investors, employees, and society at large, and what are the criticisms of marketing? (pp. 367–369)

- **Marketing** (p. 363) identifies and satisfies human needs and wants. It provides value to customers by providing benefits that exceed their costs. In turn, sellers benefit because marketing enables firms to survive.

- Businesses that are most successful in satisfying customers generate higher profits, and investors benefit from the profits earned. Employees benefit from successful marketing as well because their jobs and livelihoods are more secure.

- Society at large benefits from marketing because scarce resources are more efficiently allocated to those goods and services most desired by society.

- Criticisms of marketing include price gouging, the production of shoddy or unsafe products, and confusing and deceptive practices. The criticisms of marketing should not be taken lightly. All companies should have a code of ethics and policies in place to curb unethical behavior within their organizations.

3. What are the basic elements of a marketing strategy and the 4 Ps of the marketing mix? (pp. 369–372)

- The two basic elements of a marketing strategy are the **target market** (p. 369) and the **marketing mix** (p. 370).

- The four Ps of the marketing mix are **product** (p. 363), price, **promotion** (p. 371), and **place** (p. 367).

4. How do firms implement a marketing strategy by applying the marketing process? (pp. 372–373)

- The marketing process involves (1) identifying a need, (2) conducting market research and developing a marketing plan, (3) determining a target market, (4) implementing the four Ps of the marketing mix, and (5) nurturing good customer relationships.

- The application of the marketing process is as much an art as a science. Producing a high-quality product with a unique brand properly promoted that consistently delivers value to customers at a "fair" price when and where customers want a product are common ingredients for marketing success.

5. How do the various factors in the marketing environment influence a firm's ability to manipulate its marketing mix? (pp. 373–377)

- The **marketing environment** (p. 373) includes environmental influences, such as the competitive, economic, technological, and sociocultural environments, as well as the political, legal, and regulatory environments. Because these factors are beyond a firm's control, they constrain an organization's ability to manipulate its marketing mix.

6. **What is the marketing research process, and what are the elements of a good marketing plan? (pp. 377–384)**

- **Marketing research** (p. 378) is an ongoing process of gathering and analyzing market information to gauge changing market conditions that may suggest better ways and opportunities to provide services to customers.

- The marketing research process involves (1) defining the marketing need or opportunity, (2) collecting relevant data, (3) analyzing and interpreting the data, and (4) acting on research conclusions.

- A **marketing plan** (p. 380) is a written document that specifies marketing activities designed to achieve organizational objectives.

- Four elements emerge from all good marketing plans: (1) a clearly written marketing objective; (2) performance of a situational analysis; (3) selection of a target market; and (4) implementation, evaluation, and control of the marketing mix (the 4 Ps).

- Another type of situational analysis is looking at the 5 Cs of marketing: company, collaborators, customers, competitors, and climate.

7. **How do the buying decisions and marketing processes in B2B markets compare to those in the consumer market? (pp. 385–389)**

- In a **consumer market** (p. 385), buyers are households that purchase final consumer goods. In a **business-to-business (B2B) market** (p. 385), businesses buy from other businesses. There are many more B2B markets than consumer markets. In B2B markets, purchases are often undertaken by a small group of highly trained individuals who buy in large volumes and have a much closer relationship with marketers. B2B buyers are also more geographically concentrated and often avoid distributors.

- Consumers and businesses undertake the same five-step decision-making process when making a purchase. However, some of the influences that impact the business purchase are different.

- The marketing process remains the same for all markets: identify a need, undertake research to come up with a marketing plan, select a target market, implement and control the marketing mix, and always remember to nurture good customer relationships.

Key Terms

behavioral segmentation   (p. 384)

brand   (p. 371)

business-to-business (B2B) market   (p. 385)

consumer behavior   (p. 385)

consumer market   (p. 385)

customer relationship management (CRM)   (p. 366)

demographic segmentation   (p. 383)

environmental scanning   (p. 373)

focus group   (p. 378)

form utility   (p. 367)

geographic segmentation   (p. 383)

market research   (p. 378)

market segment   (p. 382)

market segmentation   (p. 382)

marketing   (p. 363)

marketing concept   (p. 365)

marketing environment   (p. 373)

marketing mix   (p. 370)

marketing objective   (p. 381)

marketing plan   (p. 380)

niche marketing   (p. 382)

ownership utility   (p. 367)

place (distribution)   (p. 371)

place utility   (p. 367)

positioning   (p. 382)

primary data   (p. 378)

product   (p. 363)

promotion   (p. 371)

psychographic segmentation   (p. 383)

secondary data   (p. 378)

target market   (p. 369)

task utility   (p. 367)

time utility   (p. 367)

value   (p. 367)

Self-Test

Multiple Choice   You can find the answers on the last page of this book.

1. **Which marketing era occurred during the Great Depression when manufacturers almost had to force consumers to purchase their products?**

   a. Production concept era

   b. Sales concept era

   c. Marketing concept era

   d. Customer relationship era

2. **When a car is purchased, form utility refers to the value customers receive from**

   a. owning the car.

   b. the styling and function of the automobile.

   c. ready availability and speed with which the dealer made the car available for purchase.

   d. close proximity to the car dealership.

3. **LinYee created a document that included a situational analysis and a discussion of the target market. LinYee's document is called**

   a. marketing research.

   b. a marketing mix.

   c. a marketing plan.

   d. marketing segmentation.

4. **Tenitia Reynolds opened a small community bookstore several years ago. Over time, she has developed a database that has captured her customers' purchases and reading preferences. Now, when a new book comes out, Tenetia e-mails those clients she thinks will enjoy the book based on their past purchases. Which part of the marketing process does Tenitia's actions reflect?**

   a. Conducting market research

   b. Identifying a market need

   c. Implementing the marketing mix

   d. Nurturing customer relationships

5. **Bill Wertz runs a transportation service that caters exclusively to the residents of retirement communities. Bill's business is taking advantage of which of the following marketing environments?**

   a. The competitive environment

   b. The sociocultural environment

   c. The technological environment

   d. The economic environment

6. **Which of the following is true of SWOT analysis?**

   a. The strengths and weaknesses of an organization stem from the external market environment.

   b. The opportunities and threats facing an organization stem from within the organization.

   c. An organization's strengths, weaknesses, opportunities, and threats depend on the selected marketing objective.

   d. Internal strengths reflect a company's core competencies.

7. **Market segmentation based on lifestyles, personality traits, motives, and values is called**

   a. geographic segmentation.

   b. demographic segmentation.

   c. psychographic segmentation.

   d. behavioral segmentation.

8. **Which of the following is a common criticism of marketing?**

   a. Price gouging

   b. Confusing and deceptive practices

   c. The production of shoddy or unsafe products

   d. All of the above

9. **Environmental scanning is**

   a. market segmentation according to geographic characteristics.

   b. market segmentation based on certain consumer behavior characteristics.

   c. the process of developing a unique marketing mix that best satisfies a target market.

   d. the process of surveying the marketing environment to assess external threats and opportunities.

10. **Which is NOT an example of primary data?**

    a. Census data

    b. Customer feedback

    c. Surveys and questionnaires

    d. Data collected through controlled experiments

Self-Test

1. The marketing mix consists of form, ownership, time, and place.
   ☐ True or ☐ False

2. A product is defined as any tangible good, service, or idea available for purchase.
   ☐ True or ☐ False

3. A market niche is a narrowly defined market segment.
   ☐ True or ☐ False

4. Employees benefit from successful marketing because new job opportunities are created as production expands to satisfy the growing demand for high-value products.
   ☐ True or ☐ False

5. The information gathered from a meeting with a group of potential customers to gain feedback on a product is considered secondary data.
   ☐ True or ☐ False

Critical Thinking Questions

1. Can you think of an example of how a specific organization (for-profit or not-for-profit) tried to establish a better customer relationship with you? What did the organization do? Was it effective? Why or why not? What recommendations would you make to these organizations?

2. Does ethical marketing make good business sense if it reduces profits?

3. Suppose you were hired by Apple to develop a marketing campaign for their latest iPhone. What would be the target market? List at least four characteristics and the corresponding market segment category that define the ideal customer. Repeat the exercise for a Toyota Prius and a vacation package to a luxury spa in Arizona.

4. Briefly compare the marketing environments for a pizza parlor and a flower shop. What do they have in common? What is different?

5. Think of the last major purchase you made. Discuss how sociocultural, personal, psychological, situational, and marketing mix influences impacted this purchase.

Team Time

Tobacco Wars

Divide into two teams, one to represent each group:

a. tobacco company employees; pro-cigarette advertising in magazines

b. antitobacco advertising activists

Scenario

Does a company have a fundamental right to market its products wherever it wishes? Cigarette advertising in magazines has been a topic of great controversy. The large tobacco companies provide publications with a great deal of revenue by purchasing expensive advertising space, but many antismoking groups and some magazine publishers are questioning the ethical nature of this. Antismoking groups argue that these ads appeal to children and glamorize smoking. Tobacco companies claim that they are merely making attractive advertisements with no intention of encouraging children to use their products. The European Union has banned tobacco advertisements from magazines entirely, and many U.S. publications have stopped selling ad space to tobacco companies. Do tobacco companies have the right to advertise their products as they see fit? Is it morally wrong to advertise a product that is known to cause health problems?

Process

Step 1. Collaborate with team members to discuss both sides of the issue, analyzing the arguments from each perspective.

Step 2. Prepare the most effective argument for your team's perspective, and think about counterpoints to arguments that the other team may raise.

Ethics and Corporate Social Responsibility

Subprime Mortgage Crisis

Subprime loans are home loans made available at temporarily reduced or zero interest rates that adjust or increase to much higher interest rates over time. These loans allowed many people to qualify for loans to buy expensive homes that they otherwise would not have been qualified to buy. Because of the long-standing expectation that home prices would continue to rise over time, as they have historically, and that recipients of subprime loans would be able to refinance their loans into traditional fixed-interest loans, many people thought these subprime loans would turn out to be great deals. However, when the price of homes began to fall in 2006 and 2007, it became difficult to refinance these subprime loans. At the same time, the temporary low interest rates on subprime loans were rapidly adjusting upward as specified in the loan contracts. Some people found themselves unable to make their monthly mortgage payments, and they couldn't sell their homes because they owed more than the homes were worth. Many people were forced into foreclosure and lost their homes. Foreclosures also hurt many banks, and this downturn has negatively affected the U.S. economy as a whole.

Questions

1. Do you feel that it is unethical to offer loans at low "teaser" rates that adjust upward rapidly over time to people who may not fully understand the consequences of increased house payments or allow people to purchase homes that they otherwise would not be able to afford?

2. As a bank owner, do you feel that the benefits of giving subprime loans outweigh their potential risks?

3. Do you think the banks that gave the loans should take responsibility for their payment?

4. Should the government provide assistance at taxpayers' expense to those people who received these subprime loans and now have trouble keeping their homes?

Web Exercises

1. Apple's Marketing Mix
Go to Apple's Web site and click on the iPad link. Describe Apple's marketing mix strategy: product, price, promotion, and place. How does Apple attempt to foster good customer relations? What marketing recommendations would you make to Apple?

2. SWOT Analysis
Search online for a SWOT analysis for a company such as Walmart, Target, or Best Buy. What strengths, weaknesses, opportunities, and threats would you add or delete? Why? How could the company take advantage of its strengths in terms of its marketing mix? How do the company's weaknesses impact its marketing mix? What market environmental forces do you think gave rise to its opportunities and its threats? How much control does the company have over its market environment? What recommendations would you make for the company? Why?

3. Organic Differences
Visit the Web sites of Trader Joe's and Whole Foods Market. Both companies are in the organic and health-conscious food industries. Compare the two Web sites. What marketing techniques does each site use? Do you think the companies are targeting the same type of customer? Why or why not?

4. Freebies: Long-Term Gain or Loss?
Visit Sephora's Web site. This company gives three free samples with every purchase from its Web site. Do you think that this strategy will be profitable for the company in the long run or will it cause it to lose money?

5. The Jeep Experience
The Jeep brand uses a nontraditional marketing approach by offering Jeep owners invitations to special events. Go to the Jeep Web site and research the events that this company offers to its customers. How effective do you think engaging customers in ongoing events is in getting them to be repeat buyers?

Web Case

For more on marketing new technology by targeting—and even predicting—customer needs, access the Chapter 12 Web case entitled "Focus on Apple, Inc.: Apple's Arrow Hits the Target" located in the End of Chapter Assignments section at my*biz*lab.com.

Video Case

For more on gathering and applying targeted marketing data to create a global brand, access the Chapter 12 Video Case entitled "Skechers USA: Marketing Cool Products to Cool People" located in the End of Chapter Assignments section at my*biz*lab.com.

13 Product Development and Pricing Strategies

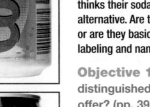

Developing Goods and Services

Evelyn and Juan each drink zero-calorie sodas made by Coca-Cola. Evelyn drinks Diet Coke, and Juan drinks Coke Zero. Each thinks their soda is better than the alternative. Are the products really different or are they basically the same with different labeling and names?

Objective 1 How is a product distinguished from a total product offer? (pp. 397–398)

Objective 2 What is product differentiation, and what role does it play in product development? (pp. 398–399)

Objective 3 What are the different classifications of consumer products and business-to-business products? (pp. 400–403)

Branding

Robin Green loves homemade bread. When her bread-making machine needed a new part, she contacted the manufacturer, and, surprisingly, was told that the company didn't actually make the machine and would not service it. The company had licensed its name to a different manufacturer! Robin felt let down by the brand she thought was so good. When you go shopping, how important is the brand of a product?

Objective 4 Why is branding beneficial to both buyers and sellers, and what are some branding strategies? (p. 403–411)

New Product Development

Jessica Smith wants to open a yoga studio in her neighborhood. She also wants to sell yoga supplies. The closest studio is 15 miles away and in poor condition, so she thinks her location would be great. What else does Jessica need to do to develop her studio? What steps are involved in the product development process?

Objective 5 What steps take place during new product development, and what is the product life cycle? (pp. 411–415)

Pricing Goods and Services

When Eugene Whitaker wanted to increase profits at the store he managed, he looked at sales data. He learned that people in his area purchasing items for newborn babies were more likely to buy premium-priced items as opposed to the more economical selections. How can the data help Eugene increase his profits? What are pricing objectives?

Objective 6 What are some pricing objectives, and how do they relate to the marketing mix? (pp. 415–417)

Objective 7 What are the major approaches to pricing strategy, and what are some pricing tactics used to launch a new product, impact price perceptions, and adjust prices? (pp. 417–421)

PEARSON **my*biz*lab**

Pricing Strategies and Objectives

You're a consultant who helps business clients price their products competitively. How well you help them succeed sets your bonus for the year. You have a full docket of appointments today. If everyone leaves happy, you'll have made the revenue to hit your bonus. Can you make it happen?

Objective 8 Test yourself using my*biz*lab.com to show that you understand the chapter objectives.

Developing Goods and Services pp. 397–403

Evelyn and her boyfriend, Juan, were ordering lunch. "I'll have a Diet Coke," Evelyn added after placing their sandwich orders, "and he'll have a Coke Zero," pointing to Juan. Evelyn laughed at Juan. "You know, they're both the same. I don't understand why you won't drink Diet Coke." "I've never liked Diet Coke. For some reason, Coke Zero tastes better. If you think they're the same, why don't you just drink Coke Zero?" he quipped back. "I couldn't imagine drinking anything besides Diet Coke. You can keep your Coke Zero, I have to have my Diet Coke."

Are Juan and Evelyn right? Are the two zero-calorie cola products produced by Coca-Cola the same, with just different labels and names, or are the products really different? Why would Coca-Cola make two very similar products? What are they trying to accomplish? ■

In Chapter 12, we saw that successful marketing requires identifying a need, using market research to determine a target market, and implementing a marketing plan that satisfies customers over the long run. This may sound easy, but it's not. Applying the marketing process is as much an art as a science. Making a high-quality product with a unique, properly promoted brand that consistently delivers value to customers at a fair price, when and where they want it, presents significant challenges to marketers all over the world.

This chapter focuses on two of the 4 Ps of the marketing mix: product and price. Chapter 14 will focus on the other two components—promotion and distribution (place). We begin with a focus on the product because all marketing begins with a product. Most businesses must regularly modify their product offerings or offer entirely new products to meet rapidly changing market conditions. The idea is to distinguish, or differentiate, your product from your competitors' products. To do this, a product should be seen not only in regard to its physical components but also in regard to the other attributes that make up the total product.

The Total Product Offer

What is the total product offer? As you have learned, a **product** is any good, service, or idea that might satisfy a want or a need. An Apple iPhone, a Toyota Sienna, a college education, E*Trade financial services, a doctor's advice, and even a Caribbean vacation package are all products. Consumers buy products for a number of tangible and intangible benefits. The **total product offer** consists of all the benefits associated with a good, a service, or an idea that impact a consumer's purchasing decision. For example, when you buy a car, you're not just buying a mode of transportation; you're also buying some intangible benefits, such as style or image. Marketers know this; when planning a total product

Colgate's MaxFresh toothpaste with Breath Strips is just one way Colgate tries to differentiate its product from the many other varieties in the Colgate family as well as from other brands of toothpaste on the market.

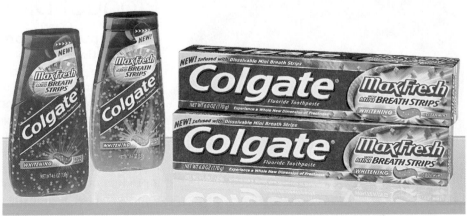

offering, they think about products on three levels: the *core product*, the *actual product*, and the *augmented product*. Each level adds more value to a product.

What is the core product?

Ultimately, a product must satisfy a basic need or want. The **core product** provides the core benefit or service that satisfies the basic need or want that motivates a consumer's purchase. For a car, that core benefit is the convenient transportation it provides. For a soft drink, it's the thirst-quenching capability. For a camera, it's the ability to capture and share memories. Notice that the core product is intangible. You can't touch it. This is because the core product is the basic *benefit* the product provides. Companies use the benefits of their products to lure customers. That is why Toyota uses "Moving Forward" as an advertising slogan. Similarly, Sprite uses "Obey Your Thirst," and camera conglomerate Kodak once used "Share a Moment, Share a Life" to draw in customers.

What is the actual product?

Of course, a product must be developed to provide the core benefit or service desired. The **actual product** is the tangible aspect of the purchase that you can touch, see, hear, smell, or taste. It provides core benefits when it is used. Consumers often assess the tangible benefits of actual products by comparing brands, quality (often associated with a brand's reputation), features, styling, or packaging. For a car, the actual product is the automobile itself. The benefits of an automobile could be numerous safety features, leather seats, or an in-car entertainment system. For a soft drink, the actual product might provide a refreshing taste, a desirable color, or a pleasant aroma. The product could even provide the "pick-me-up" caffeine buzz that consumers are looking for when they purchase some sodas. For a camera, the actual product may provide features such as an LCD screen or a lightweight design.

What is the augmented product?

The **augmented product** consists of the core product and the actual product *plus* other real or perceived benefits that provide additional value to a customer's purchase. These benefits might include customer service and support, delivery, installation, a warranty, or favorable credit terms. The value-enhancing elements of an actual product are an important part of the total product offering because they help provide a more satisfying customer experience. For a product like a car, augmented benefits might include a reasonable price, an easy payment plan, a 10-year warranty, or just the security of owning a brand-new car.

▼ **Figure 13.1** summarizes the three levels of a product. When developing products, marketers must begin with a basic customer need or want to be satisfied by a product. Then marketers develop an actual product to satisfy that need for targeted customers. Successful product developers then augment the product to create a total product offering that provides a benefit package superior to that of the competition. This is the essence of successful *product differentiation*, which we'll discuss next.

▼ **Figure 13.1**
The Three Levels of a Product
The three levels of a product define the benefits to be derived from a total product offering.

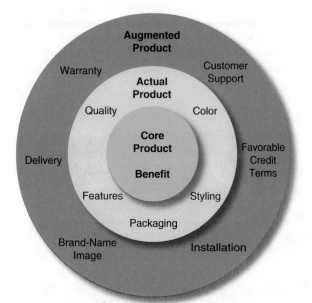

Product Differentiation

How important is product differentiation?

Product differentiation is the process of distinguishing a product from its competition in real or perceived terms to attract customers. A company can distinguish a product from its competitors by establishing concrete or intangible differences among similar products. For example, Southwest Airlines began to set itself apart from other airlines with low-cost fares and minimum hassle. It has continued to distinguish itself with a "bags fly free" campaign. Product differentiation is critical for a product's success. If a product doesn't possess qualities that make it stand out, customers will not be motivated to buy that product in lieu of a competitor's product.

How does consumer input affect product development? Companies rely on customer input and feedback to help shape their products. Listening to customers and incorporating their suggestions are effective ways to foster good customer relationships, which is a critical component in establishing repeat business and long-term success. In fact, listening to customers is one of the most important elements of sound customer relationship management. You have to know what your customers want to tailor a product offering that best satisfies their needs. As we discussed in Chapter 12, many companies have found that social media sites, such as Facebook, Twitter, and Yelp, are great ways for companies to know what is on their customer's minds—not only about their own products but about competitors' products as well, which can be equally informative. Consumer input often provides information that prompts companies to segment a large market and focus on narrowly defined, targeted customers. For example, a breakfast cereal company might find that most consumers buy its cereal because it is high in fiber. That company can differentiate its product from competing products by labeling the cereal "a good source of fiber" and target the product to health-conscious adults.

Companies might also use consumer input to differentiate their products by improving an existing product or creating an entirely new product. SC Johnson, the makers of cleaning products like Windex, Pledge, and Fantastik, found consumers were using a competing product, Lysol Disinfectant Spray, because they thought the spray killed bacteria in the air, when in fact the spray kills bacteria only on surfaces. SC Johnson used this information to create a new product, Oust Air Sanitizer, and differentiated it from competing products by stating that Oust Air Sanitizer is different because "it kills odor-causing bacteria in the air. Most disinfectant sprays are designed to kill bacteria on surfaces only."[1] Product differentiation is therefore the result of carefully segmenting markets into clearly defined targeted customers and developing a variety of total product offerings that best meet these varying customer needs—and doing it better than the competition.

Product Lines and the Product Mix

What are a product line and a product mix? Customer feedback guides product development and product differentiation. It also gives rise to the creation of a **product line**, a group of similar products marketed to one general market. A **product mix** is the combination of all product lines offered for sale by a company. For example, Coca-Cola has many product lines, including its soft drinks, energy drinks, and sports drinks, which collectively make up its product mix. Honda offers a full line of automotive products, which can be broken down into various product lines, including its cars, minivans, trucks, sport utility vehicles (SUVs), motorcycles, and all-terrain vehicles (ATVs), as well as jets, outboard motors, power equipment, and all related parts and accessories. Honda also offers a financial-services product line to dealers and their customers for the purchase or lease of Honda vehicles. Honda is involved in several other nonautomotive business activities as well. One of these product lines is the manufacture and sale of environmentally friendly home energy devices.[2] All of Honda's combined activities constitute its product mix.

Does it matter how many products are in a product line? An important marketing decision involves product line length. *Product line length* is the number of items in any given product line. Product line length is determined by how the addition or removal of items from a product line affects a company's profits. For example, the Coca-Cola Company has found it very profitable to pursue a long product line length given the huge variety of drinks it offers for sale. Although Coke is the biggest-selling soft drink in history, the company still offers 450 different types of beverages to satisfy the specific tastes of the 1.6 billion customers worldwide it serves each day.[3] Consumers who like Coke but desire a low-calorie alternative can purchase Diet Coke or Coke Zero. Consumers who want a low-calorie soda without caffeine can purchase Caffeine-Free Diet Coke. Those who do not want a soft drink can choose from the thousands of Coca-Cola beverage offerings, including fruit juice drinks, waters, sports and energy drinks, teas and coffees, and milk and soy-based beverages that appeal to the various wants and needs of the company's global consumer base.[4]

Product mix width refers to the number of different product lines a company offers. This, too, is determined by profitability. GE has hundreds of product lines, ranging from light bulbs and home appliances to jet engines and medical machinery.[5] GE aims to achieve maximum profitability by stretching its capabilities across multiple markets. Product line length and product mix width are the result of companies striving to offer differentiated products to satisfy targeted customers.

Consumer and B2B Products

What's the difference between consumer products and B2B products? In Chapter 12 we explored the differences between consumer markets and B2B markets; similarly, there are differences between **consumer products**, goods and services purchased by households for personal consumption, and **business-to-business (B2B) products** (sometimes called *industrial products*), goods and services that are purchased by businesses for further processing or resale or for use in facilitating business operations. As you might expect, consumer products are traded in consumer markets, and B2B products are traded in B2B markets.

Most products can be classified as either consumer products or B2B products. The distinction depends on their use. For example, if a homeowner purchases a lawn mower for personal use, then it would be a consumer product. If a landscaper purchases the same lawn mower but uses it in his business, then it would be a B2B product.

It's convenient for marketers to classify various consumer and B2B products differently because the buying behavior in these two categories is different. This behavior impacts how the marketer prices, promotes, and distributes the product. The shopping patterns of consumers help to establish classifications of consumer products: convenience, shopping, specialty, and unsought. Industrial products are classified by how they are used in the production of other goods, including equipment; maintenance, repair, and operating (MRO) products; raw and processed materials; component parts; and specialized professional services. Each of these types of products has unique pricing, promotion, and distribution strategies.

Consumer Product Classifications

What are the different consumer product classifications? Consumer products can be divided into four categories:

- Convenience goods and services
- Shopping goods and services
- Specialty goods and services
- Unsought goods and services

What constitutes a convenience product? Those products that customers purchase frequently, immediately, and effortlessly are considered **convenience goods and services.** Because they are normally used or consumed quickly, they are also referred to as *nondurable goods.* Gum, soap, tobacco, and newspapers are all considered convenience goods, as are common grocery items like ketchup and milk. A car wash is an example of a convenience service. These purchases are usually based on habitual behavior, meaning consumers routinely purchase a particular brand with which they're familiar and comfortable. Convenience goods and services are relatively low-priced items. They're usually promoted through brand awareness and image (which we'll discuss shortly) and are widely distributed through convenience stores or local grocery stores. Consumers make purchasing decisions for these goods based on the convenience of location and brand-name image.

What is the classification for those products that are purchased less frequently?

Some products require more effort and time for comparison and are typically purchased less frequently than consumer goods. These products are referred to as **shopping goods and services.** Consumers usually base their comparison on attributes such as suitability, quality, price, and style. Shopping goods are typically *durable goods*—goods that can be used repeatedly over a long period of time. Examples of shopping goods include clothes, shoes, televisions, cameras, stereos, bicycles, lawn mowers, furniture, and major appliances. These products are often sold at shopping centers that allow for easy comparison between stores, such as Best Buy, Circuit City, Sears, Home Depot, Kohl's, and Lowe's. Examples of shopping services include hotels and airline and other travel services. Because consumers carefully compare brands and models, companies that sell shopping services compete on the basis of price, quality, and brand-name image.

What if a consumer is very particular about the type of product he or she wants?

Sometimes buyers are willing to spend a considerable amount of time and effort searching for particular brands or styles. Customers know exactly what they want, and they will not accept substitutes. These types of unique or specialized products are **specialty goods and services.** Examples of specialty goods and services include Ferrari sports cars, Rolex watches, high-fashion designer clothing, and the services of prestigious medical and legal experts. Because there are no suitable substitutes, buyers of specialty products do not comparison shop. They already know the specific good or service they want, and they are willing to seek it out regardless of its price and location. Businesses that successfully differentiate their products to the point that they are considered specialty goods or services can set a much higher price than similar products that are considered shopping goods or services.

What about products that are purchased only when a special need arises?

Unsought goods and services are products buyers don't usually think about buying, don't know exist, or buy only when a specific problem arises. We don't usually think about or want to think about buying some products, such as life insurance or cemetery plots. These goods and services require a lot of persuasive advertising and personal selling to encourage consumers to buy products that will help them prepare for life's uncertainties. Other unsought goods and services are products that are completely new to consumers. New and innovative products, such as pharmaceutical drugs, must be introduced to consumers through promotional advertising before consumers can actively seek out these products. Emergency medical services and automobile repairs are also unsought purchases where prepurchase planning is rarely considered. In these cases, resolving the immediate problem is more important than comparison shopping

Washers, dryers, and other large appliances are examples of shopping or durable goods.

Cemetery plots and Life Insurance are examples of unsought goods and services.

based on price or other features. Notice that sales of unsought products require personal selling or promotional advertising, and price may not be an important consideration if the good or the service is urgently needed.

B2B Classifications

What are the different B2B product classifications? B2B products can be divided into five categories:

- Equipment
- MRO products
- Raw and processed materials
- Component parts
- Specialized professional services

Each of these types of products has unique pricing, promotion, and distribution strategies.

What is considered equipment? *Equipment*, also known as *installations* or *capital items*, includes all the physical facilities of a business, such as factories, warehouses, and office buildings; heavy equipment (often referred to as *production goods*); and other less costly equipment, such as computers, printers, and copiers (often referred to as *support goods*). Many of these capital items are expensive, unique, and intended to last for a long time; therefore, the acquisition process may require special negotiations involving top management and stretch out over many months or even years. Marketers frequently offer a variety of services to help sell this type of equipment, including financial assistance with the purchase, maintenance, and repairs after the sale.

How do you classify operating supplies? Products that facilitate production and operations but do not become a part of the finished product are classified as *MRO products*. These products include paper, pens, cleaning materials, tools, and machine lubricants. They are often marketed based on convenience, just like consumer convenience goods and services.

How are unprocessed products that are used to make other products classified? Unprocessed materials that are sold in their original form before being processed for use in other products, such as crops, crude oil, iron ore, and logs, are examples of *raw and processed materials*. These products are the basic inputs that become part of a finished good. Many raw products and some processed farm products, such as eggs or butter, go into the production of numerous grocery items. Raw materials like wood and processed materials like steel are used to make a variety of products, such as buildings or bridges. Raw and processed materials are usually purchased in large quantities at prices that are based on the quality of the materials.

How are parts used in an assembly process classified? *Component parts* are assembled portions of the finished product. Examples include brakes, engines, transmissions, and steering columns for a car or lumber, cement, drywall, and electrical wire for a house. Businesses purchasing component parts make their decisions based on quality and brand-name recognition because, ultimately, the quality of a business's product will be based on the quality of its component parts.

Do specialized services have a separate classification? Businesses often require the use of services, just as individuals do. *Specialized professional services* help support a firm's operations. They include advertising; management consulting; and legal, accounting, and IT services. Managers compare the costs and the quality of these specialized services with their in-house operations before deciding whether to *outsource* these activities. For example, a local grocery store owner might assess his or her ability to handle the business's financial records before hiring an outside accounting firm.

Considering the variety of types and classifications of products, it's clear that product development is an exciting yet challenging area of business. Remember Evelyn and Juan? Evelyn loved Diet Coke, and Juan preferred Coke Zero. Both products are zero-calorie cola-flavored soft drinks manufactured by the same company, but the two sodas have different flavors, marketing strategies, and targeted demographics. Coca-Cola came up with an idea to differentiate Diet Coke to appeal more to men and produced Coke Zero.[6] The can is darker to convey a bigger flavor, and ads for the beverage are male dominated, with plots built around sports like auto racing. The Web site for Coke Zero also includes a NASCAR racing game. Coke Zero shows it is important to differentiate products not only from their competitors but also to meet the needs of a broader market. As Coca-Cola showed with the development of Coke Zero, new product development can lead to great success. The key is considering and understanding the many complex factors involved in creating a differentiated product. ■

Branding pp. 403–411

Robin Green loves homemade bread and has used her bread-making machine a lot. After baking many loaves of her favorite bread, honey whole wheat, the paddles started to slip and needed to be replaced. To her surprise, when she contacted the manufacturer, she was told that the company didn't make such products nor did it service them. In fact, the company had licensed its brand name to a completely different manufacturer! The trust Robin had in this company, and its products, was tainted. Robin, like so many of us, bought a product based on the inherent trust she had in a brand name to deliver a quality product, but she didn't get quite what she expected. ■

What are the benefits of a brand? Why are some brands perceived to be better than others? How is brand loyalty built and kept? These questions are important components of another complex aspect of product development—branding. In this section, we'll discuss branding, beginning with its benefits.

Branding Benefits

What are the benefits of branding? Branding is one of the most important tools of product differentiation, and it benefits both buyers and sellers. A *brand* is a name, a term, a symbol, or a design that distinguishes a company and its products from all others. For buyers, well-recognized brands reduce the shopping time necessary to find the quality and consistency they desire in a product.

Branding also reduces the risks involved in some purchases for which buyers are unable to objectively determine quality. We rely on established brands to consistently deliver an expected level of quality. Comparing product descriptions and ingredients takes a lot longer than simply picking up your favorite brand. Consumers are also able to express themselves by buying brand names with which they wish to be identified. For example, some buyers seek prestige by buying exclusive brands, such as Mercedes-Benz, Rolex, or Dom Pérignon, or "cool" things by buying trendy items, such as UGG boots.

Branding also helps sellers define special qualities of their products, thus promoting repeat purchases as well as new sales at higher prices. Because certain brands, such as those from Kraft, are associated with quality and value, the companies with these brands are able to introduce new products quickly and at a relatively low cost. In doing so, they add length to their product lines, widen their product mix, and enhance their profitability. Marketing a product using the same brand name but in a different product category is known as **brand extension.** Because Kraft has a wide diversity in its product mix, the company can market its brand to just about any person in the world. Kraft's product line has something for everyone, whether you're "watching your weight or preparing to celebrate, grabbing a quick bite or sitting down to family night, we pour our hearts into creating foods that are wholesome and delicious."[7]

Well-branded companies are generally recognizable by a trademark. A **trademark,** a legally protected brand, can also benefit sellers by distinguishing them from competitors' *knockoff brands*, which are illegal copies or cheap imitations of another product.

Can a company's trademark legally be put on a different company's product? **Brand licensing** is an agreement between the owner of a brand and another company or individual who pays a royalty to use the brand in association with a new product, such as the bread-making machine in our opening story. Brand owners use licensing to extend a trademark or character onto different products. The Walt Disney Company is a good example. Characters such as Mickey Mouse appear on toys, books, and clothing that are not made by Disney. The NFL, the National Basketball Association (NBA), NASCAR, and Major League Baseball are also big licensors and leading retail sellers of licensed products.

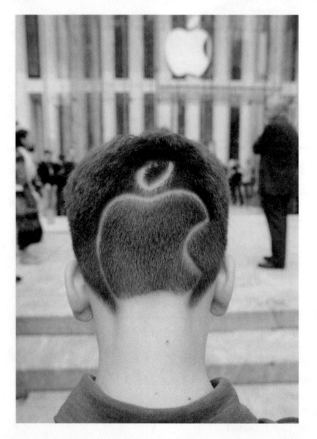

One benefit of branding for sellers is brand loyalty, such as that displayed by many Mac users for Apple products.

How does a logo help to build a brand? No doubt you can describe the logo for Nike, Mercedes Benz, Ralph Lauren, Apple, and Yahoo! These companies are easily recognized by their logos. Logos are an important element of a company's identity. They help make a company stand out from the competition, build trust and confidence about the brand, and increase customer loyalty. A good logo makes it easy for customers to associate products with a company's standard of quality, reliability, or service. When you are miles away from home and see McDonald's "golden arches" rising above the horizon, you know exactly the type and quality of food you'll be served if you go there. Logos are applied in a variety of places to help build brand image—Web sites, corporate communications, storefronts, office buildings, product labels (or the product itself), and advertising and promotional signage.

Brand Loyalty and Brand Equity

What is brand loyalty? Another major benefit of branding for sellers is the creation of **brand loyalty,** the degree to which customers consistently prefer one brand to other brands. In fact, companies hope that customers not only recognize (*brand recognition*) and then prefer (*brand preference*) but also eventually insist (*brand insistence*) on their brands. Brand insistence is the highest degree of brand loyalty. It can turn a product into a specialty good or service that can command a much higher price. Ultimately, the degree of brand loyalty depends on satisfied customers. Perhaps the most significant contemporary example of brand loyalty is the fervent devotion of many Mac users to Apple and its products.

What is brand equity? Strong brand loyalty contributes to **brand equity,** the overall value of a brand's strength in the market. Perceptions of quality contribute significantly to brand equity. Quality products are not only free from defects but also consistently perform at high levels. For example, many customers will purchase Levi jeans because of the brand's high quality and durability. This adds significantly to Levi's brand equity. *Interbrand* and *BusinessWeek* annually rank the top 100 brands in the world based on their brand equity.

Perceptions of *brand awareness* and *brand association* also contribute to brand equity. **Brand awareness** refers to the extent to which a particular brand name is familiar within a particular product category. Companies participate in mass advertising as a way to help their product's brand name become synonymous with the actual name of the product. For example, what brand first comes to mind when you think of diapers? If it's Pampers, then P&G has succeeded in its brand awareness campaigns for its disposable diapers.

Brand association involves connecting a brand with other positive attributes, including image, product features, usage situations, organizational associations, brand personality, and symbols. Hiring celebrities to endorse a product can be an effective tool for nurturing brand associations. Nike was so successful with Michael Jordan's endorsement that it launched its Air Jordan line of sport shoes. Nike later joined forces with Tiger Woods to enter the golf category with its apparel, equipment, and accessories and continued to do so throughout the Tiger Woods infidelity scandal because of the impact Woods has had on the Nike Golf brand. Disney has been successful in associating its brand with wholesome family values. The images invoked by symbols and slogans can also be very powerful brand association techniques.

What does a brand manager do? Branding has become such an important part of marketing that businesses have created brand manager (or product manager) positions within their organizations. A *brand manager* is responsible for managing the marketing mix for a specific product or product line. Brand managers attempt to increase a product's perceived value to customers to increase brand equity. Brand managers are also responsible for new product development.

Companies understand the passion of NASCAR fans, so they display their logos on cars and drivers' jumpsuits to associate their brand with the sport.

Branding Strategies

What strategies are employed in branding products? Branding strategies are important to building brand equity. There are several different branding strategies, and which one marketers choose to use is based on how they want to define their products. Is the brand meant to convey value and thriftiness or prestige and luxury? A different branding strategy would be chosen for each of these objectives. Similarly, branding strategies can differ depending on the target audience (young, old, male, female, etc.). Six types of brands emerge from branding strategy (see ▼ **Figure 13.2**):

- Manufacturer's brands
- Family brands

▼ **Figure 13.2**
Branding Strategies

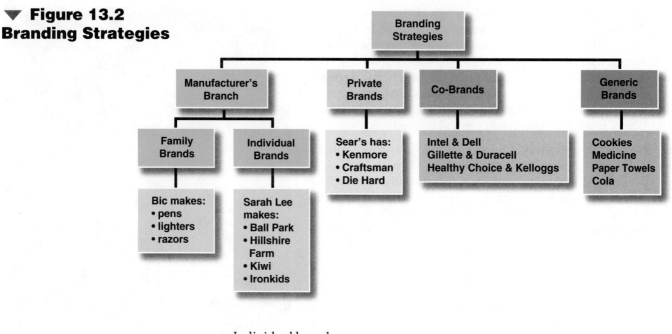

- Individual brands
- Private brands
- Co-brands
- Generic brands

What is a manufacturer's brand? A **manufacturer's brand** is a brand created by producers. Manufacturer's brands are also known as *national brands*, even though they may be distributed globally. Well-known brands, such as Levi's, Dell, Ford, IBM, McDonald's, and Bank of America, are considered manufacturer's brands. Manufacturers spend a lot of money creating, promoting, and building their brands. There are two types of manufacturer's brands: *family brands* and *individual brands*.

What is a family brand? A **family brand** is a brand that markets several different products under the same brand name. Sony home and portable electronics, Keebler snack food products, Kodak photo and film offerings, and Fisher-Price toys are examples of companies that have family brands. Consumers are more likely to try new products from an established brand that is familiar and trusted. These established companies are therefore able to penetrate new markets successfully with their brand names. Bic, most known for its disposable ink pens, successfully added to its family brand when it added Bic disposable razors and Bic lighters to its family brand. Family brands have the advantages of brand awareness and brand association. This affiliation can foster more brand loyalty and still greater brand extension. However, an unsuccessful extension can dilute an established brand name or even create a negative brand image.

What is an individual brand? An **individual brand** is a brand assigned to each product within a company's product mix. For example, Sara Lee uses individual brands among its many food, beverage, household, and personal care products. Many of these brands may be familiar to you: Ball Park hotdogs, Iron Kids bread, Hillshire Farm meat products, Prodent toothpaste, Kiwi shoe polish, and, of course, Sara Lee's frozen and packaged foods. A major advantage of individual branding is that if a new product fails, it won't damage the image of the other products.

What is a private brand? A **private brand** is a brand created by a distributor, or a middleman. These middlemen can be wholesalers, dealers, or retail stores. As a result, private brands are also called *distributor*, *wholesaler*, *dealer*, *store*, or *retail brands*. The key characteristic of a private brand is that the manufacturer is not

Retailers and Their Private Brand Labels[8]

Rank	Title	Private Brand Labels	2009 Total Sales
1.	Walmart	Equate, Sam's Choice, Great Value	$304,939,000,000
2.	Kroger	Private Selection, Comforts, Kroger	$76,733,000,000
3.	Target	Archer Farms, Market Pantry, Sutton & Dodge	$63,435,000,000
4.	Walgreens	Walgreens, Deerfield Farms	$63,335,000,000
5.	The Home Depot	Hampton	$59,176,000,000
6.	Costco	Kirkland Signature	$56,548,000,000
7.	CVS Caremark	CVS, Fieldbrook Farms	$55,355,000,000
8.	Lowe's	Kobalt	$47,220,000,000
9.	Sears Holdings (includes Kmart)	Craftsman, Kenmore, Joe Boxer, Route 66	$44,043,000,000
10.	Best Buy	Insignia, Dynex, Geek Squad	$37,314,000,000

identified on the product. Examples include Sears's line of DieHard batteries, Kenmore appliances, and Craftsman tools. These products are made by other well-known and recognized manufacturers but are sold under the private brand label. Often, the manufacturer makes special products just for the private brand. Walmart (Equate, Sam's Choice), Whole Foods (365), Kohl's (Croft & Barrow, Apt. 9), and RadioShack (Realistic, Enercell) also have their own private brands. The advantage of private branding is that an individual distributor has more control over a product's price and promotion. The competition—sometimes called the "battle of the brands"—is heating up between manufacturer's brands and private brands, as many private brands have gained national recognition.

What is a co-brand? A **co-brand** is using one or more brands affiliated with a single product. Examples include Intel and Dell, AT&T Universal MasterCard, Healthy Choice Cereal by Kellogg's, and Gillette M3 Power shaving equipment with Duracell batteries. The objective is to combine the prestige of two brands to increase the price consumers are willing to pay.

Co-branding is also used to foster brand loyalty for one product while extending loyalty to the contributing product, such as Campbell's affiliating its soup with the American Breast Cancer Association.

What is a generic brand? A **generic brand** is a product that has no brand at all. The product's contents are frequently identified by black stenciled lettering on white packages. A generic brand may mimic a branded product, but the generic brand is not associated with the branded product's manufacturer. For example, a generic brand of cream-filled sandwich cookies may look like Oreo cookies, but they are not associated with Nabisco cookies. Generic brands are typically lower in price and not advertised. Yet generic products are often made by the same manufacturer as the name brands; in this way, the manufacturer can capture both cost-conscious and brand loyal customers. Often consumers will buy generic brands for those products they use routinely and do not have a brand preference or if they understand that the product is exactly the same, such as generic drugs.

Campbell's Soup teaming up with the American Breast Cancer Association is an example of how two organizations can come together to form a co-brand.

BizChat

Brand You: Creating a Personal Brand

What do Britney Spears, Lady Gaga, and Donald Trump have in common? They all are their own brands. Each celebrity has a unique image that is as much of a brand as are Nike, Apple, and Starbucks. But celebrities are not the only ones who can create a personal brand. Everyone, including you, can create a personal brand. Personal branding is the process by which we market ourselves to others. If we develop our personal brand carefully, it can build brand equity similar to well-known corporate brands.

Business management guru Tom Peters actually coined the phrase *personal branding*. "We are CEOs of our own companies: Me Inc.," he writes. "To be in business today,

our most important job is to be head marketer for the brand called You. It's that simple—and that hard. And that inescapable."[9] Enhancing your own personal brand is important to your success; it's what will give you a competitive edge in almost everything you do.

There are a variety of ways you can create your own personal brand, and many of them are similar to the ways companies promote their own brands. For example, you can start by using social media tools, such as Facebook, LinkedIn, and Twitter. Make sure your brand image is consistent and professional with all these tools. Write a blog or have a Web site with your own name in the title or domain name and establish your brand in your e-mail address by using something like firstname.lastname@email.com. Take charge of your brand. It's the first step you can take toward your own success.

For more information and discussion questions about this topic, check out the BizChat feature on my*biz*lab.com.

Packaging

How does packaging affect a brand? How a product is packaged sends a message about a product and its brand. Think about what makes you buy the ketchup bottle that stands on its lid or single-sized serving packages of tuna. Packaging serves to contain and protect the product, facilitate use, and promote the product. Coca-Cola rolled out to select markets a new design of its two-liter bottle. The design altered the straight wall shape of the plastic bottle to a shape that mimics the iconic contour style of its glass bottles. That contoured shape was initially created in 1915 to differentiate Coke from its competitors. It was such a success that the bottle was trademarked in 1977. Effective packaging is crucial to the success of a product because customers typically see the packaging before they see the product.

How does packaging protect a product? Most products are handled several times as they are distributed from the manufacturing site to the final consumer. Many of these products need to be protected from heat, cold, light, dirt, spoilage, infestation, and many other adverse conditions. Packaging is intended to preserve and protect a product. This is the most obvious purpose of packaging. Packaging must also protect a product from tampering. Many products, such as ibuprofen or infant formula, need to be tamperproof and must meet the minimum requirements set by the FDA. The Consumer Product Safety Commission (CPSC) has also established guidelines concerning packaging that require that a manufacturer must be able to determine the exact source of the product and its components. Such labeling helps trace defects and contaminations (such as *E. coli* bacteria) to the source for a more expedient remedy.

Why is convenient packaging so important? Packaging should facilitate use and convenience. Sellers want packages that are easy to ship, store, and stock on shelves. More importantly, consumers want products that handle easily, open and reseal, store conveniently, and, for perishable items, have a long shelf life. We dislike bulky, heavy packages that are difficult to handle and open. Packages that don't reseal or result in easy spoilage are also unpopular, which is why many frozen food packages now come with resealable zipper tops.

Packages that are convenient to use and also physically attractive sell better. Heinz ketchup experienced a significant increase in sales when it began offering ketchup in a squeezable bottle. It has recently introduced a dual-function package to give users the choice of dipping or squeezing when they are on the go. Campbell's soup has responded to changing consumer tastes and preferences for greater convenience by offering pull-top lids, sippable soups, microwave soup lines, and ready-to-serve soups. Campbell's Soup at Hand line has expanded to 13 varieties, and the microwave bowl soup line now offers 10 varieties. Many sellers also offer different-sized packages dependent on frequency of use. For example, salt, sugar, and breakfast cereal packages come in many different sizes for added convenience.

How does packaging help promote a product?

Getting the consumer to notice a product and choose it from among many products on crowded shelves is extremely important. The package design, shape, color, and texture all influence buyers' perceptions and buying behavior. Luxury items, such as jewelry or high-end cosmetics, typically package their products to create an impression of extravagance, sophistication, and exclusiveness. The little blue box from Tiffany & Co. is an example of an iconic package that promotes both a brand and a lifestyle. The robin's-egg blue jewelry box has been a symbol of elegance and excitement since it was introduced in 1837. The packaging is so desirable that some consumers simply want to buy the box. However, it is an ironclad rule of the company that no Tiffany & Co. blue box can leave the store unless it encloses a purchased item.[10]

What about the environment?

A growing concern among many consumers is whether a product and its package are environmentally sound. Landfills contain discarded products and packaging materials, which often are not biodegradable. Some packaging can be considered wasteful and environmentally unfriendly. For example, some people have been critical of the excessive and wasteful packaging of products, such as Oscar Mayer's Lunchables. Consequently, many companies are going green. Increased effort is being placed on reusing and recycling and in developing new products that are eco-friendly, such as the SunChips compostable bag that is designed to fully break down in 14 weeks when placed in a hot, active compost bin. Puma is another company that has developed a new eco-friendly packaging concept for its shoes. Instead of the traditional cardboard shoebox that has been criticized as wasteful, Puma is packaging its shoes in cardboard frames wrapped in reusable shoe bags. This repackaging saves nearly 8,500 tons of paper and reduces the resources required for production and transportation.[11] Even companies that are selling services are trying to go green. For example, the Fairmont Hotels & Resorts luxury chain is advertising green luxury packages. With the help of the World Wildlife Fund (WWF), Fairmont hopes to reduce its impact on climate change by using renewable energy resources and environmentally friendly business practices.[12]

The Heinz "top-down" ketchup bottle is an example of an innovative packaging solution for the food service industry.

The Tiffany Blue color is used on Tiffany & Co. boxes, catalogues, shopping bags, brochures, and advertising to promote the idea of luxury and sophistication associated with the company and its products.

On Target *and* Off the Mark
Q-tips Brand Cotton Swabs

Branding acts as a tool to help differentiate one product from other similar products. However, what happens when the brand itself becomes the category? When was the last time you purchased a box of cotton swabs? How about Q-tips? Well if you bought cotton swabs that didn't display the brand name Q-tips, then you didn't buy Q-tips, but you probably still referred to them as Q-tips. The Q-tips brand, a genericized trademark, is a trademark or brand name that has become synonymous with a general class of product or service. Someone shopping for Q-tips may actually buy another brand of cotton swabs. The competitor's price and/or packaging could convince a consumer to choose that particular brand over the Q-tips brand. All companies want to guard against their brand name becoming a generic description for a product category because then their brand name becomes public property, which means the owner loses all rights to it! This happened to not only Q-tips but also *Kleenex, Xerox, aspirin, escalator, shredded wheat, kerosene, Jell-O, Band-Aid,* and *Thermos.* If these companies trademarked their brand names, they could have prevented them from becoming public property and preserved their product differentiation.

PepsiCo is communicating the benefits of recycling aluminum cans through its "Have we met before?" campaign. Each can displays recycling facts and messages.

The Importance of Labels

What does the government have to say about product labels? Labeling serves two functions: inform and persuade. The government has initiated several acts that regulate what must go on a product's label. The Fair Packaging and Labeling Act of 1966 requires that companies communicate specific information about their products to consumers. The Act requires that all labels include the name and place of business of the manufacturer, the packer, or the distributor and the net quantity of the contents.

Other government attempts to make labels more useful for consumers to evaluate products include the Nutrition Labeling and Education Act of 1990. This legislation requires that all nutrient content claims, such as high-fiber or low-fat, and health claims be consistent with agency regulations. Clearly, labels should inform consumers about a product, its uses, and any safety concerns. However, labels can be confusing and misleading. For example, the FDA criticized General Food's claims that Cheerios, the best-selling cereal in the world, lowers cholesterol and treats heart disease.[13] Now, instead of boasting that Cheerios "lowers cholesterol by 4% in 6 weeks," the box now announces that the cereal, "can help lower cholesterol." Businesses that wish to foster good customer relationships must be careful to label their products ethically.

Why is labeling important to establishing a brand image? Labels are also used to promote and persuade customers to buy a product. Labels can educate consumers of the features and other benefits of a product. Many companies label their products with their brand logo to distinguish their products from their competitors' products. If a label comes to represent consistent quality and dependability, then the label can perpetuate a positive brand-name image.

How are digital media and the Internet affecting branding strategies? With the Internet and its capabilities being so widespread, many companies are incorporating digital media into their branding strategies. Initially, that meant creating a Web site, but companies are now creating blogs, providing online customer chats, and placing ads in Google searches as a means to build their brands. In addition, the proliferation of social-networking sites (such as Facebook and Twitter) and geolocation applications (such as Foursquare and Gowalla) has started to cause marketing managers to rethink their strategies. Companies such as Zagats and HBO are working with Foursquare to incorporate their products into the location-based mobile application that lets users compete for points as they frequent bars, restaurants, and other sites. For example, Zagats, the restaurant rating guide, is using Twitter and placing tips and recommendations into Foursquare. Zagats is also using a new technology, called "augmented reality," in its mobile app Zagat To Go 3.0. The iPhone application merges restaurant ratings and reviews with the camera view and displays the information in the camera lens.

As media has changed over time, so have branding techniques and strategies. This new set of technology has caused some companies to rethink, redefine, and replace their prior branding practices.

Robin Green was disappointed that the brand that she chose for its quality was not at all what she bought. The next time Robin needs to buy an appliance, it most likely won't be from the same manufacturer. And, she'll be sure to check out the servicing and warranty information before purchasing anything. Branding is important for both the buyer and the seller. Making products memorable and appealing is a priority for all companies, and branding plays an important role in achieving this goal. ■

New Product Development pp. 411–415

Jessica Smith had a dream—to open a yoga studio in her hometown. At the time, the closest studio was 15 miles away and terribly rundown. Jessica formerly taught classes there but quit because it was so poorly run and maintained. There weren't enough mats for students, the locker rooms were tiny, and the paint on the walls was peeling off. So Jessica decided it was time to open her own studio. Not only did she want to teach classes, but she also wanted to sell yoga equipment. How does Jessica go about creating her new product? And what happens to the product after it's been created? ■

Developing a new product takes a lot of research and planning. It starts with an idea, like Jessica's idea to open a yoga studio, and then must go through testing, analysis, and more testing before it becomes a reality. In this section, we'll look at how products are developed and the path a product takes in the course of its existence.

New Product Development

What is involved in new product development? Introducing new products is important to the future success of many organizations. The process, which begins with generating an idea for a new product and ends with launching it to the public, is outlined in ▼ **Figure 13.3**. The process of developing new, high-quality products involves several steps:

1. **Idea generation.** Ideas for entirely new products or improved versions of existing products are often obtained by listening closely to customers or focus groups. In fact, customer complaints may signal a need for a new product. Suppliers, employees, and salespeople also generate ideas by assessing the competition and visiting trade shows.

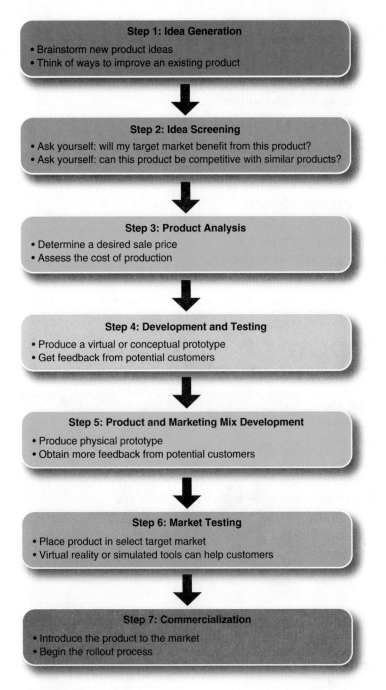

Step 1: Idea Generation
- Brainstorm new product ideas
- Think of ways to improve an existing product

Step 2: Idea Screening
- Ask yourself: will my target market benefit from this product?
- Ask yourself: can this product be competitive with similar products?

Step 3: Product Analysis
- Determine a desired sale price
- Assess the cost of production

Step 4: Development and Testing
- Produce a virtual or conceptual prototype
- Get feedback from potential customers

Step 5: Product and Marketing Mix Development
- Produce physical prototype
- Obtain more feedback from potential customers

Step 6: Market Testing
- Place product in select target market
- Virtual reality or simulated tools can help customers

Step 7: Commercialization
- Introduce the product to the market
- Begin the rollout process

▼ **Figure 13.3
The Steps in the New
Product Development
Process**

2. **Idea screening.** The objective of idea screening is to eliminate unsound concepts before devoting costly resources to their development. Screening involves estimating the level of consumer demand for a product, its profitability, and its production feasibility given the company's current technical capabilities.

3. **Product analysis.** Product analysis estimates the costs of production, the selling price, sales volume, and profitability. The costs of production depend on the features of the product deemed necessary to meet the targeted customers' needs. The selling price, sales volume, and profitability may depend on the degree of competition in the market.

4. **Development and testing.** At this stage, product ideas that survive the screening and analysis steps are analyzed further. This often begins with a physical prototype of the good. Computer-aided design systems are helpful in quickly making design changes before a physical prototype is manufactured. In the testing phase of a new service offering, management determines the details concerning staffing needs and equipment requirements to ensure the service is delivered properly. Concept testing involves soliciting customer responses to a new product idea, generally conducted through focus groups. Potential targeted customers are asked to evaluate different features, prices, packages, and a host of other factors surrounding a product. The idea is to come up with the best, most profitable total product offering.

5. **Product and marketing mix development.** Once a product has gone through initial development and testing, and business analysis indicates that there is financial merit to the idea, an initial design or prototype is developed. Previously, the design and prototype were in concept or virtual format. At this stage, a physical product is developed and introduced for additional consumer feedback to the product as well as aspects of the marketing mix, such as pricing, promotional techniques, and distribution options (retail stores, online, etc.).

6. **Market testing.** Sometimes this step is skipped if enough information and feedback has been obtained in the previous step. But often a product is placed in trial phases to test its acceptance even further. This is usually done by launching a product in a specific geographic area, aimed at a select target market. Sometimes marketers must convince distributors or store managers to make shelf space available. Some manufacturers, such as P&G and the fragrance company Coty, forgo real market testing and rely on computer-simulated virtual reality to simulate in-store environments and conduct a more controlled test.[14] Although still new, simulation tools and virtual stores are helping to reduce development costs and the time required to bring a new product to market.

7. **Commercialization.** If a product makes it this far in the process, it is ready to be launched. Commercialization is the decision to market a product. Introducing a new product can be costly due to manufacturing investments, advertising, personal selling, and other promotional activities. The returns from such investments can take time. This may explain why many companies introduce their new products in one region at a time—sometimes called *rolling out the product*.

Despite the scientific nature of new product development, a large proportion of new products still fail. In contrast to the success of Coke Zero, one of the most interesting cases of a new product failure was Coca-Cola's New Coke, launched in 1985. In an attempt to revitalize its brand, the company toyed with the formula of its popular soda and almost destroyed it. People didn't want their favorite soft drink modified, and New Coke was pulled from the shelves only three months after being introduced.[15] Coca-Cola returned to its original formula and renamed the cola Coca-Cola Classic.

The Product Life Cycle

What is a product life cycle? Once a product is developed, it begins the product life cycle. A **product life cycle** is a theoretical model describing a product's sales and profits over the course of its lifetime. During this cycle, a product typically goes through an introductory stage, a growth stage, a maturity stage, and a declining stage. The product life cycle can be applied to a specific product or an entire product category.

The Australian-made UGG boots seemed at first a fashion fad, but their warmth and comfort have continued to make them a popular choice for footwear. Time will tell how long this trend will last.

You can see how the theory works if you consider the life cycle of vinyl musical recordings. Vinyl records were first introduced in 1930 by RCA Victor but became popular in the 1950s as a replacement for the brittle and easily broken 78-rpm records. This was their introductory stage. Sales grew rapidly in the 1950s and the 1960s, representing the product's growth stage. They came in the 33⅓-rpm long playing records, or LPs, and the 45-rpm single records. In the early 1970s, vinyl records hit their maturity stage. By the late 1970s and early 1980s, cassette tapes gained wide acceptance and caused the sales of vinyl records to decrease drastically, representing their declining stage. After compact discs, or CDs, were introduced, the decline continued. Vinyl records are now sold mostly as collectors' items.

It is important to note that, like all models, the product life cycle model presents a simplified version of reality and should not be used prescriptively because of the diversity of products, environmental factors, and consumer behavior. For example, the product life of fad items like Beanie Babies can be as short as a few months; for some products, such as automobiles, a product's life can be as long as a century or more. In addition, not all products strictly follow these stages. Some products are introduced but never grow in sales, whereas others never seem to decline.

How do marketing decisions affect a product's life cycle? The product life cycle model may be useful as a general description of a product's sales and profits over time, but it should be used with caution when forecasting or predicting future sales and profits. All products don't strictly follow these stages, and the time frame involved with each stage can vary dramatically. In fact, marketing decisions can affect each phase of a product's life cycle, and knowing which stage of the product life cycle a particular product is in helps determine the appropriate marketing mix strategy for that stage. ▼ **Figure 13.4** summarizes the characteristics, marketing objectives, and strategies for each stage of the product life cycle.

Because most products eventually decline and may have to be withdrawn from the market, companies must continuously seek to develop new products to replace older ones. At the same time, marketers work hard to extend the life of existing products to milk as much profit from them as possible. Some auto manufacturers

▼ **Figure 13.4
The Product Life
Cycle Model**

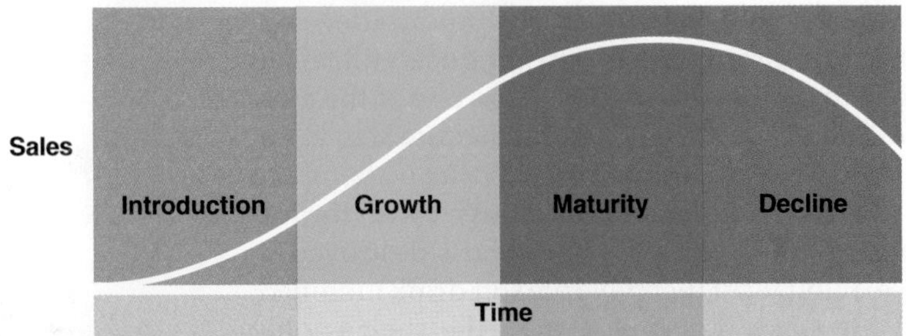

	Introduction	Growth	Maturity	Decline
Characteristics				
Sales	Low sales	Radically rising sales	Peak sales	Declining sales
Costs	High cost per customer	High cost per customer	Low cost per customer	Low cost per customer
Profits	Negative	Rising	High	Declining
Customers	Innovators	Innovators	Middle majority	Laggards
Competitors	Few	Growing number	Stable number beginning to decline	Declining number
Marketing Objectives				
	Create product awareness and trial	Maximize market share	Maximize profit while defending market share	Reduce expenditure and milk the brand
Strategies				
Product	Offer a basic product	Offer product extensions, services, warranty	Diversify brands and models	Phase out weak items
Price	Charge cost-plus	Price to penetrate market	Price to match or beat competitors	Cut prices
Distribution	Build selective distribution	Build intensive distribution	Build more intensive distribution	Go selective; phase out unprofitable outlets
Advertising	Build product awareness among early adopters and dealers	Build awareness and interest in the mass market	Stress brand differences and benefits	Reduce to level needed to retain hard-core loyals
Sales Promotion	Use heavy sales promotion to entice trial	Reduce to take advantage of heavy customer demand	Increase to encourage brand switching	Reduce to minimal level

have used discounted prices, rebates, and low-interest loans to extend the life of their models. Arm & Hammer, a company that produces baking soda, extended its product's life by advertising and *creating a new use* for its product as a refrigerator deodorizer. Home Depot and Lowe's tried to *create new markets* for their businesses by expanding into do-it-yourself training on home projects within their stores. Jell-O extended its knowledge (*extended technology*) of raw gelatin to create puddings and other snacks.

Repackaging, or using new labels or different container types, is another popular method to extend a product's life. For example, Sally Hansen, the nail care company, put nail polish in a penlike applicator that is portable and spill-proof. A company can also *reposition* its product as Oldsmobile attempted with its "This isn't your father's Oldsmobile" campaign. These strategies are not always effective, however; the Oldsmobile, for example, has been discontinued.[16]

As you've just learned, developing a high-quality product is not so much an end in itself as it is a beginning. After a product is developed, the product life cycle begins, and appropriate marketing strategies must be conceived and implemented accordingly. Jessica Smith is experiencing this now. Three years after opening her yoga studio and equipment store, she changed her marketing and pricing strategies on products that were experiencing declining sales. At the same time, she expanded offerings of her most popular classes to maximize profits during the critical growth and maturity stages. As Jessica quickly learned, a dynamic market calls for dynamic product development. ■

Pricing Goods and Services pp. 415–421

When store manager Eugene Whitaker wanted to increase profits at the store where he worked, he examined sales data. He noticed that premium newborn baby items were being purchased more often than less expensive choices. After getting approval from his supervisor, he raised the prices on all newborn-related products. At the end of the quarter, store revenues were up. Whitaker found that the rise in prices did very little to reduce the quantity of newborn-related sales, so store executives implemented a slow increase in prices over the course of the next year at other locations, and Eugene Whitaker got a raise. ■

Pricing is important to consumers and producers alike, and it is an essential component in the marketing mix. We conclude this chapter by discussing the pricing component of the marketing mix. We'll discuss promotion and distribution strategies in the next chapter.

Product Pricing and Pricing Objectives

Why is price an important component in the marketing mix? As consumers, we know a product's price means what we must pay to acquire it. Prices are sometimes called *fees*, *fares*, *tolls*, *rates*, *charges*, or *subscriptions*. From the seller's perspective, price is the only revenue-generating component of the marketing mix; product, promotion, and distribution strategies are all cost components. Therefore, price is an important factor in determining profit.

Price can also serve as a marketing tool and is often used in promotional campaigns. Trying to set the right price can be a real challenge for marketers. The price of a product has to be low enough to generate enough value to customers to motivate sales yet also high enough to enable a company to cover costs and earn a profit. Setting the right price is challenging because market conditions are always changing. As a result, companies must constantly tweak prices to remain competitive. Moreover, some companies operating in very competitive markets may have little or no control over their prices. Instead, prices are determined in the market through the interaction of demand and supply. For example, farmers have virtually no control over the prices of their agricultural commodities. These companies may therefore be called *price-takers* (not *price-setters*). However, most companies have at least some control over the prices they charge.

What are some pricing objectives? Pricing is more than simply calculating the cost of production and then tacking on a markup for profit. The price often impacts how consumers view a product and may determine whether they will purchase it. Price also helps to differentiate a product from the competition. Before a price is set, it is important to determine exactly what, beyond a general goal of achieving profit, is to be obtained by the pricing, that is, determine a pricing objective. There are a variety of pricing objectives; some of the most common pricing objectives include the following:

1. **Maximizing profits.** This occurs when price is set so that total revenue exceeds total cost by the greatest amount.
2. **Achieving greater market share.** A company's market share is the percentage of total industry sales or revenues it is able to capture. Unfortunately, achieving greater market share does not always translate into higher profits.
3. **Maximizing sales.** Maximizing sales often means charging low prices that can result in losses. Firms cannot survive for long with losses. However, maximizing sales may be an appropriate short-run objective to rid the company of excess inventory, such as last year's models.
4. **Building traffic.** Many retail stores, such as grocery stores, pharmacies, hardware stores, and department stores, may advertise a sale price on a few goods to increase traffic in their stores and build a stronger customer base. They also hope customers will purchase other, more profitable items while they are shopping for the bargains.
5. **Matching the status quo prices.** The objective of status quo pricing is simply to match competitors' prices, possibly to avoid a price war that could be damaging to everyone. The airfare wars of the past hurt every airline carrier, so they have chosen to compete on nonprice factors instead.
6. **Covering costs to survive.** If a company is struggling to build a customer base, it may choose to set prices to generate just enough revenues to cover costs. However, this is not a suitable long-term objective. Survival prices might generate sales, but they will not generate profits.
7. **Creating an image.** Some products are priced high because firms hope that consumers will associate high prices with high quality. This is the case for many specialty goods, such as luxury cars, perfume, and designer jewelry.
8. **Ensuring affordability to all.** Some companies may charge low prices to enable the poor to afford their products. For example, many governments have been involved in ensuring that staple food products, such as grains, are affordable to all.

How do you choose the right pricing objective? The most appropriate pricing objective is determined by considering the business and financial goals of a product or a company. If one of the business goals is to become a market leader and amass the greatest market share, then maximizing quantity or sales may be a more appropriate choice over building traffic; if a business objective is aggressive production growth, then profit maximization will be important. Survival and status quo pricing may be better suited when market conditions are poor or unstable or when entering a market for the first time. Understand, also, that pricing objectives will change over the life cycle of a product. Marketers must develop their pricing strategies in coordination with their product branding, packaging, promotion, and distribution strategies as well. Indeed, price is only one element in the marketing mix.

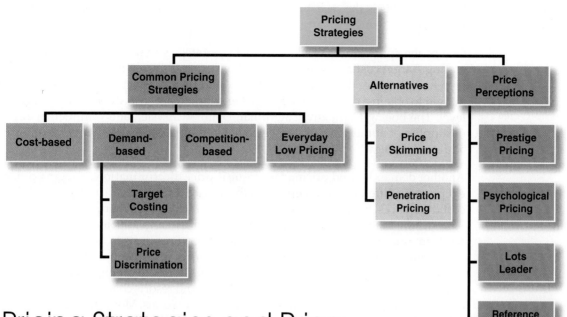

Pricing Strategies and Price Perceptions

▼ **Figure 13.5**
Pricing Strategies

What are the major pricing strategies? After determining the pricing *objective*, choosing the best pricing *strategy* to achieve that objective is next. Although there is no one right way to determine the price of a good or service, there are several strategies that sellers can use. Certain strategies work better with certain objectives, and some pricing strategies may be used at different times to fit in with changes in marketing strategies, market conditions, and product life cycles. The most common pricing strategies include *cost-based pricing*, *demand-based pricing*, *competition-based pricing*, and *everyday low pricing*. There are also several *alternative pricing strategies* and strategies that affect *price perceptions*. ▼ **Figure 13.5** outlines these pricing strategies, which we'll discuss next.

What is cost-based pricing? One of the easiest and simplest ways to price a product is **cost-based pricing.** This pricing strategy (also known as *cost-plus pricing*) is based on covering costs and providing for a set profit. Suppose you manufacture 100 units of a product at a total cost of $2,000. The average (or per unit) total cost would be $20. If you want to make a unit profit margin, or *markup*, of 20 percent, which is $4 (0.20 × $20), you would price the product at $24. Total revenue would equal $2,400; profit would equal $400, or 20 percent above costs.

There are many advantages of cost-based pricing. Besides being easy to calculate and easy to administer, it requires a minimum amount of information. However, it has several disadvantages as well. It ignores whether a price is compatible with consumer demand or expectations and the prices charged by competitors. It also provides little incentive to be efficient and hold costs down. Many pharmaceutical companies undertake cost-based pricing to recoup their expensive research and development costs associated with a new drug and earn a targeted profit level. The monopoly power granted by patents on new drugs means there is no competition, and pharmaceutical companies find little need to consider consumer demand when setting prices on drugs.

How does product demand impact pricing? Demand-based pricing (sometimes called *value-based pricing*) is pricing a good or a service based on the demand for a product or its perceived value. A high price will be charged when demand or the perceived value of a product is high, and a lower price will be charged when demand or perceived value is low. This pricing strategy assumes firms can accurately estimate the perceived value or demand for their goods or services.

Sometimes this is the case, but it's usually very difficult to do in practice. Nevertheless, many firms try.

One of the specific demand-based pricing strategies that firms employ is target costing. **Target costing** estimates the value customers receive from a product and, therefore, the price they are willing to pay and then subtracts an acceptable profit margin to obtain a desired cost. Firms then work to get costs down to this targeted level. The Boeing Company, Caterpillar, DaimlerChrysler, and Continental Teves (a supplier of automotive brake systems) have successfully used target costing as a pricing strategy.[17,18,19]

Another demand-based pricing technique is **price discrimination,** charging different prices to different customers when these price differences are not a reflection of cost differences. Successful price discrimination charges higher prices to targeted customers who are price insensitive and lower prices to targeted customers who are more price sensitive. Price discrimination requires firms to be able to successfully segment customers based on their differences in demand and price sensitivity, and it requires that a product cannot be easily resold among customers. One example of price discrimination includes hotels and resorts charging different rates based on different days of the week or seasonal variations. Movie theaters may also charge higher prices to view a movie during an evening showing as opposed to a matinee viewing time. Airline companies also price discriminate on the airfares they charge. Those who place their reservations well in advance pay less than those who book a flight on short notice. Restaurants price discriminate with early bird specials and discounted happy hour rates. Grocery stores price discriminate by offering clip-out coupons that price-sensitive customers may use to buy grocery items at lower prices. In some cases, even salespeople charge different prices to customers based on their perceived demand for big-ticket items, such as cars and furniture, so don't tell them how much you value or love their good or service! Many organizations price discriminate because it's profitable to do so.

What pricing strategy would work best in a highly competitive market? Competition-based pricing is a pricing strategy based on what the competition is charging. Revenues and costs are secondary. The degree of competition in markets affects a company's price-setting ability. As discussed in Chapter 12, competitive markets, including agricultural and raw material commodity markets firms, have little, if any, control over their prices. They charge prices equivalent to all others' prices. *Monopolistically competitive markets,* markets in which many firms compete on the basis of doing something unique, have some firms that charge higher prices if they are successful in their product differentiation strategies. Other companies may charge lower prices to get an edge on the competition. *Oligopolies,* a market with a few dominant sellers, such as those in the airline and oil industries, often avoid competing on the basis of price to avoid price wars. Instead, they compete aggressively on product differentiation and charge higher prices if their total product offerings are unique. However, periodically, a *price leader* may charge a different price and all other firms will follow with similar price changes. Finally, a *monopoly,* a market that is controlled by one dominating firm, possesses the greatest price-setting ability because there is no competition. In some extreme cases, monopolies may have captured their markets through *predatory pricing,* the practice of charging very low prices with the intent of destroying the competition. Predatory pricing is illegal, but that hasn't prevented it from occurring. Most real-world competition rests on product differentiation and the customer's perception of value. For example, Oakley, Inc., which makes sunglasses and goggles for sports and fashion, has successfully differentiated its products and can charge higher prices.

What pricing strategy offers low prices all the time? Some retail stores offer **everyday low pricing (EDLP),** a strategy of charging low prices with few, if any, special or promotional sales. Walmart has successfully used this strategy because it has been able to give the impression that its brand means everyday low cost.

Are there pricing strategies that work better with certain phases of the product life cycle?

When launching a new product, companies may need to use a different type of pricing strategy than they would on an existing product. One pricing strategy for introducing a new product is **price skimming.** It involves charging a high price for a product initially and then lowering the price over time. Price skimming coincides with the introductory stage of a product's life cycle, during which there are few, if any, competitors. The idea is to skim off as high a price as possible to recoup the expensive new product development costs. However, the high price may encourage competitors to enter the market at a lower price.

At the other end of the spectrum is **penetration pricing,** a strategy of charging the lowest possible price for a new product. This pricing strategy is designed to quickly build market share for a product. If the increased production to satisfy growing sales results in lower per unit costs, then profits can actually rise even though the price is lower. Penetration pricing is appropriate during the growth stage of a product's life cycle and when customers are price sensitive. It may also create goodwill among consumers and inhibit competitors from entering the market. Its drawbacks include the establishment of low price expectations or a poor-quality image for a brand and a company. This may make it difficult to raise prices later.

What are some strategies used to impact price perceptions?

For many consumers, a high price indicates good quality. Although this is not always the case, many consumers make this association when products are complex, do not have a strong brand identity, or are services with which they are unfamiliar. The less they know about a product, the more consumers rely on price as an indicator of quality. Businesses have to be careful not to lower their prices too much, otherwise a product may be perceived as low quality. This is certainly not the case with prestige pricing. **Prestige pricing** (also known as *premium pricing*) is the practice of charging a high price to invoke perceptions of high quality and privilege. For those brands for which prestige pricing may apply, the high price itself is a motivator for consumers. The higher perceived value because of the higher price actually increases demand and creates a higher price that becomes self-sustaining. Some people have called this the *snob effect.* Examples of this strategy include the pricing of cars made by Mercedes-Benz, Lexus, and Rolls-Royce.

Another pricing strategy that impacts price perceptions is **psychological pricing** (sometimes called *odd* or *fractional pricing*), the practice of charging a price just below a whole number to give the appearance of a significantly lower price. For example, charging $9.99 as opposed to $10.00 is an example of psychological pricing. Gas stations often use psychological pricing.

A **loss leader** is a product that is priced below its costs. Stores use loss leaders to attract customers and motivate them to buy more expensive items as well. Reference pricing is another strategy used to attract customers. **Reference pricing** refers to listing an inflated price (the regular retail price or the manufacturer's suggested retail price) that is then discounted to appear as if it is a good value. A variation of this strategy occurs when stores provide both a more expensive "gold-plated" version of a product and a lower-priced alternative. This makes the alternative appear as a bargain.

How might production be affected by pricing strategies?

No matter which pricing strategy is selected, it is important to determine how much of a product can be produced at that price level before generating a profit. A **break-even analysis**, which determines the production level for which total revenue is just

Mercedes-Benz uses a pricing strategy known as prestige pricing to invoke perceptions of higher quality and privilege.

enough to cover total costs, is useful to conduct with any pricing strategy. At the break-even point, no profit has been made, and no losses have been incurred. The first step in conducting a break-even analysis is to determine costs. There are two types of costs that make up the total product cost: fixed costs and variable costs. *Fixed costs* (sometimes called *overhead costs*) are any costs that do not vary with the production level. Fixed costs typically include salaries, rent, insurance expenses, and loan repayments. *Variable costs* are costs that vary with the production level. Examples include wages, raw materials, and energy costs. *Average variable costs* (or *per unit variable costs*) equal total variable costs divided by the production level. A convenient formula for calculating the break-even production level is as follows:

$$\text{Break-even volume of production} = \frac{\text{Total Fixed Costs}}{\text{Revenue per unit} - \text{Average Variable Costs}}$$

For example, suppose that the total fixed costs equal $600, the selling price is $24, and average variable costs are $14. The break-even volume of production is therefore $600 ÷ ($24 − $14), or 60 units. Any production level below the break-even volume will result in losses, and any production level above the break-even level will result in profits. Any changes in the fixed or variable costs, as well as changes in the price, will affect the break-even volume of production. Because of its simplicity, it is one of the more popular pricing strategies, but it does not work in all situations. When there is variable demand for a product, or a highly competitive market, other pricing strategies may be more appropriate.

Adjusting Prices

What are common types of price adjustments? Most businesses adjust their prices to promote their products. Several tactics are used, as shown in ▼ **Figure 13.6**. One way is to use **discounts,** a deduction from the regular price charged. Discounts come in many forms:

- Cash discounts (a reduced price for paying with a method that does not require processing)
- Quantity discounts (a lower price for buying in large quantities)
- Seasonal discounts (a price reduction if you buy out of season)
- Forms of allowance, such as a trade-in allowance (a reduced price if you trade your old good for a new good)

▼ **Figure 13.6**
Price Adjustments
(Tactics)

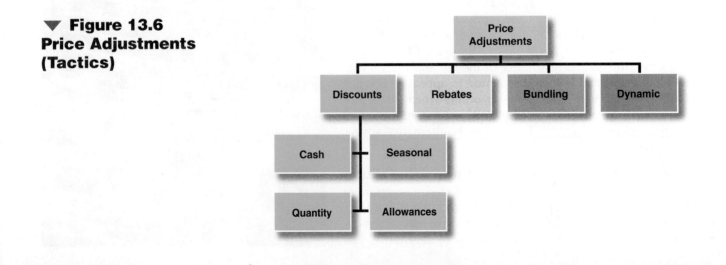

Another way to adjust prices is to use rebates. **Rebates** are partial refunds on what a customer has already paid for a product. An example is mail-in rebates, where a manufacturer gives a debit card to be used against future purchases, or may write a check to the customer after the customer provides proof of purchase.

Bundling is another type of price adjustment. In **bundling,** two or more products that usually complement one another are combined and sold at a single price. To be attractive, the single price is usually lower than the sum of the individual products' prices. Bundling is quite common in the fast-food industry, where products are bundled to make a complete meal. Bundling also occurs with cable, DSL, or satellite television sales; when a package of channels is sold at a single price; or when phone, Internet, and television plans are combined. Many vacation packages are also bundled products consisting of airfare, car rental, hotel accommodations, and other amenities bundled together.

Dynamic pricing is another price-adjustment technique. In **dynamic pricing,** prices are determined directly between a buyer and a seller, unlike the more traditional fixed pricing in which a seller sets prices. Auctions are a traditional form of dynamic pricing. More recent examples exist in e-commerce, such as eBay and Priceline.com. Dynamic pricing often results in quick price adjustments.

These are just a few pricing strategies; many others exist. Indeed, the pricing component of the marketing mix is one of the most difficult for marketers to grapple with. Although Eugene Whitaker was able to raise prices on products for newborns without significantly affecting sales, this approach might not work in all cases. In those instances, marketers must go back to the drawing board to figure out a strategy that will lead them to success. ▪

Chapter Summary

1. How is a product distinguished from a total product offer? (pp. 397–398)

- A *product* is any good, service, or idea that might satisfy a want or a need. A **total product offer** (p. 397) consists of all the tangible and intangible benefits associated with a good, a service, or an idea that impact a consumer's purchasing decision. Marketers know this. When planning a total product offering, they think about products on three levels:
  - A **core product** (p. 398) satisfies the basic need or want that motivates a purchase. Because it is the basic benefit provided by a product, you can't touch it; it is intangible.
  - An **actual product** (p. 398) is the tangible aspect of a purchase that you can touch, see, hear, smell, or taste. It provides core benefits when it is used.
  - An **augmented product** (p. 398) consists of the core and actual product plus other real or perceived benefits that provide additional value to the customer's purchase.

2. What is product differentiation, and what role does it play in product development? (pp. 398–399)

- **Product differentiation** (p. 398) is the process of distinguishing a product from its competition in real or perceived terms to attract customers.
- Customer input and feedback guide product development and product differentiation. It also gives rise to the creation of a **product line** (p. 399), a group of similar products marketed to one general market. A **product mix** (p. 399) is the combination of all product lines offered for sale by a company. Product lines and mix result from trying to tailor total product offerings to unique targeted customers.

3. What are the different classifications of consumer products and B2B products? (pp. 400–403)

- The four classifications of **consumer products** (p. 400) are convenience goods and services, shopping goods and services, specialty goods and services, and unsought goods and services.
  - Customers purchase **convenience goods and services** (p. 400), such as gum, soap, and milk, frequently, immediately, and effortlessly.
  - **Shopping goods and services** (p. 401) are products that are less frequently purchased and require that the customer spend more time and effort in comparing the products. Examples include clothes, electronics, and furniture.
  - **Specialty goods and services** (p. 401) have unique characteristics and no suitable substitutes. Examples include designer clothing or the services of prestigious lawyers.
  - **Unsought goods and services** (p. 401) are products buyers don't usually think about buying, don't know exist, or buy only when a specific problem arises. An example is funeral services.
- There are five categories of **business-to-business (B2B) products** (p. 400): equipment, MRO products, raw and processed materials, component parts, and specialized professional services.

4. Why is branding beneficial to both buyers and sellers, and what are some different types of brands? (pp. 403–411)

- Branding reduces shopping time for buyers and helps consumers express themselves. Branding helps sellers define the special qualities of their product, encouraging repeat purchases and new sales at higher prices.
- Marketing a product using the same brand name but in a different product category is known as **brand extension** (p. 404). **Brand licensing** (p. 404) is an agreement between the owner of a brand and another company or individual who pays a royalty for using the brand in association with a new product.
- For sellers, branding creates **brand loyalty** (p. 404) among consumers. Brand loyalty contributes to **brand equity** (p. 405), the overall value of a brand's strength in the market. **Brand awareness** (p. 405) refers to the extent to which a particular brand name is familiar within a particular product category. **Brand association** (p. 405) involves connecting a brand with other positive attributes.
- There are six different types of brands: **manufacturer's brands**, **family brands**, **individual brands**, **private brands**, **co-brands**, and **generic brands** (pp. 406–407).
- How a product is packaged and labeled sends a message about a product and a brand.

5. **What steps take place during new product development, and what is the product life cycle? (pp. 411–415)**

- The steps in new product development are idea generation, idea screening, product analysis, concept development and testing, product and marketing mix development, market testing, and commercialization.
- The **product life cycle** (p. 413) is a theoretical model describing a product's sales and profits over the course of its lifetime. Stages in the product life cycle include introduction, growth, maturity, and decline.

6. **What are some pricing objectives, and how do they relate to the marketing mix? (pp. 415–417)**

- Common pricing objectives include maximizing profits, achieving greater market share, maximizing sales, building traffic in stores, matching status quo prices, covering costs to survive, creating an image, and ensuring affordability to all.

- Price is the only revenue-generating component of the marketing mix. Marketers must carefully consider their pricing objectives to develop the best pricing strategy.

7. **What are the major approaches to pricing strategy, and what are some pricing tactics used to launch a new product, impact price perceptions, and adjust prices? (pp. 417–421)**

- The major approaches to pricing strategy are **cost-based pricing** (p. 417), **demand-based pricing** (p. 417), **competition-based pricing** (p. 418), and **everyday low pricing** (EDLP; p. 418).
- **Price skimming** (p. 419) and **penetration pricing** (p. 419) are tactics used for launching new products.
- **Prestige pricing** (p. 419), **psychological pricing** (p. 419), the use of **loss leaders** (p. 419), and **reference pricing** (p. 419) are pricing strategies that impact price perceptions by consumers.
- **Discounts** (p. 420), **rebates** (p. 421), **bundling** (p. 421), and **dynamic pricing** (p. 421) are common types of price adjustments.

Key Terms

actual product (p. 398)

augmented product (p. 398)

brand association (p. 405)

brand awareness (p. 405)

brand equity (p. 405)

brand extension (p. 404)

brand licensing (p. 404)

brand loyalty (p. 404)

break-even analysis (p. 419)

bundling (p. 421)

business-to-business (B2B) products (p. 400)

co-brand (p. 407)

competition-based pricing (p. 418)

consumer products (p. 400)

convenience goods and services (p. 400)

core product (p. 398)

cost-based pricing (p. 417)

demand-based pricing (p. 417)

discounts (p. 420)

dynamic pricing (p. 421)

everyday low pricing (EDLP) (p. 418)

family brand (p. 406)

generic brand (p. 407)

individual brand (p. 406)

loss leader (p. 419)

manufacturer's brand (p. 406)

penetration pricing (p. 419)

prestige pricing (p. 419)

price discrimination (p. 418)

price skimming (p. 419)

private brand (p. 406)

product (p. 397)

product differentiation (p. 398)

product life cycle (p. 413)

product line (p. 399)

product mix (p. 399)

psychological pricing (p. 419)

rebates (p. 421)

reference pricing (p. 419)

shopping goods and services (p. 401)

specialty goods and services (p. 401)

target costing (p. 418)

total product offer (p. 397)

trademark (p. 404)

unsought goods and services (p. 401)

Self-Test

Multiple Choice You can find the answers on the last page of this book.

1. The level of a product that satisfies the basic need or want that motivates a purchase is the

   a. total product offering.

   b. augmented product.

   c. actual product.

   d. core product.

2. Product mix width refers to

   a. a total product offer.

   b. a group of similar products marketed to one general product market category.

   c. the number of product lines a company offers.

   d. the number of items in a product line.

3. When companies compete aggressively on the basis of price, quality, and brand-name image because consumers carefully compare brands, these businesses are most likely selling _____ goods and services.

   a. convenience

   b. shopping

   c. specialty

   d. unsought

4. When businesses hire celebrities to endorse their products and connect their brands with positive attributes, they are focusing on enhancing their brand

   a. loyalty.

   b. awareness.

   c. association.

   d. extension.

5. A brand that markets several different products under the same brand name is a

   a. manufacturer's brand.

   b. family brand.

   c. private brand.

   d. co-brand.

6. Siobhan Clark just bought a Philadelphia Phillies jersey with player Roy Halladay's name and number on the back, as well as a hat and jacket that display the Phillies logo. The type of branding strategy used for these products is

   a. generic branding.

   b. manufacturer's branding.

   c. private branding.

   d. brand licensing.

7. In what stage in the product life cycle would you consider the Apple iPhone to be?

   a. Introduction

   b. Growth

   c. Maturity

   d. Decline

8. Stephanie Ling has been asked to conduct a break-even analysis. Rent for the building, salaries, and insurance costs are considered

   a. fixed costs.

   b. variable costs.

   c. production costs.

   d. price adjustments.

9. Rocco Valentino shops only at Walmart. Because Walmart rarely has sales, Rocco believes he'll receive the lowest price without further hassles. This type of pricing strategy is known as _____ pricing.

   a. dynamic

   b. everyday low

   c. competition-based

   d. penetration

10. Which pricing strategy sets prices just below a whole number to give the appearance of a lower price?

    a. Predatory pricing

    b. Price discrimination

    c. Target costing

    d. Psychological pricing

Self-Test

You can find the answers on the last page of this book.

1. The augmented product provides additional value to a customer's purchase.
   ☐ **True** or ☐ **False**

2. Trademarking benefits sellers by helping to distinguish their products from knockoff brands.
   ☐ **True** or ☐ **False**

3. Loss leader pricing is used to move a product quickly off the shelves.
   ☐ **True** or ☐ **False**

4. MRO B2B products are marketed much like consumer convenience goods and services.
   ☐ **True** or ☐ **False**

5. An advantage of an individual brand is protecting an established brand name from an unsuccessful product extension.
   ☐ **True** or ☐ **False**

Critical Thinking Questions

1. Why is it important for marketers to think of a good or a service as a total product offering?

2. What part of the product life cycle would a product like the energy drink Red Bull be in? What about Gatorade?

3. How are brand loyalty, specialty goods and services, and prestige pricing related?

4. Describe the pricing strategy Apple used with the iPad. Consider that the iPad launched with price differentials for wireless options. Also consider that all accessories are purchased separately. Why do you think Apple used this pricing strategy?

5. Describe the conditions when it might be appropriate to use each of the following pricing strategies: discounting, rebates, bundling, dynamic pricing, prestige pricing, psychological pricing, loss leader pricing, and reference pricing.

Team Time

Developing a Product

Divide into teams of three or four. As a team, use what you have learned in this chapter to discuss how you would develop a new product.

Process

Step 1. Begin with the first step in the new product development process: idea generation. Work as a group to decide what your new product will be.

Step 2. Proceed through the idea screening, product analysis, product development and testing, and commercialization steps. What do you estimate the consumer demand and production feasibility for this product to be? How much will it cost to produce, and what should be its selling price? How might you test-market this product? How will it be marketed? Discuss the answers to these questions as you address their corresponding steps.

Step 3. Prepare a summary of your findings and present them to the class.

Ethics and Corporate Social Responsibility

The Ethics of Rx

The pharmaceutical drug industry is an ethical minefield. The development of prescription medications is one topic among many that can present significant ethical challenges. Consider the questions raised by the following scenario. If possible, discuss your thoughts with a classmate or participate in a group debate on the topic.

Scenario

You are an executive at one of the top drug companies in the United States. At the most recent product development meeting, two teams of scientists reported that each is within one year of having a new drug ready for clinical trials. Team A is developing a drug to cure a rare but fatal bone disease. Team B is developing a drug to treat a common, non-life-threatening skin condition. To make the deadline, however, both teams need an additional $10 million in funding. You know that the company can afford to fund only one team. According to the product analysis, Team A's drug will be expensive to produce, difficult to market, and yield only modest profits. Team B's drug has the potential to yield massive profits.

Questions

1. Which team would you recommend the company fund? Why?

2. How do the potential profits of Team B's drug affect your stance, from both financial/business and medical/ethical perspectives?

3. What about pricing? How might you reconcile the need to keep the drug company profitable with the ethical responsibility to make medications affordable for those in need?

Web Exercises

1. **The iPhone as a Product**
   Go to Apple's iPhone Web site. Describe Apple's marketing mix strategy for its product and its price. When would an iPhone be a consumer product and when would it be a B2B product? What does Apple do to augment its product? What type of branding strategy is Apple pursuing? What stage of the product life cycle is the iPhone in? Is Apple undertaking the appropriate strategies, given this stage of the product's life cycle?

2. **Organic Coke?**
   Organic products are increasing in popularity. Suppose Coca-Cola came out with an organic soda product. Use the Internet to research other organic beverages and sodas. Where would this fit in Coke's product mix? How would Coca-Cola's established branding help or hurt the product launch? What kind of pricing strategy do you think it would use to introduce the product?

3. **Research a Brand**
   Choose a favorite brand of clothing or food and use the Internet to gather information about it. What type of brand is it—manufacturer's, private, individual, or other? Is it part of a brand extension? Is it associated with a co-brand or a licensing arrangement? How do packaging and labeling affect the image the brand projects? Summarize your findings in a brief report.

4. **Toothpaste Differential**
   Look at Walmart's Web site or a Web site for an online drugstore. List the various manufacturers of toothpaste. Then, under each one, list the various products they make. How are companies trying to differentiate their products from each other? How do you think consumers react to these various types of toothpaste?

5. **The Dynamics of Dynamic Pricing**
   Visit an online auction Web site such as eBay. Choose a few products and compare their prices on the Web site with their prices at a retail store. What do the higher or lower prices on eBay indicate about supply and demand? How does dynamic pricing differ from fixed pricing? What other factors must buyers take into account when purchasing products from eBay?

Web Case

For more on managing customer relations through pricing strategies, access the Chapter 13 Web case entitled "Focus on Apple, Inc.: The iPhone: Revolutionary Product or Rip-off?" located in the End of Chapter Assignments section at my*biz*lab.com.

Video Case

For more on implementing—and pricing—specialized customer demands, access the Chapter 13 Video Case entitled "MCCI: Developing and Pricing Space-Age Products" located in the End of Chapter Assignments section at my*biz*lab.com.

Promotion and the Promotional Mix

When Danny Perez started his own lunch cart business, he thought that being in a location with other lunch carts and giving away samples would generate business. Unfortunately, things didn't turn out as he anticipated the first day. How could Danny create an effective promotional strategy?

Objective 1 What is a promotional mix, and what is its function in a promotional campaign? (pp. 429–444)

Promotional Techniques: Advertising and Public Relations

Monica Pace and Steven Tham have opened their own new interior design business. They have a Web site and are using Twitter and Facebook to connect with their customers and hear what people are saying about their business. But how do they monitor online conversations? And do they need other, more traditional means of advertising? What other advertising options are best for them?

Objective 2 What are the different categories of advertising, and what role do these categories play in business and society? (pp. 432–437)

Objective 3 How are the various public relations tools essential to the marketing mix? (pp. 437–440)

Promotional Techniques: Personal Selling and Sales Promotion

Keith Jefferson works for a trucking company and is going on his first sales pitch alone. When his potential client asks a question about shipping rates, Keith freezes. He has no idea how to answer the question. What is personal selling? What traits do good salespeople have?

Objective 4 What are the steps in the personal selling process? (pp. 440–444)

Objective 5 What are the two main types of sales promotions, and what types of tools are commonly used as incentives? (pp. 444–447)

Distribution: Marketing Intermediaries

Liv Karlsen needed a book that was on the *New York Times* best sellers list for her modern U.S. literature class. The college bookstore had no more copies, and a local store of a large retail chain also had no more copies. The best Liv could do was to order the book online and pay for overnight shipping. What is the distribution process a book goes through? Are all distribution processes the same?

Objective 6 Why are marketing intermediaries and distribution channels important elements in marketing? (pp. 448–452)

Objective 7 What types of services do agents/brokers and wholesalers provide? (pp. 452–453)

Objective 8 Why are retailing and physical distribution key aspects of distribution? (pp. 453–457)

PEARSON
mybizlab

Promoting a Product

Sol Shades Inc. has been developing a new line of sunglasses for 2 years. The lightweight and super-stylish Hot Blades Shades are set to hit the market, and it's your job to create a marketing campaign. You must weigh the tradeoffs between different promotional strategies and design the best marketing mix, all while staying within your budget. Higher ups have informed you they expect big sales. Can you create a successful campaign?

Objective 9 Test yourself using my*biz*lab.com to show that you understand the chapter objectives.

Promotion and the Promotional Mix pp. 429–431

D anny Perez dreamed of having his own business. When he decided to take the leap and switch careers, he was nervous but excited. He loved to cook and wanted to get people to taste his food, but he didn't have the money to open a full-fledged restaurant. Instead, he decided to operate a food cart and was able to set up in a busy commercial area that already had several other lunch carts. Danny's son suggested he start a Facebook page and a Twitter account, but Danny didn't trust those techy things. Instead, he decided to begin by giving away samples of some of his menu items. Unfortunately, not many people took the free samples, and even fewer bought anything. In the end, he was out $400 in food the first day. Was it his food, his location, or the way the cart looked? Should he have taken his son's advice about the social media sites? ■

Danny's plan to promote his business was well intentioned, but it didn't work out quite the way he had hoped. What should he have done differently? What other options does he have? In this chapter, you'll learn about the promotion and distribution (or place) components of the 4 Ps of the marketing mix.

Promotion

What is promotion? Few products—no matter how well they are developed, priced, and distributed—will sell well if they are not properly promoted. **Promotion** involves all the techniques marketers use to inform targeted customers of the benefits of a product and persuade them to purchase a good, a service, or an idea. Promotion is designed to increase brand awareness, brand loyalty, and sales and is, therefore, one of the most visible components of the marketing mix.

Finding the best way to communicate the benefits of a product and persuade customers to buy it is a critical job of marketers. Should a product be advertised or is personal selling more appropriate? If advertising is used, is it best to advertise through newspapers, magazines, radio, television, the Internet, or another source? Beyond advertising and personal selling, what types of public relations activities might be most appropriate? These are just a few of the questions that marketers must ask themselves when promoting a product.

What are the most popular tools marketers use to promote a product? Four basic promotional tools are used to promote a good or a service: advertising, public relations, personal selling, and sales promotions. The **promotional mix** is the strategic combination of these promotional tools used to reach targeted customers to achieve marketing objectives. The elements of the promotional mix are illustrated in ▼ **Figure 14.1.** Notice that the product itself can be a promotional tool because its features may be promoted by giving away free samples of the good or service, as Danny Perez did.

Efficient organizations search for the optimal or most cost-effective promotional mix given their marketing objectives and budgetary constraints. If a firm's major

PEARSON
my*biz*lab

For an interactive, real-world example of this topic, access this chapter's **BizSkill** entitled Promoting a Product, located at **my*biz*lab**.com.

▼ **Figure 14.1**
The Promotional Mix
The promotional mix consists of advertising, public relations, personal selling, and sales promotion. The product itself can also be considered part of the promotional mix, especially if samples are given away to promote the product.

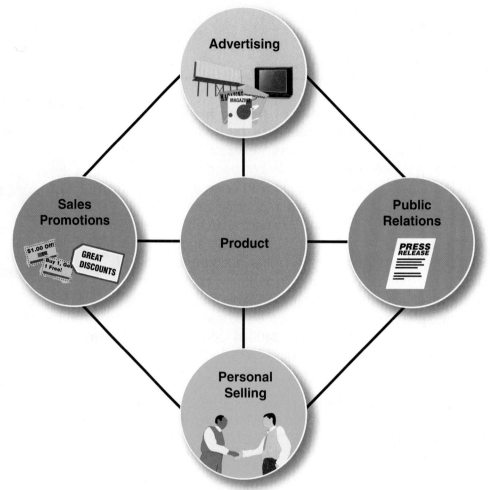

objective is to maximize profits, then, working within the constraints of its promotion budget, it will juggle the amounts of advertising, public relations, personal selling, and sales promotion until a mix is found that maximizes profits. The optimal, or best, promotional mix for a given product will vary depending on the goals of a business.

What are the steps involved in a promotional campaign? When promoting a product, it's best to plan out a promotional campaign to determine the right balance of activities and timing to increase awareness in the marketplace. Although each campaign will differ to suit the specific needs of the product, the basic steps are as follows:

1. **Identify the target market.** Recall from Chapter 12 that a *target market* is a specific group of potential customers on which to focus marketing efforts. Identifying these customers is the first step in any promotional campaign.

2. **Determine marketing objectives.** Is a business trying to maximize profits, sales, or market share? Is the goal to build traffic, brand awareness, or brand image? Is a business trying to introduce a new product or respond to an attack by a competitor? Whatever the marketing objective is, the goal should be clearly understood and measurable.

3. **Design the message.** The message should inform customers of the benefits of a business's product and be echoed by all elements of the promotional mix to give a unified message.

4. **Determine the budget.** The best combination of promotional activities can be determined by finding that mix that has the biggest bang for the buck.

5. **Implement the promotional mix.** Businesses must always integrate and coordinate all promotional efforts. For example, public relations, sales promotions, and direct marketing efforts should try to produce results at the same time advertisements are scheduled to appear.

6. **Evaluate and adjust as needed.** The effectiveness of any promotional mix depends on clearly understood and measurable objectives. Each element of the mix, as well as the entire combination of the mix, will need to be adjusted as necessary for growth, for changing marketing objectives, or to correct ineffective promotional techniques.

Billboards like the one shown here may be a part of an IMC strategy.

Integrated Marketing Communication

How do companies make sure they are consistent across the entire promotional campaign? Because a typical promotional campaign involves a variety of tools and resources, it is important to ensure that they all work together harmoniously. **Integrated marketing communications (IMC)** is a strategy to deliver a clear, consistent, and unified message about a company and its products to customers at all contact points. This strategy contrasts with allowing members of an organization to develop their own communications with customers in isolation, which could give rise to conflicting messages, consumer confusion, and a loss of sales. It is essential that all members of the marketing team—whether they are involved with advertising, public relations, personal selling, or sales promotions—work together to foster and sustain a consistent and compelling message to create a positive brand image.

Hoover, the manufacturer of vacuums and other floor care products, launched an IMC campaign to introduce several new products. The campaign included running national television advertising spots, a partnership with Cleaning for a Reason (a national organization that cleans homes for women receiving cancer treatments), interacting with consumers through Facebook and Twitter, using direct response television, and using traditional public relations.[1] To run this campaign, Hoover dedicated a team of its own employees and hired several outside agencies to handle different aspects of the campaign. Consistency of the message across all these platforms nurtures good customer relations and repeat business. In short, everyone in an organization, as well as those hired by an organization, needs to be on the same page and communicate with one voice.

Promoting a product involves choosing the best combination of promotional tools to persuade customers to purchase a good, a service, or an idea. As Danny Perez's initial experience with his food cart business shows, achieving this blend can be a challenge. Having learned his lesson, Danny is now putting careful thought into each of the steps of developing an effective promotional campaign to determine the best promotional mix for his business. ■

Promotional Techniques: Advertising and Public Relations pp. 432–440

After graduating from design school, Monica Pace and Steven Tham rented a small space in New York City and opened their interior design business. They already had several clients—friends and family connections—but they knew they had to get the word out in a more formal and broader context if they ever wanted their business to grow. Steven was in charge of the Web site and creating a fan page on Facebook. Monica loved Twitter, so she began to send little design tweets each day, but she wondered how she would monitor all the conversations that were happening in response to her tweets. Monica and Steven were also wondering if these avenues were enough or whether they needed to place ads in magazines and/or newspapers or create and distribute flyers. What kind of advertising would be best for Monica and Steven? ■

Advertising is paid, impersonal mass communication from an identified sponsor to persuade or influence a targeted audience. When we think of advertising, many of us first think of television commercials, like those during the Super Bowl. But as we shall see, advertising is much more. Advertising has come a long way since its early days when simple ads like the Morton Salt ad you see here were used. In this section, you'll learn about the roles of advertising and public relations in the promotional mix.

The Role of Advertising

What role does advertising play in business and society?
Advertising plays a huge role in business as one of the promotional tools designed to communicate with targeted customers. It is especially important in the introduction and growth stages of a product's life cycle because it helps build mass brand awareness and brand association. In the maturity stage, advertising is often used to stress product differentiation. Effective advertising also builds brand loyalty and brand equity.

Although it is often costly, advertising can lead to lower prices for consumers. The more people know about a product and like it, sales and production increase. Given the frequent economies of scale associated with increased volumes of production, consumers get lower per-unit costs and lower-priced products. Advertising can also inform consumers of the value inherent in products and educate the public in their uses. However, critics argue that advertisers are less concerned about informing or educating consumers and more interested in misleading the public into perceptions of value or qualities that may not really exist. This debate continues. It echoes the need for ethical business behavior and can explain the existence of government laws and regulations that constrain advertising and other marketing practices.

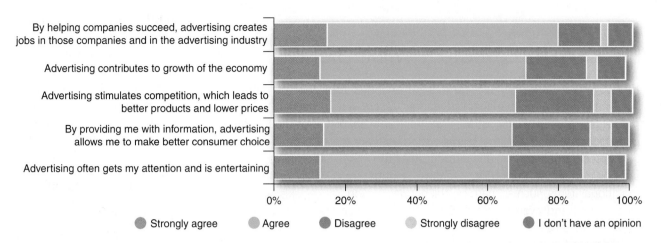

Strongly agree ● Agree ● Disagree ● Strongly disagree ● I don't have an opinion

Advertising also impacts the economy because of the huge sums of money spent on it. Google reported that its advertising services helped generate $54 billion in economic activity for U.S. businesses in 2009.[2] In addition, according to a Nielsen Company global survey, most consumers agree that advertising helps to create jobs in advertising agencies as well as related and supporting industries, which is beneficial to the economy. Moreover, consumers surveyed also believe that advertising contributes to competition between companies, thus helping to reduce costs and improve quality.[3] The results of the survey are shown in ▼ Figure 14.2.

▼ **Figure 14.2**
Nielsen Global Online Consumer Survey: Trust, Value, and Engagement in Advertising

Of course, companies spend money on advertising because it is economically in their best self-interest to do so. It doesn't just cost; it pays! For example, a business that advertises online with Google can exponentially increase traffic to its company Web site, leading to more sales.

Types of Advertising

What are the different types of advertising? In one form or another, advertising is undertaken by virtually all organizations. Different organizations use different types of advertising. The following are some of the more common types:

- **Product advertising** promotes a specific product's uses, features, and benefits. This is the type of advertising we most often think of.

- **Corporate (or institutional) advertising** focuses on creating a positive image toward an organization or an entire industry as opposed to a specific product. The campaign "Beef, It's What's for Dinner," sponsored by the Cattlemen's Beef Board and National Cattlemen's Beef Association, and the pharmaceutical industry's ads for treatments for leukemia and other diseases are examples of industry-wide institutional advertising. Government entities can also undertake institutional advertising. For example, state governments do so when they run advertisements that promote their states.

- **Comparative advertising** compares a brand's characteristics with those of other established brands. Examples include television commercials comparing toothpaste, pain relievers, and detergents.

- **Retail (or local) advertising** focuses on attracting customers to a fixed location, such as a department store or a grocery store.

- **B2B advertising** is directed to other businesses rather than to consumers. For example, Caterpillar, the earth-moving equipment company, advertises to construction companies.

- **Nonprofit advertising** focuses on promoting not-for-profit organizations, such as the Red Cross and the Nature Conservancy.

◎On Target Blendtec: Will It Blend?

How do you advertise a new blender and make it exciting? That was the problem George Wright, the marketing manager of Blendtec, faced. Wright needed to find a unique and creative venue to demonstrate the significant capabilities of the Blendtec Blender. He recognized that traditional television and print ads were becoming less effective, so he opted for online video and introduced a "fun" factor. The videos, posted to Blendtec's own channel on YouTube, feature Blendtec successfully grinding up rather untraditional items, such as marbles, cell phones, action figures, skis, an entire Thanksgiving dinner, and even the iPad. Since 2006, when it started running the demonstrations, this series of videos has collected more than 117 million views on YouTube, and demand doesn't seem to be dying down. The company is still receiving requests for what items to blend next. More importantly, sales have grown an amazing 500 percent.[4]

- **Public service advertising** communicates a message on behalf of a good cause, such as the prevention of wildfires.

- **Advocacy advertising** promotes an organization's position on a public issue, such as global warming or immigration. We are familiar with advocacy advertising undertaken during political campaigns by organizations that are independent of a political party or candidate.

- **Interactive advertising** uses interactive media, such as interactive video catalogs on the Internet or kiosks at shopping malls, to connect directly with consumers in a personal and engaging way.

- **Internet advertising** uses pop-up and banner ads and other techniques to direct people to an organization's Web site.

Types of Advertising Media

What are the different types of advertising media? Advertising media are the means of conveying a message about a product. Media conveying informative and persuasive messages exist all around us, including on the seats of grocery carts, on the sides of buses and trucks, on billboards, in magazines, in newspapers, and in brochures. Ads are also heard on telemarketing and telephone hold messages, in-store public address systems, and the radio. And, of course, we see ads on television, on the Internet, in movies, in video games, and in our mailboxes and in-boxes every day. Advertising is pervasive and has been around for many years. Some of the more traditional media for advertising include television, newspapers, magazines, radio, the Internet, and outdoor media. Outdoor media include billboards; signs in sports arenas; ads painted on the sides of cars, trucks, and buses; and even skywriting.

Beyond these advertising media, *direct mail advertising* remains one of the largest forms of advertising. You're probably familiar with direct mail advertising; you just have a different name for it—junk mail. Direct mail advertising comes in many forms, ranging from coupon offers to brochures and catalogs. However, it continues and may even grow because it is generally a very effective advertising tool.[5] Direct mail advertising allows companies to target their advertising dollars to customers who are most likely to buy their products and offer customized product offerings to these customers. Besides direct mail, the Yellow Pages are also frequently used to advertise. This medium is particularly important for small businesses.

How is social media being used in advertising? The emergence of Web 2.0 technologies—tools that allow users to connect, share information, communicate, and collaborate with each other online—has caused many companies to rethink how they can connect and communicate with their customers. Social media is a part of many IMC plans. Using Web sites such as Facebook, Twitter, YouTube, and Foursquare, companies are building customer support and gaining better insight into their customers and competitors. Companies create blogs and tweets to announce new products or corporate developments, post videos such as help tutorials and product demonstrations on YouTube, and create fan pages on Facebook that prompts interactions such as likes, favorites, and wall posts.

Best Buy's Twelpforce is a good example of using Twitter for employee to consumer interaction. Twelpforce is a service created through Twitter in which Best Buy encourages its employees to handle online customer service issues. If a customer tweets he or she has a problem with a product purchased at Best Buy, any Best Buy employee can step up to resolve the issue. Customers can then rank the employee's response. Best Buy employees are now even listing their Twelpforce ratings on their résumés as part of their job qualifications. Similarly, H&R Block posts tax tips via podcasts and Twitter and even rather amusing YouTube videos. As noted in an earlier chapter, Starbucks and Dell each have sites (MyStarbucksIdea.com and IdeaStorm.com, respectively) that allow customers to post ideas and suggestions as well as vote on which ones should be implemented.

What are the advantages and disadvantages of the different types of advertising media? The marketer's task is to find the most effective and efficient medium for transmitting his or her message to targeted customers—given marketing objectives and budget constraints. Every type of advertising media has certain advantages and disadvantages. For example, television advertising reaches a huge audience, but it's very expensive. Social media also reaches large numbers but can demand a great deal of manpower to follow and interpret the results. ▼ Table 14.1 lists some of the advantages and disadvantages of each major medium.

▼ Table 14.1

Advantages and Disadvantages of Advertising Media		
Media	**Advantages**	**Disadvantages**
Television	Good mass-market coverage; low cost per contact; combines sight, sound, and motion; good attention span	High cost; low recall; channel surfing or digital video recorders (DVRs) skip over ads; short exposure
Newspaper	Timing and geographic flexibility; good local market coverage; high credibility and acceptability	Short life span; lots of competition for attention; poor-quality reproductions
Magazine	High market segmentation; high-quality color; long life; longer attention span; high credibility	Declining readership; lots of competition for attention; high cost; long ad-purchase lead time
Radio	High geographic and demographic selectivity; low cost; creative opportunities with sound	Low attention span; short exposure time; information overload; limited coverage
Internet	Global and interactive possibilities; ease of segmentation; high audience interest; easy to measure responses	Audience controls exposure; clutter on each site; skewed demographically to surfers
Social Media	Relatively inexpensive to set up; results in immediate consumer feedback; provides access to consumer feedback on competition; builds customer relationships	Can be difficult to monitor, not a passive strategy—must be actively maintained
Outdoor	Able to select key geographic areas; low cost per impression; high frequency on major commuter routes	Short exposure time; brief messages; creative limitations; little segmentation possible
Direct Mail	High levels of segmentation; allows personalization; high flexibility; ad can be saved; measurable impact	High cost; can be rejected as junk mail and viewed as a nuisance
Yellow Pages	Inexpensive; commonly used and accessible; good local coverage and segmentation possible; long life	Costly for very small businesses; lists the competition as well

Advertising Trends

What are some important recent trends in advertising? One of the most important trends emerging from modern advertising has been the development of Internet advertising. In fact, it is one of the fastest-growing media because, in part, it allows firms to focus their advertising dollars on targeted customers. Other trends include product placement, infomercials, and global advertising.

How is advertising done online? Companies use the Internet for basic advertising functions, including spam (junk e-mail), pop-ups, banner ads, and other links found at Web sites to attract potential customers to a company's Web page. A banner ad is a graphic element that displays across the top or along the side of a Web page. Generally, when you click on a banner ad, you are hyperlinked to the sponsor's Web site. Banner ads are often more favorable to static print ads in that they can present multiple images as well as change appearances in a number of other ways in an effort to catch the viewer's attention. To get a banner ad on a Web site, the advertiser must either arrange to pay a Web site directly to post the ad on its site or pay a service like DoubleClick to post the banner on a variety of sites.

An alternative to banner ads is Google's advertising services: Google AdWords and Google AdSense. With Google AdWords, advertisers submit text-only ads to Google along with a list of relevant keywords. When a user types one of the keywords into the Google search engine, the text-only ad appears in a sidebar of the Google search results. The advertiser only pays Google when a user clicks on the ad. For example, if you are searching for a new couch and type sofa as a keyword, an advertisement from a local furniture store may appear in the sidebar. If you click on the advertisement, that furniture store will need to pay Google.

The benefits of using Google AdWords over traditional banner ads are that you pay only when someone clicks on the ad, and you receive the benefit of the millions of searches conducted on Google using the keywords that are relevant to your product rather than trying to target the specific Web sites your potential customers might visit. The potential downside to Google AdWords is that they are text-only, whereas banner ads are designed with more eye-catching graphics. Facebook has similar advertising capabilities to Google AdWords, and the pricing (at least for now) is more affordable.

Lastly, Google AdSense is a free program that enables Web site owners to earn money by displaying relevant ads on their Web sites. As an advertiser, you can pay Google to post your ad (similar to hosting a banner ad). Your ad will display only on those Web sites that are relevant to your product. For example, a blogger writing about landscaping ideas can choose to display an AdSense sidebar on his blog that might display ads from nurseries, garden supply shops, outdoor furniture retailers, and the like.

What's the benefit of online advertising? Once customers visit a company's Web site, the company can learn a lot about potential customers depending on where and how many times they click within its Web site. Businesses then attempt to interact with their customers through videos or even by starting a chat based on their perceived needs and wants. The idea is to work with customers to create a customized product offering that best meets the customers' unique tastes and preferences. If the business is able to consistently deliver high-quality value using these modern techniques, then Internet advertising can help businesses maintain positive customer relations.

What is product placement? Prominently displaying products in television shows, movies, and video games, where they will be seen by potential customers—a technique known as **product placement**—has become much more common. For example, in *Iron Man 2*, there are over 50 product placements, including Rolls Royce, Starbucks, LG, and Dick's Sporting Goods as well as the Audi R8 Spyder that was also featured in the first movie.[6] The advent of DVRs, which allow viewers to record shows and then fast-forward through ads, has driven companies to use product placement on television. An extreme example of product placement is the Apple iPad, which was featured throughout an episode of *Modern Family* that aired the night before the long awaited release of the gadget. The entire episode was about one of the characters receiving the iPad for his birthday, which was April 3, the first day of the iPad's release. A more traditional use of product placement is the prominent display of Coca-Cola glasses in front of the judges on American Idol.

Another variant of product placement is the banners of brand names, symbols, and slogans found on the walls of professional sports stadiums so that camera shots of the televised games will frequently display the banners' messages.

How are infomercials useful as an advertising technique? No doubt you've seen at least one commercial about Proactiv skin care products or with quintessential pitchman Billy Mays talking up OxyClean. Although Mays died in 2009, he was one of many celebrities hired to endorse products through **infomercials** (also known as **paid programming**). Infomercials run longer than traditional commercials, and many run as long as regular television programs. Infomercials typically appear as actual television programs, often in the form of a talk show, with little direct reference to the fact that they are actually ads. Unlike normal commercials, infomercials are designed to elicit a specific, direct, and quantifiable response from viewers. The pitches are similar to "call this toll-free number and order yours today" or "if you call within the next few minutes we will also . . . ." Infomercials often use "experts" or celebrities as guests or hosts to endorse and push their products. Infomercials have the advantage of showing the features of the advertised products in great detail. Some of the most successful infomercials include ads for the Bowflex Home Gym, Carlton Sheets Real Estate Tutorial, Proactiv Solution Acne Treatment, the Showtime Rotisserie Pro Electric Rotisserie Oven, and the Ionic Breeze Air Purifier.[7]

Billy Mays Jr. was known best as the pitchman for products sold through "as seen on TV" infomercials, such as OxyClean, Orange Glo, and Mighty Putty.

How has advertising gone global? The globalization of advertising is another important trend. Most products have to be customized to satisfy foreign customers. This means that products are tailored to meet the unique local tastes, preferences, and cultural sensitivities of foreign customers or satisfy the regulatory standards of different governments around the globe. Likewise, some advertising campaigns can be exported intact, while others have to be changed. Advertisers prefer to use the same message because it is cheaper, allows for a more globally integrated message, and allows for the pooling of talent to design the most compelling advertising message. But transferring domestically created, successful advertising messages abroad can be tricky. As we discussed in Chapter 4, marketers have to carefully consider the interpretations of their messages in the underlying cultural context of the foreign market. Increasingly, marketers are realizing that customized advertising campaigns to globally segmented markets work much better, just as domestic market segmentation is more effective.

Public Relations

What is public relations? Another important part of the promotional mix is public relations. **Public relations** is the management function that establishes and maintains mutually beneficial relationships between an organization and its stakeholders, including consumers, stockholders, employees, suppliers, the

BizChat

Product Placement: Not Just for Movies Anymore

If you watch any movie, you'll notice brand name products being used. Product placement is commonplace in television shows as well. Now with online video sites, such as YouTube, attracting so much attention, product placement agencies, such as Brandfame, have been created to connect online-video producers with the best brands for their products. Brandfame and other similar companies have found a way to capitalize on the fact that more people are spending time on the Internet. MTV was once the primary outlet for music videos, but the company prohibited the blatant display of products in the videos it would show. Now, however, YouTube, Vevo, and Hulu are the major vehicles for music videos; there are no restrictions on product placement on these Internet sites. In Lady Gaga's video to promote her single "Telephone," for example, a Virgin Mobile cell phone and Miracle Whip dressing are prominently displayed. The video was watched 62 million times on YouTube.[8] Companies are now flocking to place their products in online videos. Although some products are incorporated into videos free of charge, most are not. In fact, $3.6 billion was spent on product placement in music videos in 2009.[9] The next time you watch a music video, look for product placements.

For more information and discussion questions about this topic, check out the BizChat feature on my*biz*lab.com.

---

government, and the public in general. In other words, public relations promotes the image of a company or an individual.[10] All organizations—for-profits, not-for-profits, and even governments—are interested in public relations.

What steps are involved in developing public relations plans?

The idea behind public relations is to create and maintain a positive image of an organization in the minds of stakeholders. This begins with assessing public attitudes and perceptions of an organization. Sometimes, public opinion may be based on perceptions that have little to do with facts. Nevertheless, an honest audit of public opinion is necessary before specific public relations programs can be implemented to shape the image and reputation of an organization. Sometimes, public relations is necessary to correct or build back a corporate reputation after a significant mishap. British Petroleum (BP), Toyota, and American automobile manufacturers have all had to run public relations campaigns to build back the trust of their customers. Once an organization has listened carefully to public concerns and interests, it needs to respond by changing its behavior or correcting misperceptions. Finally, an organization needs to inform the public of any changes it has made or educate the public about the facts associated with it.

What are some common public relations tools?

Several specific types of public relations tools exist to build a positive business image. They can be classified by whether the news transmitted is controlled, semicontrolled, or uncontrolled by the organization.[11] The degree of control hinges on how and when the message is delivered.

- *Controlled messages* include corporate (or institutional) advertising, advocacy advertising, and public service advertising. A company may also disseminate annual reports, brochures, flyers, and newsletters or provide films or speakers to send a controlled message to targeted audiences.

- *Semicontrolled messages* are placed on Web sites, in chat rooms, and on blogs. In these forums, what people say about a company is not strictly regulated. Other semicontrolled messages include sponsorships of sporting events and other special events because participation by the press and stakeholders is not under the control of the sponsoring company.

- *Uncontrolled messages* generally take the form of *publicity*.

How is publicity helpful? Information about an individual, an organization, or a product transmitted through mass media at no charge is called **publicity.** Publicity has two advantages over advertising. First, it is free. Second, it is more believable because it is often presented as a news story. One example of a successful use of public relations was the Doritos "Crash the Super Bowl" campaign. This campaign invited consumers to create their own Doritos ads, with the winning ad appearing in a Super Bowl spot. The campaign successfully used public relations and the Internet to generate interest in the contest, as well as spurred sales of the product. Doritos did not use print media itself to announce the campaign; rather, the company used public relations to get the story picked up by national publications, such as *TIME*, the *New York Times*, and the *Wall Street Journal*, giving the product the exposure it needed but without the cost. Mentions of the contest were also broadcast on major morning and evening news shows, providing additional exposure. The company then used its Web site and counted on viral marketing as the videos were created and shared online. As a result, there was a 12 percent increase in sales during the month the campaign took place.[12]

Publicity, when it is positive, is a great cost savings to companies because they don't pay for publicity; it just happens. However, publicity is *not* controlled by the seller; it is controlled by the media, which can be its disadvantage. If, when, and how a news release, a press conference, a captioned photograph, an appearance on a talk show, or a staged event will be covered by the media is outside the control of public relations managers.

RONALD McDONALD
HOUSE CHARITIES

McDonald's receives a good deal of positive publicity for its Ronald McDonald House Charities.

How does a company generate positive publicity? Naturally, keeping friendly relations with the press increases the probability that a "newsworthy" story will be covered and treated with a favorable spin. Nevertheless, public relations managers need to ensure that publicity releases are timely, interesting, accurate, and in the public interest. For example, when GE launched it "ecomagination" campaign to portray itself as an environmental leader, was it sincere about the environment or was it just jockeying for a favorable marketing impression? The consensus was that GE was sincere. This may explain why the campaign won the prestigious 2006 Silver Effie Award in the category of Corporate Reputation, Image, and Identity.[13] GE's publicity releases were timely, interesting, accurate, and in the public interest.

It appears green business is good business, not just for GE. For example, Home Depot, the world's largest seller of lumber, now gives preference to vendors that offer wood certified by the Forest Stewardship Council (FSC). The FSC determines whether lumber is grown and harvested responsibly to preserve environmental integrity. Shoppers can identify FSC-certified lumber by its green tree logo. IKEA, based in Sweden, where nearly half the forests are certified, produces as much furniture as possible from FSC-certified wood. These companies received a lot of publicity when the documentary *Buyer Be Fair* first aired on public television in March 2006. You can bet these companies appreciate the publicity for their efforts.

Another example of positive publicity is the favorable press that Ronald McDonald House Charities receives for providing families with temporary living quarters while their children are in the hospital. Corporate philanthropy is generally good publicity, especially if it results in getting your name on a building, an annual event, a scholarship, or volunteer programs that are visible to the community. Many smaller companies give to local schools, hospitals, and arts programs. Some large corporations renowned for their philanthropic and charitable efforts include Microsoft, Target, Avon, HP, AOL, and Timberland.[14]

Whether motivated by publicity needs or a sense of social responsibility, giving back to the community doesn't just *cost* companies; it *pays* them. Most of us like buying products from companies if we believe that some of our money will be used to give back to the community or reward companies for doing the right thing.

How does a company respond to negative publicity? A final role of public relations personnel is managing a crisis. *Damage control* is a company's effort to minimize the harmful effects of a negative event. Negative publicity can, in a matter of days, tear down a firm's image that took decades to build up. For example, ExxonMobil still suffers from the *Exxon Valdez* oil spill accident that occurred over two decades ago. How long it will take BP to completely recover from the oil-rig explosion in the Gulf of Mexico that occurred in the spring of 2010? It is anybody's guess. BP is not taking any chances, however; soon after the explosion, it began to run spots on television explaining all the things the company was doing to help the communities hurt by the disaster recover. Sometimes, bad news doesn't come from the media but from word of mouth. In the event of bad news, a company must stand ready to react—and react quickly. No easy remedies exist for crises, but being honest, accepting responsibility, and making other ethical responses are the first steps toward regaining credibility and reestablishing a positive image.

Advertising, public relations, and publicity are important elements in the promotional mix. Monica and Steven consulted with a friend who is a public relations specialist and asked for advice on how best to get the word out about their new venture. For now, it seems they are generating just enough business with their current promotional efforts. They will continue to get the word out via their friends, relatives, and business contacts as well as work the social media sites. They can't afford to do too much more, but they also know they can't afford to do any less. ■

Promotional Techniques: Personal Selling and Sales Promotion pp. 440–447

Keith Jefferson is nervous about giving his first big sales pitch alone. He's trying to convince an electronics wholesaler to switch from its current trucking company to his company. Despite his nerves, the presentation goes well, and the client seems receptive. After the presentation, the client asks him how fluctuating oil prices will affect shipping rates. Keith has no idea what to say. How could he have been more effective with his potential client? ■

Personal selling is more complicated than simply telling a customer to buy your product. It's a complex process that involves several steps, each of which must be executed with great thought, planning, and care. In this section, you'll learn about personal selling as well as yet another promotional technique, sales promotion.

Personal Selling

What is personal selling? **Personal selling** is direct communication between a firm's sales force and potential buyers to make a sale and build good customer relationships. For example, a laboratory supplies company may deploy a representative to a research facility to demonstrate new products. Good salespeople don't just want to sell their products; they want to serve customers. A salesperson should help customers with their buying decisions by understanding their needs and presenting the advantages and disadvantages of a product. Salespeople must effectively represent their companies by establishing good customer relationships that foster repeat business and long-term company success.

Why is personal selling important?
The sales staff is often the first contact point for many customers. To build good customer relationships, a salesperson should be customer oriented, competent, dependable, honest, and likable. Good salespeople are also able to listen carefully to customer needs. They possess knowledge of a company's total product offerings and make the buying process as easy as possible for the customer. In many B2B or industrial sales, millions of dollars may be involved in a single purchase, such as buying an airplane or building an office building. You can see why businesses want nothing less than truly professional salespeople—people who can deliver carefully prepared presentations, establish rapport with customers, and negotiate details with skill. In fact, the demand for well-educated, well-trained professional salespeople today explains why some salespeople are top earners in their companies. It also explains why sales positions still account for approximately 1 in 10 jobs in the United States.[15] The unflattering stereotype of the backslapping, fast-talking salesman of the past certainly doesn't depict the modern sales consultant. Today's sales consultants are highly skilled professionals.

What are the advantages and disadvantages of having a sales force?
Obtaining and keeping good salespeople is expensive. Excluding direct compensation (salaries and commissions) and employment benefits, most sales personnel require training and tools to keep track and maintain their customers and territories. This helps explain why personal selling is the most expensive part of the promotional mix for most companies, along with the fact that sales, unlike advertising, is labor intensive and deals with only one buyer at a time. Generally, personal selling is preferred over advertising when selling a high-value, custom-made, or technically complex product. Advertising is more cost-effective when selling a low-value, standardized product that is easily understood.

What are the different types of salespeople?
There are three general types of salespeople. Of course, some salespeople, especially in smaller businesses, may be required to fulfill all three roles.

1. **Order Getters.** An **order getter** is a salesperson who increases a company's sales by selling to new customers and increasing sales to existing customers. This task is sometimes called *creative selling*. It requires recognizing customer needs and providing information to potential buyers of a product's uses and features. Many companies—such as real estate, insurance, appliance, automobile, and heavy industrial equipment firms—depend on new sales. To enhance repeat sales, salespeople stay in touch with current customers to ensure satisfaction. Salespeople also use current customers as sources for leads on new prospects. Examples of order getters include car sales representatives, real estate and insurance agents and brokers, manufacturing and wholesale sales representatives, and securities and financial services sales representatives.

2. **Order Takers.** An **order taker** is a salesperson who handles repeat sales and builds positive customer relationships. One of the major jobs of order takers is to ensure buyers have sufficient quantities of products when and where they are needed. This is especially true in B2B sales, such as selling grocery items to grocery stores or selling shoes to shoe stores. Order takers generally handle routine orders for standardized products that do not require a lot of technical sales expertise. It is becoming more common for orders to be placed electronically using the Internet, so the role of order takers is changing more toward identifying and solving problems, though some sites with live chat capabilities are using a "real" person to assist with questions and then take your order

online. Some of the same people who are order getters are also order takers. Most of us encounter order takers as retail sales clerks and cashiers.

3. **Support Personnel. Support personnel** are salespeople who obtain new customers but also focus on assisting current customers with technical matters. They are most common in B2B sales, where manufacturers assist wholesalers and retailers with the best ways to sell and promote their products to ultimate consumers. We'll discuss the role of wholesalers and retailers in greater depth later.

All salespeople, whatever their specific role at any given time, are ambassadors for a business. They need to listen carefully, act as sounding boards, and relay customer feedback to an organization. This allows firms to improve existing products or create new products to better meet customer needs and preferences. Serving customers better is a large part of what building good customer relationships and promotion is all about.

What are the steps in the selling process❓ The best way to understand
the personal selling process is to look at an example. Suppose your company sells a sophisticated GPS for use in the trucking industry. Your latest model allows trucking firms to keep track of their rigs via a password-protected Web site that features a digital map display of vehicle location and speed, engine use, refrigerated load temperature, door alarms or other motion-sensing devices that have been activated, cargo weight, and odometer reports. You can imagine the benefits of such a system for trucking companies. Although this is a B2B example, the steps involved in the selling process are essentially the same for selling a consumer product, even though selling a B2B product is usually more complex. In all cases, a salesperson has to be knowledgeable about his or her product and competitors' products.

No two salespeople are alike, and no two selling situations are the same. However, six steps emerge from all personal selling: prospecting, approaching the prospect, presenting, overcoming objections, closing the sale, and following up. This six-step personal selling procedure is outlined in ▼ **Figure 14.3.**

How are customers identified❓ The first step in the personal selling
process is to identify qualified potential customers. This is known as **prospecting.** Notice that businesses need to not only find potential customers but also identify those who are *qualified* to buy. To be qualified to buy means that a potential customer has the ability and the authority to purchase, plus the willingness to listen to the sales message. Prospecting can be a daunting task; it often involves cold calling, or approaching a prospect over the phone unexpectedly. Although cold calling can be difficult and unpleasant, it is an effective strategy for some businesses. Some salespeople find leads at trade shows, from those who have scouted a company's Web site, or, better yet, from currently satisfied customers who are willing to recommend them to others because of their superior product and service.

What is best way to approach a prospect❓ The second step of the per-
sonal selling process involves two parts: the *preapproach* and the *actual approach*. The preapproach involves salespeople doing their homework. This is especially critical if they are trying to sell a B2B product, such as a GPS device. Salespeople must learn as much as possible about their potential customers to determine their likely needs and think about how they might be able to satisfy those needs. In our trucking example, you would need to determine the people in the trucking firm who would be most interested in buying your GPS product and learn as much about them as you can. Are they currently using GPS devices? If so, what brand is it? How is your product better? You should also decide on the best approach. Should you phone them, send a letter, or make a personal visit? The timing decision of the actual approach should also be carefully planned to not catch the prospect at a busy time or at an off time in the budget cycle.

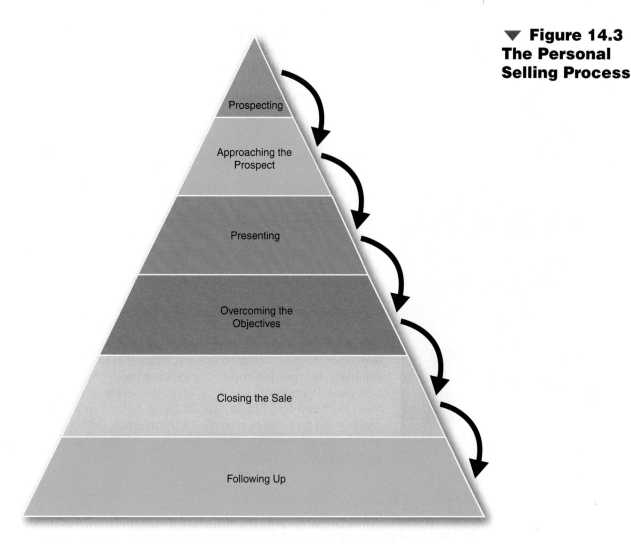

Prospecting

Approaching the
Prospect

Presenting

Overcoming the
Objectives

Closing the Sale

Following Up

In the actual approach, the idea is to meet, greet, and put the prospect at ease. First impressions are lasting impressions! This is the salesperson's first chance at building a long-lasting relationship. Good salespeople present themselves as knowledgeable and friendly professionals who are genuinely interested in serving customers. The first impression is followed by asking some questions to learn about a potential customers' needs. Then the salesperson must listen carefully to those responses. In our example, because GPS hardware and software is often complicated, you may want to remind a prospect that your product is superior, and your service is also better than that of the competition. You can offer to help install the system, train employees in its use, and offer free 24-hour service and upgrades when necessary.

How are the details of the product explained? In the actual presentation of the GPS technology, the next step in the personal selling process, you'll need to tell your product's "story" and detail how your product can help the trucking firm. You should demonstrate the product and let the prospect use it as well. Your presentation should be carefully planned using the most advanced presentation technologies that allow for the full use of multimedia effects. Most importantly, you should ask probing questions during your presentation and listen carefully to answers. Listening is more important than talking. You can't serve a customer until you fully understand his or her needs or problems.

What happens if the prospect has a problem? Objections to buying are common. Good salespeople anticipate them and are prepared to counter them. Once objections surface, you should use this opportunity to provide more information on your GPS product and turn these objections into reasons to buy. You

How to close a deal is an art learned with practice.

may invite others from your company to join in at this point to address any objections via a teleconference or a virtual meeting. This provides an opportunity to establish a rapport based on trust between you, your company, and the prospect. Overcoming objections can be the beginning of a mutually beneficial and lasting relationship.

How is the sale finalized? After overcoming objections, the next step is hopefully to close the sale and ask for a purchase. You should look for physical cues, comments, or questions that signal the time to ask the buyer for an order. You may want to review points of agreement, ask the buyer which model he or she prefers, ask how many units are needed, or sweeten the deal by offering more favorable credit terms or throwing in an extra quantity free of charge. Closing the sale is an art that is learned with practice.

What happens after the sale is made? To ensure a long-term relationship and repeat business, be sure to follow up with the customer to ensure he or she is happy with his or her new GPS product. Stand ready to promptly help him or her with any problems after the sale. Ask for feedback. Relay that feedback to your company as input for improving existing products or designing new ones. Periodically check up on customers by phone or send them birthday and holiday cards. Good follow-up service and rapport can give rise to referrals or testimonials that can be used to enhance future sales. Following up is all about building and nurturing relationships.

Sales Promotion

What is sales promotion? The final element of the promotional mix is sales promotion. **Sales promotions** are short-term activities that target consumers and other businesses for the purpose of generating interest in a product. Sales promotions encompass activities designed to inform, persuade, and remind targeted customers about a product, which have not already been undertaken by advertising, public relations, or personal selling. As consumers, we see sales promotions almost everywhere: from coupons in newspapers to rebate offers on a new car purchase, from e-mail announcements offering discounted prices on airline tickets to end-of-aisle displays of potato chips at a local grocery store tempting impulse purchases.

What are the two general types of sales promotions? Most companies' products go through a distribution system before they ever reach the final consumer. These companies encourage middlemen (e.g., wholesalers) to push their products through to end users. Any incentives to push a product through the distribution system to final consumers are called **trade (or B2B) sales promotions.** In addition, **consumer sales promotions** are incentives designed to increase final consumer demand for a product. The whole idea behind all sales promotions is to generate interest and excitement around a product. Businesses need to create a reason why stores should not only carry their products but also encourage their purchase by consumers. Companies want consumers to be so excited about their products that they seek the products out and ask for them by name. In short, companies want to create a tipping point so that all involved will opt for their products instead of competitors' alternatives.

What are some consumer sales promotional tools? Consumer sales promotions are aimed at the end users, or final consumers. Consumer sales promotions are intended to increase demand for a good or a service by providing that extra incentive to tip consumers in favor of a specific brand. Sales promotions are also aimed at providing customers with another reason to feel good about their purchases. The timing of consumer sales promotions is important to get maximum impact. They need to be strategically coordinated with other elements in the promotional mix. Here are some of the most common consumer promotional tools.

- **Coupons.** Coupons are discount certificates that reduce the price of a product and are redeemable at the time of purchase. Coupons are found in print ads, on packages, in direct mail, at checkout counters, and on the Internet. They are used to encourage the purchase of a new product or generate repeat sales. Coupons are the most common and popular consumer promotional tools because consumers like the sense of getting a bargain.

- **Rebates.** Rebates provide a reduced price if the rebate form is mailed in along with a proof of purchase. Unlike coupons, the discounted price is not realized at the point of purchase. Because most people do not redeem the rebates, they are an inexpensive way for businesses to promote sales.

- **Frequent-user incentives.** Many businesses, such as restaurants and fast-food chains, offer frequent buyer cards for a free meal or item after a certain amount of purchases. Some credit card companies encourage customers to use their credit cards for purchases that accumulate points redeemable for merchandise. Several airlines offer frequent-flyer miles that are redeemable for free tickets for additional travel. Some merchandise-buying clubs, such as Sam's Club, also offer points redeemable for cash back at the end of the year. These incentives encourage customer loyalty and repeat business.

- **Point-of-purchase (POP) displays.** These displays are strategically located to draw attention and encourage impulse purchases. Examples are items placed in racks close to checkout counters at grocery stores and end-of-aisle stacks of soft drink bottles. Studies indicate that POP displays really work.[16]

- **Free samples.** Free samples are an effective way to introduce a new product, get nonusers to try it, or get current users to use it in a new way—especially if the samples are made available where the product is sold. Most of us have sampled small portions of foods at local grocery

Consumer sales promotions, such as coupons and rebates, are aimed at end users, or final consumers.

IKEA offered "free samples" of its products by leaving displays of their furniture in several busy Paris subway stops.

stores. Some companies also mail samples of products, such as cereal and shampoo, directly to consumers. Generally it's hard to give away free samples of furniture, but IKEA, the Swedish furniture retailer, came up with an innovative way to have prospective customers sample their furniture, which also emphasized its durability. The company displayed their furniture in several busy Paris subway stops for commuters to try out as they waited for their trains.[17]

- **Contests and sweepstakes.** Many companies use contests and sweepstakes to increase the sales of their products. As a reward for participating, consumers might win cash, free products, or vacations. As an added benefit, companies increase their contact lists from the information that contest entrants supply.

- **Advertising specialties.** Companies frequently create and give away everyday items, such as bottle or can openers, caps, and key rings with their names and logos printed on them. Companies prefer to use inexpensive handouts that will yield constant free advertising when used by the recipient.

Other consumer sales promotion tools include bonuses (buy one, get one free), catalogs, demonstrations, special events, lotteries, premiums, and cents-off deals. Consumer sales promotions are becoming more common because they help segment markets and are cost-effective.

What are some trade sales promotional tools? If you want other businesses to become interested and excited about carrying your product, you must first generate in-house enthusiasm. You will need to educate your entire staff, especially your sales staff, about your product and its many uses, features, and benefits. This may require some formal training of your sales staff on how to best present your product. To generate leads, you may need to send your sales staff to trade shows equipped with sophisticated multimedia presentations, full-color brochures, shirts, hats, coffee mugs with your product logo, and a lot of excitement. You must create some internal buzz and excitement for your product before you can ever expect other businesses to be interested in carrying and promoting your product. Once your staff is energized, then you can work on creating the same level of energy and excitement for distributors. Some of the specific tools used to promote a product to other businesses include the following:

- Trade shows and conventions
- Trade allowances (deals and price reductions to wholesalers, dealers, and retailers)
- Cooperative advertising (a manufacturer agrees to pay for some of the advertising costs of the retailer)
- Free merchandise
- Sales contests (e.g., a free trip to Hawaii for those who sell the most)
- Dealer listings (ads of your product that mention retail outlets where it can be found)
- Catalogs and store demonstrations
- In-store displays
- Quantity discounts
- Training and support programs

When it comes to trade sales promotional techniques, firms have many options from which to choose. If one doesn't work, they can easily adopt new strategies until they find the best combination.

What has been the Internet's effect on sales promotion?
Technology has also had a huge impact on sales promotions. More and more companies are using the Internet to promote their products by using their companies'

▼ Table 14.2

The Advantages and Disadvantages of Promotional Tools		
Promotional Tool	**Advantages**	**Disadvantages**
Advertising	• Builds brand awareness and brand loyalty • Reaches a mass audience	• Expensive • Impersonal • Not good at closing a sale
Public Relations	• Often seen as more credible than advertising • Inexpensive way of reaching many customers	• Risk of losing control • Cannot always control what other people write or say about your product
Personal Selling	• Highly interactive communication between the buyer and the seller • Excellent for communicating a complex product, information, and features • Good for building customer relationships and closing a sale	• Expensive • Not suitable if there are thousands of buyers
Sales Promotions	• Can stimulate quick increases in sales by targeting promotional incentives on particular products • Good short-term tactical tool	• If used over the long term, customers may get used to the effect • Too much promotion may damage the brand image

Web sites to offer all kinds of deals. Moreover, many businesses post positive comments about their products and their companies on Internet blogs or publish interesting, amusing, or informative videos to generate positive publicity for their products. The idea is to create a positive image and use word of mouth to generate enthusiasm for a product and stimulate sales. In addition, podcasting allows companies to promote their products directly to targeted customers by providing audio and video feeds for download. We can expect further use of technology and the Internet for sales promotions in the future.

What are the advantages and disadvantages of the promotional mix? As you've learned, when developing the best promotional mix for a product, companies must weigh the advantages and disadvantages of each of the four main options—advertising, public relations, personal selling, and sales promotions. ▼ Table 14.2 summarizes some of these key advantages and disadvantages.

Recall Keith Jefferson? He wasn't prepared to answer questions about the service he was offering when giving his sales pitch to a potential client. As a result of his lack of preparedness, he wasn't able to land the account. In retrospect, he should have brought in someone else from the company who could answer this question or offered to get back to the client with the answer. Next time, he will also be more prepared to answer that type of question from another prospect. As Keith's story shows, determining which promotional tool to use is merely half the battle. Effective execution—whether it is an ad campaign, a public relations event, a sales pitch, or a sales promotion—is equally important. ■

Distribution: Marketing Intermediaries pp. 448–458

L iv Karlsen listened as the professor of her modern U.S. Literature class rattled off the book requirements for the new semester. Most were from the *New York Times* best seller's list, and Liv was required to have the first book read by the end of the week. After class, she ran over to the bookstore on campus to pick up the book, only to be told the bookstore had run out. Liv immediately used her smartphone to check whether any local retail stores had the book in stock. Fortunately, one of the major chain bookstores showed it in stock, so Liv rushed over, only to be disappointed again. The last copy had been sold about an hour before she arrived. Now, it seemed the only option for Liv was to purchase the book online and pay extra for overnight shipping. What is the distribution process of a book? How does it get from the publisher to bookstores? Is the distribution process the same for all products? ■

Distribution is the process that makes products available to consumers when and where the consumers want them. It is a part of a more complex and bigger system called the *supply chain*. Distribution is a very complicated but essential process in the world of business today. Most of us don't think about the transfer and storage of the products we buy—unless something goes wrong and we are unable to get the products we want, when and where we want them, like Liv Karlsen. You can imagine the challenges companies face trying to guarantee that customers have access to their products at the right time and in the right quantity and place and are handled correctly if they are returned unused or due to a defect or expiration. The distribution (or place) function of the 4 Ps of marketing is often overshadowed by the more visible product, pricing, and sales promotional strategies. In this section, you'll learn about the distribution process.

The Supply Chain and Supply Chain Management

What is the supply chain? The **supply chain** encompasses all the components—both inside and outside an organization—that are necessary to convert raw materials into a good or a service and then get it into the hands of customers. Managing the entire process of getting products out the door and eventually into the hands of final consumers is known as **supply chain management.** The Association for Operations Management states that the objective of supply chain management is "creating net value, building a competitive infrastructure, leveraging worldwide logistics, synchronizing supply with demand, and measuring performance globally."[18]

Supply chain management is a very complex and overarching process and affects nearly every part of a company's organization. It can be divided into three "flows" or processes:

1. The *product flow* traces the product itself—from raw resources to finished product and final delivery to the customer.

2. The *information flow* traces all the information about a product as it moves through the process, such as order information and delivery status.

3. The *financial flow* traces payment schedules, credit terms, and any other additional financial arrangements that may be necessary, such as title and ownership arrangements.

Technology has helped to improve the efficiencies involved in supply chain management. Software products, such as enterprise resource planning, customer relationship management, and business management software, as well as Web-based communication methods, such as instant messaging, help to coordinate the movement of goods and information. The remainder of this section concentrates on two subsets of the supply chain: *distribution channels* and *marketing intermediaries*.

Distribution Channels and Marketing Intermediaries

What is a channel of distribution? A channel of distribution is the part of the supply chain that focuses on getting the product to the ultimate consumers. More specifically, a **distribution channel** is a set of marketing intermediaries who buy, sell, or transfer title (or ownership) of products as they are passed from producer to consumer or business user. Some distribution channels involve several intermediaries, while others are shorter with fewer intermediaries.

What are marketing intermediaries? A **marketing intermediary**, formerly known as a *middleman*, is a business or person that moves goods and services between producers and consumers (in a B2C environment) or between business users (in a B2B environment). Intermediaries, therefore, pass along products from manufacturers to end users. Sometimes no intermediaries are needed, such as when you buy a dozen ears of corn from the farmer down the road. But usually many intermediaries of different types work to ensure a product reaches consumers.

What are the different types of intermediaries? There are three main types of intermediaries:

- **Wholesalers** are intermediaries that buy and resell products to other wholesalers, retailers, and industrial users. For example, your local grocery store probably purchased the Tide laundry detergent on its shelves from a wholesaler who bought it from P&G, the manufacturer.

- **Agents/brokers** are intermediaries that facilitate negotiations between buyers and sellers of goods and services but never take title (ownership) of the products traded. Examples include real estate agents and brokers, stockbrokers, and agricultural brokers. Even eBay, which never owns the various items it sells, can be considered an agent/broker because the company facilitates the transfer of ownership from sellers to buyers.

- **Retailers** are intermediaries that buy products for resale to consumers. As consumers, we buy most of our products at retail outlets, like the Tide laundry detergent from a local supermarket.

We will look at each type of intermediaries in greater detail later in this section.

Why are intermediaries necessary? You might wonder why we need all of these intermediaries and whether they serve to only drive up prices. It's certainly true that each link in the distribution channel incurs costs, and intermediaries must cover these costs and earn a profit to remain in business. However, as explained above, intermediaries add efficiency.

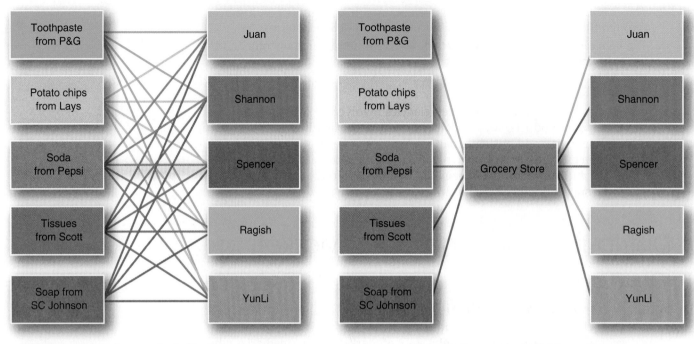

25 individual transactions required without an intermediary   10 transactions required with intermediary

▼ **Figure 14.4**
The Efficiencies of Intermediaries
The introduction of an intermediary reduces the number of exchange relationships between manufacturers and retailers.

To examine the efficiencies provided by intermediaries in the exchange of goods and services from producer to consumer, review ▼ **Figure 14.4,** which shows five consumers and five producers. Without an intermediary, each consumer would have to contact each producer to order the desired goods. Without intermediaries, if Juan, Shannon, Spencer, Ragish, and YunLi each wanted toothpaste, potato chips, soda, tissues, and soap, they would each have to go to the individual companies to get the items. That would involve 25 transactions (5 transactions for each person). Now suppose a grocery store stocks and resells each of the five manufacturers' products. Now the five manufacturers and five customers have only one intermediary (the grocery store) to deal with. Each of the manufacturers makes one trip to the grocery store to deliver the items, and Juan, Shannon, Spencer, Ragish, and YunLi each make only one trip to the grocery store to get those products. This reduces the number of exchange relationships from 25 to 10. Intermediaries therefore reduce the time and costs of providing products to customers.

In short, intermediaries are a necessary part of the process. If they are not available to do the job, someone else (ultimately the consumer) would need to perform the task of retrieving a product directly from a manufacturer. Intermediaries also help to transport and store goods and are often involved in other parts of marketing, such as advertising and relationship building. Some intermediaries even serve as interim bankers, financing inventories or giving credit. Historically, intermediaries have proven that they can perform these functions more efficiently and cost effectively than others. And, while intermediaries add costs, these costs are offset by the value added.

What are the different types of distribution channels? Not all channels of distribution are the same. As illustrated in ▼ **Figure 14.5,** the type of distribution channel used depends on the type of product being brought to the consumer. The number of intermediaries depends on whether greater efficiency or additional value is provided by adding another link to the chain in the distribution system. For example, in Figure 14.5, Jeanne buys cosmetics directly from Avon without the need for any intermediary, but when Kevin buys a Goodyear tire, the tire is manufactured at a Goodyear plant and then delivered to a Goodyear dealer, which sells it to Kevin. Adding the additional component to this channel of distribution adds value to the product because the retail shop can provide information

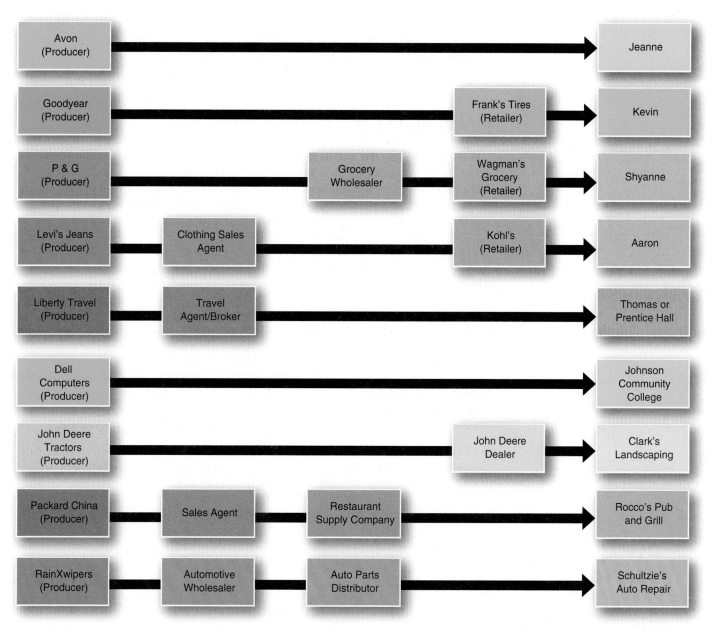

▼ **Figure 14.5
Different Distribution
Channels**

and service more easily than can the manufacturing plant and also provides convenience because Kevin lives closer to the store, not the plant.

Food products in a grocery store have a more complicated distribution system, requiring the use of brokers, wholesalers, and finally a retail store to get the products to the consumer, but all are necessary to achieve efficiency. Similar channels of distribution also exist in B2B markets. Competitive markets determine what number of intermediaries will be required to achieve the greatest level of efficiency.

How has the Internet impacted distribution? An important recent development in the distribution of products has been the increased use of **e-commerce,** buying and selling on the Internet. It is now possible for consumers to buy thousands of products online. Businesses are also using the Internet to buy and sell to other businesses. For example, customer relationship software can be purchased online and downloaded for sales to other businesses. These direct channels, such as buying Avon products or a Dell computer in Figure 14.5, bypass all intermediaries.

E-commerce is prevalent in all distribution channels, not just the direct channel. Almost all firms—whether they are manufacturers, agents, brokers, wholesalers, or retailers—have Web sites that allow customers to shop, place an order, and pay. Many sites also use interactive videos to enable customers to explore the features of products from their homes or offices. E-commerce is expected to continue to grow because of the convenience it provides.

Wholesale Intermediaries

What services do wholesalers provide? Wholesalers are intermediaries that buy and resell products to other wholesalers, retailers, and industrial users. They are different from retailers, such as Target, because retailers sell products only to final consumers. It can be confusing because of some consumers purchase products at wholesale distributors, such as Sam's Club, Costco, or Office Depot, which also sell to other businesses. One of the most effective ways to distinguish wholesalers from retailers is to remember that wholesalers *primarily* sell B2B products, while retailers sell *only* consumer products. Nevertheless, wholesalers provide a host of services to their customers, some of which are listed in ▼ **Table 14.3.**[19]

What are the different types of wholesalers? Wholesalers are technically known as **merchant wholesalers,** independently owned businesses that take ownership (title) of the products they handle. Merchant wholesalers include *full-service wholesalers* and *limited-service wholesalers*. Full-service wholesalers provide a full line of services: carrying stock, maintaining a sales force, offering credit, making deliveries, and providing management assistance. There are two types of full-service wholesalers: *wholesale merchants* sell primarily to retailers, and *industrial distributors* sell to manufacturers and institutions, such as hospitals and the government.

As intermediaries, limited-service wholesalers offer fewer services than full-service wholesalers. There are four major types of limited-service wholesalers:

- **Cash-and-carry wholesalers** carry a limited line of fast-moving goods and sell to small retailers for cash. They normally do not deliver. For example, a small fish store may drive to a cash-and-carry fish wholesaler, buy fish for cash, and bring the merchandise back to the store.

▼ **Table 14.3**

Services Provided by Wholesalers	
Service	**Description**
Bulk breaking	Wholesalers save retailers money by buying in bulk and breaking bulk packages down into smaller quantities.
Financing	Wholesalers finance retailers by giving credit, and they finance manufacturers by ordering early and paying bills on time.
Management service and advice	Wholesalers often help retailers train their sales clerks, improve store layouts and displays, and set up accounting and inventory control systems.
Market information	Wholesalers give information to manufacturers and retailers about competitors, new products, and price developments.
Risk bearing	Wholesalers absorb risk by taking title to merchandise and bearing the costs of theft, damage, spoilage, and obsolescence.
Selling and promoting	Wholesalers' sales forces help manufacturers reach many smaller retailers at a low cost. The wholesaler has more contacts and is often more trusted by the retailer than the distant manufacturer.
Transportation	Wholesalers can provide quicker delivery to buyers because they are closer than the producers.
Warehousing	Wholesalers hold inventories, thereby reducing the inventory costs and risks of suppliers and retailers.

- **Truck wholesalers** (or truck jobbers) sell and deliver directly from their trucks. They generally carry semiperishable items that regular wholesalers prefer not to carry. For example, trucks that deliver tobacco, candy, or snack food to convenience stores and restaurants are truck wholesalers.

- **Drop shippers** don't carry inventory or handle products. On receiving an order, they select a manufacturer, who ships the merchandise directly to the customer. Drop shippers assume title and risk from the time of the order to delivery. They operate in bulk industries, such as lumber, coal, and heavy equipment.

- **Rack jobbers** serve grocery stores and drug retailers, mostly in nonfood items. They send delivery trucks to stores, where the delivery people set up racks or displays within the stores. Rack jobbers retain title to the goods and bill the retailer only for the goods sold to consumers.

Because of their limited functions, these limited-service wholesalers usually operate at a lower cost than wholesale merchants and industrial distributors.

Agents and Brokers

What distinguishes agents and brokers? Agents and brokers are unique among intermediaries because they do not take title to the products traded. They merely facilitate the buying and selling of products and earn a commission on the selling price. What distinguishes agents from brokers is that agents represent the buyers or the sellers who hired them on a more permanent basis, while brokers are hired on a temporary basis.

What are some common types of agents? Three common types of agents are manufacturers' agents, selling agents, and purchasing agents.

- *Manufacturers' agents* can represent two or more manufacturers of complementary lines. A formal written agreement with each manufacturer covers pricing, territories, order handling, delivery service and warranties, and commission rates. Manufacturers' agents are often used in such lines as apparel, furniture, and electrical goods. Most manufacturers' agents are small businesses with only a few skilled salespeople. Small manufacturers may hire an agent if they cannot afford their own field sales forces, while larger manufacturers rely on agents to open new territories or cover territories that cannot support full-time salespeople.

- *Selling agents* have contractual authority to sell a manufacturer's entire product line. The manufacturer is either not interested in the selling function or feels unqualified. The selling agent serves as the sales department for the manufacturer. Selling agents are common in the industrial machinery and equipment businesses; coal, chemicals, and metals industries; and real estate and stock brokerage industries.

- *Purchasing agents* generally have long-term relationships with buyers and make purchases for them, often receiving, inspecting, warehousing, and shipping the merchandise to buyers. They provide helpful market information to clients and help them obtain the best goods and prices available.

Retail Intermediaries

What are the different types of retailers? Retailing constitutes a major sector of our economy. Although approximately a half million wholesalers exist in the United States, there are well over a million retail stores that employ approximately 15 million people.[20] You're likely familiar with retail distributors because most of your personal shopping experiences have occurred at retail stores. There are two main types of retailers: *in-store retailers* and *nonstore retailers*.

What kinds of in-store retail organizations are there?

We are all familiar with **corporate chain stores,** two or more retail outlets owned by a single corporation. Corporate chain stores attempt to realize economies of scale because their size enables them to buy large volumes at reduced prices. Corporate chains appear in all types of retailing, such as department stores, specialty stores, supermarkets, and discount stores. Specific examples include Safeway (grocery stores), CVS/pharmacy, Sears, and Walmart. But not all retail stores are corporate chains. Individually owned retail stores, sometimes referred to as "mom and pop" stores are also prevalent. ▼ Table 14.4 describes the major types of retail stores and lists some examples of each.

In response to the success of corporate chains, other independent companies have voluntarily banded together to form *cooperatives* and buy in bulk to experience other economies of scale that reduce costs. Examples of wholesalers that have banded together to buy in bulk and have agreed to common merchandising include the Independent Grocers Alliance (IGA) and True Value (hardware stores). Examples of independent retailers that have banded together and have created jointly owned, central wholesale operations include Associated Grocers (groceries) and Ace (hardware stores).

Another way to organize retailers is with a franchise, such as McDonald's, Subway, KFC, Pizza Hut, Jiffy Lube, and Holiday Inn. Recall from Chapter 5 that a franchise is a distribution system where a *franchiser* sells a proven method of doing business to a *franchisee* for a fee and a percentage of sales or profits. Franchisees are typically required to purchase necessary items from the franchiser and must meet strict rules and regulations to ensure consistency and quality.

What is nonstore retailing?

Little has drawn as much attention in modern retailing as the growth of nonstore retailing. **Nonstore retailing** is a form of retail-

▼ **Table 14.4**

Types of Retail Stores

Type of Store	Description	Examples
Specialty store	A retail store that carries a wide selection of products in one category	Gamestop, Foot Locker
Department store	A retail store that carries a wide variety of products organized by departments	Nordstrom, Saks, Neiman Marcus, JCPenney
Supermarket	Large, low-cost, high-volume grocery stores that also sell household products	Safeway, Albertson's, Kroger
Convenience store	Small stores located near residential homes that are usually open long hours seven days a week and carry the most frequently purchased convenience goods	QuikTrip, 7-Eleven
Discount store	Stores that offer lower prices by accepting lower profit margins and sell at a higher volume than department stores	Target, Walmart
Factory outlet	Stores owned and operated by a manufacturer that normally carries surplus, discontinued, or irregular goods	Nordstrom Rack, Banana Republic Factory Outlet Stores
Warehouse club	Stores that sell a limited selection of brand-name food and nonfood items at deep discounts that usually require an annual membership fee	Sam's Club, Costco, BJs

ing in which consumer contact occurs outside the confines of a traditional brick-and-mortar retail store. Of course, the Internet is a big component of nonstore retailing, but there are other forms of nonstore retailing that you commonly interact with. For example, vending machines, kiosks, and carts are convenient and inexpensive ways of providing products and services.

- *Vending machines* provide many convenience goods, such as soft drinks, at locations where they are most often desired, such as airports, swimming pools, and college dorms. But vending machines are not just for food items. Best Buy has placed vending machines stocked with frequently forgotten electronics at many major U.S. airports.

- *Kiosks* are familiar in shopping malls. Because there is much less overhead associated with kiosks, the prices of the goods sold at them are often lower. In addition to selling crafts from local artists and retailers, kiosks offer some nationally sold products, such as Rosetta Stone language systems, and cell phone retailers often choose to run kiosks rather than full-service retail stores.

- *Carts* are also an inexpensive way to sell many goods. Mostly associated with snacks such as ice cream, hot dogs, and popcorn, many complete meals are made and delivered on-site to factories and construction sites for worker convenience. Lev Ekster, founder of the Cupcake Stop, uses a mobile vending truck to bring cupcakes to people on the go.

Vending machines are not just for food. Best Buy has placed vending machines stocked with frequently forgotten electronics at airports.

Are there other types of nonstore retailing? Here are some other important nonstore retailers:

- **Telemarketing** is selling products over the phone. Sometimes the sales pitches are recorded messages. To avoid such sales pitches, many people, annoyed by telemarketers, have signed up for the National Do Not Call Registry. However, many consumers use the telephone to place orders, even though these sales may not have been solicited by phone.

- **Direct selling** is selling goods and services door-to-door at people's homes and offices or at temporary or mobile locations. Direct selling is also known as *multilevel marketing* (*MLM*) because of the marketing structure that defines the corporate strategy of many of these organizations. The sales force is not only compensated by the products sold but also incentivized to bring other sales members to an organization. When they bring in other sales members, they receive a percentage of the sales generated by the new associates, creating multiple levels of compensation. Often MLM companies are referred to as pyramid structures because of the resulting hierarchy of compensation levels. Avon and Mary Kay cosmetics, Pampered Chef kitchen products, and Herbalife and MonaVie health products are sold through MLM.

- **Direct marketing** refers to any aspect of retailing a good or a service that attempts to bypass intermediaries. It includes catalog sales, direct mail, and telemarketing. You may have bought products through a catalog, such as clothing from L.L.Bean or Lands' End. Sales from infomercials are also examples of direct marketing.

How has the Internet impacted retailing? **Electronic retailing**, or the selling of consumer goods and services over the Internet, is a fast-growing business. In fact, many small businesses have found the Internet to be the great equalizer. They can establish Web sites that offer an interactive environment, which allows for state-of-the-art multimedia to attract sales. Some small businesses are

entirely online. The increased competition from online retail sales has pushed larger, more traditional brick-and-mortar retailers to improve their Web sites to complement their in-store sales. Because more of their store traffic is online, these companies can gather information about current and potential customers to establish more personalized customer relationships. Some are able to offer customized product offerings that suit customer interests based on where a customer clicks within a company's Web site and from information gathered from search engine queries. Internet shopping also allows for companies to go global because products can be sold all over the world from a single Web site.

Retail Strategies

What are the important retail strategies? All companies that sell products need to decide how intensively they wish to cover any geographic market. Should products be sold through all available retail outlets? If so, then the company is undertaking an **intensive distribution** strategy. This is most appropriate for companies selling convenience goods, such as newspapers, soft drinks, chewing gum, potato chips, bread, and milk. Companies want these products to obtain the widest possible exposure in the market. As a result, they try to make these products convenient for purchase at as many convenience stores and supermarkets as possible.

A **selective distribution** strategy uses only a portion of the many possible retail outlets for selling products. This approach is appropriate for the sale of shopping products and durable goods, such as stereos, televisions, and furniture. Buyers spend more time comparing competitors' prices and features when buying shopping products. A sale often depends on providing buyers with information on these features to successfully differentiate one brand's product from another. Naturally, producers want to selectively determine where their products will be sold to ensure successful differentiation. Moreover, customers often want other services, such as installation, to be properly distributed. Again, producers are selective in determining outlets and may provide training to outlets to ensure the best service.

At other times, sellers want to undertake an **exclusive distribution** strategy, using only one outlet in a geographic area. This is most appropriate when selling specialty products, such as high-quality sports cars, jewelry, or high-fashion clothing. Because these products carry a certain degree of prestige, sellers often require distributors to carry a full line of inventory, offer distinguished high-quality service, and meet other exclusive requirements.

Another common form of exclusive distribution exists with franchises, such as McDonald's and Subway. Only one outlet is chosen in a given geographic area, and the retail distributors are required to meet strict quality and service standards to protect brand-name integrity.

Distribution Logistics

What do we mean by distribution logistics? **Logistics** refers to managing the flow of materials, information, and processes that are involved in getting a product from its initial raw stages to the point of consumption. Different kinds of logistics are involved at various stages of the production and distribution processes. Bringing raw materials, supplies, information, and any other goods and services from suppliers to the producer is *inbound logistics*. Managing the movement of resources throughout the production process is *materials handling* and *operations control*. Lastly, managing the **physical distribution** of produced products to customers in the quantities needed, when and where they want them, is

▼ **Table 14.5**

Benefits and Costs of Various Transportation Modes

Mode	Percentage of Freight[21]	Cost	Speed	Dependability	Flexibility in Handling Products	Frequency of Shipments	Accessibility to Markets
Railroads	15.9%	Moderate	Average	Average	High	Low	High
Trucks	75.0%	High	Fast	High	Average	High	Very High
Waterways	3.5%	Very Low	Very Slow	Average	Very High	Very Low	Limited
Airways	0.0%	Very High	Very Fast	High	Low	Average	Average
Pipelines	5.6%	Low	Slow	High	Very Low	Very High	Very Limited

outbound logistics. It is also important to properly manage *reverse logistics*, bringing products back to the producer when they are defective, overstocked, outdated, or returned for recycling. If part of the process is outsourced, then managing that process is *third-party logistics.*

The Benefits and Costs of Transportation Modes

What are the benefits and costs of various transportation modes? Transportation is often the most expensive distribution cost. To keep costs as low as possible, a company wants to choose the most economical mode of transportation—railroads, trucks, waterways, or another form. However, companies also have to consider other factors beyond cost—such as speed, dependability, flexibility in product handling, frequency of shipments, and accessibility to markets. ▼ **Table 14.5** outlines the benefits and costs of the five major modes of transportation according to these criteria. Businesses have to carefully weigh these benefits and costs in making a mode-of-transportation decision.

How does a company determine the transportation method? Businesses look at different transportation methods when receiving materials from suppliers and delivering orders to customers. A business might rely on one method of transportation or a combination of methods. **Routing** is simply the way in which goods are transported, via water, rail, truck, or air. Routing includes transporting goods to a client, transporting materials from suppliers, or any of many other combinations. Proper routing ensures that any transportation of goods, be it with a company's own equipment or through a courier, is done at a minimum of cost, time, and distance without sacrificing quality. The best way to understand all the variables of each transportation option pertinent to a specific company is to develop a comprehensive *routing guide* that provides detailed routing solutions for a company's every possible shipping situation.[22]

Warehousing and Inventory Control

How important is warehousing? **Warehousing,** or storing products at convenient locations ready for customers when they are needed, is critical for customer service. There are two types of warehouses: *Storage warehouses* store goods from moderate-to-long periods of time. *Distribution warehouses* (or distribution centers) are designed to gather and move goods quickly to consumers. For example, Walmart operates approximately 100 distribution centers in the United States. Each

Railroads are a reliable method for transporting cargo long distances.

center is over one million square feet of space (about 29 football fields) under one roof. Warehousing today uses sophisticated technologies to effectively store and distribute products.

How is inventory tracked? One of the challenges in managing a supply chain is managing inventory levels to ensure there is neither too much nor too little inventory on hand. Encountering either situation can be costly, as having too much inventory involves extra warehousing fees, and too little inventory means lost sales. As we mentioned in an earlier chapter, companies use bar codes, or Universal Product Codes, on almost all products to help identify and track products.

RFID tags are intelligent bar codes. RFID technology, although more costly than bar codes, is more versatile and provides a richer amount of information about the movement and details of a product. Companies use bar codes and RFID tags to help reduce inventory costs by generating information on a real-time basis, thus providing accurate stocking information and reordering information.

Recall the dilemma faced by Liv Karlsen? She couldn't find the book she needed for class in her college's bookstore. The bookstore is only one part of the channel of distribution for Liv's book. The channel of distribution for the book involves different marketing intermediaries, including a wholesaler and a retailer. The distribution process is not the same for all products—some are longer and some are shorter, but the process is carefully determined to be as efficient and cost effective as possible. Although it might not always work to ensure that all products are always available when needed, the distribution process ultimately adds value to the consumer. ■

Chapter Summary

1. What is a promotional mix, and what is its function in a promotional campaign? (pp. 429–431)

- A **promotional mix** (p. 429) is the strategic combination of promotional tools used to reach customers to achieve marketing objectives. It includes advertising, public relations, personal selling, and sales promotions.

- Implementing the promotional mix is part of an effective promotional campaign. Promotional campaigns involve six steps:
  - Identify the target market.
  - Determine marketing objectives.
  - Design the message.
  - Determine the budget.
  - Implement the promotional mix.
  - Evaluate and adjust as needed.

2. What are the different categories of advertising, and what role do these categories play in business and society? (pp. 432–437)

- **Advertising** (p. 432) is paid, impersonal mass communication from an identified sponsor to persuade or influence a targeted audience.

- Advertising plays several important roles in business.
  - It helps businesses build brand awareness and product differentiation.
  - It also has economic benefits, by lowering the costs and prices of products providing many jobs.

- Advertising also plays a societal role.
  - Society benefits from advertising because it informs and educates us about new and different products.
  - Advertising can also persuade us in ways that can have positive or negative social ramifications.

- Many categories of advertising emerge from marketing: **product** (p. 433), **corporate** (p. 433), **comparative** (p. 433), **retail** (p. 433), **B2B** (p. 433), **nonprofit** (p. 433), **public service** (p. 434), **advocacy** (p. 434), **interactive** (p. 434), and **Internet advertising** (p. 434).

3. How are the various public relations tools essential to the marketing mix? (pp. 437–440)

- **Public relations** (p. 437) is the management function that establishes and maintains mutually beneficial relationships between an organization and its stakeholders.

- Public relations tools consist of controlled, semicontrolled, and uncontrolled news messages. **Publicity** (p. 439) is uncontrolled and can be a powerful public relations tool.

- Damage control is the effort to minimize the harmful effects of a negative event. It is critical to respond to crises honestly to reestablish a positive image.

4. What are the six steps in the personal selling process? (pp. 440–444)

- **Personal selling** (p. 440) is direct communication between a firm's sales force and potential buyers to make a sale and build good customer relationships. Establishing and maintaining good customer relationships through personal selling is critical for a firm's success.

- Six steps are involved with personal selling.
  - **Prospecting** (p. 442) is identifying qualified potential customers.
  - Approaching the prospect has two parts. In the preapproach, the salesperson learns as much as possible about potential customers to determine their likely needs and think about how those needs might be satisfied. In the actual approach, the idea is to meet, greet, and put the prospect at ease.
  - Presenting involves telling a product's story, demonstrating its use, asking questions, and listening to customers' answers.
  - Overcoming objections involves countering customers' reasons for not buying with reasons to buy.
  - Closing the sale is when a salesperson asks for a purchase.
  - Following up is when a salesperson ensures a customer is happy with a product and asks for feedback. Following up is critical to establishing and maintaining good customer relationships that are conducive to new and repeat business.

5. What are the two main types of sales promotions, and what types of tools are commonly used as incentives? (pp. 444–447)

- **Sales promotions** (p. 444) are short-term activities that target consumers and other businesses for the purpose of generating interest in a product, which have not already been undertaken by advertising, public relations, or personal selling.

Continued on next page

- One type of sales promotion is **consumer sales promotion** (p. 444). Tools used for consumer sales promotions include coupons, rebates, frequent-user incentives, POP displays, free samples, contests and sweepstakes, and advertising specialties.

- **B2B** (or **trade**) **sales promotion** (p. 444) is another type of sales promotion. Tools used as incentives for trade sales promotions include trade shows, trade allowances, cooperative advertising, free merchandise, sales contests, dealer listings, store demonstrations, quantity discounts, and training programs.

6. **Why are marketing intermediaries and distribution channels important elements in marketing?** (pp. 448–452)

- **Marketing intermediaries** (p. 449) are middlemen in the distribution process. Wholesalers, agents/brokers, and retailers constitute the different types of intermediaries.

- A **channel of distribution** (p. 449) is a whole set of intermediaries. There are many different types of distribution channels, including consumer channels, consumer/business channels, and business channels. The type and length of the distribution channel depends on the type of product that is being brought to the consumer.

- Intermediaries are important because they reduce the costs of products to consumers by increasing the efficiency of the distribution of goods and services.

7. **What types of services do agents/brokers and wholesalers provide?** (pp. 452–453)

- **Wholesalers** (p. 449) provide many services that add efficiency to the distribution of merchandise. These include selling and promoting, warehousing, transporting, financing, and providing market information.

- **Agents/brokers** (p. 449) are intermediaries that facilitate negotiations between the buyers and the sellers of goods and services but never take title (ownership) of the product traded.

  - Manufacturers' agents represent two or more manufacturers of complementary lines.

  - Selling agents have contractual authority to sell a manufacturer's entire product line and serve as the sales department for the manufacturer.

  - Purchasing agents make purchases for buyers and receive, inspect, warehouse, and ship merchandise to buyers.

8. **Why are retailing and physical distribution key aspects of distribution?** (pp. 453–457)

- Several types of retailers exist: specialty stores, department stores, supermarkets, convenience stores, discount stores, factory outlets, and warehouse clubs.

- In **nonstore retailing** (p. 454) consumer contact occurs outside a traditional retail store. Examples include electronic retailing, vending machines, kiosks, carts, telemarketing, direct selling, and direct marketing.

- Retailers can cover their markets using an **intensive** (p. 456), a **selective** (p. 456), or an **exclusive distribution strategy** (p. 456).

- Physical distribution is one of the most expensive parts of marketing a product. In the broadest sense, it entails the management of the entire supply chain.

- Transportation options include railroads, trucks, waterways, airways, and pipelines. Careful measurement of the advantages and disadvantages of these options is important before selecting a mode of transportation.

Key Terms

advertising (p. 432)

advocacy advertising (p. 434)

agents/brokers (p. 449)

B2B advertising (p. 433)

cash-and-carry wholesalers (p. 452)

comparative advertising (p. 433)

consumer sales promotion (p. 444)

corporate (or institutional) advertising (p. 433)

corporate chain stores (p. 454)

direct marketing (p. 455)

direct selling (p. 455)

distribution (p. 448)

distribution channel (p. 449)

drop shippers (p. 453)

e-commerce (p. 451)

electronic retailing (p. 455)

exclusive distribution (p. 456)

infomercials (p. 437)

integrated marketing communications (IMC) (p. 431)

Self-Test

Multiple Choice   You can find the answers on the last page of this book.

1. Which of the following is NOT part of the promotional mix?

   a. Personal selling

   b. Product placement

   c. Advertising

   d. Public relations

2. Advertising that promotes a specific product's uses, features, and benefits is _____ advertising.

   a. corporate

   b. retail

   c. comparative

   d. product

3. Which of the following describes advantages for television as a medium for advertising?

   a. Global and interactive possibilities; ease of segmentation; high audience interest; easy-to-measure responses

   b. Good mass-market coverage; low cost per contact; combines sight, sound, and motion

   c. Short life span; lots of competition for attention; poor-quality reproductions

   d. High levels of segmentation; allows personalization; high flexibility; ad can be saved; measurable impact

4. When a company sells its product through all available retail outlets, what is its retail distribution strategy?

   a. Exclusive

   b. Intensive

   c. Selective

   d. Franchise

5. Managing the process of getting products out the door and to consumers is _____ management.

   a. wholesale

   b. retail

   c. supply chain

   d. production

6. Which type of logistics is involved in bringing raw materials, supplies, and information from suppliers to the producer?

   a. Inbound

   b. Outbound

   c. Reverse

   d. Third-party

7. Which of the following would most likely be an advantage associated with the sales promotional element of the promotional mix?

   a. Highly interactive communication between the buyer and the seller

   b. Excellent for communicating a complex product, information, and features

   c. Good short-term tactical tool to stimulate sales

   d. Reaches a mass audience

8. American Idol judges often have tall glasses on their desk featuring the name Coca-Cola. This advertising strategy is known as

   a. product placement.

   b. viral marketing.

   c. an infomercial.

   d. a direct pitch.

9. Which of the following would not be considered a consumer sales promotion tool?

   a. A 10 percent off coupon from the newspaper

   b. A $10.00 mail-in rebate

   c. A frequent buyer card

   d. All of the above

10. A giant specialty store that specializes in selling a particular product line and is staffed by knowledgeable salespeople is which type of retail store?

    a. Specialty store

    b. Convenience store

    c. Factory outlet

    d. Department store

Self-Test

True/False
You can find the answers on the last page of this book.

1. The product itself can be considered part of the promotional mix because samples of the product can be given away to demonstrate its features.
   ☐ **True** or ☐ **False**

2. Advertising can reduce the costs of production and improve quality.
   ☐ **True** or ☐ **False**

3. RFID tags are similar to bar codes except that they do not need a physical scanner to process the information.
   ☐ **True** or ☐ **False**

4. Retailers sell products to other intermediaries.
   ☐ **True** or ☐ **False**

5. The last step in the selling process is closing the sale.
   ☐ **True** or ☐ **False**

Critical Thinking Questions

1. Why might companies need to devote larger advertising expenditures to new products as compared to advertising expenditures for established brands with a larger market share?

2. How might DVRs impact media selection for advertising?

3. How has social media impacted the promotion and advertising processes?

4. Describe which distribution strategy—intensive, selective, or exclusive—would be most appropriate for each of the following products and explain why: laundry detergent, cigarettes, Mercedes sports cars, and Snickers candy bars.

5. Discuss the value created by marketing intermediaries. Is their service worth the extra costs? Why or why not?

Team Time

Developing a Promotional Mix

The company you work for, Fit Foods, is launching a new product: Shine Breakfast Bars, which are all-natural, vitamin-fortified granola bars. The company has enlisted you and your teammates to design an optimal promotional mix for this product.

Process

Step 1. Assemble into teams of four. Each team member should be assigned as the "lead" for one of the four components of the promotional mix—advertising, public relations, personal selling, and sales promotions.

Step 2. Use knowledge gained from this chapter to develop a promotional mix for Shine Breakfast Bars that integrates each promotional component. What will be the key aspects of the advertising campaign? What media will be used? What public relations tools will be used? What will a sales pitch for this product consist of? How will sales promotions be implemented?

Step 3. Summarize the key points of the promotional mix plan in a poster or PowerPoint presentation.

Step 4. Present your findings to the class for discussion.

Ethics and Corporate Social Responsibility

Just What the Doctor Ordered?

In Chapter 13, you considered the ethics involved with the pricing of prescription drugs. Now turn your attention to the promotion of these products and the ethical issues raised by such advertising. Read the following scenario and then discuss the questions that follow in a small group.

Scenario

Currently, the United States and New Zealand are the only two countries in the world that permit widespread use of direct-to-consumer (DTC) advertising for prescription drugs. Such advertising has become big business in the United States: More than $4.9 billion was spent on direct-to-consumer advertising of prescription drugs in the U.S. in 2007.[23] Some people argue that DTC advertising is unethical because it encourages the overuse of medications, preys on the elderly and/or the chronically ill, and does not fully inform consumers of the risks and side effects of drugs. Others say that DTC advertising puts the power where it belongs—in the hands of consumers—and allows people to be advocates for their own health.

Questions

1. If you were a legislator voting on a bill that proposed a ban on DTC advertising of pharmaceuticals in the United States, would you vote for it or against it? Why?

2. Is DTC advertising more appropriate for certain drugs? For example, is it more ethical to advertise cholesterol-lowering drugs or antidepressants? Why?

3. Consider the tactics used in print and television ads for pharmaceuticals. What type of style is typically employed? Why? When and/or where are the side effects mentioned? Are these ads helpful in raising awareness of certain illnesses and treatments or are they irresponsible in giving false hope and/or incomplete information about powerful medications? Explain.

Web Exercises

1. **The Perks of Internet Advertising**
Go to the Google Web site and click on "Advertising Programs." What are the benefits of advertising on Google as opposed to advertising in a nationally circulated magazine, such as *Newsweek*, a nationally circulated newspaper, such as the *New York Times*, or a national television network?

2. **Sweet Success?**
Ensuring ethical behavior is a constant challenge for all businesses, including international businesses. Visit the American Marketing Association (AMA) Web site and review its Statement of Ethics (www.marketingpower.com/AboutAMA/Pages/Statement%20of%20Ethics.aspx). What recommendations would you make to a candy company as it begins to distribute its candy in developing countries?

3. **Be a Link in the Chain**
Supply chain management is a fascinating and diverse field. Companies are spending increasing amounts on supply chain management, and many jobs and career opportunities are available in a variety of organizations. Using the Internet, research what job profiles and descriptions, career paths and progressions, and level of salaries can be earned in supply chain management. Would this be a career you'd be interested in?

4. **Personal Selling**
There are many different careers in sales. To determine whether sales is a good career path for you, use the Internet to research careers in sales. You might want to start by looking at the *Occupational Outlook Handbook* on the Bureau of Labor and Statistics Web site. What are the pros and cons of a career in sales? Describe several of the sales careers. Is this a field you are interested in entering? Why or why not?

5. **Multilevel Marketing**
Suppose you want to earn a few dollars but don't want a full-time job. Research the benefits and requirements of working for an MLM company doing in-home product demonstrations. Some companies to consider are the Pampered Chef, Amway, Discovery Toys, Herbalife, or MonaVie. How does the compensation structure work for these companies? Is this something you can make a career out of?

Web Case

For more on the positive outcomes and potential pitfalls of comparative advertising campaigns, access the Chapter 14 Web case entitled "Focus on Apple, Inc.: Mac or PC: Who Would You Rather Be?" located in the End of Chapter Assignments section at my*biz*lab.com.

Video Case

For more on turning a customer into an endorser through a unified brand message, access the Chapter 14 Video Case entitled "BMW Motorcycles: Going Down the Highway in the Ultimate Riding Machine" located in the End of Chapter Assignments section at my*biz*lab.com.

Finding a Job

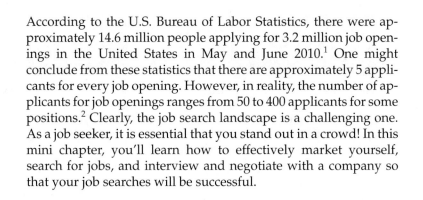

According to the U.S. Bureau of Labor Statistics, there were approximately 14.6 million people applying for 3.2 million job openings in the United States in May and June 2010.[1] One might conclude from these statistics that there are approximately 5 applicants for every job opening. However, in reality, the number of applicants for job openings ranges from 50 to 400 applicants for some positions.[2] Clearly, the job search landscape is a challenging one. As a job seeker, it is essential that you stand out in a crowd! In this mini chapter, you'll learn how to effectively market yourself, search for jobs, and interview and negotiate with a company so that your job searches will be successful.

Marketing Yourself

Standing out in a crowd requires that you sell yourself. This starts with developing a powerful résumé and cover letter.

Developing a Résumé

A **résumé** is a fact sheet that outlines your work history, experience, and accomplishments. It lets an employer know what you've done and what you want to do. There are two main types of résumés: chronological and functional. A *chronological résumé* lists jobs in order, beginning with the present. Use this type of résumé if you're staying in the same field or just getting started in the job market. *Functional résumés* detail your work history by pointing out your skills and achievements, not your titles and the companies you've worked for. This is a good type of résumé to use when you're switching fields. Your skills show employers what you can do for them because your previous job experience may not be related.

Getting Started
Before you start typing, take some time to evaluate yourself. Consider the following:

- What are your strengths and weaknesses?
- What type of skills do you possess?
- What do you want from an employer?

Navigating Career Waters

You're a senior in college, hoping to land a graphic design job after you graduate. But the economy is stormy, and everyone around you is moving back in with their parents until companies start hiring again. Never one to give up easily, you decide to pursue your career with gusto. Can you land a job, even in these tough times?

Aside from technical skills, think about your soft skills. Soft skills include personality traits and interpersonal skills, such as honesty, responsibility, leadership, and teamwork. Some employers find these traits more desirable than technical skills because technical skills can be taught, while soft skills are innate.

When you begin your résumé, remember that organization is key. Employers generally spend about 15 seconds reviewing a résumé,[3] so you need to quickly capture the attention of the reviewer. Organize your résumé clearly, with bold headings and bulleted information; no one will take the time to read a lengthy paragraph about your achievements. The following headings can help you organize a basic chronological résumé: Contact Information, Objective, Education, Experience or Work History, Skills/Interests, and References. Depending on how you format your résumé, you may or may not use all of these headings.

Contact Information

Your **contact information** is typically centered at the top of the page, with your name in the largest font. Include your mailing address, phone number, and e-mail address. Remember that prospective employers may hear your outgoing phone message, so be sure it's appropriate.

Objective

An **objective** is a short summary of the job you're seeking and how your skills will apply to that job. Objectives should be specific to the job for which you're applying. Generalized objectives don't tell a prospective employer anything about you and don't get anyone's attention.

Read the following objective and analyze it from an employer's perspective.

> **OBJECTIVE:** To employ my advertising knowledge by working for a successful company that will help me get experience to kick-start my career.

What position is the applicant applying for? This objective doesn't specify the position. It also describes what the applicant wants the job to do for him or her, not what he or she can contribute to the company. Employers already know that you want to learn and gain experience; reiterating it makes you look selfish.

A good objective is specific and short. Here's an example.

> **OBJECTIVE:** To obtain a position at Doyle and Associates as an entry-level graphic designer where my creativity and technical ability will add value to operations.

With this objective, an employer knows what position you want and why you think you're the right person to fill the opening. It also shows you're serious about the position because you took the time to tailor your résumé to this specific position.

Education

Begin your education list with your most recent educational experience. Be sure to detail your degree, major, minor, dates of attendance, and the name and location of the school. If you haven't graduated yet, list your expectant degree and graduation date. Include your GPA if it is 3.0 or higher. Including a GPA that is lower may inadvertently invite questions about your studying skills that you may not be comfortable answering, or you may be passed over altogether.

If you don't have relevant work experience, list your educational background first. If you have pertinent work experience, reverse the sections so that work history comes before education.

Experience or Work History

List your previous work experiences chronologically, starting with the most recent, and include each company's name, its location, your dates of employment, and your title or position. For each experience listed, include at least three bullet points that highlight your achievements or undertakings. You don't have to put specific dates of employment but do list the month and year. If you include the years only, you may give the impression that you have gaps in your employment history. If possible, include specific, quantifiable data about your accomplishments and how you benefited your employer.

Skills/Interests

This section should include your hidden talents or skills, such as whether you speak a foreign language or are knowledgeable about a certain software package. Also include extracurricular activities or professional organizations you belong to that relate to your career field. You don't want to restate anything you've said in your education and experience sections, so if you don't have anything to add, omit this section.

References

References can attest to your work ethic and skills and are important to have ready to go. You should have three professional references expecting to be called on to help you. If you have no professional references, obtain references from teachers, instructors, professors, clergy, and other people who know about your character. Avoid using family members and friends. Always ask permission to use someone as a reference before listing him or her. Be sure your references know you're engaging in an active job search in case a potential employer calls them. This way they can be prepared to answer questions accurately.

Employers generally won't need references until they interview you, so it's customary to include at the bottom of your résumé the line: "References are available upon request." However, if you choose to provide information for each reference on your résumé you should include for each reference the name, title, employer, contact information, the nature of your relationship, and the length of time they have known you. Including references shows that you have professional contacts with people willing to recommend you. When you are invited to an interview, bring additional copies of your references with you.

Résumé Showdown!

To get yourself noticed, you need to make your résumé pop. Look at the following two examples from the perspective of an employer who has a pile of résumés to look through. Both résumés are for the same person. Consider the strengths and weaknesses of each and which one you feel makes the best impression.

Which résumé do you think an employer would be more impressed with? Most likely the second one—right? It has a better organizational structure and a cleaner appearance. The résumé also focuses more on the candidate's achievements, rather than on her responsibilities, with specific and detailed actions and outcomes. Overall, the second résumé gives a prospective employer a stronger idea of what the candidate can offer the company.

Writing a Cover Letter

Along with your résumé, you need to include a cover letter. A **cover letter** introduces you to a prospective employer. This is an opportunity for you to market yourself by demonstrating sound communication skills. A cover letter may be more important than a résumé in the eyes of a prospective employer because it gives you

Jane Doefield
4117 Blank Street
Cincinnati, OH 45202
(513) 555-4529
Janedoefield@email.com

Education
Ohio State University, Columbus, OH, 2003–2008
BS, Biology with a concentration in Medical Technology
GPA: 2.57

Work History
Johnson and Webb, Columbus, OH, January 2008–May 2008
Intern
My main responsibilities were to organize a computerized file-retrieval system for research and create a tracking spreadsheet to keep track of tested drugs. I also worked hands-on in the lab testing cells for sensitivity to different drug treatments.

BookZilla, Columbus, OH, 2004–2007
Sales Associate
While working at BookZilla, I was responsible for stocking and straightening the magazine and stationery sections. When needed, I also worked on the cash register and sold BookZilla discount cards.

Pepe's Garments, Cincinnati, OH, 2002–2004
Sales Associate
I provided customer service by helping customers pick out garments and ringing up their purchases. I maximized sales by signing people up for Pepe's credit cards. I was also responsible for keeping an accurate sales drawer.

Skills/Interests
I am proficient in Microsoft Office and fluent in French. I enjoy playing the piano, painting, and swimming. While in college, I played on an intramural softball team.

References
Mario Rodríguez
Supervisor, BookZilla
(614) 555-7619

Andrea Zimmerman
Owner, Pepe's Garments
(513) 555-9723

Résumé #1.

Jane Doefield
4117 Blank Street
Cincinnati, OH 45202
(513) 555-4529
Janedoefield@email.com

Objective: To obtain a position as a quality-assurance technician in AIF's lab.

Education
Ohio State University, Columbus, OH, 2003–2008
BS, Biology with a concentration in Medical Technology

Work History
Johnson and Webb, Columbus, OH, January 2008–May 2008
Intern
· tested cells for sensitivity to a variety of drug treatments at a rate of 4 assays per day, enabling our department to exceed company testing expectations
· developed a tracking mechanism to organize drugs tested, preventing the inadvertent retesting of drugs, which saved our department over 10 hours of lost time per month
· streamlined retrieval process for locating researched materials, adding 5 hours of additional analysis time per month

BookZilla, Columbus, OH, October 2004–December 2007
Sales Associate
· organized and maintained periodical and stationery sections containing more than 200 items
· marketed and sold five BookZilla discount cards a week to boost sales
· provided excellent customer service while processing purchases

Pepe's Garments, Cincinnati, OH, June 2003–August 2004
Sales Associate
· assisted customers with making purchasing decisions
· used sales strategies to register customers for Pepe's credit cards
· provided customer service to achieve sales goals

Skills
· proficient in Microsoft Office
· fluent in French

References
· Available upon request.

Résumé #2.

a voice. Even if you're the most qualified person for a job, a poorly written cover letter may end your chances before anyone ever looks at your résumé. If you follow these basic tips, your cover letter may get you an interview all on its own.

Tip #1: *Tailor your cover letter to fit the job you're applying for.*

There are three main types of cover letters: an application letter, a prospecting letter, and a networking letter. An *application letter* is sent as a response to a job opening. A *prospecting letter* is sent to a company where you want to work, asking about potential positions. A *networking letter* is sent to ask for information regarding your job search.[4] Each cover letter you send out needs to be tailored to fit the job opening you're applying for or inquiring about. Look at the requirements in the ad. Find the key words and phrases used to describe the position and then describe your skills and experience using the same terms. Highlight a major relevant accomplishment in terms used by the employer. Include how you have or will address the needs of the employer. Overall, demonstrate in your cover letter that you fulfill the specific requirements the company is looking for.

Tip #2: *Indicate what you can do for the employer.*

All cover letters should explain to potential employers what you can do for them, not what they can do for you.[5] Don't tell them how the job will give you experience in a particular field. Instead, tell them how you have what it takes to perform the required tasks.

Tip #3: *Clearly explain why the company should hire you.*

After you've explained that you can do the job, discuss why the company should hire you.[6] Think about what sets you apart from the competition; remember to be assertive and descriptive. Instead of saying, "I'm flexible," say, "My years in customer service have taught me how to effectively interact with people of different ages and backgrounds. As a result, I have learned to be flexible, persuasive, and tactful. These abilities have allowed me to maintain long-term customer relationships that have boosted sales for my previous employers." Use concrete examples to show how you can be an asset to the company.

Tip #4: *Keep it short.*

Each cover letter you send out should be limited to one page with at least three paragraphs. The first paragraph explains why you are writing, whether it is to respond to a job opening or to ask about available positions. The goal of the first paragraph is to start strong and get the reader's attention. Here is an example.

> I am responding to your advertisement on Monster.com regarding an entry-level sales position. My background in customer service and advertising is a perfect fit for your company. I am interested in being part of a company that has a fast-paced environment, like ATI Corp., and feel I can be an asset to your expanding team.

The body of the letter lets the employer know your experience as it relates to the desired position. Here is an example.

> My background includes three years of experience in sales. I have extensive experience working with customers and implementing sales strategies. I have coordinated and advertised events, including fashion shows and cooking demonstrations that have boosted sales over 20 percent and led to successful product launches. I am skilled at motivating teams and have consistently met or exceeded my sales goals.

The final paragraph thanks the reader and leaves contact information. Here is an example.

> I would appreciate an opportunity to sit down with you and discuss how I can become a valuable member of the ATI Corp. team. Feel free to call me at 443-555-2728. I look forward to hearing from you. Thank you for your time and consideration.

Because your résumé states only facts, your cover letter is a valuable opportunity to highlight your skills, show a bit of your personality, and sell yourself. Consider time invested in writing your cover letter as time invested in your future.

Multimedia Portfolios and Personal Web Sites

Because résumés and cover letters *say* only what you can do, creating a portfolio to *show* what you've already done may be beneficial. Don't worry if you're not an artist or a writer; anyone can have a multimedia portfolio. A **multimedia portfolio** is a collection of work that is displayed in the form of photographs, pictures, audio clips, and video clips. The goal is to choose some of your best work for inclusion in your portfolio—papers, projects, posters, videos of presentations, or photos of you volunteering for a charitable organization. Whatever you choose, it should be your most exceptional work. You can prepare your portfolio as a display binder or save it on a portable storage device and bring it with you to interviews. You can also create your own Web site that has a list of all your accomplishments and give your interviewer the Web address to check out your work during or after the interview.

Networking is best done in person, but it can take place via the internet as well.

All these things show who you are and will help leave a mark in the mind of the interviewer. However, it takes time to create a good portfolio or an impressive Web site, so don't throw something together just to have it for an interview. The portfolio is meant to help you stand out in the eyes of the interviewer in a positive light, not hinder you by exemplifying rushed or shoddy work.

Search Strategies

When searching for a job, you need to use a variety of strategies and methods to be successful. Don't expect to e-mail a few résumés on Monday and be invited to an interview on Tuesday. In this section, you'll learn about how tools such as networking, online and newspaper job postings, recruiting companies, cold calling, college-campus career resources, and informational interviews can help you get a job.

Networking

Networking is the process of building relationships that can potentially create business opportunities. Networking is best done face-to-face, but it can take place online as well. There are numerous social-networking sites, such as LinkedIn, where you can connect with colleagues and professional acquaintances. Professional organizations also offer opportunities to connect through social networks. Other organizations hold regularly scheduled face-to-face social-networking opportunities to generate job leads.

The benefit of networking in person is that it can happen anywhere. You can meet someone while you're grabbing a cup of coffee, or you can attend a formal networking event, a conference, or a job fair. No matter where it happens, you need to know what to say and how to say it to make a good first impression. Don't mistake a networking event for a party. Remember, networking is about making business contacts, not a new best friend. The first thing you need to do is create an elevator pitch. An **elevator pitch** is a brief statement that clearly summarizes your skills and what you can offer. It's called an elevator pitch because it should be a crisp, concise statement you could make on a short elevator ride. You should focus on three or four key points and sound informal.[7] Try practicing your pitch in front of a mirror or on your voicemail.

Although you don't literally need to deliver your "elevator pitch" during an elevator ride, the pitch should be concise enough that you theoretically could.

When you attend networking events, be prepared. First of all, dress to impress. If you're going to a job fair, you may encounter people who may want to hire you, so dress the part. If others are dressed casually, you'll stand out as someone serious about your future. Don't forget to take along copies of your résumé or business cards. Before attending an event, try to find out what companies or types of companies will be there. Research the companies that interest you so you'll have more to say than, "What does your company do?" Representatives will likely be impressed by your initiative and enthusiasm for a particular job. Once you meet someone, don't ask for a job right away. Instead, if it seems appropriate, ask to meet him or her again to discuss possible opportunities.

Building a network takes commitment. You can't meet new contacts sitting around waiting for someone to call you. Get connected on some of the reputable online social-networking sites. Attend a free social-networking seminar. Check your local newspaper for conferences or jobs fairs. Enroll in classes to further your skills or meet other people with the same interests. Look for professional networking groups for people with your area of expertise. Be open to networking opportunities outside professional settings. You could meet a person who works in your desired field at the gym, at the grocery store, or in line at Starbucks. This is why it is important to always be prepared to present your pitch at a moment's notice. Finally, be patient. You can't expect to create a network overnight. It takes time, but know that after all your work, you'll have a solid group of people who can give you valuable support, advice, and perhaps the opportunity to get ahead.

Spot the Truth

Which of the following is NOT a myth related to job hunting?

a. Posting your résumé on Web sites will have employers lining up to hire you.

b. If you are in need of a job, take the first offer you get.

c. The majority of job openings are never publicized.

Answer: C. Most jobs, especially higher positions, are never advertised.[8] The key to finding out about these openings is through networking and, to a lesser extent, cold calling, which you'll learn about later in this mini chapter.

Internet Research

If you're sure of the field you want to work in, create a list of potential employers. Find each company's Web site and read about each company's history and its mission and vision statements. You want to know as much as you can about a company and the industry so that you can make an informed decision about where you want to work. You can also look online for job openings and contact information. Looking at online job postings, such as those on Monster.com, is also a popular way to look for a job. You can search these sites and then e-mail your cover letter and résumé at any time—day or night. You can also post your résumé so companies can contact you if they think you're the right fit for a job. Many people view online job sites, so openings fill fast; check sites often for new postings and make sure your résumé really stands out.

Newspapers

As with online postings, classified ads can be a starting point for your job search. Generally, the Sunday paper has the most classified job ads, but that shouldn't stop you from looking in the paper every day. Once you find a position that sounds good, research the company. Check to see whether the position is still open and send your cover letter and résumé. Newspapers don't have the same number of postings as does the Internet, but you can look at a newspaper anywhere because no computer is required.

Recruiters

Cold calling is controversial as to its effectiveness, and can end up producing mixed results.

The job of a **recruiter** is to find qualified employees to work for a company. They can work full-time for a large corporation, or they can be contracted for part-time help at multiple companies. Recruiters may get in touch with you to learn more about your capabilities or determine whether you're a good fit for a particular company. If a recruiter contacts you, be sure to ask why he or she is interested and to which companies your résumé is being sent. If the recruiter has multiple positions to fill, be clear about the types of companies and jobs that work best for you. If you don't like a strict nine-to-five schedule or a corporate atmosphere, let the recruiter know. Once you're both on the same page, you can figure out whether the job available is right for you.

You can contact a recruiter yourself if you're seeking help with your job search. His or her large pool of contacts can be useful; however, be aware that you may be one of many job seekers the recruiter is assisting. It is best to continue your job search on your own as well as with the help of a recruiter.

Cold Calling Pros and Cons

Cold calling is a method of job hunting in which you make unexpected and uninvited phone calls to potential employers to express your interest, inquire about openings, and request interviews. It's a practice that is somewhat controversial because an uninvited contact may seem off-putting to some employers but resourceful to others. If you decide to make cold calls, there are some things you should do before you start dialing. First, make a list of companies that interest you. Then make preliminary calls to obtain the name, title, and phone number of the person in charge of the department you're interested in working for. You may also be able to find this information on a company Web site. Send your cover letter and résumé directly to the person you want to impress before you make a call. Don't forget to tailor your cover letter to the specific company and position. Finally, call the people you sent your résumé to and request an interview.

This process is hard and can end up producing mixed results. An employer may view your call as bothersome or pushing, and an opportunity that could have been an option if you would have waited for the employer to contact you could then be lost. On the other hand, an employer may see your phone call as ambitious. He or she may view you as a self-starter who is motivated to reach your goals. Unfortunately, there's no easy way to tell which way the process will go. It is up to you decide whether cold calling is right for you and the situation.

College Campus Career Resources

Your college's career center can help you determine your skills and strengths, focus on your goals, explore potential career paths, and find current job openings. Most centers have manuals, informational books, and career-planning guides available. In addition, you can meet with a counselor to talk about your career goals and interests. Your counselor may administer an assessment test that can help you gain a deeper understanding about yourself. These tests don't tell you what you should do, but they can give you an idea about what kinds of preferences you have and provide career suggestions based on those preferences.

Also, check your career center's Web site for links to other informational sites that can help you. For example, the Bureau of Labor Statistics publishes the *Occupational Outlook Handbook* on its Web site, a publication that holds a wealth of information about various career fields. This is a great place to start researching a career field. There should also be listings for local job fairs and other career-related events on your college's career center's Web site. Career centers can also help you find internships that allow you to explore a career field and begin to build networking contacts. Many career centers can provide you with help writing résumés and cover letters; they also might offer seminars on proper etiquette and how to dress for success that many students find useful.

Informational interviews enable you to gain firsthand knowledge from someone who currently works in the field.

Informational Interviews

The goal of an **informational interview** is to gain firsthand knowledge from someone who currently works in the field. This gives you a chance to hear about the reality of what you think is your dream job. If you don't know anyone personally to interview, you can check your local career center or your school's alumni office for contacts. You can also contact a business directly and ask the HR office to direct you to the best person to interview. Be sure that you're interviewing the right person though. If you're just getting started, you shouldn't be interviewing the president; you should be speaking with a junior-level employee. The idea is to gain insight into what your job would be like in that field, not the boss's job.

When you meet for the informational interview, you should have a list of organized questions to ask. The following examples are general questions you would have about any job. You may want to include one or two in your interview but try to formulate questions directly related to a specific field.

- What duties do you perform daily?
- What type of degree do you need to be considered for this job?
- What types of skills are employers looking for when filling positions? Technical? Soft?
- What do you enjoy most about your job? Least?
- Do you have any advice for me if I decide to pursue a job in this field?

If your interviewee is not forthcoming and gives vague or off-putting answers, don't jump to conclusions. Set up another interview with someone in the same field. Also, although this isn't a formal job interview, you should dress professionally. An informational interview is another opportunity to network; your interviewee may be impressed with you and give your name to someone higher up or know about an opening elsewhere. Try to give the best impression possible because you never know—one meeting could turn into your dream job.

Interviewing and Negotiating

Congratulations, you've landed an interview! Interviews can be a breeze if you're properly prepared or a nightmare if you're not. The goal of the interview is to convey that you're the best person for the position, so confidence is key.

Preparation is key when it comes to interviews.

Interview Red Flags

Not all interview questions are created equal. Some are even illegal. Interviewers cannot ask questions about your race, gender, sexual orientation, religion, age, national origin, marital status, or family matters.[9] If your interviewer asks you any of the following questions or makes any inappropriate comments, it may be a red flag, a warning signal that you should look elsewhere for employment.

- Where were you born?
- How old are you?
- Are you married?
- Do you attend church?
- Do you plan on having children soon?

Preparing for the Interview

There's a lot to do before the big day, so if you have the option, give yourself a few days to prepare. Go over everything on your résumé. Be prepared to talk about anything listed, from previous jobs to your educational background. Research the company as much as you can. Look at its history, mission and vision statements, and current projects. Try to relate previous experiences to the position you're applying for, such as "While I served as vice president of the student body, I learned a lot about persuasion and compromise, which I know are two skills a marketing representative must have."

Next, practice your answers to standard interview questions, such as "What's your biggest weakness?" Think about the questions and jot down your answers. Stage a mock interview with a friend. You might feel silly, but practicing your responses will make you feel more confident.

Interview Questions

No matter which field you're in, there are certain interview questions that show up everywhere.

- What can you tell me about yourself?
- Why do you want to work here?
- What kind of position are you looking for?
- Why did you leave your last job?
- What is your greatest strength? Weakness?
- Describe a problem you faced at your previous job and explain how you handled it.
- How do you handle stress?
- What is your proudest accomplishment?
- Where do you see yourself in five years?
- How would you describe your work style?
- What motivates you?
- How do you evaluate success?

By preparing your responses ahead of time, you'll boost your confidence and give yourself a little room to relax.

Once you know what you want to say, work on looking the part. You want to make a good impression, so be careful what you choose. Because you don't know the person interviewing you, stick with a conservative look. Don't wear baggy clothes, tennis shoes, short skirts, funky jewelry, or other inappropriate attire and don't overload yourself with cologne or perfume. Also, be sure to consider the job and whether tattoos, visible body piercings, or extreme makeup will present a negative impression.

During the Interview

Aim to arrive 10–15 minutes early. Being late is a signal to the person interviewing you that you're not serious about the job. If you know you're going to be late, call and apologize as soon as you realize it. Once you arrive, give another quick apology and sit down for the interview.

When you meet your interviewer, give a firm handshake, smile, and make eye contact. Have questions prepared to ask at the end of the in-

▼ top 10 Interview Tips

1. Be confident.
2. Listen carefully to the interviewer's comments and questions.
3. Think before responding to questions.
4. Don't feel rushed. If you are uncertain about what a question is asking and want clarification, then ask for it.
5. Never interrupt anyone.
6. Answer questions succinctly yet thoroughly.
7. Avoid nervous habits, such as bouncing your leg, rolling your pen, or biting your nails; these things can be distracting and undesirable.
8. Keep a continuous yet natural level of eye contact.
9. Do not ask any questions that are clearly answered on the company Web site or in any literature provided to you.
10. Be sincere and genuine.

terview. If you need to, write them down ahead of time and take them to the interview with you. Some examples of interview questions are as follows:

- Can you describe an ideal employee?
- What kinds of growth opportunities are available?
- Can you describe the company's management style and the type of employee that fits well with it?
- What do you consider to be the most important aspects of this job?

Also, ask about the overall responsibilities of the position, the day-to-day tasks associated with it, associated travel requirements (if any), and any other questions you might have. Avoid asking directly about the salary, but if you feel it is important and appropriate to, ask about the salary at the very end of the interview.

Interview Take-Alongs

There are some things you need to take to your interview besides your winning personality. Grab a briefcase or folder and include the following items:[10]

- Copies of your résumé
- A list of your references
- A portfolio if you have made one
- Paper and a pen
- Directions
- A cell phone, in case something happens, but leave it in the car or turn it off during your interview

Negotiating a salary may be uncomfortable, but it sets the tone for your career.

At the end of the interview, if you still want the job and feel you're a good fit, say so directly. Ask the interviewer what the next step entails—a second interview, a background/reference check, and so forth—and when you can expect to hear from him or her again. Before leaving, remember to thank the interviewer for the opportunity. Following up with a personal thank-you note or e-mail is also highly recommended.

Negotiating Strategies

You aced the interview, and the company has offered you a job. Now you have to think about negotiating a salary. Negotiating may be uncomfortable, but it helps set the tone for your career. The following steps can help guide you through the negotiation process:

1. Before you negotiate, figure out a reasonable salary for the position you're interested in.
2. Using Web sites such as Salary.com, research the median salary for your profession based on your zip code, educational background, and experience.
3. Ask for a day to consider the salary offer. This will give you time to do further research and come up with a negotiating plan.
4. Don't forget that you can negotiate factors aside from salary, such as benefits, vacation time, or a more flexible schedule.
5. When you sit down to negotiate, make it clear you want the job, make reasonable requests, and have a positive attitude.

6. Sell yourself and defend your goal if you have a specific salary in mind.

7. If you succeed in getting what you want, be sure to obtain the agreement in writing. If you don't get what you want, consider how much you want the job. It may be beneficial to gain valuable experience even though you aren't getting paid what you want.

8. If you decide to turn down the offer, let the company know you are still interested in a position if something else opens up.

Marketing yourself, searching for employment, interviewing, and negotiating all present their share of challenges. Now you have the knowledge to successfully land a job that fits your skills, talents, and goals. Go for it!

Apply these key concepts by revising a new document. Go to Mini Chapter 4 in my*biz*lab.com and select Document Makeovers.

Financial Management

In an effort to remain competitive, the company that Cindy Li works for needs to launch a new device to quickly match its competitor's latest gadget. As CFO, Li was asked to assess the company's ability to pull this off. What kind of financial information does she need to pull together? What are her company's options for financing such a project?

Objective 1 What are the implications of financial management, and how do financial managers fulfill their responsibilities? (pp. 481–485)

Financial Needs

Ginny McIntyre runs a small clothing tailoring business out of her home. She is so overwhelmed with business that she doesn't have enough space for her orders and equipment. She wants to expand her business into a small shop, but she doesn't have enough money. Where can Ginny find financing for her business?

Objective 2 How do companies finance their short-term business needs through trade credit, commercial banks, commercial finance companies, and commercial paper? (pp. 485–488)

Objective 3 What is the purpose of each type of long-term financing for companies? (pp. 488–490)

Accounting Functions

Arnold Sawyer always thought he was good with figures, and for years he was able to help his niece manage the books for her catering business. Then, after an appearance on a local newscast, catering sales went through the roof. Could the company mobilize quickly enough to fill the requests? Where was the money going to come from?

Objective 4 What are the functions of corporate accounting, financial accounting, managerial accounting, auditing, government and not-for-profit accounting, and tax accounting? (pp. 490–492)

Objective 5 How is double entry bookkeeping used to maintain the balance of the fundamental accounting equation? (pp. 492–495)

Financial Statements

Mateo Morales had just received a huge bonus check. After a great deal of excited contemplation on what "big ticket item" he could purchase, Mateo wheeled in his enthusiasm and decided a more prudent action would be best. He would invest the money, so now he was trying to determine whether Google or Yahoo would make a better investment. Where should he begin? What numbers should he look at, and how should he make sense of them?

Objective 6 What is the function of balance sheets, income statements, and statements of cash flow? (pp. 496–505)

PEARSON
my*biz*lab

OBM and Financial Statements

You're the owner of a restaurant that's taken a hit because of the recession. You need to do what it takes to turn the restaurant around—and fast—or you and your employees will be out of work. Can you do it?

Objective 7 Test yourself using my*biz*lab.com to show that you understand the chapter objectives.

Financial Management pp. 481–485

indy Li had no idea how her company was going to pull this off. In the past, board members had come up with some far-reaching projects, but this one was the most aggressive by far. As a part of the strategic plan, the board was suggesting the company launch a new kind of portable handheld computer to keep up with its competitor's latest gadget. Putting this together would require significant cash and capital investments. As CFO, Cindy was asked if the company currently had the resources to pull off this venture, and, if not, what its options for financing such a project were. Cindy knew that her days would be full for the next few months. ■

Financial managers are key to the success of any company. In this section, you'll learn about what financial management entails, what responsibilities a financial manager must fulfill, and how financial managers guide their companies to success.

The Financial Manager

What is financial management? By now, you should understand that a business is created to sell a good or a service and, of course, make a profit. Producing, marketing, and distributing a product are important aspects of generating a profit. Even more important, however, is a company's ability to *pay* for the resources required to accomplish these tasks. Without financial management, there is no business! Situations like the one at Cindy Li's company can arise quickly. Without good financial controls and planning, a company will not be able to respond to unexpected challenges or planned expansion. **Financial management** involves the strategic planning and budgeting of short- and long-term funds for current and future needs. Tracking past financial transactions, controlling current revenues and expenses, and planning for a company's future financial needs are the foundation of financial management.

In most companies, the finance department has two divisions: accounting (which we'll discuss later in the chapter) and financial management. Just as you might save money to ensure that you can pay next month's rent or make plans for a big purchase such as a car or home, businesses must also plan and save. To remain competitive, businesses must make large strategic investments, such as buying or building a new factory or investing in more advanced machinery or technology. At the same time, they also must ensure that they can pay their monthly bills. Financial management involves establishing and monitoring controls to make certain the plans and budgets are monitored sufficiently so that the business can reach its financial goals.

What is the role of a financial manager? A **financial manager**, sometimes referred to as the *chief financial officer (CFO)*, oversees the financial operations of a company. Generally, a financial manager assumes the accounting responsibilities for a company. A financial manager is responsible for planning and managing a company's financial resources, including the following:

- Developing plans that outline a company's financial short-term and long-term needs
- Defining the sources and uses of funds that are needed to reach goals

PEARSON
my***biz*lab**

For an interactive, real-world example of this topic, access this chapter's **BizSkill** entitled OBM and Financial Statements, located at my***biz*lab**.com.

- Monitoring the cash flow of a company to ensure that obligations are paid in a timely and efficient manner and that funds owed to the company are collected efficiently
- Investing any excess funds so that those funds can grow and be used for future developments
- Raising capital for future growth and expansion

Although not all companies have a CFO, all successfully run businesses have some person or people designated to manage the financial needs of a company. In smaller companies, the financial manager may have other business-related responsibilities as well. Some entrepreneurs might serve as both owner and financial manager of a company.

Planning for Financial Needs

How does the financial manager plan for financial needs? A company's financial needs are both short term and long term in nature, and a financial manager must plan for both. In addition, he or she must ensure that funds are used optimally and that the firm is ultimately profitable. To meet these objectives, a financial manager oversees three important processes: forecasting financial needs, developing budgets and plans to meet financial needs, and establishing controls to ensure that the budgets and plans are being followed.

What is involved in forecasting financial needs? In most large companies, the executive management team and the board of directors formulate a strategic plan that sets out corporate goals and objectives. For example, a priority among the goals and objectives that Cindy Li's company's board of directors and management team discussed was to produce a new device to go head-to-head with a competitor's product. As the CFO and head financial manager, it was Li's responsibility to manage revenues and expenses for this plan. In addition, she also had to develop short- and long-term financial forecasts to ensure that the strategic goals and objectives were financially feasible.

Financial managers coordinate with other areas of a company to formulate answers to certain questions: How much product do we need to sell? Do we need to expand to meet demand? Do we have the resources to expand our product line? Financial forecasts are especially important when strategic goals include large capital projects, such as acquiring new facilities, replacing outdated technology, or expanding into a new product line. It's critical that such forecasts are as accurate as possible because erroneous forecasts can have serious consequences.

In developing forecasts, financial managers take many factors into consideration, including a company's current and future plans, the economy's current and future state of affairs, and the competition's current and anticipated actions. In addition, financial managers must anticipate the impact such factors will have on a company's financial situation. For example, if national economic forecasts predict a slowdown in six months, financial managers know such a forecast will affect a company in many ways. Therefore, additional planning is required during general economic downturns to handle the possibility that payments might be harder to collect or that sales could be lower. Because of the result from either or both of these possibilities, plans for expansion of buildings or equipment might have to be postponed.

How does a company know it has enough resources to meet forecasted needs? The accounting area of the finance department generates financial statements. These statements include the *income statement*, the *balance sheet*, and the *statement of cash flows*. We'll discuss financial statements in more detail later in the chapter, but for now you just need to know that together they create a financial landscape that explains where a company has been over the current and past years. Moreover, they serve as a basis for management to develop expectations of where a company will be in future periods.

Using these expectations, a financial manager develops a **budget**, a financial plan that outlines a company's planned cash flows, expected operating expenses, and anticipated revenues. An **operating (master) budget** includes all the operating costs for an entire organization, including inventory, sales, purchases, manufacturing, marketing, and operating expenses. The operating budget maps out the projected number of units to be sold and estimated income for the coming year, in addition to all anticipated costs of operating the business to manufacture and sell the estimated level of business.

How are funds made available for large projects? Another component of the budgeting process is the capital budget. The **capital budget** considers a company's long-range plans and outlines the expected financial needs for significant capital purchases, such as real estate, manufacturing equipment, plant expansions, or technology. Because capital projects are often financed with borrowed money or money raised through the sale of stocks or bonds, it is important to plan ahead to ensure that necessary funds are available when they are needed. During the capital budgeting process, each department in an organization makes a list of its anticipated capital needs. Then senior management and the board evaluate these needs to determine which will best maximize a company's overall growth and profitability. Some requests are the routine replacement of equipment or technology and may not need much evaluation. Other requests might be necessary to move a company in a new direction and should be evaluated closely.

For example, according to its annual report, Apple's capital expenditures anticipated in 2009 included "approximately $400 million for expansion of the company's retail segment and approximately $1.5 billion for corporate facilities, infrastructure, and product tooling and manufacturing process equipment."[1] Keep in mind that **assets**, which we will discuss in further detail later, are the things a company owns, which include cash, investments, buildings, furniture, and equipment.

For financial managers, ensuring that the business stays within its budget is a priority.

Addressing the Budget

What helps plan for short-term needs? **Cash flow** is the money that a company receives and spends over a specific period. The **cash flow budget**, as shown in ▼ **Figure 15.1**, is a short-term budget that estimates cash inflows and outflows and predicts any cash flow gaps for the business. Cash flow gaps occur when cash outflows are greater than cash inflows.[2] Cash flow budgets help financial managers determine whether a business needs to seek outside sources of funds beyond sales to manage anticipated cash shortages. Cash flow budgets also indicate future investment opportunities due to surges in cash inflow and whether a business will have enough cash to grow. Moreover, financial managers use the cash flow budget to help plan for debt repayment or cover unusual operating expenses.

Why is monitoring cash flow important? A company can have the best-selling product on the market, but if the flow of funds coming in and going out of is not managed properly, a company can easily fail. Monitoring cash flow is important because it measures a company's short-term financial health and financial efficiency.

Cash flow specifically measures whether there are sufficient funds to pay outstanding bills. For seasonal businesses, such as ski shops and pool installation companies, cash management is critical for carrying a business through slow months. "It's important to manage costs," says Matt Kersten, founder of Kersten Cards, a greeting card company. Eighty percent of Kersten's annual sales typically occur between July and December. "The seasonal business, regardless of size, needs to save money and resist the urge to spend when flush with cash," Kersten says.[3]

Although many investors focus on a company's profitability as an indicator of strength, a company's *liquidity*—how quickly an asset can be turned into cash—is often a better indicator. After all, companies go bankrupt when they cannot pay their bills, not because they are unprofitable. As you'll read later in this chapter, accountants also play a big role in helping financial managers monitor cash flows.

How does a company know if it's staying on budget? After a budget is developed, it must be compared periodically to a company's actual performance. It is very important that management regularly compare (the ideal is monthly) actual performance to the budget. Without such a comparison, it's hard to determine whether a company is actually performing as expected. For example, let's say you decide to save some money for one month; at the end of the month, you have $50 in your savings account. Is that good or bad? It all depends on what you originally planned to save. If you intended to save only $35 but end up with $50, that's great. If you intended to save $75, then the outcome is not as good.

The same is true with the financial performance of a company. If the actual numbers generated by a company closely match the budget, this shows that the company is fulfilling its plans. On the other hand, if the actual numbers differ greatly from those projected by the budget, this indicates that corrective actions must be taken. Businesses strive to stay on budget and fund needs through monies gener-

▼ **Figure 15.1**
Business Cash Flow

Cash *Inflows* to a Business

Revenues from sales, loans, interest, and sales of assets, etc.

Cash *Outflows* from a Business

Payment for raw materials, stock, labor, insurance, rent, etc.

ated by business operations. However, there are many situations, even with the best planning, when a financial manager needs to consider funding operations with internal cash sources or finding outside sources to fund large projects.

What must financial managers consider when seeking outside funds?

In your personal life, you most likely have different types of financing options to help you manage your financial needs. For example, you may have a credit card to pay for short-term expenses. In addition, you might also have loans to pay for bigger, long-term expenses, such as school tuition, a car, or your home. Like you, a company may have several different types of borrowing options to finance small operating costs and large projects. There are many sources of outside funds available to a company. How does a financial manager evaluate the best financing option? The financial manager must first match the length of the financing to the length of the need. Then the financial manager must evaluate the cost of obtaining the funds and determine whether it is best to finance by raising *equity*—ownership interest in the form of stocks—or issuing debt. We'll discuss both of these options later in the chapter.

Financial managers like Cindy Li have myriad responsibilities. To determine the feasibility of the company's planned launch of a handheld computer device, Cindy developed short- and long-term financial forecasts. Taking into account the state of the economy and the future plans of the company, Cindy found that while producing the new product would be challenging, it could be done. Next she would need to take a closer look at the capital budget and evaluate funding options. We'll examine some of these options in the next section. ■

Financial Needs pp. 485–490

Ginny McIntyre runs a tailoring business from her home. Her customers have been recommending her work to other people, so in the last six months her customer base has almost doubled. Her house isn't big enough to accommodate all the orders and equipment, so she wants to buy a small shop that is for sale. The location is ideal, being near her home, but the problem is that her family and friends aren't willing to help finance the expansion. What other financing options does Ginny have? ■

As you've probably heard before, it takes money to make money. When businesses, both large and small, find it necessary to expand, they must make some important decisions regarding financing. In this section, you'll learn about what options are available for short- and long-term business needs, and how business leaders decide which option is best for their companies.

Financing Short-Term Business Needs

How are the operations of a company financed?

You may recall from Chapter 6 that different forms of business ownership have varying short-term needs. It's important that all companies have a plan to finance those needs. As mentioned above, cash flow budgets are prepared to predict a company's cash flow gaps—periods when cash outflows are greater than cash inflows. When these gaps are expected, depending on the size of the business and the cash flow gap, there are several short-term sources available to help fill the temporary gap.

Short-term financing is any type of financing that is repaid within a year or less. It is used to finance day-to-day operations, such as payroll, inventory purchases, and overhead (utilities, rent, leases). Smaller start-up businesses often fund cash flow gaps by first appealing to friends and family. This is not a recommended long-term or permanent strategy because it can lead to severed relationships if loans are not paid back promptly. However, when used, it is important that both parties understand and agree to formal payment arrangements.

Another approach that many smaller businesses take to fund cash flow gaps is using credit cards. Credit cards are a good way to defer payments, but they can become very expensive if credit balances are not paid off completely every month.

Larger businesses with good credit and an established relationship with their suppliers can take advantage of another credit relationship to help bridge the temporary gap. Companies will often purchase inventory and supplies on trade credit. **Trade credit** is the ability to purchase inventory and supplies on credit without interest. Suppliers will typically request payment within 30, 60, or 90 days.

▼ Figure 15.2 Trade Credit
Using trade credit can be advantageous but always must be evaluated and monitored carefully.

Deferring payment with trade credit is a good strategy to bridge a temporary cash flow gap, and it does not tie up cash unnecessarily. Moreover, using trade credit keeps debt levels down, which is always attractive to outside investors and lenders. However, there are disadvantages associated with using trade credit. Sometimes, buyers are offered a discounted rate if they pay their creditors early. Trade credit will negate this early payment discount. Additionally, if payments extend beyond the trade credit period, delinquency penalties are charged, and, if allowed to accrue, can be very costly.[4] Financial managers must weigh the costs and benefits of paying early for a discount or paying on time without a discount so that their cash is available longer. ▼ Figure 15.2 illustrates this decision.

In addition to trade credit, often companies will rely on commercial banks, savings and loans institutions, or other commercial lenders for interim credit arrangements and other banking services.

How do commercial banks help with financial management?
Commercial banks are financial institutions that raise funds from businesses and individuals in the form of checking and savings accounts and use those funds to make loans to businesses and individuals. Small start-up businesses rely on commercial banks for savings and checking services to pay bills and store excess funds. Checking and savings accounts are a form of **demand deposit**, funds that can be withdrawn (or demanded) at any time without prior notice.

As a business develops and establishes a good relationship with a bank, the business owners may seek to open a line of credit. You can think of a business **line of credit** like credit on hand, which a manager can access at any time up to an amount agreed on between the bank and the company. The funds can be withdrawn all at once or in multiple withdrawals during the stated period. This is a common way of covering cash flow shortages, purchasing seasonal inventory, or financing unforeseen operating expenses.

Many commercial banks also offer loans for the purchase of equipment, property, or other capital assets. A **secured loan** requires *collateral*, which is generally the asset that the loan is financing, to guarantee the debt obligation. For example, if a bank were to give a loan to a company so it could purchase a building, the building would serve as the collateral. If the company was unable to pay down the loan, the bank would then take possession of the building as a substitute for the remaining loan payments. If the firm has an excellent credit history and a solid relationship with the lending institution, it may get an **unsecured loan**, which doesn't require collateral.

Are there other short-term financing options?
Sometimes, a company is unable to secure a short-term loan from a commercial bank. In these cases, an alternative source of financing is a **commercial finance company**, a financial institution that makes short-term loans to borrowers who offer tangible assets as collateral. Commercial finance companies, such as GE Capital, provide businesses with loans but are not considered banks. The credit crunch in 2009 and 2010 made it difficult for many businesses, small and large, to seek financing solutions from banks. Banks were not lending, and if they were, the requirements were very stringent. Such was the issue facing Dave Capps, owner of Capps Van and Truck Rental in Dallas, Texas. The vans, which are rented to schools and church organizations, needed to be replaced, but Capps was unable to secure financing from the lender whom he had used for the past 20 years. Fortunately, GE Capital stepped in to help.[5]

Another strategy to obtain quick sources of cash is factoring. **Factoring** is the process of selling accounts receivable for cash. This takes monies that are owed to a company by clients or suppliers, which are generally past due, and turns them to cash that a company can then use almost immediately. The factoring company pays the value of the past-due invoices to the company selling them, less a fee. Companies often use factoring to help manage their cash flow, such as making payroll or buying materials or inventory, and to keep a business going when revenues are slow or cash is low. Although more costly than collecting the invoices yourself, factoring can be an important strategy for companies to bridge cash flow gaps and is easier to obtain than a business loan.

Do larger corporations do anything differently for short-term financing?
Large corporations have the advantage over smaller start-up companies in that they have a greater ability to establish a debt (or credit) rating. Those companies who have a high-quality debt rating can issue commercial paper. When a company has a high-quality debt rating, it means it is looked on favorably by lenders as being a company that has a good or excellent likelihood of paying off its debt. **Commercial paper** is an unsecured (that is, it does not need collateral) short-term debt instrument of $100,000 or more, typically issued by a corporation to bridge a cash flow gap created by large accounts receivable, inventory, or payroll. Commercial paper comes due (matures) in 270 days or less and is not required to go through the same registration process as other longer-term debt and equity instruments, which we'll discuss next. When companies have extra cash, they may choose to buy commercial paper from other companies that need cash. The company that purchases the commercial paper will make money from the interest that is charged to the debtor. Therefore, commercial paper can be a means of short-term financing for companies in need of cash; for other companies, commercial paper can be a short-term investment.

Large capital projects, such as construction projects, often require long-term financing.

Financing Long-Term Business Needs

Why do companies need long-term financing solutions? Remember that to grow, new or small companies need expansion projects, such as establishing new offices or manufacturing facilities, developing a new product or service, or buying another company. These projects generally cost millions of dollars and may take years to complete. **Long-term financing** is needed because it provides funds for a period greater than one year. In most cases, a company will use several sources of long-term financing, even for one project.

What are the different types of long-term financing? In general, a company has two different options for long-term financing: debt financing and equity financing. **Debt financing** occurs when a company borrows money that it is legally obligated to repay, with interest, by a specified time. Contrary to debt financing, the funds for **equity financing** are generated by the owners of a company rather than an outside lender. These funds might come from a company's own savings or from a partial sale of ownership in a company in the form of stock. The choice depends on many factors, including the maturity, the size and financial worthiness of a company, the number of assets and liabilities a company already owns, and the size and nature of the project being financed.

What kinds of debt financing are available? For larger projects that demand big loans and long payment terms, long-term financing is available from financial institutions, such as insurance companies and pension funds, large commercial banks, and finance companies. Most long-term loans require some form of collateral, such as real estate, machinery, or stock. Often, as in a home mortgage, the asset being financed serves as the collateral. Large long-term loans usually have a higher interest rate because of the added risk associated with a large project and the longer term of the loan. The rate of interest is also determined by the prevailing market interest rates and the general financial worthiness of the borrower.

Are there other ways besides loans to raise funds? Loans are easiest to obtain, especially when a firm has established a relationship with a bank or other financial institution and has a good credit standing. However, there are times when loans are not obtainable or the most economical option; perhaps the rates are too high or the project requires a greater amount of financing than loans can provide. In these cases, some companies have the option to issue bonds. **Bonds** are debt instruments issued by companies or governments for the purpose of raising capital to finance a large project. We'll talk more about bonds in Chapter 16, but for now think of a bond as a type of loan; however, rather than borrowing from a bank, a firm is borrowing from investors. There is a formal contract between a firm and its investors that outlines the project, the term of the bonds, and the interest due the investors. **Secured bonds** require some form of collateral pledged as security. **Unsecured bonds,** also called **debenture bonds**, are issued with no collateral. They are backed only by the general creditworthiness and reputation of the issuer.

What kinds of equity financing are available? If a company is successful, finding long-term funding can be as simple as looking at its balance sheet for *retained earnings*, or *accumulated profits*. Using retained earnings is an ideal way to fund long-term projects because it saves companies from paying interest on loans or underwriting fees on bonds. Unfortunately, not all companies produce enough retained earnings to fund large projects. In particular, start-up businesses find themselves with few options for long-term financing. Each business owner can contribute money to a company for expansion, purchases, operations, and so forth. However, at some point the individual owners contribute as much as they can or are willing to and still need additional funds to keep their business growing.

Without an established credit history, it is difficult to obtain a loan from a financial institution. Raising capital through owners' equity is one of the few options available to a start-up operation. Offering shares of ownership in a company to the general public—in other words, "going public"—can be a great option. A company can choose to go public when it feels it has enough public support to attract new shareholders.

What kind of private equity financing is available?

If a company does not feel it is ready to go public, it may look for long-term financing in the form of venture capital. **Venture capital** is an investment in the form of money that includes a substantial amount of risk for investors. Because of the high level of risk, the group of outside investors, called venture capitalists, command an active role in a company's management decisions. Venture capitalists seek their return in the form of equity, or ownership, in a company. They anticipate a large return on their investments when a company is sold or goes public. Venture capitalists are willing to wait longer than other investors, lenders, or shareholders for returns on their investments, but they expect higher than normal results.

On Target Using Social Networks for Venture Capital

Businesses need money, and venture capitalists need investments. How do the two meet? You might find it surprising that today many connections are made online through social media sites, such as blogs and Twitter, and social networks, such as LinkedIn. For example, Chris Sacca of Lowercase Capital is always looking for new investment opportunities. In an off-chance, he sent a tweet asking if there were any "bootstrapped, profitable start-ups with founders working late on a Friday night" and, to his surprise, one replied. The connection was made, and the investment is still one of Chris' favorites.

Social media allows investors to get a sense of the personality of the start-up founders of their potential investments before sinking a lot of time and effort into cultivating a relationship. Investors use social media to find deals and create relationships with entrepreneurs so they can close the deals that seem most attractive. Searching through Twitter streams can turn up valuable insight into a company's culture and viability, as well as the individual nature of the employees. Social networks can also help forge connections between investors and founders. If an investor doesn't know the management team of the potential investment, he or she can see if there are any common connections between them. If there are common connections, they can prove to be good sources of information—even if it's only about character and business acumen.

Twitter searches can be valuable to venture capitalists to see if users are having good experiences with a product, or whether they are disgruntled. It helps to uncover the real-world problems that might otherwise be purposely ignored by a company's management team. But it's not just a one-way street. Investors also need to build their online reputations to differentiate themselves from other venture capitalists. Venture capitalists can also use the social web to build up a reputation for their investments.

How do companies choose between debt and equity financing?

Most companies use debt to finance operations, which increases a company's leverage. **Leverage** is the amount of debt used to finance a firm's assets with the intent that the rate of return on the assets is greater than the cost of the debt. Using leverage wisely is beneficial because a company can invest in business operations without losing equity and increasing the number of owners in the company.

For example, if a company formed with $3 million from five investors (who become the company's shareholders), the equity in the company is $3 million. If a company also uses debt financing to borrow $17 million, the company now has $20 million to invest in business operations without having to take on more shareholders. This creates additional opportunities for the original shareholders to make more money.

Although there is a cost to borrowing, the intention is that the project or company expansion will ultimately have a positive rate of return after paying for the cost of the debt. However, it can be risky to take on too much debt, so lenders consider how much debt a company has relative to the amount of equity (or assets) a company owns before they issue a loan. A common leverage ratio is for a company to have at least twice the amount of equity as it has debt. If a company is unwilling or cannot take on additional debt, it must consider equity financing to meet its long-term business needs. Companies aim to achieve an optimal capital structure, which refers to the optimal balance between these two forms of financing.

Businesses have a variety of options for financing their operations and expansions. Although friends and family weren't able to help Ginny McIntyre expand her tailoring business, she was able to get a loan to help her purchase a small shop. In a few years, she plans to expand her business to include more staff and additional shops. She will likely enlist the help of a commercial finance company to fund this venture. Ginny, like all business owners, hopes that securing financing for these expenditures will lead to beneficial growth and profits. ■

Accounting Functions pp. 490–495

Arnold Sawyer was pretty good at handling figures. When his niece Josephine asked him to oversee the finances for her vegan catering business, he figured he could handle it. Arnold's background was in sales, but he assumed he was smart enough to handle accounting. He used QuickBooks to create a basic bookkeeping system. Because the company had a small but steady stream of clients, the accounting side didn't seem complicated. However, after Josephine appeared on a newscast to talk about the benefits of a vegan diet, sales skyrocketed. With the significant increase in catering contracts, the workload doubled. Josephine needed to increase her staff and supplies, but the company didn't have enough cash to cover the initial costs. Arnold wasn't sure what to do. ■

Accounting is often called the language of business because it provides financial information for decision making, planning, and reporting. When companies are small, accounting can seem relatively simple. However, as a company grows and diversifies, accounting becomes increasingly complex. In this section, we'll look at the fundamentals of accounting, the types of accounting, and accounting standards and processes.

Accounting Fundamentals

What is accounting? Remember Cindy Li? She was asked to make a decision about her company's ability to finance a large project. To make an informed decision, Cindy and her staff relied on financial data that her accounting staff prepared. Similarly, Arnold Sawyer must decide how his niece's catering business will acquire the extra funds it needs to keep the business moving. Arnold will need to review the company's financial information and possibly enlist outside consultants before making a decision. Both situations illustrate how accounting helps business managers make well-informed decisions about the financial needs of a company.

Accounting involves tracking a business's income and expenses by recording its financial transactions. The transactions are then summarized into key financial reports that are further used to evaluate a business's current and expected financial status. Accounting is not just for large organizations. In fact, as Arnold Sawyer can attest, it is vital for businesses of all sizes. Accounting defines the heart and soul of even the smallest business as it helps to "account for" what the business has done, what it is currently doing, and what it has the potential to do. Although accounting involves a great deal of precision, there are also some degrees of interpretation in the process of accounting. This makes accounting both an art and a science.

⊙ Off the Mark How's This for an Accounting Goof?

In August 2007, the assessor's office in Carver County, Minnesota, made an accounting goof that affected 34,000 taxpayers across the county. One of the clerks who was entering property values into the county's database typed the value of a vacant lot as $189 million instead of $18,900. The typing error went unnoticed. Not even the accounting software the county used detected anything out of the ordinary. The county assumed it would be getting $2.5 million in property tax payments and planned accordingly. Jurisdictions in the county created their budgets with the error still in place. Taxpayers received tax estimates from the county and thought they were catching a break because the estimates included the $2.5 million payment. No one was aware of the error until the owner of the vacant lot received a bill for $2.5 million and called officials to complain. Carver County officials had to hustle to adjust budgets properly for the following year. Many taxpayers, who thought they were getting a tax cut, were livid because they actually got a tax hike.[6]

Source: Based on "Carver County contrite about tax good, but residents fuming," Minneapolis-St. Paul Star Tribune, December 12, 2007

Types of Accounting

Are there different types of accounting? Accounting is a general term, to say the least. Because different forms of business have varying needs, there are a multitude of specialty areas under the accounting umbrella. The main accounting disciplines are *corporate accounting* (including *managerial* and *financial accounting*), *auditing*, *government and not-for-profit accounting*, and *tax accounting*, as outlined in ▼ **Figure 15.3**.

What is corporate accounting? As stated in the beginning of this chapter, financial managers must make many important decisions. Some decisions may involve determining whether a company's financial assets are working most efficiently (that is, earning as much money as possible), evaluating what kind of financing strategy is best, or choosing a way to obtain needed funds. The answers to these decisions and many more are found in the reports and analyses performed by corporate accountants. **Corporate accounting** is the part of an organization's finance department that is responsible for gathering and assembling data required for key financial statements. Corporate accounting has two separate functions: *managerial accounting* and *financial accounting*.

▼ **Figure 15.3 Primary Accounting Disciplines**

What is managerial accounting? **Managerial accounting** is necessary to make good business decisions within a company. More specifically, managerial accounting is responsible for tracking sales and the costs of producing sales (production, marketing, and distribution). By doing so, it helps determine how efficiently a company is run. Moreover, managerial accountants help determine which business activities are most profitable and least profitable. Based on their analyses, management is better equipped to make decisions about whether to continue

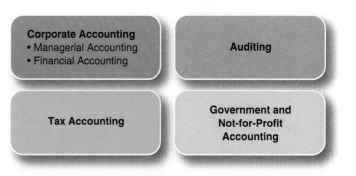

with, expand, or eliminate certain business activities. Managerial accounting produces budgets so senior management can make informed decisions. For example, a managerial accounting budget can help management determine whether it should increase staff or institute layoffs. In addition, by monitoring the activities involved in planned budgets, managerial accountants help determine and anticipate in what areas a company strays from its budgeted expectations.

What is financial accounting? Although individuals inside a company use managerial accounting to make decisions, interested parties outside a company depend on financial accounting to make financial decisions. **Financial accounting** is an area of accounting that produces financial documents to aid decision makers outside an organization in making decisions regarding investments and credibility. Investors and shareholders rely on financial accounting to help them evaluate a company's performance and profitability. Such information is generally found in key documents, such as quarterly statements or *annual reports*—documents produced once a year that present the current financial state of a company and future expectations. These documents help investors determine whether it is wise to put funds into a company. Banks and other creditors analyze financial accounting statements to determine a business's financial health and creditworthiness.

What is auditing? **Auditing** is the area of accounting responsible for reviewing and evaluating the accuracy of financial reports. Large corporations may have private accountants on staff who work in-house to determine whether a company's financial information is recorded correctly and using proper procedures. Generally, companies hire independent auditors from outside a company to ensure their financial reports have been prepared accurately and are not biased or manipulated in any way. Companies can avoid devastating budget problems, such as the one experienced by the assessor's office in Carver County, Minnesota (described in the Off the Mark box), by performing audits.

What accounting is used by governments and not-for-profit corporations? Accounting is not only for organizations that strive to make money; government institutions and not-for-profit organizations use accounting as well. **Government and not-for-profit accounting** refers to the accounting required for organizations that are not focused on generating a profit, such as legislative bodies and charities. Governmental and not-for-profit organizations need financial management expertise. Although their goal is not to make a profit, these organizations still must distribute and manage funds, maintain a budget, and plan for future projects. Government and not-for-profit organizations must also report their financial activities so taxpayers and donors can see how funds are spent and used.

Are there accountants who focus just on taxes? Paying taxes is an important part of running a business. State and local governments require individuals and organizations to file tax returns annually. **Tax accounting** involves preparing taxes and giving advice on tax strategies. The process for filing taxes can be complicated and is ever changing, so companies often have tax accountants on staff or hire a self-employed tax accountant, or an outside accounting firm, such as H&R Block or Jackson Hewitt, to prepare their taxes.

Accounting is so important to a business that accountants of all kinds are in high demand. ▼ **Table 15.1** explains some types of accountants.

Accounting Standards and Processes

Are there specific standards accountants must adhere to? For any financial information to be useful, it is critical that the information is accurate, fair and objective, and consistent over time. Therefore, accountants in the United States

▼ Table 15.1

Accountants in High Demand	
Certified management accountant (CMA)	Provides financial information to managers and other corporate decision makers "inside" a corporation and helps formulate policy and strategic plans.
Certified public accountant (CPA)	Provides financial information to stockholders, creditors, and others who are "outside" an organization. CPAs are licensed and must satisfy rigorous requirements.
Independent auditor	Provides a company with an accountant's opinion that attests to the accuracy and quality of a company's financial report. Independent auditors are not otherwise affiliated with companies for which they offer opinions.
Public accountant	Provides a broad range of accounting, auditing, tax, and consulting activities for individual and corporate clients. Not all public accountants are CPAs. Many have their own businesses or work for public accounting firms.
Private accountant	Employed by an organization for the purpose of maintaining financial control and supervising the accounting system.
Tax accountant	Assists taxpayers in the preparation of tax returns. Taxpayers can be individuals or corporations. Corporate tax accountants assist decision makers in strategic plans to minimize tax obligations.

follow a set of **generally acceptable accounting principles (GAAP)** that are standard accounting rules defined by the Financial Accounting Standard Board (FASB), an independent organization.

Although GAAP provides accountants with general rules, they are often subject to different interpretations, which can lead to problems. In 2002, Congress passed the **Sarbanes-Oxley Act**, which was created to protect investors from corporate accounting fraud in reaction to companies like WorldCom, Enron, and Tyco that made headlines and fell into financial ruin in the early 2000s due to very aggressive and fraudulent accounting practices. The act established the Public Company Accounting Oversight Board, which is responsible for overseeing the financial audits of public companies. Unfortunately, as evidenced by the fraudulent accounting practices conducted by Lehman Brothers in 2009, Sarbanes-Oxley may not be as effective as Congress had expected. Read the Biz Chat to find out more.

Biz**Chat**

Is the Sarbanes-Oxley Act Working?

The Sarbanes-Oxley Act was passed in 2002 as a reaction to several major corporate and accounting scandals that cost investors billions of dollars. The act was designed to improve corporate responsibility and accounting transparency. The question remains whether this legislation has been effective. Proponents feel that "SarbOx" has helped to restore investor confidence by strengthening corporate accounting controls. Others, however, claim that the overly complex regulations imposed by the act are not only expensive for companies to implement but also have made U.S companies less competitive internationally. Moreover, the downfall of Lehman Brothers due to fraudulent accounting practices seems to highlight the belief that it may be impossible to regulate an industry that prides itself on taking advantage of loopholes. The debate continues with no decisive and apparent "winner."

For more information and discussion questions about this topic, check out the BizChat feature on my**biz**lab.com.

▼ top
10 Accounting Scandals[7]

Rank	Company	Result
1.	Bernie Madoff	$21.2 billion cash losses
2.	Lehman Brothers	$50 billion in disguised loans
3.	Enron	shareholders lose $74 billion
4.	HealthSouth	$2.7 billion accounting fraud
5.	Worldcom	$11 billion accounting fraud
6.	Tyco	executives steal $120 million
7.	Satyam	$1.0 billion fraud
8.	AIG	$1.7 billion in improper accounting
9.	Waste Management	$1.9 billion in fake earnings
10.	Freddie Mac	$5 billion in misstated earnings

Outside the United States, other countries have their own accounting standards, which may differ from GAAP. Recently, there has been a movement toward international convergence of accounting standards. Most other countries are beginning to accept a common set of country-neutral accounting standards, which are known as *International Financial Reporting Standards (IFRSs)*. By doing so, multinational companies with operations in the United States and other countries, such as Toyota, Nestlé, and Guinness, may avoid the need to convert the financial reports prepared to meet their own country's accounting standards into GAAP specifications.

What is the accounting process? When people think of accounting, most think of the systematic recording of a company's every financial transaction. This precise process is a small but important part of accounting called **bookkeeping**. The process of bookkeeping centers on the fundamental concept that what a company owns (*assets*) must equal what it owes to its creditors (*liabilities*) plus what it owes to its owners (*owners' equity*). This balance is illustrated in ▼ **Figure 15.4** and is better described as the **fundamental accounting equation**: assets = liabilities + owners' equity.

Does the accounting equation always stay in balance? To maintain the balance of assets and liabilities plus owners' equity, accountants use a recording system called double entry bookkeeping. **Double entry bookkeeping** recognizes that for every transaction that affects an asset, an equal transaction must also affect either a liability or owners' equity. For example, let's say you started a business mowing lawns. Your initial assets are a lawn mower that is worth $500 and $1,500 in cash that you have saved and are willing to use to start the business. Your assets total $2,000. Because the cash and lawn mower were yours to begin with, you do not owe anyone any money, so you have zero liabilities. If you were to close the business tomorrow, the cash and the lawn mower would belong to you; therefore, they are considered owners' equity. The accounting statement for your lawn mowing business would look like the one in ▼ **Figure 15.5**.

Now say the business is growing rapidly. You realize you need to buy a bigger lawn mower; you also want to buy a snowblower so you can expand your business to include snow removal. Together these items cost $2,500. You don't have enough cash to buy either outright, so you have to borrow the money. Although you are increasing your assets with a new lawn mower and a new snow blower, you are also adding a liability—the debt you have incurred to buy the new

▼ Figure 15.4 The Fundamental Accounting Equation

Assets = Liabilities + Owners' Equity

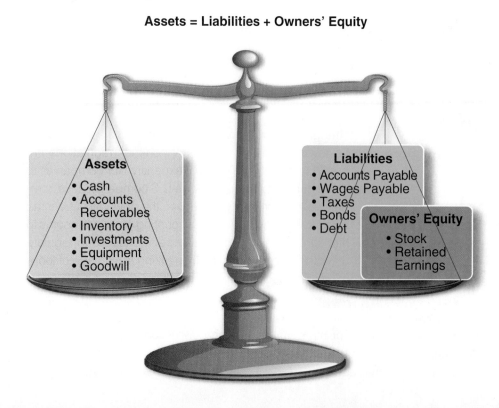

Assets
- Cash
- Accounts Receivables
- Inventory
- Investments
- Equipment
- Goodwill

Liabilities
- Accounts Payable
- Wages Payable
- Taxes
- Bonds
- Debt

Owners' Equity
- Stock
- Retained Earnings

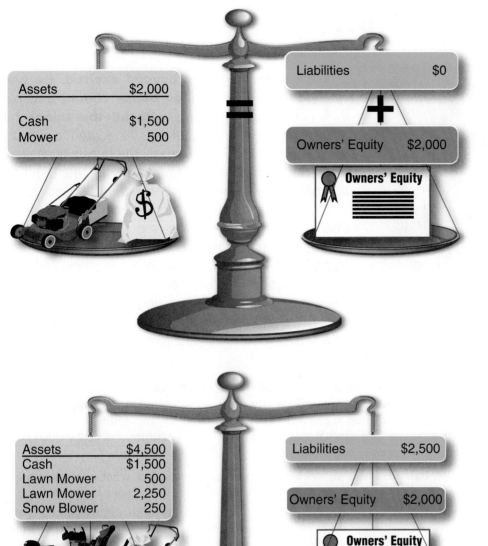

▼ **Figure 15.5**
Business with No Liability
Without any liabilities, assets equal owners' equity.

▼ **Figure 15.6**
Business with Liability
Borrowing to buy assets increases assets and liabilities.

equipment. If the business closed tomorrow, your owners' equity would not change because you could sell the lawn mower and the snow blower to pay off the debt. The accounting statement for your lawn mower business would look like the one in ▼ **Figure 15.6**.

Accounting is necessary for businesses of all sizes to help figure out what they have the potential to do. Arnold Sawyer was initially able to handle the finances for his niece's catering business, but when business boomed, he didn't know what to do. He realized he was in over his head and convinced his niece that she needed to hire a full-time accountant to handle these important matters. Having someone on staff who is knowledgeable about accounting is vital to a company's success. ■

Financial Statements pp. 496–505

ateo Morales was beyond excited. He had just received a huge bonus check, and his mind was spinning with all the things he could buy with the money: a bigger flat screen television, a long weekend trip to Las Vegas—the possibilities were endless. But then he came to his senses: Although he would love to buy those things, he knew the best choice would be to invest his bonus. Hopefully, over time, the investment would reap rewards and *then* he could buy some great things. But what should he invest in? Perhaps Google Inc. would make a great choice, but how could he know? The share value of Google was over $400. Maybe Yahoo! would be a better choice because its share value was under $20. He could certainly buy more shares of Yahoo! than Google. Was one a better investment than the other? What numbers should he look at? Where can he find the information? ■

Financial statements are the formal reports of a business's financial transactions that accountants prepare periodically. They represent what has happened in the past and provide management, as well as outsiders such as creditors and investors, with a perspective of what is going to happen in the future. Publicly owned companies are required to publish three financial statements:

- A **balance sheet** shows what a company owns and what it has borrowed (owes) at a fixed point in time and shows the net worth of a business.
- An **income statement** shows how much money is coming into a company and how much money a company is spending over a period. It shows how well a company has done in terms of profit and loss.
- A **statement of cash flows** shows the exchange of money between a company and everyone else it deals with over a period of time. It shows where cash was used.

Let's look more closely at each of these financial statements.

The Balance Sheet

What is the balance sheet used for? A balance sheet is a snapshot of a business's financial condition at a specific moment in time. It reflects what a company owns (assets), what it owes to outside parties (liabilities), and what it owes to the owners (owners' equity). At any point in time, the information in the balance sheet is used to answer questions like the following: "Is the business in a good position to expand?" "Does the business have enough cash to ride out an anticipated lull in sales?" In addition, by analyzing how a balance sheet changes over time, financial managers can identify trends and then suggest strategies to manage accounts receivable and payable in a way that is most beneficial to a company's bottom line. ▼ **Figure 15.7** is a summary balance sheet for Google as of December 2009. Summary financial statements present the data in a condensed format without a lot of detailed information.

Google Inc. Summary of Balance Sheet as of December 31, 2009 (in thousands)			
Assets		**Liabilities**	
Current Assets		Current Liabilities	
Cash and Cash Equivalents	$10,197,588	Accounts Payable	$215,867
Short-Term Investments	14,287,187	Other Current Liabilities	2,531,600
Net Receivables	3,846,121	**Total Current Liabilities**	**$2,747,467**
Inventory	n/a	Long-Term Liabilities	
Other Current Assets	836,062	Long-Term Debt	$0
Total Current Assets	**$29,166,958**	Other Liabilities	1,745, 087
Fixed Assets		**Total Long-Term Liabilities**	**1,745,087**
Property Plant Equipment	$4,844,610	**Total Liabilities**	**$4,492,554**
Other Assets	807,707		
Total Fixed Assets	**$5,652,317**	**Owners' Equity**	
Intangible Assets		Common Stock	$15,922,146
Goodwill	$4,902,565	Retained Earnings	20,082,078
Intangible Assets	774,938	**Total Owners' Equity**	**$36,004,224**
Total Intangible Assets	**$5,677,503**	**Total Liabilities and Owners' Equity**	**$40,496,778**
Total Assets	**$40,496,778**		

▼ **Figure 15.7 Summary Balance Sheet for Google Inc.**

What does a balance sheet track?

Balance sheets are based on the most fundamental equation in business accounting:

$$\overbrace{\text{Assets} = \text{Liabilities} + \text{Owners' Equity}}^{\text{Claims on assets}}$$

It is important to remember that assets (the items on the left side of the balance sheet) must always equal claims on assets, which are liabilities plus owners' equity (the items on the right side of the balance sheet). Let's look at each of these components in more detail and then see how they all fit together on a balance sheet.

Assets

Assets are the things a company owns, including cash, investments, buildings, furniture, and equipment. On a balance sheet, assets are organized into three categories: current, fixed, and intangible. These categories are listed on the balance sheet in order of **liquidity**—the speed at which assets can be turned into cash.

- **Current assets** are those assets that can be turned into cash within a year. Examples of current assets include cash, accounts receivable, inventory, and short-term investments, such as money market accounts. As you can see in Figure 15.7, as of December 31, 2009, Google had over $29.1 billion in current assets.

- **Fixed assets** are assets that have more long-term use, such as real estate, buildings, machinery, and equipment. Often, the value of a fixed asset, such as machinery or equipment, decreases over time due to usage or obsolescence. To compensate for such reduction in value over time, accountants use **depreciation** to spread out the cost of the equipment over its useful life. Depreciation helps keep the accounting equation in balance by matching the expense of the asset with the revenue that asset is expected to generate. As of December 31, 2009, Google had approximately $5.6 billion in fixed assets.

- **Intangible assets** do not have physical characteristics (you can't touch or see them), but they have value nonetheless. Trademarks, patents, and copyrights are examples of intangible assets, in addition to strong brand recognition and excellent customer or employee relations. Intangible assets are often reflected on financial statements and reports as *goodwill*. Google's goodwill and intangible assets amounted to nearly $5.7 billion.

Liabilities

Liabilities are all debts and obligations owed by a business to outside creditors, suppliers, or other vendors. Liabilities are listed on the balance sheet in the order in which they will come due.

- **Short-term liabilities**, also known as *current liabilities*, are obligations a company is responsible for paying within a year or less and are listed first on the balance sheet. They consist of accounts payable, accrued expenses, and short-term financing. *Accounts payable* are obligations a company owes to vendors and creditors. They are similar to those bills you need to pay every month, such as cable fees, credit card payments, and cell phone charges, and other obligations that are paid less frequently, such as taxes and insurance. *Accrued expenses* include payroll, commissions, and benefits that have been earned but not paid to employees. Trade credit and commercial paper make up *short-term financing*. Google had approximately $2.7 billion in current liabilities.

- **Long-term liabilities** include debts and obligations that are owed by a company that are due more than one year from the current date, such as mortgage loans for the purchase of land or buildings, long-term leases on equipment or buildings, and bonds issued for large projects. Google's long-term liabilities are approximately $1.7 billion.

Owners' Equity

What is the easiest way to think of owners' equity? Owners' equity is what is left over after you have accounted for all your assets and taken away all that you owe. For small businesses, **owners' equity** is literally the amount the owners of a business can call their own. Owners' equity increases as a business grows, assuming debt has not increased. It is often referred to as the owners' capital account.

For larger, publicly owned companies, owners' equity becomes a bit more complicated. Shareholders are the owners of publicly owned companies. Owners' equity, in this case, is the value of the stock issued as part of the owners' (shareholders') investment in the business and **retained earnings**, which are the accumulated profits a business has held onto for reinvestment into a company. The owners' equity (or stockholders' equity because it's a public company) for Google is approximately $36 billion.

Analyzing a Balance Sheet

How do I analyze a balance sheet? A lot of information about a company can be determined by its balance sheet. For example, just looking at the amount of inventory a company keeps on hand can be an indicator of a company's efficiency. **Inventory** is the merchandise a business owns but has not sold. Inventory on hand is necessary to satisfy customers' needs quickly, which makes for good business. However, there are costs associated with keeping inventory, the most obvious being the money spent to purchase the merchandise. In addition to the initial cost, storing unused inventory incurs warehousing costs and ties up money that could be used elsewhere. An even worse situation can arise if the value of unused inventory decreases over time, causing a company to lose money. This is a big concern for computer hardware companies, such as HP and Apple, whose inventory consists of computer parts and other technology-related components that can become obsolete very quickly.

For now, understand that it's okay to have a lot of inventory on hand if it's being sold quickly enough to avoid becoming outdated or spoiled. Inventory turnover varies greatly by industry, and companies must always have enough inventory to keep business moving and keep up with competitors. Google does not carry inventory.

How can I compare data from two different companies? Although looking at a balance sheet is a good way to determine the overall financial health of a company, the data presented on the sheet can be overwhelming and useless to investors if they are not organized. This is why ratio analysis is crucial when analyzing financial statements. **Ratio analysis** is a comparison of numbers and therefore is used to compare current data to data from previous years, competitors' data, or industry averages. Ratios eliminate the effect of size, so you can reasonably compare a large company's performance to a smaller company's performance. There are three main calculations one can do using information from a balance sheet to determine a company's financial health and liquidity:

- **Working capital**: Current Assets − Current Liabilities
- **Current ratio**: Current Assets ÷ Current Liabilities
- **Debt to equity ratio**: Total Liabilities ÷ Owners' Equity

Let's examine these measurements in more detail.

What measures how financially efficient a company is? One of the most important reasons one looks at a company's balance sheet is to determine the company's working capital. Working capital tells you what is left over if a company pays off its short-term liabilities with its short-term assets.

Working capital is a measure of a company's short-term financial fitness, as well as its efficiency. The working capital ratio is calculated as follows:

Current Assets − Current Liabilities = Working Capital

If a company has positive working capital (its current assets are greater than its current liabilities), it is able to pay off its short-term liabilities. If a company has negative working capital (its current assets are less than its current liabilities), it is currently unable to offset its short-term liabilities with its current assets. In this case, even after adding up all of a company's cash, collecting all funds from accounts receivable, and selling all inventory, the company would still be unable to pay back creditors in the short term. When a company's current liabilities surpass its current assets, many financial difficulties occur, with bankruptcy being the most severe. It is important to watch for changes in working capital, as a decline in positive working capital over time can be an indication that a company's financial health is in trouble. For example, a company that is experiencing a decrease in sales will have a decrease in accounts receivable (current assets).

On the other hand, situations like the one faced by Arnold Sawyer and his niece's catering company can arise when a company experiences a sudden spike in sales. It's possible to have positive working capital but not have enough immediately available to handle a large, unexpected cash need. A good financial manager and accountant must maintain a balance between having enough cash on hand and keeping the available short-term assets from being idle. Because of this, working capital can also be an indicator of a company's underlying operational efficiency.

What measures whether a company can pay its bills? Although working capital is an important measurement, it's hard to compare how efficient a company is to the rest of the industry or to its competitors, especially if companies vary significantly in size. The current ratio (sometimes called *liquidity ratio*) is a measurement used to determine the extent to which a company can meet its current financial obligations. The current ratio is calculated as follows:

$$\text{Current Ratio} = \frac{\text{Current Assets}}{\text{Current Liabilities}}$$

Google's current ratio ($29,167 ÷ $2,747) equals 10.62. The current ratio allows for better comparisons, especially when comparing a company to an industry average. For example, the current ratio for the 2010 first quarter for automotive manufacturers was 4.13.[8] During that time, Ford had a current ratio of 2.27, and Honda had a current ratio of 1.34,[9] putting both below the industry average. Having too high of a current ratio indicates a company may not be very efficient with its cash; having too low of a current ratio may indicate a company will face potential problems paying back its creditors.

Can a company have too much debt? Another way to analyze the activities of a company is to use the debt-to-equity ratio. Although leverage can be beneficial by freeing up cash for other investments, too much debt can become a problem. Companies with too much long-term debt may end up financially overburdened with interest payments. The debt-to-equity ratio measures how much debt a company has relative to its assets by comparing a company's total liabilities to its total owners' (or shareholders') equity. The debt-to-equity ratio is calculated as follows:

$$\text{Debt-to-Equity Ratio} = \frac{\text{Total Equity}}{\text{Owners' Equity}}$$

The debt-to-equity ratio can give a general idea of a company's financial leverage. As you may remember from the beginning of this chapter, *leverage* is the amount of debt used to finance a firm's assets. The debt-to-equity ratio will tell potential investors how much a company is willing to go into debt with creditors, lenders, and suppliers over debt with shareholders. A lower debt-to-equity ratio number means that a company is using less leverage and has more equity.

To get a better idea of how ratio analysis is used as a comparison tool, look at the data for two companies in the information industry, Google and Yahoo! Although the two companies are in the same industry, Google is much bigger than Yahoo!, so comparing absolute numbers is not effective. But, as shown in ▼ **Table 15.2**, look-

▼ **Table 15.2**

Industry Comparison of Balance Sheet Data for Fiscal Year 2009[*]			
	Working Capital	**Current Ratio**	**Debt-to-Equity Ratio**
Company	**(Current Assets − Current Liabilities)**	**(Current Assets ÷ Current Liabilities)**	**(Total Liabilities ÷ Shareholder's Equity)**
Google	$26,420 ($29,167 − 2,747)	10.62 ($29,167 ÷ $2,747)	0.12 ($4,493 ÷ 36,004)
Yahoo!	$2,877 ($4,595 − 1,718)	2.67 ($4,595 ÷ $1,718)	0.20 ($2,443 ÷ 12,493)

*Numbers in millions of dollars

Source: Based on Yahoo! Inc. Balance Sheet, December 31, 2009. http://yahoo.client.shareholder.com/annuals.cfm; Google Balance Sheet, December 31, 2009. http://investor.google.com/pdf/2009_google_annual_report.pdf.

ing at ratios makes the comparison more meaningful. It appears that Google has a better current ratio than Yahoo!, but the debt-to-equity ratios are about the same.

Income Statements

What does an income statement show? An income statement reflects the profitability of a company by showing how much money a company takes in and how much money it spends. The difference of money in and money out is the profit or loss, sometimes referred to as the *bottom line*. Besides showing overall profitability, income statements also indicate how effectively management is controlling expenses by pinpointing abnormal or excessive expenditures, highlighting unexpected increases in cost of goods sold, or showing a change in returns.

What are the components of an income statement? Recall that the balance sheet relates directly to the fundamental accounting equation: Assets = Liabilities + Owners' Equity. Similarly, income statements also work around an equation:

Revenues − Expenses = Profit (or Loss)

The income statement is grouped into four main categories: revenues, cost of goods sold, operating expenses, and net income, which are arranged in the following formula:

[(Revenue − Cost of Goods) − Operating Expenses] − Taxes = Net Income or (Loss)

▼ **Figure 15.8** shows a summary income statement for Google Inc. Let's look at each of these components and then see how they all fit together on an income statement.

Revenue

Revenue is the amount of money generated by a business by either selling goods or performing services. If a company has several different product lines or businesses, the income statement shows each product or division in categories to distinguish how much each generated in revenue. For example, Starbucks breaks down its revenue into two sources: retail and specialty. Revenue generated from retail sources is from sales made at all Starbucks stores. Specialty sales include sales made from its Web site and licensing fees from arrangements with Barnes & Noble, Target, and other locations, which pay for the right to operate Starbucks in their stores.[10]

Cost of Goods Sold

An income statement delineates several categories of expenses. The first category of expenses, **cost of goods sold (COGS)**, is a separate item on an income statement. COGS are variable expenses a company incurs to manufacture and sell a product, including the price of raw materials used in creating the good along with the labor costs used to produce and sell the items. For Starbucks, obviously, the costs of coffee beans, cups, milk, and sugar are included in COGS.

When you subtract COGS (or cost of sales) from total sales, the result is gross profit. **Gross profit** tells you how much money a company makes just from its products and how efficiently management controls costs in the production process. In addition, analysts use gross profit to calculate one of the most fundamental performance ratios used to compare the profitability of companies: *gross profit margin* (which we will discuss later in this chapter).

▼ **Figure 15.8**
Summary Income Statement for Google Inc.

Google Inc. Summary Income Statement as of December 31, 2009 (in thousands)	
Total Revenue	**$23,650,563**
Cost of Goods Sold	8,844,115
Gross Profit	**$14,806,448**
Operating Expenses	
Research Development	$2,843,027
Selling General and Administrative	3,651,235
Total Operating Expenses	**$6,494,262**
Operating Income or Loss	**$8,312,186**
Earnings Before Interest and Taxes	$8,312,186
Interest Expense	69,003
Interest Before Income Tax	**$8,381,189**
Income Tax Expense	1,860,741
Net Income	**$6,520,448**

Operating Expenses

Although it is certainly important to identify the costs associated with producing a product or a service, it is also important to identify **operating expenses**, the overhead costs incurred with running the business. Operating expenses include sales, general, and administrative expenses. These costs may consist of items such as rent, salaries, wages, utilities, depreciation, and insurance. Expenses associated with research and development of new products also are included in operating expenses.

Unlike COGS, operating expenses usually do not vary with the level of sales or production and are constant or "fixed." Outside interested parties (lenders and investors) watch operating expenses closely as an indication of managerial efficiency. Management's goal is to keep operating expenses as low as possible without negatively affecting the underlying business. The amount of profit realized from a business's operations (operating income) is determined when operating expenses are subtracted from gross profit.

Is operating income adjusted further? Management focuses on operating income as budgets are prepared and monitored. Some feel that operating income is a more reliable and meaningful indicator of profitability than gross profit because it reflects management's ability to control operating expenses. But, it is still not the "bottom line." Adding or subtracting any other income or expense, such as interest payments on outstanding debt obligations or earnings from investments, adjusts operating income further. Lastly, taxes paid to local and federal governments are subtracted to determine net income (or net income after taxes).

Net income is the "bottom line" and is usually stated on the very last line of an income statement. For publicly owned companies, however, net income is further adjusted by dividend payments to stockholders, resulting in *adjusted net income*.

Analyzing Income Statements

How do I analyze an income statement? One of the main purposes of the income statement is to report a company's earnings to its shareholders. However, an income statement reveals much more about a company, such as how effectively management controls expenses or how a company's profits compare to others in its industry. Specifically, the measurements that reveal this information are as follows:

- Gross profit margin
- Operating profit margin
- Earnings per share (EPS)

Let's look at each measurement in detail to understand the differences among them and how they are used to analyze a company's financial health.

How can I determine a company's overall profitability? A company's profitability and efficiency can be determined at two levels: profitability of production and profitability of operations. The **gross profit margin** determines a company's profitability of production. It indicates how efficient management is in using its labor and raw materials to produce goods. The gross profit margin is calculated as follows:

$$\text{Gross Profit Margin} = \frac{(\text{Total Revenue} - \text{COGS})}{\text{Total Revenue}}$$

The **operating profit margin** determines a company's profitability of operations. It indicates how efficiently management uses business operations to generate a profit. The operating profit margin is calculated as follows:

$$\text{Operating Profit Margin} = \frac{(\text{Total Revenue} - \text{COGS}) - \text{Operating Expenses}}{\text{Total Revenue}}$$

▼ **Table 15.3**

Benefit of Ratio Analysis*		
Company	**Gross Profit** **(Revenue − Cost of Revenue)**	**Gross Margin** **(Gross Profit ÷ Revenue)**
Google	$14,808 ($23,652 − $8,844)	62.61% ($14,806 ÷ $23,651)
Yahoo!	$3,589 ($6,461 − $2,872)	55.54% ($3,589 ÷ $6,461)

*Numbers in millions of dollars

Source: Based on Yahoo! Inc. Income Statement, December 31, 2009.
http://lyahoo.client.shareholder.com/annuals.cfm; Google Income Statement, December 31, 2009.
http://investor.google.com/pdf/2009_google_annual_report.pdf.

Gross profit margin and operating profit margin are equally important to management and investors.

You may notice they are both ratios, and, as you have learned in this chapter, ratios are best used when comparing two or more companies. Look at ▼ **Table 15.3**. Google's gross profit (revenues less cost of goods sold) for 2009 is more than $14.8 billion. Yahoo!'s gross profit of $3.6 billion seems to pale in comparison. However, you'll notice that while the two companies' gross profits are quite different, their gross profit margins are very close.

How much of a company's profit belongs to its shareholders?

The portion of a company's profit allocated to stockholders on a per-share basis is determined by calculating **earnings per share (EPS)**. Earnings per share is calculated as follows:

$$EPS = \frac{\text{Net Income}}{\text{Outstanding Shares}}$$

Again, looking at the EPS number in isolation is not completely meaningful. For example, it might seem reasonable to assume that a company with a higher EPS will be the better company to invest in than one with lower EPS. However, a highly efficient company—and potential good investment—can have a low EPS ratio simply because it has a large number of outstanding shares. Still, shareholders and prospective investors monitor EPS closely.

In some instances, the pressure of maintaining a continued growth record in net income or EPS has led management to "cook the books" or misrepresent financial information so that the business's bottom line appears better than it actually is. As noted earlier, such fraudulent behavior was the notable downfall of companies such as Enron, WorldCom, and Tyco and is the reason why the Sarbanes-Oxley Act was enacted. It's also how companies like AIG, Lehman, and Citibank spurred on the economic crisis that began in 2008. Therefore, it is best not to rely on any one financial measure and look at all the financial statements and other information as a whole.

Statement of Cash Flows

What is the statement of cash flows?

You have just looked at two important financial statements: the balance sheet and the income statement. The cash flow statement (or statement of cash flows) is the third important financial statement and provides some information that the other two financial statements do not show. The balance sheet is a snapshot of a company's financial position, and the income statement reflects a company's profitability over a specific period. A statement of cash flows is different because it does not reflect the amount of incoming and outgoing transactions that have been recorded on credit. Instead, it displays cash transactions only, similar to a checkbook register.

As shown in ▼ **Figure 15.9**, the cash flow statement organizes and reports cash generated in three business components: operating, investing, and financing activities.

- *Operating activities* measure cash used or provided by the core business of a company.
- *Investing activities* represent cash involved in the purchase or sale of investments or income-producing assets, such as buildings and equipment.
- *Financing activities* show cash exchanged between a firm and its owners (or shareholders) and creditors, including dividend payments and debt service.

Why is the statement of cash flows important? The statement of cash flows tells a story that the income statement does not. The income statement reports revenue receipts and expense payments. Because revenue and expenses often are accrued (earned but not paid), the income statement does not tell how efficiently management generates and uses cash. The statement of cash flows, be-

▼ **Figure 15.9
Summary Statement
of Cash Flows for
Google Inc.**

Google Inc. Summary Statement of Cash Flows as of December 31, 2009 (in thousands)	
Net Income	$6,520,448
Operating Activities, Cash Flows Provided By or Used In	
Depreciation & Amortization	$1,524,308
Adjustments to Net Income	−268,060
Changes in Accounts Receivables	−504,039
Changes in Liabilities	756,291
Changes in Other Operating Activities	1,287,250
Total Cash Flow from Operating Activities	$9,316,198
Investing Activities, Cash Flows Provided By or Used In	
Capital Expenditures	−809,888
Investments	−7,101,293
Other Cash Flows from Investing Activities	−108,024
Total Cash Flows from Investing Activities	−$8,019,205
Financing Activities, Cash Flows Provided By or Used In	
Sale Purchase of Stock	$143,141
Other Cash Flows from Financing Activities	90,271
Total Cash Flows from Financing Activities	$233,412
Effect of Exchange Rate Changes	10,511
Change in Cash and Cash Equivalents	$1,540,916
Cash at Beginning of Period	$8,656,672
Cash at End of Period	$10,197,588

cause it focuses specifically on cash, provides this important information. It shows whether all the revenues listed on the income statement have actually been collected.

Looking again at Figure 15.9, it is apparent that positive changes in cash flow occurred through Google's operations, and negative changes in cash flow occurred through its investments and capital expenditures. This information is useful to creditors who are interested in determining a company's short-term health, particularly in its ability to pay its bills. In addition, it signals to investors whether the business is generating enough money to buy new inventory and make investments in the business. Accounting personnel, potential employees, or contractors may be interested in cash flow information to determine whether a company will be able to afford salaries and other labor obligations.

Analyzing Statements of Cash Flow

How is a statement of cash flow analyzed? The bottom number, or change in cash and cash equivalents, reflects the overall change in a company's cash position. If it is positive, it means that a company had an overall positive cash flow. If it's negative, a company paid out more cash than it took in. Recall the balance sheet in Figure 15.7, where the first line item under current assets is cash and cash equivalents. The difference between cash and cash equivalent figures between periods is the same value that appears at the bottom of the cash flow statement for the same period. The rest of the balance sheet itemizes the broad categories that show what generated that positive cash flow.

Mateo Morales understands that it is important to carefully look at the financial statements for both Yahoo! and Google before he invests in either company. Financial statements, including balance sheets, income statements, and statements of cash flow, reveal a great deal about the health and prospects of a company. Although the abundance of numbers and figures seem a bit overwhelming, Mateo is confident that he'll be able to analyze each company and then make a good decision now that he knows what the statements all mean and how they are calculated. ▨

Chapter Summary

1. **What are the implications of financial management, and how do financial managers fulfill their responsibilities?** (pp. 481–485)

   - **Financial management** (p. 481) is the strategic planning and budgeting of corporate funds for current and future needs.
   - A **financial manager** (p. 481), often the CFO of a corporation, assumes financial management responsibilities. Financial managers generally have an accounting background.
   - Financial management includes forecasting short- and long-term needs, developing **budgets** (p. 483) and plans to meet the forecasted needs, and establishing controls to ensure that the budgets and plans are being followed.

2. **How do companies finance their short-term business needs through trade credit, commercial banks, commercial finance companies, and commercial paper?** (pp. 485–488)

   - It may be necessary to obtain **short-term financing** (p. 486) if cash flow gaps are anticipated.
   - Suppliers often offer **trade credit** (p. 486), where payment is deferred for usually 30, 60, or 90 days.
   - **Commercial banks** (p. 486) are another source of short-term financing and offer services such as **demand deposit** (p. 486) accounts, credit cards, business **lines of credit** (p. 487), or **secured loans** (p. 487).
   - **Commercial finance companies** (p. 487) are financial institutions that make loans to companies, but they are not considered banks. **Factoring** (p. 487), selling accounts receivable to a commercial finance company, is an additional way of quickly turning current assets into cash.
   - **Commercial paper** (p. 487), an unsecured short-term debt instrument issued by large, established corporations, is another means of raising funds of $100,000 or more.

3. **What is the purpose of each type of long-term financing for companies?** (pp. 488–490)

   - Large, capital-intensive projects require a different type of financing. Long-term financing is needed when companies take on expansion projects, such as securing new facilities, developing new products, or buying other companies.

   - Venture capitalists, borrowed funds, or raising owners' equity are the primary means of obtaining large amounts of long-term financings.
   - **Leverage** (p. 489) is using debt to finance a firm's assets with the intent that the cost of debt will be less than the rate of return on the financed asset. Using leverage can be beneficial unless too much debt is taken on.

4. **What are the functions of corporate accounting, financial accounting, managerial accounting, auditing, government and not-for-profit accounting, and tax accounting?** (pp. 490–492)

   - **Accounting** (p. 491) tracks a business's income and expenses by recording financial transactions.
   - **Corporate accounting** (p. 491) is responsible for gathering and assembling data required for the key financial statements.
   - **Managerial accounting** (p. 491) uses accounting information to help make decisions inside a company.
   - **Financial accounting** (p. 492) uses accounting information to guide decision makers outside a company, such as investors and lenders.
   - **Auditing** (p. 492) reviews and evaluates the accuracy of financial reports.
   - **Government and not-for-profit accounting** (p. 492) is required for organizations that are not focused on generating a profit.
   - **Tax accounting** (p. 492) involves preparing tax returns and giving advice on tax strategies.

5. **How is double entry bookkeeping used to maintain the balance of the fundamental accounting equation?** (pp. 492–495)

   - **Bookkeeping** (p. 494) is a part of the accounting process that is the precise recording of financial transactions.
   - Following the concept of the **fundamental accounting equation** (p. 494), where assets equal the sum of liabilities plus owners' equity, bookkeepers use a **double entry bookkeeping system** (p. 494).
   - Double entry bookkeeping assures that the accounts are kept in balance. For every transaction that affects an asset, an equal transaction must also affect a liability or owners' equity.

6. **What is the function of balance sheets, income statements, and statements of cash flow?** (pp. 496–505)

- The **balance sheet** (p. 496) is a snapshot of a business's financial condition at a specific time. It reflects **assets** (p. 497), **liabilities** (p. 498), and **owners' equity** (p. 498).
- The **income statement** (p. 496) reflects the profitability of a company by showing revenues and operating ex-

penses. The difference between revenue and expense is profit or loss. The income statement highlights management's efficiency at minimizing expenses while maximizing profits.

- A **statement of cash flow** (p. 496) is like a checkbook register and involves cash transactions only. It reveals important information about a company's ability to meet its cash obligations, such as salaries and accounts payable.

Key Terms

accounting   (p. 491)

assets   (p. 497)

auditing   (p. 492)

balance sheet   (p. 496)

bonds   (p. 488)

bookkeeping   (p. 494)

budget   (p. 483)

capital budget   (p. 483)

cash flow   (p. 484)

cash flow budget   (p. 484)

commercial banks   (p. 486)

commercial finance companies   (p. 487)

commercial paper   (p. 487)

corporate accounting   (p. 491)

cost of goods sold (COGS)   (p. 501)

current assets   (p. 497)

current ratio (liquidity ratio)   (p. 499)

debt financing   (p. 488)

debt-to-equity ratio   (p. 499)

demand deposit   (p. 486)

depreciation   (p. 497)

double entry bookkeeping   (p. 494)

earnings per share (EPS)   (p. 503)

equity financing   (p. 488)

factoring   (p. 487)

financial accounting   (p. 492)

financial manager   (p. 481)

financial management   (p. 481)

financial statements   (p. 496)

fixed assets   (p. 497)

fundamental accounting equation   (p. 494)

generally accepatble accounting principles (GAAP)   (p. 493)

government and not-for-profit accounting   (p. 492)

gross profit   (p. 501)

gross profit margin   (p. 502)

income statement   (p. 496)

intangible assets   (p. 498)

inventory   (p. 498)

leverage   (p. 489)

liabilities   (p. 498)

line of credit   (p. 487)

liquidity   (p. 497)

long-term financing   (p. 488)

long-term liability   (p. 498)

managerial accounting   (p. 491)

net income   (p. 502)

operating (master) budget   (p. 483)

operating expenses   (p. 502)

operating profit margin   (p. 502)

owners' equity   (p. 498)

ratio analysis   (p. 499)

retained earnings   (p. 498)

revenue   (p. 501)

Sarbanes-Oxley Act   (p. 493)

secured bond   (p. 488)

secured loan   (p. 487)

short-term financing   (p. 486)

short-term liabilities   (p. 498)

statement of cash flows   (p. 496)

tax accounting   (p. 492)

trade credit   (p. 486)

unsecured bond (debenture bond)   (p. 488)

unsecured loan   (p. 487)

venture capital   (p. 489)

working capital   (p. 499)

Self-Test

Multiple Choice You can find the answers on the last page of this book.

1. **Which formula is the fundamental accounting equation?**

   a. Owners' equity = assets + liabilities

   b. Assets = liabilities + owners' equity

   c. Owners' equity = assets ÷ liabilities

   d. Liabilities – assets = owners' equity

2. **The role of a financial manager can best be described as**

   a. outlining a company's short-term and long-term needs.

   b. identifying the sources and uses of funds for company operations.

   c. monitoring cash flow and investing excess funds.

   d. All of the above

3. **Ted Hoyt, the owner of an auto parts store, just placed a large order with his oil filters supplier. The supplier has offered Ted the ability to pay within 60 days before interest is charged on any outstanding balances. Ted is purchasing with**

   a. trade credit.

   b. a short-term loan.

   c. a demand deposit.

   d. a business line of credit.

4. **Gormley Paper Products Inc. is a privately held company with no intentions of going public or being managed by an outside group. It is looking to build a new manufacturing facility in another state. It is considering all of its financing options. Which would be a viable possibility for raising the necessary funds for the long-range project?**

   a. Issuing bonds

   b. Issuing stock

   c. Seeking venture capital

   d. All of the above

5. **Cash flow management is important for which business?**

   a. Spring Mountain Ski Shop, which operates between November and March

   b. Lederach Tea Room, which serves breakfast and lunch all year

   c. Tailwinds Airlines, which just had its first stock offering

   d. All of the above

6. **Financial accounting is responsible for**

   a. producing budgets and financial documents for corporate management.

   b. producing financial documents for outside investors.

   c. auditing corporate financial statements.

   d. preparing federal tax returns.

7. **Which financial statement shows how a company used its money?**

   a. Cash flow statement

   b. Profit and loss statement

   c. Balance sheet

   d. Income statement

8. **Hunter Wentworth is reviewing last quarter's financial statements and realized that there has been an increase in working capital. The most likely cause for an increase in working capital is a(n)**

   a. decrease in long-term liabilities and an increase in total assets.

   b. increase in current assets and a decrease in current liabilities.

   c. decrease in current assets and an increase in current liabilities.

   d. increase in long-term liabilities and a decrease in total assets.

9. **Which ratio tells whether a company can meet its short-term obligations?**

   a. Gross profit margin

   b. Current ratio

   c. Operating profit margin

   d. Earnings per share

10. **Revenues – expenses = profits is an equation that can be supported by which financial statement?**

   a. The income statement

   b. The cash flow statement

   c. The balance sheet

   d. None of the above

Self-Test

True/False   You can find the answers on the last page of this book.

1. The cash budget considers the company's long-range plans and outlines the needs for purchases, such as real estate, equipment, or expansions.
   ☐ **True** or ☐ **False**

2. Commercial paper can be a means of short-term financing for companies in need of cash, and, for other companies, commercial paper can be a short-term investment.
   ☐ **True** or ☐ **False**

3. Leverage is not a favorable financing strategy because the cost of borrowing will decrease the amount of owners' equity.
   ☐ **True** or ☐ **False**

4. Ratio analysis is conducted to better compare companies of different sizes.
   ☐ **True** or ☐ **False**

5. The income statement is analogous to a checkbook register because it records the cash generated by a business.
   ☐ **True** or ☐ **False**

Critical Thinking Questions

1. Jason worked in a deli for five years before starting his own sandwich delivery store. The business has been quite successful for two years. The quality of the service and the sandwiches has caused an increased demand for his products. Jason now thinks he needs to buy more cars to deliver the sandwiches. He is trying to determine the most appropriate way of financing the acquisition of two cars.

   a. What methods of financing should Jason consider?

   b. What information will Jason need to help make his decision?

   c. How might the financing decisions change if Jason also decided to open another store at a new location?

2. What are the key financial statements, and what is the importance of financial statements? What information do they contain? Which statement do shareholders typically find most useful? Why? What about independent contractors considering working with a firm?

3. Discuss the role of independent auditors for a company. Over the past decade, why have independent auditors been under scrutiny by the government?

4. Recall Mateo Morales. What advice would you give to him? Based on the information in the text, which might be a better investment—Google or Yahoo!? Explain your answer. Using information from current financial statements, would your answer change? Why or why not?

5. Sally owns a small women's apparel design company. Because of the poor economy, her sales have been slow, and she is barely able to make payroll. Last week, she received a surprise order for a large quantity of designs from one of her lines. She'll need to order material and other supplies but doesn't have the cash to pay. What are her options?

Team Time

Industry Analysis

Assemble into groups of four or five.

Process

Step 1. As a group, choose an industry and then have each group member pick a company in that industry. The company should be publicly traded so that financial records are easily available.

Step 2. Each group member should review the annual report and the three key financial statements for the chosen company and prepare a brief analysis of the company's financial situation. Then calculate the ratios covered in this chapter and find three other ratios that are meaningful to your analysis.

Step 3. When your report is completed, combine your information with the information from other members of your group into an industry analysis and determine how each company fits into the industry. Would the conclusions from your independent analysis change once you see the analyses of other companies in the industry?

Step 4. As a group, prepare a presentation summarizing your findings for the industry and each company in the industry and present it to the class.

Ethics and Corporate Social Responsibility

Getting to the Bottom of the Sarbanes-Oxley Act

In 2002, in the aftermath of some of the largest financial and accounting scandals in recent U.S. history, President George H. W. Bush signed the Sarbanes-Oxley Act into law. The intent of the law is to protect investors from accounting fraud.

Reports indicate that complying with the law's requirements has cost U.S. businesses tens of millions of dollars. In addition, critics state that complying with Sarbanes-Oxley has stripped CEOs of their creativity and is making U.S. companies less competitive internationally,[11] although support for the act's provisions is slowly gaining.

Exercise

Research the history behind the Sarbanes-Oxley Act as well as current compliance with the act's provisions. Then prepare a brief report summarizing your answers to the following questions:

1. What specifically are companies asked to do?

2. How might these requirements affect "CEO creativity" and international competitiveness?

3. What are your thoughts as to the need for and effectiveness of this act? Is it effective or is it causing more harm than good? Why, and what other measures, if any, do you think should be taken to address these issues?

Web Exercises

1. **Cash Flow Simulation**
   How well would you be able to manage the cash flow of a company? To find out, use Google to search for the "Cash Flow Simulation Game" and click on the Cash Flow Simulation link. Go through the tutorial and then play the simulation. Even though this is based on a company in the United Kingdom, the principle of cash flow is universal. How did you do?

2. **Balancing a Budget**
   Companies are not the only entities that must create budgets. Cities, states, and other governmental agencies must also prepare budgets, but unlike corporations, they can raise or lower taxes to help balance the budget. However, raising taxes is not always politically favorable; although lowering taxes helps get the votes, it is not always fiscally prudent. How would you do if you were just hired to close a $4 billion budget deficit for New York City? Find out by playing Balance: Gotham Gazette's Budget Game (search for it on Google).

3. **Exploring Career Possibilities**
   Visit job search sites, such as Monster, and find postings for financial managers and accountants. What are the job specifications and requirements? What companies are advertising the openings? Are these careers you are interested in pursuing? Why or why not?

4. **Securing Financing**
   Go to the Web site of a local bank and research its options for short-term business financing. What are the terms of its small business loans and lines of credit? Does it offer other commercial financing options, such as factoring? If you were going to open a small business, how would you go about financing it, based on what you learned?

5. **Analyzing Current Ratios**
   Using MSN Money (under Guided Research, Research Wizard, Comparison) or Yahoo! Finance (choose specific company, then Competitors) pick an industry (such as telecommunication services) and then two companies within the industry (such as Verizon, AT&T, or Qwest) and do a ratio comparison similar to what was done in the chapter with Google and Yahoo! Write a summary citing your conclusions from the analysis.

Web Case

For more on managerial accounting and financial management to manage the customer experience and company image, access the Chapter 15 Web case entitled "Focus on Google: A Googol of Dollars for Google" located in the End of Chapter Assignments section at my*biz*lab.com.

Video Case

For more on the challenges of financial management in an international business environment, access the Chapter 15 Video Case entitled "McDonald's: Accounting for Billions and Billions of Burgers" located in the End of Chapter Assignments section at my*biz*lab.com.

Securities and Investments

Choosing Between Debt and Equity

Joseph Cortez and Sean Hendricks were planning large capital growth for their companies. They needed capital and knew they needed outside investors for funds. Should they use bonds? Should they use stocks? What factors are involved when they make the decision?

Objective 1 What are the pros and cons of debt and equity financing? (pp. 513–516)

Objective 2 How do companies issue bonds and stocks? (pp. 516–517)

Investment Fundamentals

Lecretia Washington works hard for her money, and she knows she needs to start saving toward big goals, such as buying a new car, taking a vacation, buying a house, and, eventually, retirement. But it seems as if there is never enough money to set aside after paying her daily expenses. How can she begin to save toward achieving her long-term goals?

Objective 3 How do risk-return relationships, risk tolerance, and asset allocations relate to the fundamentals of investment? (pp. 518–522)

Investing in Stocks

When Gina Smith was young, her grandparents invested money for her Walt Disney Company stock. Now Gina is older and wants to try her hand at the stock market herself. How can she decide which stocks to buy? How can she buy them?

Objective 4 What are the different investment categories of stocks, and how does the stock trade process work? (pp. 523–526)

Objective 5 What is stock performance, and what are the factors that lead to changes in stock price? (pp. 527–528)

Investing in Bonds

Dennis Sanchez is starting to think about retirement. He's interested in making some low-risk investments that will also generate income. Dennis believes investing in bonds might be his best option. What type of bonds should he investigate?

Objective 6 What are the different types and characteristics of bonds, and how is the safety of bonds evaluated? (pp. 529–531)

Investing in Mutual Funds and Other Opportunities

Keri and Alex Young recently got married and want to start investing in their future immediately. After wedding, honeymoon, and moving expenses, they have only about $3,000 to invest. Why would mutual funds be a good place for them to begin investing?

Objective 7 What are bond mutual funds, money market funds, and equity funds? (pp. 532–535)

Objective 8 What are the advantages and disadvantages of mutual fund investments? (pp. 532–535)

Objective 9 What are other investment opportunities besides stocks, bonds, and mutual funds? (p. 535)

PEARSON my*biz*lab™

Financial Management

You've always loved dabbling in the stock market. Having received your degree, you've just been given a chance to do what you love for a living—working as a financial manager for a young company called Aireware. Can you make the right decisions to guide Aireware to financial success?

Objective 10 Test yourself using my*biz*lab.com to show that you understand the chapter objectives.

Choosing Between Debt and Equity pp. 513–518

Three years ago, Joseph Cortez secured equity investments from a venture capital group to help his company establish a presence in Europe. Since then, his company has continued to expand faster than he expected. Joseph knew that to secure the long-term success of the company, he needed to enter the Asian and Australian markets. Meanwhile, Sean Hendricks, president of an automotive dealership, was looking for capital to finance the acquisition of more dealerships. How should each company meet its financing needs? Should it issue company stock or bonds? Would one option work better for a particular company? What factors does each company need to consider? ■

As we discussed in Chapter 15, in the process of business expansion, business owners may need to raise funds to finance a large capital project. The project may involve building a new factory or a corporate office, acquiring another company, expanding into a new product line, buying updated machinery or technology, or just general expansion or added liquidity. For large capital-intensive projects or general expansion, business owners can use **securities**—investment instruments such as *bonds* (debt) or *stock* (equity).

The choice between financing large projects with debt or equity is a fundamental decision. Managers can reach the best decision by understanding the financing needs of the project itself and the impact the financing decision has on corporate earnings, cash flow, and taxes. In addition, a company must consider how much debt it already has before issuing bonds or whether it wants to dilute ownership by issuing stock. Lastly, a company must also consider external factors at the time of financing, such as the state of the bond or stock market, the economy, and the anticipated interest of the investors. In this section, you'll learn about the pros and cons of debt and equity financing and the process companies take to issue stocks and bonds.

Financing with Bonds (Debt)

Why finance with bonds? In our personal lives, when we want to buy something that costs more than what we have saved, such as a house or a car, our best option is to borrow money. We take out a loan (such as a home mortgage or a car loan) specifically to pay for the item, and that item is used as collateral in case the debt obligations are not satisfied. Similarly, when a company has a project or desired asset that it cannot finance with existing company assets, it can take out a business loan. As we discussed in Chapter 15, common lenders include banks, finance companies, credit card companies, and private corporations.

Eventually, a company's financing needs may grow beyond what these common lenders can provide. In these situations, companies may use bonds to acquire the needed funds. **Bonds** are debt instruments issued by companies or governments

For an interactive, real-world example of this topic, access this chapter's **BizSkill** entitled Financial Management, located at **my*biz*lab**.com.

with the purpose of raising capital to finance a large project. A bond consists of the principal (the amount borrowed) and interest (the fee charged by the lender for using the borrowed money). Investors loan money to a company by purchasing bonds. In return, investors often receive interest on the bonds they purchase. Although some bonds do not pay interest, all bonds require repayment of the principal.

What are the advantages of financing with bonds?

Financing with bonds allows a company to use money from investors to create or obtain business assets. By doing so, companies can finance a project or an asset rather than use (and possibly deplete) business profits, thus allowing companies to use their monies more efficiently by retaining profits for other business uses or using them to pay a return to the owners of the company. Although there are costs associated with bond financings, it is worth assuming those costs as long as the project or the asset that a company is financing will generate a greater return. In addition, unlike stocks, which we'll discuss later, financing with bonds does not dilute ownership of a company. For many companies, giving up ownership or control of a business is not a feasible or a desirable option. Unlike shareholders, bondholders have no voice or control in how a business is managed. Their only requirement is that the loan is paid back on time and with interest.

What must financial managers consider before choosing to finance with bonds?

As attractive as bond financing sounds, financial managers must consider several factors before choosing to finance with bonds. First and foremost, the cost of the loan—the rate of interest the lender will demand—is an important consideration. If the interest rate is too high, it can force the cost of the project into something that is not affordable or that just doesn't make economic sense. A high interest rate may provoke a company to consider a different line of financing or postpone the project until interest rates are more attractive.

The interest rate is determined by a combination of many factors, including *issuer risk*—whether the lender thinks a company can meet its obligations to pay back the loan. As the risk increases, so does the interest rate. Often, as you'll see later in this chapter, issuers use *bond insurance* to help lower the risk. Although there is a cost to having such insurance, the amount of money saved by having a lower interest rate is greater than the cost of bond insurance.

In addition to issuer risk, the *length of the bond term* affects the rate. Longer-term bonds have a greater chance of default, with the issuer not being able to pay principal or interest when it's due; therefore, they carry additional risk and a higher interest rate. Last, *the general state of the economy* affects the rate. Before making a final decision to issue bonds, a financial manager must also consider how this additional debt obligation affects the overall financial health of a company. From a balance sheet perspective, too much debt may impair a company's credit rating. The statement of cash flows will help determine whether there will be sufficient cash flow to repay the debt. Too much stress on cash flow can quickly launch a company into a disastrous financial tailspin.

How do companies pay back their bond debt?

As noted above, bond investors receive two types of payments: *principal* and *interest*. Most bondholders periodically receive interest payments in amounts and at the specified times arranged in the bond agreement. Most interest payments are semiannual. The amount of interest is calculated on the amount of principal outstanding and the periodic interest rate associated with the debt. So, if you held a $10,000 bond with a 5 percent interest rate, paid semiannually, you would receive $250 in interest payments twice a year. At the end of the loan period, the company is responsible for paying you the entire initial amount you invested (the principal), which in this case is $10,000.

To ensure there is enough money at the end of the loan period to pay back the principal to all the bondholders, companies annually set aside money in a **sinking fund**—

Payment Cycle of Bond Issue

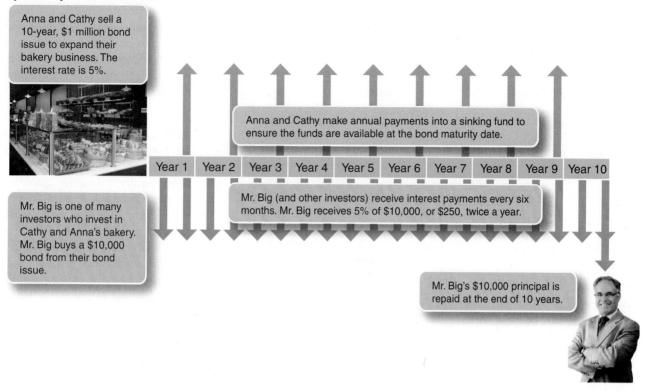

Anna and Cathy sell a 10-year, $1 million bond issue to expand their bakery business. The interest rate is 5%.

Anna and Cathy make annual payments into a sinking fund to ensure the funds are available at the bond maturity date.

Mr. Big is one of many investors who invest in Cathy and Anna's bakery. Mr. Big buys a $10,000 bond from their bond issue.

Mr. Big (and other investors) receive interest payments every six months. Mr. Big receives 5% of $10,000, or $250, twice a year.

Mr. Big's $10,000 principal is repaid at the end of 10 years.

Year 1 Year 2 Year 3 Year 4 Year 5 Year 6 Year 7 Year 8 Year 9 Year 10

▼ **Figure 16.1 Payment Cycle of Bond Issue**

a type of savings fund into which companies deposit money regularly to help repay a bond issue. ▼ **Figure 16.1** explains the payment cycle of a bond issue.

Financing with Stock (Equity)

Why finance with stock (equity) ❓ The most common forms of financing for small businesses are personal savings or contributions from family, friends, or business associates. As a business grows, venture capital or funds from angel investors are also possible sources of new capital. Eventually, however, those options are not sufficient to finance large capital needs. Companies issue stock (often referred to as *equity*) to finance long-term general funding and ongoing expansion rather than a specific project or need. **Equity** is money that is received in exchange for ownership in a business. **Stock** is a unit of ownership in a company that is sold with the intention of raising capital to finance ongoing or future projects and expansions. A **stock certificate** represents stock ownership and includes the details of the stock issue, such as the company name, the number of shares the certificate represents, and the type of stock being issued.

Are there disadvantages to financing with stock❓ The biggest disadvantage that financing with stock brings is a dilution of ownership. Especially in smaller companies, new stock owners may have a dramatic impact on the way a business operates and is managed. Shareholders do not have direct control over the day-to-day management of a company, but they do have a say in the composition of the board of directors. This means that although shareholders do not directly control how a company is managed, they do directly control who manages the company. As a result, shareholders can have a strong influence on management's decisions.

For example, companies are not legally required to pay **dividends**—payments made from a portion of a company's profits—to shareholders. However, when

▼ **Table 16.1**

Debt or Equity Financing: What Does Each Mean for the Company?	
Debt	**Equity**
Company profits are used to repay debt.	Company profits retained or paid to shareholders.
Must be repaid or refinanced. Requires regular interest payments.	No required payments to shareholders.
Company must generate cash flow to pay interest and principal.	Company is not required to pay dividends out of cash flow. Dividends, if paid, are paid out of profits.
Collateral assets are usually required.	No collateral required.
Interest payments are tax deductible.	Dividend payments are not tax deductible.
Debt does not impact control of a company.	Equity requires shared control of a company and may impose restrictions.

profits are no longer required to fund corporate growth, the board of directors or management may choose to pay dividends in an effort to increase the shareholders' rates of return. These payments are made after taxes and are not tax deductible for the company.

What are the advantages to financing with stock? Unlike bonds and other forms of debt, equity financing does not need to be repaid, even if a company goes bankrupt, so no assets need to be pledged as collateral. In addition, financing with equity enables a company to retain cash and profits rather than use the funds to make interest and principal payments. In many instances, financing with equity can make the balance sheet look stronger, as high levels of debt can be problematic to lenders and investors.

How does a company choose between debt and equity? In reality, companies use both debt and equity to finance projects and business expansion. It is important to note that although debt and equity financing can be used simultaneously, they are very different and should not be considered as substitutes for one another. Instead, they should be viewed as complementary financing; most large companies will use both types of financing.

▼ **Table 16.1** summarizes the differences between financing with debt and financing with equity. The overall goal is to strike a balance between debt and equity, take advantage of the positives of each type of financing option, and minimize the negative consequences that too much of each option might bring.

Are there guidelines for debt and equity levels? The balance between debt and equity varies according to industry and the size of a business. For example, capital-intensive manufacturing industries, such as car manufacturers, will have more debt than service industries, such as health-care providers. Other industries that are expanding rapidly but have large capital reserves, such as computer hardware manufacturers, have a minimal need for debt or equity financing. As we discussed in Chapter 15, one measure of a company's financial leverage is determined by its debt-to-equity ratio (or total liabilities divided by shareholders' equity).

Primary Security Markets

How do companies issue bonds? If financial managers decide that bonds are the best financing option, they contact a financial advisory firm for expertise. Issuing bonds is a very complex financial and legal process that requires expert advice on the marketplace, the timing of the issue, the issuing price, the structure of the bonds, and other factors. A **financial advisory firm** serves as an intermediary between a company issuing the bonds and the investors who purchase the bonds.

Before the sale of the bonds, financial advisors prepare required documents for filing with the **Securities and Exchange Commission (SEC)**, the federal agency that regulates and governs the securities industry. They also consult with rating agencies that assess an issuer's creditworthiness. The resulting credit rating has an impact on the interest rate of the bonds. Financial advisors also help set the price for the bond issue and take the lead in forming and managing a group of financial advisory firms to underwrite, or purchase, the newly issued bonds.

In addition to a managing fee, financial advisors make their money by initially purchasing all the bonds at a discounted price and then quickly selling them to investors at a higher price. These transactions take place in the **capital market**, an arena where companies and governments raise long-term funds by selling stocks and bonds and other securities. The **primary market** is part of the capital market that deals specifically with new bond and stock issues. Because it can take months or years to successfully structure a bond issue, financial advisors have time to generate interest and locate potential buyers for the bonds well ahead of the date of issuance, thus reducing their risk and ensuring the success of the initial issuance.

Do companies issue stocks in the same way as bonds?

In essence, yes, stocks are issued in the same manner as bonds, albeit with some minor differences. The first sale of stock to the public by a company is called an **initial public offering (IPO)**. Similar to the financing of a bond, a financial advisor coordinates the documentation preparation and filing with the SEC. A prospectus is one of the required documents. A **prospectus** is a formal legal document that provides details about an investment. The prospectus helps investors make informed decisions about a new investment. Financial advisors also establish the best timing for the public sale and determine the initial selling price. The advisory firm or bank, along with several other banks, forms a group or syndicate to underwrite the IPO; that is, they take the responsibility and risk of selling their allotment of the issue. The syndicate then purchases the stock and sells it back to the public.

The buyers of an IPO are generally large institutional buyers, such as insurance companies and large corporate pension plans, as opposed to individual buyers. The underwriters want to sell the issue as quickly as possible to receive a return on their purchase. Because institutional buyers are more likely to buy large quantities of the IPO, it is ultimately more efficient to sell to them than to sell the IPO in little pieces to individual investors. This is tolerable for the individual investor because buying IPOs is a risky, less desirable venture.

Companies issue shares of common stock when they need to raise capital.

Secondary Security Markets

How are stocks exchanged after they are issued?

Most investors buy and sell shares of stock in the **secondary market**, the market in which investors purchase securities from other investors rather than directly from an issuing company. As you'll read in the next section, investing in stocks requires a lot of analysis to ensure that you're making the right decision. Stocks that have been on the market for awhile are easier to analyze because you can examine their history. IPOs, by their very nature, have no historical information on which to base any analysis.

When it comes to deciding how to finance the expansion of a business, there are many factors involved, such as current debt, ownership dilution, the state of the bond and stock markets, and the interests of investors. The decision is not always obvious, as the ever-changing state of the economy determines which choice is more cost-effective. Also, business owners must decide if they are willing to compromise the vision they have for their companies by allowing stockholders to have a say in company decisions.

There is no easy answer to this question, as Joseph Cortez and Sean Hendricks discovered. After weighing the pros and cons of both options, Joseph decided to finance the expansion of his company into the Asian and Australian markets with bonds. In contrast, Sean decided that stocks were the best way to finance the ongoing expansion of his automotive company. Joseph and Sean felt confident that their decisions would help their companies achieve growth and maintain a good balance between debt and equity financing. ■

Investment Fundamentals pp. 518–523

Lecretia Washington works hard for her money, and every penny she earns has a specific purpose: rent, gas, clothing, food, and entertainment. She also is setting aside money on a regular basis. Although saving is important to her, any extra funds are often set aside to meet short-term goals, such as buying a new car or planning a vacation. Her long-term goals, such as buying a house and saving for retirement, seem long off and hard to reach. How can she save toward achieving her long-term goals while not neglecting her current needs and short-term goals? ■

Lecretia can start by opening a savings account. Depositing funds into a bank and earning interest is a good way to begin to let money make money. Because the Federal Deposit Insurance Corporation (FDIC) insures most savings accounts, you may be convinced this is a good strategy because you're guaranteed to receive your money at any time, plus interest earned. However, depending on your long-term needs, the amount your money will earn in a savings account might not be enough. While saving is important, it isn't the only way to make money. In this section, we'll discuss another way of achieving your financial goals—investing.

The Risks and Rewards of Investing

I save my money, isn't that enough? The interest rates for savings accounts and other short-term, low-risk investments are currently very low. In addition, your savings are further compromised by taxes and inflation. To reach your long-term financial goals, you'll most likely need to have your money work harder.

How can I make my money work harder for me? With time on your side, if you continue to save regularly, your savings will accumulate. How much you end up with depends on two things: time and quantity. The sooner you begin to save and the more frequently you put money into savings makes a big difference in the amount accumulated in the end. Keeping your money in a bank and having it build interest will let your savings grow more quickly than if you were to just tuck it under your mattress, but there are other options to investigate.

To illustrate the power of having your savings work for you, compare the following situations. Imagine that your grandparents began a savings account for you the day you were born. Every month, they deposit $100. On your 16th birthday, the account is worth $19,200, and you have the choice to take the money and buy a car or continue to save the money. Either way, your grandparents will stop contributing to your savings account.

As tempting as it is to buy a new car, your father explains that if you keep the money in the bank, earning 3.5 percent interest each year, and if you don't touch it until you are 65, you will have $103,604 to contribute to your retirement. Alternatively, you could buy a group of conservative stocks with the $19,200 that would earn 8.5 percent on average. When you reach 65, you would have over one million dollars—$1,045,582! What would you decide to do?

Biz**Chat**

I Can't Lose Money by Saving, Right?

It's much safer to simply save your money in a bank account than risk losing it in investments, right? Perhaps. But there are two forces beyond your control that you must consider: inflation and taxes. Even after diligent savings, there is still a distinct possibility that you might, over time, lose money due to the effects of inflation and taxes.

Let's say you saved $10 each month for three years in a savings account that earns 3 percent annually (although many savings accounts currently earn far less interest than this). If you didn't withdraw any money, at the end of the three-year period, you would have $376.21. That's pretty good considering that if you had just put the money away under your mattress, at the end of three years, you would have only $360. So, just by putting the money in a savings account, you have acquired $16.21. Or have you? Unfortunately, you have to pay taxes on that $16.21. Assuming you're at a 15 percent income tax bracket, you owe $2.43 to Uncle Sam, reducing your earnings to $13.77. Now,

consider that inflation is running at a rate of about 2.5 percent a year. That means that for every dollar you have, you lose two and a half cents every year in buying power. Therefore, had you just put $360 under your mattress, after three years, because of inflation, it would be worth only $347.18 ($12.82 eroded due to inflation). The money you invested also loses value due to inflation. After deductions for taxes and inflation, your invested money would be worth only $360.21. The entire earnings your savings has generated is almost lost because of two things you have no control over: inflation and taxes. In fact, you're almost where you started, earning only $4.29 after three years of saving!

Although savings accounts help offset the effects of inflation, they do not help you build wealth. Savings accounts are great to keep a "rainy day" account for those unexpected emergencies and short-term cash needs; however, if you are trying to save for a house, college tuition, or retirement, it would be very hard to meet your goals by investing in this type of low-interest account. To achieve big goals, you'll need to make your money work harder.

For more information and discussion questions about this topic, check out the BizChat feature on my***biz***lab.com.

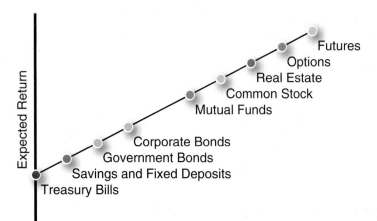

**▼ Figure 16.2
Risk-Return
Relationships**

Investment Risk

Isn't investing too risky? As the situation in the BizChat illustrates, when you invest money rather than save it in a bank, your money will have the potential to grow even more. However, investing is using money to buy an asset where there is a chance of losing part or all of your initial investment. Investing and saving are fundamentally different because of the risk involved in each process. Savings has very little, if any, risk, whereas investing has some inherent risk.

To determine whether investing is worth the risk, you must know how much risk you can tolerate. The less tolerant you are of risk, the fewer investment chances you can and should take. There are investment strategies that take on less risk than others, though keep in mind that less risky investments will present the least opportunity for return, so you might need to adjust your goals depending on your risk tolerance levels.

There is a direct relationship between risk and return for all securities, with the least risky investments offering the lowest amount of return and vice-versa. This relationship is known as a **risk-return relationship**. ▼ **Figure 16.2** shows the risk-return relationships of various investment vehicles. As you can see, the least risky investments offer the least amount of return. If reducing risk is a necessity, then you need to increase the amount of money you invest, increase the length of time to invest, or lower your expectations.

How do I know my risk tolerance? Most of us have a good idea of how tolerant we are toward risk. Your current behavior with money and other situations are indications of whether you are conservative, moderate, aggressive, or somewhere in between. There are also several tests that you can take online to help quantify your tolerance level. The bottom line to risk tolerance can be determined by answering this question: "Are my investments going to keep me awake at night with worry?" If the answer is "yes," then you need to reduce the risk level of your investments and perhaps lower your expectations accordingly. Over time, your tolerance to risk can change depending on your knowledge level and financial situation. As you become more secure financially, you might be willing to risk losing some money for the possibility of earning more. As you begin to learn more about investing, you may be more comfortable with evaluating some of the risks you will take, thus increasing your risk tolerance.

How do I start investing? Depending on how much money you have to invest, you might start investing by purchasing stock in one or two companies or by investing in a mutual fund. We'll discuss both investment options in more detail later in the chapter. As you invest, you should keep in mind two strategies that help to minimize your risk: *diversification* and *asset allocation*. Both strategies center on the notion of not putting all your eggs in one basket to avoid the possibility of losing everything because of one bad investment.

What is diversification? **Diversification** is having a variety of investments in your portfolio, such as different types of companies in different industries. For example, assume you have $6,000 to invest. You have the option of putting all your money into one company that is growing strong and has great potential for long-term advancements. You also have the option to diversify your holdings and put $1,500 into four different companies that are in four different industries.

The first option may be great if the solitary company has indefinite success, but economic factors, consumer demand, competitive advancements, and management performance can combat a company's ability to make money. If you instead invest in several companies that are in different industries, you can insulate yourself from negative influences that affect one company or one industry. You still might experience a loss, but because it's most likely not from all four investments in your portfolio, the loss will not be as significant as it would if it were your only holding. Conventional wisdom, based on these ideas, supports diversification.

What is asset allocation ? Similarly, the concept of **asset allocation** suggests you structure your portfolio with different types of assets (stocks, bonds, mutual funds, real estate, etc.) to reduce the risks associated with these broad types of investments—mostly from inflation and changes in interest rates. Studies have shown that most of an investment portfolio's performance is determined by the allocation of its assets, not by individual investment selection or market timing.[1] The allocation of assets in a portfolio depends on your risk tolerance and can change as an investor reaches certain milestones, such as getting married, paying for college tuition, or retiring. ▼ **Figure 16.3** shows how risk tolerance affects the asset allocation mix in a portfolio.

Are there rules and regulations that govern investing ? The Securities and Exchange Commission (SEC) is a U.S. federal agency created to protect investors and maintain a fair and orderly market. It governs the securities exchanges, the people who issue, trade, and deal securities and those who offer investment advice. The SEC establishes regulations that govern how companies disclose information to the investing public. In addition, the SEC governs how investment information is disclosed to investors. In doing so, the SEC controls what should be put in the initial documentation (the prospectus) of an initial bond or stock issue.

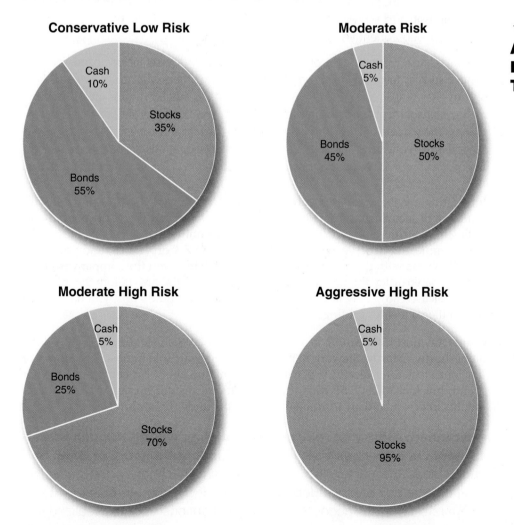

Conservative Low Risk

Cash 10%
Stocks 35%
Bonds 55%

Moderate Risk

Cash 5%
Bonds 45%
Stocks 50%

Moderate High Risk

Cash 5%
Bonds 25%
Stocks 70%

Aggressive High Risk

Cash 5%
Stocks 95%

▼ **Figure 16.3 Asset Allocation Mix Based on Risk Tolerance**

◉ Off the Mark The Madoff Ponzi Scheme

In late 2008, the securities industry was shaken by the incredible fraudulent activities of Bernard Madoff. Madoff, a former NASDAQ (National Association of Securities Dealers Automated Quotations) chairman and founder of his own investment securities company, was found guilty of running the world's biggest Ponzi scheme. A Ponzi scheme is an illegal financial arrangement in which payments are made to current investors with monies obtained by newer investors. Eventually, the scheme collapses when there are not enough new investors to cover the needs of the current and former investors. Ponzi schemes are named after Charles Ponzi, who used this type of arrangement in the early twentieth century. Madoff's Ponzi scheme is by far the largest—amounting to losses of more than $50 billion.[2] The scam was able to run for many years due to the general increase in overall market gains, which made believable the extraordinarily steady returns the fund was reporting. In addition, Madoff continued to generate interest in his fund and attract new investors by creating a general aura of exclusivity. He often intentionally deferred would-be investors who were anxious to invest after hearing the enthusiastic word-of-mouth reports of financial gains by current investors.

Reports of the investment scam began nearly 10 years prior to Madoff's arrest, when Harry Markopolos informed the SEC of his concern over Madoff's possible illegal behavior. Markopolos had determined that Madoff's remarkable results were mathematically impossible to achieve. The SEC ignored the warnings, including several further attempts in subsequent years.

The fraud impacted thousands of victims. The list is very diverse, including individual investors, such as talk show host Larry King, and many others who saw their entire life's savings disappear. In addition, many colleges, private foundations, large investment and money management firms, insurance companies, and not-for-profit organizations lost billions. The scheme also involved many foreign funds from Europe and Latin America.[3] Madoff is currently serving a 150-year prison sentence in a federal correctional facility.

In addition, the SEC prohibits fraudulent activity with regard to the offer, sale, and purchase of securities, such as insider trading. **Insider trading** is the buying and selling of securities based on information that has not been disclosed to the public. For example, suppose you own 1,000 shares of XYZ Corp. stock, and you're on friendly terms with the company's CFO. The CFO tells you the company is going to claim bankruptcy the next week, so you sell all your shares before the information is released so you won't lose your investment. If you do this, you have taken part in illegal insider trading.

One of the most high-profile insider trading cases of the past decade involved the domestic diva Martha Stewart. In 2001, Martha Stewart sold almost 4,000 shares of ImClone stock after receiving pertinent information about the company from her friend, ImClone's CEO. Stewart was convicted of insider trading and spent five months in prison and an additional five months under house arrest.

Lecretia Washington realizes that building wealth through investments is a process that takes a significant amount of time. She understands the earlier she begins investing her money, the better. So what did she do? She decided that establishing a short-term account and a separate long-term account were her best options. She also realized that she needed some professional help, so she is looking into hiring a financial advisor or a brokerage firm. What investment options would work best for you? You'll learn more about how to invest in the next section. ■

Investing in Stocks pp. 523–528

When she was a baby, Gina Smith's grandparents gave her five shares of Walt Disney Company stock. Every now and then she checks the newspapers to see how her stock is doing and over time has seen the stock price go up and down. That is all the experience Gina has had with investing. Now, having received an unexpected bonus from her first "real" job, Gina wants to do something special with it. She would like to buy more stock, but she doesn't know where to start. What kind of information should she look at to determine what is a good investment for her? ■

As you read earlier in the chapter, companies sometimes issue stock to raise funds for corporate expansion. In this section, you'll learn about the differences between various types of stocks, how stocks are bought and sold, and the factors that affect stock prices.

Types of Stocks

Are all stocks the same? There are two main types of stocks that companies issue: *common* and *preferred*. You can think of **common stock** as ordinary stock. Common stockholders have the right to elect a board of directors and vote on corporate policy. They are also entitled to a share of a company's dividends. However, common stockholders have the least priority as far as ownership and repayment in the event a company goes out of business. **Preferred stock** is a class of ownership in which the preferred stockholders have a claim to assets before common stockholders if a firm goes out of business. In addition, preferred stockholders receive a fixed dividend that must be paid before the payment of any dividends to common stockholders. Preferred shareholders, however, do not have voting privileges.

Stocks can also be categorized based on the type of company and expected growth and return of the investment:

- **Income stocks** are issued by companies that pay large dividends, such as utility companies. Investors who are looking for reliable income from their investments and not appreciation of share value invest in income stocks.

- **Blue chip stocks** are issued by companies that have a long history of consistent growth and stability. Blue chip companies pay regular dividends and maintain a reasonably steady share price. GE, IBM, and Sears are examples of companies that issue blue chip stocks.

- **Growth stocks** are issued by young, entrepreneurial companies that are experiencing rapid growth and expansion. These stocks pay little or no dividends. Investment potential is through appreciation in stock value. Growth stocks tend to be riskier than other stocks because entrepreneurial companies do not have a proven track record.

- **Cyclical stocks** are issued by companies that produce goods or services that are affected by economic trends. The prices of these stocks tend to go down when the economy is failing (in a recessionary period) and go up when the economy is healthy. Examples of cyclical stocks include automobiles, home building, and travel.
- **Defensive stocks** are the opposite of cyclical stocks. Defensive stocks are issued by companies producing staples such as food, drugs, and insurance and usually maintain their value regardless of the state of the economy.

No one type of stock is considered better than another. Investors have to decide for themselves which type of stock fits best with their financial objectives.

How do I choose which stocks to invest in ? The answer to this question begins with determining your investment goals and objectives, the time in which you have to achieve your goals and objectives, and your risk tolerance level. Once you know those constraints, you'll be better able to determine what investment strategy best fits your needs.

Many investors begin investing when they form their 401(k) retirement plan at work. This is a good way to start because the 401(k) portfolio manager has narrowed down your investment choices for you. Although there are plenty of professionals to help you, when you start investing on your own, you should research each potential investment for yourself. You can start by evaluating a company's fundamental data, such as earnings, financial statements, and key ratios (discussed in Chapter 15).

Being aware of current events in the news and changes in economic conditions that could influence a stock's price is also important. Often it's helpful to know how a company and its stock have performed in the past. You can study financial charts to compare the historical performances of multiple companies and observe trends in the data. Additionally, you might want to consider the opinions of industry analysts who independently research and analyze the investment potential of companies.

All of this information is available in newspapers, on the Internet, or in your public library. Unfortunately, it takes lots of time and research to determine what the right investments are for you. Keep in mind that if the process were easy and straightforward, we'd all be rich! In reality, there is much variability and unpredictability in the market; even with the best analysis, you still might end up with unfavorable results.

Why is it important to set goals before investing ? Assuming you can select well-run companies that you believe will generate a profit, you also need to determine what kind of company meets your investment goals and objectives. For example, depending on your age and your investment goals, you may want to invest in companies that are in their growth phase—where you'll hopefully make your money through rapid appreciation in stock value. Although such companies are more likely to have higher appreciation than more stable companies, they're also the most risky and more liable to quickly have their stock lose value, too. Someone who is 22 and just starting his or her career can "afford" to withstand temporary downfalls. Someone who is 55 may still be saving for retirement and can't endure the possibility of "starting over" if a stock does very poorly. This individual might have a mix of growth companies as well as more stable companies that have a strong history of slow but steady growth. These more stable companies generally do not experience wild swings in stock price and typically offer dividends to their stockholders.

Dividends provide another source of income to stockholders beyond appreciation in stock price. A person who is 70 years old, retired, and reliant on income from his or her investments can't afford to lose much money and is thus very risk averse. He or she would be wise to invest mostly in companies that offer high dividends and that will experience only mild swings in stock price. Regardless of these factors, the world of investing is an ongoing experience; if you choose to invest, it is an experience that you should not take lightly. You must be smart about investing and continue to do your research—even if you choose to have someone else guide you in the investment process.

How are stocks bought and sold? Before the Internet, people could buy stocks only with a **stockbroker** (or broker), a professional who buys and sells securities on behalf of investors. Brokers also provide advice as to which securities to buy and sell and receive a fee for their services. Now, because of the availability of the Internet and electronic trading, individuals have a choice of paying a broker or initiating transactions themselves for a small fee through discount brokers such as E*Trade. These discount brokers offer limited advice and guidance and are substantially cheaper than financial services firms, such as Bank of America, that offer full-service brokerage services.

Whether you use a discount broker or full-service broker, the process of buying stock is done through a **stock exchange**, an organization that facilitates the exchange of stocks and other securities between brokers and traders. Some of the largest and most dominant stock exchanges in the United States are the **New York Stock Exchange (NYSE)** and the **American Stock Exchange (AMEX)**, in which stocks are bought and sold on a trading floor or via an electronic market, and the **NASDAQ**, where stocks are only traded via an electronic market. Some securities might be too small to meet the requirements to be traded on a formal exchange. Referred to as **over-the-counter (OTC) stocks**, these securities are traded directly between professionals over computer networks or by phone. A typical trade with a broker on the NYSE is similar to the process depicted in ▼ **Figure 16.4**.

▼ **Figure 16.4 Execution of a Simple Stock Trade on the New York Stock Exchange**

1. The investor calls her broker to request a transaction.

2. I want to buy 100 shares of Acme Products Inc.

3. Broker calls floor clerk and asks for 100 shares of Acme Products Inc.

4. The floor clerk finds a floor trader who finds another floor trader who is selling Acme Products Inc. stock. The two agree on a price and complete the deal.

6. The broker calls you back with the final price. "You bought 100 shares of Acme Products Inc. for $45.50."

5. The floor trader or clerk notifies the broker that the trade has been placed.

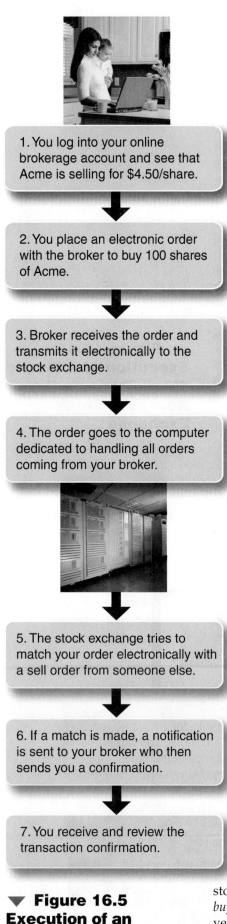

1. You log into your online brokerage account and see that Acme is selling for $4.50/share.

2. You place an electronic order with the broker to buy 100 shares of Acme.

3. Broker receives the order and transmits it electronically to the stock exchange.

4. The order goes to the computer dedicated to handling all orders coming from your broker.

5. The stock exchange tries to match your order electronically with a sell order from someone else.

6. If a match is made, a notification is sent to your broker who then sends you a confirmation.

7. You receive and review the transaction confirmation.

▼ **Figure 16.5 Execution of an Electronic Stock Trade**

Thousands of companies have issued stock and are listed on the NYSE and the NASDAQ, as well as many other smaller or international stock exchanges.[4] In fact, the NYSE handles the sales and purchases of over four billion shares every day.

Unlike the NYSE, where trades can be made electronically or on the trading floor, the NASDAQ stock exchange has always been electronic. Through the NASDAQ system, over three billion shares of stock trade hands every day via a large and immensely reliable coordinated network of computer systems.[5] As with the NYSE, you still need a broker, either online or full-service, to initiate your order. The broker will place the order electronically into the NASDAQ system, and when the order is received, the electronic exchange tries to match your buy order with a similar sell order. After the order has been executed, the broker notifies you of the successful completion of the trade. ▼ **Figure 16.5** shows the steps involved with an electronic stock trade.

How is a broker selected? The process of selecting a broker can almost be as complicated as the process of selecting a type of investment. Before you decide on a broker, the SEC suggests you do the following:[6]

- Think about your financial objectives.
- Speak with potential brokers at several firms. Ask each about their education, investment experience, and professional background.
- Inquire about the history of the brokerage firm. You can find out if any disciplinary action has been taken against a firm or a broker online through NASD BrokerCheck. Your state securities regulator can also tell you if a broker is licensed to do business in your state.
- Understand how the brokers are paid. The type of commission a broker receives might affect the advice that is offered. Also, ask what fees or charges you will be required to pay on the account.
- Ask if a brokerage firm is a member of the Securities Investor Protection Corporation (SIPC). The SIPC gives limited customer protection if a firm goes bankrupt.

Although it is ideal to start investing as early as possible, do not rush into the process. Take the time to do the necessary assessment of your own financial goals and consider the risks you're willing to take to meet those goals.[7]

Is investing in foreign companies possible? Investing is not limited to U.S. companies only; investing in foreign companies is a recommended strategy for increasing portfolio diversification and possibly obtaining higher returns. Because of increased communication abilities and the relaxation of legal barriers, investing in almost any foreign or international company is possible. There are a few ways to invest in foreign markets. Stocks of foreign countries can be traded through the London, Tokyo, or other foreign exchange markets, though it is best to use the services of a broker who specializes in foreign investments. Mutual funds and exchange traded funds, which will be discussed later in this chapter, are easier and less risky ways to add foreign investments to your portfolio.

Can I buy stocks if I don't have enough cash on hand? Sometimes investors are presented with a great investment opportunity but do not have enough cash on hand to buy the stock. In these cases, the stock can be bought with borrowed funds from a broker. This is referred to as *buying on margin*. Brokers usually use the value of other assets owned by the investor as collateral for the investment. Buying on margin is very risky and is subject to fairly rigid SEC regulations.

Changing Stock Prices

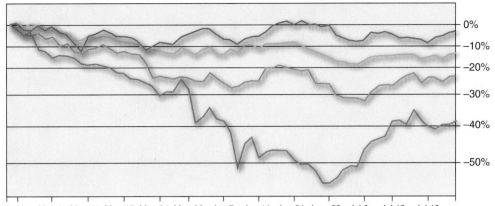

Jul 19, 2010: ■ BP 35.75 ■ XOM 58.43 ▲ AAPL 245.58 ■ DELL 13.44

2010 May 3 May 10 May 17 May 24 May 28 Jun 7 Jun 14 Jun 21 June 28 Jul 6 Jul 12 Jul 19

What causes stock prices to change? Stock prices can change rapidly. ▼ **Figure 16.6** reflects the percent change in closing prices for BP, Exxon-Mobil, Apple, and Dell over a three-month period. What is consistent among all four companies? Their stock prices change daily. There are many reasons why stock prices change, but ultimately it all comes down to the forces of supply and demand. If investors like a stock, they will buy more of it, reducing the supply and pushing up the price. On the other hand, if investors don't like a stock, more investors will sell the stock than buy it, creating a greater supply and causing the price to drop.

▼ **Figure 16.6 Percent Change in Stock Price for BP, ExxonMobil, Dell, and Apple from April to July 2010**

What is harder to determine are the influences that affect investors' attitudes toward individual stocks, causing them to favor a stock one day and oppose it another day. The reality is that despite many different theories and prediction strategies, no one theory explains it completely. In general, however, most investors will investigate if a stock's price reflects what they think a company is worth. (Stock price times total number of shares outstanding determines a company's capitalization or value.) Often, investors not only look at how a company is currently performing but also consider a company's expected future growth in anticipation of increased earnings or profits.

For example, if investors become concerned that something negative will affect a company's value, they will sell their shares and the stock price will fall. When the BP oil rig exploded in the Gulf of Mexico on April 20, 2010, the price of BP stock began to drop. ▼ **Figure 16.7** shows the overall decline in price value from late April to late June 2010 as BP struggled to contain the oil spill. Notice how the stock price and the volume of shares traded reacted to several key events, such as pressures from the U.S. government and credit rating agencies. Yet, as BP's efforts to contain the spill began to show signs of improvement, investors began to have a more favorable opinion of the company, and the stock price began to increase.

▼ **Figure 16.7 Change in Price and Volume of BP Stock from April 23, 2010, to July 23, 2010**

How do you know how well a stock is doing relative to other stocks?

Stock prices also change in reaction to broader news based on economic forecasts, industry or sector concerns, or global events. In general, financial markets have trends based on investor confidence. A **bull market** indicates increasing investor confidence as the market continues to increase in value. In a bull market, investors are

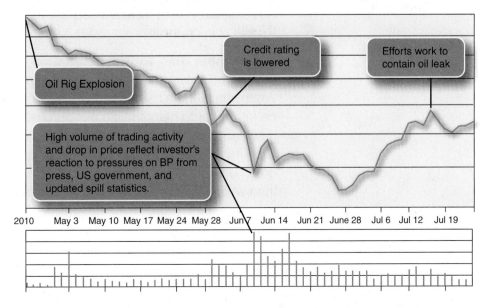

Oil Rig Explosion

Credit rating is lowered

Efforts work to contain oil leak

High volume of trading activity and drop in price reflect investor's reaction to pressures on BP from press, US government, and updated spill statistics.

2010 May 3 May 10 May 17 May 24 May 28 Jun 7 Jun 14 Jun 21 June 28 Jul 6 Jul 12 Jul 19

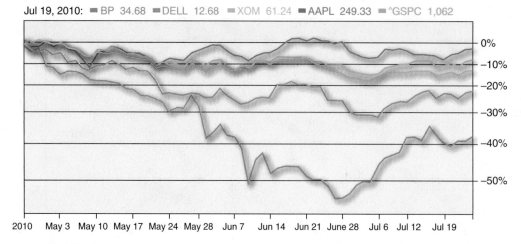

Jul 19, 2010: ▪ BP 34.68 ▪ DELL 12.68 ▪ XOM 61.24 ▪ AAPL 249.33 ▪ ^GSPC 1,062

▼ **Figure 16.8**
Price Movement
Compared to S&P 500
Average

motivated by promises of gains. A **bear market**, however, indicates decreasing investor confidence as the market continues to decline in value.

In addition, industry news can affect the performance of stocks in that industry. Notice in ▼ **Figure 16.8** that Apple, Dell, and ExxonMobil tend to move similarly to the S&P 500, unlike BP because of the Gulf Coast oil spill.

How do you know how the overall market is doing? The *Standard and Poor's 500 Composite Index* (*S&P 500*), the *DJIA*, and the *NASDAQ 100* are several benchmarks that indicate the overall health of the U.S. stock market. An **index** represents a collection of related stocks based on certain shared characteristics, such as having a similar size, belonging to a common industry, or trading on the same market exchange.

- The *S&P 500* is an index of stocks of the 500 largest companies, most of which are American.
- The *DJIA* is an index of the 30 largest capitalized public companies in the United States. Whereas the DJIA composite index initially included only those companies that had some connection to heavy industry, today that characteristic is not as prevalent. The *S&P 500* and the *DJIA* are the two most widely watched stock indexes. They are important as they often reflect, and sometimes influence, the state of the U.S. economy.
- The *NASDAQ 100* includes 100 of the largest domestic and international non-financial companies listed on NASDAQ. The *NASDAQ 100* is distinguished from the *DJIA* and the *S&P 500* by not including financial institutions in the group and including companies incorporated outside the United States.

How do I make money investing in stocks? There are several ways to earn money investing in stocks. As noted above, one of these ways is by collecting dividends. Another way to make money in the stock market is to "buy low and sell high." In other words, you buy a stock at one price, wait for that stock to appreciate, and then sell the stock at the higher price. When this happens, the investor incurs a **capital gain**. If there is a decrease in value between the purchase price and the selling price, the investor incurs a **capital loss**.

Remember Gina Smith? When Gina was researching stocks, she reviewed various financial documents, such as income statements. When she found a few stocks she was interested in buying, she used a discount broker to help finalize her purchase. By keeping abreast of industry news and monitoring stock indexes, she's able to see how well her stock is doing relative to other stocks. Recently, the price of her stock has been going up, and she's hoping that when she sells it will be at a price higher than which she originally bought the stock. ▪

Investing in Bonds pp. 529–531

Dennis Sanchez just turned 55 years old and is starting to think about retirement. He has been investing money in his company's 401(k) plan for many years and wants to do some investing on his own. Now that he is closer to retirement, he would like to receive some income from his investments. He would also like to take a less risky approach to investing his funds by diversifying his portfolio allocation. Dennis decides investing in bonds is the best way to meet both of these goals. How does Dennis know what bonds will meet his financial objectives? ■

We have previously discussed that bonds are like IOUs. As a bond investor, you're lending money to a company for a specific period at a specified interest rate. The main reasons you purchase bonds are to add a stream of fixed income or to diversify your portfolio. Bond performance usually reacts counter to that of stocks. When the stock market is performing well, bonds are generally not performing well; conversely, when the stock market is down, bonds are usually up. Because of this contrary relationship, bonds provide great diversification to a stock portfolio. In this section, we'll talk about the different types of bonds and their characteristics, and we'll discuss the risk involved in investing in bonds.

Different Types of Bonds

Are there different types of bonds? Governments and corporations issue various types of bonds, including corporate bonds, government bonds, and municipal bonds.

What are corporate bonds? **Corporate bonds** are debt securities issued by corporations. There are several types of corporate bonds.

- **Secured bonds** are backed by collateral, which is generally corporate-owned property that will pass to the bondholders (or be sold to reimburse bondholders) if the issuer does not repay the amount borrowed. *Mortgage-backed securities* are special secured bonds that are backed by real property owned by a corporation.

- **Debenture bonds** are unsecured bonds, backed only by a corporation's promise to pay.

- Another modification of a traditional bond is a **convertible bond**, which gives a bondholder the right (but not the obligation) to convert the bond into a predetermined number of shares of the company's stock. Convertible bonds generally carry a lower interest rate because the investor will benefit from investing in the underlying stock.

What are government bonds? **Government bonds** are debt securities issued by national governments. They are the safest investment because the government backs them and the risk of default is very low. Government bonds are divided into several categories based on their maturity.

- **Treasury bills (or T-bills)** are bonds that mature between 2 weeks and 26 weeks. Instead of paying interest, Treasury bills are sold at a discount, so you are paying less up front. When the bond matures, you receive the full face value of the bond. The difference between the purchase amount and the face value is the interest. For example, to buy a $1,000 T-bill, you might pay $975 up front. When the T-bill matures 26 weeks later, you would receive $1,000. The $25 difference is interest earned.

- **Treasury notes** (or **T-notes**) are bonds that mature in 2, 5, or 10 years. Interest is paid semiannually. You can hold Treasury notes to maturity or you can sell them prior to their maturity. When a Treasury note matures, you receive the face value.

- **Treasury bonds** are bonds that mature in 30 years and pay interest semiannually. When a Treasury bond matures, you receive the face value.

What are municipal bonds? Municipal bonds (or *munis*) are bonds issued by state or local governments or governmental agencies. There are two varieties of municipal bonds: *general obligation bonds* and *revenue bonds*.

- **General obligation bonds** are supported by the taxing power of the issuer, so they tend to be very safe.

- **Revenue bonds** are supported by the income generated by the project they finance.

For example, the New Jersey Turnpike Authority may issue $1 billion in bonds to finance the construction and renovation of the I-95 corridor that runs through the state. The tolls collected on that portion of I-95 would be used to pay the interest and principal of the bonds. The advantage of buying municipal bonds and government bonds is that income generated from many of them are exempt from federal income tax and, in many cases, state and local income taxes.

What are serial bonds? Municipal bonds, as well as some corporate bonds, are often issued as serial bonds. **Serial bonds** have a series of dates on which portions of the total bond mature, unlike traditional bonds that are paid back to the investor all at once on one date (the *maturity date*). Serial bonds are advantageous to the issuer because they reduce the overall interest expense of the bond issue. Additionally, serial bonds allow the issuer to time the maturity dates to the income from the project financed by the bond proceeds. Thus, for the toll road example above, serial bonds may mature as phases of the toll road are completed.

What are callable bonds? Most corporate and municipal bonds remain outstanding until their maturity date. With **callable bonds**, however, the issuer can either repay investors their initial investment at the maturity date or the issuer can choose to retire the issue early and repay investors at the "callable date." Issuers invoke the call option on callable bonds when interest rates have fallen and the bonds can be refinanced at a lower rate. To the investor, callable bonds present a degree of uncertainty and therefore carry a higher interest rate than similar non-callable bonds.

How can I tell how safe a bond is before investing? Although most bonds are viewed as a conservative investment, they are not entirely risk free. There are different types of risk that affect bonds. *Credit risk* is the risk associated with a bond issuer's ability to meet its financial obligations. As mentioned above, corporate bonds are more risky than government or municipal bonds. Before a bond is issued, it is evaluated by a rating agency, such as Moody's or Standard & Poor's, the two major rating agencies, and later assigned an investment grade. The higher the rating, the less the likelihood of default.

▼ **Table 16.2** shows the bond rating scales used by both Moody's and Standard & Poor's. To improve their investment grade, many bonds are backed by insurance policies that guarantee repayment to the bondholders in the event the issuer goes into default. Those bonds with the lowest ratings—and the most risk—are known

▼ **Table 16.2**

Bond Rating Scales Used by Moody's and Standard & Poor's		
	Bond Rating	
Risk	**Moody's**	**Standard & Poor's**
Lowest risk	Aaa	AAA
Low risk	Aa and A	AA and A
Medium risk	Baa	BBB
High risk	Ba and B	BB and B
Highest risk	Caa/Ca/C	CCC/CC/C
In default	C	D

as **junk bonds**. Because of their high risk, junk bonds offer a high interest rate to attract investors. Investors should be very comfortable with the associated risks before adding junk bonds to their portfolios.

What are the characteristics of a bond? Several characteristics define a bond: par (face) value, coupon (interest rate), maturity, and issuer.

- **Par (face) value** is the amount of money the bondholder will get back once a bond reaches maturity. Most newly issued bonds sell at par value. As noted earlier, Treasury bills sell for less than par (face) value.

- The **coupon** is the bond's interest rate. Initially, bonds had coupons that the investor would tear off and redeem to receive interest. Coupons are a percentage of par, so a coupon of 10 percent on a bond with $1,000 par value would generate $100 in interest a year. Although most bonds pay interest twice a year, some bonds offer monthly, quarterly, or annual payments. Today, interest payments are transferred electronically.

- The **maturity date** of a bond is the date on which the bond matures and the investor's principal is repaid. Short-term bonds (generally with a maturity of less than five years) have less variability and therefore a lower interest rate than long-term bonds.

Do I have to hold a bond to maturity? Although you certainly can hold a bond to maturity, many investors sell bonds, especially long-term bonds, prior to maturity. Just like stocks, after they are issued, bonds are bought and sold on the secondary market. What makes buying bonds on the secondary market very complicated is that bonds do not trade at par value but at a price higher than par (at a premium) or lower than par (at a discount). Bond prices move in the opposite direction of interest rates. So, if you are trying to sell a bond that has a coupon of 10 percent and current market interest rates are 8 percent, your bond is worth more to investors, so the price of the bond will go up. Conversely, if current interest rates are 12 percent, demand for your bond is not strong, forcing the price an investor is willing to pay to go down.

When it comes to investing in bonds, there are several things to keep in mind, such as the type of bond, the bond's risk rating, the face value of the bond, and the interest rate. Investors can determine a bond's risk based on an issuer's credit rating. One thing Dennis Sanchez could do before he purchases a bond is to review the issuer's credit rating. After doing the necessary research, Dennis would then be able to establish a diversified, less risky portfolio and receive some income. ■

Investing in **Mutual Funds** and **Other Opportunities** pp. 532–535

lex and Keri Young recently got married and want to start saving and investing for a family, traveling, and emergencies. Unfortunately, after their wedding and honeymoon expenses and buying a condo, they have only $3,000 left. Although Alex and Keri know they should have several different investments, they feel they don't have enough money to do so, and they each have their opinions as to what kind of investments to make. Alex is especially interested in investing in foreign securities but doesn't know if they make sense for them nor specifically which ones to pick. Fortunately, both Keri and Alex agree that until they know more about investing, they should use a broker or an investment advisor rather than trying to do it independently. Where should they invest their money? ■

Many investors don't have a large amount of money to invest. One of the possible options for these investors is a *mutual fund*. Simply put, a **mutual fund** is a means by which a group of investors pool money together to invest in a diversified set of investments. In this section, you'll read about different types of mutual funds, the pros and cons of investing in them, and other investment opportunities.

Mutual Funds

What is a mutual fund? Let's say you wanted to invest in the stock market but, like Alex and Keri Young, you had only $3,000 to invest. After looking at possible investments, you realize that with $3,000, you could buy stock in one or two companies only. In talking to several of your friends who are also trying to invest small amounts of money, you realize that they are experiencing the same problem. Then, as a group, you decide to pool your money and hire an expert to buy a portfolio of stocks. With this arrangement, each of you shares a proportional amount of the investment returns. If you were to do that, you would have created a mutual fund.

What are bond mutual funds? Many firms offer a number of mutual fund options. **Bond mutual funds** consist solely of bonds. Some bond funds are categorized by the type of bond, including municipal bond funds, corporate bond funds, and U.S. government bond funds. Alternatively, some bond funds are categorized by maturity, including long-term bond funds, short-term bond funds, and intermediate-term bond funds. ▼ **Table 16.3** summarizes the various types of bond mutual funds.

What are money market funds? **Money market funds** are funds that invest in short-term debt obligations, such as Treasury bills and CDs, and are quite safe. Money market funds are popular because the interest rate is often nearly double that of "regular" interest-bearing checking or savings accounts. In addition, money market funds are very liquid so you have quick access to your money, often by simply writing a check. Perhaps the only drawback of a money market fund is that the FDIC does not insure the funds. However, unlike many banks, to date,

▼ Table 16.3

	Fund Type	Investment Strategy
Bond Mutual Funds		
By Type	Municipal bond funds	Invest in tax-exempt bonds issued by state and local governments. Some municipal bond funds are further specialized in bonds issued by a particular state.
	Corporate bond funds	Invest in debt obligations from U.S. corporations.
	U.S. government bond funds	Invest in U.S. Treasury or government securities.
By Term	Short-term bond funds	Invest in bonds with maturities less than 2 years, including Treasury bills, CDs, and commercial paper.
	Intermediate-term bond funds	Invest in bonds with maturities ranging between 2 and 10 years.
	Long-term bond funds	Invest in bonds with maturities greater than 10 years.

no money market fund has ever failed. Alternatively, you can invest in a *money market savings account* through a savings bank, and, as with all bank accounts, the money in that account is insured by the FDIC.

Are there different types of stock mutual funds? Stock mutual funds, sometimes referred to as **equity funds**, are much more popular than bond or money market funds.[8] Similar to bond funds, stock mutual funds are broken down into various categories. Some stock funds invest in stocks with a particular strategy in mind, such as growth funds, value funds, and blend funds. Another popular breakdown of stock funds are those that invest in companies defined by their capitalization (cap) or size, such as large-cap funds, mid-cap funds, and small-cap funds. Additionally, there is a wide assortment of funds that center on international investments, such as global funds, foreign funds, country-specific funds, or emerging market funds. Lastly, there are sector funds that invest in companies from a particular industry sector, such as technology, automotive, banking, and health care. ▼ **Table 16.4** summarizes the various types of stock mutual funds.

Why are mutual funds so popular? Mutual funds are the best kind of investment for those who have little to no experience in investing or who might not have a lot of money to invest. There are many reasons why you should consider investing in mutual funds:

- **Diversification.** The notable advantage to investing in mutual funds is diversification. Mutual funds offer small investors a cost-effective means of purchasing a diversified portfolio. Unless you have a lot of money to invest, it's hard to buy a large variety of securities. Remember, having a portfolio of various types of securities helps to reduce risk without significantly affecting returns.

- **Professional management.** Professional management is another advantage of mutual funds. Someone who has a significant amount of investment experience manages each mutual fund. Additionally, these professionals spend all their time researching, trading, and watching the investments that make up the fund. This is likely more time than you would be able to spend if you created a similar portfolio on your own. The fund managers have great incentive to make sure their funds perform at its best.

- **Liquidity.** It is very easy to buy and sell mutual funds, so you can get to your money quickly—usually within a day. Some mutual funds, primarily money market funds, offer check-writing privileges, so accessing your money is even easier.

- **Cost.** It takes as little as $1,000 to invest in most mutual funds. Some funds charge fees with their purchase or sale, though there are quite a few good "no-load" mutual funds that are virtually free of fees and charges.

▼ Table 16.4

Stock Mutual Funds		
	Fund Type	**Investment Strategy**
Strategy Types	Growth funds	Invest in stocks of the fastest-growing companies. Often viewed as risky investments. Rarely produce dividend income.
	Value funds	Invest in stocks that are considered to be undervalued. These stocks are thought to be ready for quick appreciation. Some produce dividends.
	Blend (or balanced) funds	Invest in both growth and value companies.
By Size	Large-cap funds	Invest in companies with large (greater than $9 billion) capitalization (price times outstanding shares).
	Medium-cap funds	Invest in companies of medium capitalization—between $1 billion and $9 billion.
	Small-cap funds	Invest in companies with capitalization less than $1 billion. These companies rarely generate dividends.
International	Global funds	Invest in both U.S. and international stocks.
	Foreign funds	Invest in companies primarily outside the United States.
	Country- or region-specific funds	Invest in companies from one country or region of the world.
	Emerging market funds	Invest in companies from small developing countries. These funds are considered fairly risky.
Sector		Invest in companies from one particular industrial sector, such as technology, pharmaceutical, or automotive.
Index		Funds that try to mimic a particular index, such as the S&P 500 or the NASDAQ 100.

How do I make money investing in mutual funds? You can make money investing in mutual funds through dividends, interest, capital gains, and fund appreciation. These investment earnings are similar to those generated by individual stock holdings, although they are controlled by the fund manager and distributed to the fund owners periodically. As fund managers adjust the holdings of the fund, they sell some securities and buy others. Capital gains and losses that are incurred through selling securities are passed on to the fund owners. Your mutual fund accumulates any dividends paid by the stocks and interest paid by the bonds held by the mutual fund and periodically distributes the earnings to fund owners. Lastly, mutual funds are measured by the value of the individual holdings. This measure is the **net asset value (NAV)**. The NAV increases as the securities held by the fund increase in value. If you sell your mutual fund holding at a higher NAV than when you bought it, you will generate a profit.

What do I need to watch out for when investing in mutual funds? Although mutual funds are often deemed the "perfect" investment, like any investment, you still need to do your homework before investing. Some mutual funds, referred to as **load funds**, have additional costs (loads) that are rolled into the overall package to cover marketing and other fund expenses. The ultimate decision in buying a mutual fund should be based on its expected performance and the suitability to your investments needs. If you are given a choice of similar options, try to pick a **no-load fund**, a mutual fund that has little or no additional costs. In addition, it's also important to have a good understanding about who is managing the fund. The same individual or group of managers often runs a fund for years. However, changes happen, so you want to watch out for that. A change in management could quickly make historical fund performance statistics (what you might be using to evaluate a fund's performance before you buy) less significant.

Other Investment Opportunities

Besides stocks, bonds, and mutual funds, what else can I invest in? An **option** is a contract that gives a buyer the right (but not obligation) to buy (call) or sell (put) a particular security at a specific price on or before a certain date. Consider this example: Your uncle is selling a car that you would love to buy but can't quite afford yet. You decide to approach your uncle with a proposal. You would save your money, and at the end of three months, you would have the right to buy the car for $15,000. For accepting this offer, you will give your uncle $1,000 now. Over the course of the next three months, two situations could occur:

1. The car could be ranked one of the best cars, increasing its value from $15,000 to $20,000. You buy the car for the agreed on price of $15,000 and then sell the car for $20,000. Taking into consideration the price of the option, you net $4,000.

2. Your uncle gets into an accident and totals the car. Because you have only an option to buy the car, you're not obligated to purchase the ruined vehicle, but you still lose the $1,000 for the option.

Options work similarly in that you aren't buying the underlying asset (in our example, the underlying asset is a car; in reality, it would be a stock). Instead you're paying for the opportunity to buy the asset under certain conditions. If things go wrong, you lose the cost of the option. If things go right, you could profit. Options are complicated and can be risky. Don't confuse option contracts with stock options your employer may offer as a benefit. The stock option that employers offer gives you the right to buy a specific number of shares of your company's stock at a specific time at a set price. Stock options are used as incentives to retain and motivate employees and were discussed in Chapter 9.

What are futures? A **futures contract** is an agreement between a buyer and a seller to receive (or deliver) an asset sometime in the future at a specific price agreed on today. Usually the underlying asset is a commodity, such as sugar, coffee, or wheat. For these commodities, a price is agreed on before harvest, when the actual goods are bought and sold. Futures markets also include the buying and selling of government bonds, foreign currencies, or stock market indexes. Most holders of futures contracts rarely hold their contracts to expiration. If you hold the futures contract until it expires, you own the commodity. Instead, the contract is traded prior to expiration. If the price of the commodity increases before the contract's expiration date you make a profit. However, if the price decreases, you may lose money. The difference between a futures contract and an options contract is that an option gives you the *right* to purchase the underlying asset; with a futures contract, you have an *obligation* to purchase the underlying asset.

What are exchange-traded funds? **Exchange-traded funds (ETFs)** are a pool of stocks like a mutual fund, but they trade like stocks on the exchange. Prices of ETFs change throughout the day as they are bought and sold, whereas mutual funds are traded only at the end of the trading day. ETFs incur a fee from a broker; however, the fee is typically lower than mutual fund fees. This makes ETFs a low-cost way to diversify a portfolio.

Alex and Keri Young were glad to learn about mutual funds. Mutual funds allow them to use the limited savings they have and get the diversity they are looking for. There are still things about mutual funds that the couple is unsure about, such as which types of funds will work best for them, so they will continue to take their time, and perhaps consult an investment advisor, before making any final decision. ∎

Chapter Summary

Are you an active learner?

Go to my*biz*lab.com to master Chapter 16's content. Chapter 16's interactive activities include:
- Customizable Study Plan and Chapter 16 practice quizzes
- Chapter 16 Simulation, Financial Management, that helps you think critically and prepare to make choices in the business world
- Chapter 16 Video Exercise, Securities and Investments, which shows you how textbook concepts are put into practice every day
- Flash Cards for mastering the definition of chapter terms
- Interactive Lessons that visually review key chapter concepts

1. What are the pros and cons of debt and equity financing? (pp. 513–516)

- An advantage of financing with **bonds** (p. 513) is that it allows a company to finance a project without using other business assets or corporate profits. One disadvantage of debt financing is that if the interest rate of the bond is too high, it can force the cost of the project into something that is not affordable or that just doesn't make economic sense.
- Financing with **equity** (p. 515) allows a company to retain profits and cash in the company rather than using it to pay back debt and make interest payments. The biggest disadvantage that equity financing brings is a dilution of ownership.

2. How do companies issue bonds and stocks? (pp. 516–517)

- The steps for issuing bonds are as follows:
  - The company's financial manager contacts a financial advisor for advice.
  - Financial advisors prepare documents with the **Securities and Exchange Commission** (**SEC**; p. 517). They also help to set the price of the bond issue and take the lead in forming the group of banks that initially buy the bonds.
  - Financial advisors and bankers generate interest and locate potential buyers for the bonds before issuance.
  - A **financial advisory firm** (p. 516) initially purchases all the bonds at a discount and then quickly sells them in the **primary market** (p. 517) at a higher price.
- **Stocks** (p. 515) are issued in the same manner as bonds, with a few slight differences:
  - The first issue of stock is an **initial public offering** (**IPO**; p. 517).
  - A financial advisor coordinates the preparation of a **prospectus** (p. 517) and files it with the SEC.
  - Financial advisors also establish the best timing for the public sale and determine the initial selling price.
  - Banks form a syndicate to underwrite the IPO. The syndicate then purchases the stock and sells it back to the public.

3. How do risk-return relationships, risk tolerance, and asset allocations relate to the fundamentals of investment? (pp. 518–522)

- Various types of investments have different **risk-return relationships** (p. 520). On one hand, the least risky investments offer the least amount of return. On the other hand, the most risky investments offer the greatest return.
- Investing is not for everyone, and the level and type of investments is very personal and depends on the investor's risk tolerance level.
- Investment portfolios should be allocated or spread out among different types of investments, such as stocks, bonds, and cash, to further reduce investment risk. **Asset allocation** (p. 521) changes as investors reach life milestones; portfolios should be adjusted and rebalanced periodically.

4. What are the different investment categories of stocks, and how does the stock trade process work? (pp. 523–526)

- There are two main types of stocks that companies issue: **common** and **preferred** (p. 523). Stocks can be categorized into five categories: **income stocks**, **blue chip stocks**, **growth stocks**, **cyclical stocks**, and **defensive stocks** (pp. 523–524).
- Stocks are purchased through a **stockbroker** (p. 525) who buys and sells stocks on behalf of investors. Brokers also provide advice and receive a fee for their services.
- Stock transactions occur through a **stock exchange** (p. 525) like the **New York Stock Exchange** (**NYSE**) or **NASDAQ** (p. 525).

5. What is stock performance, and what are the factors that lead to changes in stock price? (pp. 527–528)

- Stock performance is directly related to changes in stock price.
- Stock prices change in reaction to supply and demand. Other factors that can affect stock prices include economic forecasts, industry or sector concerns, or global events. Stocks also tend to move together as a market. If the market is trending positively, it is a **bull market** (p. 527). A declining market is a **bear market** (p. 528).

6. **What are the different types and characteristics of bonds, and how is the safety of bonds evaluated?** (pp. 529–531)

- There are two issuers of bonds: governments and corporations.
  - **Corporate bonds** (p. 529) are issued by corporations and hold the greatest amount of risk. **Secured bonds** (p. 529) are backed by collateral, and **debenture bonds** (p. 529) are unsecured and backed only by a promise to pay.
  - **Government bonds** (p. 529) are issued by national governments and are the safest investment.
  - **Municipal bonds** (p. 530) are issued by state and local municipalities.
- Bonds are characterized by their **par (face) value** (p. 531), which is the money the bondholder will get back once a bond reaches maturity. Most bonds sell at par value. Bonds are also characterized by the **coupon** (p. 531), or interest rate, and **maturity date** (p. 531).
- Bonds are not risk free. The creditworthiness of the issuer is the main factor affecting a bond's risk.

7. **What is the difference among bond mutual funds, money market funds, and equity funds?** (pp. 532–535)

- **Bond mutual funds** (p. 532) consist solely of bonds. They can be categorized by the type of bond (municipal bond funds, corporate bond funds, or U.S. government bond funds). Alternatively, some bond funds are categorized by maturity (long-term, short-term, or intermediate-term bond funds).

- **Money market funds** (p. 532) invest in short-term debt obligations. The interest rate for these funds is often nearly double that of "regular" interest-bearing checking or savings accounts. In addition, money market accounts provide check-writing privileges so you have quick access to the money.
- **Equity funds** (p. 533) are categorized by investment strategy, such as growth funds, value funds, and blend (or balanced) funds. These funds are also categorized by size of the companies in which they invest, such as large-cap funds, medium-cap funds, and small-cap funds.

8. **What are the advantages and disadvantages of mutual fund investment?** (pp. 532–535)

- **Mutual funds** (p. 532) are popular investments because they provide diversification and professional management. Mutual funds are extremely liquid and fairly cost efficient.
- **Load funds** (p. 534) have additional costs to cover marketing and other fund expenses, whereas **no-load funds** (p. 534) have little or no additional costs.

9. **What are other investment opportunites besides stocks, bonds, and mutual funds?** (p. 535)

- An **option** (p. 535) is a contract that gives a buyer the right (but not obligation) to buy or sell a security at a specific price on or before a certain date. Options are complicated and therefore quite risky.
- **Futures contracts** (p. 535) are agreements between a buyer and a seller to receive (or deliver) an asset sometime in the future but at a specific price that is agreed on today.

Key Terms

American Stock Exchange (AMEX)   (p. 525)

asset allocation   (p. 521)

bear market   (p. 528)

blue chip stocks   (p. 523)

bond   (p. 513)

bond mutual funds   (p. 532)

bull market   (p. 527)

callable bond   (p. 530)

capital gain   (p. 528)

capital loss   (p. 528)

capital market   (p. 517)

common stock   (p. 523)

convertible bonds   (p. 529)

corporate bonds   (p. 529)

coupon   (p. 531)

cyclical stocks   (p. 524)

debenture bonds   (p. 529)

defensive stocks   (p. 524)

diversification   (p. 520)

dividends   (p. 515)

equity   (p. 515)

exchange-traded funds (ETFs)   (p. 535)

financial advisory firm   (p. 516)

futures contract   (p. 535)

general obligation bonds   (p. 530)

government bonds   (p. 529)

growth stocks   (p. 523)

income stocks   (p. 523)

Continued on next page

Key Terms (cont.)

index   (p. 528)

initial public offering (IPO)   (p. 517)

insider trading   (p. 522)

junk bonds   (p. 531)

load funds   (p. 534)

maturity date   (p. 531)

money market funds   (p. 532)

municipal bonds   (p. 530)

mutual fund   (p. 532)

NASDAQ   (p. 525)

net asset value (NAV)   (p. 534)

New York Stock Exchange (NYSE)   (p. 525)

no-load fund   (p. 534)

option   (p. 535)

over-the-counter stock (OTC)   (p. 525)

par (face) value   (p. 531)

preferred stock   (p. 523)

primary market   (p. 517)

prospectus   (p. 517)

revenue bonds   (p. 530)

risk-return relationships   (p. 520)

secondary market   (p. 517)

secured bonds   (p. 529)

securities   (p. 513)

Securities and Exchange Commission (SEC)   (p. 517)

serial bond   (p. 530)

sinking fund   (p. 514)

stock   (p. 515)

stock certificate   (p. 515)

stockbroker   (p. 525)

stock exchange   (p. 525)

stock mutual funds (equity funds)   (p. 533)

Treasury bills (T-bills)   (p. 529)

Treasury bonds   (p. 530)

Treasury notes (T-notes)   (p. 530)

Self-Test

Multiple Choice   You can find the answers on the last page of this book.

1. Crunchy Chips Inc. needs to invest in new production equipment to make its potato chip processing more efficient. The managers are considering financing the equipment with bonds. Which of the following is a reason why the company would consider bonds over stocks?

   a. There is no dilution of ownership.

   b. Bond holders do not require interest payments.

   c. Financing with bonds allows the company to retain profits and cash in the company rather than using it to pay back debt.

   d. All of the above

2. Jackson White is looking to raise extra capital to help expand the business operations of his company. Which is *not* a reason to raise the extra capital with stock rather than with bonds?

   a. Company profits can be retained by the company.

   b. Payments to stockholders are not required.

   c. Equity does not impact control of the company.

   d. Funds from stock do not need to be paid back.

3. What document must companies prepare and make available to investors when issuing stocks?

   a. A prospectus

   b. An initial public offering

   c. Proprietary underwriting

   d. Investor guideline sheets

4. Tracy Quinn feels she has a great investment portfolio. Because of growth in the technology sector, she has invested in Apple, Dell, Microsoft, and Google. Her investment advisor has told her she must diversify. Which strategy should she pursue?

   a. Invest in more technology companies.

   b. Invest in companies in other sectors.

   c. Purchase mutual funds that invest in technology companies.

   d. All of the above.

5. Jose Fernandez is saving toward retirement and has an investment portfolio that is reflective of Jose's risk tolerance. It was carefully put together by a trusted investment advisor. Unfortunately, the returns on the portfolio are not projected to generate the type of savings Jose desires. What should Jose do?

   a. Invest in riskier stocks that have a higher return.

   b. Lower his retirement expectations.

   c. Increase his risk tolerance.

   d. Change employers.

6. To determine how well your investments are doing relative to the rest of the market, you might compare your stock's performance to which of the following?

   a. The S&P 500 Index

   b. The NYSE

   c. The NASDAQ 100

   d. All of the above

7. Which of the following describes a security issued by a local government agency?

   a. Acme Inc. debenture bond

   b. Souderton County bond

   c. Treasury bond

   d. Fidelity bond fund

8. If you owned a $10,000 bond that had a coupon of 4.5 percent and paid interest semiannually, how much interest would you receive?

   a. $450 every six months

   b. $225 every six months

   c. $4,500 once a year

   d. $2,250 once a year

9. Which is *not* an advantage of investing in mutual funds?

   a. Mutual funds are less risky than investing in stocks or bonds.

   b. Mutual funds provide immediate diversification.

   c. Mutual fund investments are managed by a professional.

   d. Mutual funds are less expensive than buying stocks/bonds individually.

10. Which describes a pool of stocks traded on the stock exchange throughout the day?

    a. A mutual fund

    b. An ETF

    c. Futures contracts

    d. A stock option

Self-Test

1. Companies finance with either stocks or bonds but rarely both.

   ☐ **True** or ☐ **False**

2. Five years ago, Jerome bought 100 shares of Kodak at $40 per share. Last month, he sold the 100 shares at $55 per share. Jerome has a capital loss from the sale.

   ☐ **True** or ☐ **False**

3. Short-term government bonds are considered low-risk investments.

   ☐ **True** or ☐ **False**

4. Common stockholders get paid before preferred stockholders if a firm goes out of business.

   ☐ **True** or ☐ **False**

5. Because mutual funds are professionally managed, you do not need to worry about which mutual fund you invest in.

   ☐ **True** or ☐ **False**

Critical Thinking Questions

1. Before investing, you should determine your risk level. How would you define risk tolerance? What, if anything, might change your risk tolerance?

2. Discuss your life goals and how much time you have to accomplish the goals. What kind of saving and investment strategy might you need to pursue to ensure that you meet your goals?

3. The term *blue chip* applies to stocks issued by a company in excellent financial standing with a record of producing earnings and paying dividends. Stocks in companies such as GE and Chrysler were initially considered blue chip stocks. Today, stocks in companies that were not in existence when the term was coined, such as Intel and Walmart, are considered blue chip stocks. What other companies might you consider blue chip stocks and why?

4. Assume you have $25,000 to invest. Put together a portfolio of five stocks that is well diversified across several industries. What investments did you choose and why?

5. Mutual funds often compare their performance to that of the S&P 500 with the goal of "beating" it. Is this a fair comparison?

Team Time

Take This $50,000 and Invest It!

Assemble in teams of four or five students. Suppose your team is given a theoretical $50,000 that you need to invest. Your team must assemble a portfolio by selecting a minimum of 5 investments but no more than 10 investments. The portfolios should be well diversified and include different types of assets or stocks from different industries or sectors.

Process

Step 1. Your team should fill out the following charts as you conduct your research:

Name of Investment	Type of Investment	Industry/Sector

Name of Investment	Purchase Price	# Shares	Initial Value	% of Total Portfolio

Step 2. Your team should prepare a presentation outlining your investment choices. The presentation should include reasons why you included each investment choice in the portfolio. In addition, the presentation should discuss the diversification strategies you took.

Step 3. **Optional ongoing exercise.** Teams should monitor their portfolios on a weekly basis. At the end of the specified period of time, teams should determine which team portfolio has the highest value.

Ethics and Corporate Social Responsibility

Can Investments Be Socially Responsible *and* Lucrative?

Socially responsible investing describes an investment strategy that invests in companies that offer the potential for maximized gains and businesses that favor practices that are environmentally responsible, support workplace diversity, and increase product safety and quality. Some socially responsible investments also avoid businesses involved in alcohol, tobacco, gambling, weapons, other military industries, and/or abortion.

Process

1. On your own or with a partner, research several individual companies and mutual funds that would qualify as socially responsible investments.

2. In one to two paragraphs, comment on whether this type of investment strategy is a sound investment strategy.

Web Exercises

1. **Tracking an IPO**
   Go to the MSN Money Web site and find a company that recently created an IPO. Research the method of IPO allocation the company used and track its performance from the day the company went public until now. How have the stock prices changed?

2. **Ratio Differences**
   Research the debt-to-equity ratios of companies in different industries. Discuss why certain industries have a higher debt-to-equity ratio than others.

3. **Dogs of the Dow**
   Several investment strategies help investors select stocks. Dogs of the Dow is one of the most publicized strategies. Research Dogs of the Dow and describe the strategy. Would this be a good investment strategy for you?

4. **Dollar Cost Averaging**
   It is very difficult to perfectly time your investments so that you purchase when a stock is at its lowest point or sell when a stock is at its highest point. Research the investment strategy of dollar cost averaging. In a paragraph, describe what this strategy is, why it is used, and the advantages and disadvantages it has over other investment strategies.

5. **Municipal Bonds: Paving Roads and Building Schools**
   Municipal bonds are issued by local and state governments and other municipal organizations, such as school districts and toll road authorities. Conduct online research to determine the municipal bonds that the state in which you live has issued. What was the purpose behind the bond issues?

Web Case

For more on going public, initial public stock offerings, and Dutch auctions, access the Chapter 16 Web case entitled "Focus on Google: Google's Stock Starts on the Rocks" located in the End of Chapter Assignments section at my*biz*lab.com.

Video Case

For more on how investing works and how best to approach it, access the Chapter 16 Video Case entitled "The Motley Fool: Investing the Fool's Way" located in the End of Chapter Assignments section at my*biz*lab.com.

Personal Finance

People often associate discussing personal finances with calamity—trying to cover expenses after losing a job or managing a household because an illness or an injury prevents a person from working. But personal finance is a set of decisions that lets people achieve their dreams and goals—owning a home, affording college for their children, and so on.

You should begin to think seriously about your personal finances when you get your first job, if not earlier. It is most prudent to begin personal finance management from the day you receive your first allowance! The sooner you think seriously about personal finance, the easier it is to direct your earnings toward achieving your goals in life.

When an individual or a family applies financial principles in managing the ways money is budgeted, saved, invested, preserved for future life events, and protected against risks, it's called **personal finance.** In its simplest form, personal finance is about setting goals, making choices, and following through. Ultimately, as shown in ▼ **Figure 1,** you need to have a plan for reducing expenses and increasing income and assets so they begin to work for you. **Money management** is a key aspect of personal finance and generally includes the following:

- Determining what you have
- Setting goals for what you want or need
- Planning how to achieve your goals

There are several different aspects to effective money management. We begin by exploring how to create a financial plan.

Do You Need Tools to Help Manage Your Money?

Many online resources and software tools can help you manage your money. A spreadsheet program, such as Microsoft Excel, can handle simple financial worksheets and budgets, and Intuit's Quicken is a

Personal Finance

You've just gotten a new job with a starting salary of $48,000, plus benefits. You rewarded yourself with some new clothes and a vacation in Grand Cayman. It left you with $8,000 on your credit card, but you figure you can pay that off in a few months with your $4,000 a month paycheck. Can you manage your money to financial success?

popular software tool that offers more features specifically tailored to money-management capabilities. Many Web sites, such as Mint.com and MoneyStrands.com, also offer free online tools to help you track and manage your finances.

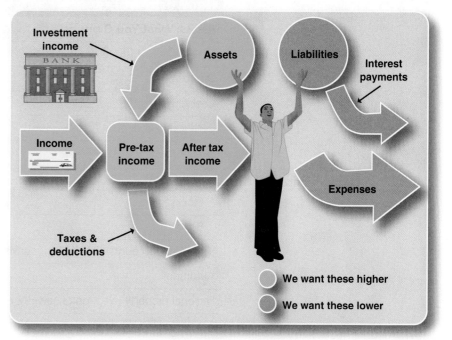

Creating a Financial Plan

Let's walk through the steps involved in creating a financial plan.

▼ **Figure 1**
**Basic Personal
Finance**

Step 1: Take a Financial Inventory

The first thing you need to do when beginning a financial plan is to *take a financial inventory*. List everything of value that you own (your assets) and then subtract from that total everything that you owe in loans and credit card balances. These are your liabilities. The remaining amount is your net worth. As shown in ▼ **Table 1,** determining your net worth is similar to a company preparing a balance sheet; it is just arranged somewhat differently. If you're young and just starting out, there might not be much to write down at first. But it's still a useful exercise. As time passes, you'll have more to add to this statement. The discipline and practice of recording where you are, even if done only once per year, will help you become more able to define your goals.

Step 2: Set Financial Goals

Next you can begin to *set financial goals*. These can be both short-term and long-term goals. Short-term goals should be measurable and realistic to complete in a time frame of less than a year, such as "I need to replace my car next year." Long-term goals can be more motivational, such as "I would like to have $250,000 in investment assets before I turn 40." Now break down the long-term goals into smaller, more manageable short-term goals. This increases the chance of achieving the long-term goals. For example, "I would like to have $250,000 in investment assets before I turn 40" could be broken down as follows: "I would like to save $5,000 each year and invest it in a money market fund that's earning 8 percent interest."

Finally, prioritize your goals by identifying them as wants and needs. Organize needs above wants and short-term goals above long-term goals. Assign short-term needs (buying a new car) as a top priority and long-term wants (a swimming pool in the backyard) as a lower priority. Choose goals that you're excited about and are determined to see come to fruition. Write these goals down in a place that you can refer to periodically to remind yourself of what you're working toward.

▼ **Table 1**

Net Worth Worksheet	
Assets: What You Own	**Value**
Cash	
Savings	
Checking account	
Certificates of deposit (CDs)	
Investments	
Mutual funds	
Stocks	
Bonds	
Retirement accounts (IRA, 401(k), pension)	
Automobile	
Personal property (electronics, jewelry, etc.)	
Cash value life insurance	
Real estate (owned)	
Total Assets	
Liabilities: What You Owe	**Value**
Student loan(s)	
Automobile loan(s)	
Credit card balance(s)	
Other loans	
Mortgage balance	
Other	
Total Liabilities	
Total Net Worth = Total Assets − Total Liabilities	

Step 3: Know Where Your Money Goes

You've figured out what you have and what you owe, and you've set financial goals. Now you need to know what you're currently spending. To start, list all the expenses you incur in a month, similar to the list shown in ▼ **Table 2.** It's easy to figure out the *fixed expenses*—expenditures that don't change from month to month, such as rent and car payments. The harder part is tracking *variable expenses*—monthly payments you have to make that may change from month to month. Gas, food, clothing, entertainment, utility, and cell phone charges are variable expenses.

You'll also need to include *periodic expenses*—items such as taxes or donations that you make but not on a monthly basis. Also, note the category of *unexpected expenses*

▼ **Table 2**

Monthly List of Expenses

Fixed Expenses	Amount	Need or Want?
Housing (mortgage/rent)		
Car payment		
Insurance premiums (health, car, renter's)		
Internet/cable television		
Savings		
Other		
Variable Expenses	**Amount**	**Need or Want?**
Electricity		
Gas/heating/oil		
Water		
Phone		
Food		
Gas		
Transportation (bus or subway fare)		
Child care		
Clothing		
Entertainment		
Other		
Periodic Expenses	**Amount**	**Need or Want?**
Taxes		
Donations		
Union/professional dues		
Unexpected Expenses	**Amount**	**Need or Want?**
Car/home repairs		
Speeding tickets		
Medical bills		
Other		

in Table 2. Although you can't determine the exact amount to fill in for this category—Will you get a speeding ticket this year?—it is important to remember that the unexpected can happen any time, and when it does, it can throw a monkey wrench into the best-laid plans unless modestly planned for.

As you create your list, you may need to track "invisible" expenses—items you don't realize you buy, such as daily lattes, candy bars or chips from the vending machine, cosmetics, or gadgets and accessories for your car. The best way to determine your invisible expenses is to create a "penny journal" that tracks your daily spending habits to the last penny. The penny journal will also help you define your variable expenses. As you continue to work with your plan, you'll be able to refine these numbers, as well as establish limits for some of the expenses.

Analyze the penny journal and expense list and identify the expenses you must cover (fixed expenses) and those that you might be able to cut back on (variable and invisible expenses). Now you're ready to develop a budget.

Step 4: Create a Budget

A budget, or a spending plan, tells you where money goes each month. The budget should be realistic in terms of the expenses you must pay. It should also include savings as a regular fixed expense. Every month, whether you think you can afford to or not, *you need to pay yourself first.* Don't fall into the trap of depositing into your savings account whatever is left over. Instead, make a conscious effort to pay yourself. Initially, your savings should accumulate so that you have a "rainy day fund" that is equal to at least one month's worth of bills. Eventually, this fund should be built up to cover three to six months of fixed expenses. This fund will cover your expenses should the unexpected happen, such as a job loss or an injury.

Once you've established a rainy day fund, your savings should go into an interest-bearing account—whether it is a CD, a money market fund, a mutual fund, or stocks and bonds. Many financial planning experts suggest setting aside at least 10 percent of every paycheck. No matter what, you should not miss making the payment to yourself. The secret to success is not so much the amount of money you save, but the persistence with which you do it.

So You Want to Be a Millionaire?

Which of the following individuals will save enough to be a millionaire by the time he or she is 60 years old?

a. A 10-year-old who puts $25 in the bank every week for 50 years

b. A 22-year-old who puts $68 in the bank every week for 38 years

c. A 40-year-old who puts $370 in the bank every week for 20 years

d. All of the above

If you chose *d*, you're right—all of these individuals with the prescribed savings plans will become millionaires before they reach 60. Notice the difference time makes in the amount each individual must contribute. The longer you have to save, the less you need to set aside. Similarly, if payment periods were less frequent (monthly instead of weekly), you would need to deposit larger amounts. The 22-year-old, for example, would need to set aside $300 (= 4 × $75) every month instead of $68 every week. What makes the difference? Compound interest. **Compound interest** is interest that is earned not only on principal but also on any interest earned previously. In a savings account, as long as you leave your money in the account and don't take out the interest you've earned, you'll benefit from the compounding effect. The moral of the story is to start saving early, save often, and don't withdraw the interest earnings!

Step 5: Execute the Plan

Tracking your expenses and setting up a budget can be tedious and time-consuming. Software packages are available to help you, such as the one shown in ▼ **Figure 2.** The real challenge is sticking to your plan, which requires discipline and persever-

Monthly Budget

	Projected Monthly	Actual Monthly
Income 1		$4,000
Income 2	$1,300	$1,300
Extra income	$300	$300
Total monthly income	**$5,600**	**$5,600**

Total Projected Cost	Total Actual Cost	Total Difference
$1,195	$1,236	($41)
Projected balance (Projected income minus projected costs)	Actual balance (Actual income minus actual costs)	Difference (Actual minus projected)
$4,405	$4,364	($41)

Housing	Projected Cost	Actual Cost	Difference
Mortgage or rent	$1,000	$1,000	$0
Phone	$54	$100	($46)
Electricity	$44	$56	($12)
Gas	$22	$28	($6)
Water and sewer	$8	$8	$0
Cable	$34	$34	$0
Waste removal	$10	$10	$0
Maintenance or repairs	$23	$0	$23
Supplies	$0	$0	$0
Other	$0	$0	$0
Subtotals	$1,195	$1,236	($41)

Transportation	Projected Cost	Actual Cost	Difference
Vehicle 1 payment			$0
Vehicle 2 payment			$0
Bus/taxi fare			$0
Insurance			$0
Licensing			$0
Fuel			$0
Maintenance			$0
Other			$0
Subtotals	$0	$0	$0

Insurance	Projected Cost	Actual Cost	Difference
Home			$0
Health			$0
Life			$0
Other			$0
Subtotals	$0	$0	$0

Food	Projected Cost	Actual Cost	Difference
Groceries			$0
Dining out			$0
Other			$0
Subtotals	$0	$0	$0

Savings or Investments	Projected Cost	Actual Cost	Difference
Retirement account			$0
Investment account			$0
College			$0
Other			$0
Subtotals	$0	$0	$0

Personal Care	Projected Cost	Actual Cost	Difference
Medical			$0
Hair/nails			$0
Clothing			$0
Dry cleaning			$0
Health club			$0
Organization dues or fees			$0
Other			$0
Subtotals	$0	$0	$0

Loans	Projected Cost	Actual Cost	Difference
Personal			$0
Student			$0
Credit card			$0
Credit card			$0
Other			$0
Subtotals	$0	$0	$0

Children	Projected Cost	Actual Cost	Difference
Medical			$0
Clothing			$0
School tuition			$0
School supplies			$0
Organization dues of fees			$0
Lunch money			$0
Child care			$0
Toys/games			$0
Other			$0
Subtotals	$0	$0	$0

Taxes	Projected Cost	Actual Cost	Difference
Federal			$0
State			$0
Local			$0
Other			$0
Subtotals	$0	$0	$0

Gifts and Donations	Projected Cost	Actual Cost	Difference
Charity 1			$0
Charity 2			$0
Charity 3			$0
Subtotals	$0	$0	$0

Legal	Projected Cost	Actual Cost	Difference
Attorney			$0
Alimony			$0
Other			$0
Subtotals	$0	$0	$0

Pets	Projected Cost	Actual Cost	Difference
Food			$0
Medical			$0
Grooming			$0
Toys			$0
Other			$0
Subtotals	$0	$0	$0

Entertainment	Projected Cost	Actual Cost	Difference
Video/DVD			$0
CDs			$0
Movies			$0
Concerts			$0
Sporting events			$0
Live theater			$0
Other			$0
Subtotals	$0	$0	$0

ance. Just cutting out one cup of designer coffee a week saves over $200 a year. Here are a few other tips for plugging leaks in your budget:

- **Pay off all unpaid credit card debt.** Carrying a balance on your credit cards is financial suicide. Most credit card companies charge more than 18 percent on unpaid balances. Therefore, pay down your credit card debt before depositing money into a savings or investment account. Also, pay your bill on time. Late fees are a waste of money!

- **If you have outstanding loans, see if you can reduce the interest rate or consolidate into a more manageable payment.** Call your bank and ask! You might be surprised at the response you get.

- **To reduce impulse buying, try using cash only.** When you use cash instead of a credit card, you immediately see the effects of your spending.

▼ **Figure 2**
Sample Budget Template
Budget templates like this one can help you set up your spending plan.

Step 6: Monitor and Assess Your Plan

You need to revisit your plan periodically and make adjustments as necessary. Look at your budget every month and make adjustments every year.

Managing Personal Credit

Credit is your ability to buy things now and pay for them later. When used responsibly, credit cards can be good things. Showing future lenders that you have a good history with credit will help you when you apply for car loans or a mortgage. But

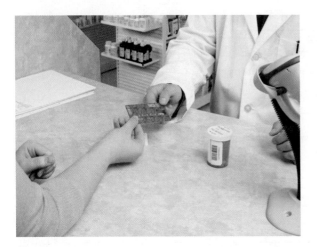

Using credit cards wisely can help you secure a car or home loan later down the road. However, reckless spending with credit cards can lead to financial disaster.

abusing credit can quickly add up to serious problems. Consider this: It might not take you very long to accumulate $3,000 on your credit card, but it will take you nearly 15 years paying $50 a month to pay it off completely! And that's if you never charge another cent! Here are a few tips to help you manage your personal credit.

Tip 1: *Check the interest rate and the annual fee.*

Credit is not free, so check the fine print on your credit card contract. Even if the initial offer is a zero or very low percentage interest rate, that interest rate will change when the promotional period ends. Make sure you understand what the new interest rate will be. Also try to find a credit card company that does not charge an annual fee. If there is an annual fee, call to find out if the issuing company will waive it. Be sure to carefully evaluate credit cards that offer airline miles or other incentives. Often, these cards charge higher interest rates and annual fees.

Tip 2: *Don't charge if you can't pay.*

Don't look at your credit card as a means of financial freedom. If you can't afford to pay cash for an item, then don't use a credit card. Think of a credit card as a short-term loan that needs to be paid back in 30 days or less. To use credit wisely, pay off the balance in full every month. Doing so allows you to keep your money earning interest longer (assuming you have an interest-bearing checking or savings account), thus making your money work for you. Some cards are beginning to encourage on-time payments. Discover's Motiva card, for example, pays you back for paying on time. Plus, like other Discover cards, it gives you a cash-back bonus on your purchases.

Tip 3: *Establish a credit history in another way.*

Although establishing a good credit history is important, you don't need to begin with a credit card if you feel the temptation is too great to charge more than you can afford. Another way to establish credit is to begin with a single store credit card or a single-purpose credit card, such as a gas card. Using these cards responsibly by making occasional purchases and paying your bill in full every month demonstrates your ability to use credit wisely.

Know Your Credit Score

If you've been using credit, then you've established a credit record. Lenders convert your credit history into a numeric score that they use when qualifying an applicant for a loan. There is no absolute number that guarantees your chances of qualifying for credit or lower interest rates, but a higher score is better. You can find out your number by obtaining a credit report from one of the three credit bureaus: Equifax, Experian, and TransUnion. Every individual is entitled to one free credit report each year from each bureau. Go to the Annual Credit Report Web site for more information. If possible, several months before applying for a big loan, obtain your credit report to make sure all the information listed is accurate. If there are errors in your credit report (which occasionally happen), you will have some time to fix them.

Car Considerations

Having a car is a top financial priority for many people. Let's look at the financial decisions and considerations involved in owning a car.

Getting Wheels

Whether you're replacing your current car or are buying one for the first time, you'll need to make several decisions. The first is whether you're buying a new car or a used car. New cars have warranties, so the manufacturer covers virtually all repairs. On the other hand, the value of a new car depreciates 20–30 percent almost as soon as you drive the car off the dealer's lot.[1] Your car loan might already be more than the car is worth before there are even 50 miles showing on the odometer! Used cars have already depreciated, so your loan is probably less and closer to the current value of the car. Don't forget that you'll need to pay for maintenance (whether the car is used or new), and depending on the age and condition of the car, the maintenance might be costly. Consider buying a "new used car," which is a car that is only a few years old, has been well maintained, and has low mileage. Sometimes, initial warranties extend to used cars, as well. In many ways a new used car is like new, although you have not had to pay for the immediate depreciation.

Buying a car requires that you make a number of decisions.

If you decide to get a new car, you have another decision: to buy (with a loan or in cash) or lease. ▼ **Table 3** outlines some of the considerations in buying or leasing

▼ Table 3

Buying vs. Leasing a Car	
Buying a Car	**Leasing a Car**
Pay for the entire cost of car.	Pay for only a portion of the car's cost.
You need to make a down payment and pay sales tax on the entire cost of the car.	You sometimes have the option to not make a down payment and pay the sales tax on your monthly payments.
You make the first loan payment a month after you buy the car.	You make the first lease payment when you sign the contract.
When you sell the car, it's at the depreciated value. Your outstanding loan obligation may be more than the depreciated value.	When you terminate the lease, you may either return the vehicle or purchase it for its depreciated value.
There are no use restrictions on mileage and no specified maintenance requirements.	Usually there are mileage restrictions (12,000 miles a year) and maintenance requirements. Turning the car in with stained carpets, dents, and dings brings on extra fees. Going over the mileage limit will mean paying extra fees.

a new car. Many people lease cars because they can get a more expensive car for less up-front cash. On the other hand, if you finance a car with a loan, at the end of the loan, you still own your car. If you continue to drive that car, you then have the money you used to spend on the loan payments to put to other uses, such as paying off debt.

Insurance and Investments

Taking care of yourself now and in the future constitutes another area of financial planning. Buying insurance and making investments are two ways you can accomplish these goals.

Insuring Your Present and Your Future

When something goes wrong, you need help to cover the costs so you can recover quickly. Fortunately, insurance is available for a variety of risks so you don't have to bear the burden of covering these costs alone.

1. **Health insurance.** Health insurance is a must. No matter how healthy you are today, a serious illness or an injury, plus any rehabilitation expenses, can be astronomically expensive. If your employer offers health insurance coverage, take it. You might have to contribute some of the cost yourself, but it's well worth it. If you're self-employed, unemployed, or not covered by your employer, investigate what affordable options you have for coverage. If you are even a part-time student, you might be eligible for a college subsidized group health plan. If you are self-employed, you may qualify for a group plan through associations and organizations you have joined.

2. **Disability insurance.** Disability insurance pays you benefits if you should become disabled and are no longer able to earn a living. Many employers offer disability insurance coverage along with their health insurance coverage. If yours does not, determine how your expenses would be met should something permanently disabling happen.

3. **Car insurance.** Most states require car insurance. There are three types of car insurance coverage: liability, collision, and comprehensive. *Liability* covers damage or injury you have caused to someone else. You should always have liability coverage. *Collision* covers damage to your vehicle from a collision with a moving or stationary object. *Comprehensive* covers damage to your car from theft, fire, or other non–collision-related accidents. If you're insuring an older car, it might not be worth carrying the cost of collision and comprehensive coverage.

4. **Homeowner's and renter's insurance.** These types of insurance protect your home and the contents inside. Homeowner's insurance also has liability coverage to protect you if someone is injured while on your property. If you have a mortgage on your home, the bank usually requires insurance. Many landlords require their tenants to demonstrate proof that they have renter's insurance. If your landlord does not, still consider it because it is affordable and will protect you in cases of theft.

5. **Life insurance.** Life insurance helps replace income lost due to your death to those who are dependent on you, such as a spouse, children, parents, or other family members. When you purchase a life insurance policy, you name the person(s) who receive your life insurance benefits as your beneficiaries. Some types of life insurance policies can act as long-term savings plans, whereas other types are strictly for protection. You might not need life insurance if you're single, with no one depending on you or your income, or if you're married, without children, and your spouse is capable of working.

Insurance policies cover natural disasters to varying degrees. Make sure you read the fine print so you know exactly what is protected in your insurance plan.

Consulting an insurance professional will help you determine your needs for many types of insurance. It pays to shop around and compare rates. Often, you can receive discounts if you carry several types of insurance (such as homeowner's and automobile) with the same company. Moreover, you should review and compare your rates every few years to make sure the rates you are paying are still competitive and your coverage is adequate.

Investing Now and for the Future

Investing your money is not without risk, although there are strategies you can pursue to help reduce these risks. Learning as much as you can about the various investment opportunities that are available to you is a useful part of your financial planning. As we discussed in Chapter 16, many types of investments exist. As you begin to build up your savings, you might choose to invest your savings in certificates of deposit (CDs) or money market accounts. As your knowledge of and comfort level with investments increase, and your amount of discretionary income builds, you might consider investing in mutual funds, stocks, or bonds.

How Fast Can Your Investment Double in Value?

The **rule of 72** is an easy way to figure out how long it will take to double your money at a given interest rate. All you have to do is divide the investment's interest rate into 72. For example, if you want to know how long it will take to double your money at 6 percent interest, divide 6 into 72 and get 12 years. The rule of 72 works well as long as the interest rate is less than 20 percent. You can also use the rule of 72 to determine the interest rate needed to double your money in a certain amount of time. If you wanted to double your money in 6 years, you would divide 6 into 72. Now you know you would need an interest rate of about 12 percent.[2]

Investing for Retirement

"There's nothing wrong with entering magazine sweepstakes - but have you folks considered any other retirement plans?"

At this point in your life, retirement probably seems a very long way off. Unfortunately, Social Security is no longer something you can rely on to fully meet your financial needs after you retire. Therefore, it is very important that you take responsibility for planning to meet your financial needs during retirement. It's best to accumulate savings for retirement by starting early and investing regularly, but other mechanisms are available to help. If you work, your employer may have a retirement plan that you can join. If you're self-employed or your employer does not offer retirement benefits, you can set up your own retirement program. Funds specifically designated for retirement, such as Individual Retirement Accounts (IRAs), Roth IRAs, and 401(k) programs, offer tax advantages to encourage you to save for retirement.

Individual Retirement Accounts

Individual retirement accounts (IRAs) are special savings accounts created by the government. The benefit of putting your retirement savings into an IRA is that you put pretax money into an IRA, thus reducing your current taxable income. You don't pay tax on money in the account until after you have retired and withdrawn the money. (The idea here is that after you retire, you will be in a lower income tax bracket and pay less tax.) You cannot begin to withdraw money without penalty from your IRA until after you have reached the age of 59½. You must begin to withdraw from your IRA when you are 70½. Despite these restrictions, you should strongly consider contributing the maximum amount you are allowed every year.

Roth IRAs

A **Roth IRA** is another type of retirement account, but it differs from a traditional IRA in several ways. Contributions to a Roth IRA are not made with pretax dollars. However, withdrawals are usually tax free, and there are fewer restrictions on when and how you can withdraw your money. Roth IRAs are restricted to individuals whose income falls below a certain level specified by guidelines established by the IRS.

Pension Plans

Pension plans are retirement plans established by your employer. There are two kinds of pension plans: defined benefit and defined contribution. In the past, most companies offered **defined benefit plans** in which you were paid a certain percentage of your salary after you had retired. To qualify, you had to work for the company for a certain amount of time. The problem with defined benefit plans is that the companies bore the risk and responsibility of having sufficient funds to meet their pension obligations.

When this became too difficult and costly, many companies switched to offering defined contribution plans. **Defined contribution plans** are the most common retirement benefit offered today. In this type of plan, your employer contributes a percentage of each paycheck that you have specified into your account. To encourage you to contribute to the plan, many companies will match your investment—

in essence giving you money when you save. The money in your account is invested for you in stocks, bonds, mutual funds, annuities, or company stock. You often have the opportunity to select the investments from a menu of choices and direct the proportion of your contributions going into each investment. Should you change jobs or leave a company before you retire, you may rollover the proceeds of your defined contribution plan into your new plan or an IRA.

401(k), 403(b), and 457 Plans

These plans are other forms of defined contribution plans. For-profit companies offer 401(k) plans, non-for-profit organizations offer 403(b) plans, and government entities offer the 457 plan. (The numbers of the plans refer to the sections in the federal tax law that authorizes the plans.)

Taxes

Everyone who earns income is required to file an income tax return. Even if you owe no taxes, you must file a return. Failure to do so will result in fines and penalties. When you get your paycheck, an estimate of the taxes you owe has already been taken out. Your tax return calculates the exact amount you owe. If not enough has been deducted from your paycheck, you pay the remainder of what you owe when you file your return. If you have had too much deducted from your paycheck, the IRS will refund the difference.

The IRS offers every taxpayer a standard deduction that reduces the amount of taxable income. You have a choice to either take this standard deduction or itemize your own deductions. Deductions include interest paid on mortgages, contributions to a tax-deferred retirement plan, contributions to charity, and a certain amount of medical expenses, to name a few. You should itemize your deductions if they're greater than the standard deduction. Generally, if you don't own your own home, you're better off taking the standard deduction. In addition, completing the tax return is much easier when you take the standard deduction!

How Much Tax Are You Paying?

Income taxes are computed on a marginal tax rate. This means that tax rates progressively increase as your income increases, and the tax rate applies to only the income in each bracket range. Remember that not all income is taxable income. Standard deductions and personal exemptions can be subtracted from what you make. These will vary depending on your personal situation. ▼ **Table 4** summarizes the tax rates for single people.

▼ **Table 4**

Personal Income Tax Rates[3]		
If Taxable Income Is at Least . . .	**But Not More Than . . .**	**Your Highest Tax Rate Is**
$ 0	$ 8,375	10%
$ 8,375	$ 34,000	15%
$ 34,000	$ 82,400	25%
$ 82,400	$171,850	28%
$170,850	$373,650	33%
$373,650	No limit	35%

If you want to know your tax bill, you can quickly estimate with these formulas. Try out an interactive Web site like MoneyChimp.com to show you the detailed calculation for your salary.

Knowing your tax bracket is important in financial planning to determine how much tax you might pay on extra income you earn or, conversely, how much tax you will save by increasing your deductions.

Managing your personal finances may sound tedious and time-consuming, but it has rewards. Remember the following tips:

- Set your financial goals.
- Make a plan to achieve these goals and stick to it.
- Pay yourself first, start early, and pay often.
- Use debt wisely and establish good credit.
- Make sure you and your assets are insured.

Soon enough you'll be on the road to financial success.

Business Plan Project Appendix

Part 1. Introduction

Business Name
What is the name of your business?

Hint: When choosing a name for your business, make sure it captures the spirit of the business you're creating. Also refer to the BizChat in Chapter 5 for tips on naming your business.

Note to students: Once you have inserted your answers in this template, delete the questions and the hints provided and leave the headings so that your business plan will look more professional.

Description of Business
What will your business do?

Hint: Imagine that you're explaining your business to a family member or a friend. It should be easy to explain, using 30 words or less.

Form of Business Ownership
What form of business ownership (sole proprietorship, partnership, or corporation) will your business take? Why did you choose this form?

Hint: For more information on forms of business ownership, refer to Chapter 6.

Ideal Customers
Describe your ideal customers. What are they like in terms of age, income level, and so on?

Hint: You don't have to go into too much detail in this part of the plan; you'll provide more details about customers and marketing in later parts. For now, simply outline the kind of customers your product or service will best fit.

Company Advantages
Why will customers choose to buy from your business instead of your competition?

Hint: Describe what will be unique about your business. For example, is your product special, will customer service be exceptional, or will your price be lower?

Part 2. The Company and Management Team
THE MISSION STATEMENT

Mission Statement
Write a brief mission statement for your business.

Hint: Refer to the discussion of mission statements in Chapter 7. Be sure to include how you will stand out from your competition and why customers will buy from you.

Ethical Issues
All businesses must deal with ethical issues. One way to address these issues is to create a code of ethics. List three core (unchanging) principles that your business will follow.

Hint: To help you consider the ethical issues your business might face, refer to Chapter 3.

Social Responsibility
A business shows social responsibility by respecting all its stakeholders. What steps will you take to create a socially responsible business?

Hint: To help you consider the issues of social responsibility, refer to the discussion in Chapter 3. Consider how you may need to be socially responsible toward your customers and, if applicable, investors, employees, and suppliers.

INDUSTRY PROFILE

Industry Description
Describe the industry and sector in which your company operates.

Hint: Industries are broad categories, such as financial, technology, services, or health care. Sectors are more specific categories within an industry, such as a sporting goods store in the services industry or computer peripherals in the technology industry. In your description of the industry and sector, discuss economic trends as well as the current outlook for the industry, including growth potential.

Opportunities and Threats
Describe the opportunities and threats that face your company.

Hint: For this section, refer to the discussion of the economy in Chapter 2. Consider external factors, such as macroeconomic matters, technological changes, legislation, and sociocultural changes that may affect the industry as well as your company. This typically is done as part of a SWOT analysis.

COMPANY PROFILE AND STRATEGY

Business Goals
What are three business goals you want to achieve in the first year? What are two intermediate to long-term goals you want to achieve in the next three to five years?

Hint: Refer to the discussion of goal setting in Chapter 7. Be as specific and realistic as possible with the goals you set. Remember the SMARTER acronym; goals should be specific, measurable, acceptable, realistic, timely, extending, and rewarding. For example, if you are selling a service, how many customers do you want by the end of the first year and how much do you want each customer to spend? If you are selling a good, what volume of sales do you hope to achieve?

Company Strengths
Describe the strengths of your company.

Hint: In evaluating a company's strengths, analyze its internal resources, including finances, human resources, marketing, operations, and technological resources. A company's strength might be its strong marketing department or a favorable location.

Raw Materials and Supplies
Explain what raw materials and supplies you will need to run your business. How will you produce your good? What equipment do you need? What hours will you operate?

Hint: Refer to Chapter 11 for information to get you started.

ANTICIPATED CHALLENGES AND PLANNED RESPONSES

Anticipated Challenges
Describe any weaknesses or potential challenges that face your company.

Hint: Consider any potential vulnerability from the competition, problems with suppliers or resources, or any legal factors that might affect the business, such as pending lawsuits or patent or copyright issues.

Planned Responses
Describe any plans you have to address these weaknesses and anticipated challenges.

Hint: Consider any resources your company can make available to address these challenges.

THE MANAGEMENT TEAM

Management
Who are the key individuals that will manage the business?

Hint: Refer to the discussion of managers in Chapter 7. Think about how *many levels* of management as well as what *kinds* of managers your business needs. In addition, outline how each manager's contribution will positively impact the business. What is it about that particular manager that will help the business succeed?

Organization Chart
Show how the "team" fits together by creating a simple organizational chart for your business. Make sure the organizational chart indicates who will work for each manager as well as each person's job title.

Hint: Most businesses start quite small. However, as you create your organizational chart, consider what your business will look like in the future. What different tasks are involved in the business? Who will each person report to in the organizational structure? Refer to the discussions of organizational structure in Chapters 6 and 7 for information to get you started.

Part 3. Marketing

MARKET ANALYSIS

Market Research
Describe your target market in terms of age, education level, income, and other demographic variables.

Hint: Refer to Chapter 12 for more information on the aspects of target marketing and market segmentation that you may want to consider. Be as detailed as possible about who you think your customers will be.

Assessment of the Competition
Describe three companies that you see as your main competitors.

Hint: For each company, describe the company's perceived strengths and weaknesses. How do you intend to take advantage of each weakness and respond to each strength?

THE PRODUCT OR SERVICE

Product Features and Benefits
Describe the features and benefits of your product or service.

Hint: As you learned in Chapter 13, a product has tangible and intangible benefits that create a *total product offer*. Describe your product on three levels, as outlined in Chapter 13—the *core product* (What basic needs or wants does this product or service satisfy?), the *actual product* (What are the tangible aspects of the product that you can taste, see, smell, touch, and hear?), and the *augmented product* (What are the perceived benefits that provide additional value to a customer's purchase?).

Product Differentiation
How will you make your product(s) stand out in the crowd?

Hint: There are many ways to stand out in the crowd, such as a unique product, outstanding service, or a great location. What makes your product special? Does it fill an unmet need in the marketplace? How will you differentiate your product to make sure that it succeeds?

Pricing
What pricing strategy will you choose for your product(s), and why did you choose this strategy?

Hint: Refer to Chapter 13 for more information on pricing strategies and tactics. Because your business is new, so is the product. Therefore, you will probably want to choose between price skimming and penetration pricing. Which will you choose and why?

SALES AND PROMOTION

Place (Distribution) Issues
Where will customers find your product or service? (That is, what distribution channels should you consider?)

Hint: If your business will sell its product directly to consumers, what types of stores will sell your product? If your product will be sold to another business, which channel of distribution will you use? Refer to Chapter 14 for more information on aspects of distribution you may want to consider.

Advertising
How will you advertise to your target market? Why have you chosen these forms of advertisement?

Hint: Marketers use several different advertising media—specific communication devices for carrying a seller's message to potential customers; each form has advantages and drawbacks. Refer to Chapter 14 for a discussion of the types of advertising media you may wish to consider.

Promotions
What other methods of promotion will you use and why?

Hint: There's more to promotion than simple advertising. Other methods include *personal selling, sales promotions,* and *publicity and public relations.* Refer to the discussion of promotion in Chapter 14 for ideas on how to promote your product that go beyond just advertising.

Part 4. The Financials

Expected Revenue
How much will you charge for your product? How many products do you believe you can sell in one year (or how many customers do you think your business will attract)? Multiply the price that you will charge by the number of products that you hope to sell or the amount you hope each customer will spend. This will give you an estimate of your *revenues* for one year.

Hint: You will use the amounts you calculate in the costs and revenues questions in this section in the accounting statements, so be as realistic as you can.

Cost of Doing Business
What are the costs of doing business? Equipment, supplies, salaries, rent, utilities, and insurance are just some of these expenses. Estimate what it will cost to do business for one year.

Hint: Insert the costs associated with doing business in the table on the following page. The following list provides some hints as to where you can get this information. Note that these are estimates; try your best to include accurate costs for the expenses you think will be a part of doing business.

Hints for each expense in the following table:
- **Rent:** What is the "going rate" per square foot for office space in your community? A real estate agent or a local SBA representative (www.sba.gov) can also be helpful in answering this question.
- **Salaries and Wages:** Refer to the organizational chart. How much will each employee earn? How many hours will each employee be needed on a weekly basis? Once you've determined the weekly cost, then expand it to a monthly cost and a yearly cost.
- **Supplies:** How much will all the computers, equipment, and furniture cost? What kinds of general office supplies will you need? Most prices for this information can be found on an office supply Web site, such as Staples.com.
- **Advertising and Other Promotions:** Refer to your marketing section. You have described how you wish to reach your customers; now you need to decide how much it will cost. If you're using television, contact the sales department at a local station. If you're using newspapers, contact their advertising department. Salespeople are usually happy to answer your questions.
- **Utilities:** These amounts will vary depending on your business and what utilities you will pay. If your business looks like an office, this cost may be similar to what a homeowner pays. However, if your business involves making a product, then the costs will be significant. An SBA representative can be a good resource.
- **Insurance:** This value will be affected by the nature of the business. More equipment will usually mean higher insurance costs. Again, contact an SBA representative for feedback.

Expenses	Expected Monthly Cost	Expected Yearly Cost
Rent		
Salaries and Wages		
Supplies: technological, equipment, furniture, other (computers, software, copy machine, desks, chairs, etc.)		
Advertising and Other Promotions		
Utilities: heat, electricity, etc.		
Utilities: telephone, Internet		
Insurance		
Other (specify)		
Other (specify)		

Start-up Costs
How much money will you need to get your business started?

Hint: Refer back to where you analyzed the costs involved in running your business. Approximately how much will you need to get your business started?

Financing
How will you finance your business? For example, will you seek out a bank loan? Borrow from friends? Sell stocks or bonds initially or as your business grows?

Hint: Refer to Chapter 15 for information on sources of short-term and long-term funds. Refer to Chapter 16 for information on securities, such as stocks and bonds.

Income Statement and Balance Sheet
Create a balance sheet and an income statement for your business.

Hint: You have **two** options for creating these reports. The first option is to use the Microsoft Word versions that are found within this student template (shown below).

*The second option is to use the specific Microsoft Excel templates created for each statement. You'll find these templates on mybizlab.com in a file called **Business Plan Part 4 Spreadsheets**. These Excel files are handy because all the calculations are preset; all you have to do is "plug in" the numbers. The calculations are performed automatically. If you make adjustments to the values in the Excel worksheets, you'll automatically see how changes to expenses, for example, can improve the "bottom line." Note that the Excel templates also include helpful hints as to where you can get the information you need to complete the balance sheet and the income statement.*

Twelve-Month Income Statement (Profit & Loss Statement)

	June	July	Aug.	Sept.	Oct.	Nov.	Dec.	Jan.	Feb.	March	April	May	YEARLY
Revenue (Sales)													
Category 1													
Category 2													
Total Revenue (Sales)													
Cost of Goods Sold													
Category 1													
Category 2													
Total Cost of Goods Sold													
Gross Profit													
Operating Expenses													
Rent Expense													
Salary/Wage Expenses													
Supplies Expense													
Advertising Expense													
Utilities Expense													
Telephone/Internet Expense													
Insurance Expense													
Interest from Loans (if applicable)													
Other Expenses (specify)													
Total Expenses													
Net Profit													

Balance Sheet

Assets	
Current Assets	
Cash in Bank	
Cash Value of Inventory	
Prepaid Expenses (insurance)	
Total Current Assets	
Fixed Assets	
Machinery & Equipment	
Furniture & Fixtures	
Real Estate/Buildings	
Total Fixed Assets	
Total Assets	
Liabilities & Net Worth	
Current Liabilities	
Accounts Payable	
Taxes Payable	
Notes Payable (due within 12 months)	
Total Current Liabilities	
Long-Term Liabilities	
Bank Loans Payable (greater than 12 months)	
Less: Short-Term Portion	
Total Long-Term Liabilities	
Total Liabilities	
Owners' Equity (Net Worth)	
Total Liabilities & Net Worth	

Part 5. The Finishing Touches
COVER SHEET AND TABLE OF CONTENTS

Cover Sheet
Create a cover sheet for your business plan.

Hint: The cover sheet should include the following:

- Basic company information (name, address, phone number, and web address)
- The company logo
- Contact information of the owner(s) and any officers (names, titles, addresses, phone numbers, and e-mail addresses)
- The date the business plan was created
- The name(s) of those who prepared the plan

Table of Contents
Create a table of contents for the plan so a reader can quickly find information.

Hint: The table of contents should include the headings of each section and the page number of the first page of each section. All pages in the document should be numbered.

Executive Summary
After you've finished your business plan, write an executive summary that contains the key points of the business plan. The summary should be brief—no more than two pages—and cover the following points:

- The name of your business
- Where your business will be located
- The mission of your business
- The product or service you are selling
- Who your ideal customers are
- How your product or business will stand out in the crowd
- Who the owners of the business are and what experience they have
- An overview of the future prospects for your business and industry
- An overview of the amount and uses of required initial financing

Hint: You've already answered these questions, so what you need to do is put the ideas together into a "snapshot" format. The executive summary is a sales pitch; it's an investor's first impression of your idea. Ultimately, you're enticing a reader to want to read more. If investors don't get excited about your business and the prospects of success from reading the executive summary, they'll stop reading and most likely not consider the plan. Therefore, as with all parts of the plan, write in a clear and professional way but be compelling about your business.

Note: Once you have created the cover sheet, the table of contents, and the executive summary, move these sections to the beginning of your business plan, with the cover sheet as the very first element.

Reference Notes

Chapter 1

1. "Company History," *YouTube*. www.youtube.com/t/company_history (April 16, 2010).
2. Peter Kafka, "YouTube Co-Founder Steve Chen Moves On, Stays with Google," *MediaMemo*, http://mediamemo.allthingsd.com/20090630/youtube-cofounder-steve-chen-moves-on-stays-with-google/ (June 30, 2009).
3. Eric A. Taub, "TV Prices Falling Faster," *New York Times*, October 25, 2008. http://bits.blogs.nytimes.com/2008/10/25/tv-prices-falling-faster/ (May 12, 2010).
4. Mark Chacksfield, "Latest Blu-ray Players Sales Up 72%," *Techradar*, May 7, 2009. www.techradar.com/news/video/blu-ray/blu-ray-player-sales-up-72—597009?src=rss&attr=all (May 12, 2010).
5. Joe Wilcox, "Microsoft, Apple Alliance at Key Juncture," *CNETNew.com*, February 22, 2002. http://news.cnet.com/2100-1040-843145.html (May 12, 2010).
6. "Bing-O: Potential Microsoft Apple Alliance," *InvestorGuide*, January 20, 2010. www.investorguide.com/article/5675/bing-o-potential-microsoft-apple-alliance-msft/ (May 12, 2010).
7. Sharon O'Brien, "Fun Facts About the Senior Population: Demographics," *About.com*. http://seniorliving.about.com/od/lawpolitics/a/senior_pop_demo.htm (May 12, 2010).
8. "100 Best Companies to Work for 2010: Top Companies: Most Diverse," *Fortune*, http://money.cnn.com/magazines/fortune/bestcompanies/2010/minorities/ (May 12, 2010).
9. Ryan Z. Cortazar, "Diversity Training Fails to Boost Minorities into Management," *Harvard University Gazette*, September 16, 2006. www.news.harvard.edu/gazette/2006/09.14/25-dobbin.html (May 12, 2010).
10. Andrea Cooper, "The Influencers," *Entrepreneur.com*, March 11, 2008. http://www.usnews.com/articles/business/small-business-entrepreneurs/2008/03/11/the-influencers_print.htm (May 12, 2010).
11. Mike Allen and Eamon Javers, "Politico, Obama Announces New Fuel Standards," May 19, 2009. www.politico.com/news/stories/0509/22650.html (May 12, 2010).
12. "About Us," *FedEx*. http://about.fedex.designcdt.com/our_company/company_information (May 12, 2010).
13. Robert Green, "This Old Computer: Upgrade or Replace?" *Robert Green's DIY*, March 17, 2009. www.rbgrn.net/content/212-old-computer-upgrade-or-replace (May 12, 2010).
14. Patty Azzarello, "How to Overcome IT's Credibility Challenges," *CIO Update*, September 25, 2007. http://cioupdate.com//article.php/3701571 (May 12, 2010).
15. Steve Ballmer, "Nashville Technology Conference," *Woopidoo! Quotations*. www.woopidoo.com/business_quotes/technology-quotes.htm (May 12, 2010).
16. "Peach State Commuters Hit Breaking Point and Opt for Mobile Working," *EON Enhanced Online News*, February 16, 2010. http://eon.businesswire.com/portal/site/eon/permalink/?ndmViewId=news_view&newsId=20100216005093&newsLang=en (April 16, 2010).
17. Jack Neff, "Beyond Online Ads: P&G Sets $4 Bil E-commerce Goal," *Advertising Age* 80, no. 29, (September 7, 2009), pp. 3–25.
18. M. P. Mcqueen, "Cybercrime Complaints, Reported Losses Increase," *Wall Street Journal*, March 12, 2010, http://online.wsj.com/article/NA_WSJ_PUB:SB10001424052748704131404575117862249387610.html.
19. "The Wawa Story," www.wawa.com/WawaWeb/pdfs/theWawaStory.pdf (May 12, 2010).
20. "The 200 Best Small Companies," *Forbes*. www.forbes.com/lists/2009/23/small-companies-09_The-200-Best-Small-Companies_Rank.html (May 12, 2010). Reprinted with permission of Forbes Media LLC © 2010.
21. "History," *CVS Caremark*. http://info.cvscaremark.com/our-company/history (May 12, 2010).
22. "Temporary Disability Insurance," *Rhode Island Department of Labor and Training*, www.dlt.ri.gov/tdi/ (May 12, 2010).
23. "About Us," *McDonald's*. www.mcdonalds.ca/en/aboutus/faq.aspx (May 12, 2010).
24. "Strange International Foods: Our Top Seven," *Independent Traveler.com*. www.independenttraveler.com/resources/article.cfm?AID=860&category=43; Erin Petrun, "Where's the Beef?" www.cbsnews.com/stories/2007/04/02/asia_letter/main2640540.shtml (May 12, 2010).
25. Robert Wolcott, "Building a Business within Wawa," Kellogg School of Management, http://hbr.org/product/wawa-building-a-new-business-within-an-established/an/KEL240-PDF-ENG (May 12, 2010).
26. "Nantucket Nectars from the Beginning," *Nantucket Allserve, Inc.* www.nantucketnectars.com/fullstory.php?PHPSESSID=996c6c936ce6351082022525b73e9fce (May 12, 2010).
27. "In Pictures: The 10 Largest Private Companies in America," *Forbes*. www.forbes.com/2009/10/28/top-10-largest-private-business-private-companies-09-top-ten_slide_11.html (May 12, 2010). Reprinted with permission of Forbes Media LLC © 2010.
28. "Limited Liability Company," *Internal Revenue Service, United States Department of Treasury*. www.irs.gov/businesses/small/article/0,id=98277,00.html (May 12, 2010).

Chapter 2

1. William Perez, "2010 Tax Rate Schedules," *About.com*. http://taxes.about.com/od/preparingyourtaxes/a/tax-rates_2.htm (March 28, 2010).
2. Jay Fowler, "12 Countries with the Highest and Lowest Tax Rates," *Zikkir Business News Digest*. http://zikkir.com/business/60403 (March 28, 2010).
3. "Denmark Tax Rates," *taxrates.cc*. www.taxrates.cc/html/denmark-tax-rates.html (March 28, 2010).
4. "The Education System in Demark," *UNI•C*. http://tilgaengelighed.emu.dk/tilgaengelighed/English/info.html (March 28, 2010).
5. Ruut Veenhoven, "World Database of Happiness," *Erasmus University Rotterdam*. http://worlddatabaseofhappiness.eur.nl (February 23, 2010).

6 David O'Connor and Christopher Faille, *Basic Economic Principles* (Westport, CT: Greenwood Press, 2000).

7 Dan Nystedt, "Wall Street Beat: iPad Spurs Technology Shares Forward," *PCWorld.com*, April 9, 2010. http://www.pcworld.com/article/193874/wall_street_beat_ipad_spurs_technology_shares_forward.html (April 11, 2010).

8 Zach Pontz, "A Year Later, Amazon's Kindle Finds a Niche, *CNN.com*, December 4, 2008. www.cnn.com/2008/TECH/12/03/kindle.electronic.reader/index.html (April 11, 2010).

9 "Microsoft Corporation," *Encyclopædia Britannica*. www.britannica.com/EBchecked/topic/380624/Microsoft-Corporation (May 12, 2008).

10 "The World Factbook: Country Comparison: GDP (Purchasing Power Parity)," *Central Intelligence Agency*. https://www.cia.gov/library/publications/the-world-factbook/rankorder/2001rank.html (March 29, 2010).

11 "Frequently Asked Questions, Question 6," *Bureau of Labor Statistics*. www.bls.gov/cpi/cpifaq.htm#Question_6 (April 12, 2010); "Frequently Asked Questions, Question 7," *Bureau of Labor Statistics*. www.bls.gov/cpi/cpifaq.htm#Question_7 (May 22, 2010).

12 "Table 1: Relative Importance of Components in the Consumer Price Indexes: U.S. City Average," December 2009. *Bureau of Labor Statistics*. www.bls.gov/cpi/cpiri2009.pdf (April 12, 2010).

13 Darryl Demos, "Understanding Productivity and the Workforce," *BNET.com*, April 2004. http://findarticles.com/p/articles/mi_qa3947/is_200404/ai_n9370350/ (March 31, 2010).

14 "Consumer Price Index 12-month Percent Change," *Bureau of Labor Statistics*. http://data.bls.gov/PDQ/servlet/SurveyOutputServlet (April 12, 2010).

15 "The U.S. Inflation Rate—1948–2007," *The U.S. Misery Index*, February 24, 2006. www.miseryindex.us/irbyyear.asp (March 31, 2010).

Chapter 3

1 "Ethics," *The American Heritage® Dictionary of the English Language*, 4th ed. (Boston: Houghton Mifflin Company, 2004). http://dictionary.reference.com/browse/ethics (April 24, 2010).

2 Ann Pomeroy, "The Ethics Squeeze," *HR Magazine*, March 2006, p. 53.

3 "Authentic Happiness," *University of Pennsylvania Positive Psychology Center*. www.authentichappiness.sas.upenn.edu/Default.aspx (May 22, 2010).

4 Renae Merle, "Boeing CEO Resigns over Affair with Subordinate," *Washington Post*, March 8, 2005. www.washingtonpost.com/wp-dyn/articles/A13173-2005Mar7.html?nav=rss_topnews (May 12, 2010).

5 Ann Pomeroy, "The Ethics Squeeze," p. 53.

6 Ibid.

7 Alyssa Abkowitz, "The Informant: I Thought I Was Bulletproof," *Fortune*, September 25, 2009. http://money.cnn.com/2009/09/24/news/companies/the_informant_mark_whitacre.fortune/index.htm (April 23, 2010).

8 "Philosophy," *Fetzer Vineyards*. www.fetzer.com/philosophy.aspx (April 23, 2010). Reprinted with permission of Brown-Forman Corporation.

9 *The Boston College Center for Corporate Citizenship*. www.bcccc.net (April 24, 2010).

10 Mark Young, "HR as the Guardian of Corporate Values at Cadbury Schweppes," *Strategic HR Review* 10 (Jan/Feb 2006), pp. 10–11.

11 "Indian Government Must Stop Refinery Expansion Until Human Rights Are Addressed," *Amnesty International*. www.amnesty.org/en/news-and-updates/report/vedanta (May 22, 2010).

12 Jennifer Alsever, "Chiquita Cleans Up Its Act," *Money.com*. http://money.cnn.com/magazines/business2/business2_archive/2006/08/01/8382241/index.htm (May 22, 2010).

13 Kate Connolly, "Brigitte, Germany's Most Popular Women's Mag, Bans Professional Models," *guardian.co.uk*, (October 9, 2009). www.guardian.co.uk/lifeandstyle/2009/oct/05/brigitte-german-magazine-bans-models

14 "Citations of Statistics Used in the Film," *BraveNew Films*. www.walmartmovie.com/facts.php (April 24, 2010).

15 "Who's Who," *The Corporation*. www.thecorporation.com/index.cfm?page_id=3 (April 24, 2010).

16 "Corporate Social Responsibility," *European Business Forum Ltd.*, Summer 2004. www.johnelkington.com/ebf_CSR_report.pdf (May 22, 2010).

17 "Chroma Wins Worldwide Award for Democracy in the Workplace," *Chroma Technology Group*. www.chroma.com/newsevents/articles/chroma-wins-worldwide-award-democracy-workplace (May 22, 2010).

18 "Being Their Own Bosses," *Chroma technology Group*. www.chroma.com/newsevents/articles/being-their-own-bosses (May 22, 2010).

19 "Citizenship," *Time Warner*. www.timewarner.com/corp/citizenship/index.html (April 26, 2010).

20 "Community Outreach," *Target.com*. http://sites.target.com/site/en/company/page.jsp?contentId=WCMP04-031700&ref=sr_shorturl_community (May 25, 2010).

21 "Global HIV/AIDS estimates, end of 2008," *Avert.org*. www.avert.org/worldstats.htm (May 22, 2010).

22 "HIV/AIDS, TB and Malaria," *DATA (debt AIDS trade Africa)*, http://www.one.org/blog/2010/04/22/africas-progress-in-fighting-malaria/ (April 24, 2010).

23 "Corporate Responsibility Report," *Intel*. www.intel.com/intel/corpresponsibility/awards.htm (May 22, 2010).

24 John Sparks, "Try Being Nice," *Newsweek*, June 26, 2006. www.newsweek.com/2006/06/25/try-being-nice.html; "About Us," *Kaplan Thaler Group*. www.kaplanthaler.com/#/about (May 22, 2010).

25 Ibid.

26 Val Lush, "Consumer Bill of Rights," *BookRags*. www.bookrags.com/research/consumer-bill-of-rights-ebf-01/ (April 24, 2010).

27 Josh Mitchell, "Transportation Department Announces Toyota Fine," *Wall Street Journal Online*, April 19, 2010. http://online.wsj.com/article/SB1000142405274870467190457519383391382400 8.html?mod=WSJ_latestheadlines (April 24, 2010).

28 "Companies in the News: Enron," *Corporate Social Responsibility News and Resources*, October 2, 2007. www.mallenbaker.net/csr/CSRfiles/enron.html (May 22, 2010).

29 "Ponzi Scheme," *Merriam-Webster Online*. www.merriam-webster.com/dictionary/ponzi%20scheme (May 22, 2010).

30 Debby Young, "Repairing a Damaged Reputation: How New CEOs Can Recover from a Corporate Scandal," *Encyclopedia.com*, June 1, 2005. http://www.encyclopedia.com/doc/1G1-133109212.html (May 22, 2010).

31 "GreenStop," *Topia Energy*. www.topiagreenstop.com/ (April 24, 2010).

32 "Malaria Prevention," *The Medical News*. www.news-medical .net/health/Malaria-Prevention.aspx (April 24, 2010).

33 Patrick Adams, "The Sanaria *PfSPZ* Malaria Vaccine, Until Recently Considered Impossible, Is Entering Phase II Trials," *TropIKA.net*, December 15, 2009. www.tropika.net/ svc/interview/Adams-20091216-Interview-Hoffman (April 25, 2010).

34 Steven Musil, "Week in Review: Google Slams China Censorship," *CNET.com*. http://news.cnet.com/ 8301-1001_3-10435702-92.html (May 22, 2010).

35 Ben Elgin and Bruce Einhorn, "Outrunning China's Web Cops," *BusinessWeek*, February 20, 2006. www.businessweek.com/magazine/content/06_08/b3972 061.htm?chan=search (May 22, 2010).

36 "Our Progress," *Interface, Inc.* www.interfaceglobal.com/ Sustainability/Sustainability-in-Action.aspx (May 22, 2010).

37 "What Is Sustainability?" *Interface, Inc.* www .interfacesustainability.com/whatis.html (May 22, 2010).

38 "Interface's Values Are Our Guiding Principles," *Interface, Inc.* www.interfaceglobal.com/Company/Mission-Vision/ Values.aspx (May 22, 2010).

39 "Groups," *Interface, Inc.* http://missionzero.org/groups (May 22, 2010).

40 Steven Musil, "Week in Review: Google Slams China Censorship."

41 "Being a Responsible Company," *Starbucks*. www .starbucks.com/responsibility (May 22, 2010).

42 Mark Young, (2006). "HR as the guardian of corporate values at Cadbury Schweppes", *Strategic HR Review*, Vol. 5 Iss: 2, pp. 10–11.

43 "Lockheed Martin Gray Matters Ethics Game," *e-businessethics.com*. www.e-businessethics.com/Game.htm (May 22, 2010).

44 "Employers Find Maintaining an Ethical Workplace Is Paramount, Especially in Tough Ethical Times," Business Wire, April 6, 2010, http://www.businesswire.com/ portal/site/home/permalink/?ndmViewId=news_view& newsId=20100406005609&newsLang=en

45 "Ethics Training in Law Enforcement," *International Association of Chiefs of Police*. www.theiacp.org/ PoliceServices/ExecutiveServices/ProfessionalAssistance/ Ethics/ReportsResources/EthicsTraininginLawEnforcement/ tabid/194/Default.aspx (April 25, 2010).

46 Megan Carpenter, "Judge Overturns Corporate Patent on Human DNA," *Washington Independent*. http:// washingtonindependent.com/80919/judge-overturns- corporate-patent-on-human-dna (May 22, 2010).

Chapter 4

1 "Remarks by the President to Vietnam National University," *Embassy of the United States, Hanoi, Vietnam*, November 17, 2000. http://vietnam.usembassy.gov/ pv11172000d.html/ (June 10, 2010).

2 "Top 10 Most Powerful People in the World," *Just Share This*. www.justsharethis.com/top-10-most-powerful- people-in-the-world/ (June 10, 2010). Reprinted with permission of Forbes Media LLC © 2010.

3 Charles W. L. Hill, *International Business: Competing in the Global Marketplace*, 8th ed. (Burr Ridge, IL: Irwin/McGraw- Hill Publishing Co., 2010), pp. 6–8.

4 Ibid.

5 Govindkrishna Seshan, "Fruit Punch," *Business Standard*, February 26, 2008. www.business-standard.com/india/ storypage.php?autono=314923 (June 10, 2010).

6 Charles W. L. Hill, *International Business: Competing in the Global Marketplace*, pp. 10–16.

7 "Tools for Trade and Trade Policy Analysis," *World Bank Institute*. www.unescap.org/tid/artnet/mtg/ gravity09_wed_ravi1.pdf (June 10, 2010).

8 Charles W. L. Hill, *International Business: Competing in the Global Marketplace*, pp. 18–24.

9 Patrick McGeehan, "Foreign Investment in City Is Growing, Report Finds," *MitchellMoss.com*. www.mitchellmoss.com/ mentions/NYTimes-27-June-08.pdf (June 10, 2010).

10 "A Massive Investment in Education to Give Queensland Kids a Flying Start," *mysunshinecoast.com.au*. www.mysunshinecoast.com.au/articles/article-display/ a-massive-investment-in-education-to-give-queensland- kids-a-flying-start,17463 (June 10, 2010).

11 "Promoting Entrepreneurialship," *Ministry of Trade and Industry*. www.regjeringen.no/en/dep/nhd/selected- topics/innovation/promoting- entrepreneurship.html?id=582899 (June 10, 2010).

12 "An Interview with Robert Reich," *92nd Street Young Men's and Young Women's Hebrew Association*, September 27, 2005. http://blog.92y.org/index.php/ weblog/item/robert_reich/ (June 10, 2010).

13 "Background Note: Cuba," *U.S. Department of State*. www.state.gov/r/pa/ei/bgn/2886.htm (June 13, 2010).

14 "The GATT Years: From Havana to Marrakesh," *World Trade Organization*. www.wto.org/english/thewto_e/ whatis_e/tif_e/fact4_e.htm (May 15, 2010).

15 "Understanding the WTO," *World Trade Organization*. www.wto.org/english/thewto_e/whatis_e/tif_e/tif_ e.htm (May 15, 2010).

16 "Doha Development Agenda: Negotiations, Implementation, and Development," *World Trade Organization*. www.wto.org/english/tratop_e/dda_e/ dda_e.htm (May 15, 2010).

17 "Rank Order: Exports," *CIA: The World Factbook*. https:// www.cia.gov/library/publications/the-world- factbook/rankorder/2078rank.html (May 15, 2010); "Rank Order: Imports," *CIA: The World Factbook*. https:// www.cia.gov/library/publications/the-world- factbook/rankorder/2087rank.html (May 15, 2010).

18 Matt Rosenberg, "Euro Countries," *About.com*. http:// geography.about.com/od/lists/a/euro.htm (June 10, 2010).

19 "Microsoft Loses Anti-Trust Appeal," *BBC News*, September 17, 2007. http://news.bbc.co.uk/1/hi/ business/6998272.stm; "Microsoft Hit by Record EU Fine," *BBC News*, March 24, 2004, http://news.bbc.co .uk/1/hi/business/3563697.stm (June 10, 2010).

20 Matt Rosenberg, "Euro Countries."

21 "About APEC," *Asian-Pacific Economic Cooperation*. www.apec.org/apec/about_apec.html (June 10, 2010).

22 "Subway Sandwiches Franchise Opportunity," *Franchise International*. www.franchise-international.net/show/ subway-sandwiches/198 (May 10, 2010).

23 "International Restaurants: A World of Opportunity," *Ruby Tuesday*. www.rubytuesday.com/franchise/intl-list (May 10, 2010).

24 "Disney Signs India Master," *Franchise International*. www.franchise-international.net/franchise/Walt- Disney-Company/Disney-signs-India-Master/1554 (June 10, 2010).

25 "Intellectual Property and Licensing," *SRI International*. www.sri.com/rd/hot.html (May 15, 2010).

26 "International Business," *Encyclopedia of Business,* 2nd ed. (Farmington Hills, MI: Thomas Gale, 2006). www.referenceforbusiness.com/management/Gr-Int/International-Business.html (June 10, 2010).

27 "FACTBOX: India retail attracts more foreign players," *Business Standard*, May 21, 2010. www.business-standard.com/india/news/factbox-india-retail-attracts-more-foreign-players/95092/ (June 10, 2010).

28 Anton Shilov, "Intel and Nokia Form Strategic Alliance," *Xbit Laboratories*. www.xbitlabs.com/news/mobile/display/20090623163122_Intel_and_Nokia_Form_Strategic_Alliance.html (May 11, 2010).

29 Tain-Jy Chen, "The Development of Taiwan's Personal Computer Industry," *Department of Economics, National Taiwan University, Chung-Hua Institution for Economic Research*, Working Paper Series Vol. 2002–15.

30 "Hyundai Is First Foreign Automaker to Install a Stamping Shop in Russia," *Infibeam.com*. http://news.infibeam.com/blog/news/2010/05/20/hyundai_is_first_foreign_automaker_to_install_a_stamping_shop_in_russia.html (June 10, 2010).

31 "Top 10 Countries with Which the U.S. Trades," *U.S. Census Bureau*. www.census.gov/foreign-trade/top/dst/current/balance.html (June 10, 2010).

32 "Sovereign Wealth Funds," *Council on Foreign Relations*. www.cfr.org/publication/15251/sovereign_wealth_funds.html (June 10, 2010).

33 Elena Logutenkova and Yalman Onaran, "Singapore, Abu Dhabi Face Losses on UBS, Citigroup (Update2)," *BusinessWeek*, March 2, 2010. www.businessweek.com/news/2010-03-02/singapore-abu-dhabi-face-10-billion-loss-on-ubs-citigroup.html.

34 C. G. Alex and Barbara Bowers, "The American Way to Countertrade," *BarterNews* 17 (1988). www.barternews.com/american_way.htm (June 10, 2010).

35 "Deaf Children Are Being Heard in Africa Thanks to SMS," *Textually.org*. www.textually.org/textually/archives/cat_mobile_phone_projects_third_world.htm (June 10, 2010).

36 "Cross Cultural Business Blunders," *Kwintessential*. www.kwintessential.co.uk/cultural-services/articles/crosscultural-blunders.html (May 15, 2010).

37 "Results of Poor Cross Cultural Awareness," *Kwintessential*. http://www.kwintessential.co.uk/cultural-services/articles/Results%20of%20Poor%20Cross%20Cultural%20Awareness.html (May 15, 2010).

38 Chris Taylor, "There's More Vacation Time on Tap for You," *CNN Money*, August 3, 2006. http://money.cnn.com/2006/08/03/technology/fbvacations0803.biz2/index.htm (June 10, 2010).

39 Ibid.

40 Ibid.

41 "Foreign Corrupt Practices Act," *U.S. Department of Justice*. www.justice.gov/criminal/fraud/fcpa/ (May 15, 2010).

Mini Chapter 1

1 Chris Anderson, "The Long Tail of Travel," *The Long Tail*. www.longtail.com (July 21, 2010).

2 "Welcome to eProcurement.ky.gov," *Kentucky eProcurement*. http://eprocurement.ky.gov/ (July 21, 2010).

3 "Welcome to TheMedica.com," *TheMedica.com*. www.themedica.com/ (July 21, 2010).

4 "B2B B2C Web Portals," *Dream Designers*. www.dreamdesigners.co.in/b2c-web-portals.html (July 21, 2010).

5 "Robert Purchese, "Eurogamer," http://www.eurogamer.net/articles/2010-10-18-steam-has-over-30-million-accounts, October 18, 2010. (November 15, 2010).

6 "What Online Sales Are Subject to Sales Tax?" AllBusiness.com. www.allbusiness.com/sales/internet-e-commerce/2652-1.html (July 21, 2010).

7 Ibid.

8 Chris Connolly and Peter van Dijk, "What Is E-Commerce Legal Infrastructure?," *Galexia*. www.galexia.com/public/research/articles/research_articles-pa04.html#Heading296 (July 21, 2010).

9 "Daily Policy Digest: Legal Jurisdiction over the Internet," *National Center for Policy Analysis*, April 29, 2003. www.ncpa.org/sub/dpd/index.php?Article_ID=5250 (July 21, 2010).

10 Julia Hanna, "Broadband: Remaking the Advertising Industry," *Harvard Business School, Working Knowledge*, September 17, 2007. http://hbswk.hbs.edu/item/5652.html (July 21, 2010).

11 "Apple Introduces iAds: "Mobile Ads with Emotion," Mashable.com. http://mashable.com/2010/04/08/apple-iads/ (July 21, 2010).

12 "Web 2.0," *Proquest Discovery Guides* www.csa.com/discoveryguides/scholarship/gloss.php (July 21, 2010).

13 Chris Lee, "'Alien' Bus-Stop Ads Create a Stir," *Los Angeles Times*, June 19, 2009. http://articles.latimes.com/2009/jun/19/entertainment/et-district19 (July 21, 2010).

14 "District 9," *The Internet Movie Database*. www.imdb.com/title/tt1136608/business (July 21, 2010).

15 "Safe Internet Banking," *Federal Deposit Insurance Corporation*, July 11, 2007. www.fdic.gov/BANK/INDIVIDUAL/ONLINE/SAFE.HTML (July 21, 2010).

16 "Adware," SearchCIO MidMarket.com. January 6, 2007. http://searchcio-midmarket.techtarget.com/sDefinition/0,id183_gci521293,00.html (July 21, 2010).

17 "Spyware," SearchSecurity.com. http://searchsecurity.techtarget.com/sDefinition/0,sid14_gci214518,00.html (July 21, 2010).

18 Rebecca Porter, "Who's Watching Your PC?" *Trial*, August 1, 2004. http://goliath.ecnext.com/coms2/gi_0199-107385/Who-s-watching-your-PC.html (July 21, 2010).

19 "Phishing," *OnGuard OnLine*. http://onguardonline.gov/phishing.html (July 21, 2010).

20 "Marketplace Safety Tips," *eBay*. http://pages.ebay.com/securitycenter/ (July 21, 2010).

Chapter 5

1 "Small Business Size Standards," *U.S. Small Business Administration*. www.sba.gov/services/contractingopportunities/sizestandardstopics/index.html (April 23, 2010).

2 "Statistics About Business Size (including Small Business) from the U.S. Census Bureau," *U.S. Census Bureau*. www.census.gov/epcd/www/smallbus.html (April 23, 2010).

3 "Table of Size Standards," *U.S. Small Business Administration*.

4 "Small Business by the Numbers," *National Small Business Association*. www.patsula.com/smallbusinessfacts/#sbgen (April 23, 2010).

5 Ibid.

6 Ibid.

7 "Small Business Resource Guide," *National Federation of Independent Business*. www.nfib.com/Portals/0/PDF/

AllUsers/IssuesElections/NFIB-Resource-Guide-111th-Congress.pdf (April 23, 2010).

8 "World Economic Outlook Database," *International Monetary Fund*, April 2010. http://www.imf.org/external/pubs/ft/weo/2010/01/weodata/index.aspx (April 23, 2010).

9 "Small Business by the Numbers," *National Small Business Association*.

10 "Select Countries," *International Monetary Fund*. www.imf.org/external/pubs/ft/weo/2010/01/weodata/weoselco.aspx?g=2001&sg=All+countries (April 20, 2010).

11 "Small Business by the Numbers," *National Small Business Association*.

12 "About Omnipod," *myomnipod.com*. www.myomnipod.com/ (April 23, 2010).

13 Keith Giard, "GM Bankruptcy Spells Disaster for Small Suppliers," *Washington Post*, May 28, 2009. http://allbusiness.washingtonpost.com/government/elections-politics-campaigns/12344120-1.html (April 23, 2010).

14 Thomas H. Klier and James M. Rubenstein, "The U.S. Auto Supplier Industry in Transition—The New Geography of Auto Production," *chicagofed.org*, May 2006. www.chicagofed.org/digital_assets/publications/chicago_fed_letter/2006/cflmay2006_226.pdf (April 23, 2010).

15 "Frequently Asked Questions," *Small Business Administration, Office of Advocacy*. www.sba.gov/advo/stats/sbfaq.pdf. (April 23, 2010).

16 Ibid.

17 "Economy: A Report to the President. *Small Business Administration, Office of Advocacy*. www.sba.gov/advo/research/sb_econ2009.pdf (April 20, 2010).

18 Ibid.

19 "Small Business Online," *entrepreneur.com*, www.entrepreneur.com/sbe/online/index.html (June 10, 2010).

20 Jason Del Rey, War Zone Start-up, *Inc. Magazine*, April 2010. www.inc.com/magazine/20100401/war-zone-start-up.html (April 24, 2010).

21 "The ASC Story," *animatedspeech.com*. www.animatedspeech.com/Story/story_founders.html (June 14, 2010).

22 Dan Tynan, "The 25 Worst Tech Products of All Time," *pcworld.com*, May 26, 2006. www.pcworld.com/article/id,125772-page,6/article.html (June 10, 2010).

23 "Bruce Freeman," *PROLine Communications, Inc.* www.prolinepr.com/html/bruce_freeman.html (June 10, 2010).

24 Jake Kilroy, "Wahoo's Has a Birthday Party (And I Get Invited)," *Entrepreneur Daily Dose*, February 27, 2009. http://blog.entrepreneur.com/2009/02/wahoos-has-a-birthday-party-and-i-get-invited.php (April 28, 2010).

25 "McDonald's Corp.," http://finance.yahoo.com/q/pr?s=MCD+Profile (June 10, 2010).

26 "Citizen Wayne—The Unauthorized Biography," *Miami New Times* 9, no. 33 (December 1–7, 1994). www.corporations.org/wmi/huizenga.html (June 10, 2010).

27 "Quotations from Famous Entrepreneurs on Entrepreneurship: Inspiring Words from the Best of the Best," *About.com*. http://entrepreneurs.about.com/od/famousentrepreneurs/a/quotations.htm (June 10, 2010).

28 "Henry Ford," *About.com*. http://inventors.about.com/library/inventors/blford.htm (June 10, 2010).

29 "Company," www.benjerry.com/company/ (June 10, 2010).

30 Adapted from Jack Kaplan and Anthony Warren, *Patterns of Entrepreneurship*, 2nd ed. (John Wiley & Sons, Inc.), p. 27; "The State of Small Business: A Report of the President,"

U.S. Small Business Administration (Washington, D.C.: U.S. Government Printing Office, 1995), p. 114.

31 Roger Fritz, "When Taking Business Risks Is Necessary," *San Francisco Business Times*, August 2, 1996. www.bizjournals.com/sanfrancisco/stories/1996/08/05/smallb2.html (June 10, 2010).

32 "Kennedy Featured in Daily Camera Business Plus Chat," *CEO Challenges*. www.ceochallenges.com/news/2008/02/29/kennedy-featured-daily-camera-business-plus-chat (June 10, 2010).

33 "Nimble and Quick: Entrepreneurs That Move, Adapt and Change Are Winners," *Nesheim OnLine*, February 3, 2010. http://nesheimgroup.typepad.com/my_weblog/2010/02/nimble-and-quick-entrepreneurs-that-move-adapt-and-change-are-winners.html (April 24, 2010).

34 "Pete's Wicked." www.petes.com/ (June 10, 2010).

35 "Lifestyle Entrepreneurs: RV-Based Businesses Can Be Going Concerns," *Entrepreneur.com*. www.entrepreneur.com/franchises/franchisezone/startupjournal/article64548.html (June 14, 2010).

36 "About Us," *LizzieLou Shoes*. http://lizzieloushoes.com/about_us.html (June 16, 2010).

37 "myYearbook Revenue at $20 Million Annually and Growing," *Mashable/Business*. http://mashable.com/2010/02/26/myyearbook-revenue/ (June 16, 2010).

38 John Case, "The Gazelle Theory," *Inc. Magazine*, May 2001. www.inc.com/magazine/20010515/22613.html (June 10, 2010).

39 "Creativity Overflowing," *Bloomberg Businessweek*. www.businessweek.com/magazine/content/06_19/b3983061.htm?chan=searchand (June 10, 2010).

40 "How Whirlpool Defines Innovation," *Bloomberg Businessweek*. www.businessweek.com/innovate/content/mar2006/id20060306_287425.htm?chan=search (June 10, 2010).

41 Jake Swearingen, "Great Intrapreneurs in Business History," *CBS Business Network*. www.bnet.com/2403-13070_23-196888.html?tag=content;col1 (April 24, 2010).

42 J. Gregory Dees, "The Meaning of Social Entrepreneurship, *Kauffman Foundation*. www.caseatduke.org/documents/dees_sedef.pdf (April 24, 2010).

43 "Meet the New Heroes: Mimi Silbert," *The New Heroes*. www.pbs.org/opb/thenewheroes/meet/silbert.html (April 24, 2010).

44 Ashley Jablow, "2010 Conference: The Business of Corporate Citizenship: Becoming a Social Intrapreneur," *Boston College Center for Corporate Citizenship*. http://blogs.bcccc.net/2010/04/the-business-of-corporate-citizenship-becoming-a-social-intrapreneur/ (April 24, 2010).

45 Josh Cleveland, "Creating a Company Culture That Engages Social Intrapreneurs," *GreenBiz.com*, June 29, 2009. www.greenbiz.com/blog/2009/06/29/creating-company-culture-engages-social-intrapreneurs (April 24, 2010).

46 Joel Holland, "Million-Dollar Partners," *Entrepreneur.com*, February 2010. www.entrepreneur.com/magazine/entrepreneur/2010/february/204718.html (June 14, 2010).

47 "Press Room," *Facebook*. www.facebook.com/#!/press/info.php?statistics (June 14, 2010).

48 "Big Bang! UC Davis Business Plan Competition," *University of California, Davis, Graduate School of Management*. http://bigbang.gsm.ucdavis.edu/ (April 25, 2010).

49 "Franchise Law: What Is a Franchise Business?" *freeadvice.com*, http://business-law.freeadvice.com/franchise_law/franchise_business.htm (April 25, 2010).

50 "2010 Franchise Business Economic Outlook," *PriceWaterhouseCoopers*. www.franchise.org/uploadedFiles/Franchise_Industry/Resources/Education_Foundation/2010%20Franchise%20Business%20Outlook%20Report_Final%202009.12.21.pdf (April 25, 2010).

51 Ibid.

52 Emily Weisburg, "101 Best Franchises to Run from Home," *Entrepreneur.com*, June 2009. www.entrepreneur.com/magazine/entrepreneur/2009/june/201848.html (June 16, 2010).

53 "Franchise Statistics for the European Union," *Franchise Europe*. www.franchiseeurope.com/top500/article/franchisestatisticsfortheeuropeanunion/4/ (April 25, 2010).

54 "2010 Low Cost Franchises," *Entrepreneur.com*. www.entrepreneur.com/franchises/lowcost/index.html (April 25, 2010).

55 "BDS Database List," *U.S. Census Bureau*. http://webserver03.ces.census.gov/index.php/bds/bds_database_list (April 25, 2010).

56 Stacy Perman, Jeffrey Gangemi, and Douglas MacMillan, "Entrepreneurs' Favorite Mistakes," *BusinessWeek*. http://images.businessweek.com/ss/06/09/favorite_mistake/index_01.htm (April 24, 2010).

57 Ibid.

58 *National Business Incubator Association*. www.nbia.org (June 16, 2010).

59 "About Us: History," *Subway.com*. www.subway.com/subwayroot/AboutSubway/history/subwayHistory.aspx (April 26, 2010).

60 "Financing Options for a Small Business: Finding the Right Funding," *StartupNation.com*. www.startupnation.com/articles/890/1/AT_FindingFundingThatsRight.asp (April 26, 2010).

Chapter 6

1 Nan Mooney, "When Good Friends Make Poor Colleagues," *Inc. Magazine*, September 2006. www.inc.com/resources/women/articles/20060901/nmooney.html/ (June 20, 2010).

2 The Devil's Dictionary, Ambrose Bierce, http://www.gutenberg.org/etext/972

3 "Tax Facts for Individuals—2010," *A/N Group Inc*. www.smbiz.com/sbrl001.html#pis10 (May 4, 2010).

4 Maureen Priest, personal phone interview by Mary Anne Poatsy, June 2008.

5 "Instructions for Form 2553," *Department of the Treasury, Internal Revenue Service*, December 2007. www.irs.gov/pub/irs-pdf/i2553.pdf (May 1, 2010).

6 "Our Story," *KaBoom!* http://kaboom.org/about_kaboom/our_story (June 22, 2010).

7 William P. Barrett, "America's 200 Largest Charities by Donations," *Forbes.com*, November 24, 2009. www.forbes.com/2009/11/22/americas-largest-charities-personal-finance-charity-09-nonprofits_land.html (June 22, 2010). Reprinted with permission of Forbes Media LLC © 2010.

8 "What Are Cooperatives?" *The Community Mercantile*. http://communitymercantile.com/whatis (June 22, 2010).

9 "About Co-ops," *National Cooperative Business Association*. www.ncba.coop/abcoop.cfm (June 20, 2010).

10 "Florida's Natural." www.floridasnatural.com/ (May 7, 2010).

11 Molly Feltner, "Delta Buys Northwest, Creating World's Largest Airline," *SmarterTravel.com*, April 15, 2008. www.smartertravel.com/blogs/today-in-travel/delta-buys-northwest-creating-world-largest-airline.html?id=2550074 (May 8, 2010).

12 Jack Henry Agrees to Buy iPay for $300M Cash, *Yahoo Finance*, May 7, 2010. http://finance.yahoo.com/news/Jack-Henry-agrees-to-buy-iPay-apf-998949144.html?x=0 (May 7, 2010).

13 Etan Viessing, "Lionsgate Rejects Icahn Tender Offer," *The Hollywood Reporter*. www.hollywoodreporter.com/hr/content_display/world/news/e3i8c42c2e07eaa0e3235cd79d5e0fbfeed (May 8, 2010.)

14 "Microsoft vs Yahoo—Hostile Take Over Explained," *Intology—Intelligent Technology News*, April 29, 2008. www.intology.com/business-finance/microsoft-vs-yahoo-hostile-take-over-explained/ (May 8, 2010).

15 Tim Arango, How the AOL-Time Warner Merger Went So Wrong, *New York Times*, January 10, 2010. www.nytimes.com/2010/01/11/business/media/11merger.html?pagewanted=1 (June 22, 2010).

16 Andrew Ross Sorkin and Duff Wilson, "Pfizer Agrees to Pay $68 Billion for Rival Drug Maker Wyeth," *New York Times*, January 25, 2009. www.nytimes.com/2009/01/26/business/26drug.html?_r=2; http://www.nytimes.com/2009/01/26/business/26drug.html (May 7, 2010).

17 Tim Arango, How the AOL-Time Warner Merger Went So Wrong, *New York Times*, January 10, 2010. www.nytimes.com/2010/01/11/business/media/11merger.html?pagewanted=1 (June 22, 2010).

18 Aaron Smith, "Time Warner to Split Off AOL," *CNNMoney.com*, May 28, 2009. http://money.cnn.com/2009/05/28/technology/timewarner_aol/?postversion=2009052809 (June 22, 2010).

19 "IBM Acquires the Business of iPhrase Systems, Inc.," *IBM*. www-03.ibm.com/press/us/en/pressrelease/7952.wss (May 8, 2010).

20 G. A. Marken, "Merger & Acquisition Wars Take No Prisoners," *Enterprise Networks & Servers*, May 2005. www.enterprisenetworksandservers.com/monthly/art.php?1457/ (June 20, 2010).

21 Susan Cartwright, Why Mergers Fail and How to Prevent It, *QFinance.com*. www.qfinance.com/mergers-and-acquisitions-best-practice/why-mergers-fail-and-how-to-prevent-it?page=1 (May 8, 2010).

22 Diane Mermigas, "Media Deal Roulette: Buy, Merge, or Fail Miserably," *Bnet.com*. http://industry.bnet.com/media/10007845/media-deal-roulette-buy-merge-fail/ (May 8, 2010).

23 "MySpace Loses $150 Million," *Xfm*. www.xfm.co.uk/news/2010/myspace-loses-150-million (May 8, 2010).

24 Diane Mermigas, "Media Deal Roulette: Buy, Merge, or Fail Miserably."

Mini Chapter 2

1 "Pizza Hut Inc.," *Funding Universe*. www.fundinguniverse.com/company-histories/Pizza-Hut-Inc-Company-History.html (July 22, 2010).

2 "Our History," *Pizza Hut Online*. www.pizzahut.co.uk/restaurants/our-history.aspx (May 21, 2008); David Gumpert, *How to Really Create a Successful Business Plan* (Inc. Publishing, 1990), p. 17.

3 Tim Berry, "Business Plan Contests Grow Up and Mean Business," *Bplans.com*. http://timberry.bplans.com/2010/04/business-plan-contests-growing-up-and-meaning-business.html (July 22, 2010).

4 "C-Crete Technologies Wins the MIT $100k Business Plan Contest," *$100K MIT Entrepreneurship Competition*. www.mit100k.org/home/mit-100k-finale-is-upon-us-may-12-7pm-kresge/ (July 22, 2010).

Chapter 7

1 "Vision," *Wikimedia Foundation*. http://wikimediafoundation.org/wiki/Vision (July 5, 2010).

2 Pete Johnson, "Best Vision Statement," *Nerd Guru*. http://blog.nerdguru.net/2008/09/25/best-vision-statement/ (July 5, 2010).

3 "About the American Cancer Society," *American Cancer Society*. www.cancer.org/AboutUs/WhoWeAre/acsmissionstatements (May 15, 2010).

4 Carter McNamara, "Strategic Planning (in Nonprofit or For-Profit Organizations)," *Free Management Library*. www.managementhelp.org/plan_dec/str_plan/str_plan.htm (May 15, 2010).

5 "Mass Layoff Statistics, *U.S. Department of Labor, Bureau of Labor Statistics*. www.bls.gov/mls/home.htm (May 15, 2010).

6 "Business Contingency Planning and Disaster Recovery Programs at Vanguard," *The Vanguard Group*. www.vanguard.com/pdf/ccri.pdf (May 15, 2010).

7 Frank Ostroff, *The Horizontal Organization* (Oxford: Oxford University Press, 1999), pp. 25–57 and pp. 102–150.

8 Thomas A. Stewart, "The Search for the Organization of Tomorrow," *Fortune*, May 18, 1992. http://money.cnn.com/magazines/fortune/fortune_archive/1992/05/18/76425/index.htm (July 5, 2010).

9 "Vineet Nayar's Scrapbook: In Search of New Leaders: Interview with Fox News," June 23, 2010. www.vineetnayar.com/interview-with-fox-news/ (July 5, 2010).

10 Vineet Nayar, "How I Did It: A Maverick CEO Explains How He Persuaded His Team to Leap into the Future," *Harvard Business Review*, June 2010. http://hbr.org/2010/06/how-i-did-it-a-maverick-ceo-explains-how-he-persuaded-his-team-to-leap-into-the-future/ar/1 (July 5, 2010).

11 "Pest Control Company Exterminates Business Problem," *Anchor Pest Control*. www.carchip.com/Product_Docs/CS_PestControl.pdf (July 5, 2010).

12 "Six Sigma: So Yesterday?" *Bloomberg Businessweek*. www.businessweek.com/magazine/content/07_24/b4038409.htm (July 5, 2010).

Chapter 8

1 Mihaly Csikszentmihalyi, *Flow* (New York: HarperCollins, 1990).

2 "Many Employees Would Fire Their Boss," *Gallup Management Journal*, October 11, 2007. http://gmj.gallup.com/content/28867/Many-Employees-Would-Fire-Their-Boss.aspx (July 7, 2010).

3 "SAS revenue jumps 2.2% to record $2.31 billion," *SAS Institute, Inc.* www.sas.com/news/preleases/2009financials.html (July 7, 2010).

4 "100 Best Companies to Work For," CNNMoney.com. http://money.cnn.com/magazines/fortune/bestcompanies/2010/snapshots/1.html (July 7, 2010).

5 Jim Goodnight and Richard Florida, "Managing for Creativity," *Harvard Business Review*, July 2005, pp. 124–131.

6 "The High Cost of Disengaged Employees," *Gallup Management Journal*, April 15, 2002. http://gmj.gallup.com/content/247/The-High-Cost-of-Disengaged-Employees.aspx (July 7, 2010).

7 Stratford Sherman and Anthony Rucci, "Bringing Sears into the New World," *CNNMoney.com*, October 13, 1997. http://money.cnn.com/magazines/fortune/fortune_archive/1997/10/13/232506/index.htm (July 7, 2010).

8 Nash Popovic, "What Really Motivates Us?" *BBC News*. http://news.bbc.co.uk/nolavconsole/ukfs_news/hi/newsid_4760000/newsid_4764500/nb_rm_4764545.stm (July 7, 2010).

9 "Strengths Based Performance Management," StrengthsManagement.com. www.strengthsmanagement.com (July 7, 2010).

10 Marcus Buckingham, *Now, Discover Your Strengths* (New York: Free Press, 2001).

11 Kristina A. Diekmann, Zoe I. Barsness, and Harris Sondak, "Uncertainty, Fairness Perceptions, and Job Satisfaction: A Field Study," *Social Justice Research* 17, no. 3 (September 2004), pp. 237–255.

12 Daniel Pink, *Drive* (New York: Riverhead Books, 2009).

13 "What Is Sociocracy: A New Power Structure for Ethical Governance," *Sociocracy in Action*. www.sociocracyinaction.ca/whatis.htm (July 7, 2010).

14 Friermuth, Donna, "Sociacracy and Consent," www.cohousing.org/cm/article/sociocracy (September 7, 2010).

15 Brian Robertson, "The Sociocratic Method," *Strategy+Business*, Autumn 2006. www.strategy-business.com/press/article/06314 (July 7, 2010).

16 Peter Drucker, "Quotation Details," *The Quotations Page*. http://quotationspage.com/quote/26536.html (July 7, 2010).

17 *Black Friday*, a 7-minute video on the *Toy Story* Blu-Ray DVD (July 5, 2010).

18 Tim Catts, "Nardelli: Driving Chrysler Off the Road?" *Bloomberg Businessweek*. www.businessweek.com/bwdaily/dnflash/content/aug2007/db2007086_385959.htm (July 7, 2010).

19 David Cho, Peter Whoriskey, and Amit R. Paley, "Pay Rule Led Chrysler to Spurn Loan, Agency Says," www.washingtonpost.com/wp-dyn/content/article/2009/04/20/AR2009042002156.html (July 7, 2010).

20 Jon Huntsman, *Winners Never Cheat: Everyday Values We Learned as Children (But May Have Forgotten)*. (Philadelphia: Wharton School Publishing, 2005).

21 "Social Responsibility," *Huntsman International LLC*. www.huntsman.com/eng/About_us/Social_responsibility/Social_responsibility/index.cfm?PageID=7426 (July 7, 2010).

22 James M. Kouzes and Barry Z. Posner, *The Leadership Challenge*, 4th ed. (San Francisco: Jossey-Bass, 2008).

23 Del Jones, "Does Height Equal Power? Some CEOs Say Yes," *USA Today*, July 17, 2007. www.usatoday.com/money/companies/management/2007-07-17-ceo-dominant-behavior_N.htm (July 7, 2010).

24 "Google Corporate Philosophy, *Google*. www.google.com/corporate/tenthings.html (May 15, 2010).

25 Venuri Siriwardane, "Zappos CEO adds happiness to corporate culture," *Zappos.com*. www.nj.com/business/index.ssf/2010/06/zappos_ceo_adds_happiness_to_c.html (July 7, 2010).

26 Ibid.

27 "Johnsonville Sausage, LLC Company Profile," *Yahoo! Finance*. http://biz.yahoo.com/ic/123/123091.html (July 7, 2010).

28 "Johnsonville Sausage Company Profile." LinkedIn.com. www.linkedin.com/companies/johnsonville-sausage.

29 Ralph Stayer, "How I Learned to Let My Workers Lead," *Johnsonville Foods, Inc.* www.wku.edu/∼hrtm/CFS-452/Readings/stayer.htm (July 7, 2010).

30 John R. Katzenbach and Douglas K. Smith, *The Wisdom of Teams* (Cambridge, Massachusetts: Harvard University Press, 1993).

31 "Six Teams That Changed the World," CNNMoney.com, May 31, 2006. http://money.cnn.com/2006/05/31/magazines/fortune/sixteams_greatteams_fortune_061206/index.htm (July 7, 2010).

32 "Teamwork Concept Questioned," *National Association of College Stores*, August 11, 2006. www.nacs.org/news/081106-teamwork.asp?id=cm (July 7, 2010).

33 Stephanie Armour, "Generation Y: They've Arrived at Work with a New Attitude," *USA Today*, November 6, 2005. www.usatoday.com/money/workplace/2005-11-06-gen-y_x.htm (July 7, 2010).

34 "What's Up with Gen Y?" *The News & Observer*, February 5, 2006. www.newsobserver.com/164/story/396500.html (July 7, 2010).

35 Anna Mulrine, "The Army Trains a Skeptics Corps to Battle Groupthink," *US News and World Report* 144, no. 15 (May 26, 2008), pp. 30–32.

36 "Six Teams That Changed the World," CNNMoney.com.

37 David Robertson and Per Hjuler, "Innovating a Turnaround at LEGO," *Harvard Business Review*, September 2009. http://hbr.org/2009/09/innovating-a-turnaround-at-lego/ar/1 (July 7, 2010).

38 J. S. Lurey and M. S. Raisinghani, "An Empirical Study of Best Practices in Virtual Teams," *Information & Management*, 38, no. 8, 2001, pp. 523–544.

39 Stephen R. Covey, *The 7 Habits of Highly Effective People* (New York: Free Press, 1989).

Chapter 9

1 "About Us," *LinkedIn.com*. http://press.linkedin.com/about (June 14, 2010).

2 Lou Adler, "Hiring and Recruiting Challenges Survey 2008 Preliminary Results," *ere.net*. www.ere.net/2007/11/09/hiring-and-recruiting-challenges-survey-2008-preliminary-results/ (June 14, 2010).

3 Michelle V. Rafter, "Unicru Breaks Through in the Science of "Smart Hiring," *Workforce Management* 84, no. 5 (May 2005), pp. 76–78.

4 Stephane Thiffeault, "Poor Reference Check Results in Damages," *McMillian Binch Mendelsohn*: *Employment & Labour Relations Bulletin*, February 2006. www.mcmillan.ca/Upload/Publication/Poor%20Reference%20Check_0106.pdf (June 14, 2010).

5 "About EEOC," *U.S. Equal Employment Opportunity Commission*. www.eeoc.gov/eeoc/ (June 14, 2010).

6 "Facts About the Americans with Disabilities Act," *U.S. Equal Employment Opportunity Commission*. www.eeoc.gov/facts/fs-ada.html (June 14, 2010).

7 "Age Discrimination" *U.S. Equal Employment Opportunity Commission*. www.eeoc.gov/laws/types/age.cfm (June 14, 2010).

8 Carter McNamara, "Employee Training and Development: Reasons and Benefits," *Authenticity Consulting, LLC*. www.managementhelp.org/trng_dev/basics/reasons.htm (June 14, 2010).

9 "Nuclear Pharmacy Opportunities with Cardinal Health," *RXInsider*. www.allpharmacyjobs.com/nuclear_pharmacy_cardinal_health_nuclear.htm (July 12, 2010).

10 "Stone City—Cold Stone Creamery," *Persuasive Games LLC*. www.persuasivegames.com/games/game.aspx?game=coldstone (May 5, 2008); "On the Job Video Gaming," *Bloomberg Businessweek*, March 27, 2006. www

.businessweek.com/magazine/content/06_13/b3977062.htm (May 5, 2008).

11 "Application Story: Pulse Inc.," *WiredRed Software*. www.nefsis.com/pdf/appstory_pulse.pdf (July 12, 2010).

12 Karen O'Leonard, "Performance Support Systems," *Bersin & Associates*, February 2005.

13 "Organizational Learning Strategies: Action Learning," *Human Resource Development Council*. www.humtech.com/opm/grtl/ols/ols2.cfm (June 14, 2010).

14 "McDonald's U.S. Training Curriculum Awarded 46 College Credit Recommendations," *McDonald's*. http://www.thefreelibrary.com/McDonald's+U.S.+Training+Curriculum+Awarded+46+College+Credit...a01389904491 (June 14, 2010).

15 Kate Hafner, "Google Options Make Masseuse a Multimillionaire," *New York Times*, November 12, 2007. www.nytimes.com/2007/11/12/technology/12google.html?pagewanted=1 (July 12, 2010).

16 John D. Menke and Dickson C. Buxton, "The Origin and History of the ESOP and Its Future Role as a Business Succession Tool," *Journal of Financial Service* Professionals, May 2010, p. 61. http://www.menke.com/esop-information/articles/pdf/origin-history-of-esops.pdf (July 12, 2010).

17 "Best Places to Work in IT—Turnover Chart," *Computerworld.com*. www.computerworld.com/html/research/bestplaces/2006/bpchart_05_itturnover.html#region (June 14, 2010).

18 "The Domestic Partnership Benefits and Obligations Act," *Human Rights Campaign*. www.hrc.org/issues/marriage/5662.htm (June 14, 2010).

19 "Google to Reimburse Tax on Domestic Partner Benefits," *Workforce Management*, July 2, 2010. www.workforce.com/section/00/article/27/25/18.php (July 12, 2010).

20 "Phoenix Enhances Employee Benefits with Paid Paternity Leave, Increased Adoption Assistance," *AllBusiness.com*, April 17, 2007. www.allbusiness.com/services/business-services/4319890-1.html (July 12, 2010).

21 "Flex-Time Workers Add Two Days to Their Workweek," *GreenBiz.com*, June 4, 2010. www.greenbiz.com/news/2010/06/04/flex-time-workers-add-two-days-their-workweek (July 12, 2010).

22 "Cisco's Telecommuting Program Boosts Productivity, Cuts Costs and Emissions," *GreenBiz.com*, June 26, 2009. www.greenbiz.com/news/2009/06/26/ciscos-telecommuting-program-boosts-productivity-cuts-costs-and-emissions?src=int (July 12, 2010).

23 "Contingent and Alternative Employment Arrangements, February 2005," U.S. Bureau of Labor Statistics," www.bls.gov/news.release/conemp.nr0.htm (July 12, 2010).

24 Alexandra Topping, "Disabled Worker Wins Case for Wrongful Dismissal Against Abercrombie & Fitch," *Guardian News and Media Limited*, August 13, 2009. www.guardian.co.uk/money/2009/aug/13/abercrombie-fitch-employee-case-damages (July 12, 2010).

25 "Work Trends: Americans' Attitudes About Work, Employers, and Government," *John J. Heldrich Center for Workforce Development, Rutgers University*. www.heldrich.rutgers.edu/sites/default/files/content/WT16_Press_Release.pdf (June 14, 2010).

26 Alam Ohnsman, "Toyota Plans Worker Buyouts, North America Pay Freeze," *Bloomberg*, February 13, 2009. www.bloomberg.com/apps/news?pid=newsarchive&sid=aU._yz1sSTP4&refer=home (July 12, 2010).

27 Carol Hymowitz, "Diversity in a Global Economy—Ways Some Firms Get It Right," *Wall Street Journal*, November 16,

2005. http://jobsinghana.com/resources/?view=198&more=106.

28 Robert Rodriguez, "Diversity Finds Its Place: More Organizations Are Dedicating Senior-Level Executives to Drive Diversity Initiatives for Bottom-Line Effect," *HR Magazine*, August 1, 2006. http:// findarticles.com/p/articles/mi_m3495/is_8_51/ai_n26968947/

29 Lisa Takeuchi Cullen, "Employee Diversity Training Doesn't Work," *Time*, April 26, 2007. www.time.com/time/magazine/article/0,9171,1615183,00.html (June 14, 2010).

30 Dave McNary, "WGA Goes on Strike: Marathon Negotiations End in Impasse," *Variety.com*. www.variety.com/article/VR1117975364.html?categoryid=2821&cs=1 (June 14, 2010).

31 "Union Members Summary, *U.S. Bureau of Labor and Statistics*, January 25, 2007, www.bls.gov/news.release/union2.nr0.htm (June 14, 2010).

32 "Strike Taking Serious Toll on LA Economy," *NPR*, December 18, 2007. www.npr.org/templates/story/story.php?storyId=17354809&ps=rs (July 12, 2010).

33 HR World Editors, "30 Interview Questions You Can't Ask and 30 Sneaky, Legal Alternatives to Get the Same Info," *HRWorld.com*, November 15, 2007. www.hrworld.com/features/30-interview-questions-111507/ (June 14, 2010).

Chapter 10

1 Karen Gottlieb, "Using Court Record Information for Marketing in the United States: It's Public Information, What's the Problem?" *Privacy Rights Clearinghouse*, January 2004. www.privacyrights.org/ar/courtmarketing.htm (July 13, 2010).

2 "Cognos Supply Chain Analytics," *IBM*. www-01.ibm.com/software/data/cognos/products/performance-applications/supply-chain-analytics/capabilities.html (June 20, 2010).

3 Mark Gentile, "Seven Principles for Effectively Managing Mobile Devices," http://advice.cio.com/mark_gentile/10480/seven_principles_for_effectively_managing_mobile_devices (July 13, 2010).

4 Michael Cocanower, "Going Digital Saves Medical Practice Money, Improves Patient Care," *PC World*, June 4, 2010, www.pcworld.com/businesscenter/article/197951/going_digital_saves_medical_practice_money_improves_patient_care.html (July 13, 2010).

5 "Communities," *Internet2*. http://apps.internet2.edu/showcase-archive.html (June 20, 2010).

6 Susan Heathfield, "Listen with Your Eyes: Tips for Understanding Nonverbal Communication," *About.com*. http://humanresources.about.com/od/interpersonalcommunicatio1/a/nonverbal_com.htm (June 20, 2010).

7 "Electronic Eavesdropping," *Encyclopædia Britannica*. www.britannica.com/EBchecked/topic/183788/electronic-eavesdropping (June 20, 2010).

8 D. DiTecco, G. Cwitco, A. Arsenault, and M. Andre, "Operator Stress and Monitoring Practices," *Applied Ergonomics* 23, no. 1 (February 1992), pp. 29–34.

9 "About Us," *wikiLeaks.org*. www.wikileaks.org/wiki/WikiLeaks:About.

10 Megan Chuchmach, "WikiLeaks Preparing to Release Video of Alleged U.S. 'Massacre' in Afghanistan," *ABC News*. http://abcnews.go.com/Blotter/wikileaks-preparing-release-video-alleged-us-massacre-afghanistan/story?id=10954929 (July 13, 2010).

11 Dan Nakaso, "$1 Tickets Crash Airline's Website," *USA Today*, June 12, 2007. www.usatoday.com/travel/flights/2007-06-12-one-dollar-tickets-crash-web_N.htm (July 13, 2010).

12 Andy McCue, "IT Failure Remains Top Cause of Business Disaster," *Silicon.com*, March 11, 2005. http://hardware.silicon.com/storage/0,39024649,39128617,00.htm (July 13, 2010).

13 Tim Elfrink, "The Biggest Identity Theft Case Ever. Right Here in Miami," *Hack Pack*. www.miaminewtimes.com/content/printVersion/2270696 (July 13, 2010).

14 Ben Worthen, "Mid-Market: The Big Upgrade to Microsoft Vista," *CIO.com*, November 16, 2006. www.cio.com/article/26664/Mid_Market_The_Big_Upgrade_to_Microsoft_Vista (July 13, 2010).

15 "Yahoo! Advertising," *Yahoo!* http://advertising.yahoo.com/advertisers/whyyahoo#Homepage (July 13, 2010).

16 Paul Sloan, "The Quest for the Perfect Online Ad," *CNNMoney.com*, April 3, 2007. http://money.cnn.com/magazines/business2/business2_archive/2007/03/01/8401043/index.htm (July 13, 2010).

17 Jim Jubak, "A 15% Raise? Try China or India," *MSNmoney*, January 5, 2007. http://articles.moneycentral.msn.com/Investing/JubaksJournal/A15RaiseTryChinaOrIndia.aspx (July 13, 2010).

18 "Offshore Outsourcing Basics," *E-business Strategies, Inc.* www.ebstrategy.com/outsourcing/basics/faq.htm (July 13, 2010).

19 David Barboza, "As China's Wages Rise, Export Prices Could Follow," *New York Times*, June 7, 2010. www.nytimes.com/2010/06/08/business/global/08wages.html?_r=2 (July 13, 2010).

20 "GM Unveils EN-V Concept: A Vision for Future Urban Mobility," *General Motors*. http://media.gm.com/content/media/us/en/news/news_detail.brand_gm.html/content/Pages/news/us/en/2010/Mar/0324_env (July 13, 2010).

21 Justin Fox, "Where Your Job Is Going," *Fortune*, November 24, 2003. http://money.cnn.com/magazines/fortune/fortune_archive/2003/11/24/353752/index.htm (July 13, 2010).

22 Jack Marshall, "Budweiser's Global World Cup Campaign Rooted in Social Media," *ClickZ.com*. www.clickz.com/3640608 (July 13, 2010).

23 Christopher S. Rugaber, "US Companies Slam China's Innovation Policies." *ABC News*, June 15, 2010. http://abcnews.go.com/Business/wireStory?id=10923064 (July 13, 2010).

24 Fara Warner, "Made in China," *fastcompany.com*, April 2007. www.fastcompany.com/magazine/114/open_features-made-in-china.html (July 13, 2010).

25 Jay Walker, "The World's English Mania," *TED Conferences LLC*. February 2009. www.ted.com/talks/jay_walker_on_the_world_s_english_mania.html (July 13, 2010).

26 Prenksy, M. (2001a). Digital Natives, Digital Immigrants. *On the Horizon*, 9(5). http://www.marcprensky.com/writing/Prensky%20-%20Digital%20Natives,%20Digital%20Immigrants%20-%20Part1.pdf

27 Digital Nation—Life on the Virtual Frontier: Rewiring Young Brains. *PBS Frontline*. www.pbs.org/wgbh/pages/frontline/digitalnation/living-faster/digital-natives/rewiring-young-brains.html

Chapter 11

1 Employed Persons by Detailed Industry, Sex, Race, and Hispanic or Latino Ethnicity," *U.S. Bureau of Labor*

Statistics. ftp://ftp.bls.gov/pub/special.requests/lf/aat18 .txt (May 16, 2010).

2 "Table 1.1.5: Gross Domestic Product," *Bureau of Economic Activity*, April 30, 2010. http://bea.gov/national/ nipaweb/TableView.asp?SelectedTable=5&FirstYear=2009 &LastYear=2010&Freq=Qtr (May 16, 2010).

3 "Workplace Trends," *U.S. Bureau of Labor Statistics*. www .bls.gov/iag/tgs/iag07.htm#workplace_trends (July 15, 2010).

4 Douglas B. Cleveland, "The Role of Services in the Modern U.S. Economy," *U.S. Department of Commerce*. http://trade .gov/td/sif/PDF/ROLSERV199.PDF (July 15, 2010).

5 "The World Factbook," *Central Intelligence Agency*. https:// www.cia.gov/library/publications/the-world-factbook/ geos/us.html (May 15, 2010).

6 Ibid.

7 Ibid.

8 Karen E. Klein, "Finding the Perfect Location," *Bloomberg Businessweek*, March 24, 2008. www.businessweek.com/ smallbiz/content/mar2008/sb20080324_098559.htm (July 13, 2010).

9 "Johnny's Lunch Menu," *Johnny's Lunch Franchise LLC*. www.johnnyslunch.com/index.php?act=menu (July 13, 2010).

10 Tim Feemster, "A Step-by-Step Guide to Choosing the Right Site," *Area Development Online*, November 2007. www.areadevelopment.com/Print/siteSelection/nov07/ stepByStep.shtml (July 15, 2010).

11 "Tata Steel Ranked World's Best Steel Maker by World Steel Dynamics," *Tata*, June 22, 2005. www.tata.com/ media/releases/inside.aspx?artid=nAIH2iibp8Q= (July 15, 2010).

12 "Business Produce Hazardous Waste," *Local Hazardous Waste Management Program in King County*. www.lhwmp .org/home/BHW/index.aspx (July 15, 2010).

13 "Business Hazardous Waste Disposal," *Pinellas County, Florida*. www.pinellascounty.org/utilities/business-waste .htm (July 13, 2010).

14 Paul Graham, "How to Be Silicon Valley," *paulgraham.com*, May 2006. www.paulgraham.com/siliconvalley.html (July 15, 2010).

15 N. Shivapriya, "India Remains World's Top Outsourcing Destination," *Bloomberg Businessweek*, July 10, 2009. www .businessweek.com/globalbiz/content/jul2009/ gb20090710_974200.htm (May 16, 2010).

16 Annie Tasker, Teva Offering to Tame Area Traffic Concerns, *Courier Times*, July 8, 2010. www.phillyburbs .com/news/local/courier_times/courier_times_news_ details/article/28/2010/july/08/teva-offering-to-tame- area-traffic-concerns.html (July 13, 2010).

17 "Florida Building a Biotech Hub: Importing Silicon Valley?" *The Academic Entrepreneur*, February 28, 2010. http://academicentrepreneur.wordpress.com/2010/02/ 28/florida-building-a-biotech-hub-importing-silicon- valley/ (May 17, 2010).

18 Jennifer C. Kerr, Mattel Fined $2.3M for Lead Paint on Toys, *USA Today*, June 5, 2009. www.usatoday.com/ money/industries/retail/2009-06-05-mattel-fine_N.htm (May 17, 2010).

19 "The IKEA Range," *Inter IKEA Systems B.V.* http:// franchisor.ikea.com/showContent.asp?swfId=range3 (July 15, 2010).

20 "Automation," *Encyclopædia Britannica*, www.britannica .com/eb/article-24854/automation (July 15, 2010).

21 Christopher W. Hart, "Create Competitive Advantages Through Mass Customization," www.spiregroup.biz/

pdfs/06-04-07%20Creating%20Competitive%20 Advantage%20through%20Mass%20Customization.pdf (July 15, 2010).

22 "Robot," *Merriam-Webster Online Dictionary*. www .merriam-webster.com/dictionary/robot (May 13, 2010).

23 David Kucera, "Computer-Aided Design (CAD) and Computer-Aided Manufacturing (CAM)," *Encyclopedia of Business*, 2nd ed. www.referenceforbusiness.com/ encyclopedia/Clo-Con/Computer-Aided-Design-CAD- and-Computer-Aided-Manufacturing-CAM.html (July 15, 2010).

24 Ibid.

25 Tim Mullaney, "An IPO That Might Print You Some Money," *BusinessWeek.com*, November 9, 2005. www.businessweek.com/the_thread/dealflow/archives/ 2005/11/vistaprint.html?chan=search (July 15, 2010).

26 "Customer-Made," trendwatching.com. http:// trendwatching.com/trends/CUSTOMER-MADE.htm (July 15, 2010).

27 "Inventory Control," *SCORE (Counselors to America's Small Business)*. www.ct-clic.com/Newsletters/customer-files/ inventory0602.pdf (July 15, 2010).

28 Jonathan Bymes, "Dell Manages Profitability, Not Inventory," *Working Knowledge for Business Leaders, Harvard Business School*. http://hbswk.hbs.edu/archive/3497.html (July 15, 2010).

29 "What Is ERP?" *techFAQ*. www.tech-faq.com/erp.html (July 15, 2010).

30 "The History of Quality—Overview," *American Society for Quality*. www.asq.org/learn-about-quality/history-of- quality/overview/overview.html (July 15, 2010).

31 "The History of Quality—Total Quality," *American Society for Quality*. www.asq.org/learn-about-quality/history-of- quality/overview/total-quality.html (July 15, 2010).

32 "Quality Quotes," *Quality and Process Improvement Special Interest Group, Society for Technical Communication*. www .stcsig.org/quality/q_quotes.htm (July 15, 2010).

33 "Continuous Improvement," *American Society for Quality*. www.asq.org/learn-about-quality/continuous- improvement/overview/overview.html (July 15, 2010).

34 "Motorola University: Six Sigma in Action," *Motorola, Inc.* www.motorola.com/Business/US-EN/Motorola+ University (July 15, 2010).

35 Roger O. Crocket and Jena McGregor, "Six Sigma Still Pays Off at Motorola," *Bloomberg Businessweek*, December 4, 2006. www.businessweek.com/magazine/content/06_49/ b4012069.htm (July 15, 2010).

36 "ISO Standards," *International Organization for Standardization*. www.iso.org/iso/iso_catalogue.htm (May 21, 2010).

37 "Discover ISO: ISO's Mame," *International Organization for Standardization*. www.iso.org/iso/about/discover-iso_isos- name.htm (May 15, 2010).

38 Stanley Fielding, "ISO 14001 Brings Change and Delivers Profits," *Quality Digest*. www.qualitydigest.com/nov00/ html/iso14000.html (May 21, 2010).

Mini Chapter 3

1 Edward G. Wertheim, "The Importance of Effective Communication," *Northeastern University, College of Business Administration*. http://windward.hawaii.edu/ facstaff/dagrossa-p/ssci193v/articles/ EffectiveCommunication.pdf (July 22, 2010).

2 Alan Chapman, "Mehrabian's Communication Research," *Businessnalls.com*. www.businessballs.com/ mehrabiancommunications.htm (July 22, 2010).

3 "E-mail Privacy," Nolo.com. www.nolo.com/legal-encyclopedia/article-29610.html (July 22, 2010).

4 Eric Horng, "No-E-mail Fridays Transform Office," *ABC News*, April 7, 2007. http://abcnews.go.com/WNT/Story?id=2939232&page=1 (July 22, 2010).

5 Evan Hansen, "Google Blogger: 'I Was Terminated,'" *CNET News.com*, February 11, 2005. http://news.cnet.com/Google-blogger-I-was-terminated/2100-1038_3-5572936.html (July 22, 2010).

6 John D. Sutter, "The Coming-Out Stories of Anonymous Bloggers," *CNN.com*. www.cnn.com/2009/TECH/08/21/outing.anonymous.bloggers/ (July 22, 2010).

7 "1 in 3 Fortune 500 Companies Have Branded Twitter Profiles," *Corporate Eye*. www.corporate-eye.com/blog/2010/03/1-in-3-fortune-500-companies-have-branded-twitter-profiles/ (July 22, 2010).

8 Ibid.

Chapter 12

1 "About Ford," *Ford Motor Company*. www.ford.com/about-ford/heritage/vehicles (May 28, 2010).

2 "Marketing," *American Marketing Association Online Dictionary*. www.marketingpower.com/_layouts/Dictionary.aspx?dLetter=M (July 16, 2010).

3 "Henry Ford Quotes," *Brainy Quotes*. www.brainyquote.com/quotes/quotes/h/henryford109833.html.

4 From General Electric 1952 Annual Report, p. 21, as quoted in Rom Zemke and John A. Woods, *Best Practices in Customer Service* (Amherst, MA: HRD Press, 1998), p. 3.

5 Nature's Way to Beautiful," *The Body Shop*. www.thebodyshop-usa.com/beauty/about-us?cm_re=Tyra_NutriganicsB2G1_Anon-_-Navigation-_-about+us (May 27, 2010).

6 "Historic Campaigns," *Ad Council*. www.adcouncil.org/default.aspx?id=61 (May 28, 2010).

7 *Ad Council*. www.mavericksatwork.com/?p=139 (July 16, 2010).

8 www.imdb.com/name/nm0095588/biol (July 16, 2010).

9 *L.L. Bean*. www.llbean.com/ (July 16, 2010).

10 Jonny Lieberman, "MyFord Touch Proves That the Shape of Things to Come Is Awesome," *autoblog*. www.autoblog.com/2010/01/07/myford-touch-proves-that-the-shape-of-things-to-come-is-awesome/ (July 16, 2010).

11 Jim Motavalli, "Surfing the Web in the Car," *Forbes.com*. www.forbes.com/2010/04/13/web-browsing-wifi-technology-security-10-autos.html (May 30, 2010).

12 Stuart Elliot, "Tropicana Discovers Some Buyers Are Passionate About Packaging," *New York Times*. www.nytimes.com/2009/02/23/business/media/23adcol.html (May 30, 2010).

13 Barb Dybwad, "10 of the Best Social Media Tools for Entrepreneurs," *Mashable.com*. http://mashable.com/2009/10/26/socia-media-entrepreneurs/, accessed May 29, 2010. Reprinted with permission of Mashable.com: Masha-ble.com http://mashable.com/2009/10/26/social-media-entrepreneurs/

14 Charles W. Lamb, Jr., Joseph F. Hair, and Carl McDaniel, *Marketing*, 7th ed. (Stamford, CT: Thomson Publishing Company, 2004), p. 33.

15 *John Deere*. www.deere.com (July 16, 2010).

16 *High Beam Research*. www.omniglot.com/language/articles/spanishtranslation.htm (July 16, 2010).

17 John Helyar, "Harley-Davidson: Will Harley-Davidson Hit the Wall?" *Fortune*. www.mutualofamerica.com/articles/Fortune/2002_08_01/fortune.asp (July 16, 2010).

18 "Rankings," *U.S. News and World Report*. www.usnews.com/sections/rankings (July 16, 2010).

19 Philip Kotler and Gary Armstrong, *Principles of Marketing*, 12th ed. (Upper Saddle River, NJ: Pearson/Prentice Hall, 2008), pp. 131–147.

20 "Sales Savvy Series for Women Entrepreneurs: #6—Gender Differences in Buying Habits," *Women's Enterprise Centre*. www.womensenterprise.ca/enews/articles/Microsoft%20Word%20-%206%20-%20Gender%20Differences%20_2_.pdf (May 31, 2010).

Chapter 13

1 "Most Frequently Asked Questions," *SC Johnson and Son, Inc.* www.oust.com/faq.aspx?oust=airSanitizer (May 14, 2007).

2 "Home Energy," *American Honda Motor Co.* http://corporate.honda.com/environment/home-energy/ (June 7, 2010).

3 "Growth, Leadership, Sustainability," *The Coca-Cola Company*. www.thecoca-colacompany.com/ourcompany/index.html (June 7, 2010).

4 "Product List," *The Coca-Cola Company*. www.thecoca-colacompany.com/brands/brandlist.html (June 7, 2010).

5 "Imagination at Work," *General Electric*. www.ge.com/ (June 7, 2010).

6 Theresa Howard, "Coke Finally Scores Another Winner," *USA Today*, October 28, 2007. www.usatoday.com/money/advertising/adtrack/2007-10-28-coke-zero_N.htm (June 7, 2010).

7 "Our Brands," *Kraft Foods Inc.* www.kraftfoodscompany.com/brands/Pages/index.aspx (June 7, 2010).

8 "The NRF Top 100 Retailers Are Private Brand Stars," *My Private Brand*, July 1, 2010. http://mypbrand.com/2010/07/01/the-nrf-top-100-retailers-are-private-brand-stars/ (July 18, 2010). Copyrighted 2010 NRF Enterprises Inc. 69694-12mcd.

9 Tom Peters, The Brand Called You, *Fast* Company, August 31, 1997. www.fastcompany.com/magazine/10/brandyou.html (July 17, 2010).

10 "The Tiffany Story," Tiffany & Co. www.tiffany.com/About/Default.aspx (July 18, 2010).

11 Harsh Paul, "Puma Gives Up Wasteful Packaging in Favor of Eco-friendly Packages," *Greenpacks.org*, April 13, 2010, www.greenpacks.org/2010/04/13/puma-gives-up-wasteful-packaging-in-favor-of-eco-friendly-packages/ (July 18, 2010).

12 Jennifer W. Miner, "Green Luxury Packages at Fairmont," suite101.com, February 7, 2008. http://luxuryresorttravel.suite101.com/article.cfm/green_luxury_packages_at_fairmont (July 18, 2010).

13 "FDA Takes Issue with Cheerios Health Claims," *MSNBC*, May 13, 2009. www.msnbc.msn.com/id/30701291/ (July 18, 2010).

14 "Shaping Retail: The Use of Virtual Store Simulations in Marketing Research and Beyond," *In-Store Marketing Institute/Advertising Research Foundation/Kelly School of Business* (Indiana University). www.kelley.iu.edu/CERR/files/09ISMI_virtualretailing.pdf (July 17, 2010).

15 Michael E. Ross, "It Seemed Like a Good Idea at the Time," *MSNBC*, April 22, 2005. www.msnbc.msn.com/id/7209828 (July 18, 2010).

16 Robert E. Cannon, "A Tutorial on Product Life Cycle," www.mrotoday.com/progressive/online%20exclusives/productlifecycle.htm (July 18, 2010).

17 Dan Swenson, Shahid Ansari, Jan Bell, and Il-Woon Kim, "Best Practices in Target Costing," *Management Accounting Quarterly*, Winter 2003, p. 13.

18 Vivian Wai-yin Kwok, "Virgin Blue Set to Challenge Qantas in Trans-Pacific Air Fight," *Forbes.com.* March 31, 2008. www.forbes.com/2008/03/31/virgin-australia-qantas-markets-equity-cx_vk_0331markets02_print.html (July 18, 2010).

19 "What They're Saying: Airline Competition Leads to Lower Fares," *U.S. Department of Transportation.* www.dot.gov/affairs/aviation080516/what_are_they_saying.htm (July 18, 2010).

Chapter 14

1 "America's Cleaning Icon Launches Integrated Marketing Campaign," *Marketwire*, May 25, 2010. www.marketwire.com/press-release/Americas-Cleaning-Icon-Launches-Integrated-Marketing-Campaign-1265555.htm (July 19, 2010).

2 Juliana Gruenwald, "Google Report Claims Wide Economic Benefits," *The Daily Dose*, May 25, 2010. http://techdailydose.nationaljournal.com/2010/05/google-report-claims-wide-econ.php (June 20, 2010).

3 "Trust, Value and Engagement in Advertising," *Nielsen Global Online Consumer Survey*, July 2009. http://blog.nielsen.com/nielsenwire/wp-content/uploads/2009/07/trustinadvertising0709.pdf (July 19, 2010).

4 "7 Awesomely Amazing Examples of Success Through YouTube," *Social Maximizer*, June 3, 2010. http://blog.socialmaximizer.com/ (June 20, 2010).

5 Frank Washkuch, "Direct Mail Volume Up 16% in Q1 as Insurance Leads Comeback," *DMNews*, June 3, 2010. www.dmnews.com/direct-mail-volume-up-16-in-q1-as-insurance-leads-comeback/article/171673/ (July 19, 2010).

6 "Brandcameo—Films," Brandchannel. www.brandchannel.com/brandcameo_films.asp (July 19, 2010).

7 Davide Dukcevich, "TV's Most Successful Products," *Forbes.com*, November 13, 2002. www.forbes.com/home/2002/11/13/cx_dd_1113products.html

8 Joseph Plambeck, "Product Placement Grows in Music Videos," *New York Times*, July 5, 2010. www.nytimes.com/2010/07/06/business/media/06adco.html (July 20, 2010).

9 Ibid.

10 Scott M. Cutlip, Allen H. Center, and Glen M. Broom, *Effective Public Relations*, 9th ed. (Upper Saddle River, NJ: Pearson Prentice Hall, 2009), pp. 1, 321.

11 Sandra Moriarty, Nancy Mitchell, and William Wells, *Advertising, Principles and Practices*, 8th ed. (Upper Saddle River, NJ: Pearson Prentice Hall, 2009), pp. 517–526.

12 "2007 Consumer PR—Doritos Crashes the Superbowl," *International Public Relations Association.* www.ipra.org/detail.asp?articleid=266 (June 20, 2010).

13 Sandra Moriarty, Nancy Mitchell, and William Wells, *Advertising, Principles and Practices*, 8th ed., p. 528.

14 Neal Santelmann, "Companies That Care," *Forbes.com.* www.forbes.com/2004/09/29/cx_ns_0929feat.html (May 15, 2008).

15 "Occupational Employment Statistics Highlights: An Overview of U.S. Occupational Employment and Wages in 2009," *Bureau of Labor and Statistics*, June 2010. www.bls.gov/oes/highlight_2009.pdf (June 21, 2010).

16 Lisa Z. Eccles, "Point of Purchase Advertising," *Advertising Age Supplement*, September 1994, pp. 1–6.

17 Paris Subway Stations Furnished by IKEA, *Huffington Post*, March 16, 2010. www.huffingtonpost.com/2010/03/16/paris-subway-stations-fur_n_501681.html (July 19, 2010).

18 "APICS Supply Chain Manager Competency Model," *Association for Operations Management.* www.apics.org/Resources/APICS_supply_chain_manager_competency_model.html.

19 Philip Kotler and Gary Armstrong, *Principles of Marketing*, 12th ed. (Upper Saddle River, NJ: Pearson Prentice Hall, 2008), p. 386.

20 U.S. Bureau of the Census, "Wholesale and Retail Trade—Establishments, Employees, and Payroll by State: 2000 and 2004," *Statistical Abstract of the United States* (Washington, DC: Government Printing Office, 2008), Table 10.13.

21 "Table 1.52: Freight Activity in the United States 2007," *Research and Innovative Technology Administration, Bureau of Transportation Statistics.* www.bts.gov/publications/national_transportation_statistics/html/table_01_52.html (July 20, 2010).

22 "Inbound Transportation Management and Control: Low Hanging Fruit and How to Grab It," *TransportGistics, Inc.*, www.insourceaudit.com/whitepapers/Inbound%20Transportation%20Management.asp (July 25, 2010).

23 Julie M. Donohue, Marisa Cevasco, and Meredith B. Rosenthal, "A Decade of Direct-to-Consumer Advertising of Prescription Drugs," *New England Journal of Medicine*, August 16, 2007. www.nejm.org/doi/full/10.1056/NEJMsa070502

Mini Chapter 4

1 "Economic News Release, Employment Situation Summary," *U.S. Bureau of Labor Statistics.* www.bls.gov/news.release/empsit.nr0.htm (July 21, 2010).

2 Kathleen Pender, "Job Seeker to Job Ratio a Stat Mashup," *San Francisco Chronicle*, July 15, 2010. www.sfgate.com/cgi-bin/article.cgi?f=/c/a/2010/07/14/BUQU1EDVF0.DTL (July 21, 2010).

3 "Résumé Development," *Ball State University Career Center.* http://cms.bsu.edu/About/AdministrativeOffices/CareerCenter/MyCareerPlan/JobSearchDocs/Resumes.aspx (July 21, 2010).

4 Allison Doyle, "Cover Letters," About.com. http://jobsearch.about.com/od/coverletters/a/aa030401a.htm (July 21, 2010).

5 Pat Kendall, "Cover Letter Tips," *Advanced Resume Concepts.* www.reslady.com/coverletters.html (July 21, 2010).

6 Ibid.

7 Allan Hoffman, "Seven Tips for Marketing Yourself," *Monster Career Advice.* http://content.comcast.monster.com/job-search-essentials/technology/Seven-Tips-for-Marketing-Yourself/home.aspx (July 21, 2010).

8 Randall S. Hansen, "15 Myths and Misconceptions About Job-Hunting," *Quintessential Careers.* www.quintcareers.com/job-hunting_myths.html (July 21, 2010).

9 Johanna Schlegel and Brian Braiker, "Inappropriate Questions," Salary.com. http://www.salary.com/Articles/ArticleDetail.asp?part=par284 (July 21, 2010).

10 Christine F. Della Monaca, "Interview Take-Along Checklist," *Monster Career Advice.* http://career-advice.monster.com/interview-preparation/interview-take-along-checklist/article.aspx (July 21, 2010).

Chapter 15

1 "Apple Inc. 2009 10-K Annual Report," p. 51, *Securities and Exchange Commission.* http://sec.gov/Archives/edgar/data/320193/000119312509214859/d10k.htm (June 25, 2010).

2 "Cash Flow Budget Worksheet Template," *Business Owner's Toolkit*. www.toolkit.com/tools/bt.aspx?tid=cfbudg_m (June 28, 2010).

3 Gwen Moran, "Out of Season: Strategies for Surviving the Downtime in a Cyclical Business," Entrepreneur.com, June 2010. www.entrepreneur.com/magazine/entrepreneur/2010/june/206604.html (June 29, 2010).

4 "6 Sources of Bootstrap Financing," *Entrepreneur.com*. www.entrepreneur.com/money/financing/selffinancingandbootstrapping/article80204.html (June 25, 2010).

5 "Dallas Keeps on Truckin' with GE Capital," *GE Reports*. www.gereports.com/dallas-keeps-on-truckin-with-ge-capital/ (June 26, 2010).

6 Herón Márquez Estrada, "Carver County Contrite About Tax Goof, but Residents Fuming," *Minneapolis-St. Paul Star Tribune*, December 12, 2007. www.startribune.com/local/west/12448481.html (July 21, 2010).

7 "The Biggest Accounting Scandals of All Time (Photos)," *Huffington Post*, August 9, 2010. www.huffingtonpost.com/2010/03/17/biggest-accounting-scanda_n_502181.html#s74418 (July 21, 2010). Reprinted with permission of the Huffington Post.

8 "Auto Manufacturers—Major Industry: Current Ratio: 3.59," *YCharts*. http://ycharts.com/industries/Auto%20Manufacturers%20-%20Major/current_ratio (July 1, 2010).

9 "Honda Motor Co. Ltd. Balance Sheet," *Yahoo! Finance*. http://finance.yahoo.com/q/bs?s=HMC+Balance+Sheet&annual (July 1, 2010).

10 "Fiscal 2009 Annual Report," *Starbucks Corporation*. http://media.corporate-ir.net/media_files/irol/99/99518/SBUX_AR.pdf (June 5, 2010).

11 Amey Stone, "SOX: Not So Bad After All?" *Bloomberg Businessweek*, August 1, 2005. www.businessweek.com/bwdaily/dnflash/aug2005/nf2005081_7739_db016.htm (July 1, 2010).

Chapter 16

1 Gary P. Brinson, Brian D. Singer, and Gilbert L. Beebower, "Determinants of Portfolio Performance II: An Update," *Financial Analysts Journal*, May/June 1991, pp. 40–48.

2 Alistair Barr and Ronald Orol, "Madoff Arrested in Alleged Ponzi Scheme," *MarketWatch*, December 11, 2008. www.marketwatch.com/story/madoff-arrested-charged-may-be-facing-50-bln-in-losses-fbi (July 24, 2010).

3 "Bernie Madoff Scandal: Where Are They Now?" *Time Magazine*, March 2010. www.time.com/time/specials/packages/completelist/0,29569,1971588,00.html (July 24, 2010).

4 "Listings," *NYSE Euronext*. www.nyse.com/about/listed/1170350259411.html (July 21, 2010).

5 "Statistical Milestones," *NASDAQ*. http://quotes.nasdaq.com/aspx/StatisticalMilestones.aspx (July 22, 2010).

6 "Protect Your Money: Check Out Brokers and Investment Advisors," *SEC*. www.sec.gov/investor/brokers.htm (July 22, 2010).

7 "Invest Wisely: Advice from Your Securities Industry Regulators," *SEC*. www.sec.gov/investor/pubs/inws.htm (May 30, 2008).

8 "Trends in Mutual Fund Investing: August 2007," *ICI.org*, September 27, 2007. http://conference.ici.org/research/stats/trends/trends_05_10 (July 25, 2010).

Mini Chapter 5

1 Suze Orman, "Buy 'New Used' Instead," *Yahoo! Finance*. http://biz.yahoo.com/pfg/e16buylease/art021.html (July 24, 2010).

2 "Compound Interest . . . The 8th Wonder!" *GreekShares.com*. www.greekshares.com/8th.php (July 24, 2010).

3 "Federal Tax Brackets," *MoneyChimp.com*. www.moneychimp.com/features/tax_brackets.htm (July 24, 2010).

Sources

Chapter 1, *Page 9,* Figure 1.1, U.S. Census Bureau, Population Projections of the United States by Age, Race, and Hispanic Origin: 1993–2050, P25-1104, 1993. http://www.georgewashington2.blogspot.com/2009/10/other-economic-crisis.html; *Page 13,* Figure 1.2, The Nielsen Company, "Global Online Survey," as cited in press released, January 28, 2008. Based on data from The Nielsen Company. *Page 15,* Figure 1-3, a, Anita\Shutterstock; b, Uwe Bumann\Shutterstock; c, Nat Ulrich\Shutterstock; d, George Doyle\Thinkstock; e, Yuri Arcurs\Shutterstock.

Chapter 2, *Page 32,* Figure 2.1, Basic Economic Principles, David O'Connor, Christopher Faille, Copyright © 2000 by Greenwood Press. Reprinted with permission of ABC-CLIO, LLC; *Page 44,* Figure 2.6, http://www.bls.gov/cpi/cpiri2009.pdf; *Page 49,* Figure 2.8, The Federal Reserve Board; Figure 2.9: Federal Reserve Statistical Release, H.6 Money Stock Measures. Released April 1, 2010, Accessed 7/10/2010 http://www.federalreserve.gov/releases/h6/Current/; *Page 52,* Figure 2-10, Historical Changes of the Target Federal Funds and Discount Rates 1971–present, Federal Reserve Bank of New York. http://www.ny.frb.org/markets/statistics/dlyrates/fedrate.html, Accessed 4/8/2010.

Chapter 4, *Page 95,* Figure 4.2, "Ford sales grow by double digits in China, Canada," *Channelnewsasia.com.* www.channelnewsasia.com/stories/afp_world_business/view/1047459/1/.html; *Page 96,* Figure 4.3, Newest data available for corporate is taken from: Fortune 500 Compare Tool," *CNNMoney.com.* http://cgi.money.cnn.com/tools/fortune/compare_2010.jsp?id=2255; newest data for countries is taken from "Economy Statistics >Gross National Income (Most Recent) by Country," *NationMaster.com.* www.nationmaster.com/graph/eco_gro_nat_inc-economy-gross-national-income; *Page 103,* Figure 4.4, "WTO Members," *Wikipedia Commons.* http://commons.wikimedia.org/wiki/File:WTO_members.svg; *Page 105,* Figure 4.5, https://www.cia.gov/library/publications/the-world-factbook/geos/ee.html.

Chapter 5, *Page 135,* Figure 5.1, www.facebook.com/press/info.php?factsheet; *Page 139,* http://www.census.gov/epcd/susb/latest/us/US—.HTM#table0; *Page 136,* Figure 5.2, "Select Countries," *International Monetary Fund.* www.imf.org/external/pubs/ft/weo/2010/01/weodata/weoselco.aspx?g=2001&sg=All+countries; *Page 137,* Figure 5.3, "Small Business Economic Report 2009," *Small Business Administration.* www.sba.gov/advo/research/sb_econ2009.pdf; *Page 138,* Figure 5.4, Shutterstock; *Page 142,* Figure 5.5, "How Small Business Owners Define Job Satisfaction," *myRetailer.ca.* www.myretailer.ca/index.php/how-small-business-owners-define-job-satisfaction. Figure 5-6, from left to right, J. Helgason/Shutterstock, Lior Filshteiner/Shutterstock, John K. Humble/Getty Images Inc. – Stone Allstock, Stephen Rudolph/Shutterstock, Claudio Bertoloni/Shutterstock, Alamy Images, Pincasso\Shutterstock, © Daniele Taurino/Dreamstime.com; *Page 153, Figure 5-7,* http://www.bls.gov/opub/mlr/2005/05/ressum.pdf.

Chapter 6, *Page 168,* Figure 6.1, "Startup Business Characteristics and Dynamics: A Data Analysis of the Kauffman Firm Survey," *Small Business Association.* www.sba.gov/advo/research/rs350tot.pdf (May 8, 2010). *Page 169,* Figure 6-2, Mika Heittola/Shutterstock, Jack Hollingsworth/Photos.com, Simon Krzic/Shutterstock.

Chapter 7, *Page 215,* Figure 7.5, "Wal-Mart SWOT," *Marketing Teacher.com.* http://www.marketingteacher.com/SWOT/walmart_swot.htm.

Chapter 8, *Page 237,* Figure 8.1, MASLOW, ABRAHAM H.; FRAGER, ROBERT D. (EDITOR); FADIMAN, JAMES (EDITOR), MOTIVATION AND PERSONALITY, 3rd, © 1987. Printed and Electronically reproduced by permission of Pearson Education, Inc., Upper Saddle River, New Jersey. *Page 239,* Figure 8.2, Based on D. McGregor, The Human Side of Enterprise (New York: McGraw-Hill 1960); *Page 348,* Figure 8.4, "Top 10 Reasons to Work at Google," www.google.com/support/jobs/bin/static.py?page=about.html&about=top10.

Chapter 10, *Page 311,* Figure 10.3, © Ted Goff/The New Yorker Collevtion/www.cartoonbank.com. *Page 314,* Figure 10.4, Pearson Education Japan.

Chapter 11, *Page 339,* Figure 11-1, Adapted from http://www.ganttcharts.com/Evolution.html. Reprinted by permission from Smart Draw, www.SmartDraw.com. *Page 340,* Figure 11.2, Created using SmartDraw, http://www.smartdraw.com/tutorials/bpm/tutorial_07.htm; *Page 335,* UF 11-1, Reprinted with permission of Blank Label Group, Inc. www.blank-label.com.

Mini Chapter 3, *Page 354,* Figure MC3-1, Adapted from "In search of a lost art: How to Write a Business Letter"; *Page 355,* Figure MC3-2, Adapted from "Written Communication" at http://www.quamut.com/quamut/business_etiquette/page/written_communication.html.

Chapter 12, *Page 364,* Figure 12.1, Adapted from http://courses.unt.edu/kt3650_1/images/img044.gif; *Page 370,* Figure 12.3, Adapted by permission of NetMBA.com.

Chapter 13, *Page 398,* Figure 13.1, http://www.marketingteacher.com/Lessons/lesson_three_levels_of_a_product.htm; *Page 412,* Figure 13.3, Kotler, Philip, Keller, Kevin Lane, *Marketing Management: Analysis, Planning, Implementation and Control,* 12th Edition © 2006. Electronically reproduced by permission of Pearson Education, Inc., Upper Saddle River, NJ, and http://instruct1.cit.cornell.edu/Courses/cuttingedge/lifeCycle/10.htm.

Chapter 14, *Page 433,* Figure 14.2, "July 2009 Nielsen Global Online Consumer Survey: Trust, Value and Engagement in Advertising," The Nielsen Company, p. 5. http://blog.nielsen.com/nielsenwire/wp-content/uploads/2009/07/trustinadvertising0709.pdf. Reprinted with permission of Nielsen Company.

Chapter 15, *Page 486,* TheSupe87\Shutterstock; *Page 497,* Figure 15.7, Google Annual Report. *Google Inc.* http://investor.google.com/pdf/2009_google_annual_report.pdf; *Page 501,* Figure 15.8, Google Annual Report. *Google Inc.* http://investor.google.com/pdf/2009_google_annual_report.pdf; *Page 504,* Figure 15.9, 2009 Google Annual Report, investor.google.com/pdf/2009_google_annual_report.pdf, Accessed July 1, 2010.

Chapter 16, *Page 520,* Figure 16.2, http://sify.com/finance/equity/fullstory.php?id=13654158; *Page 521,* Figure 16.3, http://www.statefarm.com/mutual/investors/pricing_perf/life_path/lpwork.asp; *Page 527,* Figure 16.6, "BP plc," *Yahoo!Finance.*

http://finance.yahoo.com/echarts?s=BP+Interactive#chart4: symbol=bp;range=3m;compare=dell+xom+aapl;indicator= volume;charttype=line;crosshair=on;ohlcvalues=0;logscale= on;source=undefined. Reproduced with permission of Yahoo! Inc. ©2010 Yahoo! Inc. YAHOO! and the YAHOO! logo are registered trademarks of Yahoo! Inc.; *Page 527*, Figure 16.7, "BP plc," *Yahoo! Finance*. http://finance.yahoo.com/ echarts?s=bp#chart1:symbol=bp;range=3m;indicator=volume; charttype=line;crosshair=on;ohlcvalues=0;logscale=on; source=undefined; *Page 528*, Figure 16.8, "BP plc," *Yahoo! Finance*. http://finance.yahoo.com/echarts?s=BP#chart1:

symbol=bp;range=3m;indicator=volume;charttype=line; crosshair=on;ohlcvalues=0;logscale=on;source=undefined. Reproduced with permission of Yahoo! Inc. ©2010 Yahoo! Inc. YAHOO! and the YAHOO! logo are registered trademarks of Yahoo! Inc.

Mini Chapter 5, *Page 545*, Figure MC5-1, Basic Personal Finance at http://www.planyourescape.ca/personal-finance-101-an-introduction-11, Peter Milner at http://www.planyourescape.ca.

Photo Credits

Chapter 1, *Page 2/3,* © Tony Avelar/AP Wide World; *Page 2/5,* Gregory James Van Raalte\Shutterstock; *Page 2/14,* Andre Jenny\Alamy Images; *Page 2/17,* Dean Mitchell\Shutterstock; *Page 2/20,* 15454-21DG\Comstock Complete; *Page 4,* Jeff Greenberg\PhotoEdit Inc.; *Page 9,* TebNab\Shutterstock; *Page 11,* Hartmut Schwarzbach/argus\Photolibrary/Peter Arnold, Inc.; *Page 12,* flashfilm\Thinkstock; *Page 15,* © James Leynse/CORBIS. All rights reserved; *Page 21,* AVAVA\Shutterstock.

Chapter 2, *Page 28/29,* David Lee\Shutterstock; *Page 28/32,* Jupiterimages\Thinkstock; *Page 28/39,* Photosani\Shutterstock; *Page 28/42,* Mats\Shutterstock; *Page 28/47,* iofoto\Shutterstock; *Page 33,* dundanim\Shutterstock; *Page 39,* Shiningcolors\Dreamstime LLC -Royalty Free; *Page 40,* TebNad\Shutterstock; *Page 45,* © Peter C. Vey/The New Yorker Collection/www.cartoonbank.com.

Chapter 3, *Page 60/61,* marekuliasz\Shutterstock; *Page 60/64,* SVLuma\Shutterstock; *Page 60/68,* Thinkstock; *Page 60/75,* Pablo Eder\Shutterstock; *Page 60/79,* Thomas Northcut\Thinkstock; *Page 60/82,* Ryan McVay\Thinkstock; *Page 62,* © Alex Gregory/The New Yorker Collection/www.cartoonbank.com; *Page 65,* AP Wide World Photos; *Page 66,* AP Photo/Charless Bennett\AP Wide World Photos; *Page 71,* Brave New Films; *Page 73,* © Naashon Zalk/CORBIS All Rights Reserved; *Page 80,* Topia GreenStop and Real Cafe Inc.; *Page 81,* David Young-Wolff\PhotoEdit Inc.; *Page 84,* CALVIN AND HOBBES ©1993 Watterson. Reprinted with permission of UNIVERSAL PRESS SYNDICATE. All rights reserved.

Chapter 4, *Page 92/93,* Courtesy of www.istockphoto.com; *Page 92/97,* Ciaran Griffin\Thinkstock; *Page 92/100,* niderlander\Shutterstock; *Page 92/106,* Gallo Images\Alamy Images Royalty Free; *Page 92/111,* karam Miri\Shutterstock; *Page 92/115,* JUPITERIMAGES/ BananaStock\Alamy Images Royalty Free; *Page 99,* donvictorio\Shutterstock, *Page 108,* AFP/Getty Images, Inc.; *Page 117,* Christine Schneider/Zefa\CORBIS- NY.

Mini Chapter 1, *Page 126,* Diamond Images/Shutterstock, *Page 127,* James Marshall\AP Wide World Photos; *Page 131,* top, Tim Gainey\Alamy Images Royalty Free, bottom, Lee Morris/Shutterstock; *Page 132,* http://www.cartoonstock.com/directory/p/phishing.asp.

Chapter 5, *Page134/135,* Jyan McVay\Thinkstock; *Page 134/140,* Irfan Khan\Newscom; *Page 134/147,* © Lon C. Diehl/PhotoEdit; *Page 134/152,* John Howard\Thinkstock; *Page 134/157,* Jeffrey Blackler\Alamy Images Royalty Free; *Page 146,* Jakub Mosur\Facebook, Inc.

Chapter 6, *Page 166/167,* Rob Marmion\Shutterstock; *Page 166/171,* Stephen Coburn\Shutterstock; *Page 166/176,* George Doyle\Thinkstock; *Page 166/184,* Morgan Lane Photography\Shutterstock; *Page 166/186,* Erasmus Wolff\Shutterstock, *Page 186,* bottom, Ivan Cholakov Gostock-dot-net\Shutterstock; *Page 187,*www.Cartoonstock.com.

Mini Chapter 2, *Page 198,* top, Zsolt Nyulaszi\Shutterstock, bottom, Cathy Melloan\PhotoEdit Inc.; *Page 200,* david pearson\Alamy Images Royalty Free; *Page 203,* Shutterstock; *Page 204,* Natalia Bratslavsky/Shutterstock.

Chapter 7, *Page 206/207,* Novastock/ PhotoEdit; *Page 206/212,* Digital vision\Thinkstock; *Page 206/217,* BananaStock\Thinkstock; *Page 206/222,* Goodshoot\Thinkstock.

Chapter 8, *Page 206/207,* Novastock/PhotoEdit; *Page 206/212,* Digital vision\Thinkstock; *Page 206/217,* BananaStock\Thinkstock; *Page 206/222,* Goodshoot\Thinkstock; *Page 234/235,* John Rowley\Thinkstock; *Page 234/243,* PR NEWSWIRE\Newscom; *Page 234/250,* Comstock Images\Thinkstock; *Page 241,*© Richard Cline/The New Yorker Collection/www.cartoonbank.com; *Page 242,* Galyna Andrushko\Shutterstock; *Page 245,* AP Wide World Photos; *Page 247,* © Najlah Feanny/CORBIS All Rights Reserved; *Page 249,* © Mick Stevens/The New Yorker Collection/www.cartoonbank.com; *Page 251,* © NBC/Courtesy: Everett Collection; *Page 254,* Cisco Systems, Inc. Webex Technology Group.

Chapter 9, *Page 264/265,* Creatas\Thinkstock; *Page 264/271,* Pixland/Jupiterimages/Thinkstock; *Page 264/276,* Comstock/Jupiterimages/Thinkstock/Getty Images; *Page 264/283,* Yuri Arcurs\Shutterstock; *Page 264/286,* Jose Gil\Shutterstock; *Page 272,* The Columbus Dispatch, Neal C. Lauron\AP Wide World Photos; *Page 273,* Phelan M. Ebenhack\AP Wide World Photos; *Page 278,* Scott Carson/Zuma\Newscom; *Page 279,* David R. Frazier\Photo Researchers, Inc.; *Page 284,* Photodisc/Ryan McVay/Thinkstock.

Chapter 10, *Page 296/297,* Courtesy of www.istockphoto.com; *Page 296/301,* auremar\Shutterstock; *Page 296/307,* Pixland\Thinkstock; *Page 296/311,* Comstock Complete; *Page 300,* top, Chad McDermott\Shutterstock, bottom, Ryan McVay\Getty Images, Inc.- Photodisc./Royalty Free; *Page 302,* TrAj43\Shutterstock; *Page 303,* Cico\Shutterstock; *Page 304,* iQoncept\Shutterstock; *Page 313,* top, MIRROR CHEUNG\Newscom, bottom, © Sherwin Crasto/Reuters/CORBIS.

Chapter 11, *Page 324/325,* Jimmy Lee\Shutterstock; *Page 324/327,* Comstock Complete; *Page 324/333,* Alex Segre\Alamy Images Royalty Free; *Page 324/342,* Newscom; *Page 328,* Karl Strauss Brewing Company; *Page 330,* SunPower Corporation; *Page 331,* top, Zastol'skiy Victor Leonidovich\Shutterstock, bottom, Dennis Lowe\Newscom; *Page 335,* VICTORY MOTORCYCLES\Newscom; *Page 337,* top, Rainer Plendi\Shutterstock, bottom, Ragma Images\Shutterstock; *Page 341,* Mr Zach\Shutterstock.

Mini Chapter 3, *Page 352,* Digital Vision/Thinkstock; *Page 353,* Christopher Robbins/Photodisc/Thinkstock; *Page 358,* Creatas Images/Thinkstock; *Page 359,* Comstock/Thinkstock; *Page 361,* Todd Warnock/Lifesize/Thinkstock.

Chapter 12, *Page 362/363,* Tom Wood\Alamy Images Royalty Free, Motoring Picture Library\Alamy Images Royalty Free; *Page 362/369,* WilleeCole\Shutterstock; *Page 362/373,* olly\Shutterstock; *Page 362/377,* Comstock Complete; *Page 362/385,* Digital Vision\Thinkstock; *Page 367,* Newscom; *Page 368,* CORBIS- NY; *Page 371,* Jeff Greenberg\PhotoEdit Inc.; *Page 384,* Polka Dot/Jupiterimages/Getty Images/Thinkstock.

Chapter 13, *Page 396/397,* mediablitimages (uk) limited\Alamy Images; *Page 396/403,* Worytko Pawel\Shutterstock; *Page 396/411,* Creatas\Thinkstock; *Page 396/415,* UpperCut Images\Alamy Images Royalty Free; *Page 397,* Newscom; *Page 401,* Losevsky Pavel\Shutterstock; *Page 402,* top, George P. Choma/Shutterstock, bottom, Feng Yu/Shutterstock; *Page 404,* © James Leynse/CORBIS All Rights Reserved;

Glindex

Page numbers followed by an f indicate figures, page numbers followed by a t indicate tables.

A

Abercrombie & Fitch, 282
ABS Capital Partners, 190
Absolute advantage is the ability to produce more of a good or a service than any other country, 97
Abu Dhabi, 112
Abu Ghraib prison, 78
Accountability, 251
Accountants, demand for, 492, 493t
Accounting involves tracking a business's income and expenses by recording its financial transactions, 480, 481, 490–495, 506
  audits of, 77
  corporate, 491–492, 491f, 506
  country-neutral, 494
  errors, 492
  financial, 491f, 492, 506
  fraud, 178, 308–309, 493, 494, 503
  fundamentals of, 490–491
  government and not-for-profit, 491f, 492, 506
  managerial, 491, 491f, 506
  process of, 494–495, 494f
  software for, 303
  standards for, 492–494
  tax, 491f, 492, 506
  types of, 491–492, 491f
Accounts payable, 498
Accrued expenses, 498
Accumulated profits, 488–489
Achievement, need for, 238
Ackerman, Sylvia, 324, 333
Acquisitions occur when one company completely buys out another company, 166, 186–190, 192
Action learning, 274
Active listening, 352–353
Actively disengaged employees, 236–237, 236t
Actual products are the tangible aspect of the purchase that you can touch, see, hear, smell, or taste, 398, 398f, 422
ADA (Americans with Disabilities Act), 66, 76–77, 270
ADEA (Age Discrimination in Employment Act) (1967), 270
Adidas, 19, 338
ADM (Archer Daniels Midland), 66–67, 77
Administrative trade barriers, 101, 119
Adoption benefits, 279
Adornment Expressive Accessories, 155–156
AdSense, 130, 436
Advanced Enological Closures, 146
Advantage
  absolute, 97
  comparative, 97, 98, 99, 119, 188
Advertising is paid, impersonal mass communication from an identified sponsor to persuade or influence a targeted audience, 428, 432–437, 486–487
  advantages and disadvantages of, 447, 447t

advocacy, 434
Adware, 132
B2B, 433
classified ads for, 474
comparative, 433
contextual, 130
corporate (institutional), 433
costs of, 432–433
direct mail, 434, 435t
e-mail for, 304
globalization of, 437
interactive, 434
Internet (online), 129–130, 130t, 434, 436
misleading, 432
most successful ad campaigns, 432
Nielsen survey on, 433, 433f
nonprofit, 433
product, 433
vs. publicity, 439
public service, 366, 434
reality, 314
retail (local), 433
role of, 432–433, 459
trends in, 436–437
types of, 433–434, 459
web sites based on, 128, 313–314, 314f
Advertising agencies, 74
Advertising media, 434–435, 435t
Advertising specialties, 446
Advisory boards are a group of individuals who offer guidance to the new business owner, 156, 161
Advocacy advertising promotes an organization's position on a public issue, such as global warming or immigration, 434
Adware, 132
AdWords, 436
Aesthetics, 116
Affiliated Computer Services, 207
Affiliation, need for, 238
Affiliative (laissez-faire) leaders are advisory in style, encouraging employees to contribute ideas rather than specifically directing their tasks, 244t, 245, 283
Affordability, 416
Afghan National Police, 138, 139
AFL. *See* American Federation of Labor
AFL-CIO, 287
African Americans, 137, 137f, 285
Age Discrimination in Employment Act (ADEA) (1967), 270
Age distribution, 114
Age-diversity, 283
Agents/brokers are intermediaries that facilitate negotiations between buyers and sellers of goods and services but never take title (ownership) of the products traded, 449, 453, 460
Aging population, 7–8, 8f
Aging workforce, 284–285, 290
Agriculture, 92, 100, 106
AIDS, 73
Airlines, 186, 336, 398
Alibaba.com, 138
Allaire, Paul, 220
Alliances, strategic, 109, 110t, 119
AMA (American Marketing Association), 363, 369
Amazon.com, 12, 39, 126

American Cancer Society, 214
American Customer Satisfaction Index, 226
American Federation of Labor (AFL) was founded in 1886 to protect skilled workers, 286
American Franchisee Association, 148t
American Indians, 137
American Marketing Association (AMA), 363, 369
American Motors, 116
American Red Cross, 73
American Stock Exchange (AMEX) is a stock exchange where stocks are bought and sold on a trading floor or via an electronic market, 525
Americans with Disabilities Act (ADA), 66, 76–77, 270
America Online (AOL), 188
AMEX. *See* American Stock Exchange
Amoral behavior is when a person has no sense of right and wrong and no interest in the moral consequences of his or her actions, 62
Anchor Pest Control, 223f
Andean Group, 105
Anderson, Ray, 81
Android phone, 7
Angel investors are wealthy individuals who are willing to put up their own money in hopes of a profit return later on, 158–159
Animated Speech Corporation, 139
Animation, computer, 245
Annual Credit Report Web site, 550–551
AOL (America Online), 188
APEC (Asia-Pacific Economic Cooperation), 105
Apple (company)
  acquisitions by, 190
  brand loyalty to, 405
  capital expenditures, 483
  iAds, 129
  iPad, 39, 302, 437
  iPhone, 7, 129, 211, 259, 324, 342, 345, 411
  iPod, 38, 256
  stock price changes, 527, 527f, 528, 528f
Appliances industry, 336
Apprentice training programs train individuals through classroom or formal instruction and on-the-job training, 272
Aqua Teen Hunger Force, 376
Arab countries, 116–117
Arbitration occurs when a third party settles the dispute after hearing all the issues, 287, 290
Archer Daniels Midland (ADM), 66–67, 77
Argentina, 105
Arm & Hammer, 414
Arthur Andersen, 77
ASEAN (Association of Southeast Asian Nations), 105
Asian Americans, 137
Asia-Pacific Economic Cooperation (APEC), 105
Assembly line (or production line) production is when partially complete products are moved from one worker to the next on a conveyor belt, 141, 334

information technology, 309–310
online banking and, 131
online business, 13, 132–133, 311
of personal information, 21, 131
Seidman, Dov, 78
Selective distribution uses only a portion of the many possible retail outlets for selling products, 456
Self-actualization needs include the desire to maximize your own potential through education and self-fulfillment as well as experiences of beauty and spirituality, 237f, 238
Self-direction, 142–144
Self-employment taxes, 170
Self-reporting, 72
Seligman, Martin, 64
Selling
    direct, 455
    personal, 428, 440–444, 443f, 447t, 459
Semicontrolled messages, 438
Sequencing, 339
Serial bonds have a series of dates on which portions of the total bond mature, unlike traditional bonds that are paid back to the investor all at once on the maturity date, 530
Service-based economy, 326
Service Corp of Retired Executives (SCORE) is a volunteer organization of retired executives who offer workshops and counseling to small businesses at no cost, 155, 155f, 157, 160, 205
Services are intangible products that are bought or sold, 3, 22
    communism and, 31
    in the consumer price index, 44, 44t
    convenience, 400–401, 422
    development of, 396, 397–403
    growth in, 3t
    operations management for, 332–333
    percentage of the GDP, 326, 346
    pricing, 396, 415–421
    production of, 324, 325–327
    productivity in, 46
    from restaurants, 5
    shift to, 288
    shopping, 401, 422
    small businesses and, 326
    social, 31, 45
    specialized professional, 402–403
    specialty, 401
    unsought, 401–402, 422
    web-based, 13
Seven Habits model describes habits of behavior that are exhibited by successful people, 255, 258
Sexual harassment, 64, 284
SGL Carbon, 344
Shanghai Automotive Industry Group, 312–313
Shankman, Peter, 380
Sharpen the saw metaphor, 255
Shareholders have an ownership interest in a company, 65–66, 178, 498, 503, 515
Sherman, Roger, 134, 152, 157
Sherman Antitrust Act, 39
Shoe stores, 362, 373, 374, 376, 377
Shopping goods and services are products that are less frequently purchased and require that the customer spend more time and effort in comparing the products, 401, 422
Shortage is the situation in which demand exceeds supply, 35

Short-term financing is any type of financing that is repaid within a year or less, 480, 485–487, 498, 506
Short-term liabilities (current liabilities) are obligations a company is responsible for paying within a year or less, 51, 497f, 498
Silicon Valley, 74, 329
Silver Effie Award, 439
Simulation training (or vestibule training) provides realistic job-task training in a manner that is challenging but does not create the threat of failure, 272–273
Singer Sewing Machines, 147
Sinking funds are a type of savings fund into which companies deposit money regularly to help repay a bond, 514–515
SIPC (Securities Investor Protection Corporation), 526
Sirius, 187
Situational analysis, 381, 382, 382f, 391
Situational ethics is when people make decisions based on a specific situation instead of universal laws, 61–62, 86
Situational influences, 387
Six Sigma is a statistically based, proactive, long-term process designed to examine the overall business process and prevent problems, 225–226, 343, 344
Skilling, Jeffrey, 77
Skills
    conceptual, 210
    decision-making, 210–211, 210f
    globalization and, 315
    interpersonal, 143, 208, 211, 352, 356
    life, 2, 20–21, 23
    for managers, 210–211, 210f, 227
    presentation, 352–353
    on resumés, 468
    teamwork, 255, 258
    technical, 210, 211
    time management, 210
    writing, 354–356, 354f, 355f, 356
Slosberg, Pete, 143
Small Business Administration (SBA) is an independent agency of the federal government that was formed to aid, counsel, assist, and protect the interests of small businesses, 135–136
    assistance from, 155, 155f, 160
    business plan resources, 205
    on franchising, 148t
    SCORE program, 155, 155f, 157, 160, 205
Small businesses are independently owned and operated and not dominant in their field of operation, 134–165
    assistance for, 134, 154–157, 155f, 160
    average annual revenue limits for, 136
    buying an existing business, 150–152, 151t
    the economy and, 134, 135–137, 136f, 160
    failure of, 153–154, 153f, 160
    financing for, 134, 157–159, 161
    Forbes' Best, 14
    growth of, 153–154
    impact of technology on, 138–139
    information technology for, 300
    innovation and, 136–137
    location of, 156
    reasons for starting, 139
    risks of, 134, 152–157
    service-based, 326
    short-term financing for, 486
    social media tools for, 380

starting your own, 135
structure of, 139–140
training for, 155–156, 160
workforce in, 135–136, 135f, 137–138, 137f
Small business investment companies (SBIC) are private venture capital firms licensed by the SBA to make equity capital or long-term loans available to small companies, 158–159
Smaller Business Association of New England, 136–137
SMARTER, 215f
Smartphones allow employees to access their e-mail and the Internet from virtually anywhere, 302, 356
Smart power management, 306
Smith, Bill, 344
Smith, Gavin, 286, 288, 415
Smith, Gina, 512, 523, 528
Smith, Jessica, 411
Snob effect, 419
Social audits are a study of how well a company is meeting its social responsibilities, 71
Social class, 386
Social entrepreneurs set out to create innovative solutions in the social sector; they are entrepreneurs with a social mission, 145
Social environment is an interconnected system of different demographic factors, such as race, ethnicity, gender, age, income distribution, sexual orientation, and other characteristics, 7–10, 8f, 20, 22
Social intrapreneurs build and develop ventures within a company that are designed to identify and solve large-scale social problems, 145
Socialism is an economic system where the government owns or controls many basic businesses and services so that profits can be distributed evenly among the people, 30, 31, 114, 117
Socially responsible investing (SRI) is investing only in companies that have met a certain standard of CSR, 75
Social media. *See* Social networking
Social networking describes a set of services focused on building and supporting social relationships among people, 6, 7
    for advertising, 434–435, 435t
    corporate social responsibility and, 72–73
    for customer service, 435
    digital natives and, 316
    enterprise, 306
    for a job search, 473
    for management, 211
    in market research, 380
    merges and acquisitions in, 190
    for personal brands, 408
    product development input and, 399
    production processes and, 338–339, 347
    for product placement, 438
    for recruitment, 268
    risks of, 269
    small businesses and, 138–139, 138f, 380
    technology for, 11
    viral marketing with, 130–131
    for virtual teams, 254
Social responsibility, corporate. *See* Corporate social responsibility
Social Security, 8, 44, 170
Social Security numbers, 310

Support personnel are salespeople who obtain new customers but also focus on assisting current customers with technical matters, 442

Surplus is the situation in which supply exceeds demand, 35, 112

Surveillance, of employees, 308, 309

Sustainability is the process of working to improve the quality of life in ways that simultaneously protect and enhance the earth's life support system, 81

Swartz, Mark, 78

Sweden, 31

Sweepstakes, 446

SWFs. *See* Sovereign wealth funds

Swinmurn, Nick, 138

SWOT analysis is used to determine the strategic fit between an organization's internal and external capabilities; SWOT stands for Strengths, Weaknesses, Opportunities, and Threats, 134, 214–215, 215f, 227

Synergize, 255

Synergy is the effect achieved when two companies combine, in which the result is better than each company could achieve individually, 187

System thinkers, 143

T

Tablet computers, 302, 356

Taboos, 16

Tactical plans specifically determine the resources and the actions required to implement particular aspects of a strategic plan, 215–216, 217f, 227

Tailoring businesses, 480, 485, 490

Target (chain store), 16, 72, 78–79

Target costing estimates the value customers receive from a product and, therefore, the price they are willing to pay and then subtracts an acceptable profit margin to obtain a desired cost, 417f, 418

Target market is a specific group of potential customers on which a firm focuses its marketing efforts, 253, 369–370, 372, 382–384, 383t, 430

Tariffs are a tax imposed on an imported good or service, 98, 100, 119

Task utility is when someone performs a service for someone else, 367

Tata Steel, 328

Tattoo Media, 145

Tattooes, 212

Tax accounting involves preparing taxes and giving advice on tax strategies, 491f, 492, 506

Taxation, double, 179–180

Taxes. *See also* Income tax
corporations and, 177
fiscal policy on, 48
LLCs and, 19
property, 491
retirement plans and, 554
sales, 15, 128–129
savings and, 519
self-employment, 170
sole proprietorship and, 168–170, 169f, 169t, 180
use, 129

Tax-exempt status, 184, 185

Taylor, Frederick, 241

Teams
cross-functional, 253–254
decision making by, 252
entrepreneurial, 145–146
formation of, 253
multinational, 315
in product development, 251–252
roles in, 253, 253t, 258
virtual, 254–255, 258

Teamwork, 234, 250–256, 257–258
advantages of, 250–251
best practices for, 252–255
individual's role in, 255
skills for, 255, 258
successful, 255, 258
technology and, 254–255

Technical skills include the abilities and knowledge that enable employees to carry out the specific tasks required of a discipline or a department, 210, 211

Technology refers to items and services such as smartphones, computer software, and digital broadcasting make businesses more efficient and productive, 4, 11–14, 22, 296–323. *See also* Information technology; Internet
baggage-handling systems and, 336
basics of, 317
benefits and challenges of, 296, 307–311, 317–318
benefits of, 11–12
communications, 11, 303–304, 307–308, 317–318, 356–361
competitiveness and, 98
cooperation and, 314
for the design process, 337–338, 412
ethical conduct and, 308–309, 318
globalization and, 10, 95, 119, 296
international business and, 126, 296, 311–316, 318
for inventory control, 341
management and, 309–311
marketing and, 313–314, 314f
marketing environment and, 374f, 375
new trends in, 306–307
online security and, 13
personal effects of, 21
in production processes, 336–339, 346–347
productivity and, 11, 308, 318
recruitment and, 268–269
small businesses and, 138–139
supply and, 36, 36t
supply chain management and, 449
teamwork and, 254–255
for training, 272–273
upgrades of, 310

Telecommuting is work from home or another location away from the office, 12, 65, 280, 306

Teleconferencing. *See* Remote conferencing

Telemarketing is selling products over the phone, 455

Teletraining, 273

Television, 435t

Temporary workers, 280–281

Tender offer, 187

Termination refers to the act of permanently laying off workers due to poor performance or a discontinued need for their services, 66, 264, 276, 281–282, 289

Ternary Software, 242–243

Teva Pharmaceuticals, 330

Textile industry, 97, 98

Texting, 358

Thaler, Linda Kaplan, 74

Tham, Steven, 428

Theory X posits that humans inherently dislike work and will try to avoid it if they can, 239, 239f, 243, 257

Theory Y proposes that people view work as natural and will be motivated to work as long as they are satisfied with their jobs, 239–240, 239f, 257

Theory Z suggests workers want to cooperate and be loyal to an organization, 240, 257

Third-party logistics, 457

Threat of retaliation, 102

Threats, external, 215, 215f

Three needs theory states that the main motivators are the need for achievement, affiliation, and power, 238, 257

Tieden, Lara, 248

Tiffany & Co., 409

Time, cultural attitudes on, 116

Time management skills are the ability to be effective and productive with their available time, 210

Time-motion studies, 241

Time Warner, 72, 188

Time zones, 313

Topia Energy, 80

Top managers are the corporate officers who are responsible for an organization as a whole, 208–209, 209f, 227

Topping, bob, 252

Toshiba, 43

Total product offer consists of all the benefits associated with a good, a service, or an idea that impact a consumer's purchasing decision, 397–398, 422

Total quality management (TQM) is an integrated approach that focuses on quality from the beginning of the production process up through managerial involvement to detect and correct problems, 223–225, 224–225f, 228, 343–344, 347

Toxic waste, 70, 329

Toyota, 336, 438

Toys, 332

Toy Story (film), 245

TQM. *See* Total quality management

Trade
free, 74, 92, 100, 102–106
international, 92, 97–99, 102–104, 119

Trade (or B2B) sales promotions are incentives to push a product through the distribution system to final consumers, 444, 446, 460

Trade barriers
administrative, 101, 119
benefits and costs of, 101–102, 102t
competitiveness and, 98
globalization and, 95, 119
reduction of, 102–104
types of, 100–101, 119

Trade credit is the ability to purchase inventory and supplies on credit without interest, 158, 486, 486f, 506

Trade deficits exist when the value of a country's imports exceeds the value of its exports, 112, 113

Trademarks are a legally protected brand, 108, 404, 410

Trade surplus occurs when the value of a country's exports exceeds the value of its imports, 112

Answer Key

CHAPTER 1
Business Basics
Self Test Multiple Choice
(Answers): 1. a; 2. b; 3. d; 4. b; 5. b; 6. d; 7. a; 8. b; 9. a; 10. a
Self Test True False
(Answers): 1. True; 2. False; 3. True; 4. True; 5. False

CHAPTER 2
Economics and Banking
Self Test Multiple Choice
(Answers): 1. a; 2. c; 3. a; 4. b; 5. b; 6. c; 7. b; 8. d; 9. b; 10. d
Self Test True False
(Answers): 1. True; 2. False; 3. False; 4. True; 5. True

CHAPTER 3
Ethics in Business
Self Test Multiple Choice
(Answers): 1. b; 2. d; 3. b; 4. b; 5. c; 6. d; 7. b; 8. c; 9. a; 10. b
Self Test True False
(Answers): 1. False; 2. False; 3. True; 4. True; 5. False

CHAPTER 4
Business in a Global Economy
Self Test Multiple Choice
(Answers): 1. b; 2. d; 3. a; 4. d; 5. c; 6. a; 7. d; 8. b; 9. d; 10. d
Self Test True False
(Answers): 1. True; 2. True; 3. False; 4. False; 5. True

CHAPTER 5
Small Business and the Entrepreneur
Self Test Multiple Choice
(Answers): 1. d; 2. c; 3. a; 4. b; 5. b; 6. a; 7. c; 8. c; 9. c; 10. c
Self Test True False
(Answers): 1. True; 2. False; 3. False; 4. False; 5. True

CHAPTER 6
Forms of Business Ownership
Self Test Multiple Choice
(Answers): 1. d; 2. d; 3. c; 4. a; 5. d; 6. c; 7. d; 8. a; 9. b; 10. b
Self Test True False
(Answers): 1. False; 2. False; 3. False; 4. True; 5. True

CHAPTER 7
Business Management and Organization
Self Test Multiple Choice
(Answers): 1. b; 2. b; 3. b; 4. a; 5. d; 6. d; 7. a; 8. b; 9. b; 10. d
Self Test True False
(Answers): 1. False; 2. True; 3. False; 4. True; 5. False

CHAPTER 8
Motivation, Leadership, and Teamwork
Self Test Multiple Choice
(Answers): 1. d; 2. d; 3. a; 4. b; 5. c; 6. d; 7. a; 8. d; 9. a; 10. c
Self Test True False
(Answers): 1. False; 2. False; 3. True; 4. True; 5. False

CHAPTER 9
Human Resource Management
Self Test Multiple Choice
(Answers): 1. b; 2. a; 3. c; 4. a; 5. a; 6. b; 7. b; 8. d; 9. b; 10. d
Self Test True False
(Answers): 1. False; 2. False; 3. True; 4. True; 5. True

CHAPTER 10
Business Technology
Self Test Multiple Choice
(Answers): 1. d; 2. a; 3. a; 4. a; 5. d; 6. d; 7. d; 8. b; 9. d; 10. a
Self Test True False
(Answers): 1. False; 2. True; 3. True; 4. True; 5. False

CHAPTER 11
Production and Operations Management
Self Test Multiple Choice
(Answers): 1. d; 2. a; 3. c; 4. a; 5. c; 6. d; 7. a; 8. a; 9. a; 10. b
Self Test True False
(Answers): 1. True; 2. True; 3. False; 4. False; 5. False

CHAPTER 12
Marketing and Consumer Behavior
Self Test Multiple Choice
(Answers): 1. b; 2. b; 3. c; 4. d; 5. b; 6. d; 7. c; 8. d; 9. d; 10. a
Self Test True False
(Answers): 1. False; 2. True; 3. True; 4. True; 5. False

CHAPTER 13
Product Development and Pricing Strategies
Self Test Multiple Choice
(Answers): 1. d; 2. c; 3. b; 4. c; 5. b; 6. d; 7. b; 8. a; 9. b; 10. d
Self Test True False
(Answers): 1. True; 2. True; 3. False; 4. True; 5. True

CHAPTER 14
Promotion and Distribution
Self Test Multiple Choice
(Answers): 1. b; 2. c; 3. b; 4. b; 5. c; 6. a; 7. c; 8. a; 9. d; 10. a
Self Test True False
(Answers): 1. True; 2. True; 3. True; 4. False; 5. False

CHAPTER 15
Financing and Tracking Business Operations
Self Test Multiple Choice
(Answers): 1. b; 2. d; 3. a; 4. a; 5. d; 6. b; 7. a; 8. b; 9. b; 10. a
Self Test True False
(Answers): 1. False; 2. True; 3. False; 4. True; 5. False

CHAPTER 16
Securities and Investments
Self Test Multiple Choice
(Answers): 1. a; 2. c; 3. a; 4. b; 5. b; 6. d; 7. b; 8. b; 9. a; 10. b
Self Test True False
(Answers): 1. False; 2. False; 3. True; 4. False; 5. False